The Changing Society of Tobago, 1838–1938
Volume II: 1900–1938

Also by the same author:

'The Germs of An Idea', Afterword to *Labour in the West Indies* by W. Arthur Lewis. 1939. Reprint, London: New Beacon Books, 1977.

Contemporary Caribbean: A Sociological Reader, 2 vols. Edited by Susan Craig. St. Augustine: The editor, 1981, 1982.

Smiles and Blood: The Ruling Class Response to the Workers' Rebellion in Trinidad and Tobago. London: New Beacon Books, 1988.

Uneasy Yoke: Selected Documents on the Union of Trinidad and Tobago, compiled with an Introduction, 'Tobago and Trinidad Together' by Susan Craig-James, forthcoming.

The Changing Society of Tobago, 1838–1938
A Fractured Whole
Volume II: 1900–1938

Susan E. Craig-James

Susan E. Craig-James

1 May 2025

Cornerstone Press Limited • Arima • Trinidad and Tobago

The National Library of Trinidad and Tobago Cataloguing-in-Publication Data

Craig-James, Susan E.
The changing society of Tobago, 1838–1938: b a fractured whole
WI 972.983 Cr 2 22
2 v. (p.) cm.
Volume I: 1838–1900 – Volume II: 1900–1938
9789769516038 (Vol. 2: pbk.)
9789769516021 (Vol. 2: cased)

British Library Cataloguing-in-Publication Data

Craig-James, Susan E.
The changing society of Tobago, 1838–1938: a fractured whole
Vol. 2: 1900–1938
1. Tobago (Trinidad and Tobago) - Social conditions
2. Tobago (Trinidad and Tobago) - History
I. Title
972.9'83

ISBN-13: 9789769516021 (cloth)
ISBN-13: 9789769516038 (paper)

Typeset and published by
Cornerstone Press Limited
35 San Cipriano Street, Arima
Trinidad and Tobago
West Indies
Telephone: (868) 646-4404; Fax: (868) 646-0655
E-mail: corpress@tstt.net.tt

Copy-edited by
Cornerstone Press Limited with
assistance from Savitri Pargass

Cover design by
Paria Publishing Company (1996) Limited

Imaging by Mark Lyndersay

Production for publication by
Glenda Pattenden

Printed in Malaysia by SRM Production Services Sdn. Bhd.

To my father,
Lionel Craig, and
in memory of my mother,
Sislyn Craig,
with undying gratitude
for their sacrifices
for us

Contents

Photographs

Photographs and the acknowledgements for them can be found between text pages 86 and 87, and 214 and 215.

Tables

Tables in Appendices

Tables in Appendices cont.

Box

Preface

THIS VOLUME depicts Tobago in the twentieth century. Part One, In Solitary Union with Trinidad, gives a multifaceted view of the society between 1900 and 1938.

Part Two, Supporting Data, provides the demographic and occupational analyses that undergird Volumes I and II.

Part Three, the Epilogue, offers both information and reflection on Tobago from 1950 to 2000.

Although this work is presented in two volumes, it should be seen as a whole. Volume I deals with the background period of slavery and the post-Emancipation years to 1900, while Volume II considers the whole of the twentieth century to 2000. Thus, although the title focuses on the period that is treated in greatest detail—1838 to 1938—the actual scope of the work covers 1763 to 2000.

As before, I have seized the time to write in detail. Much that is covered here is both discovery and recovery of our heritage. It will help us to understand the pathways of our past, and the ground of our being and becoming.

An island is a world. As I reflect on the Tobago-world before and after 1938, one thing is certain. Now that the norms and values that fostered respect, hard work, co-operation, trustworthiness and trust have been greatly eroded, it is clear that those norms and values were a precious part of Tobago's heritage. They were the bedrock on which human security and social order were built.

Therefore, while embracing change, our people must find ways to return to the ancient paths, if Tobago is truly to progress, and to become safe and serene again.

SECJ
2008

Acknowledgements

A WORK OF this kind is always a collective endeavour and, while those who helped are too numerous to name individually, I am grateful for the enormous goodwill which this project has received from people everywhere.

In 1983 I became excited by the records on Tobago while I was in London on a fellowship from the Nuffield Foundation to do the research for what I had hoped would be a social history of Trinidad and Tobago from the 1930s. That work was also funded by the Macleod and Collymore Foundation, Trinidad and Tobago. That research informed this work in many ways. Although, after much soul-searching, I decided to change course and to study Tobago, I gratefully acknowledge the help and the forbearance of these two foundations.

I am very thankful to the Harold Hyam Wingate Foundation, London, which awarded me a scholarship from September 1995 to August 1997, to conduct research for this work.

Although I stopped working for almost all of 1999 to focus on writing this book, I was unable to do so within that time. Therefore, I greatly appreciate the Professional Development Award from the International Development Research Centre (IDRC), Canada, which enabled me to complete the first draft of this work in 2002. I am grateful to Lloyd Best (deceased) and Kari Levitt who recommended me for the IDRC award.

In the last year of preparing this book, I received support from the Sport and Culture Fund of the Government of Trinidad and Tobago. I am truly grateful for this help.

The study of Tobago between 1838 and 1900 was the basis of my doctoral dissertation. I thank my colleagues, Carl Parris, Dean of the Faculty of Social Sciences, The University of the West Indies (UWI), St. Augustine, in 1992, and Emeritus Professor Selwyn Ryan, then Director of the Institute of Social and Economic Research (ISER), who arranged for me to spend one semester at the ISER to have time to write. I am very grateful to the late Prof. Percy Cohen, my supervisor at the London School of Economics and Political Science, for his encouragement and advice.

I received help from the Mt. Pleasant Credit Union Co-operative Society Ltd., and from Zaid and Joan Ali, Ancilla Armstrong, Gerard and Alice Besson, Annette Brice, Rex and Rhonda Collymore, Trevor Craig, Reginald Dumas, Hart Edwards, Hollis Lynch, Margaret Rouse-Jones, and Efebo Wilkinson. I specially thank Dominic and Alice Besson for designing the cover of this book.

Several people offered material, including photographs, that would be helpful for this work. Among them were Miles Almandoz, Bobby Andrews, Audrie Armstrong and her niece Alison Armstrong, Reginald Clarke, Margaret Ernestine Cordner, Nydia Bruce Daniel, Jennifer de Verteuil,

Jennifer Doyle, Reginald Dumas, Mr and Mrs A. Hatt and their daughter Patricia Hatt, Edward Hernandez, Jerome Keens-Dumas, Carlos Kendall, Gordon Lambert, Dolores Macfarlane, Sonia McLetchie, Percival Nurse, Mark and Zena Puddy, Arlene Rajnauth, Harrison Thomas, Albertha Titus, Cyril Wildman, Winston Wiltshire (Trinidad and Tobago); Alain Buffon (Martinique); David Hunt (Barbados); and Christopher Fyfe, Ben Locker, Jane McGillivray, and Sarah Micklem (UK). Many others graciously lent photographs on request, and for this I am deeply grateful; they are all acknowledged in the body of this work. In particular, I was amazed when Ms Lucille Ottley willingly offered to send her precious gold locket with the only surviving photograph of John McCall, the leading planter in Tobago until 1879.

Still others were willing to give time and energy to search for photographs. I specially thank Mrs Gloria Dilsworth of Sierra Leone and Mrs Estelle Appiah of Ghana who searched for images of Joseph Thomas Comissiong, Tobago's Collector of Customs in 1850, and William Low, Commissioner of Tobago from 1892 to 1898, respectively. We never found them, but it was worth the try.

The many people whom I interviewed were an indispensable source of information. Nearly all have now passed on. These elderly Tobagonians gave generously of their time and their knowledge, and I owe them an enormous debt. Without them, this work would have been the poorer.

In every library where I worked, the staff were extremely helpful. In the UK, I was greatly helped by the archivists at the Institute of Commonwealth Studies; the School of Oriental and African Studies; the main library of the London School of Economics and Political Science; the Foreign and Commonwealth Office Library; the Public Record Office, Surrey; Rhodes House Library, Oxford; the Royal Commonwealth Society Library, whose collection is now housed at Cambridge University Library; the National Library of Scotland; the Scottish Record Office; and the Moravian Archives. The Curator of the National Portrait Gallery in Scotland, Ms Susanna Kerr, was also particularly kind. The archivists at the Barbados Archives went beyond the call of duty, and I have always received prompt and helpful responses to requests.

I am deeply grateful to Rev. Vernon Nelson at the Moravian Archives in Bethlehem, Pennsylvania, for his interest and hospitality during my stay there in 1984, and to his successor, Dr. Paul Peucker, who has been particularly helpful. Thanks are also due to the staff of the Library of Congress, Washington, DC.

At home in Trinidad and Tobago, I owe a great debt to Mrs Kim Gransaull, Mrs Phyllis Kangalee, Mrs Kathleen Helenese-Paul, and the staff of the West Indiana Division of the Main Library, UWI, St. Augustine; in addition, the staff dealing with inter-library loans willingly and graciously served me, while Ms Floris Fraser kindly helped with bibliographical references. Ms Carol Kangalee, Mrs Gertrude James and other members of staff at the Parliament Library did everything possible to help, as did the archivist, Ms Edwina Peters, and the staff at the National Archives of Trinidad and Tobago. Ms Peters' successor, Mrs Helena Leonce, and staff were equally helpful. Ms Eintou Springer and her staff at the National Heritage Library were very gracious, as were Mrs Ann Mitchell-Gift and Mrs Cicely Gibbes at the Scarborough Library, Tobago. During his tenure as Registrar General of Trinidad and Tobago, the late Mr Edward Braithwaite afforded me every facility.

Several of these libraries and archives gave permission for the inclusion of photographs from their collections. I sincerely thank them, and have fully acknowledged these sources.

I am grateful to Canon Noel Titus, Codrington College, Barbados, who facilitated my short visit there in 1993. The Tobago church records yielded much important information. I thank Archdeacon Kenneth Forrester and Archdeacon Philip Isaac of the Anglican Church, Rev. Esther Moore-Roberts and the ministers of the Moravian Church, Rev. Sheldon Dewsbury of the Methodist Church, and Fr. Vincent Travers of the Roman Catholic Church, for granting me access to the records. The church secretaries were all very helpful.

Wherever I went, kind friends opened their doors to me. I remain eternally grateful to my adopted parents, Prof. Sidney Michaelson and his wife Kitty, both deceased, of Edinburgh; to John La Rose (deceased) and Sarah White who gave me a London home during several visits to the UK; to Jim and Ancilla Armstrong, my kind hosts in Barbados; and to Curtis and Karen Keim who befriended me in Bethlehem, Pennsylvania. Gerlinde Rambousek stood with me in the early years of the thesis. John La Rose and Sarah White were a constant source of inspiration and advice.

Prof. Lloyd Braithwaite (deceased) read the doctoral thesis on which some of this work is based, and greatly encouraged me. Vanus James gave incisive comments on some of the chapters for the thesis, and I benefited greatly from working with him on projects in 1998. Gregory Michaelson (Scotland) generously took time to read the manuscript of Volume I; I value his willingness and his comments. The comments of Jean Casimir (Haiti) helped my understanding, and I benefited from the wisdom of Eric St. Cyr for the Epilogue.

Savitri Pargass kindly agreed to check the editing, and I am very grateful for her professional work.

My profound thanks go to Robin Cohen and Bridget Brereton for agreeing to comment on this work for the cover. I specially thank them and Eric St. Cyr for standing with me as referees in my frequent applications for help.

The production of this book owes much to Glenda Pattenden (London) who guided, advised, and did the final preparations for publication. I thank her for the benefit of her great experience.

I am deeply grateful to Miriam Wilson-Edwards, the other director of Cornerstone Press Limited, for her constant help and advice over the years. She and her husband Andy wrestled with the computer analysis of the data on landownership for Volume I, and their contribution is invaluable.

Omar Romero was my first research assistant, and I am grateful for his help. My second assistant, Davindra Craig, was a rare blessing: she faithfully bore many burdens and went beyond the call of duty to make this book a reality.

Very special thanks go to Sally Sugrim for her willing excellent help with my domestic chores.

Most of the photographs received were copied by Vibert Medford; a few were done by Philip Isaac. I am grateful to them both for working with professional skill and loving care. Stein Trotman prepared the age pyramids and most of the maps. He was painstaking, gracious and excellent.

I acknowledge the help of Tarick Hosein, who painstakingly prepared the map of Trinidad and Tobago at the request of Chattergoon Kanhai and Alwyn Wharton. I also thank Harold Wall, who reproduced the map of Tobago c.1910.

The pre-publication work of scanning and enhancing the photographs was done by Mark Lyndersay. He and his wife Donna were wonderfully supportive.

I benefited greatly from the advice of Pamella Benson, Patricia Bishop, Nicholas Laughlin, Jeremy Taylor and Kevon Webster.

Many people supported this work in other ways. Mr Noel Hector at F1 Connect Limited rescued me on numerous occasions by speedily repairing the computer to ensure the unhindered progress of this book. Messrs Deenarine Radhaykissoon and Kennard McAllister did likewise with my car. I sincerely thank them all.

In the face of a spate of burglaries at our home in Tobago, Charles Jack, 'Shiloh' Jack and Gabre James gave their willing support and were very generous with their time. I am deeply grateful to them all.

I appreciate my church family, some of whom supported me in prayer daily over several years. Eletha and Doreen Baptiste, Carol Best-Aaron, Cicely Bramble, Dedra Cox, Linda Garrett (deceased), Gloria Gray, Dorcas Henry, Raymond and Wendy Herbert, Courtenay (deceased) and Glen Mayers, and Stephanie Shurland are among these kind souls. I thank Rev. Bertril and Sister Jacqueline Baird, Pastors Luis and Michelle Cave, Zaid and Joan Ali, and Norlan and Ellen Watts for their encouragement and their prayers.

Certain health care professionals helped to sustain me over the years. I am specially grateful to Dr. Garthlyn Pilgrim, Mr Ian Pierre, Dr. Rasheed Adam, Dr. Pelham McSween and Mrs Terry Romero for their gracious services.

I was deeply touched by those people who offered to help with the marketing and/or launch of this book. Among them are Annette Brice, Trevor Craig, Jacqueline Job, Emile Louis, Alake and Chike Pilgrim, Betty Davis Sylvester, and Monica Sobers-Hylton. My thanks also go to Carolyn Cooper (Jamaica), who reminded me that 'One-one cocoa full basket.'

Without my parents, Sislyn (deceased) and Lionel Craig, this work would not have been possible. I do not have words to thank them for the many ways in which they helped.

Finally, it was Almighty God through Jesus Christ my Lord who made it clear that this work and its companion volume, *Uneasy Yoke: Selected Documents on the Union of Trinidad and Tobago* (forthcoming), were a part of His will for my life. He has given grace, guidance, and waters in every wilderness. Unto Him therefore go the highest praise, the glory and the honour.

Abbreviations

ACIJ	African-Caribbean Institute of Jamaica
ACS	Agricultural Credit Society
ADC	aide-de-camp
AIDS	acquired immunodeficiency syndrome
ASJA	Anjumaan Sunnat ul Jamaat Association
BBC	British Broadcasting Corporation
BCGA	British Cotton Growers Association
BHS	The Bishop's High School
BWI	British West Indies
CADC	Crop Advance and Discount Company
CAREC	Caribbean Epidemiology Centre
CDAC	Colonial Development Advisory Committee
CEO	Chief Executive Officer
CGA	Coconut Growers' Association
CHPC	Comfort and Happiness Promotion Club
CICRED	Committee for the International Co-ordination of Research in Demography
CMP	capitalist mode of production
CNIRD	Caribbean Network for Integrated Rural Development
Co.	Company
comp.	compiler
CSO	Central Statistical Office
DMO	District Medical Officer
EC	Episcopal (Anglican) Church
EINC	East Indian National Congress
EMA	Environmental Management Authority
EMB	Empire Marketing Board
Esq.	Esquire
FS	Fabian Society
FWTU	Federated Workers Trade Union
HIV	human immunodeficiency virus

HMS	His (Her) Majesty's Ship
HMSO	His (Her) Majesty's Stationery Office, London
Hon.	Honourable
ICTA	Imperial College of Tropical Agriculture
IDRC	International Development Research Centre (Canada)
ISER	Institute of Social and Economic Research
JFC	Juvenile Farm Club
JP	Justice of the Peace
jun.	junior
LRC	Legislative Reform Committee
LSE	London School of Economics and Political Science
Ltd.	Limited
MA	Master of Arts
MBE	Member of the Order of the British Empire
MEPA	Model Ex-Pupils Association
MLC	Member of the Legislative Council
MMS	Moravian Missionary Society
MOP	mode of production
MP	Member of Parliament
MS(S)	manuscript(s)
n. (nn.)	note(s)
n. a.	not applicable
N.G.	not given
No.	number
NWSCA	Negro Welfare Social and Cultural Association
PAA	Pan African Association
PEG	Political Education Group
PEM	People's Education Movement
PNM	People's National Movement
PRDI	Policy Research and Development Institute
PWD	Public Works Department
PWPSWU	Public Works and Public Service Workers Union
RC	Roman Catholic
RMSPCO	The Royal Mail Steam Packet Company
RPA	Ratepayers' Association
SBFS	Scarborough Brotherhood and Fellowship Society
SDG	Scarborough Discussion Group
SDMS	Sanatan Dharma Maha Sabha
SEILDS	Southern East Indian Literary and Debating Society
sen.	senior
SILDA	Scarborough Ideal Literary and Debating Association
SLDC	Scarborough Literary and Debating Club
SOAS	School of Oriental and African Studies
SS	steamship
SWWTU	Seamen and Waterfront Workers Trade Union
TCPEP	Tobago Citizens Political and Economic Party
TCTC	Trinidad Consolidated Telephone Company
TDC	Tobago Debating Club
TDTA	Tobago District Teachers Association
TECA	Teachers' Economic and Cultural Association
THA	Tobago House of Assembly
TIM	Tobago Independence Movement

TITU	Tobago Industrial Trade Union
TLCC	Trinidad Literary Club Council
TLGCA	Tobago Lime Growers Co-operative Association
TLP	Trinidad Labour Party
TLSA	Tobago Live Stock Association
TPA	Tobago Planters Association
TPIWU	Tobago Peasants and Industrial Workers Union
TPPA	Tobago Peasant Proprietors Association
TT	Trinidad and Tobago
TTLCC	Trinidad and Tobago Literary Club Council
TTTU	Trinidad and Tobago Teachers Union
TWA	Trinidad Workingmen's Association
UK	United Kingdom
UNC	United National Congress
USA (US)	United States of America
UWI	The University of the West Indies
viz.	namely
Vol.	Volume
WIRC	West India Royal Commission (Moyne Commission)
WIU	West Indian Union
WMS	Wesleyan Missionary Society

Abbreviations in the Notes

ACJ	The Arthur Creech Jones Papers
App.	Appendix
Bros.	Brothers
chap.	Chapter
Cmd.	Command (Paper)
CO	Colonial Office
Col. Sec.	Colonial Secretary
comp(s).	compiler(s)
Confid.	Confidential
CQ	*Caribbean Quarterly*
Enc(s)	Enclosure(s)
encl	enclosing
ff.	following
fol. (fols.)	folio(s)
Gov.	Governor
JCH	*Journal of Caribbean History*
JDS	*Journal of Development Studies*
JPS	*Journal of Peasant Studies*
Leg. Co.	Legislative Council
Lieut.	Lieutenant
LL	*The Labour Leader*
MCR	*Tobago Metairie Commission Report*, 1891
n.d.	no date
NLR	*New Left Review*
no. (nos.)	number(s)
n.p.	no publisher or no place (of publication)

Ph.D.	Doctor of Philosophy
POSG	*Port of Spain Gazette*
PP.	Parliamentary Papers (Great Britain)
Pt.	Part
Sec.	Secretary
SES	*Social and Economic Studies*
SG	*Sunday Guardian*
TG	*Trinidad Guardian*
TH	*Tobago Herald*
TRG	*Trinidad Royal Gazette*
WD	*World Development*

MAP A **The Eastern Caribbean**

CARIBBEAN SEA

ATLANTIC OCEAN

Tobago (inset)

Charlotteville
Roxborough
Plymouth
Crown Point
Crown Point Airport
SCARBOROUGH

Trinidad

Bocas del Dragón

Gulf of Paria

PORT OF SPAIN
ST. GEORGE
Tunapuna
Arima
Piarco International Airport
Valencia
ST. ANDREW
Sangre Grande
L'Anse Noire Toco
Cumana
Sans Souci
Grande Riviere
Manantial
ST. DAVID
Manzanilla
CARONI
Couva
Claxton Bay
NARIVA
Mayaro
Bande de L'Est
MAYARO
SAN FERNANDO
La Brea
Point Fortin
ST. PATRICK
Cedros
Siparia
Princes Town
VICTORIA
Monga
Columbus Channel

Legend

Settlements •
Major towns ●
Counties
Airports ✈

Scale

0 5 10   20   30   40 Km

0   4   8   16   24   32 Miles

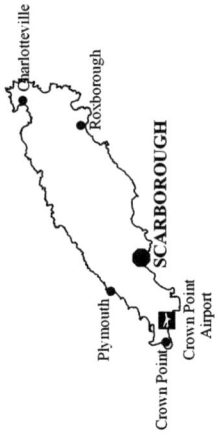

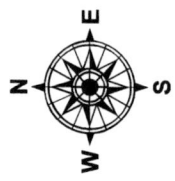

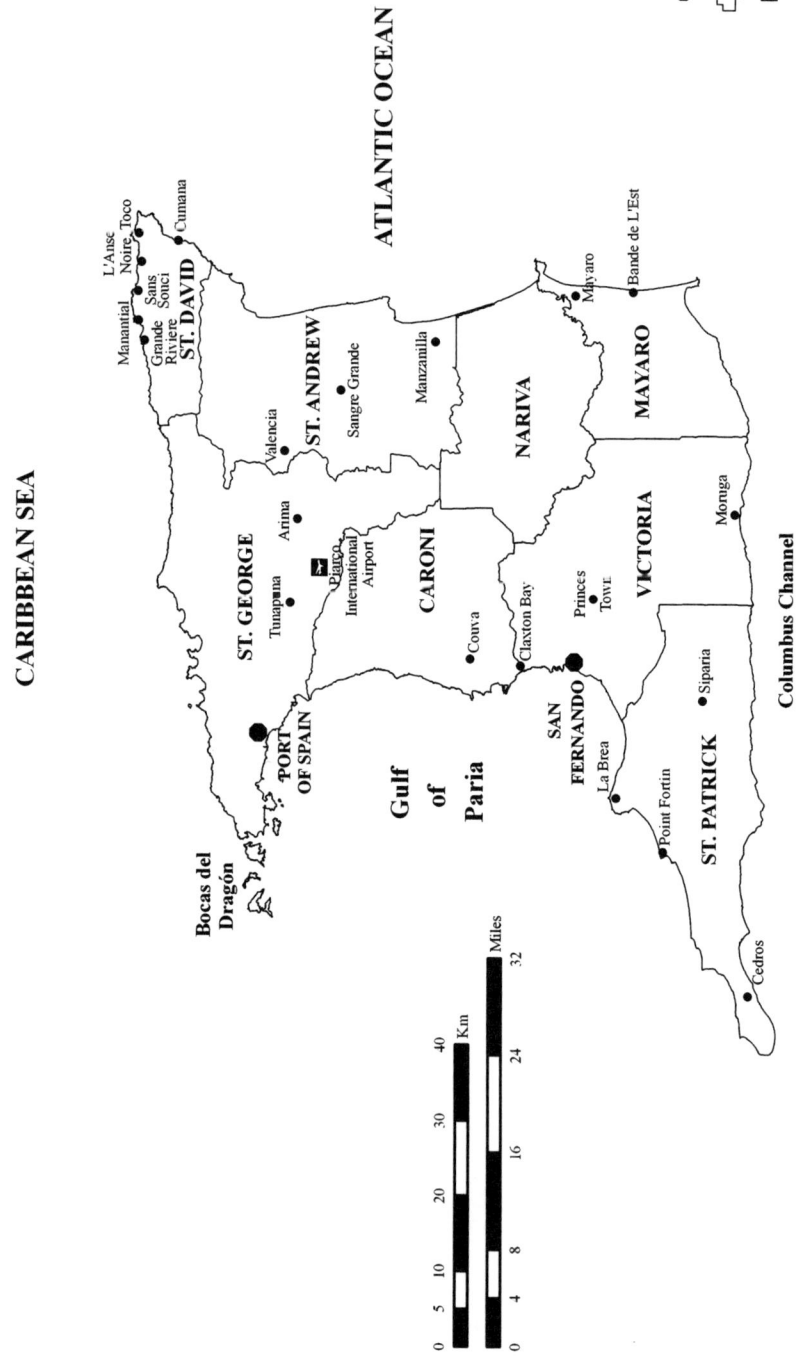

MAP B Trinidad (showing places mentioned) and Tobago

N E S W (compass rose)

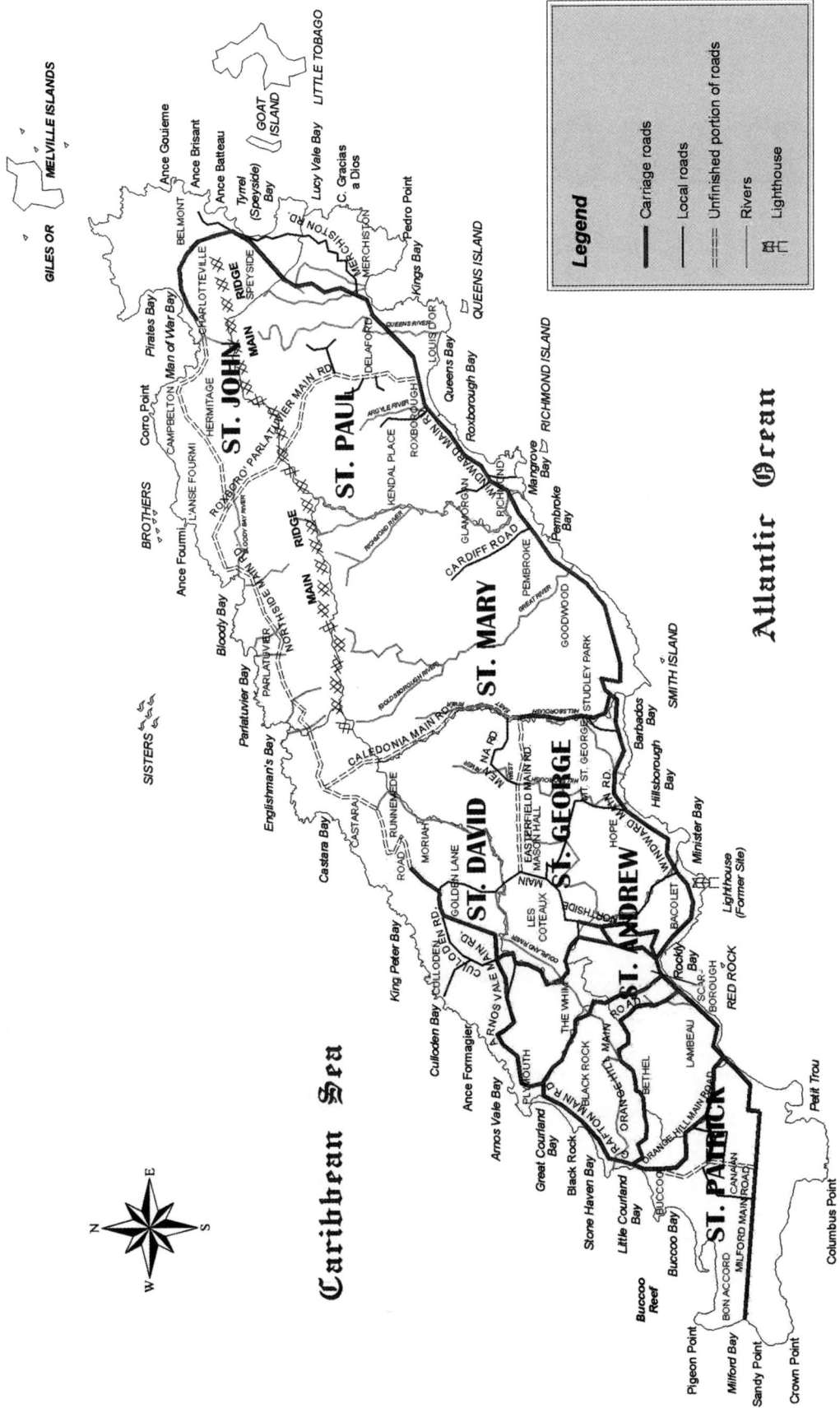

MAP C Tobago showing Parishes, Main Roads and Settlements, 1910
Based on a map prepared by Archibald Bell, Director of Public Works, Trinidad and Tobago, 1910.

TOBAGO.

1. ¾ ½ ¼ 0.   1.   2.   3.   4.

SCALE OF MILES.

ENGLISHMAN BAY.

CASTARA BAY.

25. 23. Englis

24. Englishman's
Bay.
41.

M.Dillon.

30.
Mount Dillon.

KING PETER BAY.

31.
Runnemede.

House

45.

46.

34. 35.
King Peter.
36.

Runnemede.

44. 43.
Runnemede.

42.

Woodlands
37.

43.

Indian Walk
41.

19.
Alma.

28.
Widow's
Lot.

29.
Stewart's
Lot.

30.
Mena.

Cal

House

Ance Formagier

42.

Culloden.

Golden
Lane.

38. 39. 40.

Highlands.
17.

Craig
18.
Hall.

27.
Alma.

22.
Easterfield.

21.

Retr

ARNOS VALE BAY.

24.

Arnos Vale
House

25.

Les Coteaux

St Thomas Church
Wesleyan Chapel
House

16.

COURLAND RIVER

25.
Highlands

Mason Hall-West Church
26.
Alma.

Belmont.

10. 17.

PLYMOUTH

Moravian Church

St David's Pd. Stn.

27.

23. 21. 20. 14.
ARNOS VALE

PARISH

13.
Les Coteaux

24.
Concordia.

R.C. Church
St Peters Ch.

14.
Belmont.

11.

Greenhill.

GREAT COURLAND
BAY.

Adventure

Franklyns

Providence

OF

16.

Concordia

SANDY R. ROAD

12.

House

Black Rock.

PLYMOUTH ROAD

1.

8.

Works

10.

ST. DAVID

Dunvegan

Cradley

7. Hope.

8.

Mesopotamia.

Mount

STONE HAVEN
BAY.

Courland.

Lower
Quarter

Marys
Hill.

Whim.

St. Church
M.Grace

French Fort.

Cradley
5.

Friendsfield

Works

Schools

George

Grafton

2.

Cinamon
Hill.

Montpelier

Govt. House

PARISH OF ST

LITTLE COURLAND
BAY.

Grafton
6.

3.

Orange Valley

5.

Orange

4.
Mont
pelier

Rockley Vale.

Hope.

1.

HILLSBOROUGH
BAY.

Mount
Irvine

Works

7.

ORANGE HILL ROAD

Amity

Spring

Garden

Golder

3.

B

PARISH

Prospect.

Patience Hill.

Mor. School

Bot. Station

Hall

House

2. M.

House

BUCCOO BAY.

38.

Grange

Montgomery
Mor. Ch.
Works

R.C.Church
Hope
Hill.

Garden

29.

Ordnance
Land.

Bracelet.

MINSTER BAY.

Pigeon Point.

39. 34.

OF

Buccoo.

27.

Riseland
18.
Works

17.

10.
Signal
Hill.

Lambeau.

Barleigh
6.
Castle

SCARBOROUGH

Works

2. M.

Lighthouse.

Pigeon
Point.

33.

Golden Grove.

35. 36.

New
Grange.

Carnbee

ORANGE ROAD

Sherwood
Park.

16.

Carnbee
12.

Appendage

Carnbee
Lambeau

Works

RED ROCK.

12. 11.

10.

Golden
Grove

30.

8.

BUCCOO ROAD

St Patricks Church

Sherwood
Park.
25.

St.Church
20.

Milford

41.

Bon Accord.

17.
Shirvan.

18.
19.

Mount
Pleasant.

Hampden
24.

MILFORD ROAD

22.

Sandy Point.

43.

Clapham
14.

Moravian Church
Bon Acc.

29. 28.
Works

Friendship

25.

20.
Cove.

Low lands.

16.

Cromslain
13.

Kilgwyn.

MILFORD ROAD

Lowlands

21.

Crown Point.

26.

Friendship

24.

Cove.

Petit

PARISH OF ST. PATRICK

PARISH OF ST. ANDREW

PARISH OF ST.

23.
Cove.

Trou.

Columbus Point.

GILES OR MELVILLE ISLANDS

SISTERS

BROTHERS
Ance Fourmi

Corvo Point

Telescope 32

MAN OF WAR BAY.

PIRATES BAY

36

BOBY IS. 6

Ance Gouleme 28

Wesleyan Chapel

6. Ance Fourmi 5. 51.

30 33

28

Ance Brisont

Houses

Charlotteville

Ance Batteau

Hermitage 4. 40

30 34 35

BLOODY BAY.

10.

Spey Side 3

LITTLE TOBAGO

PARLATUVIER BAY.

Stewarts Lot. 17.

St. John's Church

TYRREL BAY.

GOAT ISLAND

9. 8. 7. 50.

Trois Rivieres

21.

20. Parrot Hall. 19. Parlatuvier

PARISH OF

16. 13. 12. 14. 15. 49.

28 31

22.

27.

43. 27.

32. Lambeau

38. 29. Lucy Vale

11.

31. 37. 44. 45. 46.

ST JOHN

47. 48.

16. 29

33 35.

LUCY VALE BAY.

42. 43.

DeLaford. 2. 30. Kings Bay

34. Merchiston.

41. 42.

36. 37. Merchiston.

C. Gracios a Dios

45. 28. 32. 33.

46. 47. 48. 51. 39. 40. 20. Philadelphia 19.

13.

38.

Works

39. 49. 50. 41. 25. 26. Florida. 24. 18.

PARISH OF ST PAUL

R.C. Church

40. 24. 19. Florida. 23. Gilpin. 21. 22. Roxborough. 10. 5. House St. Paul's Church

29. 34. 35. 16. Morne D'or 18. 11. Rosebank. 9. 8. House 1. Louis D'or

39. 43. 30. 31. 36. 37. Morne D'or 15. 8. 7. Zion Hill. Wesleyan Chapel

Queens

38. McNairs. 42. 13. Bushey Park 4. Kendal Place.

ROXBOROUGH ROCK.

QUEENS IS:

PARISH OF ST MARY

32. 25. Irvine Hall. Lure. 14. 12. Cardiff 5. Richmond.

Pedro Point.

26. 11. Invergordon. Belle Garden

Hillsborough Vale.

Upper and Lower Callon. 10. Unity 9. Waterloo Pembroke Glamongan

MANGROVE BAY.

RICHMOND IS:

19. 20. Windsor Goodwood Wesleyan School

Friendship

Sturley 34. 35. Mount. Hatts Grant R.C.Church

GEORGE 36. 37. Rose 40.

BARBADOS BAY.

SMITH ISLAND.

KINGS BAY.

KINGS RIVER

WINDWARD ROAD

GREAT RIVER

MAP D Tobago showing the Estates, 1900

Source: CO 700 Tobago 11; reproduced with permission from the Public Record Office, UK.

BOX A Note to the Reader

- All unusual terms are explained either in the text or in the Notes at the end of each chapter. In addition, they are in the Glossary which precedes the Bibliography. Each term in the Glossary is printed in italics when it is first given in the text.

- There is increasing concern among Caribbean people that the language describing our history should depict us, not as victims, but as protagonists. The term 'enslaved person' is preferred to 'slave', and 'enslavement' to 'slavery'. I have tried to adhere to these conventions where possible, but at times have used 'slave' and 'slavery' with no offence intended.

- In Caribbean societies during the period of enslavement, the free people of mixed African and European ancestry were called the 'free coloured' or the 'free people of colour'. I have used these terms in their context and, since the term 'coloured' was widely used and understood in Tobago in this sense until the early twentieth century, I have used it throughout this work.

- Because much of the material in Volume I is harnessed to answer the questions posed as we seek to explain the collapse of the sugar economy in the 1880s, aspects of the economy and the political system are dealt with in more than one chapter. Each chapter has a clear Conclusion summing up its findings. To assist the reader further, a Road Map to Volume I is given in Box B on page xxvii of that volume.

- Volume I covers the period 1838 to 1900, while Volume II focuses on 1900 to 1938. Volume II meets its two objectives: it describes the changing social structure from 1900 to 1938, and it explains why all agriculture declined in Tobago in the twentieth century. In addition, Volume II examines village life and peasant production and trade; the main political issues; education, teachers and literary movements; and popular trends in secular and sacred music. These chapters are followed by a section that analyses the census data for 1844 to 1946, giving the information on demography and occupations that undergirds the two volumes. Volume II ends with an Epilogue describing Tobago society from 1950 to 2000; this depiction is supported by data from the censuses of 1960 to 2000. Abundant use is made of a range of sources, including a wealth of oral-history material.

Part One
In Solitary Union with Trinidad

The interpretation of our reality through patterns not our own serves only to make us ever more unknown, ever less free, ever more solitary.

Gabriel García Márquez

1

The Rise and Demise of the New Agrarian Order, 1900–1963

A T THE dawn of the twentieth century, a new agrarian order was being established in Tobago. The closer Union with Trinidad had been inaugurated in January 1899. The collapse of the sugar industry had made land prices in Tobago cheaper than elsewhere, and there was a growing influx of new planters, new labourers recruited for the most part from the nearby islands, and returning migrants. New crops were being grown, and landownership and land use rapidly expanded. The remotest abandoned areas were opened up to prolific cultivation for the first time since 1763, as the emergent peasants tamed the rough, hilly landscape of north and east Tobago. The Windward District became the centre of production, eclipsing the Leeward which was more suited to sugar.

By 1938, however, the general mood in Tobago was one of despondency. The harsh reality was that agriculture, on which the island had pinned her hopes of recovery, was failing. After a spectacular rise in commodity prices during World War I (1914–1919), prices fell sharply from 1920 onwards. A long depression in prices, coinciding with the period of the Great Depression worldwide, was accompanied by the spread of numerous plant diseases throughout the 1920s and 1930s. Tobago's agriculture never recovered.

The collapse of agriculture in modern Tobago is a constant source of concern to its residents. Depending on the social class and perspective of the speakers, the common beliefs are that agriculture collapsed either because of the anti-colonial politics of Dr. Eric Williams, the Chief Minister from 1956, who pronounced that 'Massa Day Done',[1] or because of the ravages of Hurricane Flora on 30 September 1963. The evidence shows that neither view is correct, since by 1930 both plantation and peasant agriculture were already in serious decline.

This chapter fulfils the third objective of this study by providing answers to the question: why did both plantation and peasant agriculture in Tobago become moribund by 1950? The argument is that Tobago suffered from two political jeopardies. First, colonialism made it a producer of primary products, and the Caribbean's small share of the global market made its producers price-takers in the world economy. Second, Tobago's status as a Ward in the colony led to its gross neglect by the central government. This double jeopardy was linked to, and compounded by, two other factors. The first was the failure to promote food-crop production, a policy that reflected the dominance in the colony of both plantation and imperial interests. The second was the political

3

ineffectiveness of all the social groupings within Tobago. Part of this ineffectiveness came from divisions of race and class. As a result, by 1930 none of the crops exported by peasants and planters in Tobago could be profitably produced, whether for the global or the Trinidad market.

The evidence and reasoning in support of these contentions are presented here.[2]

1. THE MAJOR AND MINOR EXPORT CROPS

The period 1870 to 1913 was one of rapid expansion in world trade. The British West Indian peasantry, having emerged mainly by the 1860s, benefited greatly from this expansion, particularly in the markets for crops such as cocoa, bananas, nutmegs and arrowroot. Tobago's peasants and her new planter class established themselves between 1900 and 1920, profiting from the prosperity of the times. Land use rapidly expanded. In 1930, 41,675 acres were cultivated, as opposed to 10,000 acres or less throughout the nineteenth century.[3] Cocoa, coconuts, rubber, cotton, limes, and tobacco were grown for export; and ground provisions and livestock were produced for the Trinidad market. Production and exports greatly increased between 1900 and 1920. The value of exports jumped from £14,412 in 1897 and £21,443 in 1898 to £207,740 in 1927 and £168,725 in 1928.[4] But by 1938, none of the export crops was viable.

In 1938, summing up the position in stark terms, the Tobago Chamber of Commerce told the Moyne Commission:

> The post war depressions have again caused a decline in prosperity so severe and prolonged, that Planters have depleted their reserves of capital, and Estates are suffering seriously from neglect of proper maintenance, while the effect on the Peasant Proprietor has been to reduce his income to the point where he can hardly provide the means of livelihood.[5]

Within Tobago, certain negative factors formed the backdrop of all efforts at commercial farming. The long years of sugar cultivation and poor husbandry by all users of the land in the Leeward District had leached the soils, denuded the hills, and lowered the rainfall. Severe annual drought

was normal there, made worse by no water supply apart from wells, cisterns and springs before 1925. As this chapter will show, the entire Courland River Basin was in serious need of soil rehabilitation. As early as 1909, the Governor, Sir George Le Hunte, stated:

> The South-western end of the Island, presents an object lesson of the disastrous effects of the wholesale denudation of its hills of timber, no doubt for fuel to make way for cane in the days of sugar, but now continuously burnt for grass for stock, which probably only use the lower slopes, while the fire runs unchecked to the summits. The humus in the soil is destroyed, the land becomes poorer and poorer, it loses its power of attracting the rain and of retaining it when it does fall only to form a temporary torrent in the streams at the bottom, often doing damage to roads or bridges, the springs dry up and the ultimate result is a diminished rainfall and failing water supply and this I was not surprised to hear is the actual condition there now.[6]

For these reasons, except for a few crops, productivity and yields in leeward Tobago were low.

Cocoa

Between 1870 and 1900, cocoa surpassed sugar to become the leading export of Trinidad. It became Tobago's chief crop after 1900. High world prices, high yields, and low wages led to a continued boom in the industry until 1920. So important was cocoa that in 1937 Cecil Y. Shephard dubbed its fortunes 'the financial barometer' of Trinidad and Tobago.[7]

The first factor contributing to cocoa's decline was competition from other producers, particularly Ecuador, Brazil, Sao Tomé, and the Gold Coast (Ghana), the main global exporters by 1914. Trinidad and Tobago's share of the world cocoa market declined steadily from 15.0 per cent of global exports in 1890 to 9.0 per cent in 1913 and 5.0 per cent in 1926.[8] Although the Trinidad and Tobago cocoa beans were highly valued because of their flavour, in the global market fine cocoa production fell rapidly, as manufacturers used more of the cheaper ordinary cocoa. Thus, by 1913, like all other West Indian producers, the colony was a price-taker in the global market. The price at store in Port of Spain had risen from $8.25 per *fanega* (110 lbs) in 1874 to $15.20 in 1900. On the eve of World War I (in 1913–14), it was $12.76. Prices rose to a peak of $23.92 per fanega in 1919–1920, declined to $10.00 in the following year, sank to $5.03 in 1933, and rose again by 1942 to $13.35.[9] Given that wages and other costs rose after 1920 because of rising food and other prices, most growers could not survive.

Witchbroom disease (*Marasmius perniciosus*) appeared in Trinidad in 1928, wreaking havoc in the fields at a time when low prices did not allow planters to meet the high cost of rehabilitation. In Tobago, witchbroom was first discovered at Wild Dog River in St. Paul's parish in February 1939. By 1947, in spite of a determined plant-protection campaign, witchbroom and black pod disease (*Phytophtora palmivora*) had destroyed one-third of the cocoa cultivation.[10]

Rehabilitation of cocoa holdings and replanting with high-yielding clonal varieties resistant to witchbroom were encouraged in Tobago from 1940. A demonstration station was constructed at Louis d'Or Estate (formerly Betsy's Hope) in 1948, and a propagating nursery for clonal cocoa at King's Bay was moved there in 1955. But the long years of low prices left most growers unable to rehabilitate their holdings to the extent needed to make them competitive. Although prices improved after World War II ($28.00 per fanega for 'plantation-grade' beans in 1946), production did not, owing to decreasing yields. This was partly because of senescent trees, a problem that, with time, affected Tobago, and also because of senescent *environments*, in which good cultivation practices were not maintained.[11]

Although prices rose to over $50.00 per fanega by 1950, the country's cocoa industry did not recover. Severe drought for five years after 1956 caused the loss of thousands of clonal plants, and cocoa went into steady decline, both in quantity and quality of output, thereafter.[12]

The smallest producers in Tobago were the hardest hit. And *they* were the major producers. According to Orde Browne, of the 12,000 acres under cocoa in 1939, 8,000 were in holdings less than 50 acres in size.[13] Because of inefficient methods of drying and preparing the cocoa by growers working as individuals, the small growers received lower prices since their beans were not of 'plantation' quality. To remedy this, Tobago's peasants pioneered co-operative cocoa fermentaries, with the first starting at Pembroke in

February 1929. Three co-operative cocoa fermentaries survived to 1957, but were unable to maintain high standards. In 1946 the Department of Agriculture reported on their 'continued decline' and on measures 'to revive interest' in them. Prof. C. Y. Shephard, who had visited the farms of members of the best Agricultural Credit Societies (ACS) in 1927 and had seen a uniformly high standard of cultivation and curing of beans, found a deterioration in both in 1957, because of less effective extension work. Shephard recommended village fermentaries everywhere, to raise the standard of curing and to 'restore' the reputation of Tobago's cocoa.[14] Cocoa never recovered.

Coconuts

World prices of coconuts also declined after 1920. The price per 100 lbs of *copra* fell by half from $5.52 in 1926 to $2.27 in 1933, and by half again to $1.15 in 1938.[15] In February 1936, the Coconut Growers' Association (CGA) was started to end the near monopoly of Lever Brothers, one of the leading multinational companies in the industry, and to obtain better prices by entering the manufacturing side of the industry. They began marketing nuts and copra in May 1936. Their factory, opened in Trinidad in 1938, made edible oil, lard substitute, soap and other products.

However, in 1939 Thomas H. Brinkley, manager of Courland Estates (Coconuts) Limited in Tobago, complained to the Moyne Commission that, regardless of whether the crop was used locally or exported to the UK and Colombia, UK prices were the ruling factor. Brinkley described the price-taking condition of primary producers in the global market. He stated that, while the price of copra had fallen from £25 per ton in January 1937 to £13.10s per ton in December that year, the sale of manufactured oils and fats by Lever Brothers and Unilever Limited had reached a record £190 million, partly because of higher prices for the processed product. Brinkley made it clear that the share of the market controlled by Unilever accounted for its high profits, and that the low prices to the primary producers '[could] not be attributed to any general depression.' Brinkley lamented:

The market for the sale of estates has virtually disappeared and owners can neither sell nor make a living.

In Trinidad, the CGA also complained of price-cutting by Unilever to 'kill the development of our industry, so that they should have a share in the market.'[16]

After World War II, technological innovations promoted the use of detergents and not oil-based soaps, and consumer preferences moved from saturated fats such as coconut oil to unsaturated fats. Tropical oils and fats were surpassed by competition from temperate sources. By 1972 temperate oils and fats commanded 70.0 per cent of world production and 50.0 per cent of global trade.[17]

The spread of red ring disease and the high cost of rehabilitation increased the difficulties of local growers, and coconuts became a high-risk investment in Trinidad and Tobago. Thus, as with cocoa, low prices, plant diseases, senescence, and declining yields, already prevalent by 1960, led to the progressive decline of the coconut industry.[18]

Rubber

The Tobago planters were among the pioneers of rubber cultivation in the colony, and they displayed a remarkable level of innovation in cultivating, tapping and extracting sheet rubber from latex. The fatal flaw in the process was the choice of rubber. In 1887 the Director of the Royal Botanic Station in Trinidad, J. Hinchley Hart, encouraged the growth of *Castilloa elastica*, one of the varieties that were termed 'wild rubber' in the global trade. Tobago's planters invested heavily in the new crop.

However, the British Government was disseminating the seeds of 'Para' or plantation rubber (*Hevea brasiliensis*), which had been taken from Brazil to the Royal Botanic Gardens, London, in 1876, the same year that the first *Hevea* plants arrived in Trinidad. Plantation rubber, because of its consistently high yields and the pure quality of the rubber produced, swiftly became the dominant variety in world trade. In 1905, only 174 tons or 0.3 per cent of global rubber production was plantation rubber. By 1910, *Hevea* production increased to 9.0 per cent of the world's rubber, and by 1924, it accounted for 93.2 per cent (Table 1.1). Tobago's planters began the commercial export of rubber in 1902. For the financial year 1906–1907, Tobago's rubber exports were valued at £174, rising to £1,388 in 1909.

Ironically, Tobago's planters were increasing in quantity and quality the production of wild rubber, precisely at the time when the global trade was being geared towards plantation rubber.

TABLE 1.1 World Production of Plantation and Wild Rubber, 1905–1924

Year	Total world production Tons	Plantation rubber		Wild rubber	
		Tons	% world production	Tons	% world production
1905	59,494	174	0.3	59,320	99.7
1910	80,746	7,269	9.0	73,477	91.0
1915	169,017	114,277	67.6	54,740	32.4
1920	341,135	304,671	89.3	36,464	10.7
1924 (estimated)	414,703	386,703	93.2	28,000	6.8

Source: David M. Figart, *The Plantation Rubber Industry in the Middle East* (Washington, DC 1925), 5.

Ironically too, in the expense of effort on *Castilloa*, Tobago's rubber cultivators displayed extraordinary inventiveness. In 1910 Harry S. Smith of Caledonia Estate patented a centrifugal machine for extracting rubber from latex in ten minutes without discoloration. At the International Rubber Exhibition in London in 1911, Smith also displayed a combined chisel with a thin blade 1½" wide and a sliding weight on the handle for tapping rubber. Many of the other planters—Mayow Short I, H. Tucker, S. Tucker, Thorleigh Orde, Major Edward B. Walker—also experimented with devices for tapping rubber.

At the 1911 Rubber Exhibition, Messrs Lewis and Peat of Mincing Lane remarked that Smith's rubber 'was as good as any yet produced' from *Castilloa elastica*; that the samples from Smith's Caledonia Estate and Major Walker's Easterfield 'were better than anything we have seen, either from Mexico or anywhere else'; and that Smith and his colleagues were 'teaching the rest of the world how to do it'.[19]

The planters, whose estimated investment in *Castilloa* was $100,000, had to spend large sums to cut it out and substitute cocoa and coconuts. In 1927 they stated: 'It was practically useless to substitute "Hevea" as the labour force was barely sufficient for the industries in hand.' As happened also in Trinidad, '*Castilloa* proved an expensive failure.'[20]

Cotton

In 1900 the UK depended on the USA for 85.0 per cent of its cotton supply. Early in the twentieth century, raw cotton prices were rising steadily. Shortage of supply after the short US crop of 1900 led to a revival of interest in the UK in promoting within the British Empire alternative sources of supply. In 1902 the British Cotton Growing Association (BCGA) was founded to promote imperial cotton growing, and it developed close links at the highest level with Colonial Office officials.[21]

The BCGA paid for the services of Thomas Thornton, a cotton expert, whom they attached to the Imperial Department of Agriculture in Barbados, and tried to interest growers in the BWI. In 1903, J. Hinchley Hart, the Director of the Royal Botanic Gardens in Trinidad, stated that the Agricultural Society in Trinidad had reported against the project; he offered the opinion that it would be 'opposed by the planters', and suggested that the state should encourage small cultivators by providing central ginning and packing stations.[22] The Government imported a cotton ginning and baling press, which arrived in Tobago in September 1904 and was erected on the Scarborough wharves in 1908.

By 1904, under Edward Keens' management, Dr. George Latour's Golden Grove Estate had 30 acres under cotton, with a 30-saw gin and a press for pressing cotton into bales of 500 lbs capacity. Latour grew mainly Marie Galante cotton.[23]

Early in 1908, after Thornton's contract with the Imperial Department had expired, he went to Tobago, where he bought Old Grange Estate. Thornton experimented with cotton on his own behalf and that of Dr. Gooding of Barbados, who bought New Grange, the adjoining estate, in 1909. Thornton claimed that before his arrival in Tobago to manage the Government's cotton ginnery, 'practically nothing had been done in regard to

cotton, and the Trinidad Department of Agriculture took very little interest in it, and in fact discouraged every one from taking it up.'[24]

Cotton exports from Tobago rose from 2,956 lbs valued £74 in 1905 to 12,103 lbs valued £605 in September 1908. In addition to Dr. George Latour's production on Golden Grove and Shirvan estates and Thornton's experiments on Old Grange, an experimental plot was located at Calder Hall.[25]

Thornton developed a hybrid between Sea Island cotton and native Tobago varieties. It was a high yielder, with the fibre equal or almost equal to that of Sea Island cotton. Seeds of Thornton's hybrid were distributed free to the small growers, officially estimated at 60 persons in 1911. By 1912 Thornton's hybrid was the main cotton grown in Tobago, except for two acres of Sea Island cotton.[26]

Despite these efforts, cotton did not become a major crop in Tobago. There were only two large growers—Latour and Thornton—but though their cotton was of a high quality, their profits were officially reported as being low. In 1909 cotton-stainers, red insects which stained the cotton, appeared in Tobago, and were difficult to control. Moreover, high proportions of the seeds imported for the peasants did not germinate, leaving their efforts 'largely thwarted'.[27] By 1913 Thornton left for northern Nigeria, and the ginnery was closed.

In 1917 the Acting Director of Agriculture reported on Tobago:

> Cotton of good quality was grown, but cotton-stainers proved a terrible and costly pest, and they, together with uncertain weather conditions, were the main causes which prevented the industry from being very remunerative.[28]

Limes

Limes also declined. In the 1920s 'wither tip', also known as 'blossom blight' and 'die-back' disease, appeared in Tobago. Despite serious efforts at eradication, the disease spread rapidly, and the campaign against it was abandoned in 1924. Instead, a highly resistant, prolific-bearing variety from the Philippines was substituted. In his report for 1927, the Warden noted that limes, though once prominent, had been displaced by coconuts and had 'completely disappeared partly due to the ravages of the "wither tip" and partly to the lack of a market for the raw product.'[29]

For many years officials and farmers had mooted the idea that there should be a lime factory in Tobago. In 1917 C. Henry Meaden, the officer in charge of the Botanic Station, sent out a circular to the effect that the Governor had decided that a government co-operative lime factory should be established.[30] Nothing happened, however, until the Tobago growers combined as the Tobago Lime Growers Co-operative Association (TLGCA) in June 1930, to process the lime crop of both planters and peasants into lime oil, with a small crushing plant located in the disused cotton ginnery on Scarborough wharf. In 1935 the Association purchased 4,232 barrels of limes from its 470 members, nearly three times as much as in 1931. The TLGCA was a member of the Lime Oil Producers Association of Trinidad and Tobago, which received government support in 1938: a guaranteed minimum price and assistance with buying modern mills to extract a higher percentage of the lime oil.[31]

However, these initiatives came too late. From the 1930s, molasses replaced concentrated lime juice in the production of citric acid, and the major demand was for lime oil, the price of which fell sharply, owing to competition from Mexican limes in the USA market. 'Die-back' disease, for which no cure was found, ravaged production, and Tobago's growers received a further setback when the lime factory was destroyed by fire in November of 1941.

Given the common difficulties of Caribbean producers, the West Indian Lime Oil Sales Company Limited, with membership from St. Lucia and Trinidad and Tobago, was formed in 1935 to establish an intercolonial system of collective marketing of lime oil. The West Indian Limes Association (Incorporated) was also registered in Trinidad in 1941, with membership from the Limes Associations of Dominica, St. Lucia, and Trinidad and Tobago. However, these efforts could not prevent the decline of the local industry.[32]

Finally, in 1955, the TLGCA and Industrial Cold Storage Enterprises, both of which then processed limes into lime oil in Scarborough, suspended production. The price for limes had fallen in recent years from $6.48 to $2.00 per lb. Shortly before the closure, growers sold limes for as little as 3 lbs for 1 cent. Lime oil and lime juice were again

produced by 1962, but the quantities were insignificant.[33]

Once again, the inability to overcome changing conditions on the world market caused the collapse.

Tobacco

Tobacco was cultivated on Bacolet Estate by a Port of Spain merchant, Alfred Mendes, who hired as manager Alfred Cheeks, a tobacco expert from Barbados. Mendes also purchased from other Tobago growers from c.1911. By 1911 there were some 50 acres cultivated in tobacco in various parts of leeward Tobago, particularly in Patience Hill, where 'there [were] men who ha[d] practiced the growing of this plant from boyhood'.[34] Horatio Nelson, a villager, had introduced tobacco to the Patience Hill farmers in the late nineteenth century. Thomas Thornton, the cotton expert, also raised a tobacco hybrid, which went on trial in 1911.

In 1911, under Cadman McEachrane's management, Henderson and Co. started a cigar factory which Cheeks supervised. The factory employed six persons, turning out 'about twenty thousand cigars weekly'— Cheroots, 1891s, Flor-Finas, Londres, Panetelas, After Suppers, and other brands, including Chicos, a cheaper item.[35]

Despite these initiatives, tobacco production was not sustained in the early twentieth century. By 1917, only 11.25 ounces of tobacco seeds were sold in Tobago, vis-à-vis 88.25 ounces in 1916. The fall in production was due to reduced prices and the high standards in length and quality of leaves required for the global market.[36]

In 1925, 26,779 lbs of tobacco worth £1,038 3s 1d, or 1.2 per cent of the value of Tobago's exports, were exported.[37] The comparable figures for 1916 had been 70,449 lbs worth £3,522 or 3.9 per cent of total export value. Although exports rose to 61,657 lbs in 1940, by 1950 they fell to 3,998 lbs, equivalent to £385 8s 4d or 0.1 per cent of the value of the exports.[38] In 1956 there was only one farmer with two-thirds of an acre in tobacco.

In 1957 the Government and the West Indian Tobacco Company started a Tobacco Pilot Scheme; by 1962 the crop was re-established in leeward Tobago, with 176 small farmers on 106 acres, and one estate growing 20 acres of tobacco.

The 1961/62 harvest was 78,192 lbs; but the growers complained of increasing stringency from the tobacco company in grading and pricing the tobacco.[39] Despite its resilience, tobacco remained a very minor crop.

Bananas

The commercial production of bananas in the colony was first encouraged as part of the fruit trade, which Sir William Robinson tried to foster during his administration as Governor from 1885 to 1891. It was further boosted by the efforts of an Englishman, Weldon W. Symington, whose enterprise, Symington West Indies Syndicate Limited, began shipments to the UK on 31 July 1903. The growers were peasants from Trinidad's north coast and Tobago. This trade was possible because of the coastal steamers, and the peasantry widely supported it. After Symington's death by accident in December 1904, his company continued for some time, but the export of bananas ceased in 1914.[40]

In the 1930s, because of the depressed prices of sugar, cocoa and coconuts, Trinidad's cocoa planters diversified into growing citrus fruits and bananas, but only bananas were commercially grown in Tobago.[41] Trial shipments from Trinidad were made from 1932 to April 1934, and in 1934 the Government established a Banana Board. Although bananas were easy to produce, requiring little capital expenditure on cocoa lands and giving quick returns, they succumbed to leaf-spotting fungi (*Cercospora musae*) and Panama disease (*Fusarium cubense*). In both Trinidad and Tobago, official reports noted that they were also often grown on poor soils, and that there were several rejections at the wharves because of poor reaping and handling.[42] In 1938 the Department of Agriculture wrote: 'large scale investment in this crop is not to be recommended.'[43]

The first shipments of bananas from Tobago were in 1935, but there are no consistent figures on Tobago's exports before 1950. The statistics of the Marketing Board show fluctuating shipments and a downward trend from 1950 to 1956 (Table 1.2).

In 1957 Tobago exported 579.5 short tons of bananas valued $48,427; in 1958 the tonnage was 414.0 valued $32,057; and in 1959, 339.6 tons worth $30,065.[44] The number of stems exported fell by one-half from 44,471 in 1958 to 22,401 in 1961, and an equal decline in value was officially estimated.[45]

In addition to the fact that the fruit were bruised as they were conveyed by trucks on hilly, winding roads, poor handling and packaging hindered profitability. The inconvenience of having to send the fruit on barges to Trinidad for transhipment to refrigerated ocean-going vessels was a further setback, but the leading officials thought that the small quantities exported did not justify the development of a deepwater harbour. The team of planners that visited Tobago in 1957 commented:

It would be idle to pretend that we were in any way favourably impressed with what we saw.[46]

Because of the inefficient transhipment system, banana exports from Tobago ended in March 1962.[47]

Food Crops and Livestock

At the inception of the Union with Trinidad, Tobago was popularly regarded as the 'food basket' of Trinidad, a vital source of vegetables, fruit, poultry, eggs and livestock for the Port of Spain market. Food production increased dramatically in the early twentieth century. However, Tobago faced stiff competition from Barbados, Grenada and St. Vincent, all of which had more regular communication by steamship and sailing craft with Trinidad than the island Ward. What is more, the constraints of poor sea communication prevented Tobago from exporting to the Barbados and Grenada markets, facilities which she had enjoyed before 1906.[48]

TABLE 1.2 **Shipments of Food Crops from Tobago to Trinidad, 1950–1956 (Short Tons)**

| Crops | Short tons per year | | | | | | |
	1950	1951	1952	1953	1954	1955	1956
Bananas	46	86	32	55	73	24	46
Plantains	115	65	11	38	12	9	19
Ground provisions	2,000	939	363	862	396	232	459
Corn	47	51	145	119	107	132	58
Peas	77	5	1	10	16	2	28
Total	2,285	1,146	552	1,084	604	399	610

Sources: Administration Reports of the Director of Agriculture for given years.

Note: One short ton is 2,000 lbs.

Moreover, although acreages were expanding, productivity was not. In 1926 the Director of Agriculture observed:

> There is apparently scope for much more intensive cultivation in Tobago as indicated by the fact that whereas the agricultural exports of Tobago amount to less than £4 per head of the population, those for Trinidad are approximately £8 per head, although … the percentage of the population actually engaged in Agriculture must be considerably lower in Trinidad than it is in Tobago. *The present position of Tobago is that of a community producing a great part of its own requirements but comparatively little surplus for export.*[49]

By 1938 it was clear that Tobago's peasantry had reached its 'period of saturation', to use Woodville Marshall's phrase.[50] The best evidence of this is the careful study conducted by Vernon Ferrer at the height of the wartime Grow More Food Campaign in 1943. Ferrer, a graduate of the Imperial College of Tropical Agriculture in Trinidad, had worked for nine years among the farmers studied. He examined the economic aspects of the farming enterprises of the members of the Agricultural Credit Societies (ACS), and considered the feasibility of the proposals for medium-term credit advanced by the Agricultural Policy Committee in its 1943 Report (discussed in Section 6 of this chapter).[51] In 1943 there were 18 ACS with 396 members, most of whom were farmers owning their land. Ferrer stratified Tobago into three regions, and within them interviewed 95 members or 25 per cent of the active members of the ACS. His findings provide a sound basis for understanding the peasantry's decline.

First, *the average age of the farmers was 50*; and family size ranged from 5 to 9 persons. The average number of family members helping each farm operator was 1.8, and Ferrer stated that farmers' children gave only occasional help, mainly with livestock, while seeking other occupations.[52] Among the features of cultivation, Ferrer noted the following.

1. The major implements were cutlass, hoe, spade and knife.
2. There was little crop rotation: the same crops were planted year after year, causing loss of soil fertility.
3. Because animals were often kept at home while the gardens were far off, there was little manuring of crops.

4. Internal communication was 'a subject of much acrimonious comment', since the secondary roads and traces were all unpaved and virtually impassable in the wet season. Pack animals were the means of transporting produce.[53]
5. Persons renting had insecure tenure and their practices depleted the soil.
6. Indebtedness was not a major problem; peasants showed a 'marked disinclination' to borrow, since it could impair their equity in real estate. Most borrowing was from village shopkeepers and dealers, for small advances on produce to be delivered.
7. Within the sampling regions, the highest average capital investment on peasant farms was in the south-west ($1,561), with 21.0 per cent of the investment in livestock. The average for Tobago was $1,159, with 16.0 per cent in livestock.[54]
8. Overall, only 1.0 per cent of capital invested in farms was in tools and equipment.
9. The average income of the farm operators was $228 per annum, including cash and the value of produce consumed; the average gross income per family was $462 per annum.[55]
10. Wartime prices for farm products made the average earning of $228 per annum higher than before the war, and more than could normally be expected.
11. The loans disbursed by the ACS were for not more than 12 months, with crops, livestock and other assets as collateral security. The funds were obtained at 3.0 per cent interest and lent at 6.0 per cent. In 1943 the average loan per Tobago member was $48, and was usually for crops and livestock, since the ACS were not allowed to lend for farm dwellings or purchases of land.
12. For the large majority of the farmers in the central, northern and easterly parts of Tobago, 'the amount of productive work available [was] by far too small' and, unless there were increased productive work, 'the standard of living of the average peasant [was] not likely to exhibit any substantial improvements.'[56]
13. 'Peasant economy in the Island of Tobago, therefore, exhibits marginal characteristics in

consequence of the limited resource base, and the increasing pressure of population on the available agricultural land. Improvement is likely to come only if this resource base can be widened through better use of existing land resources[,] and the level of population stabilized.'[57]

Ferrer recommended medium-term credit for up to ten years to allow farmers to buy equipment, consolidate holdings, buy cattle, refinance debts, finance permanent improvements, survey their holdings and establish clear title.[58] In a public lecture in 1944, he stated that for a peasant to have a minimum income of $30.00 per month, (s)he needed 11 acres, of which 5 acres would be in permanent crops, 5 acres in coconuts, and 1 acre in food crops; (s)he also needed to rear cows and pigs. The average peasant farm had 6 acres, mostly in permanent crops.[59]

In general, Ferrer's research showed the need for improved infrastructure and services. Above all, it highlighted the low productivity and incomes of Tobago's peasants by 1943.

The Experience of the Agrarian Crisis in the 1920s

By the 1920s, so stark were the economic realities in Tobago that the keenest observers on the island saw an impasse for both planters and peasants. The forum for discussion was the *Trinidad Guardian*, which gave prominence to Tobago's needs.

One condition that affected all residents was poor sea communications. From 1916 Tobago depended for contact with the outside world only on the SS *Belize*, the coastal steamer that connected the island with Trinidad.[60] One steamer was clearly inadequate. When the *Belize* had to be taken off the run for repairs, there was usually little official effort to secure substitute vessels, and Tobago relied on sloops and schooners instead. The villages that were without motor roads—Castara, Parlatuvier, Bloody Bay, L'Anse Fourmi and Charlotteville—suffered for want of necessary imports; but all producers were adversely affected, especially since the absences of the *Belize* lasted six to seven weeks in some instances.[61] Four other factors contributed to the agrarian stalemate in the 1920s.

First, sustained low prices for cocoa and coconuts affected all sectors of the society. Over the long term, growers were forced to consume their savings from the years of high prices, as their agrarian enterprises became non-viable. Since there was little cash in circulation, the two banks in Tobago closed their doors at the end of December 1923. Estates reduced the number of labourers hired; shops and stores reduced their staff; and, as unemployment rose, the exodus of smallholders, labourers, and young people from the middle strata was renewed. In June 1923 the *Trinidad Guardian* wrote:

In consequence of the present changed situation of the island, due principally to the very low price of produce, ... and the lack of employment, young men and women, and even whole families, have been leaving Tobago weekly for the past several months for New York, via Port-of-Spain; many of these people after spending a few weeks in the U.S.A. have sent back for their relatives and friends. The condition is serious to contemplate.

And in January 1924 the *Guardian* reported:

Business in Scarborough is practically at a standstill. In the principal stores there are just one or two clerks to be seen. The services of the others have been dispensed with. The Banks are closed. ... Tailors and shoemakers and carpenters are now living on their savings.[62]

Second, the renewed emigration highlighted the acute labour shortage on the estates. Throughout the early decades of the twentieth century the planters complained of a shortage of labour, since increasing numbers of the labouring class were becoming peasants who would offer their labour either part-time to the estates or not at all. In 1912 the Warden had stated:

There is, strictly speaking, no purely labouring class in Tobago. Most of those who work are really peasant proprietors. They are accustomed to [being] labourers who work on their own plots and who worked [*sic*] on the Public Roads or on the large estates in order to get some money to cultivate their own plots. But they do not work for others all the year round, and thus the necessity for a regular labour supply is greatly felt. ...[63]

Therefore a persistent issue for the planters was how to create an agricultural proletariat, precisely the condition that the Tobago populace wished to avoid. In the 1920s this was made more acute by renewed emigration.[64] In this context, the planters' response to their need for labour was to restrict access to land for rent and pasture, so as to reduce the options of the peasants.

Thirdly, therefore, the larger estates remained under-cultivated, for want of both capital and labour. However, as long as Tobago remained difficult to reach because of long and tedious journeys on sailing ships, it was difficult for planters to import seasonal labour from the neighbouring islands.[65] And as long as road and sea communications were so minimal, investors in large and small holdings were discouraged from settling.

The fourth area of concern—the increasingly limited access to land by smallholders—was related to the third, the under-use of estate land. It was voiced by George David Hatt, merchant and social analyst, in 1923, and by James A. A. Biggart, Tobago's first elected representative to the Legislative Council, in his Memorandum to the West Indian Sugar Commission in 1929. Both Hatt and Biggart were astute observers of Tobago's conditions.

Hatt argued that of the 16 estates with upwards of 500 acres, 'only the fringe' was cultivated, 'and yet the owners will not or cannot sell a single acre'. Moreover, the planters had combined to stop allowing the villagers to graze livestock on the estates, which had led to the demise of the livestock industry. He noted that almost all the Crown lands had been sold, and argued that the paucity of population could not be overcome unless a substantial tax were imposed on uncultivated lands and lands not in a genuine state of pasturage. If this were done, more land would become available to the state for sale to settlers, and livestock-rearing would be revived.[66]

Biggart's Memorandum began by estimating that the peasants contributed one-half of the exports. He assumed that minor industries were particularly suited to peasant methods of cultivation, because of the restricted and unsteady labour supply in Tobago. Therefore, he called for an improved system of peasant expansion and better sea communications to provide a ready market for their produce. He noted that in south-west Tobago the peasantry was constricted because of the large estates. He examined the main means whereby the smallholder or the landless could gain access to land. These were:

1. metayage, from which the 'profit borders between $3 and $6 per acre', leaving the metayer to supplement his income with food crops and livestock on his metayer holding;

2. the contract system, whereby the grower was let into possession of estate lands for five years, during which he planted cocoa or coconut trees and was paid by the owner for each tree at the end of his tenure;

3. 'free gardens, where the grower enters on the land for three years and cares the plants set out by the owner, getting only the free use of the land as his compensation.'

Biggart predicted that in the following decade, 'these systems [would] cease to exist', and there would be insufficient land for the growing of food crops and livestock, which would lead to great unemployment. Therefore the Government should acquire estates offered for sale, and resell them to peasants in five-acre plots in 'an approved land settlement scheme', in which co-operative methods would be encouraged.[67]

Other submissions to the West Indian Sugar Commission echoed the views of Hatt and Biggart. The Commission reported:

> But the most urgent plea of the memorialists was for facilities to become owners of land.

In the 1930s official reports made similar points on the hunger for land.[68]

Thus, by the end of the 1920s, poor communications, low global prices, a restricted labour market, under-use of the land by the large estates, insufficient land for peasant expansion, and lack of capital for agrarian investment were perceived in the public discourse as among the key factors preventing prosperity in Tobago. All were interrelated.

By 1933 the value of Tobago's exports had fallen drastically since 1916 (Table A1.1). For cocoa, the major crop, Figures 1.1 and 1.2 clearly illustrate that, after the sharp fall in prices from 1920, prices again dropped after 1926, while output was rising.

The estates were experiencing low productivity and profits. This also applied to peasant holdings, for reasons which Ferrer's 1943 study clinically diagnosed, while the opportunities in peasant agriculture for the rising generation were swiftly ending.

12

FIGURE 1.1 **Quantity of Cocoa Exported ('ooo lbs) and Total Value of Cocoa Exports (£), 1916–1933**

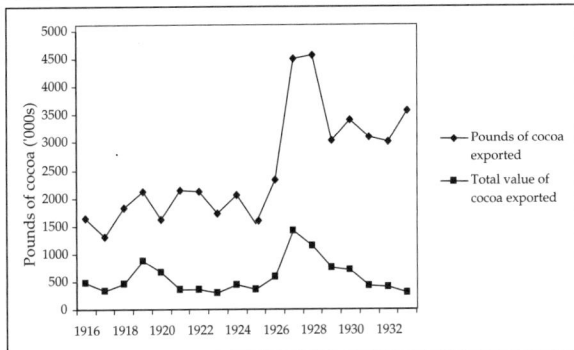

Sources: As for Table A1.1 on which this graph is based.

FIGURE 1.2 **Price per Pound of Cocoa Exported from Tobago, 1916–1933 (£)**

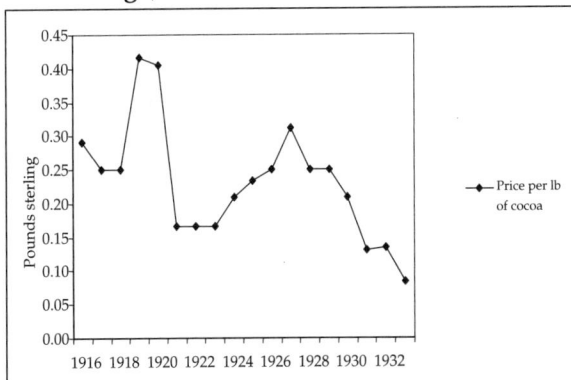

Sources: As for Table A1.1 on which this graph is based.

Tobago's Agriculture, 1950–1962

Foodstuff production fell dramatically after the war ended in 1945. Exports of ground provisions, plantains and green bananas from Tobago to Trinidad fell from 5,382 tons in 1945 to 3,593 tons in 1946.[69] There was a marked net decline in food-crop production between 1950 and 1956 (Table 1.2).

The decline in Tobago's agriculture was often discussed in the Legislative Council in the 1950s. As we show in more detail in Chapter 4, A. P. T. James, Tobago's Member of the Legislative Council (MLC) from 1946 to 1961, repeatedly called for measures to improve the infrastructure and assist agriculture, but little was done by 1956, when the People's National Movement under Dr. Eric Williams formed the first government with powers of self-rule.

Within a few months of assuming office, Williams announced plans to build the Tobago north-coast road, to end the island's 'agricultural benightedness' and enhance its tourism potential. He noted too that Tobago's 'agricultural exports to Trinidad [had] between 1951 and 1955 declined by two-thirds' and its 'imports of vegetables from Trinidad during the same period [had] more than doubled.'[70] Williams recognized that Tobago could have benefited from Colonial Development and Welfare funds provided by the imperial government, and he moved swiftly to invite a team of their specialists, who visited Tobago for two weeks in March/April 1957.

On 7 June 1957, Williams asked the legislature to endorse the recommendations of the Colonial Development and Welfare Team, and to approve an immediate approach to the British Government for funds for a development programme for Tobago, given 'the betrayal of trust' and 'the years of neglect' of the island by previous governments. He stated that the export of ground provisions from Tobago to Trinidad had declined from 118,000 lbs in 1950 to 3,083 lbs in 1955, and plantain exports had fallen from 258,000 lbs to 68,557 lbs in the same period. So meagre was production in Tobago that, while the total income tax paid in the colony was $31 million, Tobago's quota, exclusive of firms paying in Trinidad in respect of their Tobago operations, was only $133,000.[71]

Returning to the subject again in 1958, Williams compared official figures for retail prices in Trinidad and in Tobago for 1920, 1935 and 1956, and argued very correctly that the decline in Tobago's agriculture had begun 'since the end of the first World War.'[72]

As Tobago became a net importer of Caribbean foodstuff, prices of its local foodstuff rose. In 1956 the retail price index for home-produced food in Scarborough was 128, and 118 for imported food, while the indices for Port of Spain were 115 and 113, respectively (1952 prices = 100).[73]

Two reports produced in the late 1950s amply record the state of plantation and peasant agriculture. The first was the *Report of the Team Which Visited Tobago in March/April 1957*; the second was David Niddrie's doctoral research of 1958, later published as *Land Use and Population in Tobago*.[74] Both reports told of senescent coconut estates; cocoa in decline; depleted, ruinate soils, particularly in the south-west; poor husbandry by smallholders; poor marketing facilities; a potential for fisheries that was largely undeveloped; low agricultural incomes; ageing farmers; and a distaste for farming among the younger generation. According to Niddrie, young men stated that they did not wish to be 'cow-boys'. Niddrie also described the peasant holdings as mostly either 'agricultural slums on which all the crimes against good husbandry are committed', or abandoned and 'rapidly merging into the forest cover.'[75] Both reports called for the establishment of a statutory Land Authority in the Courland River Basin to rehabilitate denuded soils.[76]

Commenting on the degraded soils, the Colonial Development and Welfare Team quoted at length one of Tobago's agricultural officers:

It will be appreciated that soon (as is the case now) all the new land will be used up, and the old areas completely exhausted. The poor peasant can shift no longer, and he makes the deteriorating soil poorer, thus becoming poorer himself in the process of time. … The situation assumes the substance and form of its present state in 1956.[77]

For the Team there were several pressing concerns. One was poor feeder roads. Moreover, because Trinidad's officials were 'preoccupied' with Trinidad's needs, they recommended separate, decentralized administrative units for Tobago, to deal with agricultural credit, banana production, development of fisheries, and marketing in general, but especially of livestock and bananas. They noted that livestock production had been 'discouraged by the persistence of primitive marketing methods.'[78]

The Agriculture Department reported for 1961 on peasant production:

Yields of food crops had [sic] continued to be low and acreages planted were disappointing, despite the food crop subsidies. …

The cost of local food stuffs [sic] remained high, quantities being scarce, there being no organised machinery for proper marketing and distribution.[79]

By 1962, owing to government subsidies, the acreages under corn, pigeon peas and sweet potatoes had increased significantly, as seen in Table 1.3.

However, despite the increases in certain crops, the Agriculture Department reported that 'generally' food-crop gardens were 'poorly cultivated', and land tenure arrangements unsatisfactory.[80]

In August 1963, one month before Hurricane Flora, Dr. Williams conducted his Meet the People Tour in Tobago. Nearly every memorandum to him discussed the problem of land titles, and called for abandoned estates to be acquired for the use of peasants.[81] Nine planters offered to sell their estates to the Government. Shortly after the hurricane, the Tobago Planning Team stated that the efforts of the peasantry had been largely 'a waste of resources—land and people.'[82]

It is clear that by 1950 both plantation and peasant agriculture

TABLE 1.3 **Acres under Food Crops in Tobago, 1959–1962**

Crops	Acres			
	1959	1960	1961	1962
Plantains[a]	74	45	75	56
Bananas[a]	66	27	52	N. G.
Corn and pigeon peas	587	399	973	1,874
Other grain crops	—	—	10	N. G.
Sweet potatoes	365	475	278	1,172
Yams	110	168	102	405
Other ground provisions	126	203	213	N. G.
Mixed food crops	65	90	52	193
Green vegetables	9	18	21	N. G.
Total[b]	1,302	1,425	1,776	4,000

Sources: Department of Agriculture, Annual Report for 1961 (Port of Spain n. d.), 50; *Annual Report of the Agricultural Services for the Year 1962* (Port of Spain 1964), 75.

Notes:
[a] Plantains and bananas were interplanted with other crops.
[b] The totals given in the reports for 1959, 1960 and 1961 were 1,590, 1,543 and 1,903, respectively, probably because some items were omitted from the table.
   N. G.: Not given.

in Tobago were collapsing. There were two reasons for this. Firstly, global conditions, especially falling prices for primary commodities, contributed greatly to the non-viability of all the major export crops by the 1930s. Manufactured goods attracted higher unit prices but Tobago, as a colonial producer, was confined to primary production. Secondly, adverse conditions—poor husbandry of the soil, inadequate road and sea communications, meagre credit—caused even food production for local consumption to decline. By 1950 Tobago was a net importer of tropical food of which it had previously been an abundant exporter.

Should more have been done by the state to boost Tobago's agriculture? In the prevailing colonial conditions, was there any agrarian sector that would have benefited from more favourable state policies? Section 2 considers why state intervention was critical for Tobago's agriculture, and Section 3 examines the relevant policies of both the imperial government and the colony's dominant class.

2. THE PIVOTAL ROLE OF THE STATE IN TOBAGO'S DEVELOPMENT

After the collapse of sugar in the 1880s, Tobago's agriculture was never dominated by estates. The emergent peasants were a significant force in the production of cocoa, with at least 5,300 acres as compared to 3,100 on estates in 1938.[83] They also grew all the minor crops except rubber, while maintaining a near monopoly on food crops. Low commodity prices led to the further sale of parts of estates for small holdings and, as the Chamber of Commerce put it in 1938, 'the Planters [sic] misfortune has been the people's opportunity.' By 1938, even the planters and merchants conceded that the peasants were 'the predominant class in Tobago',[84] not only numerically but in their contribution to production and marketing. Given the high importance of the peasantry, and given their low cash incomes, initiatives by the state were crucial for Tobago's agriculture, and therefore to its general development.

Very creditable efforts were made by all the Curators of the Botanic Station, the Agricultural Advisers and their assistants, the Agricultural Instructors, and by the planters and peasants themselves to lift the standard of agriculture. From the closing years of the 1890s, Cocoa Instructors greatly helped all growers to understand how to husband the new crop, and as early as 1900, William John Sanger Tucker, a Tobago planter, received a patent for an invention to ferment cocoa.[85] In addition, the Botanic Station kept seeds and plants of ramie, sisal, onions and other crops for distribution. Moreover, in 1900 and 1901, several head teachers were trained in agriculture and chemistry, and they in turn established agricultural programmes and gardens in schools. By 1903 virtually all the schools had gardens in which the students learned the principles of good husbandry. Annual Agricultural Shows for the schools and the agriculturists were held from 1903 to 1908 and occasionally thereafter, and these competitions helped to sharpen the knowledge and skills of the participants.

Early in the twentieth century, the agricultural officers used every means to reach all levels of the population. For example, Henry I. Millen, the first Curator of the Botanic Station, read a paper on agriculture to the Tobago Debating Club in February 1902, through which he reached both farmers and teachers who had recently begun to offer agriculture as a subject in schools. Some of the popular organizations, especially the Scarborough Brotherhood, which was started in the Methodist Church in 1909, organized lectures and discussions on public issues which were well attended. Much teaching on agriculture was done under its auspices, and W. E. Broadway, the Curator, commented in 1910 that 'the backbone to some extent of the agricultural section of the community' met at the Brotherhood's meetings. He also reported that the night lectures helped to allay the suspicions of the peasants against officers visiting their plots, and resulted in improvement in peasant practices.[86] In June 1910 Broadway congratulated the Brotherhood because two of its members, Henry John and James Blackman, both employees at the Botanic Station, had become, 'after numberless failures', the first persons in Trinidad and Tobago to bud cocoa plants. John had been the first to succeed.[87]

Agricultural Credit Societies (ACS) were started in 1917, and Tobago pioneered co-operative cocoa fermentaries from 1929. Together, the ACS and the fermentaries became an effective forum for popular education on the best agrarian practices, particularly for cocoa.

Thus, much had been accomplished in extension services by 1930. But with little staff, the early momentum was not sustained. Moreover, access roads, sea communications, wharves, jetties, irrigation, agricultural credit, and facilities for breeding and marketing of livestock remained woefully inadequate. Both planters and peasants shared common problems: although there were differences and often conflicts between them, they both were subordinate to Trinidad's dominant class. In effect, neither planters nor peasants could fully achieve their economic potential.

As for the peasants, they were the group most affected by the poor infrastructure and services, but they had least influence on the Government. Although they advanced both formal and informal co-operative efforts beyond the levels reached in the rest of the BWI, the magnitude of the needs for infrastructure and services was such that they were least likely to be able to furnish them by their own efforts.

The point is that nowhere in the Caribbean could agriculture in general and peasant agriculture in particular be developed and sustained without ample state support. Lord Olivier's West Indian Sugar Commission of 1929 commented:

> ... a peasantry capable both of maintaining itself and of growing exportable produce cannot be created off-hand. It takes a long time to learn to be self-supporting, and further time to learn how to be prosperous by producing a marketable surplus. It may be said that nowhere in the British West Indies, except in Jamaica, has resolute, serious and intelligent attention as yet been given to this double problem, notwithstanding the strong recommendations of Sir H. Norman's [West India Royal] Commission [1897].[88]

Agreeing with Olivier, W. Arthur Lewis argued for state policies to support the peasantry on two important grounds.

The first was their role as producers of export crops. In 1936 Lewis stressed that though the productivity of plantation wage labourers was higher than that of peasants, the standard of living of peasants was higher, because they lost less of their output to the propertied classes through rents, interest and profits. Moreover, Lewis recognized that peasants could produce certain crops (for example, cocoa) as efficiently as estates. Therefore there was an 'overwhelming case for the pursuance of a peasant policy'.[89]

The second reason for a state policy to support the peasantry addressed their role as food-crop producers. Lewis wrote in 1955:

> In practice in most backward economies the sector which usually responds least well to growth in other sectors, and which therefore acts as a brake on all economic growth, is the agricultural sector producing food for home consumption. This is because, *when agriculture is in the hands of small farmers, the introduction of innovations depends more upon government initiative than upon the initiative of private entrepreneurs* ... To increase the output of peasants, however, requires a number of actions which are *essentially in the government sphere*; above all, considerable expenditure on agricultural research and agricultural extension, as well as expenditures on roads, rural water supplies, agricultural credit facilities, etc.

And again:

> The secret of rapid agricultural progress in the under-developed countries is to be found much more in agricultural extension, in fertilizers, in new seeds, in pesticides and in water supplies than in altering the size of the farm, in introducing machinery, or in getting rid of middlemen in the marketing process.[90]

Thus, because of the high proportion of peasants among Tobago's farmers, and because of their dual potential as efficient producers of crops for both export and local consumption, government provision of infrastructure and services was crucial if agriculture were to advance.

3. STATE POLICIES ON AGRICULTURE AND DEVELOPMENT

Trinidad and Tobago was a Crown Colony. This and Tobago's subordinate status as a Ward in the colony were the fundamental facts that determined whether and how Tobago's economic potential would be fulfilled. Despite the remarkable growth in Tobago's production and exports between 1900 and 1920, several factors combined to account for the failure of successive Governments of Trinidad and Tobago to respond adequately to Tobago's needs. These are now discussed.

Colonial Office Opinion

The prevailing ethos of the Colonial Office was a great obstacle. The 1897 West India Royal Commission urged that peasantries and crop diversification be promoted, so as to end the system of estate monoculture. However, the Commission fully recognized that the dominant planter class, concerned with getting cheap, regular labour for their estates, would oppose promotion of the peasantry. Therefore, the Commission declared it the special duty of the British Government to see that the welfare of the general public was not sacrificed to that of a small but influential minority. On the Commission's recommendation, the Imperial Department of Agriculture was established in Barbados in 1898, with specialists encouraging crop research, diversification, and dissemination of information, including education in the schools.[91]

The imperial Treasury between 1897 and 1905 gave £860,000 in grants and loans to the BWI, much of it to save the sugar industry and to settle public debts.[92] To soften Tobago's loss of status in becoming a Ward (and to appease the Trinidad legislature), the UK also granted £5,000 in support of the island's agriculture—in fact to establish the Botanic Station—for the period 1899 to 1905. In 1920 the Imperial College of Tropical Agriculture (ICTA) was established at St. Augustine, Trinidad, as a research and training centre for scientific agriculture.[93]

However, these British initiatives were minimal. On the one hand, the West Indies were not important to Great Britain. On the other, successive British Governments had little interest in spending for colonial development, before the global depression of the 1920s and the resulting unrest in the colonies forced them to do so. The dominant ideology on public spending and finance in the Colonial Office of the late nineteenth and early twentieth centuries was free trade, financial austerity and *laissez-faire*—minimal state intervention in the economy.

Lord (Sydney) Olivier, a Colonial Office official from 1882, Secretary to the 1897 West India Royal Commission, Governor of Jamaica (1907–1913), and Chairman of the West Indian Sugar Commission (1929), was a perceptive observer of British colonial policy. He stated that before the tenure of Lloyd George as Prime Minister (from 1916 to 1922), there was always reluctance to allow borrowing for development works, and 'Reproductive Expenditure' (spending that would bring increased government revenue) was upheld as a cardinal principle of public finance.[94] Hyam also records that, as early as 1905–1908, the long-term Colonial Office policy was towards 'disengagement from the West Indies by means of a federation', and that the West Indies 'were sacrificed to considerations of wider imperial policy'. Therefore, on development issues in the region, the British Government 'did little more than shuffle its feet in embarrassment.'[95]

In response to the depression after World War I and to growing colonial unrest, the imperial Colonial Development and Welfare Act of 1929 was passed. It allocated £1 million per annum to be disbursed on the advice of a Colonial Development Advisory Committee (CDAC), which would consider schemes applying for assistance. The CDAC could not initiate projects, and responded only to the proposals of the local governments. Meredith states that the CDAC, though supposedly aimed at raising colonial living standards, functioned primarily to promote and protect the commerce and industry of the UK, through facilitating access to raw materials and markets for UK investors. Industrial development was not encouraged in the colonies, and agriculture, the backbone of colonial economies, received only 6.0 per cent of the total assistance.[96] Only two Tobago projects were considered for Colonial Development and Welfare funding, and neither was successful.

The first was the application of the Tobago Producers Association to the Empire Marketing Board (EMB) in 1930 for a grant of £1,000 per annum for three years. The request was to meet 'foundation expenses in organising the ... marketing of Cocoa, Coconuts, Fruit, Grain crops, live stock and ground provisions, produced by large and small holders alike, on a co-operative basis.' The Association's main object was to 'band together the 7,193 large and small land owners and cultivators' to grade, pack, store, and market their produce. The EMB suggested that the Colonial Office refer the application to the CDAC. Nothing appears to have resulted from this, and in 1934 the Trinidad and Tobago Government agreed to lend the Association £4,530, mainly because it had the support of the largest planters.[97]

17

The second application to the CDAC was in 1931 by the TLGCA, for a grant of £500 to enable it to complete the building and equipping of its factory to process limes. In June 1930, the Association of some 84 members had begun to produce raw lime juice with a small mill, since the output of limes in Tobago, estimated at four or five thousand barrels per annum, thitherto went to waste. Although both the Governor and the Colonial Office commended the project as worthwhile, the CDAC refused the request, on the grounds that, without UK assistance, the sum needed would be forthcoming from other sources.[98]

In 1940 the British Parliament passed another Colonial Development and Welfare Act, providing £5 million per annum for the entire Empire for ten years. A subsequent 1945 Act extended the period to 1956 and increased the available funds to £120 million, and further Acts of 1949 and 1950 increased the total available to £140 million. Under the 1940 Act, a Department of Colonial Development and Welfare, headed by a Comptroller, was established in Barbados to channel aid and advisers to the regional governments. Active government and state initiatives to promote development and welfare became the avowed imperial stance.[99]

However, the shift in British strategy was merely an attempt to preserve the imperial system by changing the mode of control.[100] The British Chancellor of the Exchequer openly stated in 1940 that the Colonial Development and Welfare Acts were only a gesture 'to justify ourselves before world opinion as a great Colonial power', while the Secretary of State for the Colonies, Malcolm Macdonald, who piloted the 1940 Act, made similar remarks.[101] Indeed, all colonial reforms were concessions mainly to secure Britain's political position. One Colonial Office official minuted in 1948 that Trinidad was in need of 'drastic constitutional reform' towards 'a really democratic foundation', 'to avoid an explosion which might shake the foundations of the British position in the Caribbean.'[102]

Within the BWI, 'development and welfare' accomplished little. As Gordon Lewis puts it, development became 'a multitude of minor schemes'; and the Social Welfare Departments, in the words of Thomas S. Simey, the first Adviser to the Comptroller, were 'handy administrative dustbins in which to get rid of inconvenient governmental functions'.[103]

The laissez-faire approach, while advocating minimal state activity, was always active in the interests of the dominant class in the metropolis and the colonies. Throughout the BWI, planter-controlled legislatures restricted access to Crown land, subsidized immigration, developed roads and other infrastructure in their own interests, supported the planter class, and ensured that the burden of taxation was borne by the labouring class. Trinidad and Tobago were both apt examples of this. The high public expenditure on research, grants, loans, subsidies and other support for the failing cocoa planters between 1920 and 1940 also demonstrated this fact. The legislature in 1940 agreed to invest a further four million dollars over ten years, even though it was readily apparent that the expense would not make the majority of estates profitable.[104]

Despite the lack of interest from the UK, could local policy have been influenced to promote Tobago's interests? Chapter 4 shows how in-effective were Tobago's nominated and elected representatives in the Legislative Council. We now examine other possible sources of influence on the policy-making process.

Possible Sources of Influence on the Policy-Making Process

Concerned Governors

If the UK Government evinced no particular interest in promoting agricultural development in Tobago, neither did the dominant class in Trinidad, although a few of its members owned Tobago estates. Only a very enterprising Governor could have overridden the apathy in the dominant class concerning Tobago, but none such emerged. Lord Stanmore, formerly Sir Arthur Gordon, Trinidad's Governor (1866–1870), who had done much to legalize squatters and make Crown lands available to peasants, testified in 1910: 'it requires a very great deal of courage …, a great deal of self-reliance, to stand up against' the influence of the wealthiest planters.[105]

The Governors most sympathetic to Tobago in the first forty years of the Union were Sir Claud Hollis (1929–1936) and Sir Murchison Fletcher

(1936–1937). Of Hollis, S. M. Campbell, a Colonial Office official, minuted in 1930:

> I learnt incidentally the other day from Sir C. Hollis's ADC [aide-de-camp] that the Gov. is keen on Tobago: and it is about time some notice was taken of it.[106]

Yet there were no tangible benefits from the Hollis regime. Fletcher's tenure, begun in 1936, was abruptly ended in December 1937 by the British Government after the labour rebellion of June–July 1937, because he appeared to the planters and merchants to be weak, vacillating, and far too sympathetic to labour.[107]

Planters and Merchants

All classes and strata in Tobago were affected by its relative isolation after 1906. However, though the planters and merchants combined to seek their interests, they were unable to affect government policy significantly. The Tobago Planters Association (TPA) was founded in 1905, and both planters and merchants established a Chamber of Commerce in 1936.

The planters were mostly men of modest means. Henry L. Thornton, the nominated member for Tobago in the Legislative Council (1903–1913), applying for a special allowance to meet his expenses for attending the Council's sittings, explained that George H. McEachrane II (the previous representative, who had been refused a similar allowance) had stopped attending because of the cost. Thornton stated, 'We are a small community, a community of men of small means and incomes.'[108]

The merchants were also relatively small. Apart from Millers' Stores Limited, an English firm with branches in both Trinidad and Tobago, the shops were mainly enterprises of Tobagonians and small Barbadian, Grenadian or Trinidadian investors. The small internal market, the need to import and export through the Trinidad merchant houses, and poor communications allowed them little scope for growth and diversification. Thus, they wielded little power or influence over the colony's affairs.

Since Tobago was not regarded as integral to a long-term agricultural strategy for the colony, its planters and merchants, subordinate in means, were also subordinate in influence vis-à-vis their Trinidad counterparts. Tobago's planters had little influence in the Trinidad Chamber of Commerce,

the Agricultural Society, and other organizations which usually affected government policy. The notable exception was George de Nobriga, the owner of Lowlands Estate, who was director of several companies and a pillar of the main organizations of planters and merchants in the 1930s and 1940s. Despite his influence as Member of the Legislative Council from 1938 to 1946, between 1900 and 1946 there was no *consistent* publicizing of Tobago's needs in Trinidad forums, and little pressure to which the Government felt obliged to respond.

At the same time, the power of the *Trinidad* planters and merchants, through their representatives who were nominated *unofficials* in the Legislative Council, was enhanced after the 1903 Water Riots in Port of Spain. In those events, an angry crowd burnt down the Red House, the building that housed the Registrar General's office, the office of the Sub-Intendant of Crown Lands, and the Legislative Council. The Commission of Enquiry into the unrest noted that the riots were related to a widespread desire for representative government, and that the Government had been insensitive to public opinion. Cynically taking 'public opinion' to mean that of the dominant class, Joseph Chamberlain, the Secretary of State, advised the Governor, Sir Alfred Moloney, to defer to the unofficials in the Legislative Council, and to consult them on legislation and expenditure. Arguing that the unofficials should recognize 'the strength of their own position', Chamberlain stated that both Governors and the Secretary of State would be reluctant to override 'the convictions or even the prejudices of men of high standing and independent position'.[109]

The majority of Tobago's planters and merchants were marginal members of these highest echelons of Trinidad society. Further, since Tobago had little unrest and was not strategic to Trinidad's affairs, it was not seen as meriting special attention above other Wards with similar problems. As a result, Tobago languished in neglect.

The Intelligentsia

Tobago produced a wealth of effective writers and speakers on the island's condition, most of them teachers. The successors of the older generation of writers—George David Hatt, Mitchell J. Prince, James Biggart—in the 1930s were younger people,

19

some of them graduates of the Bishop's High School. Most of their activities are discussed in Section 7 of this chapter. The foremost was Louis Anthony Peters (1875–1954[?]), a retired head teacher who became a powerful activist, speaker and writer in all forums on behalf of agriculture. Many teachers were part of the District Agricultural Societies and ACS, in particular Fitz G. Maynard and Laurence Edwards; and Edwards helped to form the Tobago Peasant Proprietors Association (TPPA) in 1939. Others wrote articles in the pages of *The Tobagonian*, a monthly magazine appearing between 1938 and 1950. However, they had little effect on government policy.

Workers' and Peasants' Organizations

Before the 1937 strikes in Trinidad, organizations of peasants and workers were effective at raising public consciousness, but they gained little by way of reforms. In 1938 Lord Olivier testified to the House of Lords about the strength of the dominant class in Trinidad:

> There is a very strong planters' association in Trinidad. The organisation of capital in Trinidad is stronger than in any of the other West Indian Islands, and the organisation of labour is practically nil, and so the labourers are in a worse position for collective bargaining than they are anywhere else.[110]

There was only an embryonic proletariat in Tobago by 1940. The Trinidad Workingmen's Association (from 1934, the Trinidad Labour Party) under Captain Arthur A. Cipriani was the dominant labour and political organization in Tobago from 1929 to early 1937. Its strategy of giving priority to constitutional change, while raising the consciousness of workers and peasants against Crown Colony rule, produced few reforms by 1937. There was no other mobilization of peasants for political ends before the TPPA was started in June 1939, and all proposals for change were shelved because World War II broke out soon afterwards.[111]

In sum, no social group emerged with enough political influence to change the policies on Tobago.

4. GROWING OFFICIAL AWARENESS OF THE NEED TO BOOST FOOD PRODUCTION

After prolonged protests from Tobago in the 1920s about poor sea communications, a Sea Communications Committee was appointed in May 1928. It concluded that, although Tobago's agricultural exports had greatly increased since 1897, 'had a better [steamship] service been provided agricultural development would have been even more pronounced.'[112] Because of poor handling of produce, many planters shipped by sloops. The peasants remained dependent on the two government steamers, *Trinidad* and *Tobago*, which replaced the *Belize* in 1931.

It took the depression of the 1920s and 1930s to move Trinidad's officials to consider supporting the peasantry. Only in 1930 did official thinking in Trinidad first notice that peasant development and crop diversification had to be integral to the colony's progress. The 1929 West Indian Sugar Commission (Lord Olivier, Chairman), harking back to the 1897 West India Royal Commission of which Olivier had been Secretary, had made the point. Yet, between 1900 and 1930, food production had been important only during World War I. The depression of the 1920s brought starkly to the fore the issues of food supply and food security. For the first time in the century, the 1930 Administration Report on the Department of Agriculture complained of 'deplorably large sums' spent on imported food. It stated:

> ... there is far too great a tendency to neglect the growth of food crops for local consumption ... the present position is not sound.

In 1930 the landed cost of imported food was over £1.6 million, or 75.0 per cent of the value of agricultural exports for that year.[113] Later, the 1948 Economics Committee remarked:

> The need for Government interference in peasant agriculture first became apparent during the depression of the 1930's.[114]

Despite the growing concerns of the Department of Agriculture, Tobago was not seen as *integral* to the agricultural issues of the colony before 1938. Important surveys of the cocoa and coconut industries were conducted in 1930, and neither included Tobago. When the Agricultural Society testified to the Moyne Commission in 1939, it did not even mention Tobago.[115]

Between 1930 and 1938, virtually all the annual reports of the Department of Agriculture bemoaned the high cost of food imports and the low local production. By 1938, impending war in Europe made food supply and food security serious public issues, and there was more willingness to give resources to peasant agriculture generally. In this context, the decision was taken by a wide cross-section of Tobago residents to elect George de Nobriga to the Legislative Council in 1938, in the hope that, as an influential planter from the dominant class, he would be able to influence government policy in Tobago's interest.

De Nobriga's greatest success in Tobago's affairs was in getting the appointment of a committee to examine the adequacy of the coastal steamer service and to make recommendations. The committee included J. F. Nicoll, the Deputy Colonial Secretary (Chairman), and de Nobriga himself. It was appointed in April 1938, and its report was published with the short title, Tobago Coastal Service Report (hereafter the Nicoll Report), Council Paper No. 3 of 1939.

The Nicoll Committee understood clearly that its terms of reference were too narrow, and it defined the issue as the entire development of Tobago's economy, particularly in agriculture and tourism. Its members saw Tobago as strategic for the colony's food supply; and, for the first time in four decades, officials were willing to channel adequate resources for the island's development. This is the major significance of the Nicoll Report.

The Nicoll Report

The Nicoll Report was a milestone in official thinking on Tobago. It stated that transport and economic development were closely related, and that investment in the former must be accompanied by a vigorous policy to develop Tobago's resources. The Report called for diversification of Tobago's agriculture, particularly through food crops, livestock and poultry, to offset the high food imports. It showed that the colony's imports of foodstuff and animals had risen steadily from $3,205,959 in 1935 to $3,926,729 in 1937.

The Report recommended:

1. an immediate staff increase in Tobago's Agriculture Department;
2. greater co-operative marketing of produce;
3. an urgent survey of the area between Charlotteville and Castara, preliminary to construction of a road linking the two;
4. better roads and motor transport service;
5. improved accommodation for livestock on the steamers and wharves.

It also called for a new, fast steamer for passengers to facilitate domestic travel and increasing tourist traffic, while keeping the two existing vessels in service. The intention was that the coastal service should be maintained until roads were developed, after which the steamers would call only at Scarborough and King's Bay; the latter would need a jetty and storage facilities.[116]

Late in 1938, the Report of the Estimates Committee on a Comprehensive Development Programme to be carried out within the years 1939–1944 was laid before the Legislative Council. The major Tobago expenditure was to be $440,000 to upgrade the Windward Road and $680,000 to develop the Northside Road, out of a budget for roads of $3,057,500. It was the first time in 40 years that so large a share of the budget was allocated for public works in Tobago. The Estimates Committee stated that the expenditure on these roads was

intended to implement the recent recommendations of the Tobago Development Committee [the Nicoll Committee] which have as their object the acceleration of the economic development of that Island. The construction of the roads will enable the Coastal Steamers to dispense with calls at places around the Island and will open up good agricultural land.[117]

With the outbreak of war in September 1939, the Nicoll Report and the Report of the Estimates Committee were both shelved. No attempt to develop Tobago's resources on such a scale was made again until 1957, following the report of the team from Colonial Development and Welfare. Its provisions could hardly be implemented before Hurricane Flora in September 1963, by which time Tobago's agriculture had dwindled into insignificance.

After 1939 de Nobriga became quiescent in the legislature. Apart from laying petitions from groups in Tobago before the Council, he said almost nothing on Tobago's behalf, although from 1944 he was a member of the Executive Council. By 1944, it was Roy Joseph and E. Vernon Wharton, representing Victoria and the Eastern Counties in Trinidad, respectively, and Thomas M. Kelshall, a nominated unofficial, who repeatedly questioned the Government on the appalling coastal steamer service, the poor health services, and other woes of Tobago. By then, the Government's stock response was that the matters were under consideration. Ironically, on the wartime Grow More Food Campaign, Government admitted that

> until road communications and shipping facilities are improved the agricultural resources of the Island cannot be fully developed.[118]

5. WILFUL NEGLECT, 1946–1956

Had the political will existed, more could have been done sooner to support Tobago's agriculture.

At the first elections by adult suffrage in 1946, the Tobago voters returned Alphonso Philbert Theophilus James, a man of peasant origins. James conducted a militant campaign for Tobago's development. Health services, education, electricity, roads, a deepwater harbour for Scarborough, all were the subject of several demands from him. Further, on behalf of what he often called 'the Cinderella I happen to represent', on countless occasions he demanded the replacement of the coastal steamers which, by the 1950s, were regarded as 'two old tubs' and even, as the *Tobago Herald* put it, as 'two old calabashes'.[119]

In May 1948 James, L. A. Peters and an unknown third person completed a Memorandum to the Secretary of State, which James presented in person on Wednesday 2 June 1948 at a meeting at the Colonial Office, London.

This 1948 'James Memorandum' admitted that Tobago had benefited 'substantially' by its Union with Trinidad, but called for greater attention to the potential of the island. It outlined the usual catalogue of needs, and proposed dairy industries, manufacturing industries for cocoa, improved methods for fishing, fish-processing factories, and the electrification of the island.[120]

In 1950 James also influenced the County Council, of which he was Chairman, to send a resolution to the Secretary of State asking for two seats in the Legislative Council for Tobago. In 1950 too, he founded the Tobago Citizens Political and Economic Party (TCPEP). The TCPEP protested against the fact that there was no Tobago representative in the Executive Council, and called for a special Ministry for Tobago Affairs. Having waited in vain for initiatives from the local Government, James sought direct imperial aid. In August 1951 he returned to the Colonial Office to present a memorandum of the TCPEP demanding, *inter alia*, a British Government grant-in-aid to Tobago of £1.5 million.[121]

In 1956 and 1957 James told the Legislative Council that, on board ship from the West Indies in 1948, he had discussed his Memorandum with the Secretary of State, who then arranged for him to meet with Brigadier Mount, Chairman of the Colonial Development Corporation. Mount and he spoke for three hours. These officials had indicated their willingness to support Colonial Development and Welfare grants for Tobago, *if the Government of Trinidad and Tobago initiated the requests*. Although James had called upon the Government in 1949 to follow up these intimations, it had done nothing.[122]

The Chief Minister, Dr. Eric Williams, supported James' point about the Government's failure to seek Colonial Development and Welfare grants for Tobago. In 1957, in a long, impassioned address to the Legislative Council, Williams outlined the 'neglect and betrayal of trust' which Tobago had undergone since the Union. He argued that, had the Government wished to redress the Tobago situation, it could have availed itself of Development and Welfare funds, $164 million of which had been granted to the BWI after 1946 for agriculture and communications. All the Eastern Caribbean islands had received grants. However, Tobago's infrastructure, apart from the expansion of the Hillsborough Dam, started in 1947 to provide island-wide pipeborne water, remained the same until 1951 when work on the Scarborough jetty, which had begun and ceased in 1946, was resumed. Williams concluded that:

> Tobago had exchanged the neglect of United Kingdom Imperialism for the neglect of Trinidad Imperialism.[123]

The surviving records show that James and Williams were correct concerning the lack of political will in Trinidad. In 1943 the Comptroller of Development and Welfare, Sir Frank Stockdale, reporting on his department for 1940–1942, noted that Trinidad and Tobago, because of its 'satisfactory budgetary position', would receive UK funds only for BWI schemes located in Trinidad.[124] However, in 1946 the Government of Trinidad and Tobago applied for loans to finance a 10-year plan for major development works. It also received a Colonial Development and Welfare grant of $2.4 million to rebuild and extend the hospitals at Port of Spain, San Fernando, and St. Ann's, and to construct the Caura Sanatorium. The Tobago hospital received nothing.[125]

By 1951 the Government had borrowed $15 million for major development works, and had received Colonial Development and Welfare grants totalling at least $7.2 million. But the only major Tobago project from 1946 to 1951 was the Hillsborough Dam water scheme costing an estimated $1,920,000. After 1950 minimal harbour improvements for Scarborough were resumed at an estimated cost of $214,775. In 1950 a Colonial Development and Welfare grant of $1,550,000 was approved for a school building programme; out of the surplus balances from this, Tobago received new schools with land at Bon Accord, Speyside and Montgomery.[126] In 1956 Tobago still had poor health facilities, no island-wide electricity supply, and no deepwater harbour. Poor road and sea communications remained a hindrance to agriculture and tourism.

The Colonial Office response to the memoranda of James and his colleagues in the Tobago County Council and the TCPEP was to sidestep the issue. They objected to the principle and precedent of special representation for Tobago in the local and Federal legislatures, since it was inconsistent with Tobago's constitutional status as a Ward. They refused an imperial grant-in-aid on the grounds that Colonial Development and Welfare funds had already been provided for economic development.[127] In essence, the British passed the buck on Tobago to the Trinidad and Tobago authorities, whom they would not override.

The local pace of reform was so slow, however, that though gradual improvements in the infrastructure were made in the 1950s, it was a case of too little done too late. In particular, road

works and the coastal steamers were ignored until after 1956. In 1957 both coastal steamers, which had been heavily worked and badly neglected for decades, were declared unseaworthy. Large parts of their hulls could be easily broken off by hand. Williams told the Legislative Council that it was

> one of the worst disgraces in public administration which could ever characterise any country in the world. ... This is what Trinidad has done for Tobago![128]

6. AGRICULTURAL POLICY IN TRINIDAD AND TOBAGO, 1940–1956

We must now ask three pertinent questions. First, why did the Government not implement the proposals of the Nicoll Report after the Second World War? Second, given that the Government energetically put in place the development works planned for Trinidad, why did Tobago slide in its scale of priorities despite the consistent appeals of A. P. T. James and others? Third, if the global markets for primary products were largely outside of local control, why was there little sustained effort to support food-crop production? An examination of the policy documents shows a marked shift in official thinking after 1945. This, taken together with all that this chapter has argued, gives the most acceptable explanation for the demise of Tobago's agriculture by the 1950s.

The Moyne Commission and the Agricultural Policy Committee

The Moyne Commission in 1939 argued that 'the problem of the West Indies is essentially agrarian'. The population was growing faster than ever; technical advances were decreasing the need for labour and producing greater output per person; the traditional export crops could not therefore provide employment for the rapidly growing population, especially with declining market prospects. Moyne's solution was to create alternative employment in secondary industries based on agriculture, rather than to depend on primary exports. Moyne saw the need, therefore, for 'practically an agricultural revolution' to foster mixed farming, with strategies designed to move the BWI away from reliance on primary production for export. Indeed, the Report argued that the earnings from exports were merely used to import foodstuff such as milk, butter, flour and saltfish, much of which could be locally produced. Moyne did not regard industrialization as a feasible option for the BWI.[129]

Increasingly, senior officials agreed on the need to cultivate more food crops. In 1938 the Memorandum of the Department of Agriculture to the Moyne Commission analysed the estimated costs of local food production vis-à-vis imported products. Its conclusion stated that there was a 'strong economic reason', *both for the colony and for the smallholder*, to produce more food. In 1940 the Governor, Sir Hubert Young, made an impassioned statement to the Legislative Council about the need for Grow More Food and Eat More Local Food Campaigns if the colony were to meet its development expenses.[130]

These views on the agrarian question were reflected in the *Report of the Agricultural Policy Committee of Trinidad and Tobago*, published in two parts in 1943. World War II had a profound impact on Trinidad and Tobago society. Thousands of workers left sugar and cocoa estates to construct and maintain the military bases of the United States Government. Food imports could not be maintained because of the diversion of shipping to military uses; moreover, German submarines sank so many of the vessels plying to Trinidad that a food crisis arose in 1942. Therefore, in 1942 the Government announced a Grow More Food Campaign. In this context, the Agricultural Policy Committee saw the need for more 'self-sufficient systems' and for greater attention to animal husbandry.

The Committee's Report called for a complete overhaul of agriculture. It advocated land reform, mixed farming and crop diversification, forest policy, soil surveys, regional planning on a limited scale, land settlements, central experimental stations, and better extension services, credit facilities, and infrastructure such as housing, water, electricity, roads and other means of communication. The Committee aimed at establishing a 'balance between plantation and peasant farming, and specialised and self-sufficient systems of agriculture'.[131]

Tobago was not forgotten. Noting that Tobago's progress depended on production for sale in Trinidad, the Report stated:

This trade is capable of great development which cannot be achieved, however, without considerable improvement both in communications and in the facilities for accepting and storing produce or maintaining live stock at the terminal ports.

There were also detailed recommendations for the upgrading of Tobago's Stock Farm to allow it to become a rearing and breeding centre for Trinidad, Tobago, and the Leeward and Windward Islands.[132]

The views of the Agricultural Policy Committee received the full support of the Comptroller for Development and Welfare, Sir Frank A. Stockdale. Asked to advise on several matters, Stockdale insisted that the need for mixed farming was 'clearly apparent' for cane farmers and smallholders in Trinidad, and for 'some of the hill-side cultivations in parts of Tobago'. The combination of livestock and crops, which he also commended to the cocoa planters, would make for better use of the soil. He recommended the reorganization of the Tobago Stock Farm, which he called 'a farm in name only', and a number of measures to promote the rearing of poultry, rabbits and pigs, and the making of butter and cheese.[133]

The Government endorsed the 1943 Report, but did not adopt it, in the light of its clear financial implications amid low commodity prices.[134]

The Economics Committee, 1948

In the first Administration Report of the Director of Agriculture after the war (1945), the Agricultural Policy Committee Report was accepted as the ideal to which funds and efforts would be directed.[135] However, this policy approach did not last long. In September 1947, an Economics Committee, chaired by Sir John Shaw, Governor, was appointed 'to review the whole broad field of finance, economics, production and development'. The *Report of the Economics Committee* reveals a shift in thinking that coloured official policy and strategy in the early 1950s.

First, the Report gave a sober analysis of the declining importance of agriculture in the visible trade of the colony between 1936–1938 and 1943–1945. When domestic exports for those years were compared, the total value rose from nearly $31 million to nearly $47 million, while the contribution of the oil industry, averaging $19.5 million in 1936–1938, rose to $37 million, an increase of 90.0 per cent. Oil and asphalt accounted for 67.0 per cent of total exports in the first period, 79.0 per cent in the second. In contrast, in the first period, sugar and cocoa combined accounted for $8.6 million or 27.0 per cent of the value of exports; in the second, for $5 million or, correspondingly, less than 11.0 per cent. Exports of coffee had declined by about 25.0 per cent in value, and banana exports had almost disappeared. By 1946, the value of domestic exports was $58 million, of which oil and asphalt had risen to $45 million, these industries accounting for 79.0 per cent of the total exports. Sugar exports were valued at just over $6.5 million, and cocoa at $1.2 million, together accounting for only 13.0 per cent of domestic exports. Although sugar and coconut exports had risen in quantity and value, the prospects for export agriculture in general were not promising.[136]

Analysing the bleak outlook for the agricultural export crops, the Economics Committee was 'forced to the conclusion that there is no new crop which holds out sufficient promise to enable it to fill the void left by cocoa.'[137] Therefore, it advocated the boosting of sugar and citrus, the two most promising industries.

Second, the Economics Committee took the view that the BWI had developed an exchange economy, producing commodities for which they were best suited and importing the rest. Specialization and the comparative advantages of international trade offered prospects of high productivity and high living standards. Therefore, it called for increased mechanization and high productivity in export agriculture, 'a "Grow More Food" campaign *as a temporary measure* to tide the Colony over the world-wide shortage of food, and the development of peasant agriculture.'[138]

Concerning food imports, the Report noted that the main imports were cereals (especially flour), dairy products, meat and fish, mostly imported from countries whose natural and technical advantages were far superior to those of the West Indies. It also argued that, despite the successful food campaign of 1942 to 1945, food imports continued to grow in quantity and value, because of population increases and higher living standards. Its conclusion was that local production could augment but not replace imported products.

The Economics Committee proposed to develop peasant agriculture through the establishment of land settlement schemes with the necessary infrastructure and services. These, perforce, because of the high costs involved, would be possible only on a very small scale, with a limited number of new farmers. Although the Report mentioned the need for import substitution of poultry and eggs, very little was said of the peasants who were in established settlements. The Committee therefore came firmly down on the side of specialization in export staples, with only *temporary* measures to boost local food production. Its proposals reflected the fact that the political weight of the planters was far greater than that of the peasantry!

The 1948 Report laid the basis for the establishment of Pioneer Industries in manufacturing from 1950, and for the development thrust towards industrialization. This policy was intensified after the People's National Movement came to power in 1956. However, as Terrence Farrell points out, the Caribbean Governments timidly promoted industrialization—for import replacement, and not for export or for import displacement. (The latter would have required strategies to reduce *both* the final products *and* the production inputs that were imported.)[139]

It is ironic that even though the Economics Committee saw the need to produce certain manufactured goods locally, it left food consumption—even of items that could be easily and cheaply grown locally—to the workings of the global market.

In some respects, the Committee's analysis dovetailed with that of Sir Arthur Lewis, the distinguished development economist, whose ideas were used extensively in the post-war British Caribbean. Lewis, testifying to the Moyne Commission, had made the point that 'there is no crop through which the peasant can grow rich as he did on cocoa.' His view was that little confidence could be reposed in agriculture as the *sole* economic base, and that the West Indies had to use their large supplies of labour to produce manufactured goods for export. But among his recommendations was the promotion of a peasantry, a view that he had clearly stated in his 1936 paper on 'The Evolution of the Peasantry in the British West Indies', and which he repeated in his 1939 study, *Labour in the West Indies*.[140]

In his 1950 paper, 'The Industrialization of the BWI', Lewis advocated a reduction in the number of smallholdings of 5 acres or less, and the mechanization of agriculture on 50-acre farms; the resulting surplus labour would be employed in the industrial sector. However, his concern was with developing *both* agricultural and industrial sectors: an industrial programme was *essential* to agrarian improvement. In *The Theory of Economic Growth*, he argued that state provision of infrastructure and services was far more critical than the size of farm or the presence of middle men in determining peasant viability. This emphasis in his thought was noted by the Prime Minister, Dr. Eric Williams, in the 1963 Legislative Council debates on Tobago's development. In reality, however, Lewis' ideas on agriculture, like his ideas on industrialization, were never fully implemented.[141]

Once the war was over, food production ceased to be an urgent necessity. Between 1948 and 1956, agricultural policy leaned heavily towards stimulating the traditional exports, in a context where oil/asphalt and manufacturing emerged as the leading sectors. The concern of the reports from 1930 to 1943 with food supply and food security gave way to ideas on comparative advantage in international trade. Foreign farmers were deemed to be able to produce food of high quality more cheaply than local ones. Given the commitment to importing foodstuff, including fish, meat and tropical produce which could easily be locally produced, the 1948 policy regarded boosting domestic food production as only a *temporary* necessity. Therefore, it is not surprising that Tobago lost the priority ascribed to it in the 1938 Nicoll Report, and continued to be treated as marginal in the development process.

7.   INITIATIVES FROM WITHIN TOBAGO, 1935–1951

Tobago's residents did not passively submit to the effects of outside forces. Within the island, many attempts were made to influence policy changes and to improve agriculture. Besides the efforts of the MLCs and the co-operative initiatives, other ventures were started. Some failed. The more important activities are next outlined.

Public Lectures

Some of the officials tried to enlighten the people on agrarian methods. Dr. Timothy Arthur des Iles, the Veterinary Officer from November 1936, Dr. George Hilton Clarke (DMO, Plymouth), and F. D. Davies, the Agricultural Officer, started in 1937 a series of talks on nutrition, stock-rearing and related subjects. The first was convened in March 1937 by the head teachers of the three Mason Hall schools, and it attracted an enormous crowd of adults and children from Moriah, Mason Hall and nearby settlements. Des Iles continued the lectures on stock-rearing, giving advice on how to make agri-business profitable.[142]

Juvenile Farm Clubs

Des Iles' major contribution was, with the help of H. W. MacAlister, the Inspector of Schools, to found Juvenile Farm Clubs (JFCs) in the primary schools in 1938. The aim was to provide early training in breeding, care, exhibition and marketing of livestock; to stimulate love for domestic animals among school children; and to initiate them into the business aspect of stock-rearing, using a simple system of records and accounts. Ultimately, the clubs were intended to improve the economic condition of the peasants.[143]

Each member of a JFC owned or had a share in an animal, and once a term, on Farm Day, the animals were taken to school for inspection.[144] A health campaign was started for the animals, and in each club medicines were administered once per month. Students gaining over 70.0 per cent for their husbandry were allowed to exhibit their animals at an annual JFC Exhibition, first held in December 1938.[145] The movement began in 33 of Tobago's 37 schools and quickly spread to all the schools. In 1942 it spread to Trinidad where growth was also rapid (Table 1.4).

The clubs continued to grow in importance but, with good breeds not available to the public because of the deficiencies of the Government Stock Farm, these efforts failed to produce the desired effect.

In December 1946, for example, the JFC at Mt. St. George Methodist School exhibited 127 animals—cows, donkeys, pigs, goats, sheep, fowls, ducks and rabbits. However, J. Hamilton Maurice, the Inspector of Schools, commented that only one animal, a sheep, was of good breed.[146]

Marketing of Produce and Livestock

In 1936 competition from foreign livestock in Port of Spain led the Tobago traffickers to petition the Harbour Master for a 50.0 per cent reduction on freight for cattle moving between Tobago and Trinidad. The vendors claimed that it was difficult for them to make a profit. To remedy the situation, in 1938 des Iles took the initiative of liaising with the Livestock Officer in Trinidad to assist the Tobago vendors. The Trinidad officer was granted an auctioneer's licence, and animals from Tobago were sold on arrival at the quay in Port of Spain, in the hope that this would eliminate middlemen and secure higher prices for the producers.[147] However, these interim measures did not fully resolve the marketing problems.

On 16 August 1937, seven men gathered at Mt. Parnassus, L. A. Peters' home in Scarborough, to found the Tobago Live Stock Association (TLSA), with Ernest Cross as President, Victor Plagemann, Treasurer, and L. A. Peters, Secretary. Peters reported that 'the time is opportune for convincing Government that Tobago should be the meat supply centre for the Colony'.[148] The company was registered in May 1938 with a capital of $10,000 in 2,000 shares of $5.00. It planned to purchase Arnos Vale Estate for livestock farming, and also to buy livestock to ship to Port of Spain.[149] Later, in September 1938, the TLSA moved its office from Mt. Parnassus to the corner of Main and Burnett Streets, Scarborough, and it held a series of thanksgiving services in churches of different denominations.

In November 1938 the TLSA started a night market for ground provisions on Fridays and Saturdays at its office.[150] In April 1939 Peters wrote in *The People* that the TLSA proposed to end shipping and marketing to Trinidad on an individual basis, and to 'stem the import tide against which we were struggling for the last donkey number of years'.[151] Unfortunately, the records do not state how long the TLSA lasted or what it accomplished.

TABLE 1.4 **Juvenile Farm Clubs in Tobago and Trinidad, 1938–1945 (Selected Years)**

Year and place	No. of clubs	No. of members	No. of animals
1938, Tobago	33	444	395
1939, Tobago	33	701	1,007
1942, Tobago	37	1,206	Not given
1942, Trinidad	77	2,357	Not given
1945, Tobago	36	1,826	2,781
1945, Trinidad	140	5,750	7,348

Sources: Louis A. Peters, 'The Juvenile Farm Club: Its Birth and Growth and Usefulness', *The Tobagonian*, Dec. 1942, 19–20. Administration Report on the Department of Agriculture for 1942, Council Paper No. 57 of 1943, 6; *Administration Report of the Director of Education for 1945* (Port of Spain 1947), 5.

Protest over the Agricultural Credit Societies

Besides the local shopkeepers and dealers who made small advances to peasants, the major source of credit for Tobago's peasantry was the ACS. On 14 May 1937, I. A. Hope, Tobago's MLC, gave notice of a motion in the Legislative Council on the ACS. The position was that in 1933 the Government had reduced the interest rate for loans from the Agricultural Development Bank (ADB) from 7.0 per cent to 6.0 per cent, and further reduced the rate to 4.0 per cent in 1937. Most of the beneficiaries of the soft loans (30-year mortgages and generous crop advances) disbursed by the ADB were planters. In contrast, the ACS received Government funds at 6.0 per cent interest and lent to the peasants at 12.0 per cent, with compound interest charged quarterly on unpaid balances. Thus, the official policy gave much easier terms to planters than to peasants. Hope's motion asked that the interest rate for the ACS be reduced in the same proportion as that for the planters, retrospective to 1933. On 21 May 1937, the Governor promised to look into the matter, and Hope withdrew the motion.[152]

Throughout Tobago, the populace supported Hope. L. A. Peters stated: 'The wail has become Island-wide.'[153] So serious were the peasants' difficulties that from 1934 to 1938 no new loans were made to the 13 ACS in Tobago, because of prolonged indebtedness to the Government. Membership in the Tobago ACS dwindled from 524 at the end of 1932 to 242 in 1938.[154]

Despite its promises, the Government dragged its feet. In 1939 Laurence Edwards and L. A. Peters complained to the Moyne Commission about the high interest rates and the short term of the loans (one year) from the ACS. Charles Hovell, a merchant, told the Commission that the ACS had been 'the ruin' of the peasants instead of their 'friend'. Even the Government admitted to the Moyne Commission that the Tobago ACS were in 'stagnation, as far as their usefulness is concerned.' However, it was not until 1941 that the Government reduced the interest payable by the ACS for state loans from 6.0 per cent to 3.0 per cent per annum, and lowered the interest payable by members from 12.0 per cent to not more than 7.0 per cent. Laurence Edwards complained that in 1940 only $7,000 had been allocated to the ACS, an average of $1.17 for each of the island's 6,000 peasants.[155]

The Tobago Peasant Proprietors Association

The first peasants' organization was the Tobago Peasant Proprietors Association (TPPA), formed in June 1939. One of the leading organizers was Laurence Edwards, Head Teacher of Scarborough Upper EC School, who had been an important activist in literary, social and labour movements in Tobago. Edwards was the Recording Secretary, while the other officers were J. Hovell, President; S. Roberts and Hazel Fraser, Vice Presidents; George Cruickshank, Treasurer; and Aaron Howard, General Secretary.

Bypassing de Nobriga, Tobago's MLC whose policy of exacting free labour as a condition of employment on Lowlands Estate Edwards had exposed to the Moyne Commission, in June 1939 the TPPA sent a petition to the Governor through E. Vernon Wharton, MLC, a prominent member of the Agricultural Society of Trinidad and Tobago. The petition is a historic one, since its writers claimed to 'depend solely on agriculture and animal husbandry for their livelihood.'

First, the TPPA stated that hundreds of young men were willing to keep to the soil, but that conditions made dependence on agriculture 'rather precarious'. The TPPA therefore called for the following:

1. an agricultural credit bank in Tobago that would grant farmers loans at low interest rates;
2. a land settlement scheme to allow landless farmers to have secure ownership;
3. subdivision of Mt. St. George Estate, the Goodwood Crown lands and the uncultivated parts of the Government Stock Farm for sale or lease on easy terms to nearby villagers;
4. provision of shelter in Port of Spain for the livestock sent from Tobago, and expansion of marketing facilities to remove the need for middlemen;
5. expansion of the Veterinary Officer's services to cover the whole island at nominal rates;
6. improvement in roads and Crown traces to give better access to farm lands.

A branch of the TPPA at Bethel sought to acquire land in 1940. In November 1940, the TPPA also formed a Co-operative Agency to market peasant produce in Trinidad, because of the wastage of time incurred in marketing individually, and the peasants' lack of information on marketing conditions. Little is known about the success of these ventures.[156]

School Allotments

Five Windward Tobago primary schools—St. Paul's EC, Roxborough EC, Charlotteville Methodist, Goodwood Methodist and Delaford RC—pioneered a Land Settlement Scheme in 1943. The children received allotments of land for farming. They built their own tenants' huts; ran their office where discussions, lectures and trials took place; kept records; profited from the sale of their produce and livestock and, with their parents, were part of a public campaign against praedial larceny. The children used their profits to assist their parents, buy school requisites, and invest in War Savings Certificates. The main promoter of the scheme, which was supervised by the head teachers, was L. A. Peters, then the Outdoor Officer of the Food Control Department.[157]

Protests on the Ills of Tobago

The early trade unions emerging in Tobago after the 1937 labour rebellion in Trinidad were concerned about agrarian issues. In 1939 the Public Works and Public Service Workers Union (PWPSWU) put forward demands for government aid to the fishing industry, for a fish-canning factory, and for government purchase of abandoned estate lands for landless peasants.[158] In all its meetings, the union attracted people, particularly in the Leeward District, who were not government workers. Estate workers, many of them chafing under the requirement of giving two free days per week to ensure work on the other days at George de Nobriga's Lowlands Estate, were allowed to join, and the union publicly called de Nobriga's system of 'bread and swag' instead of wages 'slave labour'.[159] 'Swag' was 'chocolate tea', a hot chocolate drink made from unrefined cocoa with milk, sugar and spices. The PWPSWU also complained of the low wages paid to women for chopping and 'pulling' coconuts—2 cents per 100 in 1939.[160]

A. P. T. James, through the Tobago Peasants and Industrial Workers Union which he formed in 1946, through his 1948 and 1951 memoranda to the Colonial Office, and in numerous speeches to the Legislative Council, also brought Tobago's agrarian and other needs to public notice—with meagre results. James started the James Foundation Secondary and Commercial School at Roxborough in July 1954. He was also the patron of the Calder Hall Boys' Farm, started c.1949, of which L. A. Peters, his close colleague and an indefatigable activist on behalf of agriculture, was Managing Director.[161]

Some of the initiatives from within Tobago addressed the scarcity of land and credit. Others focused on education for adults and children, and tried to foster a love for agriculture in the rising generation. But without state-provided resources to change the harsh economic realities, little could be achieved.

8. CONCLUSION

By 1930 the writing was on the wall for both plantation and peasant agriculture in Tobago. Dependence on primary exports with falling prices, while the profitable manufacturing industries for those products were not developed locally, left farmers vulnerable throughout the long depression from 1920 to 1940. Figures 1.1 and 1.2 plainly show the relentless pressure of low prices on export values, in spite of rising output between 1925 and 1933. Cocoa production tended to fall in the 1940s, and export prices remained volatile (Table A1.2). Unable to meet the costs of rehabilitating their fields in cocoa, coconuts and limes, Tobago's farmers, large and small, succumbed to low global prices. Further, both planter and peasant suffered because of bad roads, inadequate sea communication, and deficient marketing services. The peasants in particular suffered from poor breeds of livestock and meagre, costly, short-term credit. By 1943 Vernon Ferrer's study showed that most peasants put 1.0 per cent of their investment in equipment and tools, and that, without higher productivity and ample medium-term credit, their holdings were doomed to be non-viable.

In addition, given the small population size and the growth of the peasantry, little full-time labour was available to the estates. The planters' response in the 1920s was to restrict access to land for rent and pastures, even though their properties were under-cultivated. By 1930 access to land for the expansion of the peasantry was a public issue.

The Grow More Food Campaign started in 1942 gave a temporary boost to food production. However, Tobago's exports declined sharply after World War II ended in 1945, and from 1950 Tobago became a net importer of tropical foodstuff of which it had been a net exporter. The farming population in 1943 was already ageing (average age 50 years), and the intractable problem of attracting young people to the land remained unsolved in the succeeding decades.

The long depression of the 1920s and 1930s, following World War I, forced officials to concern themselves with food supply and food security from 1930 until the end of World War II. In this context, the 1938 Nicoll Committee on the coastal steamers understood that sea communication for Tobago had to be part of a wider plan to develop infrastructure and services to support agriculture and tourism. However, the outbreak of war in 1939 prevented the implementation of their Report (Council Paper No. 3 of 1939).

29

As petroleum and asphalt dominated the colony's exports and no new profitable export crop was found, the post-war policy shifted to regard manufacturing and industry as the colony's leading sectors. Much of the new industrial thrust was towards import replacement. However, the same recognition was not given to replacement of *food* imports. Rising food imports were seen as the *necessary* result of the foreign countries' comparative advantage in global trade. There was no effective peasant lobby, and the prevailing wisdom reflected the low political importance of the peasantry in the colony's affairs. Food production and, by extension, the development of Tobago, became matters of little importance.

Once Tobago was not regarded as having rights to development equal to those of Trinidad, and once global prices and plant diseases caused the export crops to dwindle, Tobago's hope for improvement rested on its *strategic importance as a producer of food crops and livestock*. In other words, it rested on the *strategic importance of the peasantry*, the predominant group of farmers by 1938. The Trinidad officials recognized this fully for a brief moment at the start of World War II.

However, precisely in the fact that Tobago's claims for resources rested on the strength of its peasantry lay the greatest obstacles for the realisation of such claims. In the colony's affairs, peasants had little weight. Unlike workers, they had not rebelled in the twentieth century, and they were not vociferous lobbyists. What is more, in official circles even the need for local food crops and livestock was considered minimal from 1948.

One possible source of help for infrastructure and communications was the Department of Colonial Development and Welfare in Barbados, which disbursed imperial government funds under various Acts from 1940 to 1956. Despite two memoranda and two visits by the Hon. A. P. T. James to the Colonial Office, the Government refused to apply for funds for Tobago, and used the funds for which it applied mainly for Trinidad's development. The Colonial Office refused to intervene. And in the circumstances, no class within Tobago was able to influence the state.

Thus, the causes of Tobago's agrarian underdevelopment were four:

1. its colonial condition, which it shared with Trinidad, and which confined it to primary production without manufacturing of its produce;
2. its subordination as a Ward, 'a poor relation', in the colony;[162]
3. the refusal of the Trinidad elites to see the need for food production except during wartime;
4. the political ineffectiveness of all Tobago's classes and strata vis-à-vis the dominant class in Trinidad.

The last factor is closely related to Tobago's status as a Ward: *the structural arrangements of state power excluded Tobago from having a serious voice in the councils of state*. It is also related to the racial and class divisions in Tobago, which prevented concerted action between whites and blacks for better representation until 1938 (Chapters 3 and 4). Both planters and peasants suffered as a result.

From 1957 to 1963, the central government under Dr. Eric Williams sought to redress what Williams called 'the betrayal of trust and the years of neglect' by previous governments. But by 1957 Colonial Development and Welfare funding was ending, and Tobago had to rely on the colony's resources over which its leaders had little influence. From 1957 to 1963, the main increases were in tobacco, yams, corn, sweet potatoes and pigeon peas, all minor crops heavily subsidized by the state. Thus, for the most part, neither planter nor peasant was prospering when Hurricane Flora devastated Tobago on 30 September 1963.

Notes

1 *Massa*: master; general term for the planter class. Williams, *Massa Day Done* (Port of Spain 1961).

2 The argument of this chapter was outlined in Susan Craig-James, 'Milch Cow or Hard Sucking Calf? The Joining of Trinidad and Tobago and Its Aftermath, 1884–1948' (paper presented at a Conference organized by The University of the West Indies and the Policy Research and Development Institute of the Tobago House of Assembly on Tobago and Trinidad: 100 Years Together, Tobago, October 1998, mimeographed).

3 District Administration Reports for 1930, Council Paper No. 50 of 1931, 9.

4 Tobago Financial and Other Returns, 1898, Council Paper No. 102 of 1899, 18; Administration Report of the Collector of Customs for 1927, Council Paper No. 68 of 1928, 9; Administration Report of the Collector of Customs for 1928, Council Paper No. 56 of 1929, 9. See Glossary for the *pound* (£) *sterling*.

5 CO 950/757/BG/T6004: Memorandum submitted to The [West India] Royal Commission by the Tobago Chamber of Commerce, Dec. 1938, 1.

6 Address of the Governor on the Opening of the Session of the Legislative Council on 8 Nov. 1909, Council Paper No. 127 of 1909, 5; punctuation as in the original.

7 Cecil Y. Shephard, *The Cacao Industry of Trinidad: Some Economic Aspects, Pt. IV, 1870–1920* (Port of Spain 1937), 3.

8 Kathleen Phillips-Lewis, 'British Imperial Policy and Colonial Economic Development: The Cocoa Industry in Trinidad, 1838–1939' (Ph.D. thesis, University of Manitoba, 1994), 273.

9 Shephard, *The Cacao Industry, Pt. V, 1921–32* (Port of Spain 1937), Table XXIII, 29; *Administration Report of the Director of Agriculture for 1945* (Port of Spain 1946), 6; *Annual General Report on The Colony of Trinidad and Tobago for 1939–1946* (Port of Spain c.1947), 36. The price per fanega is given differently in several sources. The *Report of the Economics Committee* (Port of Spain 1949), 53, states that for 1942–44 the price was $12.25 per fanega, rising to $13.25 in 1945. All dollars in this chapter are Trinidad and Tobago (TT) currency; TT $4.80 equalled £1 sterling.

10 *The Tobagonian*, August 1947, 13.

11 See Final Report of the Committee Appointed to Enquire into the Needs of the Cocoa Industry, with Memorandum by Sir Frank Stockdale, Agricultural Adviser to the Secretary of State for the Colonies, Council Paper No. 61 of 1940. Stockdale discusses the problem of senescent environments.

12 Charles de Freitas, 'Vital Need Is to Revive Our Cocoa Industry' in *Trinidad and Tobago's Agriculture*, ed. P. N. Wilson and J. B. Stollmeyer (St. Augustine n. d.), 12–14.

13 Major G. St. J. Orde Browne, *Labour Conditions in the West Indies* (London 1939), App. III.

14 *Administration Report of the Director of Agriculture for 1946* (Port of Spain 1948), 11; Cecil Y. Shephard, 'Report on Co-operative Cocoa Fermentaries in Tobago' (Port of Spain 1957, mimeographed), 5.

15 For 1926 and 1933, Administration Reports on the Department of Agriculture for 1935 and 1936, Council Paper No. 51 of 1936, 6, and Council Paper No. 47 of 1937, 5, respectively. For 1938, CO 950/847: no. 941, Memorandum Submitted to The Royal Commission by Thomas Hepworth Brinkley, Manager of Courland Estates (Coconuts) Ltd., 7 Mar. 1939. Copra: the dried kernels of the coconuts.

16 CO 950/847: BG T6114, West India Royal Commission (WIRC), no. 941, Memorandum by Thomas H. Brinkley, Manager of Courland Estates (Coconuts) Ltd., 7 Mar. 1939. CO 950/810: Ser. 910, Coconut Growers Association Ltd. to the WIRC, Oral evidence, 8 Mar. 1939.

17 Carleen O'Loughlin, *The Coconut Industry of the West Indies*, Caribbean Development Bank Technical Report No. 9 (Bridgetown 1972), 69.

18 Ibid., 3. Department of Agriculture, Annual Report for 1961, 49. The Tobago Land Capability Survey of the early 1970s noted that 80.0 per cent of the coconut producers and 75.0 per cent of those in cocoa obtained low yields because of ageing trees. See Ridwan Ali et al., *Land Capability Studies Phase II, Report No. 8, Agriculture in Tobago* (Port of Spain 1973), 38.

19 Department of Agriculture, *Bulletin* 9, no. 66 (Oct. 1910): 219–21; 16, Pt. 3 (1917): 115–16.

20 CO 295/562/10: John B. Murray, Tobago planter, to E. R. Darnley, Colonial Office, 17 Sept. 1927, encl Memorandum on Tobago Communications, 1927; The second quotation is from Shephard, *The Cacao Industry, Pt. V*, 7. Trinidad growers responded to the demand for rubber in the USA in World War II.

21 Ronald Hyam, *Elgin and Churchill at the Colonial Office, 1905–1908* (London 1968), 452.

22 CO 295/418: no. 300, Moloney to Chamberlain, 10 July 1903, encl J. H. Hart's report, 3 July 1903.

23 *Mirror*, 27 Feb. 1904, 13.

24 CO 295/455: The British Cotton Growing Association (BCGA), Manchester, to Under Secretary of State for the Colonies, 18 Nov. 1909, encl Thomas Thornton to Hutton, Chairman, BCGA, 29 Oct. 1909.

25 CO 295/513: no. 404, Chancellor to Long, 9 Nov. 1917, encl Thomas Thornton, 'Tobago as a Field for Cotton Cultivation', 4 July 1908, 7.

26 Administration Report of the Department of Agriculture for 1911–1912 and 1912–1913, Council Paper No. 152 of 1913, with Thomas Thornton's Report on Cotton Growing in Tobago, 26; *Mirror*, 25 Sept. 1911, 5, with Acting Director of Agriculture's estimate on growers.

27 Administration Report of the Director of Agriculture, 1909–1910, Council Paper No. 115 of 1910, 9, 22.

28 CO 295/513: no. 404, Chancellor to Long, 9 Nov. 1917, encl Report by W. G. Freeman, Acting Director of Agriculture, 7 Nov. 1917.

29 Administration Report on the Department of Agriculture for 1924, Council Paper No. 52 of 1925, 23; District Administration Reports for 1927, Council Paper No. 82 of 1928, 10. The quotation is from the latter report.

30 *TG*, 13 Oct. 1917, 2. The Leeward District Agricultural Society had frequently petitioned the Government for a lime factory in the 1920s.

31 Administration Report on the Department of Agriculture for 1936, Council Paper No. 47 of 1937, 15; Administration Report of the Director of Agriculture for 1938, Council Paper No. 71 of 1939, 14.

32 'The British West Indian Limes Industry', *Tropical Agriculture* 18, no. 6 (1941): 105.

33 *Tobago Herald* (*TH*), 1 Oct. 1955, 6. Department of Agriculture, Annual Report for 1961, 48; *Annual Report of the Agricultural Services for the Year 1962* (Port of Spain 1964), 74.

34 Administration Report on the Department of Agriculture for 1911–12, 1912–13, Council Paper No. 152 of 1913, with Botanic Station Annual Report, 31 Mar. 1913, 35.

35 *Mirror*, 6 Feb. 1911, 10.

36 Administration Report on the Department of Agriculture for 1917, Council Paper No. 122 of 1918, 27.

37 Administration Report on the Department of Agriculture for 1925, Council Paper No. 60 of 1926, 8.

38 Administration Report of the Collector of Customs and Excise for 1940, Council Paper No. 33 of 1941, 3; *Administration Report of the Comptroller of Customs and Excise for 1950* (Port of Spain 1951), 8.

39 *Annual Report of the Agricultural Services for the Year 1962*, 75. Hon. K. Mohammed, Minister of Agriculture, Lands and Fisheries, *Hansard*, 27 Apr. 1961, 2715–16. The net profit per acre of tobacco in 1961 was TT $1,100.

40 Symington visited Roxborough in July 1903 to encourage farmers; *Mirror*, 1 Aug. 1903, 3. CO 295/419: no. 347, Moloney to Chamberlain, 5 Aug. 1903, and Encs. On official support received by Symington's company, see CO 295/426: no. 19, Moloney to Lyttelton, 14 Jan. 1904, and Encs; CO 295/442: no. 283, Carter to Elgin, 9 Aug. 1907; CO

295/433: folios (fols.) 88–90. On his death, see *Mirror*, 31 Dec. 1904, 11, and 26 Jan. 1905, 7.

41 By 1961, apart from the produce of backyard gardens, the only commercial citrus in Tobago was on 50 acres of Franklyns Estate; Department of Agriculture, Annual Report for 1961, 48. This cultivation had been pioneered by Duncan McGillivray, Franklyns' owner from 1878 to 1929.

42 See Administration Reports on the Department of Agriculture for 1932, 1934, 1935, 1937, respectively: Council Papers No. 33 of 1933, 14; No. 72 of 1935, 11–12; No. 51 of 1936, 8–9; and No. 50 of 1938, 68.

43 CO 950/953: Written Evidence to the West India Royal Commission, 1938–1939, Department of Agriculture Memorandum, Pt. VI, 6.

44 *Administration Report of the Comptroller of Customs and Excise for 1958* (Port of Spain 1959), 26; *Administration Report of the Customs and Excise Department for 1959* (Port of Spain 1960), 28.

45 Cyril B. Brown et al., *Land Capability Survey of Trinidad and Tobago, No. 1, Tobago* (Port of Spain 1965), Table 3, 35.

46 *Report of the Team Which Visited Tobago in March/April 1957* (Bridgetown 1957), 120. On the harbour question, see Hon. A. C. Alexis, *Hansard*, 24 Apr. 1961, 2500.

47 Brown et al., *Land Capability Survey*, 35.

48 Tobago Sea Communications Committee Report, Council Paper No. 44 of 1929, 16.

49 Administration Report on the Department of Agriculture for 1925, Council Paper No. 60 of 1926, 8; emphasis added.

50 Woodville Marshall, 'Notes on Peasant Development in the West Indies since 1838', *Social and Economic Studies* (*SES*) 17, no. 3 (1968): 252–63.

51 *Report of the Agricultural Policy Committee of Trinidad and Tobago*, Pts. I and II (Port of Spain 1943).

52 Vernon O. Ferrer, 'Some Economic Aspects of Peasant Farming in Tobago, British West Indies' (M.Sc. thesis, Cornell University, 1945).

53 Ibid., 14.

54 Ibid., 41.

55 Ibid., 46–51.

56 Ibid., 105.

57 Ibid., 105.

58 Ibid., 112–13.

59 Erasmus, 'The Peasants of Tobago', *The Tobagonian*, Aug. 1944, 5–7. The original said 0.5 acres in permanent crops; probably an error.

60 SS: steamship.

61 Sea communications are fully discussed in chap. 4.

62 *TG*, 2 June 1923, 12; 20 Jan. 1924, 14.

63 *Mirror*, 10 Feb. 1912, 1.

64 For a discussion on migration patterns, see chap. 7 of this volume.

65 See Dr. George Latour's complaints in CO 295/443:

Chairman, BCGA, to Under Secretary of State, 27 Aug. 1907, encl Latour to Atkins, Secretary, BCGA, 6 Aug. 1907; Latour to Elgin, 22 Aug. 1907.

66 George David Hatt, 'Tobago Revisited', *TG*, 11 Mar. 1923, 14.

67 J. A. A. Biggart, 'Memorandum to the West Indian Sugar Commission', published as 'Tobago Needs a Land Settlement Scheme', *TG*, 11 Dec. 1929, 6. The metayage and contract systems are described more fully in chap. 2 of this volume.

68 *Report of the West Indian Sugar Commission* (London 1930), 112. Cmd. 3517. For an example of similar official statements, see Orde Browne, *Labour Conditions in the West Indies*.

69 *Report of the Economics Committee* (Port of Spain 1948), 91.

70 *Proceedings and Debates of the Legislative Council* (*Hansard*), Budget debate, 30 Nov. 1956, 155.

71 Hon. Dr. Eric Williams, *Hansard*, 7 June 1957, 1922.

72 Hon. Dr. Eric Williams, *Hansard*, 30 Dec. 1958, 481.

73 *Report of the Team Which Visited Tobago in March/April 1957* (Bridgetown 1957), 34.

74 Ibid.; David L. Niddrie, *Land Use and Population in Tobago* (Bude, Cornwall 1961).

75 Niddrie, *Land Use and Population*, 39, 52–54. Cf. Eric Roach, describing the exodus of young men from Les Coteaux because agriculture was 'too drab and profitless', *TH*, 2 Oct. 1954, 6. Also, many of the submissions to the WIRC in 1939 spoke of the general distaste for agriculture among the young.

76 *Report of the Team Which Visited Tobago*, 97–98; Niddrie, *Land Use and Population*, 53.

77 *Report of the Team Which Visited Tobago*, 95.

78 Ibid., 62–63, 76–78, 95–97, 111–12, 121–24; the quotations are on pages 112, 121.

79 Department of Agriculture, Annual Report for 1961, 47. A Land Use Subsidy Scheme had also been started in Tobago in 1954. *Administration Report of the Director of Agriculture for 1954* (Port of Spain 1958), 9.

80 *Annual Report of the Agricultural Services for the Year 1962* (Port of Spain 1964), 77.

81 Williams, *Hansard*, 29 Nov. 1963, 525.

82 *Report of the Tobago Planning Team* (Port of Spain 1963), 4.

83 CO 950/953: Memorandum of the Department of Agriculture to the WIRC, 1939, Pt. XIIc, 7. Of the 12,000 acres under cocoa, a further 3,600 acres were unclassified.

84 CO 950/757/BG/T6004: Memorandum submitted to The Royal Commission by the Tobago Chamber of Commerce, Dec. 1938, 4.

85 *TRG*, 19 Apr. 1900, 494, describing Patent No. 26 granted to Tucker on 9 Mar. 1900.

86 Administration Report of the Director of Agriculture for 1909–10, Council Paper No. 115 of 1910, 23.

87 *Mirror*, 24 Aug. 1911, 4; 17 Oct. 1911, 8; 3 Dec. 1910, 4; 24 June 1910, 5.

88 *Report of the West Indian Sugar Commission*, 57–58.

89 W. Arthur Lewis, 'The Evolution of the Peasantry in the British West Indies' (1936, mimeographed), 41. The efficient cocoa production by the small growers in 1927, as reported by Shephard in 'Report on Co-operative Cocoa Fermentaries in Tobago', supports Lewis' point.

90 W. Arthur Lewis, *The Theory of Economic Growth* (London 1955), 279, 136; emphases added.

91 The Colonial Office supported the Department's scheme, advocating agricultural education at three levels: secondary schools and colleges and public lectures; agricultural schools with apprenticeships for St. Vincent, St. Kitts, St. Lucia and Dominica; and principles of agriculture in primary schools. Agricultural Education: Circular from J. Chamberlain, Secretary of State, to Colonial Governors, Council Paper No. 119 of 1899.

92 Phillips-Lewis, 'British Imperial Policy', 49.

93 ICTA became a part of the University College of the West Indies, today The University of the West Indies, in 1961.

94 Sydney H. Olivier, *Jamaica: The Blessed Island* (London 1936), 399–405.

95 Ronald Hyam, *Elgin and Churchill at the Colonial Office*, 457–58, 464.

96 David Meredith, 'The British Government and Colonial Economic Policy, 1919–1939', *Economic History Review*, 2nd ser., 28, no. 3 (1975): 492.

97 CO 295/583/11: no. 2, Hollis to Cunliffe-Lister, 2 Jan. 1934, and Encs; no. 510, Hollis to Cunliffe-Lister, 23 Nov. 1934; and Cunliffe-Lister to Hollis, 7 Jan. 1935. In December 1934, the Association had 111 members: 32 planters and 79 small proprietors. Administration Report on the Department of Agriculture for 1934, Council Paper No. 72 of 1935, 15. The Association mishandled its affairs, and was investigated in December 1937. In all, the Government lent it £5,030. Tobago Producers' Association Ltd.: Report of An Inquiry into the Constitution, Working and Financial Condition of the Association, Council Paper No. 22 of 1938.

98 CO 295/574/4: no. 53, Hollis to Passfield, 5 Feb. 1931, Encs and minutes.

99 John M. Lee, *Colonial Government and Good Government: A Study of the Ideas Expressed by the British Official Classes in Planning Decolonization, 1939–1964* (Oxford 1967), 39, 85–113.

100 Susan E. Craig, 'Background to the 1970 Confrontation in Trinidad and Tobago', in

Contemporary Caribbean: A Sociological Reader, ed. S. Craig, vol. 2 (St. Augustine 1982), 386.

101 David J. Morgan, *The Origins of British Aid Policy, 1924–1945* (London 1980), quoting Sir John Anderson, Chancellor of the Exchequer (later Viscount Waverley), and Malcolm Macdonald, Secretary of State for the Colonies, xxvii.

102 CO 295/639/4: Minute by Kennedy, 19 Feb. 1948.

103 Gordon K. Lewis, *The Growth of the Modern West Indies* (London 1968), 92; Thomas S. Simey, *Welfare and Planning in the West Indies* (Oxford 1946), 192–93.

104 On Trinidad, see Donald Wood, *Trinidad in Transition* (London 1968); Bridget Brereton, *Race Relations in Colonial Trinidad, 1870–1900* (Cambridge 1979); on Tobago, see vol. I, chap. 8 of this work. Government measures for cocoa included: the Mortgage Extension Ordinance, 1921; the Agricultural Relief Ordinance, 1925; the Agricultural Development Bank, 1925; grants in 1933 because of a hurricane affecting cocoa and coconut crops; Original Cocoa Subsidy Scheme, 1936; Subsidiary Cocoa Subsidy Scheme, 1938; distribution of clonal cocoa plants after 1940; and other rehabilitative measures. See *Hansard*, 29 Nov. 1940, 125–31, where several MLCs questioned the wisdom of continued assistance to cocoa proprietors.

105 Parliamentary Papers (PP.), 1910, vol. XXVII, *Report of the Committee on Emigration from India to the Crown Colonies and Protectorates*, Pt. II, Minutes of Evidence (London 1910), 351. Cmd. 5193.

106 CO 295/570/11: S. M. Campbell's minute, 17 Oct. 1930.

107 Susan E. Craig, *Smiles and Blood* (London 1988), gives details on Fletcher's dismissal.

108 Letter from Hon. H. L. Thornton Relative to the Expenses Incurred by the Member Residing in Tobago, Council Paper No. 68 of 1904, 4.

109 Report of the Commission of Enquiry into the Recent Disturbances at Port of Spain, Trinidad (London 1903), *Gazette Extraordinary*, 21 July 1903; Chamberlain to Moloney, 21 July 1904, Further Remarks on Water Riots, *TRG*, vol. 1, 1904, 4 Feb. 1904, 207. *Unofficials*: members of the Legislative Council who were not officials.

110 The Arthur Creech Jones Papers, Rhodes House, Oxford: ACJ 25/1, *Parliamentary Debates, House of Lords, Official Report*, vol. 107, no. 32, 23 Feb. 1938, Lord Olivier's Speech, 838.

111 'Tobago Peasants Make Plea for Credit Bank', *TG*, 16 Aug. 1939, 2.

112 Tobago Sea Communications Committee Report, Council Paper No. 44 of 1929, 21.

113 Administration Report on the Department of Agriculture for 1930, Council Paper No. 79 of 1931, 7.

114 *Report of the Economics Committee*, 101.

115 Cocoa Industry of Trinidad: Report by S. M. Gilbert, Assistant Director of Agriculture, Based on Recent Economic Survey, Council Paper No. 4 of 1931. The survey of the coconut industry was cited in CO 950/953: Trinidad and Tobago, vol. 3, Memorandum of the Department of Agriculture to the WIRC, 65–70. CO 950/808: BG T6059, Ser. 908, Memorandum of Agricultural Society of Trinidad and Tobago to WIRC.

116 Report of a Committee Appointed to Advise on the Trinidad–Tobago Coastal Steamer Service (Nicoll Report), Council Paper No. 3 of 1939; statistics are taken from Appendix (App.) C, 11, 12.

117 CO 295/615/3: no. 9, Huggins to Macdonald, 12 Jan. 1939; Enc. 2, Report of the Estimates Committee ..., Council Paper No. 96 of 1938; Enc H, Finance Committee minutes, *Minutes of the Proceedings of the Legislative Council*, 25 Nov. 1938.

118 *Minutes of the Proceedings of the Legislative Council, 1944–1945*, Question 68 of 1944, 109, 147–148; Question 82 of 1944, 172, 232–33; Questions 32, 33 of 1945, 261, 288, 298; the quotation is from col. 298.

119 *TH*, 20 Mar. 1954, Leader, 1.

120 Also at the meeting, called to discuss constitutional reform, were Roy Joseph, L. C. Hannays and Albert Gomes, members of the Executive and Legislative Councils. CO 295/639/5: Notes of the meeting, 5 June 1948. The document was 'Memorandum of Grievances and Complaints of the Inhabitants of Tobago, Presented to The Right Honourable Sir Arthur Creech Jones, Secretary of State for the Colonies', May 1948. The third writer may have been Cecil Louis.

121 CO 295/649/8: no. 219, Rance to Griffiths, 28 Aug. 1950, encl Tobago County Council resolution, 3 July 1950; CO 295/654/6: Rance to Griffiths, 26 Apr. 1951, encl TCPEP resolution, 29 Oct. 1950; Memorandum from TCPEP to Secretary of State, 7 July 1951.

122 A. P. T. James, *Leg. Co. Debates*, 20 Dec. 1956, 396; 7 June 1957, 1949–1951.

123 Williams, *Leg. Co. Debates*, 30 Nov. 1956, 155; 7 June 1957, 1922, 1937–1939.

124 These schemes were mainly the Central Experimental Station, the Eastern Caribbean Farm Institute, and the Central (Mausica) Teachers' College at Centeno. See Colonial Office, *Development and Welfare in the West Indies, 1940–1942*, Report by Sir Frank Stockdale (London 1943), 2.

125 CO 295/637/70711: Clifford to Call, 6 Feb. 1946; Clifford to Hull, 5 Feb. 1946, and Encs.

126 CO 295/642/5: *Memorandum Showing Progress of Certain Development Schemes in the Colony of Trinidad and Tobago up to 1948* (Port of Spain 1949); CO 295/651/1: *Memorandum on Major Capital Works of Government Showing Progress of Work in Execution and Work Proposed for 1951*, Approved by the Select Committee on Estimates (Port of Spain 1951).

127 CO 295/654/11: Minutes; CO 295/654/6: Confid.,

Griffiths to Rance, 17 Aug. 1951; Minutes; Note for the Parliamentary Under Secretary of State on Tobago Matters, n.d. [1951].

128 *Hansard*, 7 June 1957, 1924.

129 *West India Royal Commission Report* (Moyne Report) (London 1945), 422–27.

130 CO 950/953: Memorandum of the Department of Agriculture to the WIRC, Pt. III, 15. Message of Governor Sir Hubert Winthrop Young to the Legislative Council, 29 Nov. 1940, Council Paper No. 71 of 1940.

131 *Report of the Agricultural Policy Committee of Trinidad and Tobago*, Pt. 1 (Port of Spain 1943), 7.

132 Ibid., 52; Pt. II, 13–26.

133 Correspondence on Agriculture between the Government of Trinidad and Tobago and the Comptroller for Development and Welfare, BWI, Council Paper No. 23 of 1942, 5, 24.

134 *Minutes of the Proceedings of the Legislative Council*, 30 July 1943, Reply to George de Nobriga, 134.

135 *Administration Report of the Director of Agriculture for 1945* (Port of Spain 1946), 3.

136 *Report of the Economics Committee*, App. II, 74–80.

137 Ibid., App. II, 75.

138 Ibid., 75–77; emphasis added. The phrase emphasized is repeated on page 92 of the report.

139 Terrence Farrell, 'Arthur Lewis and the Case for Caribbean Industrialization', *SES* 29, no. 4 (1980): 52–75. The British were adamant that British manufacturers should supply production inputs; CO 295/651/6: Confid., Rance to Griffiths, 5 July 1950, reference to Secret Telegram no. 338 of 27 June 1950.

140 West India Royal Commission, 1938–1939, Serial No. 45, W. Arthur Lewis, 'Memorandum on Social Welfare in the British West Indies' (bound volume of documents in the Main Library, UWI, St. Augustine, mimeographed), 6–10. W. Arthur Lewis, 'The Evolution of the Peasantry in the British West Indies'; *Labour in the West Indies* (1939; reprint, London 1977).

141 Lewis, 'Industrialization of the British West Indies', *Caribbean Economic Review* 2, no. 1 (1950): 7; *Theory of Economic Growth*, 279, 136. For fuller analyses on Lewis' thought, see Ralph Premdas and Eric St. Cyr, eds., *Sir Arthur Lewis: An Economic and Political Portrait* (Mona 1991); Terrence Farrell, 'Arthur Lewis', 52–75; and Susan Craig, 'The Germs of An Idea', Afterword to W. Arthur Lewis, *Labour in the West Indies* (London 1977). Eric Williams, *Hansard*, 14 Apr. 1960, 2294–95, cites Lewis on the need for more 20 to 25-acre farms and fewer 5-acre ones; and in *Hansard*, 29 Nov. 1963, 525–25, cites *Theory of Economic Growth*, to show that Lewis' ideas on 5-acre farms had changed.

142 *People*, 27 Mar. 1937, 2, 11; 17 Apr. 1937, 2, 11.

143 Saint de Lap (probably L. A. Peters), 'Tobago Juvenile Farm Club', *The Tobagonian*, Oct. 1941, 19; Administration Report of the Director of Education for 1938, Council Paper No. 67 of 1939.

144 Albert E. Alleyne, 'Tobago Juvenile Farm Club', *The Tobagonian*, Feb. 1947, 7.

145 Hallis B. Meikle, 'Tobago's Juvenile Farm Club', *The Tobagonian*, Sept. 1939, 13.

146 Albert E. Alleyne, 'Tobago Juvenile Farm Club', *The Tobagonian*, Feb. 1947, 7.

147 *People*, 30 Jan. 1937, 5, 7; Report of the Veterinary Division for 1938, in Administration Report of the Director of Agriculture for 1938, Council Paper No. 71 of 1939, 68.

148 *People*, 21 Aug. 1937, 5; 19 Feb. 1938, 5.

149 *People*, 21 May 1938, 5; 9 July 1938, 10.

150 *People*, 5 Nov. 1938, 5.

151 *People*, 15 Apr. 1939, 10.

152 *Minutes of the Proceedings of the Legislative Council*, vol. 1, 1937, 40; *POSG*, 26 May 1937, Leader, 11.

153 *People*, 19 June 1937, 5.

154 Administration Reports on the Department of Agriculture for 1934, 1935, 1936 and 1937, and Administration Report of the Director of Agriculture for 1938, Council Papers No. 72 of 1935, 15; No. 51 of 1936, 16; No. 47 of 1937, 14; No. 50 of 1938, 16; No. 71 of 1939, 13, respectively. There were 41 ACS in Trinidad in 1936.

155 CO 950/759: Ser. 855, Laurence Edwards and L. A. Peters, Oral evidence to WIRC, 13, and *POSG*, 7 Mar. 1939, 13; CO 950/951: no. 854, Charles E. Hovell, Memorandum on Livestock Industry in Tobago. CO 950/953: Memorandum of the Department of Agriculture to the WIRC, 1938, Pt. VI, 19. Message of His Excellency the Governor to the Legislative Council, 16 May 1941, Council Paper No. 17 of 1941, Supplement, 15; Edwards, *The Tobagonian*, June 1941, 6.

156 'Tobago Peasants Make Plea for Credit Bank', *TG*, 16 Aug. 1939, 2. *Minutes of the Proceedings of the Legislative Council*, 1940, vol. 2, 29 Nov. 1940; *The Tobagonian*, Dec. 1940, 11–12.

157 *The Tobagonian*, May 1943, 7–8, 11–12; Mar. 1944, 7–8.

158 *People*, 6 May 1939, 11.

159 *People*, 27 May 1939, 7; 19 Aug. 1939, 5. See chap. 4.

160 *People*, 26 Aug. 1939, 5; 'pulling' coconuts was removing the kernel from the coconuts; it was usually women's work.

161 *TH*, 24 July 1954, 6; *The Tobagonian*, Sept. 1949, 5.

162 *Minutes of the Proceedings of the Legislative Council*, 1945, T. M. Kelshall, Question 33 of 1945, 20 Apr. 1945, 261.

2

Oral Testimonies
on Production and Trade

The methodology of social science must be … a combination of micro-ethnography, thick description and macro-empirical, historical enquiry.

Christopher Lloyd

ALTHOUGH THE remotest areas of Tobago were brought under cultivation, the farming population lived in the villages, and constructed rough 'watch houses' on their farmlands for temporary overnight stay. Many smallholders took boats and/or walked miles to get to their lands in Hermitage, St. Rose, Starwood, Pigeon Hill and other areas outside of Charlotteville. Everywhere, the names of the remote holdings spoke of the distance and the roughness of the terrain: Wild Dog, Wild Cow, Land's End, and even America!—such were the places in the woods that came under cultivation.[1]

The expansion of Tobago's peasantry, tough and resilient under difficult conditions, to become the predominant class by 1938, was accompanied by a distinctive lifestyle. Much of the cultivation and reaping of crops was done by communal labour for payment in kind—either with part of the crops or with return labour. The unique oral material collected in the 1980s for this study from some of Tobago's oldest survivors chronicles the experience of the generation born between 1890 and 1920 and that of their parents. The oral testimonies of some of these persons are given extensively on the main forms of production and trade.

This chapter relates the accounts of exchanges at the micro level among individuals and small groups, to the norms of solidarity and reciprocity at village (meso) level, and to the features of the macro economy in its global context. First, it describes the village context of social life.

1. THE VILLAGE CONTEXT OF SOCIAL LIFE

In 1900 most Tobago settlements were villages, and villages were the nuclei of the society. Chapter 7 shows that, over time, adjoining villages formed 'conglomerate' clusters, and the population of the larger villages grew at the expense of minor settlements. The suburbs to the north and west of Scarborough were mainly agrarian, although some of their residents were engaged in clerical employment, skilled trades, commerce, government jobs, and work related to the port. Because of this agrarian character, many of the village norms, particularly respect and respectability, prevailed in the Scarborough suburbs. Therefore, despite the existence of urban settlements, the ethos of the society was agrarian.

In the early twentieth century, despite continuing emigration, Tobago's villages were extraordinarily cohesive entities. This is not to suggest that there was little conflict. Social conflicts and competition were negotiated in face-to-face interactions governed by strong community norms. Where these community norms were ineffective, conflicts were settled, usually as petty crimes, before the courts. Some villagers used witchcraft and necromancy as weapons against their enemies, but such proceedings were perforce clandestine. The society developed mechanisms to mitigate and contain conflict. For example, in 'banter songs', comments were made about one's opponents, but usually indirectly; children were not allowed to take part in adults' quarrels, and were expected to treat their parents' opponents with the normal courtesy and respect; older people or people of higher status could intervene to make peace between parties; older people helped to discipline other people's children. If conflicts persisted until one of the protagonists was dying, the final mechanism was that person's *'reckonin''* when, on his/her deathbed, (s)he would voice all the wrongs on his/her conscience, and would summon the antagonist(s) and ask for pardon. (S)he would then be released, forgiven, to die in peace.

The overwhelming majority of the villagers were engaged in agriculture. Small minorities were involved in fishing, and some found work, often temporary, in the Public Works Department; but these workers usually had land or access to land which they and their families farmed.

Many families grew most of their food, reared cows for milk, and made their own butter. Some grew sugar cane and made their own sugar, using the most rudimentary sugar technology—the wood mill. This was made of a wooden pole set in a hole cut into a tree trunk. Attached to the trunk below the pole was a short platform. The canes were passed between the pole and the platform, while someone sat on the pole, working it up and down and so crushing the juice into a container below.[2] The cane juice or *cane liquor* was then boiled, usually in a *'copper'*, a large iron vessel formerly used on estates for the same purpose. Local fish was salted and dried for both consumption and sale. Coconut oil, locally made, was the main fat for cooking. Other manufactured products included chocolate balls for making chocolate tea; corn meal; preserves, baked goods and confectionery; and *farine*, a meal made from cassava that was grated and parched. Tobago was an island of agricultural producers, with food imports being mainly rice (eaten by the populace only on Sundays); wheat flour; biscuits; salt; salted meat, fish and butter; and, especially after 1920 when livestock production declined, condensed and powdered milk.

The peasants appropriated some of the estate technology from the sugar industry, and often converted the equipment to other uses. The coppers in which sugar was boiled also became vessels for parching farine or storing water. Some peasants replicated the cattle-mill rollers for grinding sugar, but did so in local hardwood to serve the same purpose.

A network of informal institutions buttressed this agrarian lifestyle. Among them was the *susu* (also called 'throw up' because the participants pooled their funds), a rotating savings group; susu was a practice of African derivation (Yoruba, *esusu*), and participation was based on mutual trust, stemming from mutual knowledge of the character of the participants. There was also the exchange of labour in sequence, in which both men and women participated—variously called *'pardners'*, *'len' han''*, 'labour', 'day fuh day' or 'day wuk'.[3] Pardners, when conducted only between kin, was called 'bredders' (brothers). Pardners was used for various aspects of peasant farming, sharecropping and house-building; it too was based on mutual trust, for one gave labour only to reliable persons who would reciprocate.

In addition, funerals were the occasion of a considerable amount of giving. Bamboo for a tent, wood for the coffin, would be cut and brought from the woods by the labour of villagers, who would also build the coffin and dig the grave. Every visitor to the home of the dead person (the 'dead house') would walk with a gift of food or money, or both. Money gifts were passed from the hand of the giver to the recipient unobtrusively, and so were called 'shake han''. Weddings were similarly the occasion for a great deal of communal help. Daily help in food and services was given to the aged and infirm, and none was left destitute.

The giving and sharing of food on a regular basis was an integral part of village life. Mrs Glycerie 'Vaso' Carrington (b.1914) recalled:

I knew that there was a thing called 'passing the bowl'. What you cook today—if you cook, well, peas soup, or if is coo coo, and you know yuh neighbour cooking something else, … so I would what you call 'pass bowl'. I cook coo coo and you might cook peas soup. I will get a bowl of peas soup from you, and I hand over a bowl of coo coo, you know?[4]

In addition, one did not visit empty-handed.

In the remote northern villages where the major transport was by boat, those who owned boats would transport without charge the produce of those who did not. In these villages, because of poor communications, the conch shell was an important means of calling for help, or alerting the village to persons in distress. For Parlatuvier, Noel Felix (b.1933) and Rachel Eastman (1928–1992) described the use of the conch shell and the strong solidary relationships in the village.

NF: De conch shell is like dis. Seh like, I livin' here, and I have family in Charlotteville dead, and deh want me to know an' ting. Dat time, 'e didn't have engine like nowadays, because boat was goin' an' sailin'. Well, you up de hill an' you hear a sound goin' like dis: 'Boooooo!' [Repeats; imitates the sound of the conch shell.] You know somebody die. A kind of mournful way.

SCJ: Oh, they had a special sound?

NF: Yes. [Repeats the sound.] You know somebody dead; everybody rushing.

SCJ: So you had a different sound for fish and for deaths?

NF: Yes. Distress.

RE: … Because if sea heavy in de bay here, and they have to pull up boats, and they want men to come to help, they blow a distress shell. If you lost in de forest, and men goin' to look fuh you in dat forest, deh blow a distress shell. If boats gone to sea, and deh didn' come back for days, boats comin' to look for you, dey are comin' to look for you wit' a distress shell.

NF: De shell goin' like dis: 'Hoo, hoo, hoo, hoo, hoo!' … Yuh deh in distress. … Yes, dat is what you will blow. And you will understand dat somebody looking—Ah tellin' you, all dese tings came from African culture.

SCJ: … if somebody is born, they used to blow for that?

RE: Nah.

NF: Nah.

SCJ: Only death, distress, and fish?

NF: Yeah.

RE: If yuh in de bush deh, on top deh, an' you hear de shell blow, you comin'. You ha' to hustle. 'Ah wonder who die? Ah hear a deat' shell, dat come from Charlottesville. Oh great, must be Cousin Annie!' Becau' you might know Cousin Annie sick. Some people who know dat deh people are very ill, dem gone now, deh en' want to know. Deh gone an' deh start packin' deh basket, deh Injin [Indian] basket, and to go to Charlotteville.[5] And is two boats, three boats, goin' up, you know.

NF: And den you find now, de boat dat bring de message, well, dem men an' ting now, like mih farder and dem now, hustlin' now. 'Cause mih farder had big boats. Pushin' down de boat and ting. Men and women goin' up in de boat to the funeral.

RE: And dat time, if you have plantain or dasheen or anyting anywhere around, you collect.

NF: You see, that was a kind of a way of relationship, when these tings occur.

SCJ: So when somebody died in the village, everybody downed tools?

NF: Yeah.[6]

In 1908 Thomas Thornton, the cotton expert, remarked:

A funeral or a wedding is a big thing to them. Nearly all the men will leave their work to assist in digging the grave, and all must go to the funeral.[7]

Even children in the villages practised co-operation in fetching water. Lionel Craig (b.1922) recalls this childhood practice at Old Road, just over a mile from Scarborough:

We used to help each other. We used to have buckets in those days, and each home had a 50-gallon drum that they used to fill up with water. We'd begin from one home, we'll fill up the water in that home, and when that home is finished we would go to another until all the barrels are filled. After the last home barrel was full, the next trip we make to the pipe, the last bucket would go to each individual home, and that bucket would be covered and set in a safe place for the next day's use.[8]

These norms of co-operation and reciprocity undergirded the formal co-operative organizations for which Tobago was distinctive. In 1917 Pembroke started the second Agricultural Credit Society (ACS) in Trinidad and Tobago. By 1940 there were 14 ACS in Tobago, increasing to 28 in 1963. Each ACS was based on a village or other settlement.[9] In 1929 Pembroke was also the first village in the colony to start a co-operative cocoa fermentary; it was followed by Roxborough in 1932, Delaford and Parlatuvier (1934), and Scarborough (1935).[10] In 1930 large and small lime growers combined to form the Tobago Lime Growers Co-operative Association, which opened a lime factory in Scarborough and promoted co-operative marketing. In that year too, the Tobago Producers Association, a co-operative led by the larger growers, was started to grade, pack, store and market copra, food crops and livestock.

By 1930 Tobago had pioneered the strongest network of formal co-operative organizations in the BWI. An expert on agrarian co-operation, Karl Walter, reporting on the subject in 1929, commended the Agricultural Adviser, F. D. Davies, 'to whom must be given the credit of establishing better economic foundations of peasant agriculture than are to be found anywhere else in the West Indies.' Walter noted that more than half the agricultural production was by the peasantry and that 'considerably more than half the cocoa is produced by the small proprietor.' He concluded that:

> With this good start in co-operative practice, Tobago may well become an agricultural business model for the rest of the West Indies and a pioneer in the social consequences of co-operation.[11]

In 1935 Sir Frank Stockdale, an agricultural expert, commented to the Colonial Office:

> Co-operative credit societies have made greater progress in Tobago than anywhere else in the West Indies, and co-operative cacao fermentaries are working satisfactorily.[12]

Strong though the thrust to co-operation was, much of it was intended to protect the dignity and the 'face' of the individual, especially in a face-to-

face society where respect was so important. Tobago's poets, especially Eric Roach, in portraying the work-worn peasants who wrested a weary living from the soil, show how strong was their sense of rugged individuality.[13] Communal uplift ensured collective survival, but shielded all, as individuals, from the dis-respect of penury and shame.

A distinct way of life, with variations from place to place, had sedimented in Tobago by 1938. Its settlements satisfied the criteria of Bender and Minar and Greer for communities: they were places in which people lived for the intrinsic value of so doing, and in which there was mutual dependence, face-to-face communication, and ordered, socially sanctioned behaviour.[14] Deviance was permitted, but within certain boundaries.

Because Tobago was a homogeneous society with strong social ties, serious crime was rare. In the early twentieth century, at almost every session of the Supreme Court, the Chief Justice was presented with a pair of white kid gloves by the senior counsel, testifying to the absence of cases for trial or appeal. Intra-village ties were strong and pervasive. For those who flouted the accepted norms, emigration was not only an opportunity but an escape.

Before 1938, when the first government school was built at Mason Hall, all the major schools were run by the churches. Even the private ones were usually started by people who were pillars of their churches. Besides the older denominations—Anglicans, Methodists, Moravians and Roman Catholics—there were Seventh Day Adventists (from 1890), London Baptists (from 1895), and the Gospel Hall Brethren from 1923. All of these denominations built churches in villages and in settlements in and near Scarborough. In the early twentieth century, sacred songs and anthems were extremely important in the repertoire of Tobago musicians, as Elder documents in the case of Charlotteville. Cantatas were frequently held as big social events.[15] In this milieu, churching and schooling combined to encourage moral upright-ness and civic consciousness.

There was a great divide between Christianity and the African-derived tradition. Many Christian ministers, representing the Eurocentric world view, denigrated all aspects of African culture, and both traditions were opposed as regards religious belief and allegiances, sexual morality and other practices.

40

Nevertheless, the two traditions coincided in many respects. The African tradition stressed co-operation and communal solidarity. The communal norms governing work and savings were based on reciprocity, trustworthiness and mutual trust. Their traditional stress on family ties and on respect for one's elders at home and in the community held vital principles for everyday life.

Thus, the dominant tradition, through churching and schooling, and the predominant one from the base of the society, through its communal values and practices, coincided in providing authoritarian and authoritative norms which the society acknowledged, albeit with varying degrees of conformity.

The village and its hinterland were the locus of work, school (for most of the population had only primary education), church, and most of the leisure. In this situation of enduring, diffuse, face-to-face encounters, most people mapped their life-world.

Extra-village networks and ties were frequent but not as intense. The agrarian economy depended on a system of trade. Village women, mainly, traded by sale and barter at Scarborough and Roxborough, in the process making friends and acquaintances from other villages and from the urban centres. Men and women from the northern villages sold and bartered produce at Plymouth. (Plymouth itself was a port of entry for small craft from Toco and the north coast of Trinidad, the destination of hundreds of migrants from Tobago.) Boatmen from Charlotteville traded and bartered fish and ground provisions for 'wet sugar' (muscovado) with leeward villagers. In addition to these exchanges based on a division of labour between the regions within Tobago, the bulk of the surplus produce was shipped to Trinidad, often with *traffickers*[16] from the villages, both male and female, as intermediaries.

Family ties, friendship, and formal organizations also linked people across settlements. Weddings, funerals, church harvests, cantatas and missionary meetings were occasions for which people from far and wide linked together. Village choirs, cricket clubs and other sporting groups, debating clubs, musicians, singers, Carnival chantwels and Speech Bands met in competition or co-operation with similar groups from other localities. Agricultural, handicraft and needlework shows also brought the schools, peasants and craftspeople

together in annual competitions. After 1915 the Boy Scout movement, and after 1925 the Girl Guides, linked young people in camps, parades and other gatherings. From 1935 the Teachers' Get Together gathered the intelligentsia annually. Newer organizations such as trade unions and political parties also held annual conventions and solidarity meetings.

Despite these numerous extra-village networks, the village with its diffuse face-to-face encounters was the core social unit apart from the family, providing social sanctions, formal and informal, that made for social order, respect for self and others, support in times of distress, and co-operation to meet mutual needs.

2. THE LABOURING CLASS AS PRODUCERS

The Taming of the North

It took extraordinary courage and endurance to convert the forest into settlements such as Bloody Bay and L'Anse Fourmi. In 1929 Amos James (1904–c.1999) decided to leave his native village, Bethel, to work as a cocoa contractor to accumulate funds to buy his own land in L'Anse Fourmi, given that all his family had was a homestead on half an acre of land. He took a contract to plant ten acres of cocoa for the L'Anse Fourmi Estate, and described how it worked.

AJ: You take up a piece of land, and you make an agreement with the owner of the land. I think the authorities had a set of rules governing that system.

So you will agree to receive a certain amount per tree, when the trees get big. They had three types of trees. So they would say, a bearing tree, a half tree and a quarter-tree. That [the latter] is a tree you just plant. A half-tree, in the case of cocoa, the one that just begin to put out branches, we call that half-tree. ...

SCJ: So you got a different rate for each stage of tree? ... And in between you planted short crops?

AJ: In those days, my dear sister, we used to get the privilege to sell our produce in Trinidad. The steamer used to come around fortnightly. We had a depot at Bloody Bay. Well, in those days, Bloody Bay was the headquarters. That is to say, there is the place where the steamer used to come in, and so a depot was built there for the people of Anse Fourmi, for whoever has anything to ship.

SCJ: So how you got your things from here to there?

AJ: Very good question. In those days, we used to carry those things on our head, or on donkeys. Almost every planter had his own donkey. Well, when one planter has more than his donkey could manage, we would help. We used to work hand in hand, eh. We used to help each other.

SCJ: So the other contractors all came from Bethel?

AJ: No. ... Some came from Grenada; some came from Canaan, some from Mt. Pleasant, some from Buccoo. Right. And that was the estate what they call the L'Anse Fourmi Estate. It was belonging to a lady by the name of Janet Stanhope Lovell. ... Some French woman.

SCJ: Tell me about these Grenadians. How did they come? … And what year did you come up here?

AJ: I came here in 1929. ...

SCJ: The Grenadians had come before you?

AJ: Yes, I met them here. Well, in those days, mind you, you come into a place with forest like this, where you goin' to build?

Now, there was the track here, they call it a bridle road. You could travel by foot, or by donkeys or horses. You come in, you take up your portion of land, and you get some stick, you get some straw, and you make yuh little hut. And you will stay in that, and do what you can on the land, until yuh produce begin to grow and so on.

... Put on galvanize. But mind you, you doing two things at the same time. But, mind you, when you first come, that is the challenge. Can I stick this type of life? Well, by reading, you see the older people used to make it. I think even in England, the people used to live in straw houses! And so we did. I live in a straw house mihself, when I was in the contract.

When I came here, I had no land of my own. I took up a contract on the lands of the estate, and there I get my bits of round wood and my straw, and make my little house. Before it was completed, I get some pieces of ... slabs. While the forest was there, men used to go and saw boards and so on, so what they didn't use, they call those slabs, and we would take our axe and we go and bring in pieces of board, and we get a ladder, and we go up there and make ourselves comfortable. But while we were there, we working on the body of the house.

SCJ: So on the slabs is where you slept?

AJ: Yes! And we used to enjoy. [Laughs.]

SCJ: At that time, you [hadn't brought] your wife and children yet?

AJ: No. When I get the house and it enclose, and we have a little floor, Ah say, 'Let her come and see, and if she's willing to stay with me, I'd be glad.' [Laughs.] It would give me the courage, you see. With the time I had to be going up and down to see them, I could be doing some advancement in the cultivation, you see?

She knew about the cocoa business before me, because her father had this cocoa contract. And she was willing, because when we married, we didn' have our own house. ... And so, when she came, and she was impressed with the field, you see, I say, 'Well, right, girl,' and so we settle down.

So while working the contract, we begin to get our own cocoa and so on, we were able to buy this piece, our own five-acre piece of land. This is the first piece of land we buy.

SCJ: How many years it took you before you got land to buy?

AJ: Eight years.

SCJ: Was that normal, or would people be able to do it faster?

AJ: In the case of the Grenadians, most of them come and buy their own lands.

SCJ: They came with money?

AJ: Yes.

SCJ: They had gone to Panama? How did they get their money?

AJ: Some of these people worked cocoa contract in Trinidad, you see, in Toco and these places. The neighbour there, I think she say she was living at Cumana, or something; and Sans Souci, L'Anse Noire.[17] So they worked cocoa contract over there, and got their money and come and buy lands here. When they gave up their contract there, the money they get for their contrac', they come over to Tobago, and buy lands in L'Anse Fourmi especially.

SCJ: And they also continued to work contract here?

AJ: No, when they came, they came on their own. They came on their own lands. So my neighbour there had a ten-acre block, you see. He come with enough money to be able to buy a ten-acre block.

SCJ: Lands up here were cheaper than elsewhere in Tobago?

AJ: Yes, you have to say that. ... Now, the lands we are owning today are lands the Government allotted to young men who fought in the 1914 War. ... The young men who went and fought in that War, when they came back, the Government had two options—to offer them five acres of land here, L'Anse Fourmi, or sixty dollars. So you could have got five acres of land in those days for sixty dollars.

... In those days, that was money! When you owned a five dollars in those days, you are a millionaire! [Laughs.] ...

SCJ: How many Grenadian families you met here?

AJ: There were the Johns up here. The Garricks. ... He had contract on the L'Anse Fourmi Estate, as well as he had his own lands. His name was Joseph Garrick. Is only those two Grenadians were [in] Anse Fourmi, but you had more Grenadians at Bloody Bay. ... You had [at Bloody Bay] quite a few. Dervis Charles, Jim Kirk, Primus, Francis. You had more Grenadians down there.

Amos James described meeting 27 families in L'Anse Fourmi in 1929, all already settled on their own lands. Of these, 1 was from Barbados, 2 from Grenada, 2 from Parlatuvier, and all the others from leeward Tobago, especially Buccoo, Les Coteaux, and Mt. Pleasant. They had all arrived five years before him, in 1924, and bought Crown lands that had initially been intended for demobilized soldiers from World War I.

These families endured hardship. The roads remained bridle paths until the 1960s when the dirt road to Charlotteville was widened for jeeps; even so, in rainy weather they would have to push the jeep out of 'a mud pool'. Bridges were pieces of wood laid across ravines, and villagers would walk to Charlotteville, Roxborough or Bloody Bay by bridle path, while travel by small boat to Plymouth and Mt. Irvine was also frequent. The village had no school until 1944. The nearest health office was at Parlatuvier, several miles away. On his Meet the People Tour of 1963, Dr. Eric Williams, the Prime Minister, remarked after his long trek on bad roads to the village, that they were 'living behind God's back'.[18]

Metayage

Between 1900 and 1940, metayage continued on the few estates producing sugar. Metayage, for many sharecroppers, was one among other economic activities. It was sometimes used as a stepping stone to acquiring land. The metayer's cane piece was called his *'cane 'ole'* [cane hole]. Samuel Adams (b.1903) was one of the few surviving metayers in the 1980s, having started working a metayer holding with his stepfather from 1911, and continuing when he grew up until 1935. He graciously described the working of the system at Orange Hill for the benefit of posterity.

SA: Well, the metayer system is that the estate owner finding the land. If you go and see a nice piece of land, you can work there. Go and tell the owner of the estate, 'I see a piece of land there, I would like to have it grow some cane.' He give you permission. You go and clean the land, and you get men and clean it, and you get men and you dig and plant. Plant potato first on that piece of land. When you dig, you plant potato and you plant your cane.

SCJ: You're planting both same time?

SA: Yes, yes, yes. ... The potato on the bank, and the cane in the middle, between the two banks.

SCJ: I see. Why they did it so?

SA: Because ... potato could kill it out, you know. Cane is a thing, when it coming small, the potato cannot be too heavy, so sometimes you had was to go and trim the potato from the cane. That's why you see, when the potato bear, you dig it out. You mould the cane then.

SCJ: So after a while, you will mould up around the cane?

SA: Yes, mould the cane. Dig the bank, you call it 'break bank'. You break that [potato] bank down and heap up and mould the cane up.

SCJ: I see. ... So you have the cane and the potato in alternate rows.

SA: Yes, that's right.

SCJ: So the estate owner didn't mind your planting the potatoes?

SA: No, no, no. Didn't mind planting the potatoes, 'gainst as you care the cane. And that was *our* benefit. The potato was *our* benefit. You get the potato for yuhself. The cane now was between you and the estate.

SCJ: Did they allow you to plant any other crops?

SA: Well, yes, you can plant little cassava. On the end bank, you plant peas.

SCJ: The last bank?

SA: Yes, quite on top, you know. In between the drains, you plant peas. But you could do anything that wouldn't interfere with the cane. And you can't plant the cassava too near. Plant them about six feet apart. Sometimes with the cassava, the estate owner self come and pull them out, with the distance.

SCJ: What about corn, you could have planted that?

SA: Yes, you could have plant corn also.

SCJ: On the potato bank?

SA: Yes, but one after the other. You plant one here. This is a row, you plant the corn here. You skip this one, you go on the next one, and you plant corn there. But very far. It may not interfere with the cane.

SCJ: Who had owned the estate at the time?

SA: At that time, it was Mr Matthew Bell Crooks.[19]

SCJ: After you plant the cane, what happens?

SA: Well, when you plant the cane, and the cane come to mature, to reap the cane, always start cut sometimes February month. To reap the cane now, you ha' to find, do all the labour.

You have to go and give help to other people. You call it 'labour'. If you have chance to cut today, they come and help you cut, and as you finish cut and grind, next man go. And so they uses to do it. And then we put hand in hand and help each other till we reap that cane.

SCJ: So len' han' was for reaping, not for planting?

SA: Well, yes, it could go for planting too, because we used to call it 'pardner'. Pardner. We all used to work together. Sometimes you get your friend to come and help you plant today. Sometimes you get men to dig, plenty men to dig; women to plant the potato. After that, you get the same thing, going partner to weed. And all this kind of thing.

SCJ: So you work pardner to dig, to weed, to reap, and then to grind?

SA: Yes. Yes. When it comes to the grind, you call that 'labour'. You call that, 'Mr Adams is cutting today, Ah goin' an' give Mr Adams a labour.' And so on. Is so we usually get on. …

Labour, yes. And then now, after you finish and you cut that cane, the estate owner give you a head carter man. You know, one carter man to cart the cane, and you have to find the other people. You usually have two carts. So you have one carter man, and you have to find now a second man for the next cart, and two leaders.

SCJ: What is a leader?

SA: To lead the cows, and to load the cart, you see. Then, the cane used to tie by bundles. … the head man when he carting, he deh on top the cart.

The same way with labour. You get all yuh people to help you, and the estate owner find the mill-feeder. One mill-feeder. To boil it, he might find one head boilerman, and a fireman. That is all they give you. And they'll find a man to pump water from a pond to cool the copper after you finish boiling the sugar. These are the only four man they used to find give you to help you wid that cane.

SCJ: In the whole procedure, what kind of work women did? You mentioned that they plant the potatoes. What else they did?

SA: Yes. Tie the cane behind the men.

SCJ: You mean when you cut, they tie it in bundles?

SA: Yes. You get three men in a row, so one woman behind three men. Next three men, one woman behind. So let's say you have fifteen men, it is three women behind the fifteen men. See, one woman here, one there, one there …

SCJ: So five women, one to three men?

SA: Well, yes, one to three men; that's right.

SCJ: So they would tie, and then the men would put it on the cart?

SA: Well, they would cut it up and men put it on the cart.

SCJ: And then when it gets to the mill, what work women do?

SA: Draw *megass* and carry bags. The megass while squeezing the cane, one man to feed the mill and one man to bag the megass from the mill, and the woman take it and throw it in the yard. Or in the megass house, you call it.[20]

SCJ: Oh, to dry. And women have to bring in the megass to stoke the fire too?

SA: Yes, of course.

SCJ: And what else they did?

SA: Well, nothing else on that occasion. That's just that. … The women dry the megass. You throw out, you come and you tote the megass from the megass house; and you get big yard; you know, the yard is big. And you spread it there to dry. And they sit down, and they tu'n it up, and they tu'n it up, until it thoroughly dry. And then you get men now, boys used to make bamboo ting. You call it—hear whey you call it—get bamboos, and you get some borris [?] tail, nail them across, and you full that, and you carry it in the magass hole, where the furnace was.

SCJ: So it's boys doing that, not men or women?

SA: Yes. Any men or so. Women could do it too, but you ha' to take it by bank, you know.

SCJ: How you mean?

SA: The *bank* is a ting make like a tray and you pack it there, and you get one person to help you lift up and you ha' to go and you throw it down. That is from the mill. Just how you take it from the mill, you can do the same thing to go in the furnace hole.

SCJ: In your time, the metayer was responsible for the building of the roads from the field to the main road?

SA: Yes, yes, yes. Well, it generally got no main road, you know, like when you have the cane in a place, you have to make a cart road, they call it, for yuhself. You see, sometimes you [?] the material, and if you get men to help you dig the road, then they [the estate owners] give you a little sugar to help, for feeding them. You got to make that road yuhself, the metayer. Then the owner come and inspect the road. If is perfect, he tell you, 'Alright, well, you can cut your cane tomorrow.' If 'e not well perfect, tell you that some place there want a little widening or so. And well, if you finish it, you come and you get chance to cut your cane.

SCJ: So you wouldn't be able to cut until you had a good road?

SA: Good road, that's right.

SCJ: And the lands you got as metayers, they were far back from the mill yard, or near?

SA: Oh, yes, plenty far. Plenty far, according to how the estate was big all over there so. You see those hilltop over there, we used to get cane all along there.

SCJ: Now when you went to be a metayer, you had to sign a written contract?

SA: No, no contract; no contract at all.

SCJ: Other people signed, or it was all by mouth?

SA: All by mouth. Just see a piece of land and you like it, ... he say, 'Alright, go along.' And you cut it down and you plant yuh cane. No signing of paper at all.

SCJ: So about how many metayers Orange Hill had?

SA: About a hundred and more metayers? ... Yes, yes, yes. 'Carse the whole estate was in cane, you know; all about was in cane. And that was the only thing for people to do.

SCJ: So how many acres you would have had?

SA: As much as you can manage.

SCJ: So if this year you could manage five, you take five?

SA: Yes, it had no limit at all. As much as you could manage. No limit at all.

SCJ: When you went in for the metayer business, were there people who were paid to plant cane for the estate?

SA: Yes.

SCJ: So they had wage workers and metayers?

SA: Yes. When I went on the estate, they had a lotta cane with men working, either by rent or some kind of thing.

SCJ: Oh, they had renters too?

SA: Yes, we used to get cows and rent land to plant yuh different provision.

SCJ: So you would be a metayer, and you would also rent provision ground?

SA: Yes.

SCJ: And other people were doing the same thing?

SA: Yes. Cow pasture. So sometimes now, in order to pay your rent, you go and work with the estate.

SCJ: To give them a few days' labour to plant their canes?

SA: Right, right, right.

SCJ: So how would they pay you? In kind, that is they would just write off your rent account, or they would give you cash?

SA: They would give you a receipt for your rent account.

SCJ: They wouldn't give you cash?

SA: No. If you overdue, like if you exhaust your rent. If the rent is three dollars, and you work for four, five dollars, you get the two dollars.

SCJ: I see. ... And about what year you were a metayer?

SA: Around when I was about twenty-five years. Well, my stepfather was first a metayer, and then I join him there. And he die and leave me there.

SCJ: So when you came here in 1911, he was a metayer, and you continued after that. And about what time you stopped?

SA: Around '35. ...

SCJ: When you finished grinding your cane, the sugar was exported, or used in Tobago?

SA: Endless that was used in Tobago, and the estate owner used to export his.

SCJ: Oh, he exported his own, his shares?

SA: Yes. Is only a few ... that oblige to take one or two barrels from you [inaudible].

SCJ: So therefore, you didn't have to put your sugar in the curing house?

SA: Yes, you could of. Put it in the curing house.

SCJ: For how many days?

SA: For as long as you can. Sometimes, you put it until you use all. As long as you can; you have no place to put it, always secure it for you. But was under lock and key. You have to make a time, the overseer used to go on Friday evening and open that lock to distribute for weekend.

The system is—the sharing of the sugar [also called *'parting'* the sugar]. You didn't ask me about that. The sharing of the sugar. As soon as the sugar boil, the estate owner take the first barrel and the second barrel for you. First part was his, second barrel is for you. And when you put your sugar in the curing house, all the molasses that carry out there, you couldn't get a pan from it for nothing.

SCJ: Even in the thirties? Even when you were in it?

SA: Yes, yes. You had was to buy from the estate. All of that is his.

SCJ: He kept the molasses?

SA: He kept the molasses.

SCJ: So you lose by putting it there?

SA: Yes.

SCJ: When it [was cured], it used to be like crystals, or like wet sugar?

SA: Well, yes. It dry, you know, when it cure. It wasn't crystal, you know. We call it dry sugar, we call it. It come brown like.

SCJ: But it wasn't like Demerara crystals?

SA: No, no, no. ...

SCJ: So when you finish sharing the sugar, about how many barrels you would get for yourself a year?

SA: Sometimes you get four, five, six, seven. Some people get—metayer small, sometimes you get two barrels for yourself. Sometime even go to one. Some persons get one.

SCJ: And then you have to go and give labour to all the people who helped you?

SA: Helped you, yes. And sometime even then, you had was to take your friends who not metayer, come and help you too, and you have to share, give them back out of that same barrel. So sometimes it come to nearly nothing.

SCJ: So for you it was worth it, being a metayer?

SA: Mmm, mm. [No.] But there was nothing else for a man to do, so that's why I used to do it. But it wasn't profitable at all. Wasn't profitable at all.

SCJ: When you got your sugar, you sold some of it?

SA: Yes, yes. By measuring it ... to people who wasn't metayer, nuh. Sell it and give dem. Sometimes women used to go all Canaan to sell sugar on deh head, with buckets.

SCJ: Oh, wives of the metayers?

SA: Yes, yes. They go and buy from the estate and go and sell.[21]

Mrs Izzy Inniss (née Jones) (*c.*1891–*c.*1987) was a peasant on her own land and a metayer on Orange Hill Estate. As in the nineteenth century, the metayers inherited cane holes (metayer holdings) from their deceased relatives. Her companion inherited a cane hole from her father, and she took another in her own right. She worked both cane holes after her companion's death, until the estate stopped grinding sugar in the 1940s.

SCJ: So when you were working the cane, what work you used to do? You used to plant?

II: Mm, mm. [No.] Me nah plant cane. ... Me used to *weed*, o' plant potato.

SCJ: And who used to help you?

II: ... Ahwe used to wuk pardner! Me a' wuk pardner wid man dem fuh come dig fuh me, fuh plant dem pitayte [potato]; an' pitayte a' beare, you nuh. Some a' dem used to pay me fuh plant dem pitayte, but afterwards dem nah pay me no mo'. Come wuk fuh me.

SCJ: When was grindin' time, who used to reap yuh cane for you?

II: Me self! Deh gie you chance fuh cut you cane, people come help you cut. Woman come 'elp you tie. Cart come tek yuh cane guh way. When dem [her friends] a' grin' [grind] you goo back guh tie deh cane. When de cane ah grin', deh come a' kerry de grin' megass guh trow um 'way.

SCJ: Women and men used to help you?

II: Yes, you have people! You have people to come grin' makash [megass]. You see, people a' come wuk fuh *sugar*.

Inniss' testimony also showed how the circumstances of international trade affected the day-to-day lives of the common people. Her father died in 1916, leaving the land where she lived to her. However, he had defaulted on taxes, and the Government's bailiff levied on her and nailed up the door to the house. She immediately took her cutlass and wrenched the door open. Desperate to get money to pay the taxes, she went to negotiate with the estate manager for the grinding of her canes, and discovered that sugar would be £5 per barrel that year (c.1919). She alluded to this below as 'five-pound year', as she described her management of labour.

SCJ: So you had to give them [those who helped her] sugar?

II: Yes, when deh work, deh come fuh work fuh sugar. Man o' woman. Stranger, arl a' Bethel, arl a' Mt. Grace, a' come help; arl at Black Rock, Plymout', come an' help. Five-pound year is a barrel a' sugar me gie 'way, when deh help me.[22]

SCJ: So how much you would have to give each person?

II: 'E have de size pan. Yuh get a long-time shilling pan. You get dat pan, yuh full it wid sugar gie *you*. If a' two day, you get two day sugar.

SCJ: How much was for one day? …

II: Yuh know long-time shilling pan? … Shilling pan. You go an' buy a shilling pan.

SCJ: It had handle?

II: Yeah, 'e get handle an' 'e ha' cover. … You full it gie. If is two day, you get two o' t'ree day, arl de way. If suh, I will gie you half-pail a' sugar. Some a' dem say deh rather half-pail a' sugar. Half-pail is 60c—2s 6d; fuh half-pail sugar; fuh half-pail sugar, deh satisfy.

SCJ: That is for how many days' work?

II: Well, deh nuh, deh nuh count seh how much day. Seh deh want half-pail sugar, yuh gie dem.

SCJ: That is if they help you real good?

II: Eh, heh. Gie dem.

SCJ: And for the shilling pan is how much?

II: If is two or three day, yuh gie dem two or three day sugar; outa de shilling pan.

SCJ: I don't understand. One day's sugar is how much?

II: One day sugar is a shilling. Is 16 cents; 8d a day to tie cane [women's work]. Man now is 30 cent.[23]

SCJ: I see. So you give them sugar that's worth 8d a day?

II: Yes.

SCJ: When was time to cut your cane, before the estate give you chance to cut, you used to have to fix the road?

II: Yes! … Ah get somebody fuh brush de road, fuh let de cart fuh pass. … When you see time, if de road nuh fix, de mananger get somebody an' fix de road; and when you see you cane grin' now, he tell yuh hoo much day you got to pay fuh pay de man fuh cutlass de cart road. [To pay for the fixing of the cart road:] I used to tek sugar—when de liquor [cane juice] come up [starts to thicken after being boiled], meh tell you Ah want a pail a' t'ick [thick] *sling* [the coagulating cane juice]; an' when you see mih get dat pail deh, leave it at de eestate deh. Put a spoon in deh. Tomorrow mornin' *fo' day* [before dawn] me guh down, tek dat pail a' sling; it turn sugar. Go down a' Black Rock go sell … sell it and get money fuh pay. Sometime deh wait 'pan you till when you done part [divide the sugar between the estate and the metayer] an' everyting; you sell, you pay up de cart. But some o' dem nah a' pay. Some a' dem man a' go wuk fuh de estate [in lieu of paying for the fixing of the road].

Referring to her need to return labour to those metayers who had helped her, Inniss stated:

Well, when a' crop time now, you a' cut cane, me come tie cane fuh you. If me nuh come a' field tie you cane back, me come kerry de bank wid de grin' makash weh de mill squeeze, guh trow it 'way.

Inniss also described how people helped her reap in 'five-pound year':

SCJ: How many acres you had?

II: Me nah a' guh by acre. Big valley carl Marcia Water; 'e have a big … mango tree down deh, an' a nex' piece a' cane 'ole by Abbey Road. Dat cane 'ole by Marcia Water a' mih farder cane 'ole. He gie de young man weh me in deh wid, an' me tek one by Abbey Road fuh mihself, facin' to de Backra House.

SCJ: So you had two cane hole?

II: Me cut two—When he sen' message fuh me to cut de Monday, 'e ha' 'orse race a' Petit Trou.[24] Ah only get two row. De lady wah a' pick cane top an' me. Tuesday, 18 *bill*![25] Eighteen bill! Ah man carl Poorman Thomas come out a' Trinidad Tuesday wid de boat a' come. … He name Poorman; an' fuh me husban' name Poorman too. … 'E had one row, only two man deh, an' he join wid dem. Me cut cane three day a' Marcia Water an' two day a' Abbey Road. [She got 18 men with bills to work for her, including Poorman Thomas.]

47

SCJ: So you used to cut cane too?

II: Mm, mm. [No.] Me only a' tie cane. An' carry bank a' de mill.[26]

Edward Peters (1904–1993), who observed the working of the metayage system, commented:

No, it was too much work. Too much work for what you was going to reap! Because I was privileged to be there the day when they was—they call that 'parting the sugar'—when they was parting the sugar. After they divide the sugar, and the estate got their portion, and the metayers got theirs, they start now to give sugar for labour. And that person got, I think, four barrels of sugar for themselves. And they share out *three barrels of the sugar* for labour, to the people who helped them *to reap the cane only*! [Raises his voice.] And to plant the cane and to take care of the cane, they have a exercise [book] cover with a list of names, that I hear them talk about, they owe labour for, to go back and pay for that, when the season come again! Have to go and help the other people! So, when you think of it, I couldn't see what they get![27]

Tobacco Farmers

In the 1880s tobacco growing had been promoted by John McKillop on Bacolet Estate. However, although it was grown there and at Friendsfield Estate, it appears to have taken hold mainly at Patience Hill, the village that was the centre of tobacco production in the late nineteenth century and the first half of the twentieth. Edward Peters (b.1904) met his father planting tobacco at Patience Hill, and relates his father's account of the origin of tobacco growing there.

EP: I'll tell you tobacco. He [his father] told me that tobacco was introduced in this area by a fella called Horatio Nelson. He first brought tobacco in Tobago. He alone was planting tobacco. Nobody else knew how to plant tobacco.

SCJ: He was an Englishman, or from Tobago?

EP: A black man. He used to employ people and plant tobacco. And after he died, a friend of my father, he say, managed to get his book, a book that this Nelson had, on the growing of tobacco, and he introduced it to my father. And both of them start practising the growing of tobacco.

So when they did succeed, the friend told him, he say, 'Well, we must tell de people, because no one man cannot pick up an industry.' So they start telling de people, and is so you see tobacco start in Patience Hill. That's why tobacco is mostly known in Patience Hill. So himself, and Gift, his friend,— It was not widespread in Tobago, because in those days, the only tobacco the people used to get was what they call the American tobacco, and dat was expensive. Just as how now the local tobacco! They used to come for it. So he used to make a few pence regularly. So he used to get a little pick-up with the tobacco, the cocoa.[28]

Horatio Nelson died in 1904.[29]

Most of the tobacco farmers worked in partnership. O'Farrell Harris (b.1908), retired tobacco farmer, described how it was done.

OH: Tobacco, Ah could say dat the women never had no hard work on the tobacco. The most they does is, when they set the nursery, they will water it morning and evening. They used to have a water can and they carry de water from the pipe, ... and wet the whole bed. And the plants grow until it come to maturity, and they remove from de bed to the place prepared for it.

An' den yuh have men dig de set of bankin'. Like I planting an acre, half a acre. Well, ... when I met mih father, he was an old man, and I used to just assist. So I got the idea and the experience from there, to grow tobacco. ...

Peas could not pay in those days. You will have to plant so much corn and so much peas, den to reap it. It was real hard work. But those people was made out of real good steel! [Laughs.]

Sometimes a man go out in his garden on mornings, he not coming back till evening; sometime near sun dusk. They were real slave people in truth, yes. Today, I see the fellas, before dey go an' scratch, they say, 'Sun hat [hot], dis hat.' Not so.

When the men were preparing to plant cane, dey used to have pardner. Dey get pardners, about twelve or how many in a gang. When dey go to dig land, man, when you look lan' suh, yuh eye tu'n! Dat de men deh dig, nuh.

But all yuh had to do, prepare meals. Make a big pot of tea, or a *pitch oil* [kerosene] tin.[30] Make some bread. Well, in dose days, we used to have a lot of *bonito* [a type of fish], you know. Well, the people used to fry bonito to go wid de *bake* [a type of bread], and den deh big chocolate tea. An' when deh drink dat, sometime when lunch time, deh doh even study lunch. Deh used to feed well, you know, and they were very strong.

SCJ: So pardners was important for the tobacco planter, the gardener and the metayer?

OH: Well, most of us go in pardner when we start planting tobacco, because it was the old men system from ever. But we come now and we form our own pardners, and plant up. So you come an' give me a day today, or three or four days, and I will give the balance of days, one for you, this one and that one, until the four days up. Then if Ah have more to dig, den deh will come again. ... And it was very encouraging, yuh nuh, because one encourage the other.

SCJ: And how you choose your pardners?

OH: People that you think alyuh can join best, can understand each other. Yes, get friendly. Or some will come and ask to come into de pardner. 'Cause men from outside sometime will come an' seh, 'Man, Ah comin' wid allyuh.' Fellas from Bethel used to come wid Patience Hill fellas here, to work at Orange Hill. And is whole day diggin'!

SCJ: So pardners was for preparing the ground, and digging banks?

OH: Yeah. Some men can cutlass partly the whole place, but it will take me a few days. So if you want it to be done in a hurry, you ask one or two other fellas to give you a cutlassin'. So they exchange labour.

SCJ: And what about reaping, you used pardners to reap?

OH: ... Well, tobacco is a family crop, really. ... We were about nine children. Well, we all used to go in the morning. We goin' an' cut grass to feed de horses. Go to the well, feed dem up, and before we go to school. And that's de motion all de time.

SCJ: And what your sisters had to do?

OH: They had to go and fetch water; sometimes two of dem would go and wet the nursery; the other two would stay home and prepare meals and so on.

SCJ: So the tobacco ... was more an independent family thing?

OH: Yes.

SCJ: And what about the gardener, the person who had potatoes, provision and so on?

OH: Well, even the same men in pardners usually work potatoes and that. Depend on if you urgent to get out; depend on how you think, nuh.

Now, if this place that you have to dig will take you five days, if you get about four men with yuhself, you do it in a day. Get de whole place to plant one time. An' when you plant one time so, it's better, because sometime you get rain; so as the place ready, you can just go and stick de plants de next day.[31]

Izzy Inniss' account of the curing process for tobacco is also instructive. Some growers had barns in which to cure their tobacco. In the 1950s a barn was a tall room, constructed with wooden walls on a base of concrete, usually with a space between the walls and the roof. Within the barn there were several rows of rafters at varying heights, on which the tobacco was hung for curing. At the base, a fire would be lit and the heat from the fire would ascend to dry and cure the tobacco. Mrs Inniss had no barn, and so hung her tobacco under the house and above the '*fireside*' in her kitchen. The fireside was usually three large stones on which pots were placed; the fuel, dried wood, was placed between the stones.

II: Me used to plant tobacco, yuh know. ... Arl down hyah suh; all by Ol' Par Road, Orange Hill; a' mih garden; plant tobacco. Ah come home, go all a' Friendship guh sell tobacco. You do well! Eh, eh! De mudder [of an acquaintance] get a barn home deh ... Well, fuh ahwe days, ahwe nuh binna get barn. You cut yuh tobacco, come heng it up eena kitchen or underneat' house. When it dry yuh trip it out, go a' Friendship guh sell dat. ... Allums, Downs an' dem used to buy. Low leaf an' long leaf.

Me an' mih brudder an' a nex' young man; one Monday marnin' get a young man come help ahwe hyah, de whole a' de yard wid tobacco. ... get barrel, put um een deh; de pickney dem ah go een a' tramp am down. When 'e done pack am out eena bag, get rice bag, put um een deh, carry am. Me one tek two bag hyah fuh Friendship, me an' mih brudder an' de odder young man, an' guh—Have fuh lef' early, fuh guh down a' Friendship guh sell.

SCJ: What is a barn? ...

II: De barn wha' dem used to get a' dry de tobacco leaves, yuh di' give it fire. Put fire inna de barn. ... De barn now open, wid de sun; an' de tobacco ah dry deh. Gie nice colour. ... Arl by Farm side, it had de barn a' dry de cocoa an' coc'nut an' ting; barn a' dry de coc'nut; dem a' put fire deh an' jes' de heat. But ahwe hyah now, you heng up arl underneat' house; yuh heng up all eena kitchen; you nuh have fuh gie am fire; 'e dry by de smoke. And the heat of de sun. Gie yuh nice colour. When you cut de tobacco now you give it some of de stick, you heng it up; get twine; heng it up wid nail. Well, de leaf now, you tek it out; you get iron hook wid twine fuh run de string an' heng it up; high dere in de kitchen. All dem wuk deh suh me do.

One of the early participants in tobacco farming at Patience Hill was A. P. T. James (1901–1962), Tobago's Member of the Legislative Council from 1946 to 1961. Calling for a committee to investigate the possibility of re-establishing sugar, tobacco and cotton, James told the Legislative Council in 1950:

> ... the first place I was permitted to work for a penny was in a tobacco plantation. I am happy to state that I planted tobacco myself and that I worked with a former member of this Council, Mr I. A. Hope, and with Mr Phillips and Mr Mendez who purchased tobacco during those years. I may assure Your Excellency that many persons who became peasants within recent years in Tobago, in my lifetime, were able to become peasants owning lands from four to twenty acres during the days of the tobacco cultivation.[32]

Tobacco went into serious decline after 1925.

Food Gardens: Division of Labour by Sex

In each field of endeavour, as for metayage and tobacco, there was a sexual division of labour. Mrs Alexandrina Watts of Mason Hall (b.1909) described the cultivation of her family's garden during her childhood.

AW: Sometimes six of them working pardner; you make a pitch oil bucket of tea fuh dem to drink. Den you go and yuh cook de big thing of food again. Full pitch oil bucket of food yuh cook, wit' big set of fish and everything, to serve them. When they finish drinking dat tea in de morning, they work until twelve o'clock; they come and they take lunch. And after lunch, they come and they work till four o'clock. Either cutlassing, o' digging, o' fallin' trees. Dat is the way they used to work the garden in those days.

SCJ: It was always men, or women in it too?

AW: Well, women doing deh cooking. Because if men working for my father, my mother had to go up and cook. She used to cook up in de garden.

SCJ: Women didn't work pardners too?

AW: Cleaning. Women will work pardner. You go an' work wid Mammy today, pickin' grass, o' mouldin' potato. ... After the men do the heavy job, and work and plant the food and everything, when to mould the potatoes, a woman will go an' work pardner with Mammy to mould. Mammy will go today, help she; an' she come back tomorrow and help Mammy. You understand?

SCJ: In other words, in the garden, certain tasks were for women; cleaning and moulding. Planting too?

AW: Yes. Sometimes, even though Mammy didn't do the planting, but she have to drop de potato slip; an'

mih father will plant it. She breaking three slips, and drop it here, drop it there all along, an' mih father will come now, just planting and planting; make it easier.

SCJ: And if is corn they planting?

AW: Well, corn, de men deh cuttin' de corn hole; and Mammy o' one of us will go and plant the corn and peas, and cover back.[33]

Noel Felix and Rachael Eastman described the sexual division of labour in planting, woodcutting and fishing at Parlatuvier in their childhood. At Parlatuvier, from the 1870s all the estates had been in black hands. Barb Stewart owned Stewart's Lot; Christmas Murphy had Parlatuvier Estate; and E. Edwards, Parrot Hall. At their deaths, the land was subdivided into portions for their relatives, and the properties were not worked as estates. All the families in the village worked their own land, some of it in the woods.

NF: As far as I get a little insight of it, long-time days were real nice, you know. ... Like, Ah have a piece of land to dig. All I do, Ah cutlassin' my land. Prepare mih land, cutlass it. If Ah bu'nin' it, Ah bu'n it. If Ah en' bu'nin' it, Ah roll it. And Ah only tell, say at least three fellas, I am diggin' next week Monday. Dis one tellin' dis other one, 'Well, Compeh [Compère] Felix diggin' next week Monday.' Awright.

And when de day meet, you see fifteen men stan' up on dat piece o' land, diggin' it; five, six women plantin' potato. Deh used to call dat de Caracas band.

RE: Den deh make dis big pitch oil pan o' chocolate tea.

NF: 'E have de women dat have three, four, pitch oil tin on de fire, an' deh boilin' dis cocoa tea. And you order—dis fella here was de chief baker, dis Carrington.

RE: But some o' dem used to bake fuh demselves.

NF: Some used to bake deh bread, but some never used to bake. You order two dollars bread. When you say two dollars bread, is a tray like dis table here so.

RE: Whole big tray o' bread.

NF: Pack up wid bread. And when deh comin', deh comin' wid deh hoe, and deh cup hang by deh side here. Dat is fuh deh drink deh Caracas.

SCJ: Caracas?

RE: Cocoa, de chocolate tea.

SCJ: Why call it Caracas band?

NF: Dat was a specie of cocoa dat came from Venezuela.

RE: De red, de reddish cocoa.

NF: Yes, deh call it Caracas. Not de white cocoa; de reddish cocoa. Dat came from Venezuela. And de long-time people, deh seh dat used to make nice tea. So deh call it de Caracas band.[34] ... Dat come from de capital of Venezuela, Caracas.

And it was a pleasure. When you coming from school, eh, you see the sun shinin' so, see how dem hoes goin' up, and deh glitterin' in de sun, and deh come down back. Yuh hear deh goin'— [Imitates the grunting of the men with each chop of the hoe.]

RE: Deh used to dig some banks. And deh used to race, eh, dat deh just make one hoe chop, an' deh make a next one, and deh call it 'de ole 'aig bank'.

NF: Ole haig bank.

SCJ: Why they call it that?

RE: Well, deh have no time to chop up dat fine. And as de man done de las' hoe chop, de women put een de potato slip.

NF: Fast as de men deh diggin', de women behin' dem plantin', yuh nuh. So when dose fifteen or twenty men done dig your piece of land today, finish plant off. Well, de women now, deh call women folk, when time to weed, deh go and deh weed after dat.

SCJ: So is women who did the weeding?

NF: Women do de weedin'. Men used to weed too, but most likely de women weedin'.

RE: Housewives.

SCJ: And on the estate, what work the women did in the cocoa?

RE: Weed.

SCJ: Weed and *samblay* [French: *assembler*, to gather]?

NF: Yes.

RE: Samblay. Deh used to pick up de cocoa when de men chook dem down from de tree. And deh uses to weed de drains.

NF: De contour drains; de drains that go through the cocoa, to lead away de water from de cocoa root, dat 'e wouldn't spoil de pods and so on.

Woodcutting

SCJ: ... Women never worked in the woods?

NF: Nah.

RE: If deh know that deh pullin' wood, deh will cook and carry fuh you.

NF: Say like, is a dry day, an' de men deh haulin' wood, deh will go on de spot and cook de food, yuh understand?

Fishing

SCJ: And women work[ed] on sea?

NF: Nah. ... In long-ago days, never; never. The men.

SCJ: But women would sell fish on the beach?

NF: They wouldn't sell the fish on the beach. ... A next thing deh uses to do again, as far as I experience. Like de men, I have my wife, Ah fishin' de whole of dis week, de whole of next week, a part of de edder week, dryin' fish and so on. And like Friday or Saturday, gone Roxborough and sell. Sell dry fish.

SCJ: She would go?

NF: Yes, she would go.

SCJ: With him, in the boat?

NF: No, walk through the woods, and go to Roxborough. ... Sometime de men follow dem halfway. Who have donkey, deh load up deh donkey, *crook* deh donkey,[35] and gone wid deh fish, and sell. ...

SCJ: How long the fish used to take to dry?

RE: ... It may take three good days to dry. Sun and fire smoke, inside o' de kitchen.

NF: Now, what I experience, our kitchen ... the dimension was something like 12 feet long and 10 feet in width. So a part, like from this upright to that upright, that was de fireside. 'E bar off, yuh understand? And deh buil' de stand an' ting, wid de fire stones an' ting.

An' when we father come wid de big snapper and grouper, he skid dem, bus' dem down, open dem out, an' take 'e knife an' he gash them. Cut dem. Deh call dat gashin' dem. An' mih mother, she used to poun' de coarse salt. Deh seh dat does brine de fish faster; 'e does dry faster. Yes, de coarse salt. And yuh sprinkle de coarse salt and pepper inside dese gash an' ting, an' yuh hang it on nails an' ting ... You put yuh nail deh, an' yuh run a stick through it, an' it open out, an' it getting' de heat and de smoke. Yuh [burning] coconut shells. Dryin' it fast, fast, fast. ... When it dry, 'e have a brownish colour, something like light brown so. Real pretty.

SCJ: So people didn't have to buy the imported saltfish?

NF: Off and on.

51

RE: 'E had de time fish would run out. ...

NF: But before, you dry a certain amount; some people used to keep a certain amount, yuh nuh.

RE: Deh keep it. And deh have a place on top de fireside called *lafter*.

NF: Lafter. Some call it de *grenne*. ... You throw yuh dry fish up deh.

RE: And look someting, yuh know what die out here? Sprats ketchin'. No net. You come down de road and you buy yuh calabash set of sprats, and you salt dat an' you dry it on a tinnin' [tin] sheet.

NF: Dose fish, after yuh tek out what yuh want to sell, yuh put de balance on top deh; deh call it *grenne top*. And when yuh cookin' an' ting, dem getting' a minor heat, keepin' dem all de time from spoilin'.

RE: Sometimes, Mammy an' dem used to t'row it in bag. Deh make purse from clot' an' den put it in de bag, an' tie 'e mout'. So, when fish scarce an' ting, deh en' getting' fish to dat 'bundant, deh cook dat.[36]

Coconut Estates

On coconut estates, according to Sidney Gibbs (1906–c.1984), the arrangement was as follows.

SG: Women had to go in the estate every morning to pull coconuts. You know what I mean by pulling coconuts? You had men cutting, and they [women] taking out the kernel from the shell; or, they had at Friendship, they had women looking after fibre. They take the husk and make fibre.

SCJ: Women did that one?

SG: Yes, women doing that. The cutting of the coconuts was done by the men. Women don't cut the coconuts.

SCJ: And men used to pick?

SG: They had men picking. But the men that were picking were not the men that were cutting. The choppers were different to the pickers.[37]

Also recalling the leeward coconut estates, Amos James described the work of men and women before 1929:

AJ: You had just a few people working on the road, and the majority used to work on the estates.

SCJ: Men and women?

AJ: Oh, yes! And you would have seen the women using their cutlass, cleaning the coconuts and—

SCJ: What was the women's work?

AJ: They used to call where the manager lived, they used to call there Great House. So you'd find women in the Great House; you will find one cooking, you will find one washing, and if he has a wife, you will find one nursing.

Then you would find some on the field. While the men working, the cart would take up the coconuts in the field and carry it in the yard. Now the time come for it to be put into copra, you will have men cutting the coconuts, and ladies taking out the coconuts. And you will find ladies in the tray, drying the copra. ...

SCJ: So in the coconut field itself, with weeding, or planting or picking, were women employed?

AJ: Yes. After the coconuts grow up, and begin to yield, the field had to be kept clean. While men were cutlassing, you will find women putting the grass around the coconut roots; we call that mulching. Or sometimes, you see them ... stringing [?] it in the row, as the case might be. And all that was to provide something for the women to do. And sometimes, you find the women too cutlassing. ... Especially on the Friendship Estate.[38]

William 'Sweetie' Pope (b.1907) worked on Belle Garden Estate planting coconuts in the 1920s.

WP: I was due to pick coconuts, 6 cent a hundred. When rain come, Ah wuk at one task fuh 30 cent, and dat is all.

SCJ: Task doing what?

WP: Cutlassin'. ...

SCJ: What work women did on the estate?

WP: Pull de coconut. When yuh cut de coconut, woman dig it out; an' den deh get donkey, and deh tote it in de copra house. ... Dat is women work. And you had one, two men used to cut. [A man] used to dry.[39]

Cocoa Estates

Albert Richardson (b.1888) worked in the first decade of the twentieth century as a labourer on three windward cocoa estates. He described both his own experience and that of his mother, Selena Marcani, a Barbadian migrant.

SCJ: You worked on Kendal Estate, Roxborough Estate and Louis d'Or. What work you did?

AR: Clean cocoa, and pick cocoa.

SCJ: All the estates were cocoa [estates]?

AR: Nuh, well, at first dey had cane, but I didn' know nutten about dat, becar I was a little boy when dey had cane. Well, afterwards, well, dey dispose wit' cane, and dey start to give out land to people to plant cocoa and coconut. By contrac'. And when dose cocoa and coconut come to perfection, dey does reckon dem, and pay de people dem who occupy dem, by de hole. An' den de estate will take over dem, an' make demselves get big. But de estate used to plant fuh demself too, yuh nuh. De estate used to plant fuh demself, along wit' contractors. By dat, de estate deh get popular wit' cocoa an' coconut. Bot' Kendal, Roxborough and Louis d'Or. ... I know about Kendal, Roxborough and Louis d'Or.

De fus' place I work after I leave school, I work at Kendal. ... Trim cocoa and pick cocoa. Den after dat, I work at Roxborough. Same ting, pick cocoa, trim cocoa; I used to brush cocoa too. And afterward, Ah spen' couple months at Louis d'Or, but not much.

SCJ: You were working on the estate because you had no lands of your own?

AR: When Ah was workin' on de estate, I had my own land. When I finish work sometimes, when I work task, I used to go at the land and work, and evening time I come home back. ... Ah work in de estate, then, right. After Ah finish work in de estate, Ah used to work in de public road, government road. ... And while workin' in de government road, Ah used to work as a saw man, sawing boa'd. Ah used to saw boa'd, you know. Well, after working in de saw pit, and working in de government road, ... well, after Ah leave de government road [on afternoons], Ah gone to mih lan'; straight away to mih land.

SCJ: What work women used to do on the estate?

AR: Well, women used to weed. And deh used to haul mould when the drainers deh dig drain, you understand? When de drainers deh dig drain, de women used to haul de mould, spread de mould through de fiel'.

Well, my mudder was a female driver. She used to drive de female dem, at Roxborough. My mudder, Selena Marcani. An' ... deh used to get twelve cents a day. Twelve cents a day. ... And she was a driver. All a' dem used to get de same twelve cents a day. Sixty cents a week, five days a week, from Monday to Friday.

SCJ: So it's only weeding and hauling mould that women did?

AR: Yes. Weeding an' haulin' moul'; an' den deh pickin' cocoa. Den samblay cocoa. After de picker pick, deh take up. And all different kind of work in de estate. ... You see, when deh picking cocoa, after de picker pick down de cocoa, de female will pick dem up, an' gadder dem, an' heap dem up one place.

An' when deh breakin' now, de male deh will break wid de cutlash, an' de female will—deh have a ting call; fuhgot what deh call it, but de ting make out of bamboo—deh used to tek dat an' chook out de cocoa from de shell. Chook out de cocoa from de shell an' put dem in basket an' bag dem up an' put dem in de cart. De estate have deh cow cart and deh mule cart, [to] *drogue* deh cocoa up to de estate dryin' tray.[40]

SCJ: Who used to dance the cocoa, men or women?

AR: Women and men. De woman dance, and men would be shovelling up. Women and men used to dance. ... When deh dance, they dry, an' after deh finish dry, dey bag dem up, hang up de cocoa an' ship dem away to Trinidad.[41]

Livestock-Rearing

Many Tobagonians owned animals for domestic consumption and for sale. Goats and cows supplied the homes with milk. Since the nineteenth century, livestock had become a form of investment, given the absence of banks between 1848 and 1880, and this continued in the early twentieth century. People of both sexes, including children, raised animals, but cows and horses were usually tended by males. Mrs 'Vaso' Carrington described how her father, Henry Livingstone Rowley, a master carpenter and independent farmer, reared his large herd of animals with the help of unpaid labour in a traditional system of shares.

GVC: We had all kind of stock: goats, sheep, horses, cows, but his trade was carpentry. ... I don't know if you ever heard of a term, giving out stock to mind and you get half and I get half, or I get the first birth and you get the second ... My father help people along and you help yuhself too. What you can't manage, you have big herd, and a person is careful and all the rest of it, and they in need, you help them too, well you give them fuh half, or first calf and second calf. ...

SCJ: And it used to work out?

GVC: People giving stock out to min', what!

SCJ: I might have heard of it but I didn't know it was prevalent.

GVC: Yes, it was, but you have to be careful. ... Tobago is a small place, and you observe a young man trying to get along and he's decent and honest—Lots of people get their own stocks and ting, helping others who ha' plenty. ... Tobago is a small place, ... but you know you really could point out an honest person that is needy and willing to do that. 'Cause some of dem darm t'ief too, you know.

SCJ: But if you could trust them and if you needed labour to help you with your stock, you could give out some of them?

GVC: Yeah. My father has done that. There was a man, … came from Patience Hill, came and married a woman in our village and lived in our village [Bethel]. [They had a lot of children] and they had things hard; he was a hard worker. And my father tested him by starting off with a calf … If you were known as anybody at all in the district where we grew, a child is born and you point out some piece of stock or something that you have for that child.

SCJ: So that is that child's cow?

GVC: That's right. Or whatever stock it is. … And so each child, they grow up owning something. So you can't manage all that. You have to have somebody, but the person you get have to be somebody honest. And he watched this man, … hard worker and honest man; that is how my father started him off, giving him stock to mind and so on. But the *first* birth is always for the person who give the stock to mind. The first birth. As you go on, the second one is yours.

SCJ: Oh, so it's alternate births?

GVC: Yes.

SCJ: And the original animal goes back to the owner at the end?

GVC: Yes, it is yours.

Public Works Department

On public roads, there were very few women workers, unlike the practice before 1887. Dalton Andrews (b.1912) described the types of work women of the labouring class did on the roads.

DA: … Like you had the public road and well, on the estate, you had women work by way of weeding, what we call samblaying cocoa, or pulling nuts—pulling copra. That is women work. On the road, it was a sort of disgrace to see women on the road.

SCJ: They didn't have water carriers?

DA: They had, here and there you meet in a gang, one woman in a gang. … There was another way, in Works Department in those days. Those days we had gravel roads; it wasn't oil roads, as now. So the women had was to go in the river with tray, and take out gravel by the yard. So we have the measure, which someone will be there to check. So the most of them would be women. Tie their waist with their

towel and get their tray. So we have men in the river bed shovelling and loading them, and there is a man who checking. So you get so many yards for yuh task. And you run competition to see who first can finish, and you know, one help the other, and all sorts of thing.

SCJ: So … those who would have been cooks or cleaners in the estate house, those who work in the estate samblaying, and pulling copra and so, and those on the public roads pulling gravel, those were the major jobs for women out of the home?

DA: Those were the major employment for women, yes; out of the home.[42]

Izzy Inniss of Patience Hill also worked on the public roads. Here is her account of her experience.

II: Me wuk like a Satan! Me in young an' me in strong, yuh know. Wuk a public road, arl Arksenscheoch [Auchenskeoch], tek am fram Wilson Road right away down to Plymout'—

SCJ: That is on the public road?

II: De driver di' name Missah Steward.

SCJ: And what work you used to do on the public road?

II: Shovel mould behin' two man.

SCJ: And what the men were doing?

II: Deh weedin'. Weedin' de road, bot' side. One man get runnin' [a distance to weed]; de edder one get runnin'. Me get behin' dem two man, shovel it up.

SCJ: And where you putting the stuff?

II: Throw de stuff over side. Sometime when 'e can't go me ha' mih tray fuh put um een deh, an' when de tray full, put um a' mih head an' go out go t'row it 'way.

Alexandrina Watts, former domestic servant and peasant, discussed how employment on the roads increased near Christmas time in the past.

SCJ: And on the roads, women worked?

AW: Just few. But the most time when women was workin' in Tobago is when around September to October, when the heavy rain come to Tobago, and the landslide come in de road, women uses to get work dat time. And there is where deh uses to spen' deh Christmas. If rain din' come down, and de landslide didn' come down, dat every woman gorn out wid deh tray to tote away de dirt from de road, because deh didn't have— [Tape ended here.] Men will shovel de dirt in yuh tray, lif' you up, an' yuh gorn to t'row it a little way up so, over a bank and so on. Dat was de major work deh had for women in Tobago. No odder work. No odder work. ... Long ago, was deh husband alone working and you wit' yuh garden, yuh go and you sell, and so on.[43]

The Features of Peasant Production

From the above accounts, we can discern four features of peasant production in Tobago.

First, in many instances, working for wages, renting pasture or provision lands, and other arrangements with the estates were combined with own-account farming. Workers on the public roads also farmed on their own account. Indeed, occupational multiplicity remained a feature of production in Tobago. Nevertheless, in the dynamics of the negotiation between planter and labourer, the labourer for the most part retained certain degrees of freedom. Thomas Thornton explained in 1908 that the labourers 'must have their provision ground' which, in the Leeward District, was often rented from the estate: 'and on this account the labourers have become more or less independent.'[44]

Second, Tobago's peasants produced most of what they consumed, and exported to Trinidad and elsewhere for cash, since there was a limited internal market for everything.

Third, there was a clear sexual division of labour in virtually every sphere of activity.

Fourth, peasant production for subsistence and sale was based on community norms and values, some of them of African origin. Foremost was the system of pardners, whereby labour was exchanged. Here, the exchange was often seen in terms of time (day fuh day) and not in terms of the monetary value to be placed on the work given. The small size and the relatively low productivity and profitability of the peasant enterprises drove the populace to sustain its co-operative activities, formal and informal. These co-operative systems, coupled with the widespread bartering described in the following section, indicate that the Tobago economy was semi-monetized until the 1940s.

The semi-monetization of the economy meant, as the metayer system of the nineteenth century had revealed, that indebtedness was often disguised. In 1936 the Wages Advisory Board observed:

the exchange of labour is widespread, there existing a sort of *quid pro quo* arrangement whereby a debtor puts in work on a neighbouring creditor's lands as value for indebtedness which he may not otherwise be able to liquidate. This accounts in a large measure for the fact that few persons appear to be indebted to any great extent, although when their statements of disbursements are compared with their actual earnings, a staggering debit balance should be carried down at the end of each fortnight.[45]

3. DISTRIBUTION AND TRADE

Three conditions shaped the distributive trades in the early twentieth century.

First, since nearly every family had cultivation of some sort, marketing within the island had to be based on a division of labour by district or region. The dry leeward areas with shallow soils and denuded hills had an abundance of sugar, coconuts, and cassava, but lacked other ground provisions such as plantains, dasheen and tannias, which grew better in the deep, fertile lands of the northern and windward villages and woods. Moreover, leeward farmers got sweet potatoes only from October to December each year, while the rest of the island had year-round crops. Some villages had fish; others did not. Buccoo and Sandy Point had sugar apples; other areas did not. These differences became the basis for trade and exchange.

Second, since sales within the island were small, the populace depended for cash on produce shipped to the Port of Spain market and the big Trinidad merchants. The system of 'trafficking' between the islands was pivotal to this process.

Third, since the ability to market frequently outside of Tobago was highly limited owing to the inadequate coastal steamer service, profits in the peasant enterprises were small; and, as in the nineteenth century, cash remained scarce. All this became the basis for a remarkable system of bartering, which made Tobago's internal distribution system uniquely different from that of Barbados, Grenada, St. Vincent and Trinidad, where barter in the twentieth century was largely unknown.

The reports on the Government Savings Bank, the only one in Tobago between 1893 and 1917, indicate the low levels of cash savings. In 1893, 93.0 per cent of the £1,598 deposited was, according to the responsible officer, from persons 'who cannot be placed in the category of poor persons'. The average deposit of poor persons was approximately 7s, while the overall average was £4 7s.[46] In 1908 there were 208 depositors with a net balance of £4,213 11s 7½d. By 1915 there were 325 depositors, up from 309 in 1914; and the 1915 net balance was £4,778 18s 7d. In 1913 there was a balance of £5,228 2s 11d for 287 depositors. In fact, the rate of savings per depositor declined from £20.3 in 1908 to £18.2 in 1913 and £14.7 in 1915. When global prices rose in World War I, the Colonial Bank and the Royal Bank of Canada both opened Scarborough branches in 1917; both closed their doors on 31 December 1923.[47]

Volume I showed that bartering was, from the era of enslavement, embedded in Tobago's culture, with rum as a common medium of exchange. After Emancipation, because of the chronic and widespread shortage of specie, wages were often paid in kind. Indeed, metayage flourished precisely because the planters could not pay wages to the entire estate labour force. The crisis of the 1880s exacerbated the lack of specie, and nearly all transactions, including sales of land and payment of court fines, were made in kind. In the early twentieth century, in the face of stringent conditions, bartering remained part of the popular mechanisms for survival, accumulation and community self-help.

To understand bartering systems, we must first address what money is. Money is used for four purposes: it is a standard of measurement, a medium of exchange, a store of value, and a standard of deferred payment.

In Tobago's bartering system there were two types of transactions. The first was 'pure barter', that is, the exchange of goods on the basis of their use value, with no monetary value placed on the items. However, as Webb notes, pure barter is rare, since 'Any single good or group of goods that are not immediately perishable and are exchanged on a repetitive basis can come to assume the properties of money.' Webb goes on to describe another use of the term 'barter', which fits the second type of Tobago transaction very aptly. Here, no actual money changes hands. Yet,

the value of goods exchanged can be expressed directly in terms of money or indirectly by the valuation of groups of goods in bundles; thus, the goods are priced either implicitly or explicitly, although the transaction may involve only goods in kind.

He also noted that valuing goods in bundles was 'standard practice' in the 'Atlantic sector of precolonial West African trade.'[48] In Tobago, as we shall see, bundles of goods, such as heaps of potatoes or fish, were often exchanged and implicitly or explicitly priced.

The term used in Tobago for bartering was '*to change*'. In discussions with those who took part in these exchanges without cash, I made every effort to find out the basis on which the exchanges were made. It is clear that, although exchanges were often made on the basis of mutual needs, a monetary value was usually placed on items exchanged. Interestingly, as Mrs Alexandrina Watts' account below shows, some of the internal marketers used 'changing' to purchase goods in one place, sold them in another, and returned to sell or barter in the village of origin. Some exchanges combined part-payment in cash and in goods. Traffickers also acquired goods by 'changing' in Tobago and sold them in Trinidad. Thus, money was clearly the standard of value or unit of account, even when its scarcity did not allow it to be the medium of exchange.

There were two official markets in Tobago, the main one being at Scarborough. At Roxborough, there was vending at the roadside and in front of the main shops, although no market building existed before 1930. Some beaches, for example Plymouth, were centres of trading between the northern and leeward villages, and regular exchanges were made between people who sold or bartered at estates and other sites.

Widespread bartering was symptomatic of the conditions described in Chapter 1: low productivity, and poor infrastructure and marketing conditions, which made peasant agriculture barely viable.[49]

Exchanging between Leeward and Windward Districts

In keeping with the regional division of labour, Charlotteville (windward) men would go by boat to Arnos Vale (John's Hill), Culloden and other leeward estates to exchange ground provisions, planks of wood and corned fish for sugar. Emeldalina Nicholson (1901–2005) from Charlotteville described the practice in her childhood.

EN: ... our people used to go down to John's Hill Bay, at Culloden way down there, to carry down fish and board an' ting, to get *sugar*.

SCJ: They would sell the fish?

EN: They carry the fish, dry fish an' ting, and board, and get sugar.

SCJ: In exchange?

EN: Mm, hm [Yes.]. … Deh get sugar fuh deh fish, deh board and—whatever deh carry, dey take sugar in exchange. John's Hill Bay. When I was a child, I know mih father and dem used to go down deh and get sugar.[50]

Mrs Mary Alleyne (1891–c.1985), who was born ten years earlier than Miss Nicholson, confirmed Miss Nicholson's testimony for the sugar-growing area around Woodlands Estate, which was also near to John's Hill and Culloden.

SCJ: In your time, you knew people who used to barter, to change?

MA: Yes, yes! Dat a' cammon ting, man! Common ting. … Well, listen me, not in de village, because most people used to get deh sugar. De 'ole a' Mt. Thomas people, ole-aged people dem, get deh cane ground, deh cane land, mih mean. An' Woodlands people dem too. So when deh mek deh sugar, deh *sellin'*, you heare. De only place where sugar used to go, Ah could tell you, Charlotteville men dem used to leave Charlotteville come down wid dem big snapper, big grouper. When deh open, dry an' everyting, come down come change fuh sugar in de estate deh. … Sometime … mih farder come home wid de big fish, weh dem guh dem change wid de sugar at de estate. Sometime Ah guh at de estate guh change de sugar fuh fish. Nuh Castara people deh; Castara people deh does come, *buy*, go back and sell. But Charlotteville people, dem boat used to come down and *change* dem big snapper—dry, well dry, yuh heare—fuh dem sugar. Dem get dem bucket sugar a' go 'ome. Get dem bucket sugar a' go 'ome, man![51]

Boats also went from leeward to windward villages, especially to Charlotteville, to barter. Dr. J. D. Elder recalled the steady contacts between Culloden, from which his father had migrated, and Charlotteville.

JDE: And so, to come up by boat from that part of the world, when my father had made good that side, was the normal thing. Our house was an entrepôt; full of Culloden. So all these men from the boat—Ben Second and all them fellas—they were sloop men; they used to build sloop and come up with cattle, with sheep and goat, and dry meat and so on, exchange for the food [ground provisions] up there. Bartering, backward and forward.

SCJ: In your childhood?

JDE: Yes, and I saw all that. *Hogsheads* of sugar—because Culloden was still grinding sugar—under our house, you know. And molasses dripping out, turning rum, and my brother and I drinking this stuff, and getting very high, for we didn't know. This is our experience as little children.

So it is this trade, bilateral trade, between *that* side and *that* side, some coming over land, and most coming by boat. When it was November time, they didn't come. Because now and again, they would try to come in November, and the sloop would founder.[52]

Exchanging within the Windward District

There were very few accounts of bartering between the villages of the Windward District. Samuel Moore (b.1902) recalled that people from 'Delaford, Roxborough sometimes, even at Kendal' used to go to his village, Charlotteville, to 'change'.

Deh bring what deh have and exchange it, but most for fish. Most for fish, because, you see, we always have een fish here. Dey had a seine, two seine, and when deh shoot deh get a lot of fish. And the men go also to sea to do trolling, as well as deep-sea banking. They catch a lot of fish, and they exchange it. … Deh used to bring in, I think, dry peas. Ah, farine! Deh used to parch farine in a big way, and so they used to bring in de farine. And so we exchange for fish an' ting.[53]

Dora Manning (b.1893), a former estate worker and cocoa contractor, recalled people going to Kendal Place from Pembroke and Goodwood with sweet potatoes and tannia, to exchange for other food crops because of shallower soils at the latter places.

You see, the land more poor to bring dasheen and all dese kind of a ting, you know. More work potato garden [at Pembroke and Goodwood].[54]

Trading within the Leeward District

As we have seen, Izzy Inniss described the way in which people from the inland and coastal villages of the Leeward District exchanged labour for sugar on Orange Hill Estate. She also discussed going to Black Rock, a coastal village, to sell sugar for cash. In the course of her interview, she mentioned 'changing' canes for fish at Courland Bay (Plymouth). There were regular exchanges between the people of the leeward uplands—

Bethel, Patience Hill, Prospect—and those of the coastal villages, as Cassie Homeward of Bethel (1911–2003) explained.

CH: Well, I know I used to leave here, when Ah come down from Moriah, Ah used to leave here, [with] one 'alf-bag of potato. I used to go in Plymouth, go and *change, change it,* fuh fish. And if dis man here come now an' [Ah] seh, 'Look mih get three heaps o' potato here now, leh me get some fish fuh mih guh down back now', he will give you, and he take de potato. *And yuh glad to get it.* Becarse you wouldn't stop in de bay from marnin' tell evenin' time, an' yuh get dat load an' 'e can't sell. Yuh see. A' suh.

SCJ: So when you got the fish, what you did with it?

CH: Well, when yuh get de fish, yuh nuh kerry 'ome yuh fish an' get am fry, an' get am fuh eat wid yuh few provision weh yuh get! Yuh glad to get it fuh yuh eat!

SCJ: So it was not to sell?

CH: Nuh, nuh, nuh fuh sell, just to eat, you see. But those people who now, get dem fish to go up and sell it, deh ha' to sell to get deh money. Because when deh buy it in de bay deh now, deh had to price dem fish to give dose people. And deh go and get it, and go and sell.

SCJ: So which was more important—trading for cash or trading by exchange?

CH: Well, those people now who buying dose fish, they have to sell back to get deh money. Sometime when de fish by de bay plentiful, you understand me, plentiful, deh will glad fuh me, as a trafficker, fuh come an' get dat fish from you. You understand me? So when you *sell* dat fish now, you have to go back and give dat man, if a' ten dollars o' how much, accordin' to weh fish you could kerry. You know?

SCJ: So you mean they would *give* you the fish, you sell it and then you carry [the money] back?

CH: Yes. But me doesn' buy fish fuh go an' sell. Me kerry anyting, mih change it, mih glad fuh get it fuh go 'ome, and mek ting. …

SCJ: In your time, changing was more important than paying money?

CH: Changin', changin', changin'. Yuh nuh ha' money fuh guh *buy.* Yuh get yuh provision an' yuh guh down an' yuh get to change fuh yuh fish, an' yuh come 'ome wid it.[55]

In Mrs Homeward's case, the exchange was based on need or use value. At the same time, she

mentioned vendors who received fish on consignment, and who were expected to return with cash for the fishermen.

Trading between the Northern Villages and Plymouth

Mrs Alexandrina Watts (b.1909) at Mason Hall described the complex transactions that her mother did between Mason Hall and Plymouth.

SCJ: … when you used to be going around with your mother, what kind of work she was doing?

AW: Well, Mammy, she was working garden. And she uses to go in de bay to get fish to sell, because my father was not very well; he got sick during dat time. And den she had was to turn round and started to work to help the chilvren. We were seven children—five girls and two boys.

SCJ: So she would go to Scarborough to buy the fish?

AW: No, Plymout'. Plymout'.

SCJ: And then, where would she sell?

AW: In the village here. When she come, she sell it here. Come back, bring it back Mason Hall and sell it.

SCJ: When she went to Plymouth, it was always cash? She was paying money for the fish? She wasn't exchanging?

AW: No, unless she exchange any fish here in the village for provision. Because Plymouth and Black Rock in those days, they didn't have any provision, like, you know, especially dasheen. Dey will have sweet potato down there, or cassava. But when it come to dasheen and yam and so on, they didn't have that around Plymouth side. So, when you change yuh dasheen here for fish, you carry it and you sell it give those fishermen. They glad to get dat!

SCJ: You sell it, you don't change it.

AW: Well, no.

SCJ: So they would have had cash to pay. What you're saying is that she would exchange in the village fish for dasheen, and carry dasheen to Plymouth and sell, to get cash to buy back fish.

AW: Yes.

SCJ: A complicated transaction!

AW: Yes, you see. When she carry it down, well, the price of the dasheen she would get here, won't be de price of de fish; because the fish will cost more; unless is *jacks* [a type of small fish], that they will sell it by the heap. One heap of jacks will value the dasheen dat she have. But if it's a big fish, dat will cost more. So they will pay her for the dasheen or the provision, and then she will buy fish from them.

SCJ: In the village here, when she is changing dasheen for fish, you just said that sometimes the fish [was] worth more than the dasheen. That means you had a money value that you put on that fish and on the dasheen?

AW: Listen, long ago, they sells fish, big fish, deh sell them by the slices. They slice them, and sell them 4c a slice for the fish. Four cents. And a heap of dasheen will cost you four cents A big calabash of jacks will value penny or four cents, and then deh give you a heap of dasheen for that.

You won't change all the fish dat you bring fuh ting, but if a poor person didn' have de money, dey bring down de dasheen and ask you to change it fuh dem.

SCJ: So changing was a recognized way of getting things that you need, if you didn't have cash.

AW: If you didn' have money. Yes.

SCJ: Besides this, you could have gone in the shop and changed too?

AW: No.

SCJ: Not even eggs or any little thing like that?

AW: No, unless the shopkeeper want some eggs, and you have few eggs, eef yuh can buy it and let you get a pound of sugar; you understand? ... Outside o' dat, dey don't do dat in de shop. But like these fish—these fishermen glad to get a solid food to eat; so they glad to get the dasheen.

And dasheen used to come from up this way most; and L'Anse Fourmi and Parlatuvier; that way used to get dasheen. But on the Low Side, yuh fin' deh getting dasheen down there now through the water from their pipe. But in those days, they had no swamp, they had no water to secure these dasheen. But up in our district, where we come from, ... up in the woods have nice place where we used to plant a lot of dasheen, a lot of yam, cassava and everything like that.[56]

Cassie Homeward (1911–2003) reported on trading between Moriah and Plymouth in her youth. People exchanged vegetables for fish in Plymouth and returned to sell the fish in Moriah.

CH: Yes, we used to go and change. People used to carry farine and change fuh coconut oil; change fuh coconut. Sometimes those Plymouth people used to leave and come up to Moriah way. We buyin' one coconut so fuh penny, and sometime you change.

SCJ: How would you know how much provision to give for how much farine?

CH: Well, deh used to put out the potato by the heap, yuh see. Eight cents a heap fuh de potato. The farine dem now, yuh get dem by de milk cup, and sell it.

SCJ: That was condensed milk [cup]?

CH: Yes!

SCJ: And how much for one of those?

CH: One o' dem deh guh give you fuh four cent.

SCJ: So you know that two of those is worth one heap of potato?

CH: Yes. ... Many times dat dose people from Moriah come down to Plymouth, yuh getting a big bonito long 'bout suh, fuh cent. Cent, yuh nuh. Now, you carry down cane. You have breadfruit, yuh kerry down breadfruit, you change it in de bay fuh *fish.* ... Plymout' bay. Dat a' all de ting does ketch. And when yuh get dem ting deh, yuh have to walk from Plymouth right on to Moriah. Those people used to lef' down dere and walk right on to Moriah to go and *sell.*

SCJ: The fish?

CH: The fish.

SCJ: And people used to pay them cash in the village?

CH: Yes, deh used to pay dem!

SCJ: So what you saying is that you used to change between Moriah and Plymouth? You would change breadfruit for fish, and cane for fish.

CH: Yes.

SCJ: When you went to the bayside to change, how would you know how much cane to change for how much fish? And how would you know how much breadfruit to give?

CH: Well, if you get 'bout three breadfruit, dis mister here now, he want it. Yuh come and say, 'Madam, I will give you fish fuh those three breadfruit.' Yuh tek it!

SCJ: Any amount of fish?

CH: Yeah, yuh tek it.

SCJ: Whatever he gives you?

CH: Yes, yuh tek it.

SCJ: ... When you were exchanging, you didn't say that this breadfruit worth six cents; you just exchanged?

CH: Mm, mm. Nuh, nuh.

SCJ: You just exchanged them—

CH: Yes, fuh fish.[57]

From L'Anse Fourmi and Bloody Bay, from the early 1930s, small boats taking ground provisions went to Plymouth and Mt. Irvine to sell. Amos James describes how it worked.

AJ: When we begin to get our little boats and so on, we used to feel good. … Well, in those days, they would go down on weekends with their provision, to Montgomery, Mt. Irvine or Plymouth. And the people in those places used to look forward to those boats coming, bringing them provisions, you see.

SCJ: Tell me about this.

AJ: Though you were shipping to Trinidad, you still had to make it possible to carry down some things for the people at Plymouth, Bethel and those places. And, you know, they get to like dasheen, man.

SCJ: So people from here went down there on weekends to sell?

AJ: With their boat, that's right. And they would come back up on Monday morning, you see. They would go down Friday, and they would stay down till Monday.

SCJ: And where would they be selling, on the beach?

AJ: Yes. Yes. The people expect them to come, yuh see. They used to have a market on the beach. They looking out for them. And if you don't bring, you disappoint them.

SCJ: And it was mostly provisions that they took?

AJ: Mm, hm. Provisions, especially.

SCJ: Was there bartering?

AJ: No, nobody bartering. Everybody buying cash. … No bartering. After they sell the provision, you know, they would go in the shop. … And you buy yuh salt, the things you will need to keep you through the week, you see. Yuh salt, yuh pitch oil and yuh matches.

SCJ: Who did that marketing on the beach, was it men or women, or both?

AJ: Men and women. There were ladies too, who used to do business by buying provision there, send it down by the boat [to Trinidad], carry it down by the boat, come back and buy again. So it was a regular business.

SCJ: And when did that start?

AJ: About three or four years after …

SCJ: You came?

AJ: Mm, hm.

SCJ: So it started in the thirties, and it continued until when?

AJ: Well, it continue until … 1963. That is when Hurricane Flora came, for we had no provision to carry again; we had no cocoa to sell again. So everyting [die down].[58]

Trading between Northern Villages

Alexandrina Watts described also trading of fish at Mason Hall, with female vendors going to Castara or Moriah to buy and returning to sell. In addition, there were men who passed at night with what was called 'boat basket' of fish.

AW: Then it have, call it *boat basket*, in the night, men will come down wit' big basket of fish. We call dat boat basket. So when they come down, you can go with a big wash-pan, an' yuh getting' it full fuh little money.

SCJ: That is when they have plenty, plenty, —

AW: Plenty, yes. [So they have to get it] off theh han'. So we call it boat basket. We seh, boat basket come down, and we gone now to buy. An' yuh getting' a quantity, you know. But those women who leave here, and go and buy a basket from them during the day, dey come back and sellin' to us penny a heap. Sometimes deh count dem; accordin' to how deh buy, deh will tell you, well, twelve of these grains for penny. And that's the way they uses to sell fish.

SCJ: So they would have had to walk?

AW: Yes.

SCJ: And the men who come in the night, they walk too?

AW: They walking, or sometimes they come down wid deh donkey. Both sides, this big boat basket, both sides. Because in the early days, they had no transport otherwise; is only cow cart they had, and is a few people had dat. We had about three people in this district had a cow cart.

SCJ: You had to be wealthier to have a cart?

AW: More or less. And even that cow cart used to help us long ago, when we go in town to sell, and coming back home; sun hot, we jump on to the back o' de cart and get a ride come home. Because is gravel, and we was bare feet. Was sharp stones and bare feet.

Yuh never wear shoes to go to town. *You couldn't afford it!* Even though yuh carry yuh shoes, yuh have to wait until yuh meet *King's Well*.[59] Yuh wash yuh foot dere. That is Cook's River. Wash yuh foot, and put on yuh shoes go eento town; when yuh come back, yuh take it off dere an' yuh walk home. Because if you get a pair of shoes now, yuh don' know when yuh goin' to get one, so you cannot afford to lick it up now by walking dat distance with it.

SCJ: So is only to church and weddings and so on, that you would wear the shoes. What about school?

AW: Bare feet, bare feet. I went to school bare feet. On mornings, when yuh finish bringin' yuh water, go and dress, and you get some of the same coconut oil, an' yuh oil down yuh foot properly, an' yuh gone up to school. I never wear shoes in school; I didn't know dat.[60]

Trading in Scarborough

The Scarborough market served a wide hinterland. Villagers went there from the north and north-west—Mason Hall, Moriah, Castara, Parlatuvier, Les Coteaux, Mt. Thomas, Woodlands—as well as from all the south-western villages, the suburbs of the town, and the nearer windward villages. In addition, traffickers collecting produce to ship to Trinidad waited in Lower Scarborough near the wharf on weekdays for vendors from the villages. Traffickers paid cash; but sometimes they benefited from the system of 'changing' by exchanging goods for goods which they sold in Trinidad. In the market, trading was a mixture of cash and exchanges in kind.

The vendors and their assistants from the northern villages would walk to Scarborough by the light of *boules di fay* (French: *boules de feu*) or *flambeaux*, bottles of kerosene with lighted cloth at the top, and arrived long before dawn. Usually they would all stop at the King's Well at Cook's River, at the entrance to Scarborough, where there was a horse trough. There they would rest, refresh themselves, put their shoes on, if any, and make their final preparations for marketing. After their sales were over, they returned there to eat bread and fish bought in Scarborough (also called '*a suit*'), or to get water to soak farine and strip pieces of saltfish or smoked herring (also called '*choir girl*') for their lunch. Often they would throw unsold ground provisions into the gully going to the river, since taking them back to the village was pointless. Sometimes they were able to 'change' provisions for goods in a shop owned by Alexander Pierre 'Black Boy' Ottley; his was the only shop in which 'changing' was allowed.[61]

Mrs Annie Caesar (b.1905) describes marketing from her village, Mason Hall, during her childhood.

SCJ: When you went to the market, you used to see people exchanging goods? How did that work?

AC: Yes. If [you] have a heap of potato, I would give you oil, salt, pitch oil [kerosene], and I would exchange you for salt; and some people would take fry fish, they would give fry fish in exchange. ... Salt, pitch oil and coconut oil.

SCJ: [You] used to exchange for provision?

AC: Yes, provision.

SCJ: And the people with the pitch oil and the salt, they were from where?

AC: Same place there in Scarborough.

SCJ: And with the coconut oil?

AC: Same place. All about. Deh will come from Canaan and all about; deh exchangin' provision for coconut oil.

SCJ: So when you were exchanging, did people put a value on the things they were exchanging? That is to say, how would you know how much coconut oil to give for how much potato?

AC: Well, according to—deh gie you; it was sold by heap. Say well, potato is 4c per heap, and coconut oil was 8c per pint. I would give you a heap of potato if you give me a pint o' coconut oil.

SCJ: You would give them a heap worth 8c?

AC: Yes.

SCJ: So in people's minds, although they were not passing cash, they had a money value that they put on what they were exchanging?

AC: That's right; that's right. Because if I give you four heaps of potato, you would give me—I would say, well, 4c. And how much your coconut oil value. Pitch oil, 4c a bottle. They would buy their pitch oil, and come to the market and exchange. You understand what I mean?

SCJ: Yes, I understand. Now, people used ... to exchange, and also used cash at the same time? They would give you part in goods and part in cash?

AC: According. ... According to the price.

SCJ: So if the price was really high, you would put part in money and part in goods?

AC: Yes.

SCJ: How important would you say this exchanging was? Would you say that people did more of their trading with cash, or they did more with exchanging?

AC: Well, I would say, well, according. Because if I carry a tray of potato, mixed provision, cassava, dasheen, tannia, and you buy your pitch oil. You would say, well, alright, you give me an amount of potato and cassava an' ting, and you will give me in pitch oil or cash. This worth a dollar. Then you feel 'e worth tuppence and twelve cents. You would give me the pitch oil or whatever it is, and I would give you the [inaudible] value, you understand?

SCJ: Trading with cash was more frequent than exchanging in your time?

AC: Nah, nah, nah.

SCJ: Exchange was more frequent?

AC: Yes. Exchange was more frequent. Sometime you go to Scarborough wit' a tray of provision; sometime you don't even get two dollars. So you had to change it up. Even the butchers used to come and exchange meat for— Beef was eight cents a pound. They would come and exchange it wit' you, and give you—I will give you provision and you will give me meat in exchange.

SCJ: And that was because they didn't have cash to buy, or because they knew you didn't have cash to buy?

AC: Sometime, you didn't have cash to buy de beef, though it was so cheap. But you go to town, yuh exchange yuh little salt, yuh pitch oil, yuh coconut oil, and yuh may geh yuh little change to come home.

SCJ: So at the end of the day, about how much cash would you have in hand?

AC: Well, yuh can't imagine. Because sometime de provision dat yuh carry to town, yuh don't get two dollars, yuh understand? De provision dat yuh carry, yuh don't get two dollars. You have to exchange it—a little pitch oil, a little coconut oil; these ordinary things fuh de home. Becau' yuh can't bring it back. Yuh can't bring back provision to meet provision. You just change it over.

SCJ: You could have changed in any shops in town?

AC: No. Buy. You had to buy.

SCJ: Could you change in the village here? You couldn't change with your neighbour?

AC: No. No, because everybody have …

SCJ: … And in the shop, could you go and change at all in the village?

AC: No.

SCJ: So changing was only in the market.

AC: In the market. You had to go and buy in the shop.

SCJ: Was it possible to go to other villages, like say, Castara, and change?

AC: Nuh, nuh, nuh, nuh, nuh, nuh, nuh! They have up there. I can't go up there and change, because they have no need. People from Parlatuvier used to bring down their provision and carry it in the market. And Castara. People from Castara used to walk wid deh tray on deh head, because in dose days, we hadn' motor car and so on. So they had to walk wid deh tray, beginning quite night time to meet into Scarborough to change, to go and sell deh little ting.

SCJ: It was not easy.

AC: NO, IT WASN'T EASY AT ALL! …

SCJ: A while ago, you said that it was your mother and your grandmother, who would go to the market; and you. Was it always women who went to the market?

AC: No, men used to go too.

SCJ: Men used to carry things to change and sell?

AC: No, not from here. The men used to take the provision from Castara and Parlatuvier [the more remote villages] and go, but deh wife used to go and sell it fuh dem.

SCJ: Oh, so the men were just going to carry load?

AC: Yes.

SCJ: I see. And then, when they reached to town, what they had to do?

AC: Deh wife, well deh jus'—and deh used to carry it by de bag, from Castara and Parlatuvier. When deh reach, de wife take it and deh sell in de market.

SCJ: So market vendors were always women, except for butchers?

AC: Ye-e-s!

SCJ: So it was women selling the pitch oil and salt?

AC: Yes, yes. Yes.[62]

Mrs Agnes Sandy (1870–1987) was 114 years old at the time of the interview. She described going before school on mornings from Moriah to Mason Hall to sell breadfruit, and selling produce to traffickers on the Scarborough wharf.

AS: … Mason Hall nuh ha' time fuh change. Me used to go down deh a' marnin' fuh sell breadfruit, an' come back fuh go a' school. Come back befo' time fuh go a' school. Me used to put down de beef [?] tray a' road deh. 'E nuh wort'. 'E can' meet. [She never had enough to sell.]

... Yuh know me meet a' town, guh sell a' town. [For example:] Yessiday evenin' mih pick wan bag a' green peas, mih meet a' town dis marnin'; put am a' mih head, sell am a' de wharf a' town an' come back ... Mih nuh walk! ... A' ahwe head we used to put load, an' meet a' town seven a' clock o' eight a' clock. ... [Because of the sale to traffickers on the wharf:] Yuh nuh badder [bother] go up a' market.

Sometime when yuh a' come back, yuh deh a' Concordi, yuh heare Moriah bell a' ring fuh school.[63]

SCJ: You go on the wharf?

AS: Yes, every trafficker deh deh a' wait fuh yuh.

SCJ: Deh buyin' it to carry to Trinidad?

AS: Mm, hmm. [Yes.]

SCJ: So you used to get cash money?

AS: Yes. Provided you meet trafficker. We used to be happy.

SCJ: You never carried your things to Trinidad?

AS: Yes, one time. ... Mih husban' come out a' Plymout' come heah. Mih buil' boat, mih wuk seine; all ting. Mih wuk, yuh nuh. Mih never siddown. He 'in dead lef' two boat an' all lakka dat give me. Mih 'in min' plenty stock. ... De trafficker come. If deh hear mih ha' stock, deh meet hyah dis mornin', buy am, goo weh tinight. 'E nuh hard. Tobago nuh hard, lika how de people lazy![64]

Mrs Jane Ann 'Edna' Thomas (1894–2003) recalled selling in Scarborough in her childhood. Her parents were metayers and smallholders at Les Coteaux.

SCJ: When your parents took their produce to town to the market, did they use to get cash, or get goods? Did they use to exchange goods for goods?

ET: No. Sometimes, you get tannia, and the man who selling beef in the market deh, will come and he will exchange meat for you for food; you give him de food and he give you meat.

But when you go in the market, you put out de load on de ground and sell, and when you finish sell yuh load, you get yuh cash in yuh hand, and yuh go in Mr Ottley shop; ... you buy yuh matches, yuh salt, yuh everyting; you pack up yuh basket and come home.

You walking from Les Citteaux. Our parents walk it, and we come back and walk it with our children too. Walk from Scarborough to Les Citteaux with a heavy load. And you walking from Les Citteaux village to Scarborough with that heavy load. Now, we get good ease; we get de bus to carry us; we get dem boys with car and ting. Walking from Scarborough to Big River

down there. It didn't have no bridge; you walking through the water. Is after de olden-days people deh get old now, Public put a bridge down there; the same bridge where you a' pass deh wid car, people used to come from town, put deh foot inside de water deh, take cold. We ketch we tail![65]

Mrs Keziah Solomon (1915–1995) lived at Bethel as a child. She described her experience of marketing in Scarborough.

KS: ... We used to leave here on Saturday morning, *fo' day mornin'* [before dawn], go into town, meet de people dem at Moriah an' ting; we exchange our coconut fuh *provision*, like dasheen o' banana, yuh know; these sorts of ting. But very cheap. Corn an' ting, we used to kerry een an' exchange. Boil yuh coconut oil. Deh come an' deh take yuh coconut oil, deh gie you dasheen, o' plantain. Anyting you want. Becar I do dat already; mih mudder used to sen' me to town. Yes.

SCJ: Now, when you went to town to do this, when you exchanged your coconut oil, you had a value that you put on the coconut oil, to say, well, this worth 8c, and so I must get 8c worth of dasheen?

KS: Mm, mm [No]. 'E have no value. You give dem a bottle of coconut oil, and they gie you certain amount of provisions.

SCJ: So how they will know how much to give you for that bottle?

KS: Well, they will sort it out, you know wha' Ah mean? Becau' if dey give you three dasheen, and they say, Alright, take dat, and two ripe plantain, o' two green plantain an' ting, we don't charge them. We gie dem de bottle o' oil, an' deh give you de provisions.

SCJ: But you are saying no money value is put on the provision or on the oil?

KS: Mm, mm; mm, mm. [No.]

SCJ: You used to do this with particular people, or just anybody?

KS: De people who I know come from Windward side, from Moriah and so.

SCJ: That is people you got to know over time?

KS: Yes. Who Ah know, over time.[66]

Although traffickers between Tobago and Trinidad generally dealt in cash, at times some of their transactions were through exchanges without cash. Noel Felix and Rachael Eastman recounted what obtained in Parlatuvier.

RE: When we go in de market, in Scarborough. ... Now, Parlatuvier didn't get farine, and well, deh had coconut, but not so much, eh. And deh uses to go into town wid deh provision. Deh didn' get it sell out, deh exchange it. You give me farine. 'Cau' down deh en' have dasheen and plantain an' dese tings, suh deh exchange plantain fuh farine. ... Suh deh exchangin' coconut oil from Scarborough. De people at Plymout' an' Les Coteaux and dese places would bring een farine and coconut oil. Canaan. Canaan was coconut-oil area. And de most tings deh does plant down deh is—potato deh used to plant, eh. And dey would exchange for dasheen, 'cau' dat don' bear down dere.

SCJ: But people didn't use to come in here to barter?

RE: Yes, the traffickers.

SCJ: They would barter, bringing what, farine and so?

RE: Yes, people used to come in and sell farine ... and wet sugar.

SCJ: In exchange for provision and dry fish?

NF: Yes.[67]

The grandmother of Harold Nymn (1896–1986) was a market vendor, most of whose exchanges were by 'changing'. Nymn recounts how little cash she accumulated as a result.

SCJ: In your time, you remember much bartering taking place here?

HN: Ah! Yes, as I told you, with my grandmother. She didn't have any money. A shilling was a big lot of money. But she never carried any money to the market, but she'd carry her calabash, her ginger beer, her grapefruit. What you used to call it? Forbidden fruit. Those are the things she will carry. But she will bring back farine, salt, perhaps a potato or two, a plantain, something like that. And may have a sixpence in her pocket, or a threepenny piece, after.

SCJ: She would have sold a few things?

HN: Yes, after those other things, she would bring back a sixpence, and people will tie up that sixpence. She wouldn't spend that sixpence, in this sense. She wouldn't carry that sixpence the next day. Next week, she may bring back a shilling, or nine pence.

SCJ: So cash was scarce?

HN: It was scarce because a labourer's pay was a shilling. I worked in a store at a shilling a day. I used to get seven shillings a week, first job. Miller's Stores.[68]

Nymn also described the transactions of his father, a boatman who sold fish on commission for the women who brought it in trays on their heads from Plymouth to Scarborough.

HN: He was a boatman, and a fish-seller. ... When I say a boatman, he used to get passengers come from the boat in a little boat go out, and a sixpence a head to bring them in to the jetty, and carry them from. While he never had a boat, but he worked on a boat as that. And then, after that, he would sell fish for the people who bring in their fish from Plymouth to the market; and he would sell on a commission basis. From the trays. ... If he had six trays, if he sell from you two pounds, and somebody come, he takes the next tray, and he takes the next tray. And the lady there; the tray owner is there. And he putting that money, he putting that money, and the lady there. So when the trays are finished, they divide, and they give him his commission. And sometimes, fish is left, and they give him a piece. So we were well fed, in that sense.

SCJ: Every time you mentioned a tray, you said, 'the lady'. Was it that women were the main fish vendors?

HN: Women! *Women* used to bring in the fish from Plymouth! The seine would catch the fish at Plymouth. Whether these women, whether they buy it from the seine, but they bring it in. It was women, no man. *Hardly* a man will bring in fish on he head coming. Is women; he wife will have to do dat.

SCJ: That's interesting. And the market vendors would have been more women too? You mentioned your *grandmother* selling.

HN: Yes. The market vendors would have been more women; selling in the market would have been more women. Today, is man and woman; but in those days, it was more woman come to the market. The husband might come wid her, but he is not the man in the forefront. It was more or less the women.[69]

As Cassie Homeward's testimony above about 'changing' at Plymouth showed, many of these women obtained their goods on credit, and had to return with cash to the fishermen.

Confectionery and Baked Goods

One of the important forms of employment for women in the suburbs of Scarborough—Darrell Spring, Rockley Vale, Calder Hall, Morne Quiton and nearby settlements—was the making of snacks, baked goods and confectionery. Most of them sold as itinerant vendors to householders in the town, in addition to positioning themselves near the market on market days. Mrs Eileen Guillaume (1916–2004) described them.

EG: Quite a number of them, ... they made things like starch cake, and cakes and pone, and things like that, and come in to Scarborough to sell. ... Well, people worked on the roads, yes, they had Public Works employment. The men worked on the roads and the women—well, they were in the home; but there were a few who made confectionery and so on—cakes. Some of them were every day; and some of them you know when they gonna pass. We had some good old names there that we looked forward—. People will tell you about Miss Marcelline and her tart. People looked out for Miss Marcelline when she comin' down. She was more on the Calder Hall area there now. And then on the other side, we had a lady we called Miss Diddy, and her nice starch cake and sugar cake. ... Persons looked forward to that, to buying from them.[70]

George Leacock (1915–2005) described, first the activities of his grandmother Emma Gordon, and then those of the other female entrepreneurs.

GL: She learned these things from these people who were around here, that was attached to her mother. And really, they used to put over these nice candies, especially you see the shaddock skin? Pink and white. Then they used to make the coconut fudge. Coconut tart was the famous ting. Cassava and corn pone, most. And heavy *leaven* bread. [Flour mixed with water and left in a calabash to ferment was the leaven or rising agent used in baking.] We didn't know nutten 'bout yeast bread. Heavy leaven bread. Very nice heavy leaven bread. And the coconut sweet bread. And you know what they used to do too? ... They had a lot of that here—cashew nuts. But they never used to do it in this high-style way, you know. Bunnin' dem. And quite a lot of guava jelly; but they didn't know anything about guava cheese. Guava cheese lately come in here. Guava jelly and stew guava.

SCJ: But those things were not bartered in the market?

GL: No. You'd find just a few of the upper class of people would buy those for cash. ... Most of them used to be buying it to send away. They'd come and give my Granny a order for two dozen bottles of jelly. Sometime they used to bring their own containers. Those people used to be having like their biscuits and all this sort of thing coming from away ...; and their special sets of candies and ting. They used to bring the tins for her to make it and pack them inside there. ...

Well, the next class of people before the poor people. Those were the people—they did a lot of baking, making local ... bread, pone, pudding. You had people around the area; ... I'd say the outer part of Scarborough—Calder Hall, Glen [Road]—they were noted within the area for certain things. For instance,

like Old Road, there was a special lady there who was noted for pone. Potato pone and corn pone. Then in Calder Hall, you had a lady there, she was Miss Reid, particularly for *bregedeh* and coconut tart. Bregedeh is like a bread baked flat; like a *roti*, but roughly about a inch thick. But it had quite a lot of ingredients like butter and coconut juice and thing, and you could just eat that just so. Very nice. A leaven bread with coconut juice and plenty butter. Glen Road was noted for cashew cakes, starch cakes, sugar cakes, right. Ginger beer—they didn't know nothing 'bout mauby, you know—and sorrel.[71]

Trafficking between Tobago and Trinidad

The smallholders shipped their produce to Trinidad. There were three ways in which this could be done. Some shipped their cocoa directly to George F. Huggins or Alstons and Company, the large cocoa merchants, who posted payment to the senders within a few weeks. Others used the services of Mr A. Halfhide, a middle man who travelled from port to port on the coastal steamers to ship on behalf of growers. The third means, particularly for food crops and livestock, was through a large number of traffickers or speculators, male and female, who bought produce in the villages or in Scarborough and sold wholesale or retail in Port of Spain.

Emeldalina Nicholson from Charlotteville (1901–2005) worked as a trafficker, baker and storekeeper simultaneously. She describes her trafficking from 1930 to 1940.

SCJ: So everybody used to ship their produce to Trinidad?

EN: Yes, to Trinidad. People would come and buy provision from us and ting, but the cocoa we used to ship to Trinidad. And when we get pigs, they used to come and buy pigs, cows, goats. Everything they used to come and buy. And some of our people used to traffic too, you know. Because when I come years after, I did trafficking a lot.

SCJ: You were a trafficker?

EN: Yes, I did trafficking a lot.... From 1930, Ah traffick a lot till '40. From den, Ah ease up, and Ah doing business, baking and then Ah had a big store.

SCJ: In Charlotteville?

EN: Ah have a big business place in Charlotteville. It is there now. ...

SCJ: There were a lot of women traffickers?

EN: Plenty of us used to traffick. Some at Scarborough way. Plenty woman used to ... plenty woman! Down by Low Side, deh used to speculate wid peas, corn, coconut, sorrel, sugar apple, pumpkin. They used to get those plentiful. Well, where the airplane is there, that whole area used to be sugar apple. Well, deh cut dem all down. And pumpkin. Well, deh cut dem all down and buil' the airplane [airport] about there. A good many acres of land out dere.

Used to get different people, and sugar apple and pumpkin. One man will sell seven dozen pumpkin, and how much boxes of sugar apple. Then they used to plant plenty corn, plenty peas, plenty cassava. Then deh used to mek plenty cassava farine, plenty farine! And get plenty cassava. Den deh had a world of coconut too. Deh used to mek fibre, as goin' in mattresses. Dat was a direct trade in Tobago.

After Flora, all dese tings cut off. Den you see, deh mek de airport an' ting, sell away plenty a' dose lands dat was ting. Den de Government must be buy dem over an' ting. And after dat Flora came in, and after dat, de worl' change up. From Flora came, de worl' change. A different world. More scravishing fuh de wealth, mo' wicked an' everyting. A *new* world of wickedness!

SCJ: Now, let me ask you this. Every week you used to be on the boat going to Trinidad?

EN: Our boat [at Charlotteville] was coming every other week. ... But on the town side, they used to get their boat every week.

SCJ: So those women used to go to Trinidad every week?

EN: Yes. You get some going every week. Some go this week, next week; they used to travel.

SCJ: And you used to go every other week?

EN: Every other week Ah used to go.

SCJ: You used to buy in Charlotteville and sell in Port of Spain. ... When you go to Port of Spain, you sell wholesale or retail?

EN: The people in the market will buy from us, and then they go and sell.

SCJ: So you sold wholesale.

EN: And—when I go, a sister of mine was in the business place. We had a business, and that sister was in the business. And I trafficking. And Ah used to bake.

SCJ: When you [were at] home?

EN: Mm, hm. Bake bread. ... I used to get six half-bags of flour every steamer, and work out dat. Every week, six half-bags.

SCJ: So when you [came] to Trinidad then, you used to buy your flour and everything?

EN: Everything, everything. I buy this week, Ah go, Ah bake, den Ah gather money; ... Ah come down, and when Ah come down, Ah work an' Ah go up Tuesday, and from Wednesday morning, Ah bake bread, bake de whole week till de next week. Till Thursday morning come. And after dat Ah go again. Every other week Ah used to travel.

My sister was in de shop, de business place. We used to sell all kinda ting in de business place, and den we used to sell clot' and—all sorta ting. Well, after Ah finish wid de parlour business, I used to sell hats, shoes, drugs, all sarta ting.

SCJ: So you used to come down to Trinidad for that too?

EN: Ah used to come down, yes. Every month Ah used to come down to Trinidad and buy mih stock and go up, and sell, and buy mih stock and go up. Ah had a good business.

SCJ: The trafficking wasn't hard for you?

EN: Is work. Ah get accustom to mih hengin'; me en' study dat.

SCJ: How many days you had to go around to get the stuff in the village?

EN: No. 'E come Tuesday morning, the people bringing deh tings.

SCJ: Oh, they used to bring it for you?

EN: And they buy—on the depot, and they buy there. We don't go about people place. De people deh bring deh goods down in de depot, and we buyin'. Dat wasn't so hard!

SCJ: Well, that is much easier than if you had to go from house to house to buy.

EN: No, no, no. We don't ha' to go noway. If dey have fowls deh bring it. Well, if deh have fowls in de week suh, deh bring it. Who have pigs, you go round. ... If Ah get pigs, Ah wasn't kerry it to Trinidad, Ah will sell it wholesale.

SCJ: Sell it to other traffickers who like to traffic in pigs?

EN: Have a man who used to kill pigs to mek po'k, Ah used to sell mih pigs give 'im. Ah used to sell mih pigs give 'im. Ah not worryin' mihself to kerry pigs—nah! Ah kerryin' *provision*. Ah used to kerry fowls. It was difficult wid dat fowl business, hear, but I used to kerry fowls. Sometimes I get eight, six fowls, Ah kerry dem. But when it come to pigs, Ah don't kerry dem. Ah kerry pigs one and two times, but it don't value me to kerry pigs. When Ah get mih pigs, Ah 'ranging, ... Ah sell it give Mr Richard. He does kill pigs on Saturdays. Sell it give him.[72]

Edward 'Pappy' Peters was also a trafficker, but he specialized in pigs.

SCJ: ... You became a trafficker! You would sell on the wharf in Trinidad, or in the market?

EP: On the wharf.

SCJ: As soon as you land, you get sale, from butchers and so?

EP: Yes.

SCJ: So you had to go around to get—

EP: That's it!

SCJ: So where you would get transport [to get around]?

EP: I used to jump on mih bicycle. If I tell you ... Ah could remember one morning, I wake here, and Ah lef' home before tea, because I told de wife I was going to come back fuh tea. Lef' here de morning about half past five. Ah went Buccoo Point was to buy a hog down there. When I got to Buccoo Point, somebody told me about a pig at Plymouth. Ah went Plymouth. When I went Plymouth, I was told about a pig at Castara. I reached Castara. [Laughs.] On de bicycle!

SCJ: So you mean you didn't get the one in Buccoo, and you didn't get the one in Plymouth?

EP: Ah get de one at Plymouth. Ah didn't get the one at Buccoo. Ah got two at Castara. And when I reach back here, is nine o'clock de night.

SCJ: But how you bringing the pigs?

EP: Can't bring dem. Does leave dem. Now, when you buy a pig—like I bought those pigs at Castara. Mark dem; I put my mark on dem. And just now, I ha' to look for a transport man, a man dat have a truck. And tell him, 'Well, I have two pigs at Castara, so and so place; so and so person yard. Mark so and so.' He would go and collect those pigs, at the day the steamer would be leaving, and he would bring dem in Scarborough for me. When I reach in Scarborough, Ah pay 'im his money for the transportation right there, and collect my pigs. And that's the way we does it.

SCJ: So you only shipped from Scarborough?

EP: Only from Scarborough.

SCJ: In those days, the boat wasn't going round the island again?

EP: No, it wasn't going round again. Yes, that was the game.

SCJ: A lot of people did the trafficking?

EP: Oh, yes! Plenty people.

SCJ: So it wasn't just that those who produced sold in Trinidad, but the traffickers would buy up things and carry down to sell as well. But you didn't like trafficking in things like peas, provision, and so?

EP: Well, I used to try a little, because I find I wasn't lucky wid dem kinda ting. 'Cause most time I buy de peas and so on, yuh go, yuh get very little more than what you pay for it. Never worth the while.[73]

Observers' Comments on the Bartering System

Mrs Olga Comma Maynard, educator, writer and poet, went to Tobago for the first time in 1936, after her marriage to Fitz G. Maynard, a Methodist head teacher stationed there. She observed bartering in the Scarborough market until 1941 or 1942. When asked if bartering was a common means of exchange, she stated:

OCM: Yes, yes! In 1936, when I went—

SCJ: You met bartering?

OCM: Yes, ma'am. It's the first time I had seen it. I'd stand up and hear, 'Me want twenty cents coals.' This is the person who wants the coals standing in front of the coals-seller. She would hand her a bottle. She would give her coconut oil. Then she would go to another one. And it was the same throughout the market. And it was fascinating! I used to go on Saturdays, and spend a lot of the time that I should be minding my own business, looking at this thing.

SCJ: So this was in 1936 you saw this?

OCM: 1936. I never went to Tobago before.

SCJ: How long after that do you think it continued?

OCM: Oh, about four or five years after.

SCJ: And you had not known this in Trinidad at all?

OCM: No. Neither had I seen it in St. Vincent or Grenada. Tobago was the first place I saw that. Because instead of bringing money to the market, they brought coconut oil. Lily—our Lily—used to bring milk from the Whim. The woman who worked with us, Mrs Noray, she brought bottles of milk, but she didn't carry home money. She carried home cooking oil, tannia, plantain and so on, in exchange for her milk. ...[74]

Lionel Mitchell, educator and community activist, went to Tobago in 1924 from Trinidad where he was born, and remained there for the rest of his life. Mitchell stated that he knew bartering from 1924 in the Scarborough market.

LM: That was in the early days. Yes. In the market. Only in the market. People will bring coconuts, and people will bring potatoes. I know this. And they would swap coconut for potatoes. The reason being that the areas with the coconuts were not areas in which they had potatoes. So they would carry potatoes to market, and rather than sell and buy coconuts, they swapped. And they had a better chance of getting coconuts if they had potatoes to offer. I have coconuts, but I would want some potatoes. I have no guarantee that when I sell, I would get money to buy the potatoes. By time I go there, the potatoes finish. So therefore, I will take my coconuts to the fellow over there. And as soon as he see that, he know that I am trading coconuts; he goin' put aside an amount of his potatoes to swap with me.

SCJ: Now, when they did this, was there a value being placed on what is being exchanged?

LM: That is always between the two people, so that the value would vary. Sometimes the fellow with the coconut would come off; sometimes the fellow with the potato would come off.

SCJ: But the value that is being put is a monetary value? That this is worth 10 cents, so you are giving 10 cents worth of coconuts ...

LM: I don't think so. I think what mattered then was, 'What does this mean to me?' ... What can I do with these potatoes? I have all the coconuts in the world, but I can't get along except I have potatoes. Therefore, the potatoes are of importance to me, and even if the fellow tries to pinch me, and make me give him a potato over or so, is alright. I want potatoes. ...

SCJ: So that in the market there were two modes of exchange, one with cash, and one with barter?

LM: Mm, hmn. Yes, yes. It's barter, yes, but barter based on what it means to me; the value it is to me. I have no way of assessing how much money it should give me, because it might give me so much money, and I might not be able to get what I want over there.

SCJ: So which was the predominant mode of exchange, predominant in the sense of more prevalent? Was it the cash?

LM: Cash. Yes, oh, yes. Is only one or two isolated cases, where the conditions necessitated, that you used the barter.

SCJ: This is in '24?

LM: Yes, when I came here in '24. ...

SCJ: You knew barter in Trinidad?

LM: No. Remember I came here at 18 years. They didn't have any barter there at all [in Port of Spain].

SCJ: ... Most of the people who sold in the market were male or female?

LM: Female, for the most part. Mainly, some men bring the thing to the market and then leave it there with their wives.[75]

Features of Exchanges within Tobago

The above accounts of trading within Tobago indicate that there were three basic types of transactions. First, there were exchanges with money as medium, which was the dominant mode. Second, there were exchanges without cash, based on need and use value, in which both parties gained what they needed. Third, although the element of use value often remained, there were exchanges based on the implicit use of money as the unit of accounting, though not always the medium of exchange. In some instances, payment for one bundle of goods was both in cash and in kind, which underscored the use of money as the unit of accounting. The second and third types were both very widespread and long-term, especially in the Leeward District and the northern villages, and were important in exchanges between windward and leeward villages.

The system of 'changing' and exchanges in kind at the micro level was tied to the macro level of the economy, described in Chapter 1, and to village and communal forms of solidarity. Bartering in Tobago occurred because the colonial economic arrangements resulted in low levels of accumulation of wealth and a lack of specie on the island. This had several implications.

In the first place, many exchanges, including those of labour for labour, were implicitly forms of credit. Indebtedness in kind freed up available cash for other needs; it also allowed peasants to pool resources such as labour that could raise productivity.

Secondly, exchanges without cash were based on, and in turn reinforced, interpersonal ties and obligations. Where there is a medium of exchange, there is no *necessary* continuing relationship between the parties exchanging. However, in certain instances where there is no medium of exchange, the parties remain under various forms of obligation to each other. The clearest examples of this are the exchange of labour, the system of rearing livestock with labour that was paid with animals, and the selling of fish granted on trust to be sold in Scarborough. The *susu*, a rotating credit and savings institution, also depended on trust and personal relationships. Therefore, the informal credit systems presupposed interpersonal ties, trustworthy character, and continuing obligations. They also reinforced such ties and obligations.

Thirdly, bartering was essential to the well-being of the poor. *It was the poorest residents who took part in the system of 'changing'.* Several of the respondents acknowledged that bartering was necessary, since to wait for buyers for their goods would have been futile, because of the general scarcity of cash. It is interesting that some of the market vendors exchanged blue, salt and kerosene, basic items needed in the home. In this way, the person without cash to go to the grocery could still procure imported necessities through 'changing'. Also, the person with food items could save scarce cash by 'changing' them for imported items. Therefore, for the poor, bartering was a means of maximizing utility, avoiding lack of sales, meeting consumption needs for both local and imported goods, and even procuring goods for sale or barter in another series of exchanges. It also fostered interpersonal ties and intra- and inter-village exchanges and solidarity.

In this context, though outright destitution was rare, and though the population amply fed itself, for most of the populace it was very difficult indeed to accumulate wealth.

Fourthly, bartering was a clear indication of the fetters on Tobago's production and marketing. As Brunner and Meltzer point out, the use of a medium of exchange allows the household to economize on the resources needed to acquire and enjoy a diversified basket of goods and greater leisure. It also fosters the expansion of trade.[76] Therefore, bartering reflected, and contributed to, the marginal state of Tobago's economy. Thus, it is not surprising that, after having no commercial bank between 1847 and 1881, Tobago got two banks in 1917 when prices were high, and both closed in 1923, when prices were low. No commercial bank returned to Tobago until 1950, when Barclays Bank opened after a spate of robberies in Scarborough in October 1948. Besides these, the only formal bank from 1893 to 1950 was the Government Savings Bank whose deposits per capita, as we have seen, were small.

4. CONCLUSION

The Tobago labouring class that rapidly became a peasantry in the early twentieth century strove to create a viable agriculture under tough conditions. For most people who did not emigrate, the village was the locus of school, work, worship and leisure. Enduring face-to-face contacts and their accompanying norms and sanctions were the bedrock on which production and exchange were based. Building on communal ancestral traditions, the villagers established systems of co-operation and exchange, which allowed them to take advantage of regional and sexual divisions of labour, and to survive with respect and dignity under increasingly bleak conditions.

For the labouring class, though there was little destitution and food was plentiful, there could be only low levels of wealth accumulation, in an economy in which strong fetters had been placed on prosperity. The low global prices for commodities after 1920, coupled with plant diseases, whittled away at the profitability of the peasants' enterprises. Poor communication of all kinds, inadequate marketing systems, and meagre credit compounded the difficulties. These factors drove the peasants to co-operate for credit, savings, labour, processing and marketing; the planters were also impelled to form producer and marketing co-operatives in the face of the many obstacles. By 1930, out of desperate necessity, at all social levels, Tobago had developed some of the most vibrant co-operative institutions in the British West Indies.

The oral history recorded here shows that a sexual division of labour was integral to production on estates and peasant holdings and to marketing. There was also a division of labour across villages and districts, depending on natural resources, soils, and climatic conditions, and this allowed for complex systems of exchanges between them.

Exchanges in kind, with money often the unit of accounting but not the medium of exchange, were widespread. These exchanges had implications for credit and indebtedness, for the money supply, and for the obligations of those who relied on exchanged labour, communal savings, and other facilities based on interpersonal trust.

Bartering between the members of the peasantry was a strategic means of community self-help, support and survival. By helping each individual to meet his/her needs, these efforts helped to maintain personal dignity and respect, while raising productivity. They also fostered inter- and intra-village ties.

Thus, individual exchanges at the micro level, communal norms of solidarity at the village (meso) level, and the wider macro economy were all thoroughly interrelated. They also reflected the difficulties under which the peasantry laboured in the early twentieth century.

Notes

1 Wild Dog and Wild Cow are in the hills north and east of Roxborough, respectively; Land's End is near Parlatuvier; America is north of Kendal Place.

2 Wood mills were also called 'batty mills' (vulgar slang for 'bottom mills'), since they were worked by the posterior of the person riding the pole. See photograph in the first set of Plates in this volume.

3 The system was known by various names: in Grenada, *maroon*; in Haiti, *coumbite*; in St. Lucia, *coup de main*; in Trinidad, *gayap*.

4 Glycerie 'Vaso' Carrington, b.1914, interview with author, 20 Jan. 2007.

5 Injin baskets: Amerindian baskets. The spellings of Charlotteville are in keeping with the verbatim record.

6 Rachel Eastman (1928–1992) and Noel Felix (b.1933), interview with author, 18 May 1983; Felix' emphasis.

7 CO 295/513: no. 404, Chancellor to Long, 9 Nov. 1917, encl Thomas Thornton, 'Tobago as a Field for Cotton Cultivation', 4 July 1908, 3.

8 Lionel Craig (b.1922), telephone conversation with author, 20 Mar. 2007.

9 *Report of the Tobago Planning Team* (Port of Spain 1963), App. B. The first ACS was started at Diego Martin, Trinidad, in October 1916.

10 District Administration Reports for 1929, Council Paper No. 58 of 1930, 9.

11 CO 295/570/11: no. 393, Hollis to Passfield, 26 Sept. 1930, encl Excerpt from Karl Walter's Report; Karl Walter, 'Revival in the West Indies', in *Year Book of Agricultural Co-operation*, ed. Horace Plunkett Foundation (London 1930), 19–20.

12 CO 295/583/11, File 36808: no. 510, Hollis to Cunliffe-Lister, 23 Nov. 1934; Stockdale's minute, 18 Jan. 1935.

13 Eric Roach, *The Flowering Rock: Collected Poems 1938–1974*. Leeds: Peepal Tree Books, 1992.

14 Thomas Bender, *Community and Social Change in America* (New Brunswick, New Jersey 1978), 3–13; David W. Minar and Scott Greer, eds. *The Concept of Community: Readings with Interpretations* (London 1970), x.

15 See chap. 6 below and Elder, *Folk Song and Folk Life in Charlotteville*.

16 Traffickers were people who bought produce in Tobago and took it to Trinidad to sell wholesale or retail there. The term also refers to similar trade in other islands. It does not connote illegal selling as in the English usage.

17 These are villages on the north and north-east coasts of Trinidad.

18 Amos James (1904–c.1999), interview with author, 24 July 1992.

19 Matthew Bell Crooks died on 27 June 1921; *TG*, 30 July 1921, 2.

20 *Megass*: also called *bagasse*, and in Tobago *makash*; the tough fibrous residue of the sugar cane after the juice has been expressed. Megass was taken on trays called *banks* to the mill yard where it was dried in the sun and then stored in the megass house, from which it was carried to the furnaces to be used as fuel during the process of boiling cane juice to make sugar.

21 Samuel Adams (b.1903), interview with author, 3 Jan. 1985.

22 One hogshead of 13 hundredweight (cwt) minimum contained 8 barrels; a barrel of sugar would have weighed at least 182 lbs. One cwt equalled 112 lbs.

23 One English penny (abbreviated: d) was 2 cents in Trinidad and Tobago currency; 8d = 16 cents.

24 Throughout the nineteenth century and until 1930 when Shirvan race course was opened, horse races were held on Petit Trou beach at low tide.

25 A bill was a tool with a long wooden handle and a long concave blade, used for digging, cutting and pruning. It was one of the commonest tools on

Tobago (and BWI) sugar estates from the days of enslavement to the early twentieth century.

26 Izzy Inniss (c.1891–c.1987), interview with author, 9 Jan. 1985.

27 Edward Peters (1904–1993), interview with author, 28 Sept. 1984; Peters' emphases.

28 Edward Peters, interview, 28 Sept. 1984.

29 Horatio Nelson was buried at Montgomery Moravian Church on 1 Mar. 1904. See Moravian Church Records: Montgomery Moravian Church, Burial Register, 1878–1914.

30 One kerosene tin held four gallons of liquid.

31 O'Farrell Harris (b.1908), interview with author, 16 Feb. 1985.

32 Trinidad and Tobago, *Hansard*, 14 Apr. 1950, 784. I. A. Hope, MLC from 1932 to 1938, was a Scarborough merchant; Mendes (the usual spelling) owned Bacolet Estate and also grew tobacco.

33 Alexandrina Watts (b.1909), interview with author, 2 January 1985.

34 Caracas band: the group of pardners who drank chocolate tea made from the Caracas cocoa.

35 A crook was a wooden device placed on the back of a draught animal to enable it to carry loads which were tied to the crook; the word was also used as a verb, as in the sentence to which this note refers.

36 Noel Felix and Rachael Eastman, interview, 18 May 1983.

37 Sidney Gibbs (1906–c.1985), interview with author, 29 May 1983.

38 Amos James, interview, 24 July 1992.

39 William 'Sweetie' Pope (b.1907), interview with author, 29 May 1983.

40 Drogue: used as a verb in the Tobago vernacular to mean to carry heavy loads; derived from droghers, coasting vessels which transported cargo between Scarborough and the outbays.

41 Albert Richardson (b.1888), interview with author, 24 May 1983.

42 Dalton Andrews (b.1912), interview with author, 16 May 1983.

43 Alexandrina Watts, interview, 2 January 1985.

44 CO 295/513: no. 404, Chancellor to Long, 9 Nov. 1917, encl Thomas Thornton, 'Tobago as a Field for Cotton Cultivation', 4 July 1908, 3. As land hunger increased, this degree of independence is likely to have decreased in the Leeward District, which compelled some workers to give free labour on Lowlands Estate; see chaps. 1 and 4.

45 Report of the Wages Advisory Board (1935–1936), Council Paper No. 88 of 1936, 33.

46 A. L. Marshall to William Low, Report on the Transactions of the Tobago Branch of the Government Savings Bank for 1893, 8 July 1894, *Tobago Gazette*, 13 July 1894, 114. £1 sterling equalled TT $4.80; 20 shillings made £1.

47 Annual Report of the Chief Manager of the Government Savings Bank for 1909–1910, Council Paper No. 96 of 1910, 2–3; Report on the Working of the Government Savings Bank for 1913–14, Council Paper No. 135 of 1914, 3; Report of the Chief Manager of the Government Savings Bank for the Nine Months Ended 31 December 1915, Council Paper No. 76 of 1916, 3–4.

48 James L. A. Webb, Jr., 'Toward the Comparative Study of Money: A Reconsideration of West African Currencies and Neoclassical Monetary Concepts', *International Journal of African Historical Studies* 15, no. 3 (1982): 455–66; Harold Schneider, *Economic Man: The Anthropology of Economics* (New York 1974), chap. 5. I am grateful to Alain Buffon, 8 Apr. 1984, for helping me to understand bartering; and to Curtis Keim, Bethlehem, Pennsylvania, who kindly shared this material in the summer of 1984.

49 Vernon O. Ferrer. 'Some Economic Aspects of Peasant Farming in Tobago, British West Indies, and the possible function of medium-term credit in the rehabilitation of low-income farming areas in Trinidad and Tobago' (M.Sc. thesis, Cornell University, 1945).

50 Emeldalina Nicholson (1901–2005), interview with author, 26 June 1996; Nicholson's emphasis.

51 Mary Alleyne (1891–c.1985), interview with author, 23 May 1983; Alleyne's emphases.

52 Jacob D. Elder (1914–2003), interview with author, 24 May 1983; Elder's emphases. Hogsheads: large wooden casks in which sugar was shipped.

53 Samuel Moore (b.1902), interview with author, 25 May 1983.

54 Dora Manning (b.1893), interview with author, 13 May 1983.

55 Cassie Homeward (1911–2003), with Ivan and Jane Taylor and Irene Cadiz, interview with author, 8 Jan. 1985; Homeward's emphases.

56 Alexandrina Watts, interview, 2 January 1985.

57 Cassie Homeward, interview, 8 Jan. 1985; Homeward's emphases.

58 Amos James, interview, 24 July 1992.

59 The King's Well at Cook's River, the north-western boundary of Scarborough in the early twentieth century, was one of the few sources of water for the townsfolk before 1925.

60 Alexandrina Watts, interview, 2 January 1985; Watts' emphases.

61 Ottley was the father of Carlton Ottley, the social worker and historian discussed in chaps. 3 and 5.

62 Annie Caesar (b.1905), interview with author, 8 Jan. 1985; Caesar's emphases.

63 The bell could have been at Mason Hall, which was closer to Concordia than Moriah.

64 Agnes Sandy (1870–1987), interview with author, 16 July 1984.

65   Jane Ann 'Edna' Thomas (1894–2003), interview with author, 18 July 1992.

66   Leopold Solomon (1906–1999) and Keziah Solomon (1915–1995), interview with author, 17 Mar. 1985.

67   Noel Felix and Rachael Eastman, interview, 18 May 1983.

68   Harold Nymn (1896–1986), interview with author, 12 May 1983.

69   Harold Nymn, interview, 12 May 1983; Nymn's emphases.

70   Eileen Guillaume (1916–2004), interview with author, 29 Apr. 1983.

71   George Leacock (1915–2005), interview with author, 30 and 31 Aug. 1985. Roti: a flat, soft bread of Indian origin, in which is folded curried meat or seafood and/or vegetables.

72   Emeldalina Nicholson, interview, 26 June 1996; Nicholson's emphasis.

73   Edward 'Pappy' Peters, interview, 28 Sept. 1984.

74   Fitz Gerald Maynard (1900–1984) and Olga Comma Maynard (1902–1998), interview with author, 31 May 1983.

75   Lionel P. Mitchell (1905–1992), interview with author, 22 Apr. 1983, 27 Sept. 1984.

76   Karl Brunner and Allan H. Meltzer, 'The Use of Money: Money in the Theory of an Exchange Economy', *American Economic Review* 61 (1971): 784–805.

3

Tobago's Social Structure
in the Early Twentieth Century

To UNDERSTAND Tobago's social structure, one must view the society from many angles. Chapter 2 described village life, the crucible in which the people were shaped. This chapter outlines the main contours of the social structure. In turn, its analysis must be linked with those of Chapter 4 on political issues, and of Chapter 8 on the occupational structure.

Essentially, the society was transformed after the sugar crisis of 1884. The old alliance of coloureds and whites in the dominant class ended, owing to the decline through death and emigration of the prominent coloureds, and the rise of a new planter class that was mainly white. The middle strata were also transformed, mainly through emigration of the coloureds and the upward mobility of the rising members of the labouring class. The labouring class, now largely small landowners, continued to work in a multiplicity of occupations, and its prevailing tendencies varied by district.

While the composition of the classes and strata changed, race and colour distinctions remained strictly drawn, and this chapter describes the ways in which these distinctions marked social life.

Gendered differences formed part of the structuring of occupations and opportunities over time. These issues will be discussed only briefly here, since the data on gender and occupations, as revealed in the censuses, are fully examined in Chapter 8.

The most important social change was that Tobago between 1900 and 1940 became *a society of landowners*. This raised the general level of security and well-being, and softened the dividing lines between planter and labourer. By 1946, although wage earning had been expanding with the decline in agriculture, 61.2 per cent of those officially defined as gainfully employed were wage earners (vis-à-vis 72.2 per cent in Trinidad (Table A3.9)); and wage earning was always combined with other sources of income. Increasingly, as agriculture declined, state employment in the Public Works and other departments became far more important than estate labour.

1. ECONOMIC ACTIVITIES

The old sugar planters were in rapid decline. Those, like Thomas Blakely, who could invest in other crops, did so. Blakely and others formed a syndicate to convert his Calder Hall Estate to Tobago silk grass (*Furcroea cubensis*), a type of sisal hemp which, it was hoped, would fetch high prices in London. However, the project failed because, to keep the scutching machines fully

73

operational, silk grass, like sugar, needed large economies of scale. A few of the old planters survived in the rump of the sugar business, but only two estates, Mt. Irvine (Usine Ste Marie) and Auchenskeoch, had vacuum pans by 1903. In 1922 two of the twelve estates continuing in sugar had steam engines, and one had an oil engine; the others limped along with the old cattle, wind- and water-powered mills.[1] Some of the sugar produced was exported; but 'wet sugar' and 'wood sugar', as the different grades (and shades) of muscovado were called, were extremely popular in Tobago and on the north coast of Trinidad, where many emigrants from Tobago lived.[2] Sugar cultivation on estates was done by metayage, although written contracts were rare. The old sugar planters were ageing, and their demise in the early years of the twentieth century marked the definitive end of an era.

In 1943 Les Coteaux, the last of the northern sugar estates, ended sugar cultivation, while Orange Hill continued to the closing years of the 1940s.[3]

In the wet windward and northern areas, the chief crops were cocoa with coconuts and rubber, the latter being grown on some 11 estates by 1910.[4] The spread of cocoa was accomplished through the 'contract' system, whereby small growers contracted to plant specified acreages of estate land in cocoa for a fixed period, at the end of which they were paid for each tree.

In leeward Tobago, cocoa was grown where soil and other conditions permitted; coconuts and livestock replaced sugar during the 1920s. Many of the leeward estates converted to coconuts by allowing villagers to grow food crops rent-free on particular acreages. As the tenant-at-will cleared the land, the estate owners planted coconuts between the crops. Once the long fibrous roots of the coconut took hold, the food crops were robbed of nutrients, and the tenant would be obliged to move to another plot, after having cared for the coconut plants.

The axis of the economy turned towards the fertile valleys of the Windward District and the northern areas, reversing the leeward thrust of the previous sugar economy. As a result, there was a small redistribution of the population, as migrants from several leeward villages, where little land was available for purchase, moved to Bloody Bay, L'Anse Fourmi, Roxborough and Charlotteville.[5]

Roxborough was declared a town in 1927, and Charlotteville and Moriah developed into lesser townships. Plymouth attracted coastal trade between Toco in Trinidad (where there were large numbers of Tobago migrants) and Tobago, and between the northern and leeward villages.

The hospitality industry, which women from the middle strata had pioneered in the closing years of the nineteenth century, began to expand. In 1924 Harry Hislop Tucker, owner of Speyside Estate, opened Tobago's first hotel, Speyside Inn, also called Speyside on Sea Boarding House. Burleigh House, owned by Captain R. J. Link, opened its doors in 1927 in Lower Scarborough, and by 1929 Aberfoyle Hotel at Bacolet was well established. Fontanebleau (*sic*) Hotel, less costly than the others, opened in October 1926 in Scarborough. By 1939 Bacolet and Welbeck guest houses were the other main establishments. In 1945 the list included the Savoy, the Royal, the Tobago Country Club and Samuel's Guest House. The advent of regular commercial air travel to Tobago from November 1940 onwards meant that the major increase in visitors occurred after World War II. However, even in the early years of the twentieth century, Tobago attracted at Easter and August large numbers of holiday-makers from Trinidad; each year, two or three yachts owned by wealthy Europeans or North Americans also called. Like agriculture, tourism suffered from poor roads and communications.

Tobago's beauty attracted the growing motion picture industry. *Robinson Crusoe* was filmed there in 1926, followed by *Piccadilly Incident* (1946), *Fire Down Below* (1956), *Heaven Knows Mr Allyson* (1957) and *Swiss Family Robinson* (1959).

One of the most beautiful sights in Tobago is the coral reef off the coast at Buccoo. In 1934 certain boatmen began to remove the sea eggs and other encumbrances, so that visitors could see the coral without being harmed. Cecil Anthony, while still a boy, started with a homemade mask, working with his father Fedi Anthony and Sullivan Dillon; these were the pioneers of this aspect of tourism.[6]

Goat races at Buccoo on the Tuesday after Easter were started in the 1920s. According to a newspaper report, their founder was Samuel Callender of Bethel, a former overseer on Grafton Estate. By 1930 the races were well organized.[7]

2. TOBAGO'S SOCIAL GROUPINGS, 1900–1938

The Dominant Class

By 1920, of the old planter families from before 1884, only a few members remained in the planting business.

Among the whites, there were Duncan McGillivray with Franklyns Estate; H. R. Hamilton with Greenhill and Blenheim; Florence McCall with Lucy Vale which was uncultivated; and the Davidsons of Scotland with Grafton.

The planters from the old coloured families were Matthew Bell Crooks and others with Mary's Hill, Orange Hill, and Amity Hope estates; R. Crooks

with Crown Point; D. L. Yeates with Milford; George R. Agard with Indian Walk; and Clarence W. S. Phillips, a relative of Agard's, with Buccoo. W. S. Ward held Smithfield; the heirs of Gordon Turnbull Macdougall I retained their hold on Adelphi, while the Des Vignes and Keens families owned Castara and the small Craig Hall Estate.

From the ranks of the blacks, the heirs of Alexander Nora Henry held Golden Lane Estate; Mrs Laura Todd, daughter of Craig Castella, still owned Providence; and Samuel Peterkin, son of Theodocia Peterkin, retained ownership of Dunveygan. Thus, only 18 out of 116 estates (including Bird of Paradise Island) remained with the families of planters who had survived the collapse of 1884 (Table 3.1).

TABLE 3.1 **Tobago Estates: Owners and Cultivation, 1920**

Owners	No. of planters	Sugar and other crops	Cocoa	Coconuts	Cocoa and other crops	Uncultivated	Other	No. of estates
Estates of old planters								
Whites	5	—	—	—	4	1	1	6
Coloureds	6	3	2	1	—	1	1	8
Blacks	4	1	2	—	—	1	—	4
Company	—	—	—	—	—	—	—	—
Unknown	—	—	—	—	—	—	—	—
Subtotal	**15**	**4**	**4**	**1**	**4**	**3**	**2**	**18**
Estates of new planters								
Whites	29	10	9	3	19	0	1	42
Coloureds	12	2	4	4	4	1	0	15
Blacks	9	2	4	1	2	0	0	9
Company	9	3	4	7	6	0	1	21
Unknown	11	1	5	2	1	2	0	11
Subtotal	**70**	**18**	**26**	**17**	**32**	**3**	**2**	**98**

Source: Calculated from C. B. Franklin, comp., *The Trinidad and Tobago Year Book for 1921* (Port of Spain 1921), 204–206.

Even the rising owners from within Tobago in the 1890s did not survive in the estate business by 1920. Of those who were mentioned in Volume I, Chapter 9, the remaining ones were Luke Toby, a butcher, who still owned Hampden Estate; and E. Edwards had Parrot Hall. By 1940 there were only 10 old planter families, owning 13 out of 112 estates, excluding 4 owned by the Crown.[8]

For the most part, the planters were migrants to Tobago from the late 1880s onwards. Most were whites, owning either as sole proprietors or as syndicates and companies from Trinidad or the UK. In 1920, 9 firms owned 21 estates; in 1940, 7 firms had 16 estates (Tables 3.1, 3.2). Trinidad firms like Gordon Grant and Company, besides owning, also held mortgages over several Tobago estates. A few of the new planters were members of Portuguese families doing business in Tobago from the 1890s. Thus, in 1920 Alfred Mendes owned Friendsfield Estate; he and his brother Francis Mendes owned Waterloo (Goldsborough), Bacolet and Invergordon; Ignatius Ferreira owned Johnsville; and Mary de Freitas (née Des Vignes), Mount Dillon. [9]

The price of land in Tobago in 1907 was £2 per acre; in Grenada, £20 to £30 per acre. Therefore, among the migrants, there was a small important group of black or coloured estate owners, most of whom were from Grenada. In 1911 Cyril Wildman, a coloured Grenadian, arrived in Tobago and bought Lady Smith Estate near Moriah. The Blackburn family arrived in the same period and purchased The Ochills, a property in the hilly woods some distance from Mason Hall. J. Raebourne bought Mt. Pelier Estate. The black

Grenadian planters included Attiste Mark, a butcher who bought The Heim, Mrs Purser's small estate at Craig Hall; Thomas McKenzie Joseph, who purchased Highlands in 1913; Thomas Francis St. Louis, buying Woodlands, also in 1913; and O'Reilly and Juliana Noel who bought Les Coteaux in 1918, and whose descendants still own the remnant of the estate. [10]

By 1920 the leading white planters were Robert Smith Reid with Hermitage and Campbelton, and his son, Kenneth Reid with King's Bay; the Turpins with Charlotteville; Mayow Short I, a pioneer of rubber cultivation, with Richmond; Robert Archibald, owner of Roxborough and Inverawe; Thorleigh Orde, manager of Louis d'Or (Betsy's Hope) and Bloody Bay; John B. Murray, a Scotsman, with Kendal Place and Florida; [11] and Henry (Harry) S. Smith with Caledonia.

TABLE 3.2 **Tobago Estates: Owners and Cultivation, 1940**

				Estates of old planters				
Owners	No. of owners	Sugar and other crops	Cocoa	Coconuts	Cocoa and other crops	Uncultivated	Other	No. of estates
Whites	3	—	—	—	3	1	—	4
Coloureds	5	2	2	1	—	1	1	7
Blacks	2	1	1	—	—	—	—	2
Company	—	—	—	—	—	—	—	—
Unknown	—	—	—	—	—	—	—	—
Subtotal	**10**	**3**	**3**	**1**	**3**	**2**	**1**	**13**
				Estates of new planters				
Whites	29	6	11	5	21	1	3	47
Coloureds	12	4	6	3	4	1	0	18
Blacks	9	2	5	1	1	0	0	9
Company	7	3	3	7	3	0	0	16
Indian	1	0	0	0	1	0	0	1
Crown	1	0	2	0	0	1	1	4
Unknown	8	0	4	1	2	0	1	8
Subtotal	**67**	**15**	**31**	**17**	**32**	**3**	**5**	**103**

Source: Calculated from C. B. Franklin, comp., *The Trinidad and Tobago Year Book for 1941* (Port of Spain 1941), 171–173.

The new planters were not wealthy. Cyril Wildman described how greatly they profited from increased prices for cocoa and coconuts during World War II.

SCJ: So these white people from England and Scotland, they kept coming even in the twentieth century?

CW: Yes, '20, '21, '22, all the way up. ... They used to come and settle. Some of them died leaving a lot of mortgages. And when the German war started, cocoa went up and they paid off their debts. They had to thank the Germans. Coconuts went up.

SCJ: Coconuts as well? Cocoa and coconuts?

CW: Yes. Cocoa was forty dollars a bag, and coconuts was twenty dollars a pound for the big nuts.

Wildman stated that although there were a few black and coloured planters, 'they all looked up to the other man, to the Englishman and the Scots' who were at the top of the society, controlling 'the stores, and buildings and estates, and everything.'[12]

Balls and other public activities for the 'respectable' were no longer held at the Court House, as in the heyday of the old planters (since the new administration divided up the space for offices and other amenities). The social spheres of white (and near white), brown and black became increasingly distinct. The old close alliance between coloureds and whites in the dominant class was in effect broken.

In general, the merchant houses of the late nineteenth century ceased to exist by 1920. The firm of S. B. Isaacs and Company, which had existed since *c*.1850, closed at the end of March 1906. By 1920, the businesses owned by the McCalls, Pantings, Blakelys, Robertsons and other traders were all defunct. The main new merchants were Millers' Stores Limited, an English firm, which opened at the former McCall property in the Market Square in November 1900; George David Hatt (with two stores); Isaac A. Hope with businesses in Scarborough, Moriah, Roxborough and elsewhere; Captain William Hovell, former sea captain from Barbados, who settled in Tobago as a produce and dry goods merchant; D. Hope Ross and Company, another English firm; and the grocery and spirit shops of the Ferreira, de Freitas, de Souza and Dias families. The first major Chinese business was started at Mt. St. George in 1911 by a 'wealthy Chinaman', Ho-Chi, who dealt in cocoa and other goods.[13] A few Syrian–Lebanese businessmen, among them Abraham Morales, arrived from 1916, and in the 1930s there were a small number of Chinese grocers and storekeepers. Most of these Syrian–Lebanese and Chinese families remained in business. However, within the next 30 years, most of the business houses existing in 1920 ceased to exist.

The merchants and planters became increasingly distinct, a process that had begun in the last two decades of the nineteenth century. In 1920, among the planters only the Agard family (Scarborough merchants), William S. Ward, Thomas McKenzie Joseph (with one 'cocoa shop'), Attiste Mark (with two village 'cocoa shops'), and the Noels (with one estate shop) had businesses.[14] With the exception of the firms that owned estates, the overwhelming majority of the planters had only their planting business.

Besides planters and merchants, the remaining segments of the dominant class were officials and professionals. From the beginning of the closer Union with Trinidad, the senior officials in Tobago were transferred elsewhere, and all heads of departments were recruited from Trinidad. The administration was highly centralized, with even pay sheets for teachers and public workers being made up in Trinidad—to the great inconvenience of the Tobago public. The Public Service in Tobago (and the teaching service), though very small, became a stepping stone for promotion (or isolation) for officers from Trinidad.

Like the senior officials, the professionals were few. There were usually at most three lawyers practising in the Tobago courts. There were only three District Medical Officers (DMOs) in 1900, and it took the dysentery epidemic of 1912 to prick the conscience of officialdom to increase the number to four. There was no resident dentist until the 1930s; and usually there was one senior engineer.

Thus, the dominant class consisted largely of planters. All its segments were subordinate to their Trinidad counterparts. By 1940, because of the downturn in agriculture, the planters were in decline.

The Middle Strata

The middle strata were also transformed. Volume I showed that there were two blocs, comprising coloureds and upwardly mobile blacks in commerce, landowning, teaching, clerical and supervisory positions. Master mariners, master masons and other senior artisans also formed part of the middle strata. Between 1900 and 1938, the middle strata underwent two contradictory processes of contraction and increase.

Contraction came from the extraordinary emigration of the generation born in the 1880s to both black and coloured families of these strata, even though overall rates of population growth were rising in the early twentieth century. The children of the Webbers and of many of the coloured families left for the USA, UK, Trinidad, British Guiana, Maracaibo and elsewhere. In some instances whole families departed. World War I also accelerated the emigration process, since some of the young men went to the war. There is no evidence of a permanent return migratory movement.

A good example of the high level of emigration is the family of Sinai Josiah Gordon, one of the rising black businessmen in the 1880s, who had eight children: four boys and four girls. One went to Canada, three to the USA, two to Trinidad, one to Maracaibo, and only one of them, Ann Evelina (Mrs Cordner), remained in Tobago by 1928. She later emigrated to Trinidad.[15]

So important was the migration that in June 1923 the *Labour Leader's* correspondent remarked:

School teachers, mercantile clerks, tradesmen, all are packing: and their wives and children are getting ready.

In July 1923, referring again to the 'American exodus', the *Labour Leader* noted that assistant and head teachers were not to be had for employment.[16]

In Scarborough in particular, many families sold their property and left. Ruth Wilson (1886–1987) came from a family living in the upper town. Her relatives were mainly artisans; both she and her grandmother were seamstresses. She describes the exodus from her environs in Scarborough, the selling of many properties, and the influx of people from the country, bringing the traditions that the middle strata in Scarborough had always frowned upon.

I never heard my mother, grandmother, grandfather, father, not one, call the name of obeah. Since I have grown up and my grandmother died, and the place done away, and everybody around seem to sell their property, and the country people came in and buy, all in obeah.[17]

Similarly, Jules Crooks (1903–1993) commented on the old Scarborough families:

But the majority of those people sell their property and go. Most of the people that live around here now is either Trinidadian or people from the country, you know.[18]

Increases in the ranks of the middle strata came from three sources, all mainly black, as the Tobago coloureds underwent major decline.

The first was the expansion of landowning, which created hundreds of farmers independent of the estates. Some of these independent landowners were migrants from Grenada and St. Vincent.

The second area of growth was the expansion in commerce, as the peasant enterprises spawned increased trade with Trinidad and elsewhere. 'Cocoa shops' with licences to trade in cocoa, coconuts and other licensable produce came into being; a few were owned by the merchants, but most were in the hands of small shopkeepers. In 1900, 25 licences were granted to 21 owners; in 1920, the number of produce licences was 27, doubling to 53 in 1930, but declining to 32 in 1940.[19] Most of the small cocoa-shop proprietors were also independent cocoa cultivators. Several 'traffickers', male and female, also emerged, buying livestock and produce from the villagers to ship to Trinidad on the coastal steamers. Sea captains working sloops between Trinidad, Tobago and sometimes Barbados, conducted an important area of commercial activity. Some of these captains, like Victor Belmar, Alfred Macdonald and Captain Martineau, originated in Grenada or Carriacou. The changing character of the society and the growth in tourism, which became most apparent in the census of 1946, led to increases in restaurants, 'snackettes' and like activities, some of them owned by women (Chapter 8).

The third source of increase in the middle strata was the expansion in education and of the teaching service. In addition to the increase in access by 1912 to primary education (Chapter 7), private secondary schools were started after 1900. In 1925, at the request of Thomas J. Baldwin and James A. A. Biggart, Bishop Arthur Henry Anstey of the Anglican Church, assisted by Archdeacon Herwald W. Davies, started The Bishop's High School (BHS), which widened opportunities for secondary schooling for the children of the rising peasantry.

Some of the independent landowners in the middle strata were themselves employers of labour. In 1942, referring to the scarcity of labour because of the attraction of the nearby American Base at Charlotteville, Cyril Turpin wrote that:

> 'big' petty proprietors like Archie Lewis, shopkeeper[,] Dearson Moore, ... old Captain Nicholson and his family, Mrs Alitia Williams (the richest villager), old carpenter John Lewis (who built the Methodist Chapel), old Murray (whose brother burnt down the 'Great House' ...) ... had to take off their footwear and in their born boots [bare feet] dance their own cocoa last crop ...[20]

Thus, the groups we have called the middle strata were, as in the nineteenth century, heterogeneous. Some were employers, others were salaried. Many had several sources of income. Despite the heavy emigration, these strata expanded, mainly because of upward mobility of black people.

The Labouring Class

There was a significant influx of migrants to Tobago in the early twentieth century. Some of the migrants were East Indians, recruited after their indentureship in Trinidad; most were from Grenada and St. Vincent, often travelling to Tobago after having accumulated the funds to buy land by working in Panama, Trinidad and elsewhere. They established a strong landowning presence at Charlotteville, Kendal Place, Belle Garden, Grenadian Hill near Roxborough, and Bloody Bay. Returning Tobago migrants from Venezuela, Panama, Trinidad and elsewhere also bought land: five or ten acres of cocoa became one of the prime ambitions of the populace.

For the labouring class, the period was one of rapid change. Owing to the opening up of Crown lands after 1887, and the sale of estate lands to labourers and metayers, landownership and land use expanded rapidly. By 1939 there were 4,940 owners of properties of 1 to 5 acres, and a further 1,403 owning land 6 to 10 acres in extent, up from 3,670 and 214 owners, respectively, in 1897. This was an increase in the total number of smallholders of 63.3 per cent, while the increase in the owners of 6–10 acres was 555.6 per cent.[21] Even the Chamber of Commerce admitted in 1938 to the Moyne Commission that 'the predominant class' 'responsible for producing half the exports of the Island' was undoubtedly the peasantry.[22]

Although landowning became prevalent, large numbers of the labouring class also made themselves available to the estates. This was particularly so in the Leeward District where opportunities for acquiring fertile freeholds became more limited.

In the Windward District, the planters used several incentives to obtain labour. Some recruited Grenadians and East Indians to live in estate barracks. Some sold land to workers through small fortnightly deductions from the wage. The most important strategy was the 'contract' system. As a further incentive, sometimes the planters allocated small plots for purchase by those with cocoa contracts, the cost of the land to be deducted from the value of the cocoa trees at the end of the contract. Dalton Andrews (b.1912) explains:

> The estate will give the labourers [on contract] maybe five acres of land, ten acres of land; and within 5, 6, or 7 years that will come into fruition. While they are working that, the estate land, the estate will give them another piece for themselves. So they working two pieces of land; they working one for themselves. At the expiration of the contract, to take away the contract, they deduct the money from the contract for the land. ... So while he is working the owner's land, he coulda still work his land. ... Is estate land, but that estate land is marked out for him. He's buying it, but he hasn't the money to pay.[23]

By these means, those who had not returned from overseas with ready money could accumulate to purchase their own lands. Even those with land often had to supplement the returns from their holdings with work either on estates or in the Public Works Department (PWD).

However, the dynamics of the negotiation between planter and labourer gave certain degrees of freedom to the labourer, especially given that before 1920 plantations were expanding rapidly in relation to available labour. The labour shortage and the growth of smallholdings therefore strengthened the labourers' position. In 1908, even in the Leeward District where the constraints on buying smallholdings were greatest, rented land for gardens was a concession won by the labourers. Thomas Thornton, himself a planter, wrote that the leeward workers depended on their gardens because 'no regular wages have been paid', and because of this 'the labourers have become more or less independent.' He cautioned that any person starting an estate must understand the characteristics of the labourers: 'They must have their provision ground' which was a kind of 'storehouse'.

They dig their provisions as they require them, and when they have dug out provisions for the day, they put in fresh plants, so that they have almost always something to draw upon.

Thornton stated that only when the estates were worked 'on regular estate lines' (that is, paying regular wages without allowing rented gardens) would the labour supply improve.[24]

Over time, the situation of the labourers, and therefore their bargaining power, changed. In 1915 when, because of wartime food scarcity, the Government undertook to rent Crown lands for food crops, there was no demand for such rentals in Tobago, because of the large number of small proprietors. However, ten years later, as younger cohorts of school-leavers emerged, the demand for land became acute. In an article published posthumously in March 1925, George David Hatt (1865–1924), reflecting on the 'large number of natives of both sexes' who had settled in New York 'to such profit', expected emigration to increase, 'especially now that suitable land at a moderate rate is unobtainable.' By 1935 I. A. Hope, the Member of the Legislative Council (MLC), told the Council that, because of the ending of cocoa and coconut contracts, 'land for the growing of food crops and of fodder for the raising of live stock has become a difficult problem in Tobago'. In 1939 Major G. St. J. Orde Browne reported that the outlook for boys leaving school was 'depressing and discouraging'.[25]

Since estate agriculture was not thriving, there was little paid employment in the 1930s. In 1939 there were 602 males and 187 females employed as labourers on cocoa estates, and the figures for coconut estates were 458 and 141, respectively, making a total of 1,388 workers. These constituted only 14.0 per cent of the 9,945 gainful workers at census 1931.[26]

Besides the most prevalent commercial activities of the labouring class (trafficking to Trinidad, market vending, itinerant vending, and small shopkeeping), there were three other major sources of employment.

The first was in the skilled trades: virtually every boy on leaving primary school was sent to learn a trade; every young woman was expected to know how to sew. The skilled trades occupied large numbers of both males and females, the most important being sawyers, carpenters, joiners, dressmakers and tailors, bakers and confectioners.

The second main source of employment was fishing, which occupied men, although women formed part of the marketing complex for the fishing industry.

Thirdly, there were the public works, and the cadre of lightermen, stevedores and other water-side workers who took passengers and goods on and off the vessels that called in the harbours. The Public Works Department (PWD) became the main source of regular cash earnings in Tobago by the 1930s.

As in the nineteenth century, the majority of workers, whether on estates or in the PWD, were not proletarians: virtually all had land which they and their families worked, and there was seldom complete dependence on paid employment of any kind. The Warden noted in 1935 that

> 95 per cent of the labouring population own or rent land, owning from quarter of an acre (2 lots) to 20 to 25 acres, the ratio of land available to population being about an acre to a man, a woman and a fraction of a child.[27]

A committee of the Wages Advisory Board stated in 1935 that only 'a decided minority' relied solely on earnings from working on the roads or the estates. Most wage earners engaged in gardening, stock-rearing, fishing, basket-making or other activities, which cushioned them from the low daily wages, which for males ranged from 30 to 60 cents and for females from 24 to 30 cents.[28]

Orde Browne reported in 1939 that nearly all the PWD workers were also agricultural producers. However, he noted that 'a limited number of skilled and unskilled workmen', mainly employed in the PWD, were 'dependent on regular wage-earning for their support'. He was careful to add that,

> Were additional land available for occupation on easy terms, some of these people would apparently be glad of an opportunity to establish themselves in a position which would give them some alternative means of support.[29]

Thus, although the overwhelming tendency was towards own-account activity and avoidance of dependence on wages alone, opportunities for landowning had become more restricted.

80

Clear tendencies can be discerned within Tobago. In the Leeward District where land was scarce, by the 1930s the poorest workers had fewest options. This explains why George de Nobriga of Lowlands Estate could impose a regime of two days' unpaid work per week for workers who wished to work the rest of the week. In the windward and northern villages, the incidence of survival by only farming, fishing and related activities was greater. However, after 1920 the viability of such enterprises was low, and the rising generation increasingly resorted to emigration.

The strategic importance of the PWD as the most widely available source of waged labour in the 1930s meant that it became the centre of the emerging labour movement in Tobago by 1938. It also meant that, over time, a large section of waged labour in Tobago would become directly dependent on the resources of the state.

3. CONTOURS OF RACE, COLOUR AND GENDER

Anti-Black and Anti-White Sentiments

Racist attitudes permeated the entire society, beginning with the colonial administration. In 1900 the highest official in Tobago, the Warden, James Tod Rousseau, applied for promotion to the governorship of Christmas Island or one of the West African colonies. At the Colonial Office, as they decided to reject his application, C. P. Lucas minuted:

> He is highly spoken of, but his colour may be against him for high appointment outside the West Indies.[30]

Within the dominant class, although the black planters were respected, in general they did not move in the circles of the whites, who had closest ties with their fellow whites. Carlton Ottley, historian and social analyst, remarked:

> Well, they wouldn't mix with them at all. They would form another group apart. They wouldn't mix with the white people. The white people wouldn't invite them to a party or anything of the sort. As a planter [sic], they would form another social grouping.[31]

In 1912 an unfortunate incident demonstrated the strength of underlying racial antagonisms.

George Swale Alefounder, an Englishman, was the owner of Studley Park Estate; he was an epileptic. On 2 August 1912, he was driving home when he found the road blocked by a buggy, occupied by George Wiltshire (painter), Arthur Wiltshire and Joseph Payne (plumber). According to Alefounder's brother-in-law, W. A. Farmer, Alefounder called out: 'Now then boys let's get by'; to which the answer was, 'You want to get by do you, you "white son of a bitch"!' Alefounder lost his temper and struck the speaker across the face with his horsewhip. He was belaboured with blows, lost much of his vision, and had to be operated on for a brain tumour.

At the trial on 30 August 1912, the Warden–Magistrate, E. C. Eliot, could not refer such a serious matter to a higher court, because Alefounder had started the assaults. All parties were found guilty. Alefounder was fined £5, George Wiltshire, £10, and the other two defendants, £5 each. Alefounder wrote to the Colonial Office, admitting to hitting one of the 'niggers' first, but thought that the others were not justified in beating him.[32]

Another example of the strength of racial exclusiveness occurred in 1913. Esmé Howard, a British aristocrat and diplomat involved with the syndicate owning Louis d'Or and other estates, wrote to Lord Harcourt, the Secretary of State, to complain that the only doctor within 18 miles and the only Government doctor in the Windward District was 'a mulatto who has not, I believe, a very good reputation.' He continued:

> The planters … have practically boycotted him as they cannot bear to have a coloured man as doctor for their wives and daughters. Much as I should wish to regard the coloured man as a man and a brother, I quite sympathize with their point of view.

Howard recommended that in remote districts with many white residents, the whites 'might fairly claim special consideration and get a white man appointed as District Medical Officer.' Harcourt, his fellow member of the Crabbet Club in London, replied that the suggestion that white men be singled out for remote districts

> would, I fear, merely have the effect of debarring them from promotion to appointments in the more populous districts which are of course the most profitable & therefore the coveted rewards of service. I fear that nothing can be done.[33]

In 1915 James A. A. Biggart stated that colour prejudice was 'rampant in the island and may soon reach breaking point.'[34] As a result of these tensions, in recruiting for World War I, Captain Mayow Short I complained of the attitudes of the 'country people':

> They say 'it is a white man's war,' and the Negro must not go—showing the narrowness of their minds.[35]

The refusal of some of the labouring class to fight for King and Empire is understandable.

In the final analysis, racial prejudice contributed to the political ineffectiveness of the planters. In February 1925, the first general elections in Trinidad's history, and the first in Tobago since 1874, were held with a limited franchise. Before that, Tobago had been fitfully represented on the Legislative Council (Chapter 4). By 1925 Tobago had been marginalized into being a backwater, its main connection with the outside world being one coastal steamer which was frequently docked without notice. This was one among many burning issues; but ironically the planters—the only persons that the Governor would nominate to the legislature—could not afford to accept such nomination even to plead their own cause, precisely because infrequent communications would keep them in Trinidad for too long. Therefore their perennial approach to the need for representation was to call for a Commissioner–Warden who would sit in both Legislative and Executive Councils, and who, by having authority over all departments within Tobago, would have higher responsibility than the other Wardens. This was consistently refused, firstly because neither the Trinidad dominant class nor the British officials wished to raise the administrative status of Tobago. Secondly, any such official would also be stranded in Trinidad because of infrequent communications, and another official would have to do his Tobago work.

The general elections of 1925 were an opportunity to improve the level of representation. However, Sir Horace Byatt, the Governor, reported that outside of Port of Spain it was difficult to arouse 'even a moderate interest' in the elections among the whites:

> From various sources I gathered that Europeans of status and substance, who might well be regarded as desirable members of the Legislature, felt very generally an indisposition to come forward and hazard the white man's prestige by risking defeat at the hands of an Indian, a coloured, or a black opponent, *and I found this feeling particularly strong in Tobago during a short visit there.* At an interview, the European planters of that Island, while stating that none of them could sacrifice the interests of his estate by prolonged absence in Trinidad, urged strongly that Tobago needed a special representative in Council to watch over and protect Tobagonian interests. My suggestion that this would shortly be assured by the presence of an elected representative was by no means well received, and the field was left open to two candidates of African origin, one a druggist [James A. A. Biggart] and one a storekeeper [Isaac A. Hope].[36]

After the elections, the Tobago Planters Association (TPA) failed to convince Byatt to appoint a Commissioner–Warden. Therefore, in July 1925 the TPA wrote to the Colonial Office to make its case. They called for the Commissioner–Warden to be both the social and the official head of Tobago, and asked that he 'not be a local man, but a man from England, or at least from another Colony, who would have no outside interests.' However, Byatt argued that Tobago had greatly benefited from its Union with Trinidad; that the proposed Commissioner–Warden, in order to attend meetings of the Executive Council, would be absent from Tobago each week from Thursday to the following Tuesday, and another official would have to perform his duties. What is more, Byatt stated that the planters' own attitudes were their undoing.

> At the recent election no European came forward as a candidate from Tobago, and the planters have themselves very largely to blame, both now and formerly, if they are not satisfied with their representation.
>
> Tobago now has an elected member of the Legislative Council [James Biggart] who is specially active in bringing the interests of the Island before the Legislature.

The Colonial Office officials supported Byatt.[37]

Thus the exclusiveness and the prejudices of the white planters worked against their own interests.

The Swan–Peters Affair

Perhaps the most socially explosive case of interracial conflict occurred in 1937, not long after the June general strike in Trinidad which marked a watershed in the colony's history.[38] Louis Anthony Peters (1878–c.1958), one of Tobago's finest teachers, had retired c.1933 after 35 years' service. He had been among the first group of teachers to be trained in agriculture and chemistry in 1900, and he was a lifelong promoter of agriculture and livestock-rearing. In addition, Peters was a musician, a playwright and actor, an activist on behalf of labour, and a celebrated debater. When he emerged in 1936 as a creative journalist, 'the LAP', as he was popularly called because of the initials of his name, easily became one of the most loved and respected people in Tobago. Late in August 1936, Peters began a column in Standard English on 'The Sister Isle' in *The People*, a 'little newspaper' edited and published by Leonard Fitzgerald Walcott of Belmont, Port of Spain, since 1933. *The People* was a voice of dissent, and the mouthpiece of the growing labour movement in Trinidad and Tobago. On 6 March 1937, Peters began a column in the Tobago vernacular called 'Suzie & Sambo', in which his characters discussed the social issues of the time. The first articles were devoted to the levying on animals and on cooking pots which were lifted off the fire in Tobago, because their owners had defaulted on taxes and water rates; 'Suzie & Sambo' also commented at length on Tobago's 'Governors', its officials who were dubbed 'pseudo-Governors' in Peters' articles in English. On 26 June 1937, 'Suzie & Sambo' first appeared with a cartoon of the two characters, which added to the column's attractiveness and popularity.

In 1937 a young Englishman, Sub-Inspector G. Cable Swan, was in charge of the Tobago Constabulary. On 19 June, the day the Trinidad strikes—in which two policemen were killed—started, Peters' article in *The People* discussed Swan's going fishing at night, with 'his favourite prisoner' carrying a lighted flambeau (a bottle of kerosene with a lighted cloth at the top). Swan was displeased, and was reported to have wished he had imprisoned Peters.[39] On 14 August, under the headline 'Prison Scandal', Peters wrote in full the story of Sempha Reid, a former prisoner, who stated that he had been taken on mornings for two weeks to Swan's house when Swan had no cook, to cook, wash baby's clothes, and iron. Reid also stated that he had often been called out at night to catch fish and crabs for the Sub-Inspector, and would be taken back to his cell at midnight 'wet to the skin'. Reid had asked Peters to take up the matter with the authorities and, in this capacity, Peters had written to Swan to inform him of their intention. Peters alleged that when Reid had gone to see Swan on the matter, Swan had put a dollar in his hand 'and told him to go and keep quiet'. Peters questioned Swan's fitness for high office, and called for his punishment and removal.[40]

Swan responded violently. On Thursday 19 August 1937, he invited Peters to the police station to hear his side of the story. In Peters' words:

> As soon as I entered the office he rushed at me from behind the door and gave me a severe blow on my head with a cane incased [*sic*] in leather. Then he said: 'I have called you, you swine, to flog you.'

According to Peters, Swan continued to beat him with the cane, while he backed out of the office, protecting his head and face with his hands. Swan ordered him out of the Constabulary yard 'and threatened to use his rifle on me if I was not quick in leaving.' Among the eyewitnesses was a police Sergeant.[41]

The People immediately demanded Swan's suspension and trial before an independent court, and Peters laid charges of assault and battery against Swan.

The Tobago public rose up in protest and telegraphed their displeasure to the authorities. Swan was ordered to Trinidad. At a mass meeting in Scarborough on Saturday 21 August, Noble Charles, Thomas J. Baldwin, Lee St. Louis and Peters, all leaders of the nascent labour movement, 'explained in unmistakable terms the seriousness of the insult offered by Mr Swan to the people of Tobago', and immediately a public subscription was taken in support of Peters.[42]

In full flight, Peters continued his offensive on 'the weaklings of the Civil Service' who were sent to be heads of department in Tobago, and referred to Swan as 'a mere stripling'. His article of 28 August had the headline, 'A Dumping Ground for Dunderheads, Noodles and Upstarts Is The Sister Isle'.[43]

Large crowds 'from every nook and corner of the island' gathered at the Scarborough Court House on Tuesday 7 September 1937 for the trial before R. E. J. Paul, Tobago's magistrate. Henry Hudson Phillips, a distinguished attorney practising in Trinidad, was Swan's lawyer; Adrian Cola Rienzi, then a leader of the Trinidad labour movement, appeared for Peters. Swan's lawyer argued that his youthful client had been goaded by 'the indignity and humiliation' suffered from Peters' pen. Rienzi called for peremptory imprisonment because Swan showed no regret. Swan was convicted 'after a scathing vocal castigation', and was fined $48.00 or three months' hard labour, with another $24.00 for costs and compensation.[44]

Neither Peters nor the public was satisfied with the verdict. *The People's* editorial on 18 September stated that the sentence was too lenient and that Swan ought to have been dismissed. It argued that when a semi-literate man had attacked a white official shortly before, the guilty man had been sent to prison. But though Swan had decoyed Peters and attacked him, 'when the guilty party is a white police officer' the fine was only £10. The editorial warned against tolerance of such 'barbarian exhibitions'. When Swan was dismissed in September 1937, *The People* wished him 'Happy Riddance' under the headline, 'Swan Sings His Swan Song'.[45]

Interestingly, Peters' 'Suzie & Sambo' column survived until 1940, while the one in English did not.

Once again, as in the 1880s, the power of the press was demonstrated in Tobago's political life. Had it not been for Peters' restraint, a serious riot with racial overtones could have occurred in Tobago, especially in the volatile political climate following the June rebellion in Trinidad. With his keen sense of the central issues involved, Peters diagnosed the incident as showing the 'very urgent need for reform', for experienced heads of departments in Tobago, for a magistrate trained in the law, and for separation of the judiciary from the general administration. With his even keener sense of communication, Peters chose to see the beating as an 'anointing' for public service, 'to protect the weak from the strong, the oppressed and down trodden from the oppressor, the starving poor from the heartless rich.'[46]

Exceptions to the Rule of Separation

In spite of the great distance between the white planters and the rest of the society, there were individuals within the dominant class who, by vocation and employment, interacted with the middle strata and the poor. The clergy and some of the officials, especially those of the Agriculture Department, were in this group. Many of them selflessly served the community, at times risking their own lives to do so.

Among them must be mentioned Canon Sydney Russell Browne of the Anglican Church who died in 1912 of typhoid, after working long hours to minister to the sick and suffering in the great dysentery epidemic of 1912, and Rev. Theodor Liley Clemens of the Moravian Church. Browne, a native of York, England, served 16 years in Tobago; at his death, he was deemed 'a friend of the poor, the fatherless and the widow, the desolate and oppressed.' Clemens, in the course of his long service from 1888 to 1923 with only short breaks, was one of the most influential men in the island, both with the populace and with the authorities. He took part in every committee or meeting that called for better conditions in Tobago, and boldly spoke out on the negligence of the Government as the prime cause of the high mortality in the dysentery epidemic. At a meeting in Scarborough on 18 September 1912, Clemens, after having buried some 90 victims of dysentery, pointed out that in England there was 1 doctor to 1,000 people, while in Tobago for a population of over 20,000 there were only 3 doctors. Referring to the many requests for a fourth DMO, he said, in opposition to the Warden and other members of the clergy:

> If the Government had responded to the appeal made twenty years ago the mortality would not have been so great.[47]

Among the agricultural officers who willingly gave lectures and demonstrations, helped with co-operatives, and went to the villages at night to attend meetings were H. I. Millen, the first Curator of the Botanic Station (1900–1908), who died in office; W. E. Broadway (1909–c.1914); and F. D. Davies, who arrived in 1915 and served over 20 years. Broadway was awarded the MBE in 1934.[48]

The Planters' Changing Political Strategies

In 1905 the Tobago Planters Association (TPA) was formed; its members were near white or white. After various contentions with the *Mirror's* correspondent, Mitchell J. Prince, over the TPA's desire to have Crown lands granted to indentured Indians because of the alleged laziness of the Tobago worker, the TPA refused to allow the press to cover its meetings, and it became increasingly exclusive.[49] Throughout its existence, the TPA held its ground against constitutional reform that would empower the labouring class. Instead, from 1922 it constantly argued that the best representation for Tobago would be a Commissioner–Warden, who would have direct influence on the executive. Both the Colonial Office and the local Government refused to countenance this move.

However, the sheer force of circumstance had a sobering effect, since all Tobago's residents needed to unite in the cause of development. By 1938 the TPA was defunct, and most of its members had joined the Chamber of Commerce which was started *c*.1936. The Chamber embraced people of all races and shades. In 1938 the leading planters and merchants formed an informal coalition with the political activists of the middle strata to elect George de Nobriga unopposed. Between 1946 and 1956, as Tobago's neglect in the country's affairs remained unchanged, the white planters were among the wide cross-section that supported A. P. T. James, a man of humble, black, peasant background, in his push for Tobago's development.[50]

Middle Strata and Labouring Class: Dividing Lines of Colour and Culture

The social distance between the middle strata and the labouring class was jealously guarded in Scarborough and its environs. Mrs Eileen Guillaume, social worker, who belonged to the middle strata in Scarborough, stated:

> To me, the estate owners were in a class by themselves. Then you had another set, the people might have been merchants, or they might have been professionals—lawyers and doctors—they would be in another strata. And then you had another strata, the people would be civil servants and teachers. And then come a little lower down, you have your shop assistants, and maybe other persons not working, in

the home and so on. And then you came down to your domestics, and then to your labourers. … But you see, colour carried a great weight. That was the greatest divider—colour and shades of colour.[51]

Carlton Ottley, historian and social worker, belonged to one of the prominent coloured Scarborough families. Lengthy though his remarks on Tobago society are, they are an important statement by a perceptive insider, and they are given here in full, since he particularly wanted this researcher to know and record his analysis for posterity. Ottley identified the major cleavage between the middle strata and the labouring class as one of culture. The former adhered to a strict Victorian code; their manners and mores were European; the latter indulged in Africanisms. Superimposed on culture, he stated, was a divide between town and country, with town symbolizing all that was 'civilized', and country the opposite.

> *CO:* … You see, what happened is that there were two real social classes, apart from the 'white people', as we called them. There were two social classes. One was the people who lived in and around Scarborough. They were known as the town people; and the other people, who lived outside of that, were known as the country people. And they lived separate and distinct lives; their whole social pattern of life was separate and distinct. And it didn't matter; it was not a question of wealth either. Because the country people were known particularly as 'black people', and although the town man could be as black as ink, he wasn't a black person at all, to the people who lived in the town. He was a town man, he was a Scarborough man.
>
> And therefore, one of the things that I remember very well was the fact that no one from the town, or no person who belonged to the town could marry into the country, marry a country girl or a country boy. You had to marry within the town. The town becomes the class there.
>
> So I was particularly aware of this on two occasions. On one occasion, [a relative] married a girl from [a village], a nice decent girl, well trained by the missionaries and everything, but the family never accepted her. As a matter of fact, we always, and the whole family, called her 'Miss —'; wouldn't call her 'Auntie' at all. She was completely boycotted. And then I remember a [relative] later on marrying a girl from [a village]. Nice decent girl; not accepted; not accepted into the family circle, because she was a country girl. You couldn't be a country girl and marry a town boy. This was *verboten* [forbidden], as they say. Not allowed. You had to marry in town. …

So that you actually had, and to a certain extent it still exists, as I said, two separate social institutions, two classes, the town people and the country people. So that they found that the town people were more addicted to the foreign culture; they accepted the foreign culture, and didn't have wakes and reel dances and things like that. You didn't find that in Scarborough. You had to go to the country in order to find that. They would have the wake, but they wouldn't have the reel dance and so on. They'd probably have the wake.

SCJ: They would have bongo?

CO: No, no. Town people didn't have bongo and things like that; nothing African. They were completely Europeanized. They didn't have obeah either. If the town man wanted an obeah man, he had to go to the country. You couldn't find an obeah man in Scarborough. You had to go to Mt. St. George.[52]

Sharp though the division between town and country was, there were also strict social lines between middle strata and labouring class within the environs of the town.

SCJ: But town people were themselves internally stratified?

CO: Yes, they were. Because they were stratified into those who had become complete Victorians in their lifestyle, and those who had not. The upper middle class in Scarborough, well, the middle class in Scarborough, were as poor as the others in Scarborough, the working people, or what we would call the working class. They did the same agricultural labour on their land, on their plots of land, they went to church like the others and so on; but, as I said, they were Victorian in their attitude.

SCJ: What sort of jobs they would have held? Petty civil servants?

CO: There wasn't much opening for civil servants in Tobago in those days, you know. They would be butchers, petty shopkeepers; as I say, some civil servants, a few; one or two civil servants; they would largely be farmers, cultivating their land. They would not be labourers. They didn't work on the estates. They would cultivate their own land and so on, sell their animals. They would be traders, traffickers to Trinidad; you know, bring the animals down, and so on ... But the others would be labourers on the wharf, labourers on the estates and so on.

But it was a distinct class, I mean distinct division. ... The middle class wouldn't openly come out and abuse their neighbours, for instance, whilst the others would stay by the steps and let the neighbour have all the cuss words in the world. And of course the middle class would, they would have tea, for instance, they would drink tea in the afternoon like the masters, as we say, masters. They would dress their children like little Lord Fauntleroy. They would probably send them to a private school instead of sending them to the ordinary schools; they would want to send them to a private school, even though they didn't have the money to pay. So that, as I said, although they were as poor as the others, it wasn't based on wealth at all, and it wasn't based on occupation either. It was just based on social norms, different social norms altogether, different ways of behaving. ...

And of course, the middle-class children weren't allowed to play with the others. Though they were neighbours, they weren't allowed to mix and play at all. ... the black-people children were not allowed to play with the middle-class children. They shut them off altogether.[53]

Ottley also stated that the low incomes of the middle strata made them highly dependent on unpaid domestic labour provided by relatives and others from the labouring class.

CO: We remained at the Fort [the area near Fort King George]. We had a closed circle at the Fort. We were surrounded by working-class people ... who were lower-class people to us, and we never ventured out from that closed circle. Even though she was a town girl, if she was from the other circle, we wouldn't marry her. We would have to marry within our closed middle-class range. And the working-class people didn't visit us either. They couldn't come in the house, and if they came, they had to go in the back and remain there. Although we were all catching the devil. We didn't have any money; we didn't have anything.

... You wouldn't find a middle-class woman going to the river or to the well for water; she would have a boy, she would have a yard boy, some affiliate that she had taken on to 'mind', you know, and he would do all these tasks, look after the animals and so on; and she would have a maid to cook, somebody to wash the clothes, and so on. Again, sort of hangers-on. They didn't pay them any salary; they just took the young girl or the young boy to 'mind' them, as we say; and they then became a part of the household, and did the menial tasks in the household.

SCJ: So it was unpaid labour?

CO: It was unpaid labour, yes. We used to have a maid and we used to have a yard boy, and they were never paid. They were fed and clothed, fed and clothed, and they laboured there until they became men and women; probably after that they set out, you see. But we didn't have to pay for labour. And of course, the yard boy had to look after the animals, feed the pigs, and so on, you know.

Peasants, *c.1910. Reproduced by permission of the Syndics of Cambridge University Library.*

Peasants going to market, *c.1920. Photograph courtesy Patricia Hatt.*

Liley Clemens and Thomas Thornton, cotton planter in Tobago from 1908 to 1913. Miss Clemens was the daughter of Rev. Theodor Liley Clemens and his wife Mary, Moravian missionaries to Tobago (1888–1917).
Reproduced with permission from the Institute of Commonwealth Studies, University of London.

'Four shilling per annum houses', 1939. The sum of money refers to the taxes paid for the house each year. The structure at left, made with undressed board, is the kitchen. Such houses usually comprised 'room an' hall' (one bedroom and a small living room), with the kitchen separate, and were typically built by the poorest peasants.
Photograph by P. S. H. Lawrence. Reproduced with permission from the Foreign and Commonwealth Office Library, UK.

Farm Day for the children in the Juvenile Farm Clubs.
Reproduced from CO 298/180 with permission from the Public Record Office, UK.

Izzy Inniss née Jones (1891–*c*.1987), retired metayer, peasant and market vendor.

Below left: Alexandrina Watts (b.1909), retired peasant and market vendor.

Below right: O'Farrell Harris (b.1908), retired tobacco and food-crop farmer.

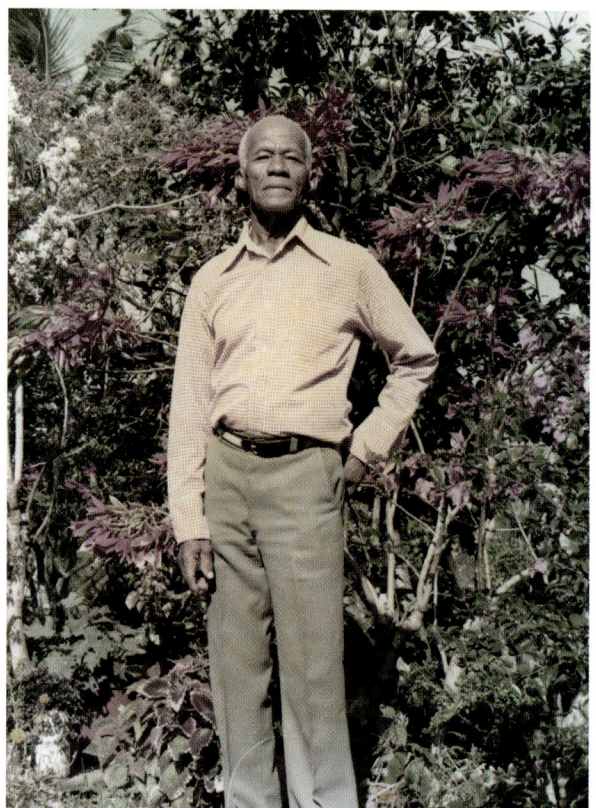

Amos James (1904 –*c*.1999), farmer,
Methodist lay preacher, and
community activist.

Agnes Sandy née Stewart
(1870–1987), retired peasant and
market vendor, in 1984.

Dalton Andrews (b.1912) and his
wife Ruth (b.1913). Mr Andrews is
a retired mason, farmer, small
manufacturer, and trade union and
village council activist. Mrs
Andrews was her husband's
partner in business. In 2005 they
were the oldest couple in Tobago.

Ivan Taylor (1900–1993), his wife Jane (1912–1989) at left, and Irene Cadiz (b.1911). Mr Taylor was a peasant; Mrs Taylor had been a teacher until her marriage, and thereafter a peasant and housewife. Ms Cadiz was a peasant.

Below right: Sidney Gibbs (1906–c.1985), retired hospital store-keeper.

Below left: Annie Caesar (b.1905), peasant, market vendor, and former domestic worker.

Photographs on this and the preceding two pages by Susan Craig-James.

An adze, a tool used by carpenters, joiners and other wood-workers.

From left to right: rip saw used by woodcutters and sawyers; cutlass in its sheath with the user's belt; gullet; 'grass knife'; axe. These were tools commonly used by the peasantry in Tobago.

Photographs by Susan Craig-James with permission from George Leacock, owner of the Scarborough Heritage Parlour.

CHOCOLATE MILLS.

Chocolate mill, used for crushing cocoa beans into a paste. *Reproduced with permission from the Archivist, The National Archives of Trinidad and Tobago.*

Below: Leopold Solomon (1906–1999), carpenter and musician, demonstrates the use of his corn mill, which was over 100 years old in 1985. Such mills were used to make corn meal. *Photographs by Susan Craig-James.*

Above: Oven made of dirt and grass with its door (front left) and a 'cokyea' or 'fex' broom made from the spines of coconut branches, leaning on the oven at right. The broom is used to sweep the ashes from the oven. The life of a dirt oven is usually 40 years. *Photograph by Philip Isaac.*

Right: Two coral water filters, or 'drip stones' as they were called in Tobago, placed one on top of the other, with the filtered water falling into the bucket below. These water filters were usually imported from Barbados. *Photograph by Susan Craig-James with permission from George Leacock, owner of the Scarborough Heritage Parlour.*

Boiler from an estate that had had a steam mill in the days of sugar production. This is one of four boilers that were used for storing water at the home of George David Hatt (1865–1924), Scarborough merchant, and family, at Cinnamon Hill, since there was no pipeborne water. *Photograph by Susan Craig-James with permission from Lloyd Hart.*

The children of Simeon Henry at Mason Hall, using their wood mill to squeeze the juice from sugar cane, 1985. This is the lowest level of technology for expressing the juice from the sugar cane, and it was used only by peasants. Wood mills were also called 'batty mills' (vulgar slang for 'bottom mills'), since they were worked by the posterior of the person riding on the pole that squeezed the canes. *Photograph by Susan Craig-James, with permission from Mr Henry and family.*

Pulling a seine at Plymouth in the early twentieth century.
Photograph courtesy Patricia Hatt.

Roxborough, Tobago's second town, *c.*1930. *Photograph courtesy Patricia Hatt.*

Detail of the eastern façade of Charlotteville Rest House. Rest houses were government buildings for the use of officials while on public business. The architecture of this house and of the post office and telephone exchange in the picture above is typical of public buildings built in Tobago in the early twentieth century. *Photograph by Susan Craig-James.*

Thomas McKenzie Joseph, planter and businessman, and family. Joseph was one of the Grenadians who bought Tobago estates in the early twentieth century. He arrived in 1913 and bought Highlands Estate. His daughter Leelyne (later married to Herbert Adam Dixon Phillips), is standing at far left. *Photograph courtesy Anna Phillips and Diane Laguerre.*

Speyside Inn, also advertised as Speyside on Sea Boarding House, was built by Harry Hislop Tucker, owner of Speyside Estate, *c.*1923. It was opened in 1924. A part of the estate's water wheel can be seen to the left of the picture. *Photograph courtesy Patricia Hatt.*

Sinai Josiah Gordon (1855–1926), tailor, shopkeeper, manufacturer of aerated drinks, violinist.

Below is a photograph of one of Gordon's letters to Mrs E. E. Fraser, Barbados (3 October 1908), negotiating for the purchase of the property now owned by the telephone company on Main Street, Scarborough. Gordon's home was on the site of what is now the car park opposite to the telephone company. *Reproduced with permission from Margaret Cordner.*

The Tobago Cricket Club sometime between 1920 and 1925. By 1920 cricket clubs proliferated in Tobago. The Tobago Cricket Club was composed mainly of men from the dominant class. Only some of its members can be positively identified. Standing: left, Lewis de Nobriga; second from left, Dr. George Hilton Clarke; far right, H. McKenzie. Middle row, left to right: Frank Latour, Harold Kernahan, L. J. Sorzano (Warden and Magistrate), Joe Clarke (Assistant Inspector of Schools). Front, seated on the ground: left, Hilton Thomas; and right, W. Haynes, vice captain of the team. Photograph by J. Keens-Dumas. *Reproduced with permission from the Institute of Commonwealth Studies, University of London.*

The Sister Isle

Continued from Page 5

A LITTLE NONSENSE NOW AND THEN

WILL DRIVE DULL CARES AWAY. TRY IT

Sambo—Gal Oh! Yo ya're how dem ah kill pellice mans ah Trinidad ?

Suzie—No me no ya're. Weh dem do ?

Sambo—Nigga people Ha now say dem money no nuff Pellice try fo keep dem quiet and dem fight apen.

Suzie—Me sorry fo ya're. An' weh dem no pay de people mo money ?

Sambo—Dat no can happen ah Tobago. Yo see dem no know how fo run Bobull Club ah Trinidad. Ef we bin got Oil Fields ober yah, by now me bin done rich.

Suzie—Rich wah. Sense yo say ah go married me 'yo no eben ge me one cent fo buy up me tings.

Sambo—No mo dat yo ha full up yo mind. Yo no member me tell yo say me want fo buy one lime estate. Ef the Lime Factory brug up, me can morgage the estate and dem bank de money. Ef me bank am now in ah me name dem go know me club binness...

Suzie—Me no understand nutting bout bank. 'gi me de money leh me hold am.

Sambo—Oh yes, so yo tink me name Mr Jack Ass. Oman shet yo mout an don' tark yo nonsense. Ah 'ope yo leff nice food fo me.

Suzie—(aside) Me mus coax am because me really want de married. (Aloud) Yes me darling Sambo yo dinner dey ah table tay,

Sambo (After dinner) Suzie Gal me ha some ting fo tell yo but me frecken yo go tark. Ah yo 'omans got so much tongue.

Suzie—Darling tell yo sweet gal. Yo know say me can

SUZIE & SAMBO

keep secret.

Sambo—Well come close. Win sef mussen ya're. Dem higher authority ah set trap fo Jimbo. Dem ya're say e' buy motor-car wid Bo-bull money. Dem eben know de number ob de car. Ef dem know weh me know, hell go roll but me sware no fo tark.

Suzie—Who name Jimbo ? He join the Club too ? Weh he no bin buy Gubna Sancho car. As he ah go weh next month, 'e want fo sell am. He ax young Mc School fo buy am fo $400.00,

Sambo—(Aside) Me Gad oh how dis omans ah ya're people binness so. (Aloud) Jimbo tek out de license in Marcus name but dat no ge help am, Ef Mr. Shinglo no mo han' am up, jail go pick am up.

Suzie—Ef e no get mo den 14 days, dem no go sen' am

ah Trinidad and Soft Grave say dem ah treat prisoners la-ka gentlemans in Tobago jail.

Sambo—Listen no, me no ah tell yo nuttin' mo. Last week me tell 'yo bout Miss Tom, and yo talk. Ebbrev body say me wrong fo talk out Club Secret.

Suzie—Ef yo can't' trust wid one lilly ting la-ka dat how yo go married me ?

Sambo—Cmans don't be chuppit. Dat different. Well me ah go try yo fo de last time.

Dem ah go sem' people fo find out all bout de Predit Society binnis. One mans from Delaford write say he know all 'bout de money binniss. His Excellency know all 'bout the binniss now.

Suzie—Ah dat yo no bin want fo tell me ? Well leh me tell yo, me ya're say Joe no want fo married to Lizzie agen. Sense he ya're say me an yo ah buy up de wedden tings. He say painting job no ah pay.

Sambo—Ef yo bring up dis married tory to me again. Yo go sorry. Wen yo see omans busy busy 'bout married only de ring dem want not de mans. Joe 'e bung fo married.

Suzie—Ah right Sambo dear. No fret, Wha 'bout coppers dis week ? Only ge me a few cents fo run de 'ouse. Me go try wid dat. aside) Lard leh 'e married me.

Sambo—Now me see yo ha sense Ef yo behave yo-sef

me go married next month, jist after Gubna Sancho go weh. Weh yo no buy some ah 'e furniture, me ya're say e' ah sell dem cheap,

Suzie—Me go find out 'bout dem...ah dat mek me lub me Sambo laka fly lub sugar, (aside) Lard leh 'e no mo put de rign pan me finger.

Our Labour Troubles

Continued from Page 7

serf and an economic serf he must remain all the days of his life. The Boer cannot tolerate the idea of Blackmen being allowed to hope that while toiling for their white employers, they may lay by something as a foundation upon which to build a future in which they should not be obliged to toil so hard and so hard and so continuously.

South African bosses come to Trinidad with their consciences dulled by cultivation in the vile atmosphere of Boer hatred for the Black Race. It is a pity they do not seem to appreciate the fact that methods and conditions that obtain in the land that was Oom Paul's cannot be conducive to peace in a place like Trinidad. Here the Black man has long been taught to regard himself as a free British subject entitled to all the rights and privileges which belong to British citizenship. Our laws and everything that goes to regulate life here have made the European standard of life our own. To this fact the colony owes the prosperity of its commerce and the flourishing condition of its trade with those countries that produce commodities for European use. It is obvious that the European standard of life we have been taught to live calls for the European standard of pay,

Yes, law and order must be maintained. This is the duty of Government backed by law abiding citizens. But it is equally incumbent upon Government to see the grievances righted which caused the disorders. And if South African bosses must continue to come to Trinidad, it will be the bounden duty of Government to keep a constant eye upon their doings and their methods. The West Indian Negro cannot be forced into conditions of labour as they exist in South Africa. This must be clearly understood. You cannot treat an intelligent people whose civilization is European in the same way you deal with a backward community without causing trouble. It is safe to say in this matter 'Black is white' in the West Indies.

Now the working-class people couldn't afford this. As a matter of fact it was from a working-class home you would draw your unpaid labour from. And they, of course, economically they were useful because, as I said, they had to feed the fowls, cut the coconut for the fowls, and feed the pigs and so on, and actually produce. So they actually allowed the middle-class people to live a little bit above the level of the ordinary working-class person.[54]

The above illustrates how the very closeness— socially, financially and geographically—of the middle strata to the labouring class prescribed the enforcing of a strict social distance by the middle strata. Their comforts and social standing depended on the avoidance of menial tasks through the use of black domestic labour in return for food and shelter. Underlying this division were lines of colour and culture. The residents at the Fort were largely coloured, while domestic workers and labourers were usually black.

Gender

Chapter 2 described the sexual division of labour in all areas of economic production. Chapter 8 discloses that gender inequalities were embedded in the economic structure and in the basis of capitalist accumulation in Tobago, insofar as the census data capture those realities. In 1901, because of the sexual imbalances in the population, women formed the backbone of the estate labour force and constituted 59.0 per cent of the working force. Wages at all levels were lower for women than for men; higher proportions of women than men were concentrated at the base of the occupational structure; and opportunities for upward mobility were fewer for women than for men. However, there was a marked withdrawal of women from waged work after 1921, to the extent that in 1931, 52.6 per cent of the female working force stated that they were in unpaid domestic work, up from 13.3 per cent in 1901. The figure for 1946 was 60.3 per cent.[55]

Gender must be seen as a significant factor interacting with social class in any meaningful analysis of Tobago society. Yet, given the importance of household production, female involvement in trade, and too little information on other aspects of gender relations, no clearer statement than the above can be made.

4. OTHER ASPECTS OF SOCIAL LIFE

One of the important ways in which the people of Tobago met each other and met groups from other islands was through sport and recreation. By 1925 cricket was the dominant sport at all social levels, although swimming and boat racing were also very popular in Scarborough and the villages near the sea. Lawn tennis and polo were played largely by the dominant class. Horse races supported by all classes continued to be held at Petit Trou beach until 1930, when a race track was opened at Shirvan Park; the dominant class still controlled the Tobago Race Club. By 1930 there were also popular horse races on Roxborough beach. From c.1925, goat races were organized on the Tuesday after Easter at Buccoo, and by 1930 they were a major attraction.[56] Boxing became popular among men from c.1927; it was usually held on Saturday nights in the Scarborough cinema. By 1932 there was also a Tobago Cyclists Club.

The cricket clubs in Scarborough were still stratified by colour, with the Tobago Cricket Club (TCC), started in 1906, attracting, for the most part, members from the dominant class, while Sunbeam, its main rival, had mainly men from the middle strata. The only Ladies Cricket Club noticed by the newspapers before 1930 comprised women from the dominant class. However, people from all the villages participated in cricket. In 1924 a combined team from Parlatuvier and Bloody Bay travelled 42 miles by open boat and walked 12 miles to Scarborough to play against the TCC's second team.[57] In 1908, 8 clubs competed for the Merchants' Cup in first-class cricket; by 1931, in addition to the Le Hunte Cup competition, there were competitions at Windward for the Murray Cup and the Dr. Jarrette Cup. Some 16 clubs were listed as participants in the three competitions; another 7 were named in 1932, and a further 3 in 1934, including the Public Works Department Cricket Club. Most of these clubs had their own grounds.[58] In addition, there were several clubs that were not in the competitions. The schools also had cricket clubs.

Although the first World Cup competitions in football were held in 1930, before 1925 football was unknown in Tobago. Through the influence of Rawle Jordan, the first Principal of BHS, who had been captain of the Codrington College team in Barbados, the first football match was played on

26 December 1925. In 1926 the TCC formed a section called the Tobago Football Club, captained by Jordan, and Sunbeam Cricket Club, by then the champion club in Tobago, started Sunbeam Football Club, captained by one Mourad. Football quickly attracted the youths in schools and those who were becoming involved in the Scout movement. Thus, by 1931 there were Scouts Cricket Clubs in both the first and second divisions, and a Scouts Football Club; BHS also had a football team by 1931, by which time there was also an Inter-School Football Cup competition.

The outstanding sportsmen (no distinguished females appear in the records on sport at this time) in the period 1920–1935 were H. McKenzie (batsman and bowler) and Harold Daniel (batsman) in cricket. Also excellent were Conrad Abbott and Emil Morales, both involved in cricket and cycling; but both these men died in 1928. Aubyn Crosby was another very good cyclist.

In 1900 the Church Lads Brigade already existed in the Anglican Church, and the Boys Brigade in the Methodist Church. Both of these organizations were very vibrant in the early twentieth century, and their members held frequent marches and parades. Their leaders had military titles, such as 'Captain' and 'Lieutenant'.

The first Boy Scout troop in Tobago was started by W. Howard Bishop, Principal of the Collegiate School, in 1915. After Bishop's departure, a Mr Macpherson became Scout Commissioner, assisted by a Mr Souter; both were employed at Miller's Stores.[59] By 1922 the movement appeared to be dormant. After 1925, however, the Scouts and Guides were extremely vibrant movements. The First Tobago Boy Scouts was started under Scoutmaster T. Vincent Mitchell, with his brother Lionel P. Mitchell as Rovermaster, in 1923. The first Guides began under Captain Ann Evelina Cordner, their founder, and Lieutenant L. Wyllie, c.1925. By 1931 there were 13 Scout troops and at least 4 companies of Guides, all of them attached to schools where teachers—such as the Mitchell brothers, Joseph I. Greenidge at Delaford, Fitz Maynard at Roxborough, Samuel Sandy at Speyside, and Ann Cordner, L. Wyllie and Una Collier in Scarborough—had founded and nurtured the groups. The movements promoted exchanges with other groups in nearby islands, and fostered discipline, discussion, public speaking, and other social graces and skills.

These social activities provided opportunities for people to meet and appreciate each other, although they did not alter the boundaries of class and colour.

5. CONCLUSION

By 1938 the transition that Tobago had undergone from the 1880s was coming to an end, as the new agrarian order declined. Although the main contours of the social structure remained, all the major social groupings had been transformed. All were subordinate to the Trinidad dominant class.

The dominant class was mainly white, and the previous alliance between white and non-white within it was broken. The black planters had stronger social ties with the middle strata than with the white planters. As Tobago became marginalized in its intercourse with the rest of the world, the merchants were few, and their businesses relatively small; most planters were not also merchants. Senior professionals were very few, and the Public Service remained minuscule. Thus, the majority of the dominant class were white and near-white planters.

The middle strata changed in composition: coloured families declined, mainly through emigration, while there were increases through the expansion of the teaching profession and the rise of black independent farmers, many of whom also engaged in commerce as shopkeepers.

The labouring class was heterogeneous. In the early twentieth century, its members combined wage labour on estates or on public works with landowning and/or efforts to acquire land. By 1930, however, several factors produced changing conditions. Owing to the contraction of estate labour because of depressed global conditions, there were far fewer opportunities for waged labour. Only 1,388 persons (or 14.0 per cent of the gainful workers at the 1931 census) were employed on cocoa and coconut estates in 1938. At the same time, restricted access to estate land for purchase meant that the peasantry could no longer expand, and the generation of school-leavers in the 1930s faced scant opportunities for landowning or for making a decent living from agriculture. Land reform became a public issue from the end of the 1920s.

There was a twin process of 'levelling down' and 'levelling up' in the society. On the one hand, there was a class of planters whose viability was severely compromised by 1938; and were it not for improved commodity prices during World War II, their decline would have been swifter. Their influence in the councils of state was extremely limited. On the other hand, by 1938 there had been a general 'levelling up' in the rest of the society, since most families owned land and nearly every wage earner, whether on the estates, in the PWD or elsewhere, had other sources of income.

Therefore, social class divisions between employer and labourer were not as sharp as they were elsewhere where a proletariat dependent exclusively on wages existed. This explains why no strikes occurred in Tobago in 1937, despite the prevailing low wages.

There was also no outright destitution in the society, because locally grown food was plentiful, and communal practices undergirded the poor in the villages.

But as peasant agriculture contracted in the depression of the 1920s and 1930s, both emigration and employment in the PWD assumed growing importance by the end of the 1930s. World War II, by raising commodity prices and the demand for food and livestock in Trinidad, brought temporary benefits to the peasants. However, their long-term decline continued after the war ended.

Social distance based on race, colour and cultural boundaries remained important features of the society. However, by 1938, the exclusiveness of the whites was giving way, at least in politics, to the need to combine with all other residents on the development issues. The coloureds in the middle strata, enjoying a kind of genteel poverty, continued to maintain in the private sphere a strict social distance from the black labouring class.

Though organized recreation and sport increased, the basic contours of class and colour remained unchanged.

Gender differences were woven into the fabric of the society. All production was based on a sexual division of labour, and employment patterns, as captured by the census data, showed marked gender inequalities among persons in paid employment. Most women in the working force withdrew from work for wages by 1931. However, given the importance of household production, the role of women in the distributive and other trades, and the lack of information on many other spheres of gender relations, no clear conclusions can be drawn.

Notes

1   *TG*, 31 Dec. 1922, 12.
2   'Wet sugar' was very dark brown; 'wood sugar' was a lighter brown.
3   Lyttleton Noel (b.1909), owner of Les Coteaux Estate, unrecorded conversation with author, 24 May 1999.
4   *Rubber in Trinidad and Tobago* (Port of Spain, 1911), App. 3, 14.
5   See chap. 6; Elder, *Folk Song and Folk Life*, notes the influence of migration into Charlotteville.
6   C. Cruickshank to editor, *TG*, 9 Aug. 1960, 8.
7   *TG*, 8 May 1930, 3. There were also goat races in British Guiana at the time.
8   C. B. Franklin, comp., *The Trinidad and Tobago Year Book for 1921* (Port of Spain 1921), 204–206; and *The Trinidad and Tobago Year Book for 1941* (Port of Spain 1942), 171–73.
9   Franklin, *Year Book for 1921*, 204–206.
10 Cyril Wildman (1892–c.1984), interview with author, 5 May 1983; Mary Alleyne (1891–c.1985), interview with author, 23 May 1983; Frank St. Louis, unrecorded conversation with author, 22 June 1983; Lyttleton Noel, 24 May 1999. Mrs Purser was the widow of Dr. William Allen Purser, the missionary doctor and musician who had died in 1895. On Dr. Purser, see vol. I, chaps. 7 and 9.
11 Not to be confused with John Baptiste Murray (c.1848–c.1897), teacher, and sometime manager of Pembroke Estate, who was a son of Brutus Murray.
12 Cyril Wildman, interview, 5 May 1983.
13 *Mirror*, 30 May 1911, 4.
14 The term 'cocoa shop' is explained on page 78.
15 Margaret Ernestine Cordner, daughter of Henry and Ann Cordner, unrecorded conversation with author, 9 May 2002.
16 *LL*, 23 June 1923, Supplement; 7 July 1923, 9.
17 Ruth Wilson (1886–1987), interview with author, 5 Jan. 1985.
18 Jules Crooks (1903–1993), interview with author, 24 Apr. 1983.

19 *TRG*, 1 Feb. 1900, 181; 12 Apr. 1900, 468; 15 Jan. 1920, 50; 18 Mar. 1920, 250; 16 Jan. 1930, 37–40; 27 Mar. 1930, 205; 2 Oct. 1930, 698; 11 Jan. 1940, 39–40, 14 June 1940, 686.

20 Turpin Family Papers, Cyril to Charles Turpin, 19 Aug. 1942.

21 Report of a Committee Appointed to Advise on the Trinidad–Tobago Coastal Service, with Appendices (Nicoll Report), Council Paper No. 3 of 1939, 4; CO 295/384: no. 16, Jerningham to Chamberlain, 10 Jan. 1898, encl S. W. Knaggs to Col. Sec., 26 July 1897.

22 CO 950/757/BG/T6004: Memorandum submitted to the Royal Commission by the Tobago Chamber of Commerce, Dec. 1938, 4.

23 Dalton Andrews (b.1912), interview with author, 16 May 1983.

24 CO 295/513: no. 404, Chancellor to Long, 9 Nov. 1917, encl Thomas Thornton, 'Tobago as a Field for Cotton Cultivation', 4 July 1908, 2–3.

25 *LL*, 4 Mar. 1925, 10; *Minutes of the Proceedings of the Trinidad and Tobago Legislative Council*, vol. 2, 16 Oct. 1936, 75; G. St. J. Orde Browne, *Labour Conditions in the West Indies* (London 1939), 125. Cmd. 6070.

26 Calculated from Orde Browne, *Labour Conditions*, App. III, App. IV, and from Table 8.8.

27 Report of the Wages Advisory Board (1935–1936), Council Paper No. 88 of 1936, 31.

28 Ibid., 33.

29 Orde Browne, *Labour Conditions*, 124–25.

30 CO 295/400: Rousseau to Under-Secretary of State, 29 May 1900; Lucas' minute, 31 May 1900.

31 Carlton R. Ottley (1914–1985), interview with author, 8 June 1983.

32 CO 295/480: Capt. E. C. Tryon, MP, to Harcourt, 19 Nov. 1912, encl Farmer to Tryon, 6 Nov. 1912; CO 295/481: no. 31, Le Hunte to Harcourt, 18 Jan. 1913, and Encs; Alefounder to Colonial Office, 25 Sept. 1914. Alefounder died in England in July 1915.

33 CO 295/489: Private, Howard to Harcourt, 19 Dec. 1913; Harcourt to Howard, 3 Jan. 1914. Howard in 1929 was British Ambassador to the USA.

34 Quoted by Brinsley Samaroo in 'The Trinidad Disturbances of 1919–20: Precursor to 1917', in *The Trinidad Labour Riots of 1937: Perspectives 50 Years Later*, ed. R. Thomas (UWI, St. Augustine 1987), 28. The issue of the *Mirror*, 16 Aug. 1915, quoted by Samaroo, survives neither on the British Newspaper Library's microfilm nor in the collection of the National Archives of Trinidad and Tobago.

35 *Mirror*, 6 Sept. 1915, 5.

36 CO 295/554: Confid., Byatt to Amery, 10 Mar. 1925; emphasis added.

37 CO 295/555: no. 331, Byatt to Amery, 23 July 1925, encl M. Short, Chairman, TPA, to Amery, 1 July 1925.

38 See Roy Thomas, ed., *The Trinidad Labour Riots of 1937*, and Susan Craig, *Smiles and Blood*.

39 *People*, 19 June 1937, 5.

40 *People*, 14 Aug. 1937, 5.

41 *People*, 21 Aug. 1937, 2.

42 *People*, 28 Aug. 1937, 11.

43 *People*, 21 Aug. 1937, 5; 28 Aug. 1937, 11.

44 *People*, 11 Sept. 1937, 2. The currency is Trinidad and Tobago dollars; $4.80 = £1 sterling.

45 *People*, 18 Sept. 1937, 6; 25 Sept. 1937, 7.

46 *People*, 18 Sept. 1937, 4; punctuation as in original.

47 *Mirror*, 17 Sept. 1912, 1; Browne was mentor to George Horatio McEachrane III, later a Canon of the Anglican Church, and Browne's encouragement caused him to enter Holy Orders; *Mirror*, 28 Sept. 1912, 5. For Clemens' statements on the epidemic, see *Mirror*, 21 Sept. 1912, 7.

48 MBE: Member of the Order of the British Empire.

49 For 1905, see *Mirror*, 26 June, 11–12; 15 July, 17; 26 July, 11–12; 11 Aug., 19; 23 Oct., 8; 21 Nov., 2–3.

50 Victor Wheeler (d.2005), one of James' close colleagues, interview with author, 13 Mar. 2001.

51 Eileen Guillaume (1916–2004), interview with author, 29 Apr. 1983.

52 Carlton R. Ottley, interview, 8 June 1983.

53 Ibid.

54 Ibid.

55 See Tables A3.5, A3.8.

56 There were goat races in the then British Guiana in the 1920s also.

57 *TG*, 28 June 1924, 5.

58 *TG*, 28 Mar. 1931, 3; 31 Mar. 1931, 3; 25 July 1931, 16; 26 Apr. 1932, 13.

59 *TG*, 19 Nov. 1921, 12.

4

Political Issues
in Tobago,1900–1950

TRINIDAD AND Tobago was a Crown Colony. Therefore, the fight for self-government was the most important item on the political agenda of the country from 1900 to Independence in 1962.

Five issues confronted Tobago in the first fifty years of the Union with Trinidad. All were related to the colonial state and its policies. They were also all interrelated. The first was adequate representation in the councils of state. The second was complex: the need for decentralization of the administration, transfer of decision-making power to the island, and popular control over the organs of the state. The third was the provision of infrastructure and services. Fourth was the need to respect the rights of workers. The fifth was an appropriate development strategy for Tobago.

The colonial state will be considered in the context of these issues, after the national struggle for constitutional reform is discussed.

1. MOVEMENTS FOR CONSTITUTIONAL REFORM

Under the Constitution, the Governor, representing the British Government, held supreme sway. He was advised by an Executive Council of nominees, mainly *ex officio*. The Legislative Council in 1900 was composed of nominated unofficials, officials *ex officio*, and the Governor who had an ordinary and a casting vote. Most of the unofficials were planters and merchants. From 1886 the Colonial Office had permitted a majority of unofficials to control the Finance Committee, but these arrangements simply reinforced the power of the planters and merchants.

The Trinidad Reform Movement having failed in two campaigns (1885–1886, 1892–1895) to gain elected membership of the Legislative Council, the struggle for constitutional reform was taken up in the twentieth century by several organizations. Indeed, the period 1900 to 1962 was one of continued demands for increasing measures of popular representation and greater devolution of power to the majority in the society.

The Ratepayers' Association (RPA), an organization led by professionals but supported by all classes, was formed in September 1901 to monitor the Government's spending of taxpayers' money after the Port of Spain Borough Council, the main forum of popular representation, had been abolished in 1899. Its leaders included Emmanuel M'zumbo Lazare and Edgar Maresse-Smith, both lawyers. The activities of the RPA culminated in the Water Riots in Port of Spain on 23 March 1903, when 16 people were killed, 45 wounded, and the Red House, the seat of the Legislative Council and several Government offices, was burnt down. As a result of the Water Riots, Cyrus Prud'homme David was made the first black unofficial in the Legislative Council in 1904, followed by Dr. Stephen Moister Laurence in 1911. The Commission of Enquiry into the Water Riots found that the objections to the proposed Port of Spain Waterworks Ordinance, which sought to introduce metered water and other measures to prevent wastage, were the major cause of the riot. However, it was widely acknowledged that the events were in part a protest for representative institutions.[1]

Another organization pushing for change was the Pan African Association (PAA), established in Trinidad as branches of the PAA founded in London by Henry Sylvester Williams, a lawyer from Arouca, Trinidad, who spearheaded the first Pan African Congress in London in 1900. Williams visited Trinidad in mid 1901, and large crowds attended his meetings. This gave impetus to the PAA, which started branches in Couva, Claxton Bay, Manzanilla, Sangre Grande and the chief towns. The PAA was short-lived, however, many of its members gravitating to the RPA.[2]

The strongest anti-colonial organization after 1906 was the Trinidad Workingmen's Association (TWA). Founded in 1897, the TWA protested to the 1897 West India Royal Commission against Indian immigration which, it argued, undercut African labour and served only the class interests of the planters. From 1900 to 1906, the TWA was dormant, but its leaders revived it in May 1906 and called in 1907 for an elected Town Council for Port of Spain. Their protest failed, and a wholly nominated Town Board was appointed in 1907. The TWA spearheaded the strikes of longshoremen and stevedores in 1919 and early 1920, which led to a series of strikes on sugar and cocoa estates, and on the railways in Trinidad. In Tobago, there were strikes on estates and in the Public Works Department. The strikes arose from escalating prices and low wages after World War I; but they were fuelled by strong anti-white feeling as a result of local conditions, newspaper reports of riots in Liverpool and Cardiff, and the heightened race consciousness of the black soldiers returning from World War I, who had suffered severe discrimination under white officers. In Tobago, low wages, the rising cost of living, and race consciousness were undoubtedly factors in the situation.

Captain Arthur Andrew Cipriani (1875–1945), a Trinidadian of Corsican descent, who had earned the love and respect of the soldiers under his command in the theatre of war, was invited to join the leadership of the TWA in 1919. The TWA called for a West Indian Federation with Dominion Status, the Constitution enjoyed by the colonies ruled by whites—Canada, Australia and New Zealand. Under Cipriani's leadership, 'Agitate, Educate, Confederate' became the rallying cry. The TWA forged good relations with similar organizations across the BWI, and became, to quote Selwyn Ryan, 'undisputably the dominant left-wing political force in the British Caribbean'.[3] Strong links were established with the British Guiana Labour Union and with T. Albert Marryshow in Grenada. In 1929 Marryshow asked Cipriani for an outline of his labour programme, which was used to found in November that year the Grenada Workingmen's Association, the successor to the Grenada Representative Government Association. In September 1929 Cipriani addressed, at Gouyave, Grenada, a meeting of some 5,000 people, which passed a unanimous resolution in favour of self-government.[4] In 1932 Cipriani's slogan in Tobago was:

No Federation without Self-Government and no Self-Government without adult franchise.[5]

From early in the century, the TWA also established strong ties with the British Labour Party. In 1926 it formed a Fabian Society (FS) in Trinidad. W. Howard Bishop, the editor of the *Labour Leader* and a leader of the TWA, was Secretary of the FS, and Cipriani, the President.[6]

In 1921 the Legislative Reform Committee (LRC), a middle-class organization, was formed in Trinidad to press for representative government. By then, throughout the BWI, Representative Government Associations and other popular organizations such as friendly societies had agitated enough to persuade the Colonial Office in 1921 to send out a Commission under the Hon. Major E. F. L. Wood, Parliamentary Under-Secretary of State for the Colonies, to enquire and make recommendations.

The Wood Commission found Trinidad and Tobago to be 'more difficult than ... any other colony', because of the racial complexity and divisions in the society. In favour of reform were the LRC, representing the middle class and the peasantry; the TWA, representing labourers, clerks and workers in skilled trades; and the East Indian National Congress (EINC), concerned about protecting the interests of Indians, which asked for communal representation and a franchise giving the vote to taxpayers; the EINC was opposed to educational tests to determine voter eligibility. Against reform were the Chamber of Commerce speaking for the merchants, the Agricultural Society for the planters, and a deputation of East Indians, who wanted only nominated membership of the Legislative Council.

The Tobago Planters Association (TPA) also opposed constitutional reform to promote greater democracy. It called for Tobago to be administered through a Commissioner and not a Warden. Wood ignored their view, on the grounds that those were issues for the Government of Trinidad and Tobago in the first instance.[7]

On the recommendation of the Wood Commission, a limited franchise with property qualifications for both voters and candidates was conceded to Trinidad and Tobago from 1925. The Legislative Council was to comprise twenty-six members, twelve of whom were to be officials; seven of the thirteen unofficials were to be elected, and six nominated by the Governor, who was to have an original and a casting vote.

A local Franchise Commission was selected in 1922 to make recommendations for implementing the Wood Report, and the Tobago nominee was Robert Smith Reid, planter. Reid argued that, since Tobagonians had had no experience of government and were ignorant about the franchise and the legislature, only local government bodies such as village and town councils were appropriate. He therefore called for high voters' and candidates' qualifications (incomes of £150 and £500 per annum, respectively). M'zumbo Lazare, one of the champions of reform, dubbed him 'an Anti-Reformer'; and the Tobago correspondent of the *Labour Leader* opposed his

> unpardonable offence of estimating very cheaply, the people of this island as a whole, in stating that Tobagonians were not able to appreciate the Franchise.

The Commisssion recommended much lower voter qualifications.[8]

The electorate in 1925 for the entire colony was 21,794, or 6.0 per cent of a total population of 365,913 at the 1921 census; for Tobago, it was 1,800 out of 23,390, or 7.7 per cent.[9]

Although Cipriani was extremely popular at the elections of 1925, by 1937 his influence in the colony had waned for four major reasons.

First, in 1931 he was persuaded to oppose a Bill permitting divorce, which he had earlier supported, and this led to his outright condemnation by many members of the TWA, including W. Howard Bishop, his close comrade.

The second factor was one of strategy. In 1932 a Trade Union Ordinance was passed, but it did not permit to workers the right to peaceful picketing or immunity from actions in tort. Refusing to register under it on the advice of the British Trade Union Congress, the TWA changed its name in August 1934 to the Trinidad Labour Party (TLP). Its strategy was to struggle for increased political representation for the masses. However, Cipriani misunderstood the importance of organizing labour to safeguard the interests of workers per se, and by 1936 more radical elements emerged from within and without the TLP, who were to have a decisive influence on the course of political and industrial events. In 1936 Adrian Cola Rienzi (born Krishna Deonarine), an Indian lawyer, and Tubal Uriah Butler, a Grenadian worker in the oilfields, founded the Trinidad Citizens' League which began to mobilize workers in south Trinidad. Butler also founded in 1935 the British Empire Citizens and Home Rule Party, again based in the south, particularly in the oilfields. From within the TLP, the San Fernando branch and the members in the oil belt developed a radicalism that went far beyond that of Cipriani. In Port of Spain, the National Unemployed Movement was started early in 1935, conducting marches on behalf of the unemployed. Its leaders, Jim Barrette, Christina King, Elma Francois, Bertie Percival, Rupert Gittens and others, formed later that year the Negro Welfare Social and Cultural Association (NWSCA). The NWSCA agitated on the betrayal of Ethiopia by the metropolitan governments in the aftermath of the Italian invasion of 1935, and fought for better local industrial and political conditions. One group from the NWSCA entered the trade union movement after the strikes of 1937 and started the Public Works and Public Service Workers Union (PWPSWU), which superseded Cipriani's TLP in Tobago and became, by 1940, the most important union there.

The third reason for Cipriani's loss of popularity was his signing in 1936 of the Report of the Wages Advisory Board. Since 1925 he had fought in the legislature for a minimum wage. When, finally, a Wages Advisory Board was set up, it called for a minimum weekly standard of $3.13 for manual workers in Port of Spain and $2.57 for those in rural districts and Tobago, while, ironically, deploring the absence of thrift. The Report was nicknamed the 'Bloomers Report', since it outlined the acceptable amount of underwear and other garments that workers and their families could afford on such wages.[10]

The fourth factor discrediting Cipriani was his refusal to support the 1934 strikes in the sugar belt and the 1935 hunger marches organized by Butler, Bertie Percival and others in the oilfields. His popularity finally crumbled in 1937, when he distanced himself from the island-wide strikes in Trinidad.

The strikes and rebellions of 1937 in Trinidad formed part of a wave of similar activity in the BWI, beginning in St. Kitts and Trinidad in 1935, continuing in Trinidad and Barbados (1937), Jamaica (1938), and Antigua and British Guiana (1939). There were also minor strikes and disturbances in St. Vincent (1935) and St. Lucia (1935, 1937). There were rumours of a general sympathy strike planned for Monday 28 June 1937 in Tobago, and the Naval Commodore sent to quell the rebellion reported 'sporadic unrest' there. HMS *Exeter* was dispatched to Tobago on 27 June 1937, to 'nip this in the bud' by presenting a show of imperial power; its sea plane distributed leaflets, and no strikes occurred there.[11]

In response to the labour rebellions, apart from local investigations, the British Government sent the West India Royal Commission (Chairman, Lord Moyne), which held sittings in the region in 1938–1939. Its analysis of prevailing conditions could not be published in full in 1940 during World War II, so damning were they about British rule. The Moyne Report called, inter alia, for 'representative' government (that is, greater elected representation in the legislature though not full elected control over the executive); gradual progress to universal adult suffrage; adult education; agricultural diversification; promotion of the peasantry; social welfare; and other reforms.

On the basis of recommendations from a local Franchise Committee appointed in 1941, the Government conceded universal adult suffrage to elect 9 out of an 18-member Legislative Council. The first elections under universal suffrage were held in 1946. Advisory County Councils were also started in 1946.

Most of the submissions from Tobago to the 1941 Franchise Committee favoured gradual change and not immediate adult suffrage; self-government was held to be a remote goal. The Tobago representatives on the Committee were the Warden, Henry Meaden; George de Nobriga, planter, company director, and MLC; and Louis A. Peters, retired teacher, journalist and political activist. De Nobriga signed the rider insisting on property qualifications for candidates to the legislature, thinking it 'preferable to hasten slowly in any scheme which involves the extension of the franchise'; both he and Peters signed the Majority Report, which called for the granting of the franchise to all who were aged 21, not legally incapacitated, and able to understand spoken English, which would have excluded some of the East Indian population. Kenneth Reid, owner of King's Bay Estate, submitted that he viewed with

> misgiving too great a lowering of the Franchise qualifications and even more, the lowering of the qualifications for membership of the Legislature— after all the man with a stake in the Country is likely to make a better Legislator than the 'man of Straw'...[12]

Reid's father, Robert Reid, had expressed similar misgivings to the Franchise Commission of 1923.

Although Tobagonians were aware of these developments, apart from the TWA/TLP which had widespread support there from the 1920s, no organization emerged within the island before 1937 to articulate strong views on Crown Colony rule. Several persons did so as individuals writing in the press, usually anonymously. But Tobago's development crisis was undoubtedly the central issue of public concern. In this context, protests against the continued neglect of Tobago were also protests against British rule. The most telling one was the refusal of the majority in 1914 to have any celebration for the centenary of Tobago's final cession to Britain in 1814. Several Tobagonian emigrants, however, formed part of the early BWI struggles for workers' rights and for self-government.[13]

Constitutional change for Tobago before 1946 therefore owed more to these broader national and regional political movements than to the initiatives of organizations and spokesmen within Tobago. The only strong political organization in Tobago by 1930 was Cipriani's TWA/TLP. Cipriani's eclipse by 1937 therefore left room for new initiatives, in which the concern was increasingly with Tobago's big needs: strong political representation in the councils of state; decentralization and devolution of power to the island; improved infrastructure and services; respect for the rights of workers; and the all-encompassing development crisis. These will be considered in sequence.

2. POLITICAL REPRESENTATION IN THE LEGISLATIVE COUNCIL

Nominated Members of the Legislative Council

Throughout the period January 1889 to February 1925, Tobago's representation in the Legislative Council was weak. All the representatives, in keeping with the 'pure' Crown Colony system, were nominated. Besides the Commissioner for Tobago *ex officio*, the first nominee in 1889 was John McKillop, the lessee of Bacolet Estate, who had been very sympathetic to the interests of the metayers in the conflicts of 1884 to 1891. He declared himself bankrupt in 1893 and was replaced by George Horatio McEachrane II, Ebenezer Henderson's partner, who ran Henderson and Co. after Henderson's death on 28 September 1890.[14]

Because of poor sea communications, McEachrane's attendance from 1893 to April 1898 was irregular. In his maiden speech to the Legislative Council in 1893, he asked that matters related to Tobago should be discussed in two special sessions per year, so that the Tobago MLCs could participate without undue expense and loss of time; his proposal was ignored.[15] Re-appointed in 1898 to the Legislative Council, McEachrane was absent from all sessions between May 1898 and 5 July 1900; however, he made representations to Trinidad in writing, but not in person.

McEachrane continued to absent himself from the Council until April 1903, when Henry Lushington Thornton, an Englishman who had bought Cocoawattie (formerly Alma) Estate with Humphrey Sworder in 1900, was nominated to represent Tobago.

Thornton attended some meetings, but because of the poor sea communications between Tobago and Trinidad, resulting in long absences from his estate, he ceased to attend from c.1906 to 1913. In his absence in England for a year between August 1904 and August 1905, no replacement was appointed. Thereafter, because no Tobago planter or merchant was willing to devote the time and expense to sit in the Legislative Council, there was no representative residing in Tobago. Instead, from February 1913, the Governor nominated one individual in the Council to speak on Tobago's interests; the first was Mr Moodie from San Fernando. After complaints by the Tobago Planters Association about the lack of representation of Tobago on the 1919 Road Development Committee, Thorlief L. Orde, manager of Louis d'Or Estate, was asked in 1920 to serve temporarily in the Legislative Council, but he declined because, owing to the schedule of the steamers, it would have been necessary to spend four to six days away from home for each meeting. A. H. Cipriani, a merchant resident in Port of Spain who owned coconut estates in Tobago, was then asked to regard himself as a special representative for Tobago.[16] However, Cipriani became bankrupt in 1923 and had to withdraw from the Council. When the Wood Commission arrived in 1922, therefore, Tobago had had no resident MLC for almost a decade, and very little representation for nearly 30 years.

The 1925 Elections and James Biggart as MLC

The campaign for the first elected representative for Tobago in 1925, coming as it did after over two decades of mounting discontent at the neglect of the island's administration, was keenly fought.

James Alphaeus Alexander Biggart (1877–1932) was a chemist and licensed druggist.[17] His father, William Thomas Biggart, was a carpenter; his mother, Sarah Eliza Biggart (née Murray) was a daughter of Brutus Murray (1797–1887), the former metayer who had owned Pembroke Estate.

Biggart first appeared in the official records in 1903 when, after protesting unsuccessfully to the Government about having to travel to Trinidad to sit the druggists' examinations in 1900, he appealed to the Colonial Office. The London officials agreed with him, and the druggists' exams were held in Scarborough. Biggart passed his examination in 1905 with over 90 per cent of the marks, by which time he had been a dispenser for some 13 years. In 1899 he had been owner of the only pharmacy in the Windward District. Biggart bought The People's Pharmacy in Scarborough in 1906 and started The People's Store from 1908.[18]

As a public activist, he had been involved in a wide range of activities for two decades. From 1904 he had organized, or been signatory to, virtually every protest on steamers, roads, education and other conditions in Tobago. In 1911 he was President of the Scarborough Literary and Debating Club (SLDC), and of the Scarborough Brotherhood, a vibrant organization formed in 1909 for intellectual and social improvement. Biggart, an Anglican, was pharmacist to the Heart and Hand Friendly Society started by the St. Andrew's Anglican Church, from its inception in January 1906. In 1914 he was secretary to the Anglican Guild of St. Mary in his native village, Pembroke. He was also a member of the Vestry and a Churchwarden at St. Andrew's Anglican Church, Scarborough, for several years. In 1920 he was the first President of the Scarborough Club, a society formed for recreation and literary pursuits. He was a member of the committee responsible for the Tobago Public Library, which started on 2 July 1922. Biggart was among those who persuaded the Right Reverend Arthur H. Anstey, the Anglican Bishop, of the need for a secondary school for boys and girls in Tobago, which led to the founding of the Bishop's High School in 1925.[19] In addition, he was co-founder and Permanent Secretary of Tobago Star Lodge (No. 8869, Oddfellows; founded January 1912), while his wife, Marie Antoinette Biggart (née Murray; herself a granddaughter of Brutus Murray), was the leader of the women's branch of Oddfellows, positions which they held for several years.[20]

Moreover, he was President of a rising cricket club, Stingo, the champions in the Tobago tournament in 1912. With George David Hatt, merchant, Thomas Haynes Hendy, Scarborough shopkeeper, and William Hovell, a master mariner and Scarborough merchant, Biggart led in 1919 a protest against the abolition of the post of Clerk of the Peace. Their protest was successful and the post was restored.[21] Biggart was also the moving spirit behind the establishment of a Leeward District Agricultural Society in Scarborough in 1923, there being already one at Windward.[22] He was thus well known in many circles.

What motivated this remarkable level of activity? Something of Biggart's vision can be seen in his speeches before the SLDC, of which the surviving newspapers offer a small sample. On 8 March 1910, Biggart presented the first paper to the newly formed SLDC on 'The progress of the negro [sic] race in spite of difficulties.' Reporting on the meeting, *The Mirror* stated:

> In well chosen language Mr. Biggart for nearly an hour rivetted [sic] the attention of his hearers while he endeavoured to convince them of the progress the negro [sic] race had made in the West Indies and in America. A subject of this kind requires careful handling, even at this distant time from slavery, and Mr. Biggart was fortunate enough in the construction of his sentences to steer clear of everything that savoured of bitterness of feeling against the oppressors of the race. His appeals to perseverance in the onward movement of the race were manly and vigorous and elicited hearty applause from his hearers.[23]

Despite Biggart's concern for the advance of his race, his was a wider vision, seeing the people of Tobago as part of the onward march of mankind towards its fullest potential. When he became President of the SLDC, in his inaugural address on 11 April 1911 he declared:

> The world is preparing for a great crisis, the universal emancipation of the human intellect from the slavery of ignorance.
>
> This is the silent, steady but sure revolution which is working in society and it is upon those who are now young that the conduct of this mighty movement will devolve.
>
> Let the question with you, fellow members, be: Shall I use the highest and most ennobling faculties with which the Creator has endowed me, or shall I abuse them?
>
> Shall I strive to elevate myself to the highest point of which my nature admits, or shall I permit myself to wallow in worst [sic] than brutal ignorance?
>
> Shall I, as some inferior creature in creation's scale, skulk from the highways of life and strive to forget

and be forgotten? Or shall I, big with emulation, attempt to out-distance my compeers in the race of progression?

By all means, gentlemen, let us endeavour to live at an intellectual elevation commensurate with the nobility of our nature and the opportunities our situation has afforded us, ever remembering that self-help is the only efficient aid, that it must be by our own toil, struggle and upward marching that we shall eventually reach the height of our aspirations, that it is by resolute, untiring diligence, unintermitting [sic] study and unconquerable perseverance and grit that we are enabled 'to bring the mind up to our own esteem.'[24]

While staunchly seeking Tobago's well-being, Biggart, like many from the middle strata, was staunchly pro-British and loyal to officialdom; and on most labour issues he was conservative. In November 1909 he was a founding member of the Empire League which promoted loyalty to King and Empire. In 1911 the League wanted to decorate Scarborough, celebrate Empire Day, and foster knowledge about the Empire to fit the children to become 'loyal subjects to His Majesty the King, and good citizens of the Empire.'[25] Both the Scarborough Brotherhood and the SLDC were willing to affiliate to the Empire League. When the SLDC held its meeting of 23 June 1911 at Biggart's Hall (Biggart's building which he had turned over to public use for a library and meeting house of the SLDC), portraits of King and Queen and flags and banners festooned the hall. The Warden noted that 'in that humble portion of his Empire', the King would find 'hearts as true as in the British Isles themselves.'[26]

Biggart's manifesto presented him as a son of Tobago, identified with its interests. It stated his concern for daily sea communication with Trinidad, new roads and better road maintenance, a secondary school for girls and boys, extension of Scarborough jetty, erection of a new jetty for Roxborough, and a Borough Council for Scarborough. Mitchell J. Prince chaired the meeting in Scarborough on Wednesday 10 September 1924 to nominate Biggart. Biggart also held meetings at the major population centres, including Castara, all of which aroused immense popular support, with villagers attending by boat from the northside villages of Parlatuvier, Bloody Bay and L'Anse Fourmi, which had no motor road.[27] Clearly, although most of the populace were not eligible to vote, they displayed great political excitement, as occurred in the election campaign in Port of Spain.

The other candidate in 1925, Isaac Arbuthnot Hope (1865–1956), was a coloured merchant and building contractor, with businesses in Scarborough, Mason Hall, Moriah, Roxborough and on the north coast of Trinidad. In the 1880s he had been a merchant's clerk at John McCall and Company. While Hope was respected, his social activities were mainly in the Methodist Church, where he was the Senior Circuit Steward in 1925; he was also a pillar of the Scarborough Brotherhood. Hope had the backing of the TWA in Trinidad, which promoted him as the Labour candidate, while portraying Biggart as a Liberal, prone to take no firm position on matters relating to labour, especially since he had opposed the strikes of 1919 in Tobago.[28] Captain Cipriani and Howard Bishop, the editor of the *Labour Leader*, the weekly associated with the TWA, went to Tobago in October 1924 to support Hope's campaign. Exceptionally large crowds attended two meetings at Scarborough and Moriah, but the meeting planned for Roxborough was cancelled because of rain.

At the Scarborough meeting in support of Hope, the convener was George Horatio McEachnie, solicitor (later Hope's son-in-law). L. A. Peters, then Head Teacher, Mason Hall Roman Catholic (RC) School, was the first speaker. Cipriani and Bishop backed Hope because they thought that, unlike Biggart, he would have the courage of his convictions, and would not be what Cipriani dubbed 'an elected unofficial official'. They were also critical of Biggart's emphasis on his being a full-blooded Negro, but Biggart's supporters denied that colour was important in the election.[29]

Hope presented his views in a letter to the electorate with the title, 'The Hour and the Man'. The 'principal planks' of his platform were technical education for boys, and old-age pensions as the solution to the problem of poor relief.[30]

Out of an electorate of 1,800, only 547 voted, and 6 of these ballots were spoilt. Biggart won the elections by 363 votes to Hope's 178.

The Governor, Sir Horace Byatt, was no liberal. To secure the precedence of the whites over the incoming elected representatives in the new Legislative Council, since it would be 'somewhat embarrassing' [sic] to place men like the distinguished lawyer, Sir Henry Alcazar, 'below some unknown member returned by a country constituency', he appointed the nominated members before the elections.[31] In his biographical notes on the newly elected members, Byatt expressed disrespect for all except Charles Henry Pierre and Thomas Meade Kelshall. Of Biggart he stated disparagingly:

> Physically he is short of stature and heavy of appearance, and his mentality might be somewhat similarly described. A man of parochial ideas and limited outlook, whose utterances are not always lucid. While I feel that Tobago might have produced a more able representative, I must record that Mr. Biggart is staunchly loyal to the British Government and that he exerted a most useful moderating influence during the riots in Tobago in 1919.[32]

In this context, as the sole spokesman for Tobago, despite his persistent efforts, Biggart had little chance of being effective in the Council.

Biggart was one of a committee, including T. H. Hendy (teacher and small businessman, from Barbados), G. F. Samuel (pharmacist, from Trinidad), C. Hatt (merchant), D. Robertson, H. I. McNish (teacher, from Trinidad), H. Massy, I. B. Wilson (merchant, from Grenada), T. McKenzie Joseph (planter and businessman, from Grenada), Samuel I. Bonnett (planter, Adventure Estate, from Barbados), A. Toby McIntosh (storekeeper, insurance agent, from Trinidad), T. Jerome Baldwin (teacher, from Trinidad), that convened a large public meeting at the Court House on 19 January 1926, to press for the conversion of Scarborough and its suburbs to a Borough with a Borough Council, which would enable the burgesses to manage the town's affairs. They also called for an extension of the town's boundaries. The Executive Council refused the request because it was not satisfied that the financial responsibilities would be successfully undertaken, especially since over half the revenue projected by the petitioners was to be derived from the general revenue.[33]

In the February 1928 elections, Samuel I. Bonnett contested against Biggart and lost. Biggart represented Tobago until his death on 11 August 1932.

During his tenure as MLC, Biggart tirelessly made representations for Tobago's needs. He pleaded extensively for roads, bridges, improved jetties and ports, post offices, a Scarborough fire service, better schools, improved health services, and better telephone and sea communications; but most of his representations to the Government went unheeded because of their alleged cost, or because it was thought that other districts had more pressing claims.[34] Biggart was also concerned with the protection of animal and bird life. He and the West India Committee drew attention to the fact that the Government was not caring for the birds on Bird of Paradise Island, which had been conveyed to the state by the heirs of Sir William Ingram in 1909. Because of his efforts, provision was made for the protection of the birds. His major achievements were the construction of a market at Roxborough, the erection of a bridge over the Louis d'Or River, and the agreement of the Anglican Church to start the Bishop's High School (BHS).[35] In the face of opposition from the churches in Trinidad, he also won the Government's agreement to make BHS an assisted school affiliated to Queen's Royal College, the leading state-run boys' college.

His contemporaries greatly valued his prodigious efforts, especially since attending meetings of the Legislative Council cost him many days' stay in Trinidad because of poor steamer communications. In December 1926, at the first BHS Speech Day, Rawle Jordan, Principal, said of Biggart:

> From the opening of the school he has been most zealous in doing everything which might contribute towards its progress. ... When, after the lapse of years, we who are present this evening have sought fresh fields and pastures new, and generations yet unborn shall find in their midst a great and flourishing institution sprung from this, they will reflect that next after His Lordship the Bishop, their reverent gratitude will be due to the Hon. Member for Tobago.[36]

At his death in 1932, a reporter stated that he had 'risen so high in [the] affection and esteem' of Tobagonians. On 1 August 1934, I. A. Hope, on behalf of the Emancipation Centenary Committee, unveiled at St. Andrew's Church, Scarborough, a plaque that stated in part:

> A token in Memory of the Hon'ble J. A. Biggart first Elected Member for Tobago 1925–1932.[37]

It was a fitting tribute to one who had fought to emancipate Tobago from ignorance and inequity. Yet there is still need to honour and to keep alive the memory of this man, who led by upright example in unremitting public service, a faithful advocate for better conditions for his people.

I. A. Hope as MLC

After Biggart's death, I. A. Hope was returned unopposed at the by-election in September 1932. At the general elections on 28 January 1933, Hope won with 346 votes against John King, representing the TWA, with 117.

Although Hope presented Tobago's case on several important issues to the Legislative Council, he was usually overruled or ignored. Among the problems he raised was the annual disruption of the Tobago coastal steamer service from 1935 until the opening of the deepwater harbour in Port of Spain in 1939, through the use of the steamers as tenders to the ocean-going liners that brought tourists in the winter season. Hope protested that the *St. Patrick*, a steamer owned by the Government for north and south trips in the Gulf of Paria, could have been used instead.[38] He called for an extended jetty and other improvements at Scarborough wharf; better facilities for landing at the outbays; and for the repair of the road from Parlatuvier to Charlotteville 'to make it a safe bridle road and so bring the rich and fertile cocoa lands in that district nearer to both labour and capital'.[39] In April 1936, Hope also advocated an extension of the Government Stock Farm to government property at Mt. St. George, east of Scarborough, for the convenience of Windward stock-rearers who would have a shorter distance to travel with brood stock. Consideration of this was deferred for the reason that a resident Veterinary Officer would be appointed later that year, but the proposal was not implemented.[40]

One of Hope's most popular acts was his exposure in May 1937 of the high interest rate charged by the Agricultural Credit Societies (12.0 per cent at compound interest) vis-à-vis that charged by the Agricultural Bank, which had lowered its rate in 1933 from 7.0 per cent to 6.0 per cent. It highlighted the way state funds were used to support the large planters, the main users of the Agricultural Bank, while the peasantry in dire need were paying higher rates of interest.[41]

In the 1930s Hope served on the Board of Management of BHS; he supported the Breakfast Sheds and the literary and debating societies, and gave generously to sundry worthy causes. He also donated the I. A. Hope Shield for the best school choir in the colony *c.*1937.

The Mandate to George de Nobriga

Hope's tenure as MLC having proven unsuccessful at improving Tobago's infrastructure and services, by January 1938 a new coalition emerged within Tobago to seek what was hoped would be stronger representation. The consensus of support went to George de Nobriga, planter, managing director of Trinidad Consolidated Telephone Company, Electric Ice Company Ltd., and Tobago Plantations Ltd.; and director of several other companies. De Nobriga was an outstanding tennis player, a race horse enthusiast, and a lover of golf; he had been responsible for the purchase of the Maraval Golf Course in Trinidad.

In the elections of 1938, he was returned unopposed, after Samuel Ignatius Bonnett, a black Barbadian who owned Adventure Estate, was disqualified on nomination day because of irregularities in his papers. De Nobriga's manifesto called for improved raising and breeding of livestock among peasants, fast and regular sea communication, improved facilities for tourism, better marketing arrangements for Tobago's produce, and better roads, both in width and surface.[42]

The committee that secured de Nobriga's nomination included the planters and all ranks of the middle strata. They sponsored a large public meeting in Scarborough early in 1938 at which Kenneth Reid, a windward planter, presided. De Nobriga was presented with an illuminated Address, describing on one side Tobago as it was; on the other, Tobago as it should be. It had been prepared by L. A. Peters and executed by the Scarborough nuns. Ministers of all denominations, senior officials, teachers, planters and businessmen were all present. Hope supported de Nobriga and handed over to him copies of *Hansard* covering his tenure as MLC.

The Tobago District Teachers Association prepared a Teachers' Mandate, which T. J. Baldwin, Laurence Edwards, Hallis Meikle and John Donaldson delivered to de Nobriga in March 1938. It called for free school meals for necessitous children, a Schools Medical Officer for Tobago, a farm and industrial school for post-primary children to be established 'with haste', improved salaries, accommodation for teachers, and grading of schools, since under the 1935 Code there were no A-grade schools in Tobago.[43]

Although the planters, merchants and some segments of the middle strata supported de Nobriga, among the labouring class he was unpopular. He was the owner of Lowlands and Cove estates where the workers consistently complained of having to work one or two days free per week as a condition of their employment. The practice was immortalized in a folk song that still survives, as sung by Jonathan Scott (b.1934):

De Nobriga day
De Nobriga day, Oh, Oh, Oh, Oh!

Chorus:
Ahyuh nuh heare weh massa say
Wensday a' come a' nutten day
Ahyuh nuh heare weh massa say
Wensday a' come a' nutten day.

You have fuh wuk whole day
You have fuh wuk whole da-a-a-ay
Chorus

When freedom a' guh come?
When slavery a' guh do-o-o-one?
Chorus[44]

Complaints about the practice were widespread. In 1939 Laurence Edwards submitted a statement to the Moyne Commission signed by Alteno James, a worker who had started at Lowlands in January 1937, who claimed that after his first fortnight's work, he had been paid four days short, and had been told that that was the rule on the estate. By the time James was fired on 13 September 1937, he had worked 58 days without pay. He was also evicted from the holding he rented, and was refused rented pasturage for his cow. Edwards quoted Archdeacon H. R. Davies, who had arrived at his school when James was giving his statement, as saying that 'all James has told me is true and that there are several other cases of a similar nature.'[45]

The labour policy at Lowlands was mentioned in the Memorandum of the Industrial Adviser, A. V. Lindon, to the Moyne Commission:

It is understood that on this Estate Monday is not regarded as an ordinary working day, and the labourers, if they desire to work do so upon their own volition on the understanding that no wages would be paid but that food would be provided.

Questioning him on this statement, Sir Walter Citrine, President of the British Trade Union Congress, said: 'This is getting dangerously near

truck [*the truck system*]', to which Lindon, who was unwilling to offer an opinion, replied,

Definitely very near, but it is one of those interesting examples we are looking at.[46]

In 1939 estate workers asked to be allowed to join the Public Works and Public Service Workers Union, claiming that for

2 days in the week, they have to work (not for pay) but for bread and tea; given as remuneration, they term it 'Swag' and if they refuse, well: the remaining 3 or 4 days of the week—no work and the price ranges from 18 cents per day for Cart-leaders (smallre [*sic*] men) to 45 cents per day for able bodied fellows ...[47]

Cyril Wildman, a cocoa planter, stated that the cocoa planters would sell to the owners of Lowlands the siftings from their cocoa, which would be made into balls, grated and boiled in a 'copper' (formerly used for boiling sugar) to make 'chocolate tea' for the workers; 'swag' was the chocolate tea.[48]

For these reasons, de Nobriga was not popular with the labouring class; but he was backed by the rest of the society because he was highly influential, since he was director of several important companies and organizations.

In 1937 de Nobriga was managing director of the Trinidad Consolidated Telephone Company (TCTC) and also of the Trinidad Electricity Board. Writing to Sir Alexander Roger, the head of the TCTC, he defined the island-wide strikes as 'a racial problem rather than an economic one', and called for imperial troops to be stationed in Trinidad, so that a show of strength would forestall future upheavals:

The black man respects authority but it must be backed up with strength with a fair measure of benevolence.[49]

In the Legislative Council, de Nobriga's strategy, judging by the few questions he raised during his tenure, was to use his personal influence to accomplish his ends. He pressed for a new enquiry in 1938 into the steamship service, asking for a faster and bigger ship to ply between Trinidad and Tobago, independently of the existing service. He also argued for treating the service as a public utility and not a paying concern. A committee chaired by J. F. Nicoll, the Deputy Colonial Secretary, was appointed in April

1938, and its report with the short title of Tobago Coastal Service Report was a milestone in the thinking of officials concerning Tobago (Chapter 1). However, with the outbreak of war in September 1939, all proposals were shelved. After 1940 de Nobriga said very little on Tobago's behalf.

The 1946 Elections and A. P. T. James

At the first elections by universal adult suffrage in 1946, the voters returned Alphonso Philbert Theophilus James (1901–1962; nicknamed 'Fargo' after a type of heavy-duty truck), a Tobagonian of peasant origins. James began as a pupil teacher before migrating from Tobago in 1927 to La Brea, Trinidad, the site of the Pitch Lake, then leased to the Trinidad Lake Asphalt Company, a subsidiary of the New York and Bermudez Asphalt Company. In Trinidad he first worked as a stevedore. In 1941 he became a contractor for labour with the United British Oilfields of Trinidad at La Brea, and subsequently for the Lake Asphalt Company and the subsidiary of the New York and Bermudez Asphalt Company in Guanoco, Venezuela.

James' native village was Patience Hill, a stronghold of the TWA. It is not surprising, therefore, that his political career in Trinidad began as a member of the TWA at La Brea, where he quickly became the branch Secretary; but he supported the 1935 hunger marches which Cipriani opposed, and finally left the TWA. In 1937 he established and presided over a branch of the Federated Workers Trade Union (FWTU), one of the first labour unions, at La Brea, until December 1939, when the members asked him to become the branch Secretary. In April 1937, months before the June strikes, James led a deputation to the management of the Lake Asphalt Company to argue for a pay rise because of the high cost of living. Although he had no initial success, James kept up a dogged campaign and, at the end of April 1937, the company agreed to raise wages by 1d per hour. After that, James succeeded in several negotiations with the company, and was dubbed 'Butler No 2' by the workers.[50] James also became Vice President of the FWTU. With the active support of Uriah Butler, the main leader of the Trinidad strikes of 1937, he won the Tobago seat in 1946.

James' appeal was threefold: he was a champion of the interests of labour and peasants; a black man from the grassroots; and a Tobagonian, unlike some of his rivals. Dalton Andrews, a shop steward in the Tobago Peasants and Industrial Workers Union (TPIWU) which James formed late in 1946, observed:

> What Fargo brought to us was that all these years, it was the upper-bracket man who represented us, and we didn't know them. We didn't know Mr Hope, right. We didn't know—you understand when I say we didn't know. And we didn't know Mr Biggart, because they was the upper-bracket people. And moreso, we didn't know Mr de Nobriga, which was a kinda white. So Fargo brought this to us that the time has come when your own son of the soil—though Biggart was a son of the soil—your own son of the soil, who knew the wear and tears of yuh life, who fetch water with buckets, who went down in the gully, ... who got his little education like any of you, and I am here to represent you.[51]

The 1946 elections were keenly fought in Tobago. George de Nobriga defended his seat against A. P. T. James; Raymond Hamel-Smith (Progressive Democratic Party); Captain Robert H. Harrower, a Canadian who had retired to Tobago; George F. Samuel, pharmacist, who contested as an Independent; and Laurence Edwards. Harrower was backed by the Citizen's League Party in Trinidad. Edwards, a remarkably able head teacher, had been a pillar of the Tobago debating movement since 1921. As Leeward District Organizer for the TWA, he had started its first sections in Tobago, had taken an active part in the 1925 election campaign, and had been a labour and political activist for some 21 years; he was supported by the progressive United Front in Trinidad.[52] James, with 4,014 votes, defeated his nearest rival, Edwards, with 1,625; Harrower got 942 votes and de Nobriga, 580. At least four of the candidates had support from groups based in Trinidad.

James won again in the 1950 elections with 4,529 votes, defeating Laurence Edwards, his closest rival, with 3,021 votes; Bevan Archibald, a planter, with 810 votes; Egbert Taylor, businessman (704); and Mrs Pearl Bailey with 252. Bailey later became James' staunch supporter. Seventy-five per cent of the Tobago electorate voted, in one of the highest polls in the country's voting history.[53]

In the Legislative Council, James contributed greatly to the fight for self-government. He implacably opposed the principle of nominated membership of the Council. He was regarded by the Governor, Sir John Shaw, as a consistent member of the Opposition Bloc in the Legislative Council (Dr. Patrick Solomon, Victor Bryan, Chanka Maharaj and James himself), who were 'publicly and unequivocally committed to the cause of government by an executive chosen from a wholly elected single-chamber legislature.'[54] Thus, James stood firmly within the anti-colonial movement in the country from 1946 onwards. In 1949, he was a Vice President of the Caribbean Socialist Party, whose President was Dr. Solomon.

From 1946 James conducted a militant campaign for the development of Tobago—'the Cinderella I happen to represent', as he often put it. He called for special representation of Tobago's interests in the Executive Council, but this was ignored. When the legislature for the West Indies Federation was being considered in 1949, he proposed special representation for Tobago as a distinct unit; this too was unsuccessful. Until 1960, he fought for an increase of the members from Tobago in the Legislative Council from one, which it had been since 1925, to two. This was granted for the 1961 elections. Increasingly, as every effort to win policies favourable to Tobago failed, James stressed that Tobago was a separate island with distinct needs, and should be a separate unit within the West Indies Federation. In 1960 he founded the ill-fated Tobago Independence Movement (TIM) on this platform, but this contributed greatly to his losing the 1961 elections to Arthur N. R. Robinson, an Oxford-educated lawyer, candidate of the ruling People's National Movement.[55]

On countless occasions James called for the replacement of the coastal steamers. In addition, he proposed the construction of the Northside Road from Castara to Charlotteville for wheeled traffic, to bring fertile lands into cultivation. Health services, education, the need for a deepwater harbour at Scarborough, all were the subject of several of James' demands.

While Biggart and Hope had seen the need for infrastructure and services, by 1938 it was clear that a comprehensive development plan was needed for Tobago. Like the Nicoll Committee, James went further than simply itemizing needs:

he spelled out a holistic programme for Tobago. Chapter 1 has already discussed the 1948 James Memorandum and another from the Tobago Citizens Political and Economic Party, which James took to the Colonial Office in 1948 and 1951, respectively. All James' efforts were largely ignored. The major improvement was the construction of the Hillsborough Dam from c.1947 to facilitate an island-wide pipeborne water system. In 1952, the water supply was turned on; and Scarborough received electricity in that year. But the coastal steamers, the need for rural roads, the terrible conditions at the Scarborough hospital, and the intractable problem of rehabilitating agriculture, all remained in abeyance by 1956.[56]

3. DECENTRALIZATION OF ADMINISTRATION AND DEVOLUTION OF POWER

From the inception of the closer Union in 1899, the administrative arrangements were unsuitable for Tobago's needs. There were four overlapping issues. First, record-keeping and decision-making even at the most trivial level were centralized in Trinidad. Second, the corollary was that little discretionary power was vested in the administrators in Tobago. Third, within Tobago, offices were often combined, which left a few individuals unable to cope with too many responsibilities. Fourth, many of the services to the population suffered as a result of the above, and from the need to decentralize within Tobago. For example, the people of the distant windward and northern villages often had to walk over 15 miles each way to call a DMO to examine the bodies of their dead relatives and give a death certificate. Between the visits of the DMO, persons falling sick had to be carried on stretchers on foot for several miles to reach medical help. The debates over the post of Warden–Magistrate amply illustrate the problems of over-centralization, little discretionary power and combined offices.

The Warden–Magistrate

The Warden was the sole Magistrate on the island, but before 1938 the incumbent was never legally trained. From the beginning, popular opinion in

Tobago favoured the separation of the two posts, but this view was ignored. Yet, whenever the Magistrate had to give evidence in court in his capacity as Warden, a Magistrate had to be brought from Trinidad to try the case. In the early years of the Union, the Warden–Magistrate was also Inspector of Schools, Sub-Registrar, Commissioner of Supreme Courts, and Commissioner of Affidavits. In the first decade of the Union, the Warden's deputy usually filled the position of Sub-Receiver, Sub-Collector, Postmaster, and Harbour Master. As M. J. Prince noted wryly in 1902, 'combined offices [did] not necessarily mean combined forces.'[57]

Given the infrequent visits of the heads of departments domiciled in Trinidad, and the lack of jurisdiction of the Warden over any of the officers other than those in his departments, there were widespread complaints about inadequate supervision and poor service to the public by officials, many of whom had been transferred from Trinidad as a stepping stone in their careers.

In 1901 James Tod Rousseau, the first Warden, complained that the Tobago Warden should be given higher status with greater independence of action and decision-making powers than other Wardens, arguing that this had been the intention of the 1897 Royal Commission and also of Sir Hubert Jerningham, during whose tenure the Union was inaugurated. He stated also that, given Tobago's isolation and lack of telegraph facilities, the Warden should be able to decide on urgent matters within the jurisdiction.

All the heads of departments in Trinidad disagreed, some noting that Tobago was no more isolated than parts of rural Trinidad, while others thought that public works and police were outside of the Warden's competence. The Collector of Customs, R. H. McCarthy, saw Rousseau's position as retrograde:

> The powers sought by Mr Rousseau for the Warden are quite inconsistent with the ideas which underlay the annexation of Tobago; they would logically bring about the loosening of the union between the two Islands; they would tend backward not forward.

Sir Alfred Moloney, the Governor, agreed, suggesting that Rousseau be moved from Government House, which was to be reserved for the Governor, Chief Justice, and heads of departments on official visits. The Colonial Office

officials concurred with the local administration, and the Secretary of State in reply stated:

> Tobago is now an integral part of the Colony of Trinidad and Tobago, and the Warden of Tobago should be in the same position as any other Warden in the Colony.[58]

Moloney reversed his opinion in 1904. Having made Rousseau Sub-Intendant of Crown Lands to reorganize the Lands Department after the Red House, where the records were housed, was destroyed in the Water Riots, he requested that Rousseau serve as Warden, Tobago, at £600 per annum (his salary as Warden previously had been £500), with £100 allowances, and with the right to occupy Government House when it was not needed for the Governor's use. The Colonial Office officials agreed to the salary increase, 'in spite of [Rousseau's] ambition to be regarded as Governor of [Tobago]', but not to the residence, fearing that Rousseau would be encouraged to ask for increased powers and for a higher salary to upkeep the house.[59] However, Rousseau managed to gain local permission to live at Government House rent-free, but in 1907 was asked to pay a very small rent of four shillings per annum.[60]

Although the issues raised about the status and powers of the Warden were interpreted in the light of Rousseau's ambitions, they remained to dog the Tobago administration for decades to come. The fallacy of believing that a close Union was the same as excessive centralization in Trinidad also remained to bedevil relations between Trinidad and Tobago for the rest of the century.

After Rousseau's death in October 1910, the new Warden was an Englishman, E. C. Eliot. The Governor, Sir George Le Hunte, asked for approval to change the title of the Tobago Warden and Magistrate to 'The Commissioner', with no change in executive or judicial responsibility, although Tobago was 'the most important Ward in the Colony and the position of the Warden [was] one of greater responsibility than the others'. To discourage 'centrifugal tendencies', the Colonial Office agreed to the title 'Commissioner and Warden', on the understanding that the title would be purely honorary, as was the case with the Commissioners of Carriacou and the Bahamas Out-Islands.[61]

The difficulties under which the Warden laboured were well illustrated in the administration of H. P. C. Strange, who was appointed in 1913, on transfer from the post of District Commissioner of Corozal, British Honduras (today Belize).

In 1915 Strange's clerk, Arthur L. Marshall, reported the loss of the key to the iron chest in the Warden's office. The duplicate key had to be sent from Trinidad, which took *ten days* because of the steamer's schedule. When the chest was opened, the sum of £94 19s 4½d was missing, and the local authorities brought disciplinary charges against Strange and Marshall. Marshall was suspended from duty, although there was insufficient evidence for criminal charges. Strange was asked to pay by surcharge £44 15s 10½d, this being the amount less £50 8s 6d improperly received by the clerk for deposits on Crown lands. The authorities made an example of Strange, although his personal honesty was never questioned.

At the Executive Council Committee's enquiry into the matter, Strange stated:

No doubt if I had nothing to do but look after taxes nothing of the kind would have occurred. But my position there is not an easy one. I have to fill a large number of offices of a very diverse nature. My judicial work has been very large indeed. It has very largely increased in both courts [Scarborough and Roxborough]. I have also been at a disadvantage in having to deal with a large number of legal gentlemen at all times in court and that takes up a great deal of my time. One has to listen to them, and examine their arguments later on in the privacy of one's office to see whether ... they are trying to get at a man who has no legal training.

In addition, in the Warden's office there was only one clerk. The pressure of work there was so great that the Chief Ward Officer, who should have been out in the districts often, had to spend nearly all his time in office to check the Taxes Roll of over 6,000 entries. 'I have been working under very heavy difficulties since I have been there.'

In the circumstances, given the failure to show dishonesty on the part of either officer, the view in the Colonial Office was that Marshall, who had been in the service since 1879, should not be dismissed, but retired on a reduced pension, and that no note should be made against Strange, who obviously was overworked. However, since Marshall had been twice before the Executive

Council for misconduct, he was dismissed, with the Colonial Office allowing the responsibility for the decision to be local.[62]

Strange appealed to the Colonial Office, which allowed him to pay £20 of the missing amount and, if the balance could not be paid from the Public Officers Guarantee Fund, agreed to sanction a vote from the revenue for the balance. Because of their remoteness from the circumstances of Tobago, the London officials had not realized that the chest could not have been opened under ten days, owing to the schedule of the steamers! His Honour Mr Justice Blackwood Wright, a Judge of the local Supreme Court, wrote in his private capacity to explain that the chest was opened at the first opportunity. Like many of the senior officials in Trinidad, he felt that Strange deserved no blame, for he 'is a most deserving painstaking official; but not a lawyer & the post he holds can only be properly held by a lawyer as there is so much litigation in Tobago.'[63]

Strange was clearly unable to cope. In May 1914, an anonymous author, Homo, writing in the *Mirror*, commented:

he came, he saw but he has not conquered the work of his offices and it is predicted that he never will.

In June 1914 Homo reported that Strange was unable even to keep order in the courts, and commanded no respect. In one instance, a barrister had slapped a solicitor for using violent language in the court 'and Mr Strange sat impotent.'[64]

Despite all this, the Government did not separate the posts of Warden and Magistrate.

In 1919, on the recommendation of a committee established to review the Civil Service, the post of Clerk of the Peace, Tobago, was abolished. In effect, it meant increased burdens on the Warden–Magistrate, and great inconvenience to the public, who could not be seen by the Magistrate on court days in both Roxborough and Scarborough, when he and his clerical assistant were busy. It could also involve a miscarriage of justice, since litigants would have to give partial evidence to the Magistrate who had to adjudicate, issue summonses and try the cases. A petition spearheaded by James Biggart, Thomas Hendy, William Hovell and George David Hatt, Scarborough businessmen, called for the decision to be rescinded. In Trinidad, the Civil Service Committee and the Governor, Sir John Chancellor, upheld the decision until the

Warden–Magistrate, L. J. Sorzano, explained that the Clerk of the Peace, usually a Justice of the Peace, was indispensable to his work.[65] Only then was the decision rescinded.

Appearing before the Wood Commission in 1922, the TPA asked for a Commissioner–Warden for the island, a request which they repeated locally in 1925, and sent to the Secretary of State after it was rejected by the Government. They also asked that the person to be appointed Warden on the retirement of L. J. Sorzano be a member of the colony's Executive Council. They argued that because of Tobago's history and its comparative isolation, it should not be treated as other Wards in the colony, but needed a social and official Head with authority over officers of other departments, who could both voice Tobago's needs at the executive level and settle urgent matters without delay.[66] The TPA's unspoken assumptions were two. First, they hoped that greater powers for the Warden would procure an administration more amenable to their views. Given that the Warden was appointed by the central government, this might not necessarily have resulted. Second, they would not countenance any expansion of the democratic process. Nevertheless, the planters clearly saw the need for devolution of power to the administration in Tobago.

In 1937 the Governor, Sir Murchison Fletcher, decided to reform the Tobago wardenship. He noted that the Wardens in Trinidad collected taxes and performed specified duties, but had not been given 'general charge over the affairs of their districts.' The administration was centralized and the Warden 'thrust into the background, and his authority has been diminished'. For Tobago, therefore, he wanted to have a Warden with greater executive powers, 'represent[ing] the Governor in his district, and hold[ing] a position of authority accordingly.' He also asked for approval to separate the posts of Warden and Magistrate.

The Colonial Office was very amenable to his request, coming as it did after the strikes of June 1937. Beckett minuted, 'I think there can be no doubt that *Tobago* needs a Commissioner', but doubted that the tendency to centralization could be reversed in the colony, which was a small place with big commercial interests. Sir Henry Moore was doubtful and asked for more information,

since they did not want to have either the Warden or his subordinate officers under-occupied.[67]

Unfortunately, the period September 1937 to March 1938 in which the Colonial Office considered the matter was also the time in which Fletcher was removed from office. Unfortunately too, Tobago's problem was but a particular state of the general condition in the colony. Refusal to address the general problem of over-centralization made it easy for Tobago to be ignored.

The Acting Governor succeeding Fletcher, J. Huggins, recommended that the decision to appoint the proposed Commissioner be reversed:

I have come to the conclusion ... that this change of title will give rise to difficulties for the reason that a Commissioner, once appointed, would be immobilised in Tobago which for obvious reasons is undesirable. I see no reason why Tobago should not continue to be in charge of a Warden who could be transferred to another County when Government finds it convenient to do so, the more particularly as the Commissioner would have the same powers as a Warden so that the change is one in title only. The change would, however, connote in the minds of the public a difference in status between the Commissioner and the wardens and that is particularly undesirable in view of the efforts which are being made to give effect to the recommendation of the Unrest Commission that the influence and status of the District Administration should be improved. ... I accordingly recommend that the new post of Commissioner which has not yet been filled should be abolished and a post of Warden on the same salary scale substituted.

The London officials agreed. The Tobago Warden received no greater powers, and all that was conceded was the appointment of a separate Magistrate—after almost 40 years.[68]

Calls for Popular Control over the Administration

From the inception of the Union, there was a growing demand for popular control over the administration from the middle strata, the older members of which had never forgotten the loss of their political rights which Crown Colony had brought in 1877.

Not long after the Union, in July 1902, Mitchell J. Prince began the call for a Local Road Board to manage the roads, given that the District Officer,

Edward Matthias Macdougall, was in charge of the whole island, doing the clerical, administrative and supervisory work without any assistance whatsoever. Macdougall, a Glasgow-trained engineer, was extremely diligent, and received much public commendation for his excellent service. Prince's demand was the first call for some measure of popular control over the administration.

On Wednesday 23 September 1903, a meeting of planters, merchants, professionals and peasant proprietors held at the chambers of Thomas Reeves Blakely, barrister and solicitor, petitioned for a Local Road Board. Edgar Maresse-Smith, the Trinidad solicitor who then owned Les Coteaux Estate in Tobago, was the chairman. Maresse-Smith had been one of the leaders of the Reform Movement in Trinidad in the 1880s, and was a prominent member of the PAA; he was also prominent in the RPA that had led the protests ending in the Water Riots, and he was arrested and tried for incitement to riot late in 1903; moreover, he was a pillar of the Trinidad Crop Advance and Discount Company (CADC) that had been founded by Sir John Gorrie to assist smallholders.[69] Prince was the secretary of the meeting.

In 1904 Maresse-Smith published the full correspondence with the authorities resulting from the September 1903 meeting. The call for a Local Road Board was a counter to the high-handedness and unresponsiveness of the Trinidad officials. The petition stated that the roads were 'in a deplorable condition', and asked for Tobago to be defined as a Road Union and for a Local Road Board to be established, as in other Wards. The Government refused.[70]

In newspapers like *The Mirror* and *The Labour Leader*, George David Hatt and Mitchell J. Prince, from 1900 to their deaths in 1924 and 1925, respectively, and L. A. Peters from 1936 in *The People*, called for reform of the administration to give greater local autonomy and popular democracy, and to separate the functions of Warden and Magistrate. In September 1902, Prince called for a Town Board to manage Scarborough's affairs. Homo, an anonymous writer, was one of those advocating a Town Board in 1907.[71] Much of this went unheeded over the years.

In January 1926 Biggart and others took up the call for a Scarborough Borough Council. In 1936

the matter was again broached with Sir Murchison Fletcher, the incoming Governor, but Scarborough's population was hardly 1,000 people, and Fletcher suggested an Advisory Board, which was duly named but never functioned. A Borough Council for Scarborough was an issue about which the Tobago trade unions agitated after 1937, but without success.[72]

It took the labour rebellions of the 1930s to shift the ground in favour of greater popular representation. The wave of strike activity throughout the BWI led to adult suffrage in 1946, in which year advisory County Councils were also elected for the first time by adult suffrage. In 1952 they were given executive powers for minor road works and maintenance of cemeteries, playgrounds and other public facilities. The councillors challenged the power of the Wardens, stating that the latter should be responsible to the County Councils.[73]

The Tobago County Council from 1946 to 1956 was one of the pillars of support for A. P. T. James. Many of its members had been stalwarts of the TWA/TLP, the Agricultural Credit Societies, and the TPPA; and some, like John Edwards (Chairman of the Roxborough branch of the Public Works and Public Service Workers Union in 1938), had also been members of the early trade unions. The ubiquitous L. A. Peters, one of the authors of the 1948 James Memorandum, was the first Secretary of the Tobago County Council; John Edwards was its Chairman.

The members of the County Council elected in 1950 staunchly supported James. Some of them formed the core of James' Tobago Citizens Political and Economic Party, the leaders including Pearl Bailey, Barnabas Quamina, William Stewart, Lloyd St. Louis and Dalton Andrews. James also had as strong supporters several female village activists in the Windward District, many of whom formed the early Village Councils after 1944. From 1946 the Tobago County Council had become an important political base for all parties that would win support in Tobago.

By 1950, after decades of simmering discontent, little had been achieved to grant greater popular representation or transfer of power to Tobago. The Scarborough Advisory Council never functioned. The idea of a local Road Board for Tobago was never realized, and the island gained limited control over roads only as part of the general devolution of power to County Councils which occurred from 1952. The other major changes were the provision of a Warden's Office at Roxborough, and more postal agencies and health centres in the villages. However, the need for decentralized administration was again posed by the Colonial Development and Welfare team of experts which visited Tobago in 1957; and, despite the historic call by Arthur N. R. Robinson and Dr. Winston Murray for internal self-government for Tobago in January 1977, it remained an issue of popular contention for decades to come.[74]

4. INFRASTRUCTURE AND SERVICES

For decades, yaws, malaria, dysentery and syphilis were the scourge of Tobago.

Under the Trinidad Yaws Ordinance (No. 9 of 1896), a Yaws Hospital was built in Tobago and opened on 18 April 1902; it was closed in 1920, and treatment was given at patients' homes, which encouraged more people to seek help by avoiding the stigma of going to the Yaws Hospital. By 1930 the disease was brought under control. Malaria was common, but by 1950 it too was under control.

Dysentery was endemic, with an average mortality of 20 deaths in the latter half of each year from 1907 to 1912. Contaminated water was one of its causes. The water supply was from wells, rivers, ponds and cisterns, and there was perennial hardship in Scarborough and the Leeward District in the dry season. In 1903 pipeborne water was taken by gravity from Darrell Spring, near Scarborough, to four standpipes in the lower town. The rest of the island remained without pipeborne water. In 1912 a dysentery epidemic began in the south-western and northern villages, spreading eventually throughout the island. In all, there were 3,179 cases and 466 deaths in six months. Its causes were attributed to prolonged drought in the preceding six months, lowered vitality of the population, 'primitive and insanitary methods of disposal or rather lack of disposal of human dejects', accumulations of manure heaps and other refuse near to houses, prevalence of flies, and contaminated wells and other water supplies.[75] Only after the epidemic was serious consideration given to providing pipeborne water, and for the first time the 1913

Estimates provided for one qualified Sanitary Inspector for Tobago. This was not enough, given the difficulties of travel and the people's ignorance of good hygiene. In 1927 waterworks at Greenhill were formally opened to serve Scarborough and part of the leeward area, 27 square miles in extent with a population of 12,000, but the supply had been available to many areas from 1925.[76]

Acquired and congenital syphilis was also prevalent. In 1918 Dr. Lennox Pawan (the renowned microbiologist who isolated the rabies virus in 1931 and developed a vaccine for rabies) was struck by 'the relative preponderance of sickness and death among infants due to congenital syphilis', which was popularly called 'marasmus' or 'marasma'. Pawan noted that

among the grand-parents of the present day in Tobago it is known as the 'Trinidad Sickness' which seems to represent truly the source of the infection and the mode of travel.

The spread of syphilis could also be traced from Scarborough to the villages. In 1919 he again adverted to the 'extensive prevalence of syphilis' in his district.[77]

In 1924 Dr. Hubert Bishop was hired to conduct a campaign against hookworm in Tobago. He and his staff went to every home on the island, diagnosing and treating all residents. Gerald O'Keiffe, the calypsonian, composed a long ballad on the success of the campaign.

The hospital was renovated in 1904 to provide accommodation for 42 patients, including beds for 2 private patients; this was an upgrade from the previous 25 beds in open wards. However, there was no ongoing upgrading of facilities, and in 1944 an official report stated that the water supply was insufficient, there was no disinfection plant, no laboratory or related equipment, no physio-therapy department, and no X-ray machine. The kitchen and laundry were both 'hopelessly inadequate, insanitary and out-of-date.'[78] The first ambulance arrived in Tobago in 1930.

As late as 1930, Tobago still had no resident dentist. Dentists from Trinidad made periodic visits, sometimes six months apart, but in July 1920 no dentist had served for over one year. After much publicity in the *Trinidad Guardian* on the subject in the late 1920s, in 1930 the Government decided to provide a dentist who would attend to school children without cost.[79]

A market shed for Scarborough, much needed to protect the vendors from the elements, was completed in 1906, amid great contention over the unpopular decision to place it in the Market Square in the upper town, rather than in a more spacious location in Lower Scarborough. Most of the square remained uncovered, and the majority of vendors sold in the open air at the sides of the shed with their goods on the ground. The square was not paved until after 1956.

One of the major complaints was the absence of street lights in Scarborough. Acetylene gas lights were placed at Scarborough bay by 1909. In November 1911 new lights were erected in Scarborough, but these seem to have been short-lived. In 1914 oil lights were installed in a small area of the town, for which a 2.0 per cent property tax was imposed on the urban proprietors. The lights malfunctioned from the beginning and, when repeated submissions produced no improvement, in 1922 the disgruntled residents asked for their removal and the repeal of the Ordinance.[80] Street lights were not placed in Scarborough again until 1952.

Electricity arrived in Tobago in 1925, but it was installed mainly in government offices and at the quarters of some officials at Fort King George. Widespread access to electricity in the south-west occurred only from 1952.

The telegraph, using the newer wireless system and not the cable technology, was installed late in 1905 and became operational from 2 January 1906, but it connected Tobago directly only with a station in north Trinidad. Messages had to be relayed to Port of Spain and the rest of the country. Telephone lines were installed to connect the police stations and certain of the government offices by 1909. In the rural areas, the poles were of bamboo and they sometimes sagged in rainy weather, bringing the wires into connection with passing traffic.

Harbours and jetties were wanting. Passengers and cargo had to be lifted ashore by boatmen, since there was no harbour at which steamers could safely dock. In 1925 James Biggart stated:

> In no other civilised country, are passengers—male and female—lifted in the arms of seamen, who must wade waist deep in water to carry them ashore.[81]

In 1900 the roads were poor, with few bridges; travel was difficult in rainy weather and many lost their lives trying to cross swollen rivers and streams. Some of the main roads were crossed by drains as much as three feet wide and two feet deep, which were locally called 'dips'. In 1931 the Windward Road between Speyside and Charlotteville was made fit for motor traffic, but the road from Charlotteville westwards to L'Anse Fourmi, Bloody Bay and Parlatuvier was still a bridle path, overgrown with tall grass and bushes. Thus, communication with the villages of Parlatuvier, Bloody Bay and L'Anse Fourmi was mainly by boat. As for Castara, the first time a motor car entered the village from Moriah was in February 1922, but the road was so subject to landslides that in the succeeding years few vehicles made the journey. By 1940 there was still no wheeled traffic on the Northside Road between Moriah and Charlotteville, and the bridle path was 'in some places only three feet wide with fallen trees, overhanging branches, fallen telephone wires', and unbridged rivers.[82]

In the early years of the Union, road improvement works were undertaken. Although Tobago received no allocation under the first Road Development Scheme of 1903, a series of 'string' bridges was built to convey pedestrians and horses over the streams and rivers. In 1904 a suspension bridge for wheeled traffic, built under the direction of Edward Macdougall, Tobago-born engineer, was erected over the West Blenheim River. A steel bridge was completed over the Courland River near Plymouth in 1912; the master mason for this work was Daniel Macmillan of Patience Hill. Every year in the rainy season, the villagers east of the Louis d'Or (or Delaford) River were cut off from the rest of Tobago when the river was in flood, because there was no bridge. After much delay and disputing about the cost, a steel bridge was built at Louis d'Or in 1930. The grateful populace regarded the building of these bridges as historic events.

Between 1906 and 1916, under the administration of Sir George Le Hunte, Governor, and Mr A. E. Hitchins, District Engineer, a considerable amount of road work was done, and several difficult corners were removed. Both Macdougall and Hitchins, a native of Jamaica, received public thanks, when they were transferred, for their strenuous efforts to improve the roads, bridges and other infrastructure. By 1948 the northern villages from Castara to L'Anse Fourmi were accessible by jeep. Secondary roads and Crown traces remained unmetalled and well nigh impassable in the rainy season.

Much of Trinidad was similarly without good road communications in 1900, hence the need for coastal steamers. However, in the last two decades of the nineteenth century and the first two of the twentieth, there were concerted efforts to extend the railways in Trinidad and to provide feeder roads linking major estates and settlements to the rail stations. During the depression of the 1920s, construction of new roads ceased and minimal maintenance work was undertaken. By 1928, because of improving revenues, a continuation of the colony's Roads Scheme was approved by the Executive Council and adopted by the Finance Committee. Under this new Roads Scheme no main roads in Tobago were improved. Three minor roads—Cardiff and Branch Road, Pulteney Hill Road and Cameron Canal Road—serving 160 proprietors in the windward parishes, were upgraded at an estimated cost of £7,500, while the total estimate for upgrading roads in the colony was £140,709.[83] Tobago's trifling allocation was a drop in the bucket.

Because of improved roads in Trinidad, by 1938 that island no longer needed the coastal steamers, except for a steamer that went north and south on the Gulf of Paria from Port of Spain to Cedros. In contrast, poor sea and road communications became the pivotal issue on which Tobago's development turned.

5. SEA COMMUNICATIONS

Tobago Isolated

Before 1889 Tobago had been linked to the outside world by the vessels of the Royal Mail Steam Packet Company (RMSPCO) which called once per month, by the merchant ships of A. M. Gillespie and Co. and John McCall and Co., and by intercolonial schooners, sloops and other small craft. In addition, in the early 1880s Gillespie had introduced two English lines of steamers, and McCall brought an American line.

Between 1889 and 1899, although Tobago's imports and exports were conducted for the most part through Port of Spain, there were still direct links with the BWI, North and South America and, via Barbados, with Europe. From October 1889 to 1896, the Government entered into a contract with Messrs Turnbull, Stewart and Company for a steamer connected with the fruit trade to ply around Trinidad to New York, calling at Tobago fortnightly. The Royal Mail steamers also called fortnightly, en route from Trinidad to La Guaira, Venezuela; sometimes Margarita was included in the itinerary. From the latter half of 1903, however, direct links with Venezuela ended; and Tobago was served by Royal Mail intercolonial steamers going to and from Grenada, St. Vincent, and sometimes Barbados, to Trinidad.[84] From July 1900 to July 1906, the Canadian steamers of Pickford and Black visited Tobago twice monthly, to and from British Guiana. In addition, in the 1890s and the first decade of the twentieth century, sloops from Grenada and Carriacou opened a regular, prosperous trade between Tobago and Trinidad. Direct trade with Barbados became infrequent, although schooners run by sea captains from Carriacou—the *Sibyl* (Captain Belmar) and the *Royal Sovereign* (Captain Martineau)—still worked the Barbados route.

In March 1901 the first coastal steamer dedicated to the Trinidad–Tobago run, the *Kennet*, arrived and began calling at Scarborough only, until her sister ship, the *Spey*, arrived in October 1901, after which each provided a weekly service around Trinidad and Tobago, respectively. Tobago's steamer, the *Spey*, was fitted with passenger cabins and an ice chamber between decks for the transport to Port of Spain of fresh fish caught off Tobago.

All these facilities for travel and trade meant that between 1900 and 1905, Tobago enjoyed its best sea communications of the twentieth century. There were easy connections with the Caribbean, the Americas and Europe. In addition, the coastal steamers put 15 outbays in Tobago in connection in alternate weeks with 5 northern and 6 southern Trinidad ports besides Port of Spain.

But from 1905 these varied connections ceased. The Royal Mail intercolonial steamers ceased to call in August 1905, and this cut some of the ready links with the northern islands. To make matters worse, in July 1906, the Canadian steamers were also withdrawn, because Pickford and Black complained that Grenada, St. Vincent and Tobago were unremunerative ports. The Royal Mail and

Canadian steamers, which had connected Trinidad, Tobago and Grenada, allowed Grenadian traffickers, who had travelled to Port of Spain to sell goods, to return home via Tobago, where they would purchase large amounts of foodstuff to sell in Grenada. As one resident put it in 1906,

> It is a market day here whenever those steamers call on their return voyage, as the labourers in the country invariably flock into Scarborough to sell their provisions to the Grenadian traffickers who always take this route for that purpose. By this means a good little trade has been silently springing up, and mutually profitable to all parties engaged in it.[85]

After 1906, apart from a few sloops, Tobago's sea links for more than 50 years were the coastal steamers travelling to Trinidad.

The loss of both the Royal Mail and Canadian steamers was disastrous for Tobago. As her residents saw their growing isolation from the intercolonial and North Atlantic traffic, sea communications became a constant source of agitation and complaint. The Scarborough merchants and other residents petitioned for the resumption of service, first from the Royal Mail intercolonial packets, and then from the Canadian boats. Their argument in 1906 was that 'several large and small proprietors of Grenada' had acquired Tobago properties and were travelling between the islands to develop their estates; and that the trade which had been developing with Canadian ports would be destroyed. The companies' position was that the passengers and goods shipped from Tobago were insufficient to warrant the stops; and the Government did not wish to increase the subsidy. George H. McEachrane II, the former Tobago MLC who spearheaded the protest, reasoned that where the volume of trade and traffic was large, there was no need for a subsidy, since such assistance was intended to help places like Tobago develop their resources by trade with the most favourable markets. McEachrane pointed out that before 1889 Tobago had been 'well served by unsubsidised bottoms' connecting her with the BWI, the UK and the USA. However, no doubt recognizing that the Trinidad and Tobago legislature would be unsympathetic, he asked that the petition go to the Secretary of State instead—to no avail.[86]

The loss of the intercolonial links put fetters on Tobago's development. Dr. George L. Latour, who had bought Golden Grove Estate, complained in 1907 that it took him six days to travel from Grenada to Tobago. He had had to travel via Trinidad, where he had waited four days to get the *Spey*, while the Canadian ships used to make the journey overnight in fourteen hours. Travel by sloop or schooner was also difficult:

> I sent Indian labourers from my cacao estates to Tobago on a Thursday in a schooner, and they only reached Tobago on the following Monday. Even the cotton seed I wish to ship to the Factory at Barbados must first be shipped to Trinidad.

Latour also stated that Samuel Franco, a Grenadian who had bought three large Tobago estates, had attempted the Grenada–Tobago journey by sloop, only to drift at sea for 28 days to the Spanish Main.

Latour had hoped to transfer labourers to Golden Grove from Grenada, given a scarcity of labour in Tobago, while hundreds of Grenadians were leaving for work on the Panama Canal. He explained:

> ... labour for the cotton industry can only be obtained from Grenada where cotton is known (Carriacou is in the Government of Grenada), and it chimes with the Cacao cultivation. Cotton crop begins when the Cacao crop is over. We can bring labourers over and reap the cotton crop. But with experience I have just mentioned it is impossible unless there is direct communication.

The cost of the new arrangement was also greater. The Canadian steamers charged 4 shillings per labourer and £1 for first-class passengers, while the schooners, which were infrequent, charged 10 shillings per labourer.[87]

The view of the Colonial Office was that Government should run the coastal service only as a last resort, on the grounds that public officials lacked experience, and the service would incur risky costs out of the loan funds which had been granted for road development.[88] The decision stood.

A Royal Commission on Trade Relations between Canada and the West Indies sat in 1910. No witness from Tobago appeared before it 'owing to the difficulties of communication', but several written memoranda were submitted. Given that by then Tobago's link with the outside world was only through Trinidad, the Commission called for the renewal of service to Tobago by the Canadian boats, subsidized by the Government of Trinidad and Tobago.[89] It never happened on a permanent basis.

Powerful Allies in Trinidad

The coastal steamer service to Tobago continued to slide downwards in quality and frequency. The *Spey*, a vessel of only 300 tons, which rolled and pitched at sea, was replaced in 1912 by the *Jamaica*; and both this and the *Kennet* were replaced by the *Belize* and the *Barima*, larger vessels, in 1914 under a new ten-year contract with the RMSPCO.

In December 1915 there was another protest, this time over the proposal of the RMSPCO to remove one steamer and perform its contract for half the subsidy. By then, one steamer had indeed been withdrawn. The influential Finance Committee of the Legislative Council unanimously resolved:

> That this Committee is of opinion that the withdrawal of one of the steamers from the Coastal Service has resulted in great inconvenience and loss to the North, South and East Coasts of Trinidad and to the whole island of Tobago, and the time during which the Government permitted its withdrawal, under special and exceptional circumstances, having elapsed this Committee urges upon the Government the necessity of calling upon the Contractors ... to return it at once to the service contracted for.

The Finance Committee further resolved that any modification of the terms of the coastal steamer contract 'would be detrimental to the interests of Trinidad and far more so to those of Tobago, and that it would be false economy to attempt any saving of money in this direction.'

The Finance Committee was backed by the Trinidad Chamber of Commerce, the Tobago Agricultural Society and the Tobago Planters Association. The Acting Governor, S. W. Knaggs, saw this as 'strong opposition', and the full service was duly restored on 1 January 1916. However, the RMSPCO's argument was that the coastal service to the northside of Tobago was unprofitable, its calls at Mt. Irvine, Plymouth, King Peter Bay, Castara and Parlatuvier having yielded in 1915 only $4 to $8 average in freight charges per bay. The Colonial Office, persuaded by the Company's claims, asked that the objectors reconsider their attitude in view of the grave shortage of tonnage during World War I.[90]

Although the withdrawal of the *Barima* in 1916 was justified as being in support of imperial interests, the steamer was not removed for the war effort. Writing to Sir George Fiddes at the Colonial Office in 1916, the RMSPCO explained that the British minister in Morocco had complained that there was only one ship used in the Morocco trade; they proposed to use the *Barima* there. However, he added:

> Of course, if there be any other service in which the Government consider the relieved ship will be of more use, we shall be perfectly agreeable to follow their wishes.

Further,

> Broadly, the position is that the vessel is not really needed where she is and is very much wanted in various other directions where she can be useful.

At the same time, the Foreign Trade Department wrote to Fiddes, asking for the *Barima* to help improve British trade with Morocco.

In Trinidad, the Finance Committee, persuaded that the release of the *Barima* would genuinely assist the war effort, given the shortage of tonnage worldwide, agreed to surrender it, but asked that a small steamer, of a class not needed for imperial purposes, be substituted. However, Tobago was so low in Britain's priorities that the Colonial Office agreed with the RMSPCO's proposal, without putting them under any pressure to provide a substitute. A copy of a letter to Sir Owen Philips of the RMSPCO survives. It asks for an official letter stating that the *Barima* would be employed on a service which the Foreign Trade Department considered most important, and giving the assurance that she would be available for any service the British Government considered more important. It continued:

> Your letter might also contain a promise that you will use your best endeavours to find another small steamer for Trinidad, if you can.[91]

Thus, the Trinidad and Tobago coastal service was served by the *Belize* alone from 1916 to 1931.

The RMSPCO wanted to withdraw from the Trinidad and Tobago coastal service altogether, since it claimed to be incurring loss; and was willing to pay the penalty of $3,000 rather than continue the contract. By then, the laments of the Tobago planters had made it clear to the Colonial Office officials that any stoppage of service would mean the complete dislocation of all Tobago trade and business.[92] The Company's only concession was that the Secretary of State would be consulted before a decision was taken.

Moreover, because the *Belize* was a vessel of 1,000 tons with capacity for some 7,000 bags of freight, its hold was seldom full, and the RMSPCO used this as an argument against the need for the steamer. However, the Tobago planters claimed that the *Belize* sometimes carried 5,100 bags.[93]

The Acting Governor, S. W. Knaggs, explained the serious inconvenience that would occur if the coastal service were reduced. Though the postal services could be maintained with one steamer,

> there can be no doubt that the withdrawal of the other must deprive the people of Tobago and the coastal districts of Trinidad of many of the freight and passenger facilities which they have up to the present enjoyed; and as the Commissioner–Warden of Tobago informs me in a recent report 'a curtailment of the service would fall more heavily on the peasant than on the estate owner, and would certainly discourage the cultivation of provisions and the raising of stock for the Trinidad market.'[94]

As long as the Trinidad coastal service was needed, her cocoa and coconut planters used their influence in the planters' organizations and the Chamber of Commerce to press their claims for the service. By 1919, however, as the road network in Trinidad was developed, much of the coconut and copra, thitherto carried to Port of Spain by steamer, was taken by lorry to the rail stations for transport to the city. Along Trinidad's south coast, sloops had a near monopoly on coastal transport for the estates. Thus, after 1925 most of Trinidad did not need the coastal service.

There were two implications for Tobago of a reduced need for the steamers in Trinidad. Firstly, with diminished freight, the RMSPCO was anxious to raise the rates of freight and passenger fares, or the Government subsidy, or both. Both courses of action were recommended in 1918 by a Committee comprising the Auditor General, Director of Public Works and Collector of Customs, after reported losses of £8,460 in 1916 and £9,314 in 1917, borne by the British Government under the Liner Requisition Scheme. The increased subsidy was paid from 1 January 1920.[95] Secondly, the protest from Tobago about the steamers would not be given the weight it had received when the dominant class in Trinidad supported it strongly. The second became a fact of life.

This became clear in 1919, when a Committee established to consider development strategies for the colony, which had no Tobago representative,

recommended that, at the end of the current contract with the RMSPCO in 1923, the Government should establish and maintain the coastal service with a single steamer of 500 to 600 tons in the first instance, without cabin accommodation, giving only daylight service; a second steamer to be added if warranted by the traffic. The Tobago Planters Association (TPA) protested, pointing out the absence of Tobago representation on the Development Committee, and the need for health, water, sanitary inspection, and wharf facilities in Tobago. The TPA argued that the proposal was short-sighted, given the growing output of cocoa and coconuts from Tobago indicated in the Committee's report, and they were supported by the *Trinidad Guardian's* editorial of 19 June 1919.[96]

From the official viewpoint, the problem was cost, and whether the Tobago service was a public good of sufficient necessity to warrant a continued subsidy. For the officials, to restore the pre-1916 service with two steamers of large capacity was out of the question, and the most that Sir John Chancellor, the Governor, could promise was that with lower demand from Trinidad, Tobago would be better served.[97] The promise was not kept.

On 9 April 1920, the Legislative Council adopted the report of the Development Committee, and the Government began to seek a private contractor to assume responsibility for the coastal steamer service on the expiration of the RMSPCO contract in 1923. The hope was that by the end of 1921 the roads in Trinidad linking the ports of the south and east coasts to the railways would be complete, so making the service around Trinidad unnecessary.[98] Tobago's roads were no priority.

Thus, by 1919, as Trinidad's need for coastal steamers was minimal, her planters and merchants lost interest in the subject, and support for Tobago declined.

Official Unconcern about the Tobago Steamers

Late in 1921 Tobago's planters began discussions with the Clyde Steamship Company of the USA to arrange for a regular steamship service to link Tobago with the Caribbean and North America. This came to nought, largely because of the relatively small freights from Tobago, and its people continued to rely solely on the *Belize*.

With one steamer only from 1916, the service to Tobago was infrequent and unstable. Tobago's northern villages were served once per fortnight by the *Belize*, which called once per week at Scarborough. Tobagonians also underwent the repeated frustration of having the *Belize* withdrawn from service for repairs twice per year, with short or no notice, and often without prior provision for a replacement steamer. Sir Selwyn Grier, the Acting Governor, wrote in September 1929:

> I must admit that I have considerable sympathy with the complaint from Tobago where regular steamer communications have been interrupted by the docking of the Belize.[99]

When, on the night of 31 October 1924, the *Belize* ran aground off Toco on Trinidad's north coast, Tobago was without service for 132 consecutive days. Matters reached a head after repeated interruptions of service as the *Belize*, by then an ageing vessel, needed frequent repairs, which left Tobago for several weeks without steam service. Early in 1927, the *Belize* was off the run for over two weeks. Then during six weeks in July–August 1927, Scarborough received only one steamer call, and the outbays received none. As a result, a delegation of Tobago planters went to the Colonial Office in 1927, thinking, mistakenly, that the Governor, Sir Horace Byatt, was sympathetic to their cause, and would interrupt his holiday in Edinburgh to journey to London to give it his support.

Byatt, instead, wrote privately to E. R. Darnley at the Colonial Office:

> Tobago's revenue is far from meeting its needs & the deficit is found by Trinidad. Among other things Trinidad provides a steamer which is much too large & costly for the job.

Byatt proposed, privately, to get a regular call at Tobago by a Canadian line of steamers, dispose of 'the white elephant', the *Belize*, and replace it with one small and inexpensive auxiliary schooner for inter-port work around Tobago. However, he felt that the schooner was not strictly necessary:

> As it is, every little Tobago planter takes his stuff to the nearest spot on the beach & expects the steamer to call and pick it up: he *will not* make use of the excellent roads which lead to the port, yet is always asking for more & better roads & bridges. Murray himself [John Murray, owner of Kendal Place Estate, the leader of the delegation] is on the main road only 12 miles from Scarborough, & a Ford lorry shared between 3 or 4 of them is what they ought to use, as I have told them.[100]

Ironically, Byatt seems to have forgotten that he himself had had to wait for hours at the swollen Louis d'Or River in July 1925, because his car could not cross over.[101] Referring to the low profitability of Tobago's estates, Byatt described Murray as 'one of the very few prosperous planters in Tobago'.

The deputation was duly received by E. R. Darnley at the Colonial Office on 14 October 1927, having presented a memorandum dated 17 September 1927. They denied that Tobago was financially dependent on Trinidad, given the indirect and incalculable benefits of the Union to the latter. In the hope of receiving fortnightly calls from the Canadian steamers, they conceded that the *Belize* was too large, and asked for two smaller, cheaper vessels of about 600 tons each; they also conceded that sleeping accommodation could be dispensed with. The planters called for a local commission to investigate the question.

Darnley was favourably impressed with the reasonableness of their demands, and recommended the appointment of the commission, if only to ventilate the strong feelings expressed:

> This would be well worth while, even if no improvement could be made. ... I think we should point out that the Government of Trinidad has a great responsibility for securing for Tobago conditions favourable to development, that Trinidad would reap considerable advantage from the prosperity of Tobago, and that the matter appears to be one which ought not to be entirely dependent upon calculations of the revenue derived from and the expenditure incurred in Tobago.

However, the influential Sir Samuel Wilson, who had been Governor of Trinidad and Tobago from 1921 to 1923, and who was then Permanent Under-Secretary of State for the Colonies, minuted agreeing with Byatt, and argued that the Tobago planters exaggerated the advantages from their having better communications:

> ... don't attach too great weight to the argument that Trinidad will reap considerable advantage from an increase in Tobago's prosperity.[102]

Thus, the Governor and some of the senior London officials were not disposed to take seriously the need for better steam communication for Tobago.

In the 1920s some of the planters and merchants found a way out of the impasse by chartering sloops, given that because of poor conditions at the outbays, their produce and goods were often mishandled or damaged on the *Belize*. As late as 1938, the Nicoll Report found that 5.0 per cent of Tobago's cargo was transported by sloop. In 1929 several residents considered buying a motor launch to connect Tobago with Toco in Trinidad daily, but this came to nought. Probably because of the large investment involved, the general perception was that the coastal service had to be run by the state and was not one in which planters, merchants and peasants could invest. In fact, it was a vicious circle. Low prices, productivity and profits left Tobago's producers with little room for investment in steamers, and altogether dependent on an administration that regarded them as too small to matter.

The Tobago Sea Communications Committee was duly appointed in May 1928, under the chairmanship of Hon. M. A. Murphy, Director of Public Works, and its Report was laid before the Legislative Council as Council Paper No. 44 of 1929 (hereafter the Murphy Report). Of the six members, Henry Meaden (Warden), James Biggart (MLC) and Kenneth Reid (planter) were intimately connected with Tobago.

The evidence before the Committee stated that sea links with only Trinidad restricted opportunities for labour and investment from other BWI territories, as well as for exports of food crops and livestock to Barbados. They concluded that capital was more likely to be attracted if there were better steamship services, but were sceptical about the alleged strangulation of Tobago's development in the light of the phenomenal increase in its exports since 1899. However, the evidence clearly showed that because of infrequent steam communication (once per week for Scarborough, once per fortnight for the outbays), Tobago's exports were unable to compete in the Trinidad market with those of Barbados, Grenada and St. Vincent, which were linked to Trinidad by schooners, sloops and steamers daily.

Referring to the question of whether Tobago could be served by more lorries, they stated plainly that though roads were shown on the map, road travel was extremely difficult:

> The roads of the island are narrow; many of them are located on precipitous hill sides and follow tortuous routes; their surfaces have never been constructed to carry heavy loads and fast moving traffic, and while in some instances such traffic could be borne intermittently, yet it would be a misconception of the position to assume that transport by sea could be entirely replaced by transport by land.[103]

In the circumstances, they decided that it would be too costly to develop the Northside Road beyond Moriah for wheeled traffic. Instead, they recommended the replacement of the *Belize* by two smaller vessels.

In the meantime, the West India Committee, the planters' traditional ally, began to ask questions of the Colonial Office and to publicize the matter in its *West India Committee Circular*.[104] More embarrassing were the Parliamentary questions posed by Hon. E. Ramsden on 27 February 1928, and especially by Dr. H. P. Morgan, originally from Grenada, who raised the matter on 6 and 20 November, 4 and 11 December 1929, and 10 February and 2 July 1930, after the *Belize* had been withdrawn for seven weeks of repairs without adequate replacement service.[105]

The Government dragged its feet. Even the calls by the Canadian steamers on which the TPA rested its hopes were slow in coming. Two years after the delegation of October 1927 to the Colonial Office, and only when the *Belize* was docked for another extended period, the Canadian National Steamships were asked to call at Tobago on their north- and south-bound voyages to Demerara once per month. By then, George F. Huggins and Co., the local agents for the Canadian line, had requested additional markers and a buoy in Scarborough harbour costing £3,000, as well as a subsidy of £50 per call. Observing these developments, Robert Reid, one of the more prosperous Tobago planters, wrote to Sir Samuel Wilson in September 1929, supposing him to be willing to use his influence to aid their cause:

> One is forced to the conclusion that there is now a deliberate intention to cut out Tobago from the Canadian W. I. Contract ... it is self evident that Trinidad Merchants would probably lose part of their Tobago trade, inward & outward, if the Island is served by Steamers to & from external markets.

Only when Tobago's inhabitants cabled the Colonial Office asking for an enquiry into this 'ruinous interference with trade, business and postal arrangements' was the Canadian service inaugurated with two calls per month late in September 1929.[106] However, the service was unpunctual, and the vessels were cargo ships without shelter or amenities for passenger accommodation. Moreover, they did not reach the outbays. Inadequate though the *Belize* was, it was preferable to the Canadian service.

Poor steam communication, coupled with over-centralization, meant that many land transactions in Tobago in the early twentieth century were not registered, since to do so involved one or more trips to Trinidad. This has had long-term adverse effects on land titles in Tobago until today.

The Trinidad merchants were the only group that benefited from handling all of Tobago's imports and exports. The system placed Tobago's consumers and producers at a disadvantage, because of high transhipment costs. One observer noted in 1929:

> Tobago merchants have to pay the ocean rate to Trinidad [for imports]. Then they must pay the high rate from Trinidad to Tobago … A cargo landed in Tobago direct, saves on the ocean rate, saves on the inter-island rate, and, passing through its own Customs, is delivered straight to the warehouse.

Goods exported via Trinidad paid an extra 30 cents per bag of cocoa, copra or coconuts, plus cartage to storage.[107]

The new coastal steamers, the *Trinidad* and the *Tobago*, arrived early in 1931, but they soon proved woefully inadequate for the increasing volume of passengers and freight. Passenger traffic rose from 10,000 in 1932 to 33,000 in 1944, nearly 27,000 of whom were deck passengers, for whom there was little seating; freight traffic doubled.[108] The over-crowding and squalid conditions on the steamers, poor embarking and landing facilities, and primitive conditions at the outbays, were all a hindrance to the public, to agriculture and to the tourism potential of Tobago. Both ships were withdrawn from the Register of Lloyd's of London in 1935, just before their first quadrennial survey was due; and no systematic survey and main-tenance was done for the next 22 years. Despite repeated complaints, the *Trinidad* and *Tobago* remained in service until they had to be declared

not seaworthy in 1957. The Government displayed a remarkably callous disregard for human life.[109]

6. LABOUR POLITICS IN TOBAGO, 1919–1940

Throughout the first four decades of the twentieth century, the PWD and the estates were the main employers of labour. The mercantile sectors and the state bureaucracy outside of the PWD were small.

The 1919 Strikes

On 15 November 1919, a series of strikes broke out in Trinidad, starting with stevedores in Port of Spain, and eventually involving scavengers and workers on sugar and cocoa estates. The main causes were racial antagonisms, the discontent of re-turning demobilized soldiers, and the rising cost of living in relation to pre-war rates of pay.

On Saturday 6 December 1919, a market day, the cartermen in the Tobago PWD struck in Scarborough for higher wages. They marched through the town seeking to get the stores to close. The officials closed the spirit shops about 9 a.m., but thereafter until 10.30 a.m., according to L. Sorzano the Warden, 'the mob had complete possession of the town'. The crowd was deter-mined to close all shops, the market, and all government installations, including the Telephone Exchange and the Wireless Station. The small police force—Sub-Inspector H. Cavenaugh, one sergeant, one corporal and six men—received arms and went to protect government buildings. But they were pelted with bottles and stones.[110]

Although James Biggart tried to pacify the crowd and the Warden–Magistrate read the Riot Act, the police were stoned with missiles, in response to which they fired on the crowd. Nathaniel Williams died. The wounded were Henry Niblett, Samuel Emmanuel, Sylvester Chevalier, Albertha Critchlow and May McKenzie, all from Scarborough or its suburbs.

Twenty-two persons—store clerks, government senior and clerical staff, demobilized soldiers and one minister of religion—were quickly appointed Special Constables as a second line of defence to augment the police. The police and the Warden retreated to the police station, but they 'were stoned from the backs of the houses all the way'. The third line of defence, a British man-of-war, was despatched to Tobago the same day.[111]

Meanwhile, according to Cavenaugh, there were strikes at 'several' estates. All except Friendship Estate had no acts of disorder. Resulting from the strikes, the average wage was raised from 36c to 50c per day. Cavenaugh stated:

> I am satisfied that the unrest is due to low wages—36c is exactly what a labourer was getting before the war and now, taking two articles, salt fish 18 cents a pound and rice 9 cents, he cannot make two ends meet.

Cavenaugh also believed that the Trinidad strikes triggered the Tobago ones, because 'agitators' from Port of Spain had arrived on 2 December and posted a notice 'warning people to strike and not be slaves'.[112]

The Senior District Engineer, L. G. Scheult, on 10 December stated that while the Scarborough carters, carpenters and labourers returned to work after negotiations with the officials, 'the strike fever has spread to Charlotteville, Moriah, Parlatuvier, Mason Hall and Plymouth and work along these Sections is practically suspended.' Scheult noted:

> With regards to the wages obtaining here I find them rather low i.e. 36c to 40c for men and 18c to 20c for women the lower rates being by far the more usual ones.
>
> As I understand that the labour question is already a difficult one in Tobago I am of opinion that we should do something to attract a permanent and a better class of labourer and would be glad to have your authority to make a general increase of 3d in the present wages *and will do my utmost to increase the tasks proportionately.*[113]

Short strikes also broke out at Bon Accord and Hope estates in August 1920.[114]

The harsh reality was that the increases in prices of commonly consumed goods over pre-war prices were greater in Tobago than in Trinidad. The Wages Committee, 1919–1920, gave the differences in the increases as shown in Table 4.1.

The Wages Committee in 1920 noted that Tobago, like rural Trinidad, had the highest price increases; they estimated that if costs had risen by a ratio of 2 : 1, the daily minimum wage for a male worker should be 68 cents. In fact, the pre-war wages of 16 to 36 cents per day for men, and 12 to

18 cents per day for women had increased to ranges of 36 to 50 cents, and 18 to 37½ cents, respectively, far lower than what was equitable for the workers.[115]

TABLE 4.1 **Increases in Prices of Consumer Items after World War I**

Item	Per cent increase over prices before World War I	
	Tobago	**Trinidad**
Foodstuff	141	140
Fuel, lights, coal, blue, soap, starch and smokers' supplies	159	91
Local fruits	317	115
Household equipment	194	156
Clothing	197	199
Medicines	162	135
Tools	204	148

Source: Wages Committee, 1919–1920, Preliminary Report, Council Paper No. 125 of 1920, i.

Because the Tobago estate or road worker did not fully depend on the wage, Albert A. Cipriani told the Committee:

> it might be said almost that the labourer of Tobago hires himself out in order simply to supplement the income he earns from his business as a peasant proprietor, gardener, or small stock raiser, and his economic position therefore cannot but be incorrectly determined if viewed from the angle of his wage earnings alone …

Henry Meaden, the Assistant Warden, also commented that the labourers' standard of living was due, not to increased wages, but to increased *prices* for their vegetables, livestock and other produce.[116] The implication was also true: were it not for food gardens, livestock, fishing, trafficking, and the many forms of co-operation practised, the Tobago labourers and their families could not survive on wages paid in the island.

Indeed, the villagers' widespread landowning and their ability to augment income through livestock and fishing formed part of the planters' calculus on wages paid, and on their policy as regards selling land. For example, Cyril Turpin, one of the owners of Charlotteville Estate, stated in a confidential memorandum on their policies in 1929:

> The proprietors have unanimously agreed on this point, *viz.*, that should there be positive indication of a strike by local labour during the harvesting season because of the rate of wage offered …, the manager is authorised hereby to indenture on neighbouring islands for temporary gangs at enhanced rates of wages with passage allowances rather than have the local doctrine of evolution upset, say, the domestic cocoa cart and cause to be introduced unhappy fantasies within the precincts of the household.
>
> If the surplus labour of other coastal villages is engaged some time ahead by prearrangement, there may be no occasion to bring in force the [above] labour scheme reserved for crises.

In another letter, Turpin advised in 1926:

> The villagers may say what they like but the fish will always hold them on the spot. They will say that if they cannot get a freehold parcel they will not stay but the fish will hold them near Man of War Bay. They will say that they have toiled many years and wish to emigrate to some place where they can own their land and finish their years without having to work, but the fish will hold them.[117]

Describing the experience of Mason Hall villagers, Henry Shade (b.1910) stated that land was available for rent and pasture only from Adelphi and Dennett estates. The other planters had a set policy of cutting off alternatives, so that the villagers would have no choice but to give steady work to the estates:

> The white people … they not renting garden give you, they not renting pasture give you. They plot not to give you no garden, not to rent no pasture fuh you. You must just come and work for them. We pass through real trouble here.[118]

Cipriani and the TLP

Artisans were an important section of the labouring class, the few with 'master' certificates having been trained under the Board of Industrial Training at establishments in Port of Spain. They were among the first organized workers.

In July 1929 the TWA sent Comrade Seizont to mobilize support in Tobago. By then, Laurence Edwards and others had begun to organize artisans, workers and peasants. In December 1929 a section of the TWA began at Bethel, with Isaac Sandy, President; David W. Cowie and Samuel

Thomas, Vice Presidents; James Layne, Secretary; and the other officers being John Alfred, Winn James, and Joseph Romeo. Earlier, in November 1929, the Moriah Section had been formed, with Lloyd St. Louis as President; H. Philips, Vice President; and Thomas P. Warner, John I. King, and J. Norah among the officers. At the same time, three other sections were applying for permission to affiliate.[119] By December 1929 there were over 500 members in Tobago.

In January 1930 there were TWA sections at Bethel, Bloody Bay, Canaan, Glamorgan, Lambeau, Mason Hall, Moriah, Parlatuvier, Plymouth, Roxborough and Scarborough. One of the strongest sections was at Bethel/Patience Hill where Daniel Macmillan, a master mason, Nelson Duncan, Edmund Scipio, Henry Chance, and women like Betsy Solomon, the parents of the generation born between 1900 and 1920, were among the staunchest activists.[120] Patience Hill and Bethel were later to be strongholds of support for A. P. T. James, who himself began in politics as a TWA member.

When Cipriani arrived in Tobago on 28 January 1930, his mission was to affiliate 16 TWA sections and to solicit signatures for a monster petition to the UK for self-government in Trinidad and Tobago. The reception committee included Comrade Leighton, President, Scarborough Section; Laurence Edwards, Secretary of the Mason Hall Section; L. J. Keith and George F. Samuel of the Scarborough Section; J. St. Louis of Moriah; J. Trim, Canaan; N. Williams, Plymouth; H. Frederick, Belle Garden; and T. J. Baldwin, Vice President, Scarborough. Baldwin, then the Principal of Trinity School, read the welcome address. Edwards was a head teacher; Samuel, a druggist; and St. Louis, a scion of the family owning Woodlands Estate. Such was the groundswell of support that a large crowd, comprising some 5,000 people, awaited Cipriani's address.

Cipriani went throughout the island, and in Charlotteville 1,000 people were reported present at the meeting to affiliate a section of the TWA. When Cipriani arrived in Tobago there were 945 TWA members; another 1,390 were added during his short stay.[121]

One of the high points of the TWA in Tobago was the visit of Cipriani and T. Albert Marryshow, leader of the Grenada Workingmen's Association, in September 1933. Over 1,000 members and well-wishers gathered at the jetty on 21 September to greet the visitors, who spoke all over Tobago, calling for workers' rights, West Indian Federation, and popular representation. 'The clarion call is sounded for Federation and the right to govern ourselves.' In every district, thousands gathered to hear the visitors; and Laurence Edwards invited Marryshow to address the students at Scarborough Upper EC School. The *Tobago Times* reported:

> It was a week of a blaze of glory and colour to the worker. Everywhere could be seen a riot of red in profusion, red banners, red rossettes [*sic*], red attire of females etc.[122]

Despite the support from Edwards, Baldwin, L. A. Peters, George Samuel, Barnabas Quamina, head teacher and President of the Parlatuvier branch, and a few others from the middle strata, the TWA remained, in the words of *The People*,

> mostly confined to the Labouring Classes, those in better situations keeping generally aloof.[123]

Despite the vibrant beginnings of the TWA/TLP in Tobago, the organization quickly declined for at least three reasons.

First, there were quarrels both within and between branches. Because of this, the Plymouth and Charlotteville branches were the subject of much adverse comment in the press. In July 1935, 'A Worker' writing under the title 'Progress or Strife—Which?' stated that the Scarborough branch had only eight members. Later that month, reporting on a visit of Shaffie Mohammed and Charles Piontkowski, TLP officials from Trinidad, he cited the need to 'rehabilitate' the Tobago branches, because of serious internal conflicts. Piontkowski, on his departure, wrote that he had perceived in the rank and file 'a considerable lack of interest and consequently a dwindling in membership', though the crowd support at meetings was high. In September 1935, C. B. Mathura and Shaffie Mohammed returned to Tobago. Addressing the sections and mass meetings, they called for co-operation among members and loyalty to the TLP. But none of this stopped the decline in interest.[124]

Second, most Tobago workers were not proletarians depending on the wage alone for survival. Therefore, although there were grievances about work conditions on estates and in the Public Works Department, a proletarian consciousness was not well developed. Many of the early TWA members, especially in the Windward District,

were independent farmers with substantial holdings: Joseph Caruth, Rudolph Davidson, Hazel Fraser, and Leoni Hercules among them. H. L. A. Cordner and James T. Arthur, two of the windward activists, were teachers. Many TWA members were pillars of the ACS and were concerned about conditions of peasant agriculture. For example, in July 1930, the sections at Canaan, Bethel, Hope, Les Coteaux, Mason Hall and Moriah called for a Produce Depot in Scarborough to help 'working men to get ready sales at fair prices for their crops'.[125] And as Chapter 6 shows in detail, because there was little proletarian consciousness much of the time in some sections of the TWA was spent singing sacred songs and organizing choir competitions, to relieve the monotony of meetings. The TLP also gave priority to self-government and not to industrial issues. For all these reasons, no serious strikes occurred in 1937 in Tobago, when there were widespread labour rebellions in Trinidad. The Warden reported in 1937:

> about four small strikes occurred on estates, but I am informed that these were organised more in sympathy with the Trinidad strikes than because of any real grievances. There were no disturbances.[126]

Thus, there was no proletariat and little proletarian consciousness, despite the widespread support for Cipriani, Marryshow and the movement for self-government.

The third reason for the decline of the TLP in Tobago is its decline in Trinidad, especially after 1935, when there was increasing protest against Cipriani's strategies.

Although membership in the TLP was declining, on 28 March 1937 the Scarborough Artisans Section was affiliated to the TLP. Its founders were T. J. Baldwin (President) and Samuel Peterkin, singer and musician; L. A. Peters was a staunch member, having previously been Secretary to the Mason Hall Section of the TWA. The TLP announced its 'rebirth' with a march on 24 May 1937. But by November 1937, as trade unions began to be formed, the popularity of the TLP waned, and many of its activists joined the trade unions, in defiance of Cipriani. The meetings to start the Tobago branches of the Public Works and Public Service Workers Union (PWPSWU) were held at Peters' home. In November 1937 Peters himself referred to:

the now dying (or is it already dead) Labour Party and its young and vigorous successor, The Trade Union. ... The Labour Party in so far as Tobago is concerned is now peeping into its grave.[127]

The Early Trade Unions in Tobago

The Tobago branch of the PWPSWU began on 10 Oct. 1937, with Atrill Arnold, Peters' son-in-law, as chairman, and for some time it continued to meet at Peters' home. By January 1938 Peters had also formed the Tobago Industrial Trade Union (TITU) with himself as President; the executive included Ernest Cross, T. Pilgrim, Samuel Peterkin and Joseph Henderson.[128] In mid 1939 the TITU had branches at Bethel–Sherwood Park, Plymouth and Scarborough.

Trade unionism expanded, but mainly among workers in the PWD, on estates, and in the fledgling tourism industry. The PWPSWU, the largest union, quickly spread; by September 1940 the working branches were at Belle Garden, Bloody Bay, Castara, Charlotteville, Delaford, Parlatuvier, Roxborough and Scarborough. The PWPSWU also started a Domestic Section for domestic and allied workers in 1939, and Eileen Ramsay was its Assistant Organizer and Secretary.[129] Among the leading female members in 1940 were Alma Cudjoe, Iris Daniel, Louise Douglas, Delcina Jordan, Flora Rodney, Magdalene Scotland and Albertina Wright.

Workers on the docks and the steamers were also organized. Rupert Gittens, one of the national leaders of the PWPSWU, was Educational Director to the Seamen and Waterfront Workers Trade Union (SWWTU) and, with the assistance of L. Holder, Assistant Organizer of the PWPSWU in Tobago, he started a Tobago branch of the SWWTU in April 1939. Peter Holder was the Chairman, the other officers being Norman Campbell, Sylvester Martin, Conrad Roy and Duncan Saul.[130]

Many of the early unionists, both rank and file and leaders, were former members of the TLP; among the latter were Atrill Arnold, T. J. Baldwin, H. L. A. Cordner, John Edwards, Laurence Edwards, Samuel Peterkin, L. A. Peters, and George F. Samuel. Lionel Mitchell, head teacher, bandmaster and scoutmaster, was among the supporters of the early trade unions. When the PWPSWU formed a Recreation Club in Scarborough in 1940, Mitchell

led its orchestra section. All these men were from the intelligentsia.

Chapter 8, Table 8.7, shows that in 1931 for the first time the census recorded open unemployment of 718 persons or 4.8 per cent of the working force. As agriculture and livestock-rearing waned, waged employment became crucial. As a result, on 15 March 1939, the PWPSWU held a large workers' march (of 300 men) to the PWD to protest against the PWD policy of hiring men six days per fortnight and of contracting out work, which gave only sporadic employment to some workers, and subjected them to loss of seniority for their gratuity and pensions. After the march, united groups of workers, according to *The People*,

> unemployed, hungry, destitute and otherwise, kicked up a rumpus and asserted that this system was bringing them down to the dust ....[131]

Even though trade union membership expanded among wage earners, in some areas members were often artisans, peasants and small businessmen. At Charlotteville in 1942, Cyril Turpin, planter, noted that the PWPSWU leaders were Philip (Sonny) Moore (Secretary and Treasurer), Samuel Perry (Chairman), George Dick, George Garnett Moore,

> and others of that ilk, mostly tradesmen (carpenters, masons, painters, speculators, Traffickers etc) who do nothing for the cultivation of the Estate.

He also stated:

> None of the Charlotteville Branch of the Union do or will do Estate work, i.e. cultivation of the fields and reaping of the crops,

and all had their own land.[132]

Because of the agrarian base of the members, and because the early trade unions were concerned with all facets of life of the working people, the Tobago unions were pressure groups on a wide range of issues. On 19 January 1940, the PWPSWU wrote to the Governor, complaining of the roads and bridges in a 'very dangerous state of disrepair'; of broken-down telephone lines on the way to Parlatuvier; and of the hardships experienced by the people of Castara who had to walk several miles for medical services. The union called for these conditions to be rectified, and for the Scarborough jetty to be modernized to facilitate the landing of passengers and cargo.

On 9 June 1940, the PWPSWU 'and other representatives of every district and village of Tobago' held a conference in Scarborough. The conference passed a wide range of resolutions. It called for government regulation of estate wages; expansion of public works to relieve 'mass unemployment'; increase in the number of Tobago's representatives to the Legislative Council; assistance to the fishing industry; free grazing grounds; more modern telephone, sewerage, transport and lighting systems; and a recreation ground at Charlotteville. In addition, it pledged support for the trade union movement and the fight against Fascism and 'wholesale murder and aggressions on small nations and peoples'; it called for laws to protect domestic workers and for an increased minimum wage for them; and pressed for a survey of abandoned lands to protect the rights of the Crown and the small taxpayer.[133] The union also called for a Borough Council for Scarborough.

From 1946 A. P. T. James organized the Tobago Peasants and Industrial Workers Union (TPIWU), which was based at Roxborough, and which mobilized the workers on the Hillsborough Dam project. Gaskynd Granger, a Guyanese-born labour activist, Dalton Andrews, and Philip Moore were among the main organizers.

7. DEVELOPMENT STRATEGY FOR TOBAGO

By 1938 Tobago was at a critical juncture, as had been the case after the collapse of sugar in the 1880s. Chapter 1 discussed the many initiatives that were taken by those who sought a strengthening of the livestock industry, a boost for the peasantry, and enhanced training in agriculture, to reverse the agrarian crisis. The 1938 Nicoll Report advocated a comprehensive approach to development. A similarly comprehensive programme, which had received the widespread endorsement of Tobago's residents, was the James Memorandum of 1948. All these proposals hinged on state intervention in the economy, especially since such a high proportion of Tobago's farmers were peasants. Given the political structures, the perennial response of the state was grossly inadequate. This led to the irreversible decline of Tobago's agrarian economy.

8. CONCLUSION

The only political organization to gain widespread popular support in Tobago in the 1920s was the TWA/TLP, led by Captain Arthur Cipriani. The major political issues were over-centralized administration, the need for power to be vested in organs within Tobago, the lack of popular participation in the political process, the need for respect for workers' rights, and the feeble response of the Government to the need for infrastructure, services and overall development.

Politically, on the issues of over-centralization, little devolution of power and the need for popular involvement, Tobago was a special case of the general condition of the colony; and the colonial powers, in keeping with their colonizing role, conceded change only under severe pressure.

Economically, Tobago was again a special case of the general. It exemplified in starkest terms the agrarian crisis that beset the BWI in the 1930s. Although Tobago had much in common with the rest of the region, its political relationship with Trinidad gave it little access to the state resources so sorely needed for infrastructure and services. In particular, poor communications hindered the flow of capital, labour, goods and services. Ironically, they also prevented Tobago from being competitive in the markets of its 'Sister Isle', vis-à-vis producers from Barbados, Grenada and St. Vincent whose goods arrived daily, while goods from northern Tobago reached the market once per fortnight or at even longer intervals. Because Tobago was confined to importing and exporting through Trinidad alone, high transhipment costs raised the living expenses of its people and lowered their profits. Tobago's loss through the coastal-steamer arrangement was gain to the Trinidad merchants who handled Tobago's imports and exports. Thus, the Union with Trinidad put serious fetters on Tobago's already fettered development.

The difficulty of communicating with Trinidad in the context of the high level of centralization of state functions had a long-term effect on land-ownership in Tobago. Even today many families have no legal titles to their land holdings, because their relatives did not travel to Port of Spain to register wills, deeds and other transactions.

In response to the engulfing crisis, the closing years of the 1930s were a time of tremendous organizational activity. As part of this upsurge, the new trade unions organized workers in the PWD, on the estates and docks, and in the hotels. However, most workers were not proletarians depending on wages alone. Therefore the early trade unions, like the TWA before them, concerned themselves with a range of issues for the well-being of the people. Since agriculture was declining, wage labour was becoming important for survival, as the 1939 trade union march 'for bread and butter' disclosed.

In addition to the new trade unions, the Tobago Live Stock Association and the Juvenile Farm Clubs were formed in 1938, while the Tobago Peasant Proprietors Association began in 1939. All these were part of the impetus to retrieve the situation.[134]

A. P. T. James was the most militant of the Tobago MLCs, and the first to offer firm opposition to Crown Colony rule, calling for a legislature that would be wholly composed of elected representatives. His was an informed, thoughtful position on the development plan that was needed for Tobago. Having failed to interest both the British Government and the local one in Tobago's plight, he demanded separate recognition of Tobago as a unit within the colony and within the West Indies Federation.

The growing frustrations within Tobago fed the Tobago nationalist movement which coalesced around James in the late 1940s and 1950s, and which had support from all levels of Tobago society, including the white planters.

In the face of increasing official unconcern with Tobago's affairs, Tobago nationalism was to emerge with even greater strength in the last quarter of the twentieth century.

Notes

1 Brinsley Samaroo, 'Constitutional and Political Development of Trinidad, 1898–1925' (Ph.D. thesis, University of London, 1969); Bridget Brereton, *A History of Modern Trinidad, 1783–1962* (London 1981).

2 Owen C. Mathurin, *Henry Sylvester Williams and the Origins of the Pan-African Movement, 1869–1911* (Westport 1976), 94 ff.

3 Selwyn Ryan, *Race and Nationalism in Trinidad and Tobago* (Toronto 1972), 30.

4 Brinsley Samaroo, 'The Trinidad Disturbances of 1917–20: Precursor to 1937', in *The Trinidad Labour Riots of 1937: Perspectives 50 Years Later*, ed. R. Thomas (St. Augustine 1987); *LL*, 28 Sept. 1929, 3; 11 Nov. 1929, 5.

5 *TG*, 30 June 1932, 6.

6 *LL*, 30 Apr. 1927. The Fabian Society was named after Quintus Fabius Maximus surnamed Cunctator (The Delayer), a Roman general who was famous for his delaying tactics. Fabians believed in gradual social reforms.

7 *Report by the Hon. E. F. L. Wood, MP, on His Visit to the West Indies and British Guiana, December 1921–February 1922* (London 1922), 22–23, 82. Cmd. 1679. See also Section 3 of this chapter.

8 Franchise Commission Report, Council Paper No. 90 of 1923, 19; *TG*, 28 Nov. 1922, 9. Voters had to fulfil one of the following conditions: own property with an annual rateable value of not less than £12 10s in the cities or £10 elsewhere; pay similar sums in rent; occupy property assessed at not less than 10s per annum; have an annual income of not less than £62 10s; or be paying this amount for board and lodging. Men who qualified could vote from the age of 21, women from the age of 30. Ibid., vi. *LL*, 13 Jan. 1923, 5.

9 CO 295/554: Confid., Byatt to Amery, 10 Mar. 1925, Sub-Encs nos. 1, 5.

10 Report of the Wages Advisory Board (1935–1936), Council Paper No. 88 of 1936, 4, 7.

11 CO 295/599/13 Pt. 1: Secret Naval Cypher, Commodore Commanding South American Division, 29 June 1937. CO 295/599/14 Pt. 2: Commodore to Sec. of Admiralty, 9 July 1937; cf. *Trinidad and Tobago Disturbances, 1937, Report of Commission*, 1938, 68.

12 Report of the Franchise Committee of Trinidad and Tobago, Council Paper No. 35 of 1944, 141 and *passim*.

13 The list includes A. R. F. Webber (1880–1932), West Indian nationalist, labour activist and writer, who became a Member of the Legislative Council of British Guiana. Arnott Stanley Henderson (1887–1954), a son of Ebenezer Henderson (1852–1890), was an accountant and manufacturers' agent. He helped to spearhead the protest in Trinidad for shorter shop hours in 1909, which resulted in the closure of shops after 1 p.m. on Saturdays from 1910: Petition to Governor and Legislative Council for Shorter Hours of Labour

for the Clerks of Port of Spain, Council Paper No. 141 of 1909; Report of the Select Committee of the Legislative Council on Shorter Hours of Labour for the Clerks of Port of Spain, Council Paper No. 22 of 1910. Henderson was a prolific contributor to the newspapers, especially *The People*, the most important organ representing labour's views in the period 1933–1939. He testified before the Trinidad and Tobago Disturbances Commission, 1937, as Vice President of the newly formed Federated Workers Trade Union, and also in his personal capacity before the above Commission, the Moyne Commission, and the 1941 Franchise Committee. Stanley Duke, an accomplished musician, was an activist of the Negro Welfare Social and Cultural Association in Port of Spain. Dalton Andrews was a Butlerite activist in Point Fortin, Trinidad, in 1937 and its aftermath. Several of the young clerks in the oilfields—Len De Paiva, Vincent Bowles among them—became members of the Marxist study groups of the late 1940s in Port of Spain, and formed part of the Workers' Freedom Movement, a Marxist group founded in 1948.

14 For Henderson, see vol. I, chaps. 9 and 10.

15 George Horatio McEachrane to Trinidad and Tobago Legislative Council, 31 July 1893, as reported in *The News*, 5 Aug. 1893, 2; reprinted from Trinidad *Daily News*, 1 Aug. 1893.

16 CO 295/526: Confid., Chancellor to Milner, 12 Feb. 1920; CO 295/527: Confid., Chancellor to Milner, 26 Mar. 1920.

17 Anglican Church Records, Tobago: Parish of St. Mary, Baptismal Register starting 1857, 104, no. 35, baptism of James Alfred Alexander Biggott (*sic*), 5 Aug. 1877. This source gives his date of birth as 6 June 1877. It seems that he preferred the Latin version of his second name, Alphaeus.

18 CO 295/418: no. 226, Moloney to Chamberlain, 9 June 1903, enclosing Petition of J. A. Biggart, Pembroke, to Secretary of State for the Colonies, 17 Feb. 1903. *Mirror*, 24 Apr. 1906, 13; 21 Dec. 1908, 23.

19 *People,* 26 June 1937, 9. Biggart emphasized always the need to educate girls as well as boys.

20 The women's branch of Oddfellows was Tobago Gleaner Lodge No. 60 (Household of Ruth), founded in 1916.

21 CO 295/521: no. 214, Chancellor to Milner, 15 May 1919, and Encs; CO 295/528: no. 255, Chancellor to Milner, 21 May 1920, and Encs.

22 *LL*, 22 Sept. 1923, 4; 29 Sept. 1923, 18.

23 *Mirror*, 12 Mar. 1910, 5.

24 *Mirror*, 19 Apr. 1911, 4.

25 *Mirror*, 16 Nov. 1909, 6–7; 6 May 1911, 6.

26 *Mirror*, 3 July 1911, 8.

27 *LL*, 13 Sept. 1924, 9; 16 Sept. 1924, 7; 8 Nov. 1924, 9.

28 See Section 6 of this chapter. In 1925, the *Labour Leader* castigated Biggart for objecting to the eight-hour day in the Leg. Co., and for wondering what would happen with his cook, butler and maid if such a measure were introduced; *LL*, 23 May 1925, 7. At the same time, Biggart wanted equal rates of pay for PWD workers in Tobago and Trinidad; *LL*, 17 Mar. 1925, 4. Biggart regarded Tobagonians as conservative in politics because 'they were a community of proprietors ... of hard working capitalists employing labour even if only on a small scale.' *TG*, 8 Aug. 1929, 7.

29 *LL*, 1 Nov. 1924, 4–5; *TG*, 14 Sept. 1924, 8.

30 *TG*, 14 Sept. 1924, 10.

31 CO 295/554: Confid., Byatt to Amery, 17 June 1925.

32 CO 295/554: Confid., Byatt to Amery, 11 May 1925.

33 CO 298/143: Executive Council Minutes, 4 Mar. 1926; 6 May 1926.

34 CO 298/143: Executive Council Minutes, 1926–28; Leg. Co. Minutes, 1925–32.

35 *TG*, 13 Aug. 1932, 1.

36 *TG*, 19 Dec. 1926, 16; Principal's Report at the first Speech Day of BHS.

37 *TG*, 16 Aug. 1932, 2; *TG*, 5 Aug. 1934, 24.

38 *TG*, 6 Mar. 1937, 8, 11, and C. E. R. Alford, 'Might is Right', *TG*, 1 Apr. 1937, 6.

39 *Minutes of the Proceedings of the Legislative Council*, vol. 1, 1934, 16, 22; vol. 1, 1936, 22, 30; vol. 1, 1937, 29, 40.

40 *Minutes of the Proceedings of the Legislative Council*, vol. 1, 1936, 44, 49.

41 *Minutes of the Proceedings of the Legislative Council*, vol. 1, 1937, 40, 47; *POSG*, 26 May 1937, 11; *People*, 5 June 1937, 5. This is discussed in chap. 1.

42 *The Tobagonian*, Sept. 1938, 9; *TG*, 8 Jan. 1938, 1, 15.

43 *TG*, 24 Feb. 1938, 7; 10 Mar. 1938, 7, 11.

44 Jonathan Scott (b.1934) was not aware of the significance of the song; interview with author, 1 Sept. 1985.

45 CO 950/759, BG/T6006: Serial No. 855, Memorandum to WIRC by Laurence Edwards.

46 CO 950/813, BG/T6064: Serial No. 913, Government Memorandum on Labour Statistics to WIRC; oral evidence, 7 Mar. 1939. The truck system: forms of employment in which consumption is tied to the work contract directly or indirectly, so causing workers to get into debt.

47 *People*, 27 May 1939, 7.

48 Cyril Wildman, interview, 5 May 1983; Edward Peters, interview, 28 Sept. 1984.

49 CO 295/599/14, File 70297 Pt. 2: Roger to Bowyer, Colonial Office, 27 July 1937, encl excerpt from de Nobriga to Roger, 5 July 1937.

50 André Phillips, *Governor Fargo: A Short Biography of Alphonso Philbert Theophilus James* (Scarborough

1993); *People*, 30 Nov. 1940, 8, for FWTU and quotation.

51 Dalton Andrews, interview, 16 May 1983.

52 For more on the 1946 elections, see Ryan, *Race and Nationalism*, chap. 4; Brereton, *History of Modern Trinidad*, 192–98.

53 *District Administration Reports for the Year 1950* (Port of Spain 1951), 53.

54 CO 295/639/5: no. 8, Secret, Shaw to Creech Jones, 28 May 1948.

55 *TG*, 17 Apr. 1961, 3.

56 For some of James' interventions on agricultural and other policy, see *Leg. Co. Debates*, Oct. 1949–July 1950, *passim*.

57 *Mirror*, 31 Mar. 1900, 3; 15 July 1902, 3.

58 CO 295/404: no. 424, Moloney to Chamberlain, 26 Sept. 1901, Encs and minutes; no. 316, Chamberlain to Moloney, 23 Oct. 1901.

59 CO 295/426: Confid., Moloney to Lyttelton, 10 Mar. 1904; quoting minute by H. C. Bourne, 26 Mar. 1904.

60 CO 295/440: Confid., Jackson to Elgin, 2 Mar. 1907. In 1908 Rousseau applied for the post of Administrator, St. Kitts/Nevis or Dominica, not wanting 'to be left stranded in a backwater'. CO 295/445: no. 199, Knaggs to Crewe, 12 June 1908, encl Rousseau's application. His debt to the Archibald brothers, which he completely cleared in 1910, may have militated against his promotion; he died on 28 Oct. 1910. CO 295/458: Confid., Le Hunte to Crewe, 25 May 1910; CO 295/460: no. 399, Le Hunte to Harcourt, 3 Dec. 1910.

61 CO 295/480: Le Hunte to Harcourt, 24 Sept. 1912, Grindle's minute, 27 Sept.; Lambert to Le Hunte, 3 Oct. 1912.

62 CO 295/497: no. 89, Le Hunte to Harcourt, 5 Mar. 1915, and Encs, especially Enc 12, Executive Council Committee Enquiry, n.d. CO 295/498: no. 188, Le Hunte to Harcourt, 15 May 1915; Grindle's minute; Harcourt to Le Hunte, 16 June 1915.

63 CO 295/498: no. 229, Le Hunte to Harcourt, 16 June 1915, encl Strange's memorial and Private, Wright to Grindle, 18 Nov. 1915.

64 *Mirror*, 19 May 1914, 1; 15 June 1914, 10. Homo (Latin) means ' a man'.

65 CO 295/528: no. 255, Chancellor to Milner, 21 May 1920, encl Sorzano's report.

66 CO 295/555: no. 331, Byatt to Amery, 23 July 1925, encl TPA to Amery, 1 July 1925.

67 CO 295/601/14, File 70334: no. 535, Fletcher to Ormsby-Gore, 22 Sept. 1937; minutes by Poynton, Beckett, Moore; Beckett's emphasis.

68 CO 295/607/1, File 70334: Confid., Huggins to Macdonald, 3 Dec. 1938; Confid., Macdonald to Huggins, 27 Jan. 1939 (draft).

69 Maresse-Smith was the Chairman of the CADC, which was dissolved in 1902 for want of capital,

and because of the peculation of some of its leaders. On the Reform Movement, see Henry A. Will, *Constitutional Change in the British West Indies, 1880–1903, with Special Reference to Jamaica, British Guiana and Trinidad* (Oxford 1970); on the Water Riots, Brereton, *History of Modern Trinidad*, 146–53. On Sir John Gorrie, see vol. I, chap. 6 of this work.

70 *Mirror*, 15 July 1902, 3; 25 Sept. 1902, 7; 28 Sept. 1903, 11.

71 *Mirror*, 26 Feb. 1907, 9.

72 'Tobago and Popular Representation', *LL*, 30 Jan. 1926, 3; *People*, 28 Nov. 1936, 7; 6 May 1939, 12.

73 Lulworth D. Punch, *A Journey to Remember (39 Years in the Civil Service)* (Port of Spain 1963), 160.

74 *Report of the Team Which Visited Tobago in March/April 1957* (Bridgetown 1957); A. N. R. Robinson, Motion for Internal Self-Government for Tobago, *Hansard*, 14 Jan. 1977, and debate on it.

75 CO 298/97: Report by the Surgeon-General on the Epidemic of Dysentery in Tobago in the year 1912, Council Paper No. 11 of 1913, 3–5.

76 District Administration Reports for 1926, Council Paper No. 53 of 1927, 12.

77 Annual Reports of the Medical Inspector of Health and the Medical Officers of Health on Health Conditions in Trinidad and Tobago for 1917, Council Paper No. 121 of 1918, 44–45; Administration Reports of the Medical Inspector of Health, Medical Officers of Health and the Port Health Officer for 1918, Council Paper No. 101 of 1919, 48.

78 Report of the Committee Appointed to Enquire into the Medical and Health Policy of the Colony, Council Paper No. 65 of 1944, 35.

79 *TG*, 30 Mar. 1930, 5.

80 *Mirror*, 29 Nov. 1911, 1; CO 295/542: no. 105, Wilson to Churchill, 3 Mar. 1922.

81 *TG*, 28 Feb. 1925, 7.

82 A. E. S. Mondezie, organizer for the PWPSWU, *People*, 21 Sept. 1940, 4.

83 CO 295/565/7, File 56492: no. 229, Byatt to Amery, 16 June 1928, and Encs, especially Director of Works to Col. Sec., 7 Mar. 1928.

84 The Royal Mail transatlantic steamers connected with the intercolonial ones at Barbados.

85 *Mirror*, 23 Aug. 1905, 2; 17 July 1906, 3.

86 CO 295/437: no. 259, Clifford to Elgin, 21 Aug. 1906, encl petition, 28 July 1906; Private Secretary to Inhabitants, 13 Aug.; and McEachrane to Clifford, 15 Aug. 1906.

87 CO 295/443: Chairman, British Cotton Growing Association (BCGA) to Under-Secretary of State, 27 Aug. 1907, encl Latour to Atkins, Secretary, BCGA, 6 Aug. 1907; cf. Latour to Elgin, 22 Aug. 1907.

88 CO 295/468: Confid., Harcourt to Le Hunte (draft), 30 Jan. 1912.

89 Royal Commission on Trade Relations between Canada and the West Indies, Council Paper No. 123 of 1910, 30, 34.

90 CO 295/504: no. 91, Knaggs to Law, 4 Jan. 1916, and Encs; Telegram, Law to Knaggs, 2 Feb. 1916.

91 CO 295/504: Telegram, Knaggs to Law, 19 Feb. 1916; RMSPCO to Fiddes, 23 Feb. 1916; Nugent, Foreign Trade Department, to Fiddes, 23 Feb. 1916; unsigned letter, Colonial Office to Philips, RMSPCO, Feb. 1916.

92 CO 295/504: ERD's (Darnley's) minute, 2 Aug. 1916, on visit by T. L. M. Orde; CO 295/506: no. 274, Chancellor to Law, 14 July 1916.

93 CO 295/522: no. 426, Gordon to Milner, 25 Sept. 1919, Sub-Enc C, M. Short, Tobago Planters Association, to Editor, *TG*, 17 June 1919.

94 CO 295/504: no. 88, Knaggs to Law, 26 Feb. 1916.

95 CO 295/517: Confid., Chancellor to Long, 26 Oct. 1918; Sub-Enc 2, RMSPCO to Auditor General, 13 September 1918. CO 295/525: ERD's minute, 2 Apr. 1919; Philips, RMSPCO, to Grindle, Colonial Office, 4 July 1919, and Encs. Report of the Committee appointed by the Governor on 15 August 1918 to Consider Representations by the Royal Mail Company on Its Loss on the Coastal Service and to Advise, Council Paper No. 43 of 1919; Secretary, RMSPCO, to Under-Secretary, Colonial Office, 5 Nov. 1919.

96 CO 295/522: no. 426, Gordon to Milner, 25 Sept. 1919, and Encs, especially Sub-Enc A, Development Committee: Preliminary Report, Council Paper No. 50 of 1919; Sub-Enc D, *TG*, 19 June 1919.

97 CO 295/526: no. 13, Chancellor to Milner, 9 Jan. 1920.

98 CO 295/531: no. 661, Chancellor to Milner, 30 Dec. 1920.

99 CO 295/567/9: no. 377, Grier to Passfield, 18 Sept. 1929.

100 CO 295/562/10, File 36628: Private, Byatt to Darnley, 16 Sept. 1927; Byatt's emphasis.

101 *TG*, 2 Aug. 1925, 12.

102 CO 295/562/10: Minutes by Darnley, 21 Oct., Wilson, 27 Oct. 1927.

103 Tobago Sea Communications Committee Report, Council Paper No. 44 of 1929, 17–18.

104 CO 295/563, File 56429: Darnley to Aspinall, 4 Dec. 1928; CO 295/567/9, File 66494: Aspinall, West India Committee, to Under-Secretary of State, encl *The West India Committee Circular*, no. 810, 17 Oct. 1929, Leader on Tobago Sea Communications.

105 United Kingdom, Parliamentary Debates, House of Commons, 1928, vol. 214, 5; 1929–1930, vol. 231, 1060; vol. 232, 502–503, 2384; vol. 233, 471; vol. 235, 41. Vols. 231 to 235 were for 1929–1930.

106 CO 295/567/9, File 66494: Reid to Wilson, 14 Sept. 1929; Telegram, Grier to Passfield, 13 Sept. 1929.

107 *TG*, 27 Sept. 1929, 6.

108 Governor's Address to the Legislative Council, Council Paper No. 4 of 1945, 11.

109 *Report of the Commission of Enquiry on the Administration and Cost of the Government Steamship Service between the Islands of Trinidad and Tobago* (Port of Spain 1957).

110 CO 295/526: Confid., Chancellor to Milner, 24 Jan. 1920, Enc 1, Sorzano to Chancellor, 7 Dec. 1919; Enc 5, Report of Crown Solicitor, 20 Dec. 1919.

111 CO 295/526: Confid., Chancellor to Milner, 24 Jan. 1920, Enc 1, Sorzano to Chancellor, 7 Dec. 1919.

112 CO 295/526: Confid., Chancellor to Milner, 24 Jan. 1920, Enc 3, Cavenaugh to Inspector General of Constabulary, 11 Dec. 1919.

113 CO 295/526: Confid., Chancellor to Milner, 24 Jan. 1920, Enc 4, L. G. Scheult, 10 Dec. 1919; emphasis added; punctuation as in the original.

114 *TG*, 21 Aug. 1920, 2.

115 Wages Committee, 1919–1920, Preliminary Report, Council Paper No. 125 of 1920, 18; also App. 4, lxv.

116 Wages Committee, 1919–1920, Preliminary Report, Council Paper No. 125 of 1920, 18; also App. 4, lxvi.

117 Turpin Family Papers: Cyril Turpin, Kampala, Uganda, Confid., Memorandum on the Administration of Charlotteville Estate, Its Cultivations etc., 25 Dec. 1929; Cyril to Charles Turpin, 14 Apr. 1926. Viz.: namely; italics added.

118 Henry Shade (b.1910), unrecorded conversation with author, 20 July 2005.

119 *LL*, 11 Nov. 1929, 5; 28 Dec. 1929, 5.

120 Leo and Keziah Solomon, interview, 17 Mar. 1985.

121 *LL*, 8 Feb. 1930, 9.

122 *Tobago Times*, 23 Sept. 1933, 3; 30 Sept. 1933.

123 *People*, 30 Sept. 1933, 6.

124 *Tobago Times*, 13 July 1935; 20 July 1935.

125 *LL*, 12 July 1930, 10.

126 District Administration Reports for 1937, Council Paper No. 82 of 1938, 10.

127 *People*, 13 Nov. 1937, 5; 20 Nov. 1937, 8.

128 *People*, 29 Jan. 1938, 5, 9.

129 *People*, 23 Sept. 1939, 5; 21 Sept. 1940, 4.

130 *People*, 29 Apr. 1939, 2.

131 *People*, 25 Mar. 1939, 10; 1 Apr. 1939, 9.

132 Turpin Family Papers: Cyril to Charles Turpin, 19 Aug. 1942.

133 *People*, 7 July 1940, 7; 20 July 1940, 11.

134 For discussion on these, see chap. 1.

5

Education, Teachers
and Literary Movements, 1900–1950

WHEN TOBAGO joined Trinidad, the education system needed investment and improvement. By 1950 primary education had advanced considerably. By then too, Tobago's residents and its emigrants had produced a remarkable corpus of literary and cultural work. In particular, the synergy between the Tobago intelligentsia and the teachers and officials from Trinidad and elsewhere had helped to create a vibrant intellectual and political life on the island. Their endeavours were part of the Caribbean quest for self-definition, cultural assertion and nationhood in the anti-colonial fervour of the time. They also contributed to the rise of today's Tobago nationalism. This chapter traces these movements.

1. TOBAGO'S EDUCATION SYSTEM

Primary Schools

In 1900 there were 28 assisted denominational schools and no government schools in Tobago; a few of the church schools were not assisted. Most of them were in need of better buildings, equipment, and training for the staff. The old buildings came to be regarded as 'slum schools'.

The first state school was Mason Hall Government School, built in 1938. By 1940 there were 36 primary schools.

The teachers, brought under the Board of Education in Trinidad in 1899, found the new arrangements a mixed blessing. Whereas the old Tobago administration could not afford to pay the salaries of pupil teachers and the system had to be discontinued in 1891, the pupil-teacher system was fully implemented. The schools received larger government grants. However, the Trinidad regulations were very stringent. Moreover, the salary scales and allowances in Tobago, always lower than those of Trinidad before the Union, initially remained lower, on the grounds that the cost of living in Tobago was lower.

To qualify for state assistance, each school had to have a certificated head teacher, and the threat of reduction of salary or loss of employment hung like the sword of Damocles over those without certificates. In 1900, ten teachers were granted temporary certificates until July 1902 to give them time to sit the examinations; six others were given permanent certificates because of long meritorious service; a few who refused to prepare for examinations were dismissed. A further five teachers were given temporary certificates for 1902 to 1903, on the understanding that if they did not succeed at the June 1903 exams, 'they must cease to be employed in schools under the control of the Board of Education'.[1]

Thus, the teachers emerging from the old system were under pressure to succeed, although there were no model schools and no training institutions on the island.

In 1900 there were no Class I teachers in Tobago; one, Ernest Taylor (Mason Hall Wesleyan School), was in Class II; and a further six—Thomas Jerome Baldwin (St. Mary's EC), J. D. Williams (Scarborough EC), Samuel T. W. Charity (Ebenezer Wesleyan), J. S. Spiers (Mt. St. George Wesleyan), S. M. Green (Montgomery Moravian), and S. George (Patience Hill RC)—in Class III. The transition from Pupil Teacher to trained certificated Class I status was slow for the Tobago teachers. For the years 1900 to 1905, 1 person passed in Class II and 10 in Class III. Failure rates were high, especially at Class II level.[2]

Tobago teachers gained Class I certificates for the first time in 1915—B. A. Thomson and T. J. Baldwin at Whim EC and Scarborough Wesleyan, respectively, followed in 1916 by T. L. Stephenson (Moriah Upper Moravian), who had studied at the Mico Training College, Antigua, before 1899.[3] By 1920 there were 8 Class I teachers, 6 in Class II, and 22 in Class III. Although there was a growing number of female teachers serving as infant teachers and sewing mistresses, among the certificated the only female was Ann Evelina Gordon in Class III.[4] The upward route through a long series of examinations was a difficult one, which is why from 1924 the senior teachers decided to help their juniors prepare for the teachers' examinations.[5]

Because of the shortage of trained teachers in Tobago, many of those in the service before 1899 had come from other Caribbean territories—among them, S. E. Thibou and Jacob Walters from Antigua, Robert Adam Edwards and Thomas Weekes from St. Kitts–Nevis, and Ernest Taylor and M. B. Smart from Grenada. After the Union with Trinidad, senior teachers were recruited from there.

Among the Trinidad teachers who distinguished themselves in Tobago between 1900 and 1940 were Thomas Jerome Baldwin, Egerton Blizzard, Eric Cameron, George T. Daniel, W. Dolly, John S. Donaldson, Laurence E. Edwards, H. I. McNish, Ernest E. Quinlan (originally from St. Lucia),

Ivan B. J. Rouse, Cuthbert M. Tull and Garrick Warner. Lionel and Vincent Mitchell arrived in 1924. They were the sons of John James Mitchell, a Tobagonian who had been schoolmaster and catechist at Delaford RC School in the closing years of the nineteenth century, and his wife Louisa, also a teacher; John Mitchell had founded the Roman Catholic school at L'Anse Noire on the north coast of Trinidad, and his wife, a Class I certificated teacher, later became the principal.[6] Fitz Gerald Maynard, originally from St. Lucia, was transferred from Trinidad on two stints from 1922 to 1929, and from 1936 to 1944.

The teachers from other Caribbean islands quickly integrated themselves into the society; some married Tobagonian women. Among these were Thomas J. Baldwin, Lionel Mitchell and Jacob Walters, who made Tobago their permanent home. As educators in schools which until 1938 were all denominational, the teachers were usually lay readers, catechists, and some also Sunday School superintendents, commanding an extraordinary prestige in the society. Many of them were musicians—Donaldson, Lionel Mitchell, Rouse, Thibou, Walters—and they trained choirs and taught instrumental music.

From 1903 an annual Schools Show was held, at which there were exhibits of agricultural produce, needlework, handicraft, and other artefacts from the schools. Because connections by sea from the north coast of Trinidad were easier with Tobago than with other parts of Trinidad, the schools from Toco, Manantial, L'Anse Noire and other north-coast villages sent their exhibits to Tobago. The peasants participated as well, and the competition was extremely keen.

In the early twentieth century, there were also private primary schools. One was run by Emmeline Scobie, one of the owners of Deal Fair Estate, a part of which was sold to the Government for the Botanic Station. Another was owned by Ann Evelina Gordon (later Mrs Cordner), a daughter of Sinai Josiah Gordon, Scarborough businessman. A third was run by Mrs Nelly McCall, the wife of John George McCall, son of the former sugar plantocrat, John McCall.[7] In 1941 Mrs Olga Comma Maynard's Nelson Comma Junior School (named after her father who had served as Tobago's Inspector of Schools for six months in 1924) existed in Scarborough.

126

The statistics in Table 7.9 amply demonstrate the expansion in primary school enrolment. In the light of this, the great thrust in private education turned towards secondary schooling.

Improvement in Primary Education

In 1930 F. C. Marriott, the Director of Education, returned from a trip to Tobago and reported his dissatisfaction with the Tobago schools. There were too many denominational schools; the majority were inefficient; their standard was lower than that of the Trinidad schools; their buildings were dilapidated, their furniture in disrepair and inadequate; attendance was poor; and children often started school so late in life that they reached the school-leaving age (15) when they were still in the classes for children aged 11 or 12. Despite initial opposition from the denominational boards, the Government proposed to replace three schools at Mason Hall with a state school. So high-handed was their approach that, addressing a meeting attended by the Governor, James Biggart, the MLC, vowed to oppose them if they showed such disrespect for the efforts of Tobagonians and their forefathers; he felt that Marriott was seeking to impose his will 'by forced methods'. This led Marriott later to describe Biggart as talking 'arrant nonsense', and Biggart responded that Marriott, by his poor advice to the Government, had also been talking 'arrant nonsense'. Biggart called for a Tobago representative on the Board of Education, which was refused, but the Government agreed to his request for a resident Inspector of Schools, an appointment that they had stopped making since the end of 1924. He also argued for more apparatus and support for the denominational schools.[8]

Despite the weaknesses in the system and the lack of opportunities for technical and vocational education, to most observers the standard of the Tobago primary schools had risen by the end of the 1930s.

In 1937 St. Paul's EC School, Delaford, under Ivan B. J. Rouse, Head Teacher, won the prize for the best school choir in Trinidad and Tobago, and became the first winner of the I. A. Hope Shield for that competition.[9]

The first student of a Tobago school to win a Government College Exhibition was Ray C. Gill of Pembroke EC School under Lindsay Francis, Head Teacher, in 1923. However, it was the practice for parents to remove their children to Trinidad schools just before the exhibition class, and several Tobago boys won exhibitions from Trinidad to St. Mary's College, one of the leading colleges for boys. In 1943 James Cross of Tobago placed first in the College Exhibition examinations from a Port of Spain school, having first attended Scarborough Methodist School.[10] Others entered the Port of Spain colleges as fee-paying students. It was therefore a signal achievement when two students from Scarborough Upper EC School under Laurence Edwards—Audrie Armstrong and Beatrice MacAlister—won two of the ten Government College Exhibitions in 1938.

In 1938 too, Hallis Meikle at Scarborough Methodist School under Fitz G. Maynard won the colony's Little Folks' Challenge Shield; the school also won the Little Folks' Challenge Competition. The Shield had been won only once before in Tobago, in 1924, also at Scarborough Methodist, under Cuthbert Tull. In 1939 the best candidates in the second and third year of the pupil teachers' examinations were from Tobago. The crowning glory was the capture of the Madoo Medal for highest efficiency in the colony's schools by Mason Hall Government School under Benjamin J. Sealy in 1941 and 1942.

Assessing the schools in 1940, Fitz Maynard stated that the buildings, equipment, and standard of the teachers had all improved; he noted the teachers' high involvement in community life, and the *esprit de corps* among them. Tobago schools even competed for a Civility Cup, so that good manners would form part of the fabric of social life. It was clear to him that 'if nothing else has improved in Tobago, the schools definitely have.'[11] In the process, a generation of Tobago-born teachers was being raised up to fill the senior positions.

The Tobago students who had their early education at home and attended Port of Spain colleges were usually very successful. The first Tobago-born Island Scholar in the twentieth century was Norris O'Connell Blanc, son of Dr. Edwin G. Blanc, Tobago's senior DMO. Blanc won his award in 1916, studied medicine in Ireland, graduated in 1922, and later served in Tobago.

Secondary Schools

Before 1925 all the secondary schools were private. Geraldine Prince (1874–1916), the daughter of Mitchell J. Prince and his wife Judith, had been educated in England from 1886. There she trained at the Royal College of Music, qualifying as a pianist, violinist and vocalist. In June 1900, on her return to Tobago with her parents—who had been teaching at Constantine, Grenada—she and her father opened a secondary school on Main Street, Scarborough. The subjects taught were English Language and Literature, Scripture History (*sic*), English History, Geography, French, Drawing, Elementary Latin, Arithmetic, Algebra, Euclid, Singing, Music and Hygiene. Their intention was to prepare students for the Oxford and Royal College of Preceptors examinations. Later, because of declining health, Miss Prince confined herself to teaching only music at her home in Rockley Vale. Both these establishments catered exclusively to the children of the planters, merchants and professionals: 'all the first-class people', as George Sinclair (b.1905) put it.[12]

By 1904 Joseph Francis Henry (1859–1945), a brilliant linguist, historian and mathematician, having returned from Grenada, founded the Middle School, the most important secondary school in Tobago until its closure c.1920.[13] Henry was one of the venerable 'Mico men' (trained at the Mico Training College, Antigua) of the nineteenth century, and was nicknamed 'The Bookworm'. His school was also on Main Street. Henry's school attracted children of the planters, merchants, professionals, shopkeepers, butchers, and the more prosperous of the labouring class. Henry was the only teacher, managing students at primary and secondary levels. He taught English, French, Latin, Geography, History, and Mathematics.[14]

Both Miss Prince and Henry were black educators. Their schools were places where people of all colours, albeit those who could afford their fees, met and interacted.

The third private secondary school, The Collegiate School, was started by W. Howard Bishop jun. at Cook's River, Scarborough. It began in May 1915. In that same month Bishop received a commission from the District Commissioner for Boy Scouts to start three patrols in Tobago; the Tobago Boy Scouts No. 1 Troop began under his leadership, with a Mr Carrington as the Assistant

Scoutmaster. In the Cambridge Local Preliminary Examinations of December 1915, history was made when Neville W. Robertson became the first student to succeed from a Tobago school, passing with distinctions in English and Algebra, and 'Good' in Arithmetic, Geography, Latin and French. Before that, successful Tobago candidates had all gone to Trinidad schools.[15] By June 1916, the Collegiate School was offering two scholarships: the Duncan Scholarship granted by Dr. Charles Frederick N. Duncan, a native of Plymouth and a former Moravian teacher, who had become a medical doctor in the USA; and a Cambridge Scholarship, the first of which would be awarded on the basis of the July 1917 Cambridge Local Preliminary Examinations. Bishop stated in 1916 that an article by Dr. Duncan appearing two years previously in the local newspapers, lamenting the absence of a good secondary school in Tobago, was 'the fulcrum on which the lever was placed for the establishment of the Collegiate School.'[16]

By January 1918, the School had moved to Springbank, Wilson Road, Scarborough, and had begun to offer tuition for the London Matriculation, Preliminary Law and Druggist examinations, along with private tuition in commercial subjects including Shorthand and Bookkeeping.[17]

Bishop may have been the W. Howard Bishop who had been assistant teacher of the Middle School, Georgetown, British Guiana, under Hon. A. A. Thorne, headmaster; who had started the Middle School in Tunapuna, Trinidad, in June 1906; and who co-founded and edited the *Labour Leader*, an organ of the labour movement, in Port of Spain, from 1922 until his death in January 1930.[18]

Thomas J. Baldwin, after retiring from the Methodist schools where he had been one of the able head teachers, started the Scarborough Intermediate Private School. Its commencement date is uncertain but it existed in 1927 and was finally closed on 31 January 1930. Another school founded by Baldwin, Trinity School, which taught elementary, secondary and commercial subjects, existed in 1934 and 1937, but its commencement and closing dates are both uncertain.[19]

All these private secondary schools were relatively short-lived. When, in response to a request from James Biggart and Thomas J. Baldwin, the Right Rev. Arthur Henry Anstey agreed to found a secondary school in Tobago in 1925, it was an incalculable boon to the island. Before that, most of the secondary graduates had had to attend Port of Spain schools at considerable expense for fees, board and lodging. Rev. Herwald W. Davies, who was responsible for the Tobago schools of the Anglican Church, helped to implement the idea.

The Bishop's High School (BHS), a co-educational institution, opened with 22 pupils on 14 September 1925. Rawle Jordan, MA, a Barbadian graduate of Durham and Cambridge Universities, was its Principal for the first 21 years. From 1925 his deputy was John Ottley, a Tobago-born graduate of St. Mary's College, Port of Spain. In 1926 Ottley was the first Tobagonian to win the Bishop Neville Gold Medal for Classics, by passing first in Latin and Greek, and also in Latin and Greek History.[20]

In 1926, in the face of opposition from other denominations, Biggart won the Government's agreement to allow the BHS to be affiliated to Queen's Royal College, the leading state secondary school in Port of Spain. The first home of BHS was Peru Cottage (renamed Coney Gatha in 1926), a former boarding house. In 1937 it was housed at a new building, Sans Souci, until 1956 when it was moved to the present site at Mt. Marie. In 1950 its junior departments were housed at Fairfield, another former boarding house.

The BHS opened up opportunities for the children of the peasantry. The school began as a fee-paying institution, but there were in 1925 four Bishop's Scholarships, and in 1927 the first Island Scholarship was awarded. The former were open to Anglican children of either sex; the latter to all Tobago children; both were awarded on the basis of competitive examinations in the Tobago primary schools. In 1931 the Methodist Church awarded one annual scholarship to BHS also.[21] In 1938 Dr. Sylvan Bowles, a migrant to the USA who had become a dentist, awarded two scholarships to BHS for children from the primary schools. The first winners were Arthur N. R. Robinson (His Excellency the President of the Republic of Trinidad and Tobago (1997–2003)) from Castara Methodist School, and Laurence Douglas (Hope EC School). Bowles increased the number of scholarships to six in 1941. When tertiary education became the pressing need, after 1947 the Bowles Scholarships were awarded to finance the university education of able graduates of BHS.

Technical and Vocational Education and Training

Agriculture and some forms of handicraft were taught at primary schools and at the BHS. However, since there were no technical and vocational institutions in Tobago, most of the learning was by formal or informal apprenticeships. Most teachers were recruited as pupil teachers. Male artisans who desired to be certified as masters in their fields had to be examined by the Board of Industrial Training in Trinidad. By the 1930s, virtually all the applicants residing in Tobago were carpenters, masons, joiners or tailors. Because of the agrarian base of the society, fitters, machinists, welders, mechanics and such artisans were rare. A few men became pharmacists, usually under the tuition of the DMOs and other pharmacists.

For women, the opportunities for upward mobility were limited. Baking, confectionery-making, dressmaking and teaching had been the main avenues for personal advancement in the late nineteenth century, and these skills were learnt mainly by apprenticeship to others. Secretarial work, based on knowledge of typing, shorthand and bookkeeping, became important in the twentieth century; so did nursing. For both of these, apart from the efforts of the Trinity School which taught commercial subjects in the 1930s, training was in Trinidad. Female teachers were paid less than their male counterparts, and female teachers and nurses had to resign after marriage. By 1932, five Tobago nurses had won the colony's Gold Medal for Nursing: Connie Anderson, Olive Gordon, Gwendoline James, Serene Nelson and Margaret Pearl Ottley.

2. THE LITERARY, DEBATING AND DISCUSSION CLUBS

The Birth of Literary Clubs in Trinidad

The literary activities in Tobago were part of the Caribbean movement for popular self-expression, nationhood and decolonization. Their roots were native to Tobago, but they were influenced by the cross-fertilization that came from the interchange of people between Trinidad and Tobago after 1899.

Throughout the nineteenth century in Trinidad there had been reading clubs, the forerunners of the Public Library which began in 1851. At the end of the century, the ones patronized by the upper class were the Queen's Park Book Club, of which S. W. Knaggs, a senior clerk in the Colonial Secretary's office, was the Secretary, and the Commercial Newsroom, run by the Chamber of Commerce, with 'the best English newspapers and magazines and many French and other foreign journals'.[22]

Education was spreading, and several more clubs emerged in the growing townships, including the Tacarigua Magazine Club, of which M. J. Murray was the Secretary. By 1892, the Belmont Literary Association (T. Jason Burkett, President) existed, and in 1893, the Port of Spain Literary Association (President, Alexander Miller) started at the Victoria Institute.[23] In 1897 Pamphyllian Club was formed for 'Intellectual Improvement and social intercourse'; two years later, it had 24 members, described by the *Port of Spain Gazette* as 'all young men of respectability and many of them in the Public Service', and from 1903 it published its own journal.[24] By 1900 Amity Club, established in August 1899, met weekly, alternating at Arouca and Tacarigua, teaching shorthand and bookkeeping, and having a debating society and cricket club associated with it. The President was Rev. W. M. Springer, BA. A few dramatic clubs had also emerged in Port of Spain, among them the Wilberforce Dramatic and Minstrel Troupe at Belmont, the Trinidad Dramatic Club, Duvenny Dramatic Club, and the Port of Spain Theatrical Club, whose President was the popular anti-colonial lawyer, Edgar Maresse-Smith. St. Joseph also had a Theatrical Club, led by Arthur P. L. de Coteaux. Choral societies and minstrel troupes emerged in all the major townships.[25]

In 1901 more clubs existed, among them the Model Ex-Pupils Association (MEPA), comprising graduates of the Model School, the foremost primary school in the city, later called Tranquillity Boys Intermediate School. In central Trinidad, there was the California Literary Association (President, E. P. Morgan); at San Fernando, an Oriental Debating Association (President, Charles FitzPatrick); and at Williamsville, a Young Men's Literary Association (President, J. Wallace). Debating was embraced at the highest echelons of the society with the formation on 8 January 1902 of the Trinidad Debating Club, in which the prominent professionals and the colony's elite took part.[26] Debating clubs were formed in the colleges.

By 1920 the Century Literary and Debating Club which was closely linked to the MEPA, and the Moulton Club, started at Moulton Hall Methodist School by Fitz Gerald Maynard in 1919, were among the foremost in Port of Spain. In San Fernando the Southern East Indian Literary and Debating Society (SEILDS), whose nucleus included Dalton Chadee, Jules Mahabir, and Rev. Dr. F. J. Coffin, began in 1919. Most of the members of the SEILDS were graduates of Naparima College. Its junior branch was formed in December 1937. Prior to that, in 1916 an East Indian Literary and Debating Club was started at Woodbrook, Port of Spain, at the Canadian Mission to Indians (Presbyterian) school. The club's first debate was on 'Should Indian marriages be made legal', and its plans included 'An Evening with Mother India'; short papers were to be read on 'The Indian in Trinidad' by C. B. Mathura (later a journalist and an important figure in the labour movement); 'A History and the Derivation of the Hindi Language' by P. Akal, the school's head teacher; and 'News of India for Indian Contemporaries' in Hindi by P. Ramcharan. Cyril Burkett, who later founded the *Tobago Times* (1933), read a paper on 'Industry' at the first meeting.[27] By 1934 there was also a Chinese Literary Association in Port of Spain.[28]

The literary movement, a forum for gaining self-knowledge and continuing education, attracted the young educated, most of whom were later to become the leading professionals of the colony.

In November 1917 the Trinidad Literary League was formed, with Dr. Stephen Moister Laurence as President. Its leading officers were W. Douglas Inniss, T. H. Williams, E. B. Grosvenor, Cyril W. Price and G. C. Catto. It sought to prepare the people, to quote Selwyn Cudjoe, for 'the wider duties of citizenship'.[29] However, it does not appear to have been able to weld the clubs into a solid colony-wide organization, as did its successor, the Trinidad Literary Club Council (TLCC), started in 1925 by Mrs Marcelline Archbald, who had founded The Young Ladies

Literary and Debating Association at San Fernando in 1921. Mrs Archbald, a Methodist, had been for many years a member of the Wesley Guild where public speaking was practised, and by 1931 she was an accredited lay preacher of the Methodist Church. The Tobago clubs affiliated in 1931. The TLCC's first President was J. Hamilton Maurice, educator, who later was Director of Education in Dominica before eventually becoming Minister of Education in Trinidad and Tobago. Its first Secretary was W. A. M. ('WAM') James, a journalist and an indefatigable pivot of the literary movement until his death in 1938.[30]

On Sunday 3 July 1932, the *Trinidad Guardian* started a weekly page devoted to the literary clubs, which were seen as 'the moulding ground for our future legislators', politicians and leaders.[31] One article on the TLCC stated that the movement was no longer only for the benefit of teachers and social workers:

Today that selfishness of aim has given way to the wide-spread [sic] demand for the promotion of knowledge in every class[,] sect and creed.[32]

After seven issues, however, the page lapsed until it was restarted on Tuesday 11 September 1934. The *Guardian* had also donated a challenge cup for the clubs' annual competition and, because of this weekly page, there was heightened interest in the movement. Given that teachers were the bulwark of the literary movement, the *Guardian's* Teachers' Page, also started in 1934, attracted news on the literary clubs, and both pages published poetry, short stories, book reviews and other essays by fledgling writers. There was also a page devoted to Indian News and Views; some of the articles were in Hindi. When, from 14 August 1938, the *Guardian* started a special literary page on Sundays conducted by Albert Gomes, a young writer and politician, controversy from the Sunday page spilled over into the pages devoted during the week to teachers and debating. As debating was honed into a fine art, the halls where the clubs met throughout the colony overflowed with people, who went by the busloads to follow the debates.

By May 1934, such was the impact of the movement that the Grenada Literary Club was one of the affiliates to the TLCC, and permission to join was granted to clubs in Demerara (British Guiana), St. Vincent and Venezuela.[33]

In 1935 the Mayor of Port of Spain, the Hon. Garnet McCarthy, donated a silver cup named after himself for an annual competition among the clubs. This competition was followed with the keenest excitement. The first winners of the Garnet McCarthy Cup (1935–1936) were the Forest Reserve Club, followed by Tableland in 1936–1937 and Alpha Club of Tunapuna in 1937–1938. In 1935 too, the TLCC started a General Knowledge competition among its affiliated clubs for the H. O. B. Wooding Cup. This too was keenly contested. The TLCC also formed a strong junior section, with clubs in many of the primary schools; it held a recitation competition among the junior affiliated clubs.

In May 1938, after a committee headed by Maurice recommended a change of name and constitution, the Council became the Trinidad and Tobago Literary Club Council (TTLCC), organized into seven regions, each with a committee conducting its affairs, and each sending delegates, both *ex-officio* and elected, to the Council's executive. J. Hamilton Maurice and W. A. M. James were again the first President and Secretary, respectively, of the TTLCC in 1938, with George Daniel as Tobago regional convener. The re-organization of the TTLCC gave a tremendous impetus to the literary club movement. By early 1938, fifty-two clubs were affiliated and the numbers were rapidly growing. Several of the adult clubs had juvenile branches, and many of them published their own club magazines. From 1932 the TLCC itself produced a magazine, edited in 1938 by Beryl Archbald Crichlow (later Mayor of San Fernando and the first female Mayor in the BWI), Marcelline Archbald's daughter.

By 1938, as Dr. Stephen M. Laurence told the assembled delegates at the 13th Annual Conference of the TTLCC,

The tide of the literary movement in the Colony is now at the flood.[34]

It was a fitting assessment of the enormous popular interest evinced by the movement.

In addition to the phenomenal local growth of the movement, there were efforts to start a BWI regional association. In 1916 T. A. Marryshow, editor of *The West Indian*, member of the St. George's branch of the Grenada Literary League, a champion of the popular struggle for West Indian Federation and self-rule, and later the founder

(1929) of the Grenada Workingmen's Association, visited the Century Literary and Debating Club and the MEPA in Port of Spain, and discussed a proposed union of the BWI literary societies.[35] Mrs Archbald also went on several teachers' excursions to other islands, to interest their people in a West Indian Literary League.[36] Delegates from British Guiana, Grenada, St. Kitts–Nevis, St. Vincent, and Trinidad and Tobago met informally at St. George's, Grenada, in August 1937 and agreed to this proposal. Lindsay E. Francis, then Head Teacher of San Fernando EC School and President of the TLCC, presided; Francis and W. A. M. James travelled to St. Vincent in August 1938 to discuss the proposal there. The West Indian Literary League was formed c.1947 with Fitz G. Maynard as its first President.

Teachers, clerks, pharmacists, journalists, chauffeurs, 'bespoke' tailors and other skilled artisans were the core of the literary movement. The clubs were an extraordinary means of adult education. They saw themselves as schools, and each term they published programmes with a wide range of activities, which they called their 'syllabus'. Their development was autonomous. Although the clubs were usually a-political, the TLCC declared itself in 1931 to be staunchly in favour of West Indian Federation, and Captain Cipriani was their patron.

The literary clubs were the training ground in public speaking, organizational skills, and analysis of social and political issues for many who later became County Councillors, legislators and Cabinet ministers. Many of their members were in the forefront of the anti-colonial struggles at home and abroad. Tito Achong (Mayor of Port of Spain, 1941–1944); Arthur Busby (later Chief Magistrate); Learie Constantine (famous Test cricketer; later Minister in the Trinidad and Tobago Cabinet, his country's first High Commissioner to London, member of the Board of Governors of the British Broadcasting Corporation (BBC), and, as Baron Constantine of Nelson (England) and Maraval (Trinidad), Member of the British House of Lords); John Donaldson (later Minister of Education and Culture); Malcolm Nurse (later George Padmore, the Pan Africanist who helped to organize the historic 1945 Pan African Congress at Manchester, England, and who became an adviser to President Kwame Nkrumah of Ghana); Evan Rees (later a Judge and finally the country's first Ombudsman);

George Richards (later Attorney General); Lionel Seukeran (later Member of Parliament); Arnold C. Thomasos (later Speaker in the Trinidad and Tobago Parliament for 20 years); and Hugh Wooding (later Chief Justice of Trinidad and Tobago and Pro-Vice Chancellor of The University of the West Indies) are only a few of the illustrious persons who formed these early societies.

Several of the clubs did social work—they visited prisons and other penal institutions; they put on concerts, lectures and debates in the House of Refuge, the leprosarium and other places. From 1925 the Young Ladies Association at San Fernando held an annual examination, to select promising students for scholarships to secondary schools. From 1932 one of their scholarships was tenable at BHS, the first winner being Victor Bruce (later Governor of the Central Bank of Trinidad and Tobago). An outstanding club in social work was the Optimist Club, which visited institutions, including the Blind Welfare Institute. In 1934 it had some 50 members, sighted and unsighted; at least one of its executive was unsighted. Women were prominent in this club, among them Thelma Bastien, Mrs Besson, Lucille Padmore and Mrs Swanston.[37]

The literary and debating clubs were not always appreciated by the iconoclasts of their time, who saw in them a suffocating smugness and mimicry of European culture. They were accused of debating topics of little relevance to the society. Albert Gomes, writing in *The Beacon*, remarked in 1933:

> The very atmosphere of the 'literary' club reeks of an unctuousness, a stupid formality and a hypocrisy, from which any man or woman of true artistic sensibilities would flee in disgust.

The *Tobago Times* also quoted *The Beacon* as having accused the clubs of 'excessive formality', 'commonplaces of speech', 'platitude', 'rhetorical monstrosities, [and] cringing sycophancy'. Early in the 1940s, the Why Not Discussion Group of young radical, anti-colonial men and women, deliberately avoided becoming a debating club, deciding instead

> to break away from the accepted pattern of sterile debate and excessive formality with which our cultural activities have been for so long shrouded ...[38]

In contrast, Prince Ferdinand, then President of the La Brea Literary and Debating Club, in 1938 saw the clubs in the context of the very limited educational and other opportunities. Ferdinand called them 'sheet anchors against mental degeneracy', and 'the sphere of unfoldment and self-discovery' for many distinguished persons.[39]

Lionel Frank Seukeran, former teacher, businessman, trade unionist, member of the San Fernando Borough Council, and later Member of the Legislative Council and the Parliament, led the champion debating team in 1933, and later won a trophy for being the country's best orator. Here is his testimony on the Literary League:

The Trinidad and Tobago Literary League was perhaps one of the most dynamic movements in the annals of Trinidad's history over the years 1928, '30, right on to '40, '45, and it was spearheaded by some of the finest and most cultured men, to wit, people like Hamilton Maurice, Fred Ferdinand, [Ivan B. J.] Rouse, and quite a few others.

It was a training ground, in my opinion, for almost all the men who … had made a mark politically, whether it was at County Council level, or City Council level, or Legislative member. As a matter of fact, … it was the training that I had in the literary field that put me at such *ease* in Parliament, in so much so that when I entered the House and spoke for the first time in Parliament, the standard was regarded so high, that the editorial in the *Guardian* expressed the hope that the standard set by me would have been followed by other Members of Parliament for the years to come. I felt perfectly at ease in the Parliament of Trinidad and Tobago, because I had done more serious work in the literary field than I had to do for the Parliament. My rivals in the literary field were sharper, people who worked harder, more discerning, more conscientious, so that one had to be prepared to the *hilt*. Whereas in the Parliament, you met people of such mediocrity that you didn't have to bother; you knew you were right at the top from the very start. …

In my own time I can recall men like Wilfred Best, J. V. Bastien, Harold Telemaque. These were all my contemporaries against whom at one time or the other I was pitted. And each one of these men is a living symbol, and perhaps the greatest testimony to what the Literary League did for them and for the country in those years. …

When we met at one of the debates, the whole table was lined with 40, 50 volumes to substantiate your arguments, so *seriously* did you apply yourself. I believe that every time I did a debate … or Wilfred, or Bastien, or Telemaque, or any of the boys may have done it, or [Arnold C.] Thomasos, the Speaker, against whom I have been pitted, whenever any one of us made that research, it was sufficient to pass a Bar

examination. That was the amount of work one put in, in a debate.

So that if the era of good English, well-prepared speeches, and devotion to the cause of literature is over, as I might well lamentably state, it is because people have given up the finer things of life, seeking the pleasures that are pedestrian.[40]

The Great Debate on the Constitution, 1949

Throughout the 1940s, the anti-colonial movement in Trinidad and Tobago agitated for an end to the Crown Colony system with its nominated majority. Each concession from the British led to further demands for a Constitution granting self-government.

On 2 February 1949, the most famous debate of all was held at Queen's Royal College, Port of Spain, on the proposed Constitution which failed to give control over decision-making to the elected element in the legislature. Dr. Patrick Solomon and Jack Kelshall opposed the Constitution, and Albert Gomes and Canon Max Farquhar spoke in its favour.

The Governor and the social elite were there; and so were the populace. Crowds thronged the hall and the grounds. The debate was broadcast live on radio and beamed to other West Indian colonies. The whole country listened. Solomon and Kelshall, expressing the popular desire for self-government, won the debate.

The speeches were published verbatim in the daily press. At Calypso Ville in Port of Spain, the calypsonians formed a forum to give their rendition of the debate on the new Constitution. King Radio played Gomes; Small Island Pride, Farquhar; Lion, Solomon; Tiger, Kelshall; and Attila played Sir Gerald Wight, the chairman, while Invader took the role of the Colonial Secretary with whom Kelshall, according to Solomon, had 'wiped the floor'. Such was the impact of the debate in the shaping of the national consciousness that Canon John Ramkeesoon remarked:

Every class, creed, colour and race, ranging from the top to the bottom of our diversified community was represented. … Not the least merit of such an occasion was the fact that all sorts of conditions of people were pressed together for a couple of hours, talking, listening, applauding, disagreeing and forming

133

judgements on a question of the utmost importance to them all.[41]

The debate on the Constitution was the crowning point in the impact of debating as a means of popular education.

Literary Clubs in Tobago

The Early Movement, 1900–1920

As in Trinidad, the late nineteenth and early twentieth centuries ushered in a flowering of intellectual activity, in keeping with the growing thrust to self-knowledge and self-determination. The Tobago Debating Club (TDC), the brainchild of Rev. G. Taitt, Curate of St. Andrew's Anglican Church, Scarborough, was started in February 1901. It began with 36 members, and both membership and interest grew in the first years of its existence. Its first President was the Warden, James T. Rousseau; its Vice President was Rev. Sydney R. Browne of St. Andrew's, and its Secretary–Treasurer, Rev. Taitt. Among its leading members were Mitchell J. Prince, educator, senior lay preacher in the Scarborough Methodist Church, and correspondent for *The Mirror*; Dr. Edwin Blanc, the senior DMO; and Duncan McGillivray, planter and store manager.[42] The TDC discussed a variety of issues, ranging from the benefits of emigration to Trinidad versus continued residence in Tobago, to the system of road-making in Tobago, to the life and works of Lord Lytton. On 9 January 1903 Edgar Maresse-Smith, a radical democrat, lawyer and accomplished debater himself, delivered a paper entitled 'Tobago, Past and Present' to the TDC.[43] W. C. Nock, the Acting Warden, became its President in 1903 when Rousseau returned to Trinidad after the Water Riots, and in 1907 Rev. Taitt was the President.

The literary movement received a great impetus in the ensuing years, mainly in the larger settlements and townships. In June 1908 the Roxborough Men's Association was formed, and initially it met weekly; its programme included lectures, papers and debates. Samuel T. W. Charity, the Wesleyan head teacher, was Vice President.[44] The Association was followed by two groups in 1909.

The first was the Scarborough Brotherhood, formed in July 1909 under the auspices of the

Methodist Church, but open to people of all faiths. By August 1910 it had more than 100 members, with an average attendance of 60–70 people at its meetings. The Brotherhood organized debates such as the very lively one on the topic, 'Has Tobago improved socially by the annexation to Trinidad?', which was held on 4 April 1916; Mitchell J. Prince, speaking for the negative, won.[45] The Brotherhood from 1911 expanded its activities to several of the villages, and opened its membership to all who could be called 'useful member[s]' of society. By 1920 its members came from 'most villages in Tobago as well as Scarborough'.[46]

In 1911 the Brotherhood organized a 'monster petition' for an agricultural bank for Tobago. It opened its platform to the agricultural officers for lectures on crops, pest control and other issues, and so became an important forum for agricultural education and promotion of the best practices. Its members were the backbone of the peasantry. More than that, it invited officials and others to discuss the pressing development issues facing Tobago, and moved from the plane of discussion to that of action. It sent memorials and protests about all the needs of Tobago to the Government. For example, when I. A. Hope delivered a paper on the coastal service most acceptable to Tobago in November 1910, the Brotherhood sent its recommendations to the Government. In the same month, they discussed the need for schooling for the children at the Yaws Hospital, and by January 1911, provision was made for teaching the children there. In April 1918, it formed the Scarborough Agricultural Credit Society. The need for more DMOs and better health care, the high infant mortality, and many other issues were raised with the Government. The Brotherhood also had a music class which women attended; however, the newspaper accounts do not say whether women took part in the regular meetings.

In the 1920s the Brotherhood was known as the Scarborough Brotherhood and Fellowship Society (SBFS). In 1928 it had some 160 members and was regarded by a newspaper reporter as 'the largest Society in Tobago'. Its leading members included James A. A. Biggart; Albert Collier (accountant); W. H. Gamble (senior public servant); Sinai J. Gordon (businessman, violinist); Charles A. Hills; Isaac A. Hope (merchant, and Tobago's MLC

(1932–1938)); Archie Cornelius John (educator and musician); Harold Nymn (wireless operator); Charles Louis Plagemann (market clerk and businessman); Mitchell J. Prince; James E. Roberts (planter and businessman); and James White (lighthouse keeper and signalman). In 1931 Harold Nymn was President of the SBFS.[47]

The second organization was the Moriah Literary and Debating Club, which was started *c.* August 1909. It met fortnightly, and its moving figures were T. Z. Stephenson, the Moravian head teacher; H. S. Warner, also a teacher; D. E. Philip; and J. W. Campbell.

The Scarborough Literary and Debating Club (SLDC), was formed on 25 January 1910. Its members overlapped with those of the Scarborough Brotherhood and included James A. A. Biggart who spearheaded its founding, Mitchell J. Prince, Louis A. Peters, Herman Simmons, and Super Sergeant Millington; the incumbent Warden–Magistrate was always the patron. In April 1912 Biggart devoted one of his Scarborough buildings, 'Biggart's Hall', to be a public reading room, library and meeting place for the SLDC. Important debates and discussions were held under its auspices. The SLDC still existed in 1915. However, in December 1920, the Scarborough Club, devoted to recreation and literary pursuits, was founded, and Biggart, Peters, and George H. McEachnie, solicitor, were its leaders.[48]

In addition, under the auspices of the churches, there were several groups which promoted literary and intellectual pursuits. In the Methodist churches, the Wesley Guilds were the main forum, and one was started at Mt. St. George on 16 November 1903. By 1906 Rev. W. L. Broadbent had started libraries in Mason Hall, Mt. St. George, Goodwood, Roxborough and Scarborough, and books were distributed to the Sunday and Day Schools. From 1930 the Tobago Wesley Guilds competed in debating for the Guild Challenge Shield.[49] Among the Anglicans, in 1904 Canon S. R. Browne started branches of the Church of England Men's Society and the Women's Help Society in Scarborough. There were also a reading room and a circulating library open every evening of the week. These societies were to have lectures, debates and entertainment, and 'Has Tobago benefited by annexation or not?' was among the topics scheduled for debate in 1904. The Men's Society aimed to organize 'so that the questions

of the day, and others of vital importance to the Church, may be adequately discussed by its members.'[50] Among the Moravians, a Christian Endeavour Society for women, led by Miss Patience Guy, and a Mutual Improvement Society for men, with W. Osborne as director, existed at Bethesda in 1914.[51] Thus the churches, besides having major responsibility for formal public education, had a profound influence on civic consciousness and intellectual life.

The Early Writers, 1900–1925

Some of the members of these early debating and discussion clubs were gifted writers, although the avenues for this expression were few. The press therefore became an important forum for news and views. In 1898 Loraine Geddes Hay, Tobago's former Treasurer and its first Commissioner after 1889, who had published in 1884 a *Handbook of the Colony of Tobago*, issued a revised edition entitled *A Handbook of the Island of Tobago*. Edward C. Eliot, the Warden, prepared a book called *Illustrated Tobago* in 1911; it was expected to have photographs taken by a resident, along with pictures made available by the West India Committee and the Royal Mail company.[52] Mitchell J. Prince in 1916 published a booklet entitled *Tobago in My Own Time* which, unfortunately, does not seem to have survived. As correspondent for the *Mirror*, a daily newspaper published in Port of Spain until 1917, and for the *Labour Leader*, a weekly which was closely associated with the TWA, Prince wrote extensively and well, though usually anonymously.

George David Hatt (1865–1924), a Scarborough merchant, was a fine social analyst and amateur historian. Posthumously, the *Labour Leader* published an essay, 'Tobago, British West Indies: Robinson Crusoe's Isle', in which he discussed the activities in the 1780s of the famous naval captain, John Paul Jones, and recounted other historical events.[53] From 1899 to 1909, Hatt was a regular contributor to the *Mirror*, analysing statistics to show that there was a serious labour shortage in Tobago, praising the policy of expanding the peasantry, calling for good steam communications, reviewing government policy since the 1880s, and trenchantly criticizing policies that did not promote Tobago's well-being. In particular, Hatt was always careful to state that Tobago's prosperity was due to Commissioner Low's policy of land distribution to the labouring class in the 1890s, and not to the Union with Trinidad. In 1908 he addressed the issue of infant mortality. Of 700 babies born in Tobago per year, only 250 survived for more than one year; Hatt attributed much of this heavy loss to parental ignorance. He therefore distributed 150 copies of a publication called, 'Hints about baby, by a trained nurse', and called on the Warden to provide a brochure to help mothers.[54] In the 1920s, Hatt wrote extensively in the *Trinidad Guardian* on the scenic beauty of Tobago and on issues of the time. He served on many committees that struggled for better conditions, and was a highly influential figure in Tobago's affairs.

Many of the articles on Tobago that survive reveal the strong and growing discontent with its neglect by Britain and Trinidad. Outstanding among them are those by an anonymous writer, Homo. Three articles, entitled 'What Has Tobago Done?', appeared in June and July 1914. In the first, Homo analysed the incompetence of the Warden, H. P. C. Strange, in performing his duties as Magistrate, and called for a qualified barrister for the latter post. Homo demanded an urgent 'infusion of new blood in almost every department'. The second article appeared on 9 July 1914, dealing once again with Strange's incompetence as Magistrate. Homo complained that the Tobago people were taxed directly and indirectly at the same level as those in Trinidad, contributing to several public facilities 'without obtaining an iota of benefit' from them. The most important were the assisted secondary schools and the Government Training Schools, all of which were in Trinidad. By then, no Tobago nominee would accept the position of MLC because of the infrequent sea communications, and the Governor had appointed a Mr Moodie from Trinidad to represent Tobago. Homo recommended that Moodie press for secondary schools for boys and girls in Tobago, which would atone for 'his past sins of omission'. Later that month, Homo returned to the subject, arguing that since government officials 'have a wholesome dread of the searchlight of public opinion being turned on them through the medium of an independent and fearless press … every effort should be made to expose their short-comings.' He recommended that Strange be transferred to Trinidad, and called for better supervision to restrain the officials 'who

are shuffled off from time to time on poor Tobago.'[55]

Homo's piece 'On the Civil Service in Tobago' was a frank and scathing analysis of Tobago's administration in 1916. Appraising the performance of each senior official by name, he commented on the little work done by officials who behaved like 'demi tin-god[s]'—eating, drinking and smoking during working hours, and complaining of overwork—and the need for a Commissioner with oversight of the work of all the departments. In other words, Homo called for devolution of authority from the central government to Tobago. 'On the Civil Service' began:

> It must be apparent to every resident of this Island-Ward who takes an intelligent interest in its progress that a fundamental change should be made in the administration of its affairs if the people are to receive the benefits of the ever-increasing taxation imposed on them by an unsympathetic Legislature composed of men who take not the slightest interest in the welfare of the island and its inhabitants.

When Sir John Chancellor, the new Governor, paid his maiden visit to Tobago in October 1916, Homo wrote an open letter to him, inviting him to read his previous article.[56]

Similarly strong language was used in 'Tobago Yesterday and Today' and 'Tobago's Needs: An Appeal with a Demand', both by Vice Versa, who wrote about an 'impending crisis' on the island in 1923. In the second article, moving from the tone of lament in the first ('Oh Tobago! Tobago!! It is now that I weep for Thee'), the writer called for unity among Tobagonians, and demanded that only Tobagonians should staff the water scheme planned for the Leeward District.[57] By 1920, the neglect of Tobago had paved the way for a rising sense of Tobago nationalism.

The Literary and Debating Movement after 1920

The teachers from other Caribbean islands were an important leaven for the musical and literary life of Tobago. Laurence E. Edwards helped to foster the growth of literary and debating associations. Edwards, popularly called 'Laurence of Arabia', arrived in Tobago in 1919 as an Assistant Teacher at Belle Garden EC School, after which he was promoted to become Head Teacher of Adelphi EC

School. Late in 1922 he founded the Mason Hall Literary and Debating Society, and organized the Mason Hall–Moriah League to embrace literary groups which he hoped to form in nearby villages. In January 1923 a Moriah branch of the League began, with Lloyd St. Louis, President; C. Swalls, Vice President; and W. Stuart, Secretary. The members of the League wrote papers, debated and discussed. Often the judges would be solicitors and other educated people working in Tobago. At one debate in June 1923, the topic was, 'That the confederation of the British West Indies would be more beneficial to the inhabitants than is the present system of Government.'[58]

In 1924 a Tobago Literary and Debating Association was formed in Scarborough, the main mover being Cuthbert Tull, then Head Teacher at the Methodist School. Tull was the Secretary, with T. J. Baldwin as President and H. McNish, Vice President; and the committee included Ernest E. Cross, Fitz G. Maynard, Vincent Mitchell and Luther A. Roberts. All except Cross, a druggist, were teachers.[59] In this initiative, only Roberts among the leaders was from Tobago. On 11 July 1926, another debating club was started in Scarborough, with H. McNish as President, and the *Trinidad Guardian* reported that 'most of the teachers are members of it'. It was probably the Scarborough Literary and Debating Society, which existed in 1927.[60]

The only club for women in the 1920s was Unity Club, started late in 1921 in Scarborough for education and recreation. Its President was Bernice Plagemann; its Secretary, Edwina Biggart. The press reported little about its activities, apart from its concerts.[61]

Although these societies of the 1920s do not seem to have lasted long, by the 1930s literary and debating societies existed island-wide. In 1930 there was a Plymouth Literary Club, with Rev. J. H. Clark as President. At Roxborough in 1934 there was a lively debating club, of which the chief activists were C. B. Blake, C. Jack, J. Hercules, C. Nimblett, J. Rameshawr and L. Roberts. They met weekly, and their activities included poetry reading, lectures, impromptu speeches, debates and essay writing.[62] By 1935 there were also similar clubs at Charlotteville, Glamorgan, Pembroke (led by Adam Edward, head teacher), and Delaford (led by C. Blake, head teacher). Moriah's club (led by Messrs Stephenson and Percy, Moravian teachers) was active in 1938. In 1935 a Canaan Literary and Debating Club was formed with 22 members; and W. H. Stewart, Moravian head teacher, was President. In 1936 F. G. Maynard, then Scarborough Methodist Head Teacher, founded the Methodist Ex-Pupils Debating Club, which became one of Tobago's best clubs.[63] BHS had a debating society, as did some of the primary schools, where the teachers and senior students were the main activists; by 1943, one school, Roxborough EC (G. Warner, Head Teacher), published a school newspaper. The Wesley Guilds in the Methodist churches continued to be forums for reading, discussion, debate and writing.

Some of the branches of the Trinidad Workingmen's Association (TWA) also had literary sections. For example, in 1930 the Mason Hall TWA considered whether the work of Marcus Garvey had had a wider influence and was calculated to do more good for the human race than that of Booker T. Washington.[64] Many of the topics discussed revealed an interest in history and current affairs.

The leading club with some of Tobago's best debaters, meeting at Peru Cottage, the location of BHS in the early 1930s, was Scarborough Ideal Literary and Debating Association (SILDA), founded on 10 March 1931 by Laurence Edwards. Its motto was 'Let your guiding motives be truth, freedom and general upliftment.' SILDA's members were, as Eileen Guillaume put it, of 'one class': teachers and civil servants. They included Badroul Armstrong, Eileen Armstrong (later Guillaume), Cyril Burkett, Cecil Comma, Irma Dalrymple, George Daniel, Nydia Bruce (later Daniel's wife), Jules de Freitas, Dorothy Hislop (later de Freitas' wife), Cecil Donaldson, John Donaldson, Laura Dove, George Irvine, Carlos Kendall, the Lyons sisters—Olga, Pearl and Gertrude, Joseph Mangatal, Fitz Maynard, Hallis Meikle, Lionel Mitchell, Victor Noel, Rupert Nurse, the Ottley brothers—George, John and Carlton, Eric and Peter Roach, Elfreda Ross, Flora Wilhemina Ross (later Jordan), Olive Sawyer, Norma Spencer, Harold Telemaque, Henry and Walter Williams, and George C. Young. Many were graduates of BHS.

SILDA was divided into houses—Owens (after Jesse Owens the African-American athlete (1913–1980), who won gold medals in the 100-metre, 200-metre, broad jump and 100-metre relay competitions at the 1936 Olympics in Berlin);

Cullen (after the African-American writer Countee Cullen (1903–1946), who was one of the pillars of the Harlem Renaissance in the 1920s); and Aggrey (after Dr. James E. K. Aggrey (1875–1927), a Christian educator and social worker from the then Gold Coast, who was one of the founders of Achimota College, Ghana).[65]

SILDA's 'syllabus' included musical evenings, recitations, impromptu speaking, debates, short papers, visits to the cinema, mock trials and ladies' and gents' evenings.

Its first patron was Rawle Ramkeesoon, the resident Inspector of Schools between 1934 and 1936, after which Dr. George Hilton Clarke replaced him until Clarke's death in 1941. From 1935 SILDA offered the Jubilee Challenge Shield for English composition in the Tobago schools, and this annual competition was keenly contested.[66] On 1 January 1937, Rodney St. Rose, a graduate of BHS, published the first issue of a small quarterly magazine, *The Gem*, under SILDA's auspices. His list of members and friends of SILDA totalled 101 people.[67]

SILDA had several internal competitions. In 1933 an essay competition on the subject of 'Self-Government' was sponsored by George F. Samuel, a Scarborough druggist. The managing director of the *Trinidad Guardian*, Major C. Lionel Hanington, also sponsored another essay competition on 'How I Would Improve the Island of Tobago' in December 1934. Both of these were won by Rodney St. Rose, with Hallis Meikle in second place for the former, and Joseph T. Mangatal for the latter.[68] Although many of SILDA's members were ardent anti-colonialists, the group as such had little discussion on the political issues of the day. SILDA faded out in the 1940s, when many of its activists were transferred to Trinidad or went abroad to study.

In September 1939 Laurence Edwards started the Jenny Lind Club, named after the excellent Swedish singer (1820–1887); it was intended to bring together pupil teachers of all denominations. Jenny Lind was the counterpart to the Tobago Amateurs, a cultural group of young men, which had also been formed in the 1930s, but about which little is known. Jenny Lind was exclusively a women's club, which combined debating with sport, dance and choral singing. Eileen Guillaume, a former member, said:

We did sport, athletics, cricket. We did our debating society; we used to give concerts; we did some cookery. We did all sorts of things. We were [a] real sort of cultural group, and we were one of the foundation groups in the Women's Federation in Tobago. So we had a varied programme; home improvement and everything.[69]

A small group of teachers and other prominent persons around Scarborough formed in 1937 the Comfort and Happiness Promotion Club (CHPC), which met on Sundays at Mt. Parnassus, the home of L. A. Peters. George Frederick Samuel, an extremely well-read pharmacist, was a member, as was Thomas McKenzie Joseph, planter and businessman. T. Jerome Baldwin, retired Methodist head teacher and Principal of Trinity School, was Dean of Discipline; Laurence Edwards of Scarborough Upper EC School was Recording Officer, and Peters, Senior Recording Officer; John Donaldson was its Musical Director. The main activities of the CHPC were debates, discussions, lectures and musical evenings; they also honoured Tobago students, teachers and others, who were successful in scholastic and other pursuits. It was a forum of adult education for young people with primary education.[70]

Some time in the 1940s, a discussion group was started at BHS; on leaving school, some of its members formed The Scarborough Discussion Group (SDG), which met at Fairfield in the late 1940s. In 1947 Joseph Fernandes was President and Arthur N. R. Robinson, Secretary. Eileen Armstrong, Georgina Crichlow, Leslie Gray, Basil Pitt, F. Daniel Reid, Eric Roach, Iris Henry (later Roach's wife), Cynthia Robinson, and O. Warner were among its chief activists. They had a lively dramatic section. Recalling these groups in which he had participated, Robinson stated in 1959 that the SDG 'met regularly to talk over and to study the problems of the day', but that they thought only in 'economic and social terms', not considering political initiatives for Tobago's welfare. The SDG wanted to 'break away from the routine of the average literary group'. According to Robinson, they would take a theme and discuss it from various angles, at times preparing speeches of ten minutes each; visiting speakers were also invited to address them on the topic. Prominent among their concerns were conditions in Tobago:

The chief problem they saw in Tobago was stagnation. All the young people were either leaving or thinking of leaving.

The SDG aimed at forming a buying and selling company, their general tendency being towards co-operatives as the way forward for the Tobago economy and people.[71]

From May 1944 the Government started adult education classes in six population centres, partly resulting from a campaign in Trinidad spearheaded from 1938 by the Citizens' Committee, led by Richard E. Braithwaite, Alexander Brown and C. V. Gocking. Discussion groups were organized at several centres to equip adults for responsible citizenship, given that the end of colonial rule was near. At the Scarborough centre, the only one in Tobago in 1944, the Adult Education Discussion Group became a forum for understanding Tobago's development needs and how they could be overcome. Prince Ferdinand presided, and participants included James Dove, C. McFarlane, D. Ottley and E. Stewart.[72] By 1948 there were centres at Mason Hall, Bon Accord and Charlotteville; the latter was replaced by one at Roxborough.

Thus, as part of the growing intellectual and political ferment in the closing years of the colonial era, debates and discussion groups formed the pivot of intellectual life in Tobago.

All the resident Inspectors of Schools, themselves pillars of the literary–debating movement, assisted its progress in Tobago. Besides Rawle Ramkeesoon, mention must be made of Egbert B. Grosvenor (1931–1933), who arrived in Tobago while still President of the TLCC; W. H. MacAlister (1936–1940); J. Hamilton Maurice (1941–1947), the first President of the TLCC; and Prince Ferdinand (1947), who became Social Welfare Officer, Tobago, in 1948, and who for many years had been President of the La Brea Literary and Debating Club. All these men took part in, and supported, the literary and debating movement.

Around 1944, the Tobago Youth Council was formed, with affiliated local groups. Among its leaders were Victor Bruce, Jacob D. Elder, and Basil Pitt, all of whom were later to distinguish themselves in public life. Although the Tobago Youth Council affiliated with the Trinidad Youth Council, it did so as a separate and distinct body, and remains so until today.

The debating movement continued into the 1950s but, as happened in Trinidad, after the TTLCC celebrated its 25th anniversary in 1950, the movement waned in significance in the following decade. Like a comet, it had come across the skies of the BWI, as part of the cultural awakening that went with the quest for education and self-determination. It had served the purpose of popular education and preparation for civic duties and, as colonialism ended and its leading participants entered larger spheres of social responsibility, the literary and debating movement became a spent force.

3. TEACHERS, SOCIAL REFORM AND THE BIRTH OF THE PNM

The Tobago District Teachers' Association

In 1922 the Tobago teachers united to form a branch of the Trinidad and Tobago Teachers Union (TTTU), but by the end of the decade it had become dormant. Its revival as the Tobago District Teachers' Association (TDTA) in 1935, with Ernest Lyons as its President, enhanced the vibrancy of intellectual and social life. In 1937 Fitz Maynard became the President, with John Donaldson, Secretary. Donaldson had been the main mover in the revival of the TDTA. Nydia Bruce, George Daniel, Laurence Edwards, Lionel Mitchell and Harold Telemaque were among the leading members of the TDTA, whose plans included the founding of a circulating library and a short course in music by John Donaldson.[73] The TDTA as an organization and teachers as individuals were central to numerous initiatives in the 1930s.

The first was in handicraft. In 1929 Lionel Mitchell returned to training college to specialize in music and handicraft. As Head Teacher of Scarborough RC School from 1930, he pioneered handicraft and also taught the subject to teachers. In March 1937 he presented a paper on 'Handwork in Schools' to the TDTA. The lecture, and a remark by the Inspector of Schools, W. H. MacAlister, that handwork in Tobago schools was 'a joke', prompted the TDTA to host a handwork show, using local materials as far as possible. The show, held at BHS in April 1938, and the first organized by Tobago schools on their own, was a huge success, with an exceptionally high standard of creativity and execution in the exhibits, which included needlework done on the spot.[74] Similar exhibitions were held in April 1939 and subsequent years.

The second innovation was in music. Spearheaded by Donaldson, the TDTA from the mid 1930s organized singing competitions in the Tobago primary schools, usually in August. The test pieces were a local composition, a Negro Spiritual and a classical European piece. The songs performed in 1937 were 'Boca Chimes' by John S. Donaldson, 'Old Kentucky Home' and 'The Harp that Once through Tyra's Hall'. Dr. George Hilton Clarke, Mrs Lucy Latour-Link and Mr Adrian Latour were the judges.[75]

Thirdly, the TDTA dealt with education reform. It organized its first Teachers' Week in August 1935, during which ten lectures on an impressive range of pedagogical and educational issues were given. In 1936 another Teachers' Week was held, this time with eight lectures. The first All Tobago Teachers' Conference took place in July 1937. Out of this came a 'minimum scheme' for Tobago schools, worked out by a committee of teachers. The conference became an annual affair called 'Teachers' Get Together', lasting a weekend, with lectures, discussions on educational matters, a cricket competition between windward and leeward teachers, dinner and dance. The high standard of the lectures and the well-organized proceedings were a credit to the teachers; and the conferences attracted much public interest. Donaldson had proposed the conferences.

At each conference, the TDTA emphasized the urgent need for an agricultural and industrial school at post-primary level, to stop the steady exodus of the young from the island, and to teach them business skills.

The TDTA also established pupil-teacher training centres at Scarborough and Roxborough, together with a night school to prepare candidates for the teachers' and the Cambridge School Certificate examinations.[76] In this, they continued a tradition begun under Nelson Comma, Inspector of Schools, in 1924, and carried on by subsequent Inspectors, where classes to train teachers for their exams were taught by senior teachers.[77]

Some of the teachers on their own initiative founded evening continuation classes in their schools, as did Eric Cameron at Delaford and Lionel Mitchell at Scarborough from 1933.[78] In addition, spearheaded by John Donaldson, a Tobago Teachers' Benevolent Fund was started to provide for widows and orphans; by October 1939 it had 100 members.[79] It was managed by a board consisting solely of teachers and the Inspector of Schools.

The Tobago teachers also mobilized public opinion in support of education reform in the colony. In 1935 they submitted a petition signed by 1,200 taxpayers, objecting to several provisions in the new Education Code. In particular, they opposed the admission of children to school at age 5 and not before, and the school-leaving age of 14 or 15, without pre-schools or continuation schools.[80] In March 1938 the TDTA gave to the Tobago MLC, George de Nobriga, a Teachers' Mandate, outlining reforms needed for the teaching service and for the benefit of the general public.

The fourth major initiative came from Dr. Timothy Arthur des Iles, the veterinarian who was appointed to Tobago in November 1936, and W. H. MacAlister, Inspector of Schools; the TDTA supported it fully. Recognizing the decline in stock-rearing, des Iles formed Juvenile Farm Clubs (JFCs) in the primary schools in 1938. The aim was to provide early training in breeding, care and marketing of livestock, and to initiate children into the business aspect of stock-rearing. Ultimately, the clubs were intended to improve the economic condition of the peasants. Every Tobago school was affiliated, and the movement spread to Trinidad.[81]

The fifth activity was a 10-day educational tour of Trinidad which the TDTA conducted for 20 Tobago teachers in May 1939.

In nearly all these matters, the TDTA led the way in the country. It was the only District Association to run its own exhibitions, hold its own annual conferences, and host educational outings for teachers.[82] In addition, led by Dr. des Iles, the Tobago schools pioneered the JFCs.

Besides all this, as individuals the teachers served in executive positions in the District Agricultural Societies, helped with the Agricultural Credit Societies, promoted the public library, assisted with clubs for cricket and football, participated in the organization of Boy Scouts and Girl Guides, tutored the upcoming pupil teachers, worked in the peasant and labour organizations—and much more. One of the important areas in which they contributed leadership was the founding of Breakfast Sheds. On 10 July 1933, Dr. George Hilton Clarke, with the assistance of Mrs Tull, wife of Cuthbert Tull, Mason Hall Methodist Head Teacher, and Mrs Theodora A. Grosvenor, wife of Egbert B. Grosvenor, Inspector of Schools, started the first Breakfast Shed in Tobago in Mason Hall, to give hot, nourishing meals to children who often went to school without lunches. The first meals were served in the Tulls' home. The Breakfast Sheds in Tobago were inspired by similar activities led by Miss Audrey Jeffers and the Coterie of Social Workers in Trinidad, and Miss Jeffers in 1934 gave guidelines for the Scarborough Breakfast Shed, which was founded under Dr. Clarke's presidency on 17 September 1934.[83]

Donaldson, TECA, Tobago, and the Birth of the People's National Movement

One of the most loved of the teacher/activists in Tobago was John Shelford Donaldson, born of Tobagonian parents in Trinidad in 1905. Donaldson served in Tobago from 1933 to 1942 as Head Teacher of Patience Hill RC School, and exercised an enormous influence on the society. He was a pivotal figure in SILDA and the TDTA, and spearheaded the singing competitions in the Tobago schools, the annual teachers' conferences, the Benevolent Fund for teachers, and much more. He was at the centre of the Tobago centenary celebrations of the Emancipation from slavery in 1934. He was also one of a group that started the Tobago Negro Welfare League in September 1934. Members included Thomas J. Baldwin, Cyril Burkett, Laurence Edwards, S. McNeil, Harold Telemaque, and H. Young. All except Burkett, a journalist, were teachers. The League planned to get public support to send two youths to the Tuskegee Institute, USA, to study agriculture.[84]

Donaldson was transferred to Trinidad in 1942. Despite the fact that it was his lot, because of his outspokenness, to be posted to remote schools, he became a moving force in the Teachers' Economic and Cultural Association (TECA), which he and his close friend, De Wilton Rogers (1906–1984), formally registered in July 1942. TECA had existed since 1939. The Tobago Teachers' Benevolent Fund was transferred to TECA in 1942.

Donaldson and Rogers had a long, close and fruitful relationship in teaching and public life. Together, they had founded the Thistle Debating Society, which became one of the most formidable clubs in the country in the 1930s.[85] Among Thistle's offshoots were a writers' guild called the Quill Club, and a Reading Circle. Rogers had been a frequent visitor to Tobago in the 1930s, and had been Tobago's representative on the executive of the TTTU. Rogers edited *Thistle* magazine and was sometime sub-editor of the *Teachers' Journal*, the organ of the TTTU. He was also a perceptive sociologist and a prolific creative writer. By 1947 he had a growing corpus of work, which included *Lalaja*, *Chalk Dust* (novels); and *Blue Blood and Black*, *Trickidad*, *Silk Cotton Grove* and *Parson Bailey* (plays).

TECA, a lineal descendant of the Thistle club, was a very vibrant organization, somewhat bolder and more radical in its demands than the TTTU. Under Donaldson and Rogers, TECA organized a biennial music competition in all the primary schools from 1945 to 1951; this was a forerunner of the country's Music Festivals founded by Helen May Johnstone in 1948. Understanding the need to press for equal pay and fair conditions for female teachers, TECA mobilized the women and held annual women's rallies from 1940 to 1952. From January 1947, *Teachers' Herald*, from which Alexander Brown, its founder–editor, had retired in 1946, became TECA's organ.

Rogers was very conscious of the need for the middle class to join with the workers and peasants in the struggle for betterment. Addressing SILDA on the topic 'Education at the Cross Roads' in 1934, he explained that the teacher was the 'grand factor' in the current situation. He declared:

> The middle class intellectuals must form the leaven of the masses; if they keep themselves isolated then they are courting not only the doom of the third estate, but their disaster also.[86]

TECA worked in keeping with this analysis. In 1950 TECA formed the People's Education Movement (PEM), intending to develop a mass base, mobilize the population, and recruit members. In 1950 too, they invited Dr. Eric Williams, historian, who was then employed at the Caribbean Commission's secretariat in Port of Spain, to be consultant to TECA. Donaldson and Rogers decided to launch the PEM in Tobago on 16

March 1950. From 15 to 30 March, they trudged through the entire island, delivering 19 open-air lectures, with further discussions in homes and halls. Donaldson spoke on the economic position of the country; gambling and prostitution; production and productivity as the only remedy; and on TECA. Rogers' topics included: the education we need; the long thread of liberty; what slavery left in its wake; the Negro in world history today; and what is being done around the Caribbean. They were very well received, and a mass recruitment of members began. In 1951 Donaldson and Rogers returned to Tobago for another round of discussions, this time to find out what part the PEM could play in the society.

Why did they decide to launch the PEM in Tobago? Both Donaldson and Rogers understood the political value of their accomplishments in and out of the TDTA. Donaldson in particular was well known and highly respected. Moreover, Tobago was a relatively homogeneous society with a cohesive village structure; in each village, certain persons and families formed the core of the village networks and, if won to the cause, could influence the others. Therefore Tobago was the centre of their reforming thrust.

TECA's Women's Rally was held in Tobago in April 1951. By then, the Government had conceded equal pay for female teachers, and both Donaldson and Rogers received scrolls at the Rally. Donaldson was acclaimed for 'his stand against the many discriminations which beset our sex', his greatness as a teacher, his 'sterling qualities', and 'the part he played in the emancipation of women teachers'. Rogers was praised for 'self-sacrifice', good leadership, and for having 'guided the emancipation of women teachers from the bondage of inequality.'[87]

Both in Tobago and in Trinidad, the PEM established regional secretaries, who had voluntary workers to assist them with mobilizing. This quickly gave a mass base to the organization. In Tobago, influential people supported. Rogers states:

> Men like James Robinson, father of A. N. R. Robinson, T. J. Baldwin of the Baldwin dynasty, Albert Alleyne, the Fredericks of Pembroke, the Rowleys of Bethel, Richard James, Nicholson of Charlotteville. These … were veritable foundation members of the People's Education Movement. It cannot be disputed that, when the Roll of Honour is unfurled, Tobago

residents with their blood, sweat and tears, would be the foremost names to flutter in the breeze.[88]

In 1955, it was the PEM that sponsored a series of Eric Williams' public lectures, so making him known to the mass public. The first, Williams' historic lecture on *My Relations with the Caribbean Commission, 1943–1955*, took place on 21 June 1955. It attracted some 20,000 people, reflecting the powerful network at all social levels that the teachers, the literary movement, and TECA–PEM had built. At the end of his address, Williams announced his decision to 'let down my bucket' with the people of the West Indies in the fight for self-determination. Over the next six months, the PEM sponsored 52 lectures by Williams, which produced a monster petition for constitutional reform.

As the groundswell of popular support grew, the PEM leaders formed the Political Education Group (PEG). Its leaders included W. J. Alexander, Cecil Alexander, Felix A. Alexander, Donaldson, Rogers, Donald Pierre (all former stalwarts of TECA), Donald Granado (former Thistle member), Eric Williams and Miss Wong Shing. The PEG lasted only a few months before being disbanded to give way to the People's National Movement (PNM), the party led by Dr. Williams which formed the government in 1956 and led the nation to Independence in 1962. All the above people, Fitz Maynard, Arthur N. R. Robinson, Harold Telemaque, and many other educators and/or stalwarts of the debating movement were among the founding members of the PNM.[89]

Donaldson became the Minister of Education and Culture in July 1959. During his tenure in office, arrangements for free secondary education were finalized; and he concluded the Concordat, an agreement between state and religious bodies on policy regarding state-assisted schools.

On 14 May 1961, after delivering a lecture in honour of the centenary of the great Indian poet, Rabindranath Tagore, Donaldson died in a car accident. The nation and the Caribbean mourned. His was one of the largest funerals ever seen in the country, and thousands of mourners thronged the streets of the capital. At the sitting of the Legislative Council on Friday 26 May 1961, his fellow debater, Lionel F. Seukeran, then an Opposition member of the Council, placed the following tribute to Donaldson in the Council's record:

No more with us; no more.
  How hath the hand
Of heartless Death been
  mercilessly laid:
But yesterday it was we
  watched him stand
And speak his conscience,
  honest, unafraid,
Nor once by carping critics'
  tongue dismayed.

He was a man. To him in
  Providence fell
The challenge and the
  opportunity
To mould the tender mind;
  this he did well.
This land, thank God, again
  shall never see
Ambition, talent, chilled by
  penury.

Farewell, O friend, farewell.
  Thy task is done;
Lo! Ours yet lies before us.
  Grant that He
Who nerved thy arm for
  every victory won,
Will strengthen us no less;
  will ever be
With us who shape a nation's destiny.[90]

In Donaldson's lifetime *The Nation*, the PNM's organ then edited by C. L. R. James, had called him:

a leader in thought, a great patriot, a fearless pioneer, and a relentless opponent of Colonialism and all that it stands for, and above all a man of scrupulous honesty and unimpeachable integrity.

At his death, James wrote:

He died as he had lived, working to the last in the cause of humanity.[91]

Rogers died in 1984, rejected by Dr. Williams and disillusioned by the performance of the PNM in power.

It is clear that, because of the efforts of Donaldson and the teachers who served Tobago, Tobago had a strong input into the nationalist movement of the 1950s and the birth of the PNM.

4. TOBAGO'S WRITERS IN THE MAINSTREAM OF CARIBBEAN LITERATURE

The emergence of West Indian fiction in the early twentieth century was marked by the publication of literary magazines, such as *Trinidad* (two issues 1929, 1930), edited by C. L. R. James and Alfred Mendes; *The Beacon* (1931–1933, and one issue in 1939), edited by Albert Gomes in Trinidad; *Bim* in Barbados; *Kyk-over-al* in Guyana; and *Focus* in Jamaica. In Trinidad and Tobago, the 'little newspapers', such as *The People* (Leonard Walcott, editor) and *Teachers' Herald*, edited from 1933 to 1946 by Alexander Brown, a retired head teacher, became forums for publishing local writings. *New Dawn*, a left-wing paper, also appeared from November 1940 to March 1942. *Teachers' Herald* in January 1947 became the organ of the TECA, founded in 1942 by John Donaldson and De Wilton Rogers. At the same time, Ernest Quinlan, having returned to Trinidad from Tobago, published *A Teacher's Annual* from 1936. The organ of the TTTU, *The Teachers' Journal*, started in 1915, still appeared in the 1930s. All over the region, the teachers were gaining in organizational strength, and in 1935 the West Indies and British Guiana Teachers Association was formed. We have already shown the pivotal role of the *Trinidad Guardian* in giving exposure to the teachers, the debating movement and the local literature of the time.

Several less-known magazines with literary content, often ephemeral, also emerged in the first half of the twentieth century in Trinidad, in addition to the publications of the literary clubs: *The Trinidad Literary Magazine*, 1919, which attracted 'some of the colony's best thinkers' as contributors; *The East Indian Weekly*, edited by C. B. Mathura, 1928; *The Caribbee*, a monthly magazine edited by A. T. Pollonais, with which Mrs Beatrice Greig was associated, *c*.1934; *The Mercury*, for which Tito P. Achong (later Mayor of Port of Spain) was a prominent writer, *c*.1934; *The Humming Bird*, edited by A. E. James, *c*.1936; *The Westind*, a quarterly magazine edited by R. V. Hogan for the Paramount Club, appearing late in 1936; *West Indian Comment*, a literary magazine edited by Leonard Pereira from December 1938; *The Private School Journal*, edited in Port of Spain by J. Claud McNish from *c*. September 1939; and *The Civil Service Review*, first appearing in

143

September 1939, to which the contributors were said by Alexander Brown to be the best educated young people, mostly men. Jean de Boissiere edited *Callaloo* in the early 1940s, and in 1943 published a book of over 100 local recipes, entitled *Cooking Creole*. Dennis Jules Mahabir, the moving figure behind the Minerva Club (founded 1940) and its magazine *Minerva Review*, edited the *Observer* (previously known as *The Statesman* (1940) and *The Spectator* (1940–1941)) with Martin Sampath and S. M. Rameshwar until 1945. When the Trinidad and Tobago Youth Council was formed, it published from 1946 a magazine called *Youth*, with poetry and fiction by its members. Even within the schools there were literary efforts: *Tranquillity Boys Annual* first appeared in July 1934, and the literary club at Queen's Royal College produced *The Royalian* in 1932. Some of the writing was stylized, stilted and self-conscious, as is common with new writers; but it spoke of a great desire for self-expression.[92]

From the ranks of the teachers, apart from John Jacob Thomas who died in 1888, one of the earliest writers was Joseph Augustus de Suze (1847–1941), who taught from age 21 for 56 years at the school now known as Rosary Boys' RC School, Port of Spain. De Suze was the first teacher to write geography and history books on the colony. He published *Trinidad and Tobago* in 1894, a *Columbian Geography of the World*, 189?, and *Little Folks' Trinidad*, 1901. Both the *Columbian Geography* and *Little Folks' Trinidad* became standard texts in the primary schools.[93]

By the 1930s some of the leading members of the debating movement were writing and publishing their own work. Prince Ferdinand, for example, published *A Handbook of Civilization* (193[?]) and *A Guide to Life* (1938). The most famous book for schools was Wilfred Best's *The Student's Companion* (first edition, 1958), a compendium on good English and general knowledge that is still treasured by generations of students worldwide.[94]

The intelligentsia in and from Tobago were very much part of these literary currents. Fitz Maynard, Harold Telemaque and others contributed to the Teachers' Page and the literary pages of the *Trinidad Guardian*. From 1936 L. A. Peters was a correspondent for *The People*, as were Samuel Peterkin, singer, guitarist and labour activist; Hobson Smith, a teacher and occasional writer of poetry from Moriah; and Hallis Meikle, another teacher, who sometimes wrote in the *Guardian* and in *Teachers' Herald* on issues affecting Tobago's development. Meikle went on to study, and publish on, the Tobago dialect and folklore.[95] Many others—J. D. Elder, Carlton Ottley, Eric Roach, Thomas and Harold Telemaque, to name a few—studied the folklore, as their contributions to *The Tobagonian* (discussed below) show. Peters, besides being, as we have seen, a creative populist journalist, composed songs, and was the author of at least one play, *Charity*, which was staged by the Mason Hall RC Sunday School in March 1944.[96]

From 26 August 1933 to c. October 1935, *The Tobago Times*, a weekly newspaper, was published first from Scarborough, and in its later issues from Port of Spain, by Cyril Burkett, a champion debater, originally from Trinidad. It was the first Tobago newspaper since the demise of *The News* c.1894, and in its short life it supported the Trinidad Labour Party under Cipriani, and highlighted many of the burning issues for Tobagonians. It also held an essay competition for Tobago's primary schools on 'Toussaint L'Ouverture' in 1935.

In October 1938, A. Toby McIntosh, a Scarborough store owner and insurance agent, began publication of *The Tobagonian*, a substantial monthly magazine. The co-editors were Rawle Jordan, Principal of BHS from 1925 to 1946, when he became Principal of the Grenada Boys' Secondary School; K. I. M. Smith, another BHS teacher; and Reverends G. N. Davis and J. H. Clark. *The Tobagonian* existed until c. May 1950, and most of its editors were not of Tobago origin. They were concerned, however, to 'rous[e] the residents of Trinidad and Tobago from their lethargy' concerning Tobago, and 'to encourage a West Indian Literature and literary appreciation among our people'. The magazine's pages were open to literary talent from all quarters.[97]

Contributors included Alfred Cruickshank, a Trinidad poet; Jacob D. Elder, teacher, later to become Tobago's leading anthropologist and ethnomusicologist, who wrote essays on Tobago's development needs, short stories and poetry. His twin brother, Esau Elder, also a teacher, wrote poetry. *The Tobagonian* featured Fitz Maynard, with a teachers' column and occasional essays; Thomas Telemaque and his brother Harold, with songs, poems and essays; George Daniel, with essays and occasional poetry; Nydia Bruce Daniel, Isabel Wilson and Basil Pitt, with poetry; Olga

Comma Maynard (poetry and short stories); Hallis Meikle, L. A. Peters, Archdeacon Davies, and Arnott Stanley Henderson, then Vice President of the Federated Workers' Trade Union, with essays and social commentary; and Carlton Ottley with historical articles. Henderson was also a frequent contributor to *The People*, *Teachers' Herald* and the *Trinidad Guardian* on social and political issues. Much of their work revealed a concern for Tobago's history, folk traditions and development needs.

Carlton R. Ottley (1914–1985), while working as a clerk in the Tobago Registrar's office, studied the island's history, and produced a series of 52 articles for the *Sunday Guardian* from 15 May 1938, some of which were reproduced in *The Tobagonian*, and later in *Tobago Herald*, a monthly newspaper that he and his brothers issued from October 1953 to October 1956. In 1945 Ottley published the first edition of *The Complete History of the Island of Tobago*, which was revised and reprinted as *The Story of Tobago* (1973). In all, Ottley wrote at least 13 books on the history, dialect and folklore of both Trinidad and Tobago. In 1944 he joined the Social Welfare Department, was trained in Jamaica, and returned as Rural Welfare Officer, Tobago, from 1945. In April 1946, during his tenure in office, the *Tobago Welfare Magazine* appeared, its motto being: 'The place does not make the man, rather the man makes the place.'[98] In 1947 he was granted a two-year British Council scholarship to Liverpool University; he returned in 1949 to become the Head of Education Extension Services and, from 1950, the Director of Community Development. He was the moving spirit behind the Trinidad and Tobago Arts Festival, which was his brainchild in 1950, and which was staged biennially from 1954. Shortly before his death in 1985, he was the President of the Trinidad and Tobago Historical Society.[99]

Olive Sawyer (1914–1997) and Eileen Guillaume (1916–2004), former members of SILDA and graduates of BHS, joined the Social Welfare Department and distinguished themselves as social and community development workers. Mrs Guillaume was the author of 'A Study of Community Development in Trinidad and in Great Britain with Special Reference to the Work of Women' (c.1955).[100]

Harold Moses Telemaque (1909–1982) was one of the first class of students who entered BHS in 1925. He wrote occasionally for the *Trinidad Guardian*, and was a frequent contributor to *Teachers' Herald*. Telemaque published, with Alfred M. Clarke, a joint collection of poetry entitled *Burnt Bush* in 1947. The collection was dedicated to 'The New West Indian'. He also published another volume of poems, *Scarlet*, c.1950. By then Telemaque resided in Trinidad, whither he had been transferred in 1941, first to Port of Spain and then to Fyzabad, where from 1947 he was the first Head Teacher of the Fyzabad Intermediate EC School, one of four secondary schools founded by the Right Rev. Arthur Henry Anstey.[101]

Telemaque's poetry was aired on the BBC's *Caribbean Voices* programme produced by Henry Swanzy, in 1949, and he himself read poems on the programme in that year. His work was published in several Caribbean and other journals—*Bim*, *Kyk-over-al*, *Caribbean Quarterly*, *The West Indies Literary Magazine*, the Jamaican magazine *Now*, and *Freedomways* (USA). His poems have been translated into Czechoslovakian, German, Russian, Spanish and Swedish. In 1973 the Tobago Central Library published a mimeographed collection of 'Poems by E. M. Roach and H. M. Telemaque', Tobago's major poets. Telemaque was also a hymn writer and, having served as a lay minister since 1941, he was ordained a Deacon of the Anglican Church in 1980, two years before his passing in 1982.[102]

Another distinguished Tobago writer—poet, playwright, journalist and essayist—was Eric Merton Roach (1915–1974), who also was a frequent contributor to *Teachers' Herald* under the pseudonym Merton Maloney. Roach had been educated at BHS, and was a strong participant in the literary movements of the late 1930s and 1940s. In the 1950s he wrote occasional articles for the *Tobago Herald*, and eventually joined the staff of the *Trinidad Guardian*. In 1960 Henry Swanzy, who helped to publicize the work of many West Indian writers through the BBC, described him as 'the purest poet of them all'.[103]

Roach studied the Tobago folklore and wrote on the slave legends, his most famous piece being the poem, 'Ballad of Canga' (1955), which was translated into Sranantongo (Surinamese Creole language).[104] In 1956 he won a calypso competition on the West Indies Federation, composing under the pseudonym, Lord Troubadour.[105] He wrote three plays—*Letter for Leonora* (1966), *Belle Fanto*

145

(1967) and *A Calabash of Blood* (1971*)*. In an autobiographical essay published in 1975, the year after his suicide, he reflected on his response to BHS, which left the students 'exoticized natives', 'knowing absolutely nothing of ourselves, our country, its history and circumstance.'

> ... I loved to read and so afterwards discovered, as adventitiously as did Columbus himself, the Caribbean, its several peoples, my own tribe particularly, its origins and the tragic history that flung us on the islands. It was this self-acquired knowledge of my own time and place and circumstance that turned me round again and taught me to bless the school and the two clerics of the English middle classes (Bishop Anstey and Archdeacon Davies) who founded it in 1925, and through us, gave our island a place in our two-island country and the world.[106]

His poems were published posthumously as *The Flowering Rock: Collected Poems 1938–1974* (1992).

Nydia Bruce Daniel (1917–2001) resided in Trinidad from 1948. She continued to write poetry, and at her death had a corpus of some five hundred poems, most of them unpublished.[107]

Jacob Delworth Elder (1914–2003) was born at Charlotteville, and became a school teacher from 1928 through the pupil-teacher system. He was a frequent contributor to *The Tobagonian* on development needs, but one of his most touching pieces was a poem, 'Mymba', on a proud peasant woman who refused to accept her old-age pension because

> I don't want no gubna [Governor] monny,
> never me to beg me bread.

Elder was, with Basil Pitt and Victor Bruce, a leader of the Tobago Youth Council in the late 1940s. In 1950 he was research assistant to Dr. Gordon Gladys Fry, an ornithologist studying Tobago's birds. In 1951 he was assistant to Andrew Pearse, and went through Tobago collecting songs and other aspects of the folk culture.

Having migrated to Trinidad after 1955, Elder was a founder of the Ethnographic Society of Trinidad, and also of the Caribbean Folk Singers, one of the country's early folk choirs. Later, with Alan Lomax, he studied the folklore of several Caribbean islands. Elder also researched the cultural traditions of western Nigeria. His doctoral thesis from the University of Pennsylvania is 'Evolution of the Traditional Calypso of Trinidad and Tobago: A Sociohistorical Analysis of Song

Change' (1967). His numerous publications include *Song Games from Trinidad and Tobago* (1965; revised 1973), *From Congo Drum to Steelband* (1969), *The Yoruba Ancestor Cult of Gasparillo* (1969), *Folk Song and Folk Life in Charlotteville* (1971), *Ma Rose Point: An Anthology of Rare Legends and Folk Tales from Trinidad and Tobago* (1972), *African Survivals in Trinidad and Tobago* (1988), *Folksongs from Tobago* (1994); and sundry articles, especially 'Kalinda: Song of the Battling Troubadours of Trinidad' (1966). With Alan Lomax and Bess Lomax Harvey, he also published *Brown Girl in the Ring: An Anthology of Song Games from the Eastern Caribbean* (*c.*1997). He was the moving spirit behind the Tobago Heritage Festival which started in 1988, and he inspired a conference on Tobago's culture, held in 1984. Among Dr. Elder's many awards and honours are an honorary doctorate from the University of Sheffield (1998) and an award from the Friends of the Tobago Library (1999).[108]

Fitz Gerald Maynard (1900–1984) and Olga Comma Maynard (1902–1999) spent only a relatively short period of their lives in Tobago. However, Fitz' impact on Tobago's social life was formidable, and both of them as writers formed part of the thrust to Caribbean self-definition and self-knowledge that marked the period. Olga Comma in 1929 published *Carib Echoes*, a collection of short stories and poems, her first book.

> The idea behind it was that I felt a desire to *share* some of the things I enjoyed around me. Other than that, there was a lack of written local stuff. There was a lack of stuff that you heard only from legendary sources. Folk tales for instance. It was not the fashion to write folk tales. I've never seen one written before then. ... I wanted to share whatever was *within* me, and most of the stuff would be written, and kept, according to my father, under the bed. And I made up mih mind to *share it*. But it became a hobby. I didn't buy any bicycle, I didn't buy anything. I did nothing at all, except write in my spare time.[109]

In all, nine editions of *Carib Echoes* were published, the last in 1988, each with a new collection of poems, some in the vernacular, and short stories. Each held the hope of attracting 'the younger generation of readers to the charm of their immediate surroundings.'[110] *Carib Echoes* was spontaneously welcomed and used by the colony's teachers in the schools, and the third edition (1934) was officially adopted by the Department of Education as a text for schools.

146

Many of her poems were learnt and recited in schools, at local gatherings, and by other poets, for example, Harold Telemaque.[111] Comma also contributed an article on Trinidad folklore to the anthology, *Negro* (1934), edited by Nancy Cunard, a daughter of an English baronet; *Negro* was banned in Trinidad and Tobago as a seditious publication, because of its advocacy of communism. She went on to co-author with Fitz Maynard *The New Road*, a Civics source book for Social Studies (1961, updated 1985), and to write *The Briarend Pattern* (1971), the story of the Coterie of Social Workers founded by Audrey Jeffers and others in the 1920s.

Mrs Maynard spent from 1936 to 1944 in Tobago, where she started the Nelson Comma Junior School for young children; and Tobago was the subject of many of her finest poems. At age 90, she published her autobiography, *My Yesterdays*.

Levi A. Darlington (1906–1938), a Tobagonian from Delaford residing in Belmont, Port of Spain, published a book of poems, *Calliope*, shortly before his death in 1938. Darlington had been a teacher in the Harmon Seventh Day Adventist School, Tobago, had been ordained as a minister of the African Methodist Episcopal Church, and had been appointed Pastor of the Fountain Mission, San Juan, Trinidad. He left preaching for literature, preferring to be a lecturer on social and political issues, pamphleteer, poet and debater. In 1932 he was President of the San Juan Literary and Debating Club. He also founded the Thespian Club, a similar society, and he was a frequent contributor of articles to *The People*. His best-known play, *The Seven Great Monys*, was performed in Port of Spain in 1935 by the Quill Club, directed by Cecil Cobham. At his death, three poems were written in memoriam—'A Poet Passes: To the Memory of Levi A. Darlington' by Eric Roach, under the pseudonym Merton Maloney; 'Levi Darlington' by Alfred M. Cruickshank; and W. H. Carrington's 'Levi A. Darlington'.[112]

Darlington was also a frequent contributor to *Teachers' Herald*, whose editor, Alexander Brown, was a pivotal figure in giving exposure to the young Tobago writers, many of whom were also teachers. In its pages, Darlington entered into a long philosophical debate on first causes with Dr. M. A. Forrester and A. Llewellyn Noel, which began late in 1937 and continued until March 1938. George Thomas, a teacher from the Anglican

school, Kingstown, St. Vincent, also participated, indicating that *Teachers' Herald* was read in other BWI territories. In 1938 a fascinating debate arose because of the objections of some writers to the trenchant literary criticism of Albert Gomes in the literary page which he edited in the *Sunday Guardian*. Some of the discussion was conducted in the pages of *Teachers' Herald*, and Darlington published 'What Is Poetry?', on poetry and the critic's role, in the October 1938 issue. The first issue of *West Indian Comment* in 1938 also included posthumously one of his short stories.

From the ranks of the dominant class, Thorlief Orde, son of Harry Orde of Louis d'Or Estate, published in London in 1929 a book of poems called *Louis d'Or*, the title of one of his poems. It would seem that Orde lived abroad; he was not a participant in the local literary movements.[113]

Samuel George Thomas Peterkin was Tobago's most popular poet/musician from the 1890s until his death in September 1954. He is discussed more fully in Chapter 6. Peterkin's family owned Dunveygan Estate, a nutmeg and cocoa property which was uncultivated by 1920.[114] He was a clerical worker, and he identified with the interests of the labouring class. Peterkin was an early activist of the TWA/TLP, President of its Mt. St. George branch in 1934, and a founder of the Artisan Section of the TLP in March 1937. Given the impetus to trade unionism emerging from the strikes in Trinidad of June 1937, Peterkin was instrumental in forming both the Tobago Industrial Trade Union, of which he was a Secretary, and the Scarborough branch of the Public Works and Public Service Workers Union, late in 1937. By 1938 he was Educational Director of the latter, and one of its chief negotiators in industrial disputes.

Peterkin celebrated Tobago in two long ballads (Chapter 6), and he used his literary skills to advance the cause of labour. On the occasion of the visit by Captain Cipriani and the Honourable T. Albert Marryshow to Tobago in 1933, he published a poem to honour them for their commitment to labour and to the ending of Crown Colony rule.[115] This was followed by another, calling on workers to read *The People* and to 'co-operate or perish'; and yet another, 'Demonstration and Conference at Scarboro', to mark the demonstration of PWD workers from all over Tobago on 15 March 1939 to protest against irregular work on the roads.[116] Peterkin also promoted a night school for workers' education. Thus, his literary/musical work celebrates Tobago, while showing a commitment to self-rule and to justice for the labouring class.

Most of these writers wore a mantle of responsibility, not only for their own self-expression but for the collective aspirations of the people from whom they had sprung. Eric Roach, as we have seen, saw their role, at least in part, as giving their island a place in the country and in the world. Harold Telemaque, writing in 1940, insisted that the artist and critic

> must not spare himself in the search for universal truth. He must find himself and then be himself. True art is never produced on a conscious basis.

At the same time, the artist must portray for his readers

> their own joys, their own sorrows, their hopes, their aspirations, their creeds, the spirit of their times.[117]

They were authentic Caribbean voices expressing, in scholarship, social analysis, literature and song, the stirrings of Caribbean nationhood.

From the end of the 1930s, a steady exodus of the young educated occurred. After 1945 most of the Tobago writers, debaters and literary activists, native and adopted, departed from the island on transfer, for work, or for study. The nucleus of teachers, clergymen and other professionals that supported *The Tobagonian* suffered severe attrition. In 1954 Andrew Pearse, then Director of the Local Studies Department of the Extra-Mural Department, University College of the West Indies, began a research project on Tobago's anthropology, involving many of the students.[118] A course on Current Affairs was also run by the Department. But the 'critical mass' of the calibre that had sustained the activity of the 1930s and 1940s was not there. Thus, the 1950s saw the waning of literary activities and publications on the island, along with the demise of the debating society movement.

5. CONCLUSION

The first fifty years of the twentieth century were a time of considerable intellectual and creative activity in Tobago. Although Tobago produced few newspapers, the press continued to be a powerful medium for popular self-expression, protest, and solidarity with various causes. Tobago's writers contributed to all the major literary and political media in the country.

Throughout Tobago's history, there were contradictory tendencies towards both social division and social integration. Cross-cutting ties bound people together, despite the dividing boundaries of race, colour and class. At least two of the private secondary schools run by black teachers catered to the 'respectable' of all colours. Music, drama and literary pursuits also provided nodes, as it were, at which the lives of whites, browns and blacks intersected. Several of the teachers, journalists and clerical workers staunchly supported the nascent labour movement within Tobago and in the country at large. And the gross neglect of Tobago became a rallying point for all races and classes by 1938.

Access to primary education increased in the early twentieth century, and average attendance also improved. In general, the standard of the schools had advanced enormously by 1938. The founding of the BHS in 1925 was a major milestone, opening up new opportunities, especially for the children of the poor. The spread of Eurocentric education produced among the educated many who turned their talents to seeing themselves and the Caribbean with new eyes. Colonial education cradled anti-colonialism.

The literary, debating and dramatic movements that swept through Trinidad from the closing decades of the nineteenth century to the mid twentieth century reflected the growing quest for self-knowledge and self-determination of the generations after slavery and indentureship. They met the need for post-primary education by providing their own autonomous programmes and syllabuses countrywide. Their impact was extraordinary.

In Tobago, those movements had their own indigenous roots. After 1920 the presence of such dynamic leaders as John Donaldson, Laurence Edwards and Fitz Maynard provided a new thrust. They built on the efforts of venerables like James Biggart, Samuel Charity, George David Hatt, Archie Cornelius John, Mitchell J. Prince and L. A. Peters of the older generation, and those of the rising group of graduates of the Tobago primary schools, BHS, and some of the Port of Spain colleges. Women like Nydia Bruce Daniel, Eileen Guillaume (née Armstrong), Olga Lyons and Elfreda Ross were prominent members of this new generation of speakers and writers.

The result was an enormous and lasting impact on the literary, artistic and scholastic life of the country. John Donaldson's music competitions in the primary schools were an important initiative, while the country's Arts Festivals were the brainchild of Carlton Ottley. J. D. Elder inspired the Tobago Heritage Festivals.

Moreover, these leaders intervened to push for reform in education, nutrition, agriculture, youth affairs, labour relations, and much more. Many of them were pillars of the labour movement and the anti-colonial nationalist movement of the 1940s and 1950s. And Tobago formed a central, strategic stream in the popular nationalist groundswell that led to the birth of the PNM under Eric Williams.

By 1938 the main issue in Tobago was the island's development crisis. Forty years of closer Union with Trinidad had produced profound and widespread discontent, and all the discussion groups of the late 1930s and the 1940s focused on the island's development needs.

When we consider that Tobago had few cars, few telephones, little public transport, and no widespread electricity supply before 1952, that so much was accomplished with so little speaks of the undaunted and unstinting efforts of a whole generation in the process of nation-building. Certainly, where public debate, social activism, and artistic creativity were concerned, the period 1930–1950 was Tobago's finest hour.

Notes

1 *TRG*, 6 Sept. 1900, Board of Education minutes for 28 Aug. 1900, 1071–1072; *TRG*, 14 Aug. 1902, Board of Education minutes for 29 July 1902, 1062.

2 *TRG*, 14 June 1900, 710; 13 June 1901, 866; 12 June 1902, 795; 12 June 1903, 717–19; 12 May 1904, 812–13; 8 June 1905, 933.

3 C. B. Franklin, comp., *The Trinidad and Tobago Year Book, 1917* (Port of Spain 1917), 145–52.

4 C. B. Franklin, comp., *The Trinidad and Tobago Year Book, 1921* (Port of Spain 1921), 373–83.

5 *TG*, 5 Oct. 1924, 19.

6 *Mirror*, 20 July 1912, 4.

7 It is difficult to derive clear dates for the existence of these schools from the oral record.

8 In the pages of the *Trinidad Guardian*, see Marriott's report, *TG*, 1 July 1930, 1; Biggart's first objection, 12 July 1930, 6; Col. Sec.'s response to Biggart's requests, 29 Aug. 1930, 1; Biggart on Marriott, 31 Aug. 1930, 5. In addition, there were several articles by Tobago observers, commenting on the needs of the schools. See *TG*, 20 July 1930, 5; 27 July 1930, 5; 10 Aug. 1930, 5; 17 Aug. 1930, 5; 31 Aug. 1930, 5.

9 *TG*, 14 Jan. 1938, 13. Isaac A. Hope, like Dr. George Hilton Clarke who donated a cup for cricket in the schools of the whole country, resided in Tobago.

10 *LL*, 8 Sept. 1923, 8. By 1923, 6 Tobago boys had attended St. Mary's College, Port of Spain. In 1938 William Koo, who had attended Scarborough RC School, won from Nelson Street RC School, Port of Spain, first place in the St. Mary's College entrance exams. See on Koo and Cross, respectively, *The Tobagonian*, Sept. 1938, 30–31; Dec. 1943, 9.

11 Maynard, 'Tobago Schools', *The Tobagonian*, Sept. 1940, 8, 12. *Esprit de corps*: (French); pride and mutual loyalty in a group.

12 *Mirror*, 18 June 1900, 7; 17 July 1916, 12; George Sinclair (b. 1905), unrecorded conversation with author, 17 Feb. 1985.

13 Retired Matron Kadah Henry, Henry's great-niece, telephone conversation with author, 28 June 1999; Cecil Sandy (1917–2004), unrecorded conversation with author, 17 July 1999; Irma Crosby (1907–2003), unrecorded conversation with author, 17 July 1999; *Mirror*, 9 July 1904, 12.

14 Harold Nymn (1896–1986), interview with author, 12 May 1983; Irma Crosby, interview with author, 20 July 1992. Both were past pupils of the school.

15 *Mirror*, 31 May 1915, 4; 15 Apr. 1916, 10. On Mitchell, see *The Tobagonian*, Sept. 1947, 9.

16 *Mirror*, 5 June 1916, 7.

17 *TG*, 5 Jan. 1918, 9.

18 *Mirror*, 30 Nov. 1906, 9; 6 Dec. 1906, 9; 9 July 1907, 8. Bishop was also a journalist for both the *Mirror* and the *Trinidad Guardian*, and wrote at least two books, *Ex Post Facto* and *The Magnificent Province*,

according to *LL*, 18 Jan. 1930, 5. *San Fernando Gazette*, 10 Sept. 1894, 3, citing the Demerara *Echo*, 11 Aug. 1894, announced the inaugural meeting for A. A. Thorne's school. Thorne had taught at Harrison College, Barbados, and held the BA degree from Durham University, UK.

19 *TG*, 2 Feb. 1930, 8; *Tobago Times*, 28 Apr. 1934, and 4 Aug. 1934.

20 *TG*, 19 Dec. 1926, 16, reporting on Mr Jordan's Principal's Report at the first Speech Day, 14 Dec. 1926; *TG*, 28 Mar. 1926, 5.

21 The offering of the scholarships depended on the availability of funds and the standard of the students. The numbers therefore varied from year to year. Sometimes they were not awarded.

22 R. J. Lechmere Guppy, comp., *The Trinidad Official and Commercial Register and Almanack for 1890* (Port of Spain 1890), 48.

23 James H. Collens, comp., *The Trinidad Official and Commercial Register and Almanack, 1893* (Port of Spain 1892), 75; *The Trinidad Official and Commercial Register and Almanack, 1894* (Port of Spain 1893), 82.

24 *POSG*, 9 Mar. 1899, 5; *TRG*, vol. 2, 15 Oct. 1903, 1372.

25 Mole Bros., comps., *The "Mirror" Almanack and General Commercial Directory of Trinidad and Tobago for 1901* (Port of Spain n.d), 166.

26 Mole Bros., comps., *The "Mirror" Almanack and General Commercial Directory of Trinidad and Tobago for 1903* (Port of Spain n.d), 133.

27 *Mirror*, 21 Nov. 1916, 7. An East Indian Literary and Debating Club also existed in St. James, Port of Spain, in August 1916; I am not sure if it was the same club. Vishnu Noujardi and Leonard Daniel were among its speakers; *Mirror*, 6 Sept. 1916, 5.

28 *TG*, 18 Oct. 1934, 7.

29 C. B. Franklin, comp., *The Trinidad and Tobago Year Book, 1918* (Port of Spain 1918), 233; quotation from Selwyn Cudjoe, 'Glimpses of Our Literary Past', *Trinidad Guardian 80th Anniversary Supplement*, 31 August 1997, 88.

30 W. A. M. James was an Antiguan; his only child was Horace James, who became an acclaimed actor.

31 *TG*, 3 July 1932, 19.

32 *TG*, 10 July 932, 17.

33 Marcelline Archbald, *TG*, 18 Sept. 1934, 7.

34 *TG*, 31 May 1938, 7.

35 *Mirror*, 24 May 1916, 5; 12 July 1916, 5.

36 Marcelline Archbald, letter to editor, *Teachers' Herald*, Nov. 1939, 21–23.

37 *TG*, 25 Sept. 1934, 7.

38 Gomes, 'Literary Clubs' (*The Beacon*, June 1933; reprint in *From Trinidad: An Anthology of Early West Indian Writing*, ed. R. W. Sander, London, 1978), 29–30; *Tobago Times*, 16 Sept. 1933; Why Not

Discussion Group to H. Stannard, *Teachers' Herald*, Feb. 1944, 22.

39 Prince Ferdinand, 'The Place of Clubs in Society', *TG*, 13 Oct. 1938, 13.

40 Lionel F. Seukeran (1908–1992), interview with author, 9 June 1975; Seukeran's emphases.

41 Patrick Solomon, *Solomon: An Autobiography* (Port of Spain 1981), 121–22, for first quotation; Jack Kelshall Papers: newspaper cuttings, *TG*, 3–13 Feb. 1949; *TG*, 6 Feb. 1949 for Ramkeesoon.

42 *Mirror*, 14 Feb. 1901, 13–15; James H. Collens, comp., *The Trinidad and Tobago Year Book, 1903* (Port of Spain 1902), 92.

43 *Mirror*, 14 Feb. 1901, 13–15; 8 Oct. 1901, 3; 18 Nov. 1901, 7; 20 Dec. 1901, 7; 15 Jan. 1903, 11.

44 *Mirror*, 10 July 1908, 11; 28 July 1908, 12.

45 Archie C. John, like Prince a venerable teacher, argued for the affirmative.

46 *TG*, 25 Sept. 1920, 9.

47 *Mirror*, 3 Sept. 1909, 4; 6 Nov. 1909, 5; 9 Aug. 1910, 4; 13 Aug. 1910, 4; 7 Nov. 1910, 2; 19 Nov. 1910, 4; 20 Jan. 1911, 4; 24 Aug. 1911, 4; 10 Feb. 1914, 1; 10 Apr. 1916, 12; *TG*, 28 Apr. 1918, 5; *LL*, 31 Mar. 1925, 4; *TG*, 12 Aug. 1928, 22; 9 Apr. 1931, 3.

48 James H. Collens, comp., *Trinidad and Tobago Year Book, 1915* (Port of Spain 1915), 152; *TG*, 19 Dec. 1920, 7; 26 Feb. 1921, 10.

49 *Mirror*, 29 Nov. 1904, 13; 18 Apr. 1906, 13–14.

50 *Mirror*, 29 July. 1904, 2.

51 *Mirror*, 17 Jan. 1914, 10.

52 *Mirror*, 17 July 1911, 8.

53 *LL*, 4 Mar. 1925, 3. For discussion on John Paul Jones, see vol. I, chap. 3 of this work.

54 *Mirror*, 7 July 1908, 14–15.

55 *Mirror*, 15 June 1914, 10; 9 July 1914, 1; 31 July 1914, 1. An earlier article under the pseudonym Homo had appeared in *Mirror*, 26 Feb. 1907, 9; it supported payment by instalments for Crown lands, and called for a Scarborough Town Board or independent authority under the Warden.

56 *Mirror*, 4 Sept. 1916, 7; 23 Oct. 1916, 6.

57 *LL*, 7 July 1923, 6, 7; 28 July 1923, 2.

58 *TG*, 10 Dec. 1922, 15; *LL*, 27 Jan. 1923, 11; 23 June 1923.

59 *LL*, 11 Oct. 1924, 4, 13.

60 *TG*, 18 July 1926, 15; *TG*, 17 Dec. 1927, 12.

61 *TG*, 1 Jan. 1922, 5.

62 *Tobago Times*, 12 May 1934; 22 Sept. 1934. The names are spelt as reported.

63 *People*, 13 Apr. 1935, 10; 12 Nov. 1938, 5; *Tobago Times*, 16 Mar. 1935; *POSG*, 6 Feb. 1937, 6.

64 *TG*, 26 Nov. 1930, 6.

65 I am immensely grateful to Professor Christopher Fyfe, formerly of Edinburgh University, for the gift of Edwin W. Smith, *Aggrey of Africa: A Study in Black and White* (New York 1930).

66 *TG*, 2 Feb. 1937, 6.

67 I am grateful to Mr Carlos Kendall, who was a member of SILDA and a public servant in Tobago in 1934–39 and 1960–64, for a copy of *The Gem*.

68 *The Gem*, First Issue, Jan. 1937, 2.

69 Mrs Eileen Guillaume, interview, 29 Apr. 1983; unrecorded conversation, 22 Apr. 1983.

70 *People*, 24 July 1937, 2; 23 Oct. 1937, 10; Eric Ottley (1910–1986), former member of CHPC, interview with author, 12 Mar. 1985.

71 *Nation*, 13 Mar. 1959, 7; unrecorded conversation with Eileen Guillaume and George Young, 22 Apr. 1983.

72 *The Tobagonian*, June 1948, 7; July–Aug. 1948, 7.

73 *Tobago Times*, 28 Sept. 1935. In 1922 L. A. Peters was President of the Tobago branch of the TTTU and Egerton Blizzard, Vice President.

74 *TG*, 12 Apr. 1938, 11, 14; 15 Apr. 1938, 13.

75 *People*, 7 Aug. 1937, 8.

76 F. G. Maynard's Speech Day report, Scarborough Methodist School, *TG*, 20 Dec. 1938, 13; *TG*, 1 Aug. 1939, 13; *People*, 22 Oct. 1938, 2.

77 *LL*, 11 Oct. 1924, 4. The first tutors in 1924 were Cuthbert Tull, H. McNish, L. A. Peters, F. Skinner, E. Lyons and Miss B. Plagemann (Needlework).

78 On Cameron, *The Tobagonian*, Aug. 1941, 14; on Mitchell, *Tobago Times*, 7 Oct. 1933.

79 *Teachers' Herald*, Oct. 1939, 22–24.

80 *People*, 12 Jan. 1935, 5.

81 Saint de Lap, 'Tobago Juvenile Farm Club', *The Tobagonian*, Oct. 1941, 19. See also chap. 1. Dr. des Iles also gave two scholarships to Roman Catholic children to attend Pamphyllian High School, a private establishment in Port of Spain.

82 Fitz Maynard, 'Tobago Schools and Teachers', *The Tobagonian*, Sept. 1940, 8–12.

83 *People*, 22 July 1933, 5; *Tobago Times*, 2 June 1934; *TG*, 25 Sept. 1934, 3; cf. Olga Comma Maynard, *The Briarend Pattern: The Story of Audrey Jeffers OBE and the Coterie of Social Workers* (Port of Spain 1971).

84 *Tobago Times*, 15 Sept. 1934; 3 Nov. 1934.

85 Among its members were Donald Granado (later a Cabinet Minister and Ambassador), R. W. Hogan (a credit union leader), C. W. Alexander (later Deputy Speaker), his brother F. W. Alexander (later a Cabinet Minister), and Clement Payne, a labour activist who took part in the 1937 Trinidad strikes, and whose speeches triggered the Barbados strike of the same year.

86 *Tobago Times*, 25 Aug. 1934; also published in *TG*, 18 Sept. 1934, 7.

87 On Donaldson, *Nation*, 7 Aug. 1959, 9; on Rogers, De Wilton Rogers, *The Rise of the People's National Movement, Vol. 1, In the Beginning* (Trinidad n.d.), 8.

88 Rogers, *Rise of the People's National Movement*, 21.

89 *Nation*, 7 Aug. 1959, 9; Rogers, *Rise of the People's National Movement*, 37–41, 58; Selwyn Ryan, *Race and Nationalism in Trinidad and Tobago* (Toronto 1972), 106–110, including footnotes on those pages; Fitz Maynard, 'Loss to Trinidad of Truly Great Christian Gentleman', *TG*, 27 May 1961, 8. See also Andrew Carr, 'PNM Reminiscences', *Nation*, 29 Apr. 1960, 2; 13 May 1960, 2; 3 June 1960, 2; 17 June 1960, 2; 1 July 1960, 2.

90 Lionel Seukeran's poem in memory of John Shelford Donaldson, *TG*, 20 May 1961, 1; also *Proceedings and Debates of the Legislative Council (Hansard)*, 19 May 1961, 3011–3012.

91 *Nation*, 7 Aug. 1959, 9; 19 May 1961, 2, for quotations; Solomon, *Solomon: An Autobiography*, 194–96.

92 For notices of each, respectively, see *TG*, 3 May 1919, 7; Harry Partap, 'The East Indian Experience in Media Development, 1845–1995', in *In Celebration of 150 Years of the Indian Contribution to Trinidad and Tobago*, ed. K. Ramchand, B. Samaroo et al. (Port of Spain 1995), 187; *Sunday Guardian* (*SG*), 16 Sept. 1934, 23; *SG*, 8 July 1934, 19; *People*, 15 Aug. 1936, 12; *Teachers' Herald*, Oct. 1936, 35; *SG*, 18 Dec. 1938, 23; *Teachers' Herald*, Oct. 1939, 37; Nov. 1939, 37; Jan. 1943, 19; Jan. 1946, 30; *TG*, 15 July 1934, 21; 17 July 1932, 19. Beatrice Greig, a Canadian, had been joint editor of *The Beacon* and one of the founders of the TTLCC.

93 For more on John Jacob Thomas, see vol. I, chap. 9. In 1932 De Suze received the Member of the Order of the British Empire (MBE) for his service to education. *SG*, 28 Feb. 1932, 19.

94 Wilfred Best, *The Student's Companion* (1958; reprint, 2nd edition, London 1963).

95 Hallis Meikle, 'Tobago Villagers in the Mirror of Dialect', *Caribbean Quarterly* (*CQ*) 4, no. 2 (1955): 154–60; 'Mermaids and Fairymaids or Water Gods and Goddesses of Tobago', *CQ* 5, no. 2 (1958): 103–108.

96 *The Tobagonian*, March 1944, 20. Peters also produced and acted in *Experience*, a morality play staged in Scarborough in 1929; *TG*, 4 May 1929, 6. The author is not given. Chap. 6 has one of his songs.

97 *The Tobagonian*, Sept. 1938, 3; Dec. 1938, 4.

98 *The Tobagonian*, April 1946, 15. His *Complete History* was revised as *The Story of Tobago* (Port of Spain 1973).

99 Fitz G. Maynard, interview with author, 31 May 1983; cf. Heather Roberts, 'The Life and Work of C. R. Ottley' (Caribbean Studies thesis, UWI, St. Augustine, 1992).

100 Eileen Armstrong, 'A Study of Community Development in Trinidad and in Great Britain with Special Reference to the Work of Women' (presented for the Associateship of the University of London Institute of Education, *c*.1955).

101 The schools founded by Bishop Anstey were: The

Bishop Anstey High School for girls, Port of Spain (1921); The Bishop's High School, Tobago (1925); The Bishop's High School for Boys, Port of Spain (1937); the Fyzabad Intermediate EC School for girls and boys (1947), today Fyzabad Anglican Secondary School. Interestingly, in 2007 Telemaque's daughter, Ms Claire Telemaque, is the Principal of this school. The school for boys existed in 1945, but did not survive; *Teachers' Herald*, Mar. 1945, 6.

102 Anne Marie Baird-John, 'The Life and Times of Mr Harold Moses Telemaque' (Caribbean Studies thesis, UWI, St. Augustine, 1992).

103 Quoted in *SG*, 8 Jan. 1961, 7.

104 'Legend at Golden Lane', *TH*, 16 Oct. 1954, 2; 'Ballad of Canga', *CQ* 4, no. 2 (1955): 165–68.

105 *TH*, 15 Sept. 1956, 4.

106 Eric M. Roach, 'Growing Up in Tobago', in *David Frost Introduces Trinidad and Tobago*, ed. M. Anthony and A. Carr (London 1975), 157–58.

107 Nydia Bruce Daniel (1917–2001), interview with author, 19 July 1996.

108 Jacob D. Elder (1914–2003), interview with author, 20 April, 21 May 1983; for 'Mymba', *The Tobagonian*, Dec. 1948, 14.

109 Fitz and Olga Maynard, interview, 31 May 1983.

110 *Teachers' Herald*, Oct. 1944, 23.

111 Olga Comma Maynard, *My Yesterdays* (Port of Spain 1992), 61.

112 See, respectively, *Teachers' Herald,* Nov. 1938, 4; *People*, 5 Nov. 1938, 2; *The Tobagonian*, Dec. 1938, 34. Roach's poem also appeared in *The Tobagonian*, Jan. 1939, 36.

113 *TG*, 10 Dec. 1929, 6; Thorlief Orde, *Louis d'Or* (London 1929).

114 C. B. Franklin, comp., *The Trinidad and Tobago Year Book for 1921* (Port of Spain 1921), 205.

115 *People*, 30 Sept. 1933, 4.

116 *People*, 7 Oct. 1933, 11; *People*, 25 Mar. 1939, 9.

117 Harold Telemaque reviews *Glory of Youth*, poems by James R. Best, *Teachers' Herald*, Mar. 1940, 13–14.

118 The Andrew Pearse Papers are a special collection in the Main Library, UWI, St. Augustine, Trinidad and Tobago.

6

Popular Trends in Secular and Sacred Music in Tobago, 1900–1940

TOBAGO HAD a distinctive culture and unique folk traditions. The musical repertoire was extremely wide. By 1900 the main dances were bele, bongo, reel, jig, quadrille, lancers, pique, and paseo. These and the accompanying instruments have been studied by Dr. J. D. Elder, and will not be discussed here.[1]

By the 1920s the cultural world of Tobagonians was rapidly changing. Many migrants who had gone to Curaçao, Maracaibo, Panama, Trinidad, and other parts of the pan-Caribbean region were returning home, some with money to build better homes and to purchase land. Demobilized soldiers who had seen war in Europe and elsewhere during World War I had returned. Sometimes these travellers brought new musical instruments that swiftly became popular locally. Migrants to Tobago from Grenada also brought their traditions.

The motion picture industry, started at the turn of the twentieth century, had become one of the world's largest industries. In 1919 a cinema was opened in Tobago, and the population took great pleasure in the silent movies. In 1926 the film *Robinson Crusoe* was made in Tobago with mainly local actors, and its availability from 1927 created great excitement in the island. Talking movies reached the colony c.1930, and cinema became an even more important form of popular recreation.

The gramophone was another major influence, bringing music from other parts of the world. In particular, it brought from the USA jazz which, by 1925, had come into its own. So steeped were the younger generation in the jazz music emerging in their time that in 1926, when M. A. Wetherell filmed *Robinson Crusoe*, the young men who acted in it, when asked to do a war dance depicting cannibals, danced what Wetherell called 'the eccentricities of jazz and the Charleston' instead.[2] As we shall see, one stream of popular music-making among the younger men and women was the emergence of music bands influenced by jazz.

On several aspects of the popular culture of Tobago in the early twentieth century there is little written. For example, returning migrants from Trinidad brought many of that island's popular arts: Carnival, stick fighting, calypso, and the *tamboo bamboo* (percussion instruments made of bamboo). Little is known about the involvement of Tobago's folk artists in these activities in the early twentieth century.[3]

Further, the 1930s saw in Trinidad the phasing out of the tamboo bamboo with the invention of the steel pan, today the national instrument of Trinidad and Tobago. Musicians in Tobago were early participants in the steelband movement, but there is still no history of the beginnings of the movement there.

Church music was a strong feature of life at all social levels, the result of both churching and schooling, and Tobago developed a tradition of church and village choirs rendering sacred music. This too has been little studied, apart from Elder's interesting discussion in *Folk Song and Folk Life in Charlotteville*.[4]

The Carnival arts (especially the music), the early steelbands, the choirs rendering sacred music, and other popular musical activities will be discussed in this chapter.

By 1938 Tobago's changing musical styles were influenced by its own traditions, by the global mass media, by returning migrants from the pan-Caribbean region, by immigrants from Grenada, and by internal migration within Tobago. The major aspects of these changes are here considered, using oral material that is at times fragmentary.

Although some of the popular art forms were adopted from Trinidad (where the Carnival traditions had been influenced by many streams of migration from the nearby colonies), the calypso blended into older Tobago folk-song traditions. By 1900, there were many folk songs that, by being repeated at play, work, wakes, reel dances and other occasions, formed a known corpus of music. However, folk songs were constantly being created, in the sense that for every major new event, new social commentary in song would emerge, sometimes incorporating older tunes and lyrics. Village musicians were also creating music for the entertainment of their relatives and communities. Banter songs, which commented on other people's foibles, formed part of the musical repertoire. Therefore, songs like calypsoes existed in Tobago long before the Union with Trinidad. Thus, the conscious adoption of some of the Trinidad styles, and the emergence of *chantwels* (calypso singers) with their 'singing bands' were grafted onto deeply rooted local song traditions.[5]

1. STRING BANDS

At the turn of the twentieth century, among the most common musical instruments were the tambourine, made with goat skin, and the violin;

they were the accompaniments at reel, jig and other folk dances. In addition, almost every village and town had kettledrum-and-fife bands, which accompanied marches and processions. But string bands became even more popular. The main instruments were violin, guitar, cuatro and fife (flute). Rohlehr states that Venezuelan-type string bands grew in popularity in Trinidad in the 1890s.[6] Whether Tobago's musicians adopted them from Trinidad is not known.

Newspaper reports show how widespread the string ensembles were. In the growing township of Roxborough, at a musical and dramatic performance by St. Paul's Amateur Theatrical Company on 11 February 1903, Prince Stewart's string band played. Charles Baird was the leader of a string band in May 1905, and its existence was again recorded in November 1915. In January 1906 there was one at Mason Hall, and it still existed in June 1913. In April 1906 the Scarborough string band was due to make its debut. It was led by E. Beard, conductor; and by 1911 its members included Messrs C. Beard and Jemmott (flutes), J. Beard and S. McFarlane (violins), Leason and E. Beard (cuatros), Paul Mathew (bass), and Herman Simmons (mandolin). Simmons, a popular composer and singer, was the son of a master mariner, Captain Walter Simmons (1837–1909), a native of Bermuda who had settled in Tobago from 1858. He was also the director of a minstrel troupe in 1912, and became the leader of Simmons' string band, which in the years 1912 to 1915 enjoyed great popularity. The Mt. Grace string band in 1910 was led by William James. Lambeau also had one in 1916, led by Mr Moses; and another existed at Plymouth in 1913. The origins of the bands led by R. Lyons and one Sylvestre are not known, but both played at events in 1913. James Baird, an organist, also led a band, whose existence was recorded in 1913 and 1915. Another popular group was that of Hidey Forbes, a master carpenter; it existed in 1915 and 1916. Slaney's String Band, named after Arthur Daniel (also known as Slaney) existed in 1922. The last one appearing in the newspapers was Albert Alleyne's string band at Charlotteville in 1945. These bands travelled to several villages to play for concerts, celebrations, bazaars, fairs and other popular entertainments.[7]

By 1938 string bands were rapidly giving way to larger ensembles with a wider range of instruments, which were regarded as 'jazz bands'.

The most famous of the string band leaders was Samuel George Thomas Peterkin (d.1954), guitarist, composer, singer, poet and, in the 1930s, activist in the Tobago labour movement. Peterkin was the son of Samuel T. Peterkin, shopkeeper and lessee of Concordia Estate, and his wife Theodocia, the owner of Dunveygan Estate in the 1880s after her husband's death. From the closing years of the nineteenth century Sammy Peterkin, as he was popularly called, was a favourite entertainer because of his 'comic ditties'. In 1913 he was the director of the St. James String Band and Minstrel Company, St. James being the Anglican parish in which his village, Whim, is situated.[8] For several decades, Sammy was one of Tobago's foremost singers, though accounts vary as to whether he was a chantwel leading a Carnival band. He is remembered for his exquisite songs, and his expertise as a guitarist who could play the guitar behind his back. In particular, Peterkin composed two long ballads describing journeys around Tobago. The first ballad recounts a trip around the coast on the *Kennet*, one of the two Royal Mail coastal steamers connecting Tobago with Trinidad from 1901; the second describes a journey around Tobago by land. They are remembered as 'The Island Songs'. Both of them, treasures of the folk tradition, are given in full in Section 2.

2. CARNIVAL AND CARNIVAL ARTISTS

Growing Interest in Carnival, 1900–1930

In the closing years of the 1890s, Carnival in Scarborough was the preserve of the labouring class, and costumes were cheap. It was heavily frowned upon by the 'respectable' and the churches. However, in 1902, the *Mirror's* correspondent, Mitchell J. Prince, saw the Metropolitan Band, with 'high-class dress and attractiveness' and 'decent bearings [sic] throughout', singing 'several popular patriotic songs'. Prince observed:

The people here have taken to a practice which was more or less unknown to Tobago, and which was condemned wholesale a few years ago. This heritage have we from Trinidad.[9]

The next year, Carnival was held on a larger scale in Scarborough and its suburbs. On the Monday, masqueraders 'representing some of the learned professions' paraded until night. But on Carnival Tuesday, crowds of people from the country flocked to town, and five bands paraded in the Market Square, 'surrounded and followed by a large concourse of people' so numerous that it was impossible to cross the streets. The bands were Starlight Social Union, Shamrock, White Rose Social Union, Sweet Evening Bells and Birds of Iere. Starlight won on dress, while White Rose won for singing. Each band had a king and a queen, and some also had a princess. Starlight was described as follows:

The 'Queen's' costume was of light blue tinsel gauze net over white silk, and decorated with sequin trimmings, gold stars with a round of feather trimming which continued onto the long train, held by two waiting maids. Her crown was of sequins, with a fall of sequin chiffon, edged with lace. The 'King's' costume was of white silk, decorated with sequins and a robe of white satin, while the entire band was a mixture of blue and white silk. The banner was of blue silk with silver letters, and prettily decorated with artificial roses of blue and white paper. Streamers of white silk ribbon with rosettes were attached to it, and it was carried by girls.

Prince remarked:

Although it must be confessed that the prejudice in Tobago against this pastime is very strong, yet it is quite plain that if they conduct themselves in the future as they did this year they will win a large majority over to their favour.[10]

Interest in the Scarborough Carnival fluctuated between 1904 and 1920, and in some years (1907 to 1909), there was no parade.[11] In 1920, while Scarborough's Carnival was dull, at Charlotteville where there were two demobilized soldiers from World War I, one of whom had earned the Military Medal, the revellers had a Peace Song celebrating the end of the war, accompanied by a string band and chorus.[12]

Cyril Wildman, who arrived in Tobago from Grenada in 1911, recalled no Carnival in Moriah and its environs. However, according to him, by 1914 there were more masqueraders in Scarborough, in part because of the influence of Grenadian migrants who were used to Carnival.[13]

In the earliest years of the century, chantwels and masked bands often developed separately. Some villages had chantwels but no disguise bands. Others had disguise bands but no chantwels. In Scarborough and its environs, where disguise bands existed, the evidence does not clearly show that all had chantwels. There the most popular singers between 1900 and 1915 were Sammy Peterkin and Herman Simmons, who were leaders of string bands but were not chantwels, at least not in the first two decades of the century.

In the Windward District also, where the earliest Carnival bands were at Roxborough and Delaford, Henrietta Arthur (1899–1984) recalled that the chantwels emerged later than the masked bands. In 1907 she was a bridesmaid in the Delaford band, which had no chantwel.

HA: Dey used to have decent carnival. It had a man and a woman disguise as—well dressed, neatly dressed, and have girl holdin' up deh wreath, deh dress tail, you know. It have guards, if you please. When Ah say guards, the king and queen marchin', and den it have another fellow now, have to guard the road. Nobody cannot interrupt dem. And deh march right into Roxborough.

SCJ: And that was the Delaford band. You remember the names of [the] people who used to play?

HA: Yes, one woman called Peggy McKenna and a fella called Dursey Stewart, the king; and she was the queen. And den a fellow called Boxer Macmillan; he was the guardman fuh dat ban'. [14]

After 1915, where disguise bands emerged, they tended to do so as singing bands with chantwels.

When George Leacock (1915–2005) arrived in Tobago in 1923, he had been used, though a child, to taking part in Port of Spain Carnivals. This is his account of Carnival 1924 in Scarborough.

Well, the next morning is Carnival Monday morning. They never had holiday for Carnival in Tobago, you know. But what they used to get is that the children were afraid to come out to meet up with this devilish action, and they all stayed home. ... And I went around, I came down the road, all down by Scobie parlour [in Lower Scarborough], and we watching, we saw not one ... thing; nothing at all.

And when it reach about ten o'clock in the day, I saw some boys coming down the Burnett Street; it wasn't pitched. And they were coming from—they say Morne Quiton. ... And they had a thing like a stretcher, made with bag, and a stuffed *bobolee* [large effigy made of cloth and stuffed with rags, intended to be beaten] on it, what we call *bobolee* on Good Friday. And about ten of them. And they had one or two pitch oil pans and a bottle. And some pieces of cardboard

with some holes bore in it, tie behind here. No hat. Flour down all their face, and ting. And dey comin' down de road.

Tell mih sister, Ah say, 'Look a band comin' down deh. Leh we go and see, nuh.' Dis is in actually 1924, you know. A band coming down de road, boy. Fus' time Ah see a band in Tobago. You want me sing de song for you?

Mih bredder dead, Oh, wup, wup
Mih donkey wan' water, wup, wup
Mih bredder dead, Oh, wup, wup
Mih donkey wan' water
Mih carry am a' river
He dry up de river
Mih carry am a' pipe
He bruk up de pipe
So give me a penny
Fuh pay for de pipe
Mih bredder dead, Oh
Mih bredder dead.

That is what I ketch; dat. And Ah follow dem all round back and round the town. And nobody en' givin' dem nothing more than a penny. [15]

Interest in Carnival grew throughout Tobago. By 1928 the advent of private motor buses as a means of public transport permitted larger crowds to travel to Scarborough to see the masqueraders and to attend public dances there. By 1931 Roxborough was an important windward centre for Carnival activities. The *Trinidad Guardian* reported that there were 'bands of Red Indians, Blue Indians, Bats, Stick-men, etc. Many people from the villages of Goodwood, Pembroke, Glamorgan, Belle Garden and Delaford gathered at Roxborough'. [16] By 1931 too, Carnival celebrations at Charlotteville had grown big enough to cause all work to cease. The *Trinidad Guardian* reported:

Most of the younger generation had seen it in Trinidad and have transported this foreigner into Tobago. [17]

The Rise of the Chantwels and the Singing Bands, 1915–1940

By 1925 a clear pattern had been established. The core of the Carnival was 'singing bands' of musicians, singers and masqueraders, led by chantwels. The instruments were flute, violin, cuatro, banjo and guitar, with a chorus to back up the chantwel. All the members wore a disguise designed by the chantwel and his colleagues.

Not every settlement had a chantwel and singing band. Where they existed, each village or settlement (and the Scarborough suburbs such as Darrell Spring, Rose Hill and Bagatelle were like villages) usually had one chantwel; but even when there were several, they belonged to one band. Because the village was the social nucleus, the village backed the band, and the band represented the village. Elder notes for Trinidad that this community base of the bands strengthened communal loyalties, and fostered the growth of versatility in dramatic art.[18] It did the same in Tobago.

In each settlement, the chantwel and his group would organize a makeshift tent made of bamboo uprights and surrounded with plaited coconut fronds. Coconut branches formed the roof. The seats would be made of bamboo. Each tent had a king and a queen. In the weeks before Carnival, the chantwel and band would practise, and on certain nights villagers paid six cents per person to attend; in some villages, attending the practice was free. The singing was often either call-and-response songs, or songs with choruses, which would be sung by the members and followers. Usually on Carnival Monday night, the bands crowned their king and queen within their tents, followed by the sharing of food.

On Carnival day, the chantwel with his singing band would serenade the planters and the biggest shopkeepers in the village, or the nearby villages, to be repaid with refreshment and money. On Carnival Tuesday, those within walking distance of Scarborough serenaded in the stores and shops where, in 1923, George Frederick Samuel, a druggist who owned Nyall's Drug Store, started a competition for the best song; the first competing bands were White Rose, Metropolitan and the Mason Hall band.[19] Often businessmen would pay for the best song in praise of their business.

In Scarborough there would also be impromptu competitions for supremacy between the chantwels, who would sing or '*shant*' against each other wherever they met. Much of their art continued the traditional banter songs and satires that so incisively commented on the class structure and on the foibles of the villagers themselves. In the Carnival tradition, when the singers threw witty barbs at each other it was called '*picong*' (from French *piquant*, prickly). By the 1930s, a formal competition was held for the best song and also the best picong. The judging was sponsored by the Scarborough stores, and was usually held in the upper town. In the 1930s the space in front of the administration building on Jerningham Street was the site of the judging. On Carnival days, each band had a guard, who would ensure that nobody disrupted the band. Usually, this man would be a champion stick fighter, who had learned his art in Trinidad.

The interviews for this study provide ample evidence, though sometimes fragmentary, that social commentary, picong, ballads recounting events or describing places, road marches (jump-up music to enliven the singers who had to walk long distances), praise songs pandering to shopkeepers or planters, and boasting songs which told of the physical prowess of the singer or the band, were all part of the Tobago repertoire.[20]

Tobago's early calypsoes were not recorded, and most of them do not survive. For lack of information, the early calypsonians not discussed below include the leading Charlotteville singers before 1922—Manny Wheeler (a regular Carnival visitor to the village), Quintin Hackett and Samuel Greenidge; those at Castara—Frederick Eastman, Captain Edwards and Baker Alleyne; and Frederick Osmond at Culloden.[21]

Social Commentary

Jane Ann 'Edna' Thomas (1894–2003) recalled that 'old Trummy Scotland' was the Les Coteaux chantwel in her childhood *c.*1906, singing what she called 'cariso songs'. 'Cariso' was one of the terms for the Trinidad calypso between 1850 and 1920.[22] Thomas' father, James Demas, was himself a composer, guitarist and concertina player, who had temporarily migrated to Trinidad *c.*1899 to work. She remembered two of Demas' songs, composed after his return from Trinidad in the first decade of the century.

The first song ends with '*sans humanité*' (French: without humanity), a typical ending in certain types of Trinidad calypso.

ET:

Woman is a nation, they are very deceivin'
Each and every one
When dey want to squander yuh labour
So dey say, 'I love you forever.'
When yuh money done

Dey hate you lika poison
Santi manité [*Sans humanité*]

[Imitates the sound of a cuatro.]

Dey playin' de cuatro dat time.

SCJ: Cuatro, not fiddle and not tambrine [tambourine]?

ET: All mixed together.

SCJ: They had all those with it too—tambrine, fiddle and cuatro?

ET: Yes.

The second song by James Demas was a commentary on the returning migrant who squanders his money with fast living.

A young man come from Trinidad
Smoking all de fancy girls
Drinking all de common rum
Wey causin' to break him down
Nobody to love 'im now
Because he is broken down

A young man come from Trinidad
Drinking all de common rum
Nobody to love him now
Because he is broken down.[23]

At Mason Hall the Carnival disguise band and the chantwels emerged together in a singing band. There was neither masquerade nor chantwel until Bobby Franklin, 'Papa Choonks' (also known as 'The Black Prince'), and Andrew Jack started to sing *c.*1918. They had all lived in Trinidad, and Choonks and Jack helped to groom a younger generation of singers, including Franklin's son, George Franklin. Eric Ottley was a member of this group of singers. At Carnival 1920, Jack sang on the December 1919 strikes in Scarborough. Alexandrina Watts (b.1909) recalled one stanza, and Annie Caesar (b.1905) recalled a part of the chorus.

If you all can remember
When de war broke out in de town
Everybody arm wid bottle and stone
Policemen arm wid bayonet an' gun
An' de benefit arrive
Was a deat', an' agony

Chorus
On the 8th of December
We all can remember
When de war broke out
Bottles and stones …[24]

Sislyn Craig (1921–1996) was in her youth the queen in the Mason Hall singing band. She recalled parts of two songs by George Franklin. The first, sung *c.*1936 after Mussolini's invasion of Ethiopia in 1935, said:

What does Mussolini know about Africa?
He wants to claim Addis Ababa
He's in this world like a rolling stone
He lives on nothing that call his own
He's a parasite to humanity
He wants to rob our forefathers' country …

The second song (1937) was on the abdication of King Edward VIII from the British throne on 10 December 1936 to marry Mrs Wallis Simpson, a divorced commoner. Two of the verses were:

1935 we had Jubilee
This year she's in big calamity
He has brought England to subjection
Setting examples to all nations
No one could have faced such great disaster
Not even Stanley Baldwin, Prime Minister
British subjects must all agree
And lend them their sympathy

Chorus
We must extend our sympathy
To the ex-King and his family
We must extend our sympathy
To the ex-King and his family
As a mother she was bound to mourn
When he abdicated the throne
British subjects must all agree
And lend them their sympathy.[25]

In the 1920s the chantwels in Scarborough and its suburbs were Zadoc Bedlow (born in Trinidad) and his son, George Bedlow, at Rose Hill; 'Zita' Collins with Iron Duke band at Darrell Spring; Edwin Peterkin (Sammy's son) at Rockley Vale; and Gerald O'Keiffe with Allies band in the upper town near Rose Hill. After O'Keiffe emigrated in the 1930s, David Harris and Claude Saunders sang for a few years in Scarborough.[26] O'Keiffe, the choirmaster in the Methodist Church and a clerk in Bonanza Store, was a master of social commentary as well as of picong. He is remembered for one of his songs on World War I, which used the letters of the alphabet to describe the events of the war. Only a fragment survives, as sung by Jules de Freitas (1906–1991):

A stands for Allies
We fought side by side

B stands for Belgium
Britain as well
C stands for Canada
Sent soldiers to fight …[27]

The pipeborne water supply for Scarborough and the Leeward District was started in some settlements in 1925, and James Biggart was elected as MLC at the elections of February that year. O'Keiffe won the Scarborough calypso competition in 1926 with this song, recalled by George Leacock:

Tobago is an island come from afar
Getting as bright as a morning star
Water works came down from Greenhill
Down to Canaan land
Mr Biggart selection
Was a grand celebration
Santi manité.

And he went on shanting with other verses in between of different topics that happened in the course of the year, you know?[28]

Vincent Bruce, the Moriah chantwel, after the invasion of Ethiopia by Mussolini in 1935, sang a warning to the British, that the impending world war would have staggering dimensions. Mrs Cassie Homeward (1911–2003) sang it.

Dungar Benjaman, yuh hear de alarm?
War! We in 'Hopian [Ethiopian] war!
Dungar Benjaman, yuh hear dere are war?
War! We in 'Hopian war!
Wire up to England
Tell Kitchener
To care de soldiers
War in France
Dis is de war
To stagger da whole worl'
Sanda manité [Sans humanité]

Dungar Benjaman, yuh hear dere are war?
War! In 'Hopian war!
Dungar Benjaman, yuh hear dere are war?
War! In 'Hopian war!
Wire up to England
Tell Kitchener
To care de soldiers
War in France
Dis is de war
To stagger da whole worl'
Sanda manité.[29]

The reference to war in France may have been to Hitler's invasion of the demilitarized zone of the Rhineland on France's eastern border in March 1936. Interestingly, William Shirer states that Hitler's Rhineland coup was 'more staggering and more fatal' than was understood at the time.[30]

Picong

The chantwels turned their merciless gaze on their fellow villagers and townspeople. For example, Sammy Peterkin sang about several young women who, instead of going to choir practice at night, held rendezvous with their lovers at a building in Lower Scarborough called the Watch House.

One Friday night
Dressed all in white
See how they run
They mesmerize any gun
[The names of the women followed.]

Chorus
You see that watch house a' bay dey
You see that watch house a' bay dey
You see that watch house a' bay dey
A' he a' de instigator.[31]

Peterkin himself was on the receiving end of picong that reflected the dividing lines of colour in the society. Peterkin was black. The unknown singer therefore considered it presumptuous for one of his colour to court a mustee, a near-white woman.

Peterkin an' all a' look mustee
Peterkin an' all a' look mustee
All yuh look 'pan Peterkin
Look 'pan am
He an' all a' look mustee.[32]

From Rockley Vale, Wilfred Caesar, better known as Sugar Wilfred, sang the following song about a man who stole lumber and other materials from Government House and was arrested for the offence. George Leacock remembered it.

Early in de mornin' just before dawnin'
Police lay han' on —
Early in de mornin' just before dawnin'
Police lay han' on —
Lots of lumber lying at ease
Till de lorry dat came to seize
Three pounds he had to pay
Or a month in Baroom Bay [prison]
Santi manité.[33]

In the Windward District, among the chantwels at the end of the 1920s were Hardtime and Willy Boucher. Elton 'Bob Hope' Arthur (b.1920) re-called one instance in his boyhood (1929) when one of the Boucher brothers shanted in picong against a chantwel called Huggins.

> One of the fellow competing against the other. Now, Huggins was singing against Boucher, so he want to bring down Boucher. So he is telling the population—Boucher wife name Obstal, suh he want to tell the population that Obstal say she tired eating rock fig [a type of banana] all the days. So he start on the stage like this. He say:
>
> > Obstal declay
> > That she tired eating
> > Rock fig all de day.
>
> That is as far as I could remember. And de whole crowd jumpin' up now, dat he let down Boucher … You know rock fig was a ting, if you are a rock fig eater, you down to earth [very poor], in those days. So when a fella would cuss you and tell you only naked rock fig yuh wife eatin', dah's a big joke. … like de stage nearly break down wid laugh, you know.[34]

According to Dalton Andrews of Belle Garden, the leading chantwels from Pembroke were 'a fella called Dalgo' and 'the Hamiltons, those sisters, about two or three sisters', who used to 'shant' against each other.[35]

Extemporaneous composition was part of the repertoire of these village singers, as this picong by Andrew Jack at Mason Hall shows. Jack had gone to I. A. Hope's shop in Mason Hall on Carnival day to serenade in exchange for money. Hope's manager, Allenby, a Barbados-born Methodist Local Preacher, told Jack that, since he preached against Carnival, he would not encourage it by funding him. Instantly, Jack replied in a song remembered by Alexandrina Watts:

> De Bajan [Barbadian] at Hope store
> He low like a louse
> I don't know what to say
> We went on Carnival day
> And dis is what he have to say
> He preach against it
> So he can't encourage it
> Santa manité.

This song dates from early 1921 or before, since Allenby resigned at the end of November 1921.[36]

Ballads

Gerald O'Keiffe sang several long ballads, chronicling current events. One was on the house-to-house campaign conducted by Dr. Hubert Bishop against hookworm during 1924. One of his greatest surviving songs is a ballad of seven stanzas on 'The Disaster of the *Belize*', when the steamer ran aground at Toco on the night of 31 October 1924. Sidney Gibbs remembered most of four stanzas and Lionel Mitchell, the chorus:

> The *Belize* has just came down from dock
> And everything was quite up to mark
> She went round the island that week
> Doing her duties quite complete
> Then on Thursday night, sad to say,
> She sail out Rockley Bay …
> Santi manité
>
> It was on October the 31st at night
> Calm, serene, and with bright moonlight
> When about an hour of twelve o'clock
> The people on board felt an awful shock
> They say that the *Belize* went on a reef
> And there she'll have to sleep
> They got a great uproar
> Not a man could go ashore
> Santi manité
>
> Women and children must go down first
> Men and crew must stay for the last
> The air was filled with mourning and weeping
> Sad to say, I believe, to be witnessing
> Children going leaving their father
> Lovers going leaving their lovers
> Husbands not in life
> Can't get a kiss from their dear wife
> Santi manité
>
> After time, I learnt to understand
> The men had a chance to go on to land
> The mechanics on board tried to patch her up
> But success was far from crowning their effort
> When she returned to Port of Spain
> The Governor said, 'No more steamer again.
> To go back to Tobago, you would have to
> Embark as a sailor.'
> Santi manité
>
> *Chorus*
> The disaster of the *Belize*
> Cause Tobagonians at large to grieve
> The disaster of the *Belize*
> Cause Tobagonians at large to grieve
> Hampering the products of businessmen

Having people worried from end to end
Proprietors don't know
When to bag up dey cocoa.
Sans humanité![37]

The best-loved of the ballads were Sammy Peterkin's Island Songs, which were not sung in the context of Carnival, but were perennially enjoyed in all seasons. The earlier one on the sea journey around Tobago is presented first, as sung by Noel Felix (b.1933) who learned it from his father, Eddie Felix (1881–1973), a renowned violinist and Peterkin's close friend. The *Kennet* and the *Spey* were the two coastal steamers plying between Trinidad and Tobago from 1901 to 1913. That such a long poem was transmitted entirely from memory is a testimony to the high regard in which it was held, and to the extraordinary power of the oral tradition.

Just an hour's run from Iere [old name for Trinidad]
Reach at break of day
Under de SS *Kennet*
Sister ship to *Spey*
Come to tour dis little island
Crusoe loved the best
Took her anchorage up at Scarborough
For a journey west

It was afternoon on Tuesday
We left Rockley Bay
Auchenskeoch in just ten minutes
Was in full display
Though Columbus Point now sighted
We had ceased to fight
Bay of Cave [Cove?] is close to Lowlands
Scarborough lost in sight

Gaskynd Bay had lovely breakers
We saw Killigwyn [Kilgwyn]
Anxious eyes were pleased with Crown Point
Where Crusoe Cave was seen
But a large boatload of cargo
Caused us to delay
As we lay abreast the depot
Into Milford Bay

Pigeon Point seemed now declaring
Don't you pace too fast
All you think of Buccoo corals
Long as life should last
But the zigzag current brought us
Facts we can deplore
As we drove some precious cargo
On Mt. Irvine shore

Grafton, also called Stonehaven,
Had a doubtful calm
Later, Courland town of Plymouth
Was the next alarm
There we had no big importance
So we made no stay
Roundin' up de church, Bethesda,
There we saw Back Bay

Heavy seas began to grumble
Up at Arnos Vale
And a place called Killiecrankie
Had a perfect gale
Turtle Bay and small Ma Lucy
Was the next to glance
And the heavy weather blowin'
Made Culloden prance

From Woodlands to King Peter
There we got some stock
Gordon Bay and Bullman Harbour
And a large sunk rock
When we roundin' up Castara
A little rain came down
So we called at Englishman's Bay
Bay of less renown

Parrot Hall and Parlatuvier
Came right in the line
Bloody Bay was noted, kicking,
Almost like a shine
L'Anse Fourmi behaved more quiet
Though we passed outside
Brothers and the rocky Sisters
Wrestled in their pride

Hermitage a moment later
Whisper, peace be still
We got charmed at Man-of-War Bay
Over Charlotteville
Though the Giles and Melville alarm us
What a madding sea!
Starwood Bay and Belmont calm us
Coming on the lee

Just as here the special interest
Far as eyes could reach
Tyrell Bay is now revealing
Speyside pretty beach
Delaford exposed the chapel
Where the people pray
And we lay for thirty minutes
Anchored at King's Bay

Another place of special interest
Far as we could note
Betsy Hope was ranking viewing

Foremost from the boat
But the most important Roxborough
Turned out lower down
Argyle and Morocco River
Seventeen miles from town

Kendal Place, of course, had beauty
Which we saw full well
Mangrove Bay have better anchorage
Garden of the Belle
Richmond Bay outside Glamorgan
We remain a while
Pembroke had some dreadful breakers
In a fearful style

We took muscovado sugar
In at Waterloo
Studley Park gave us a signal
And some coconuts too
Leaving there we arrive lower
To a place of fame
Hope and Blenheim showed their colours
Hillsborough by name

Bacolet with bay called Minister
With its waters green
Little rocks around the coastline
Rudely intervene
Through the channel, back to Scarborough
Rockley Bay did smile
So we terminate our journey
Round Tobago's isle![38]

Sammy Peterkin's second ballad on Tobago describes the island from the standpoint of a traveller by land. It was written before 1930, since it mentions the 'bridgeless river' at Louis d'Or; and probably before 1915, since L'Anse Fourmi is still 'virgin soil'. This song is reproduced with the kind permission of Ms Alison Armstrong, who received the typewritten words from her late father, Samuel Armstrong.

Tobago Inland Route

Crusoe's dear little island
I've circled east and west
Since then a special critic
Sent me an inland test
And just to please his fancy
I'll start at Charlotte Ville
The public highway leads me
To the foot of Pigeon Hill

Bark Hill, Observatory
Where walking power's tried

And Trois Rivières decides it
Soon as you reach Speyside
Up Lambeau Hill you're wending
And down again King's Bay
Passing Merchiston you're wonted
Delaford to stay

The local road to Windsor
You'll notice as you pass
And soon the bridgeless river
Called Louis d'Or you'll cross
Roxboro', Argyle, and Kendal
Belle Garden once a shine
But you won't see the Zion Hill
Thro' Rosamond's incline

From Richmond to Glamorgan
The Cardiff Road, Pembroke
And Waterloo's wide streamlet
With its majestic look
Goodwood is like a desert
And so is Studley Park
Mount St. George, Hope, John Dial
And Bacolet you'll mark

I had an inclination
At Caledonia Road
To take snapshots of Green Hill
And Easterfield's abode
But hastening on to Scarbro
And then the Lower Bay
I found a second Lambeau
Where Burleigh Castle lay

From Auchenskeoch a pathway leads you
To Sherwood Park
From there to Carnbee's Appendage
Is visible til dark
But soon as radiant sunlight
[Gives?] you a brighter view
You're sure to see the seaward track
That we call Petit Trou

Lowlands and Little Hampden
All on the seaward wing
From Bethany [to?] Buccoo
Hear Bethel Church bells ring
Cove, Shirvan and the Granges
All very near abreast
The little road to Bower
By Golden Grove out west

Now Friendship on the sea line
Canaan on the other side
And Killigwyn is central
When Tyson Hall is 'plied
From Bon Accord to Milford

Way down to Pigeon Point
The cave of Robinson Crusoe
Is at the other joint

Step back and take enquiry
Of the other spots you didn't see
I'm sure you will at Riseland's Hill
Gain notoriety
Prospect, Hopestan, Mt. Irvine
'Ringe Hill, Amity Hope[39]
And Patience Hill, via Ararat
Shew Grafton in the slope

Pleasant Prospect, Stonehaven,
Then Plymouth near the stream
Adventure and Bethesda
A lovely morning's gleam
Roselle, that's just ascending
The brow of Mary's Hill
Now take the north-east pathway
St. James the Whim there still

The high road [thro'] Dunveygan
Exposes Arnos Vale
Les Coteaux facing Golden Lane
Culloden in the dale
But go to Mount Grace summit
And look the other way,
There stands the old Mt. Pelier
Spring Gardens far away

Then Harmony Hall adorning
The east of Providence
I scale the heights Concordia
To view the land from thence
I see the old and new forts
Friendsfield and Calder Hall
Cinnamon Hill, Mt. William
And Cradley last of all

Now as I swerve Adelphi
I go to Mason Hall
To Petrie Hill or Alma
Widow, Belmont and all
Craig Hall is right of Highlands
Where Courland river cools
'Tween Indian Walk and Ladysmith
A road to Woodlands spools

Moriah takes my fancy
And specially Fair Hill
Hooghly Bush is rough enough
King Peter's rougher still
From Runnymede, Des Vignes Road
Mt. Dillon's winds blow chill
But ere you reach Castara
There's a second Patience Hill

I pass the fisher's village
Which leads to Tucker's Dale
And Englishman's rude harbour
Is blowing quite a gale
Then comes a spot quite dreary
The village Parrot Hall
Here many a weary foot will rest
As ev'ning shadows fall

You will, amid the sunlight
Embrace Parlatuvier
And find a second Widow there
As upward you will steer
I drank of that small river
That runs in Dead Man's Bay
And you will feel persuaded
At Bloody Bay to stay

This war-famed seat of action
Once glorious in its days
From here you'll see the Ance Fourmi
On virgin soil you'll gaze
St. Rose in due succession
With crops of tender age
But Telescope has scenery
And reveals the Hermitage

From Campbelton the breakfast time
Is always mid-day hour,
Where here recuperating
There's oft a heavy shower
As soon as that is over
We terminate this route
For here comes the Man-o'-War Bay
Right where I started out.

So now to you, dear critic
I leave you to digest
My geography poetic
Of judges you are best
I claim no rank as poet
Such laurel's hard to win
I'm just your humble servant
S. G. T. Peterkin.[40]

The last stanza is a charming piece of mock deference to the critic who had challenged Peterkin to compose on an inland journey.

Road Marches

Road marches kept the members of the singing bands lively, since they went many miles on foot on Carnival days.

In the leeward villages there was a cluster of chantwels in the 1920s and 1930s. Phillip Mills sang at Plymouth and Donald Job at Black Rock. At Patience Hill the leading chantwel was Noah Caesar. Caesar was a master of extemporaneous singing, and unfortunately his song on the Ethiopian war of 1935 survives only in small fragments. One of his road marches, probably near World War II, was recalled by Leopold Solomon:

Bidim bim
We go march to Berlin
Bidim bim
We go march the queen [of the singing band] home
Bidim bim
We go enter Berlin
Bidim bim
We go march the queen home. [41]

At Bethel the singing band in the 1920s was White Rose. Its members included Evelyn Percival and Reuben Adams. Its surviving road march is this, as sung by Mrs Jane Taylor (1912–1989):

White Rose Band is on de way
Enemy, try an' clear out de way
I don't care what de people say
White Rose boun' to rule de day. [42]

Some time in the 1930s, the Mason Hall band, then known as Shannon, placed first in the Scarborough calypso competition. Shannon's road march (its composer unknown) was:

I don't know
In fact
I don't care to know
The number
Of my enemies
When Shannon
Gain the victory. [43]

Advertisements and Praise Songs

In Scarborough there were often contests between calypsonians vying to sing the best song on the business places; the winner would receive a small sum of money. Eric Ottley, who assisted George Franklin, the chantwel who succeeded Andrew Jack at Mason Hall, described a contest in Scarborough between Papa Choonks and Franklin on Cross' Drug Store, owned by Ernest E. Cross. Papa Choonks won with this song:

There's a lovely pharmacy
Nice and neat, Burnett Street

Everybody knows the boss
Who is he? Mister Cross
Cross's Drug Store leads the way
Purity, courtesy, on display
To prove the truth of what I say
Go to Cross Drug Store.

George Franklin's song was:

Mister Cross is an honourable boss
And his medicine no one can surpass
He has saved the lives of many a citizens
With his pure and excellent medicines
We are proud of his presence here
So let us help him in his career
Go to Cross' Drug Store
Which is situated—Main Street, Tobago. [44]

Phillip Mills, Plymouth chantwel, sang in this genre on Mrs Eleanor Alefounder's house, which she built at Grafton Estate (bought in 1932/33). Mrs Keziah Solomon recalled it.

The prettiest building they have in Tobago
Just in Venture [Adventure?]
Down by Grafton
Hip, hip, hoorah
Miss Alefounder have de prettiest building
In Tobago. [45]

Boasting Songs

Two of the road marches above are also songs in which the chantwel, on behalf of the group, declares against all enemies. A striking song in this genre was composed by Eugene Nedd of Mason Hall, who gave it to George Franklin and Eric Ottley. Ottley recalled two stanzas.

I come, I come from the mountains of light and strong
I come, I come from the mountains of light and strong
Anyone want to compete with me
They must first prove their dignity
For men look at me
And bow down in agony
Santi manité

Out of the darkness have I emerged
And the stillness of my voice have heard
I am a warrior, a terror I'm also called
Anyone want to compete with me
They must first prove their dignity
For men look at me
And bow down in agony
Santi manité. [46]

George Leacock recalled a chantwel called The Mighty Pretender, surnamed Bradshaw, from Whim, who sang the following *c*.1926:

Who's dat carlin' my name
Singin' in vain
Ahwe don' know
Who's dat carlin' my name
Singin' in vain
Ahwe don' know

That is the chorus hitting back.

Dis is The Mighty Pretender
Coming to blow dem down
Santi manité
De Mighty Pretender
Coming to blow dem down.[47]

Gordon Rohlehr, writing on the 'Oratorical', *sans humanité* calypsoes like the first of the boasts above, noted their 'self-annunciation', in that the singer announced his presence and gave himself extraordinary significance, in contrast to the humble reality of his social and political life. At the same time, his command over words enhanced his prestige in his community. Both aspects of this were real in Tobago. George Franklin often used his dictionary to compose in the oratorical style, and several Scarborough people stated that Gerald O'Keiffe attracted the middle strata to his band, because his education allowed him to sing in good English. Jules Crooks, who was a member of O'Keiffe's band, recalled:

And of course, he [O'Keiffe] used to write his calypso, and then he take his ... dictionary ... and some of the words that he have written dey, he look in the dictionary, the meaning; and he put in the big word. So when he singing calypso, and he give you English dey, well, some people don't know the meaning.[48]

Singing Bands and Their Disguises

George Leacock, with assistance from his wife Cecile, described the costumes he saw in the singing bands in the 1920s:

GL: The only difference in the bands is the colours. But every band actually dressed the same way. You know in Robin Hood wear? A balloon pants, a bodice with a string. ... Everybody in bars of different colours, red, green, yellow. And a collar around the neck. And a corn straw hat, covered with satin; turn up on one side, da' is de chantwel, and a big plume, like Robin Hood. And a wire mas' face. And he must have a little wand in his hand. A stick wrap with pretty flowers and ting. Wrap round, you know. And stockings.

And in those days *watchekongs* [canvas shoes with rubber soles] were just six cents, because those watchekongs used to come from Hong Kong. You go at Millers' dey, you pick up any watchekong for six cents a pair. They used to cover those watchekongs with satin, making it look like a court shoe. So that was the kind of a dress. Every chantwel ... dress the same way. Every band the same way, but just different colours.

You had a band like White Rose ...

CL: The hat turn up on one side, and the robe, the cloak.

GL: The ... shawl. That's all.

SCJ: The chantwel had the cloak, or everybody?

GL: The chantwel alone had the cloak, and everybody—you see the English way of carrying this collar? The collar around the neck here, very wide, with a frill right round. And a star glass here, and a half-moon glass here.[49]

By the 1930s, however, some chantwels, like George Franklin, wore a velvet cape and a shirt with honeycomb smocking; sometimes all the followers had the same kind of embroidery, done by women from the village.

Of all the bands, O'Keiffe's, because it attracted 'the cream of Scarborough'—the middle strata—was particularly exclusive. Therefore, there were usually people holding ropes around the band to cordon it off from non-members.[50]

Other Masqueraders and Other Carnival Activities

There were bands of Wild Indians and individuals playing *Jab Jab* (French, *le diable*: devil) with whips, long tails and coloured costumes on Carnival days, but they were relatively few. Bethel produced Wild Indians in the 1930s, as did Plymouth, Canaan and Scarborough. Moriah had a sailor band.

Stick Fighting

As increasing numbers of returning migrants came from Trinidad, stick fighting became a part of the Tobago Carnival, but did not take place in all the villages. All the leading stick players had lived in Trinidad.

In the Windward District, William 'Sweetie' Pope recalled that there was an annual stick-playing contest at Hazel Fraser's shop in Roxborough: 'Kendal 'gainst Roxborough; Roxborough 'gainst Betsy Hope. All de way suh.'[51] At Bloody Bay, the leading stick fighters were Hardtime George, Feddie George and Headman Tobias.[52]

In Charlotteville, stick fighting existed before 1922, as Samuel Moore (b.1902) recalled:

SM: Dere were one or two men [in stick fighting]. See like de old men who grew in Trinidad, and deh accustom with this; La Brea and—Bande l'Est, Princes Town, Ah think, and ... Moruga, Manzanilla and Mayaro and those places and thing there; Princes Town. All dem fellas deh grow up there. 'Cause dose are places where they play the stick. ... And so dey come een ... and den de Speyside fellas used to come over here, and make ting, and deh exchange. But no big fightin' or so, yuh know. Dey used to enjoy demselves.

SCJ: You remember some of the leading stick fighters?

SM: Yes. ... An uncle of mine, his name was Archie Lewis. You find Ralph Alleyne; William Alleyne. You got a fella belonging to Hermitage, deh call him Vanburgh Espinanza—I don't know. Bud Espinanza. Benny Murray. My father used to play too. Deh call him William Moore. Eliezer Jack, Diamond Jack—brothers. And Quintin Hackett, who used to sing de calypso. And de same [Samuel] Greenidge [chantwel] Ah talk about. And Eddie Christmas. Quite a lot of dem.

SCJ: So all of these people had gone to Trinidad, and brought back the traditions with them—the chantwels, and the stick fight?

SM: Yes, yes, yes. ... Deh spen' a little time deh. Most of the men used to work in the pitch; asphalt, yes. They work on the Pitch Lake, yes, La Brea; they got their experience there. And so they come back home.[53]

The best known of the stick players in the Scarborough Carnival were Jimmy Reid of Bagatelle, Johnny Archer of Old Road, and William Billy ('Fisherman Brush') of Plymouth. These fights took place in an open space in Lower Scarborough. George 'Colonel' Holder (b.1911) was eyewitness in 1927 to a fight in which Archer lost an eye. Stick fighting was prohibited in Scarborough for several years thereafter, but it still occurred in the 1950s. A common Kalinda song that accompanied the stick fights was learnt in Trinidad also:

Mooma, Mooma
When Ah dead bury me
When Ah dead bury me
Bury me in red, white an' blue

Today, today
Today is the grand Carnival
Today is the grand Carnival
Tomorrow is me son funeral.[54]

Maypole Dancing

One of the enduring practices brought to Tobago by the Grenadian workers on estates and in Scarborough businesses was maypole dancing. George Leacock recalled that from 1932 onwards the maypole band appeared each year.

The king, the queen; and they plait the maypole in all different forms. They make it like a Christmas tree; they make it like a cone. They do all sorts of things. *Very pretty*, you know![55]

Another recollection of this custom came from Leo and Keziah Solomon, who saw it played by Tobago children in Bethel, Black Rock and Plymouth. Leo Solomon was the guitarist accompanying Donald Job, a Plymouth chantwel, whose song was the same as the White Rose road march quoted on page 164, except for the change of name.

LS: Some girls will be playing, and they will be going round and plaiting the ribbon round the pole. One person stand up and hold the pole; might be two, if one is not a strong person. Two persons stand up and hold the pole, and the children go round and pass in between one another and plaiting the pole, so when they reach down to the end of the ribbon; when it reach to the top, they will stand up and everybody will dance and dance. ...

Maypole band is on de way
Enemies, try and clear out the way
I don't care what the people say
Maypole bound to rule de day.

KS: If you heare cuatro going down in 'eaven! Nice!

LS: An' Ah crazy clean on dat guitar, especially when de sun hot so! Fella up de road deh had a banjo, used to play de tenor banjo, called Willy Cruickshank. Man, he's a *terrible* banjo man. Oh jeez! When de sun hot so, de banjo cryin', man, 'e bawlin'! Oh je-e-ez! Bawlin', man! Crying, man! Ah had to open up dat guitar to keep down dat banjo, you know. 'Cau' de fella who playin' de cuatro, he wasn' so hip wit' it. I had to open dat guitar, man.[56]

Speech Bands

The speech bands were a traditional Tobago art form that found a place in the Carnival. The villages that they sprang from included Bethel, Culloden, Les Coteaux, Mt. Thomas, Parlatuvier and Plymouth. Not all villages had speech bands. Usually, each speech band built its own bamboo-and-coconut-branch tent for its practice and its contests with visiting speech bands. All their members were male, accompanied by tambourines, fiddles and steel triangles. They drew on older speech traditions, but each year they wrote their speeches and practised them. Sometimes the speeches alluded to topical events. At the end of each speech, the orator would say, 'Draw yuh bow, Mister Fiddler.'

Two bands would meet. Each band had a roster of characters, who came forward to give their speech and their acts in a certain order. Therefore, the Robins of one band would be followed by the Robins of the other in a competitive exchange of speeches. The usual order, regulated by the band's Commander, was Robins, Pupule or Devil, Creator, Sealy, Norway, Hero Conqueror, Lord Wallace, Lord Hampton, Duke of Wellington, and the King. Sometimes Hero and Conqueror were separate characters. Alfred Smart (b.1915) recalls:

> After the King come in, then you get Valentine, which is his son. And you get Doctor too. The Duke will kill his son, and he lie down there as if he's dead. The Doctor will come now, and the Doctor will go round and make all sorts of *simmy dimmy* [antics]. 'Doctor, Doctor, try yuh best. Doctor, Doctor, try yuh best.' Deh playing the violin, you know.[57]

Noel Felix, who used to play King in the Castara–Parlatuvier speech band for the Prime Minister's Best Village competition in the 1960s, gave examples of some of his speeches, which are in the style recalled from his boyhood in Parlatuvier. The lead players in the speech band at Parlatuvier where he grew up were Levi Duncan, Eric Phillip and George Irvine.

> Pink and blue
> Was nothing new
> England flag dat was reigning
> Was red, white and blue
> My case was judge by lawyer Kalloo
> Ah scorn de nation
> To speak to a blue-foot bwoy like you.

Den seh:

> You draw yuh bow, fiddler!

And de tambrine start to play. A next one say:

> Ah tell you, stop
> And if you don't stop
> I put you in my lap
> And I give you seventy-seven slap
> An' Ah feed you on nutten else
> Mo'e dan naked cassada pop.

Dat is cassava porridge, called cassada pop. Yes.[58]

The Carnival arts gave space to various kinds of speechifying: in the speech bands, in picong, oratorical calypsoes, and the performances accompanying masquerades. Mastery of language won respect from the hearers. These arts built on a long tradition of oratory in the New World that, according to Roger Abrahams, is an African retention. Rohlehr states that such bombastic oratory had African, European and local antecedents.[59]

Abrahams makes three significant points. First, concerning Plymouth, Tobago, he argues that 'the spirit of cooperation dominates' and guides the way in which authority in the speech bands is shared by the King and the Commanders. This study supports his perception about the strong communal norms. Throughout, the individual artist was always integral to the group and acting on its behalf. Secondly and in consequence, even though chantwels and speech-makers distinguished themselves as virtuosos, the very means of competition became a means of co-operating within and between villages; in Abraham's words, 'Conflict becomes a positive mode of socialization.' Thirdly, these oratorical arts showed clearly that the speakers used a range of speaking styles in the continuum between the Creole vernaculars and Standard English. Respect and status were bound up with bombastic eloquence and mastery of Standard English. The Carnival arts therefore reflected that, in the process of creolization, individuals and groups took part, as well as they could, in both ends of the linguistic continuum.[60]

Decline of Carnival and Singing Bands

After World War II, the Tobago Carnival declined. Many of the youthful chantwels emigrated in search of work; some joined the Police Force and could no longer take part in those activities. Even Mason Hall, which had a vibrant singing band, ceased to have Carnival after 1945.

By the end of the 1940s, there were very few bands in the Scarborough Carnival, and scores of Tobagonians went to Trinidad to see the masquerade. In 1952 a group of them returning on the boat took the decision to improve Tobago's Carnival. They were George Leacock, a businessman, C. P. Roberts, a teacher, and Henry Smith, owner of Brown Betty restaurant and bar. On the advice of George Ottley, the Warden, they formed a Carnival Development Committee.[61]

But Tobago's Carnival remained miniscule by comparison with Trinidad's. As the calypso art form evolved, the singing bands became extinct, and the individual artists who excelled made their way to the calypso tents of Trinidad.

3.   THE EARLY STEELBANDS

The steelband was invented by underprivileged young men in Port of Spain, Trinidad, in the 1930s. The first instruments were dustbins, discarded oil drums, biscuit tins and paint pans; today the main instruments are oil drums. The immediate predecessor to the steelband was the tamboo bamboo band, in which various sizes and lengths of bamboo were struck to give different tones. The tamboo bamboo instruments were rhythmic, with varying tones, but they could not play tunes.[62] In Tobago, tamboo bamboo bands existed in the 1930s at Belle Garden, Charlotteville, Les Coteaux, Plymouth, and elsewhere.

According to Alford Paul (b.1934), the first steelband was started at Les Coteaux in 1943, under the influence of a visitor from Trinidad.

In 1943 a man came from Trinidad. And we called him the Robust Man, because he had some cuts on his neck. ... And he brought with him a paint pan, those four-gallon paint pan that it have four notes. He used to rent an apartment inside of the village, and on evenings he would bring this down between his legs in front the door and he would play different things. ... And I as a young guy, a schoolboy, with others, we'll go and dance to his tunes and look at him and so forth. But I remember the Christmas night of 1943, we took to the street with this man, and we gather all sort of old iron and old pan, and all these things, and we beat tunes. We wasn't in unison, but we had the

timing and the rhythm, and we beat all over the village in the night, man, ... until abut midnight.

That was the beginning of steelband in Les Coteaux and, I can guarantee you, in Tobago. Because this is 1943 December we talking about.

The man left very early in 1944. ... And in 1944 it was a little dormant with the steelband.

But I can remember in 1945, when we had VE Day, Victory over Europe, that's the end of the 1939–45 war, we took to the street. And we were a little more united. Gather all different pans, some with notes on them, and we marched through the village VE Day, up and down ... and we sang ... 'Hitler dead, war done!'

My big brother [Japheth Paul] was four years older than me; he started to develop the steelband here in Les Coteaux. Putting notes. And I took up the pan and started to beat the pan. Some of them, you call it ping pong [tenor pans], we used to beat it with the raw stick.[63]

[Japheth] organized the steelband in the village. There were about six of us. I was the smallest one and I had the smallest pan. We started to play tunes. ... We didn't carry a name, but ... I inscribed on my pan, Pearl Harbour.

The first Carnival after the war was in February 1946. Mr Paul described it:

And in Scarborough there were two or three main steelbands. Lucky Jordan—that was the town band; the leader was Christopher Gaskin. And then there was Rhythm Tigers; that was further up Wilson Road. ... and then there was Fair Valley steelband from Moriah ... led by two Saunders brothers. ... They played mas; they played red Ju-Ju [African warriors]; ... and Lucky Jordan, they were the black Ju-Ju.[64]

Lucky Jordan were more improved than the other steelbands, because Christopher Gaskin, the leader, came from Trinidad. ... I understand he used to be in Alexander Ragtime Band [acclaimed as the first steelband in Trinidad]. So he had ideas. And he came and he tuned pans. He came to Les Coteaux when my big brother was alive, and he helped him.[65]

Thus, by 1946, at least four steelbands existed independently in Tobago, each under the impetus of men who had returned from residence in Trinidad, where the movement had started.

Side by side with these developments in the early 1940s, some of the Tobago bamboo bands were innovating to transform themselves into bands with a variety of instruments, as happened at Plymouth, according to George 'Josey'

Richardson, a respected pioneer of the Tobago steelband movement. He described Desperadoes at Plymouth before 1947:

A guy named Humphrey James, Urban Archer, Humphrey's brother, who was Christopher James, Russell Ford, Seaton Sandy and Egent Yorke. These fellas, they had what you call a bamboo band. They had things like bamboo flutes [homemade fifes], locally made. They even had pieces of bamboo, which shape like saxophones; you know, they cut holes in it and put these cigarette paper over them. They used even combs. And they started a little orchestra. There was another fella, I must mention his name, because he was very outstanding; he used to play the drums or traps, as we call it. His name is Lecinth Roberts. ... well, that is how we started, you know, and these boys used to have a few engagements, even in dances.

And then they used to have—well, they had the regular orchestra drums, because there was an old string band, which break up after a time, and they gave these boys the drums and so on. And they used to use that.

Well, this guy, Lecinth Roberts, he used to play that. They had a lot of engagements ..., because there was no other band or anything in the village, whether string or otherwise; that was the only thing.[66]

Thus, in addition to the earliest steelbands, there were transitional bands with bamboo instruments, which incorporated other instruments and innovated, using bamboo to produce both rhythm and melodies. Richardson recalls Desperadoes at Plymouth, Invaders at Lambeau, and Casablanca at John Dial as the three transitional bands. Interestingly, they all had the names of early steelbands in Port of Spain.

After the death of Japheth Paul in December 1948, Alford Paul became the captain of the Les Coteaux band, which called itself North Stars from 1951. In 1950, in preparation for the Carnival, he got advice on pans from Invaders steelband in Port of Spain, then led by the celebrated pannist Elliott ('Ellie') Mannette, and they received pans from Cross Fire steelband, also in Port of Spain, led by Sterling Betancourt, another hero of the steelband movement. Paul established a strong relationship with Betancourt thereafter. 'And there I developed more and more the art of steelband.'

Between 1946 and 1950, several new steelbands emerged without bamboo instruments. Paul

recalls the following, besides Fair Valley, Lucky Jordan, Northern Star, and Rhythm Tigers, the bands that had existed before 1946: Casablanca at John Dial, led by the Collett brothers; Desperadoes from Plymouth, which became a full-fledged steelband by 1947 under Lytton 'Bomber' Stewart, a teacher; Black Swan at Whim, led by Hucill Edwards; and Tokyo from Mt. Grace, led by Hubert Peterkin, also known as 'Tokyo'. Renwick Prescott was a leader of Tokyo also.

In the '40s Tokyo was the best steelband in Tobago. They were the best. Sidney Thomas [one of the leading members of Tokyo] was a steelband man par excellence. I learn a lot from him. ... 70 per cent of that band were teenagers. Under 20. They were the best. They were *far* ahead of us![67]

George 'Josey' Richardson is a founder of two of the steelbands of the 1950s. From 1947 he had lived in Trinidad at St. James, where he had become a member of Tripoli steelband. On his return to Tobago, he founded Tripoli steelband at Plymouth in 1950. A few former members of the Plymouth bamboo band joined Tobago's Tripoli, but in general, younger men were the mainstay of the band. Richardson also founded Katzenjammers at Black Rock c.1952.

The steelband movement spread rapidly among young men in their late teens and twenties. According to Alford Paul, in the early 1950s, besides the ones named above, there existed the following in their respective settlements: Boys' Town in Lucy Vale; Eastern Syncopators, Goodwood; Elite Boys, Scarborough; Free French, Canaan; Harmony Kings, Speyside; Invaders, Lambeau; Red River, Roxborough; Sputnik (today Redemption Sounds), Bethel; West Side Symphony, Patience Hill. There were also bands at Buccoo, Castara, Delaford, Glamorgan, Mason Hall and Mt. Pleasant.

In general, because of the cohesive village structure of Tobago, the bands were not associated with gang warfare, violence and police brutality, as occurred in Trinidad. There was stigma against the steelbands in some districts, usually because their instruments were noisy, but the movement became an important channel for the musical creativity of one segment of the young. They embraced the pans more readily than the traditional tambourine-and-fiddle music of their grandparents and the string bands of their parents. Traditionally, the accompaniment at weddings was tambourine and fiddle, with a steel triangle. Alford Paul describes how initially the steelband eclipsed the older instruments at Les Coteaux:

> What happened, the steelband took over from that string band and also from the tambourine. At one time the tambourine was dormant, you know. People never used to bother with the tambourine. When people getting married, we [North Stars steelband] played bachelor's night and marched them the day. Tambourine became dormant for a long, long time. And the string band went out.[68]

Thus, steelbands became one stream of modern music that captured the imagination of the young.

Some villages with singing bands had no steelbands, and some with steelbands had no singing bands; some also had no speech bands. Les Coteaux, like many villages, had neither singing band nor chantwel in the 1930s and 1940s, but it had an excellent speech band and it developed an early steelband. The patterns were affected by the history of each village, and by the gifts and influence of individuals returning from Trinidad.

4. FROM STRING BANDS TO MODERN ENSEMBLES

The musicians born between 1900 and 1915 grew up with the African drums, tambourine, fife, string instruments, and the music of the traditional dances. Many of them spoke of these older dances as the tradition of their parents and grandparents. However, as young men, they gravitated to the string bands. By 1930 the string bands were undergoing transformation. Wind instruments such as the clarinet, saxophone, trumpet and trombone had been known in Tobago through the Constabulary Band when it went each year from Trinidad, and had occasionally been seen at church concerts.[69] In the 1920s jazz music came into its own in the USA, and the clarinet, saxophone and trombone became attractive to young Tobago musicians. By 1930 these instruments became more available to the populace, owing to return migration from Curaçao, Maracaibo and elsewhere.

George Leacock described how the change occurred in Rockley Vale.

> There was a fella from Plymouth who went away to Venezuela, and remained there for many years. That is

about 1931, thereabout, and when he came back to Tobago—I can't remember his name, you know—he had the people in Tobago going. He brought a brass-plated saxophone from Maracaibo, and he raised a band in Plymouth. ...[70]

> I can't tell you what the band was, but he was the leader of the band. And you know I like these things, so I used to follow him. And he used to come to town more or less on pay days, and centre himself at Dias' rum shop, with these few fellas with the cuatro and guitar, and serenade. It was very unusual. That was the first start.

> Well, after that, my brother [Talbot Leacock]—he is now a resigned Sergeant—he and this same Marse Jim Hamilton and a few other Rockley Vale boys got together and formed a band. ... Jimmy Best, he played the bass. Then we had my brother played the ukelele banjo. ... And we had Sugar Wilfred [Rockley Vale chantwel] playing a cuatro, and somebody else playing a guitar—can't remember. And we had one Macdougall blowing a fife. Well, Stanley Duke, he also used to blow a fife. He was in that band too. ... and they called it Mayfair Jazz Orchestra. And they started playing with their fife, and ukulele, and bass and violin.

> Well, they started a kind of economical saving between the band. And my brother, he bought after some time, for himself, a tenor banjo; something looking very nice. And with the savings of the band from playing, they ordered a drum and traps quite from Jettel—that was the name of the company in the UK. And they sent down a drum and traps set-up, but not a very big one; and they paid something like one pound extra for marking the name on the drum—Mayfair Jazz Orchestra.

> The next thing, they ordered from the same firm a clarinet. Well, Stanley Duke, they set aside his flute, and they gave him the clarinet. Well, that was the property of the band. Macdougall dey blowing his flute, but he still jealous of Duke playing the clarinet. The next thing they ordered was a tenor saxophone. Well, the clarinet now was handed to Mac[dougall], and Duke had the saxophone. Well, that was the first time Tobago ever saw—plus the fella from Plymouth—a saxophone, a drum and traps, and a clarinet. Other than seeing them once a year when the Police Band come here. So that was the first jazz band that had those instruments in Tobago.[71]

Another important Scarborough band was Jazz Hawks, started in the early 1930s by Arthur Winter (later the Trinidad and Tobago Harbour Master). Winter was an outstanding trumpeter and, after a visit to Tobago at Easter 1932 by Jazz Hounds, the leading Trinidad music band led by Bert McClean, he formed Jazz Hawks, 'with Reginald Toby, and a whole side of good, elite boys. And they had it swinging.'[72] Among the Jazz Hawks was Rupert Nurse, a teacher at BHS from 1932 to 1936, who was the band's leader in 1936. Nurse was later well known as a bass musician in the UK.

Thus, the youthful musicians, some of them migrants to Tobago, were swiftly embracing the new instruments and new styles which included, according to Leacock, 'jive and the rocking boat'.[73] Even though the repertoire of these new music bands was wide, the fact that some of them declared themselves to be jazz bands shows that they had been influenced by the emergence of jazz in the USA.

Outside of Scarborough, similar developments were taking place. In 1928 Branford Williams (b.1910), a chantwel, started Thrilling Star, one of the leading music bands, at Patience Hill when he was still a teenager. The members were Leo Solomon, cuatro; Lionel Louis, ukelele banjo; Valley Phillip, alto saxophone; Kernell Samuel, trumpet; Joseph Williams, clarinet; Dennis Roberts, trumpet, 'but he was a guitar man'; and Dennis London and Taylor Wood on the kettle drums and cymbals. Branford Williams played the tenor sax and sometimes the fife.[74]

At Mason Hall, Tom Shade started Tom Shade and His Boys c.1938. Tom started on the clarinet and later played the saxophone; his brother Henry was a saxophonist. The other members, all young Mason Hall men, were Gerald Adams, saxophone; Harthorne Adams and Herbie Dennis, trumpet; Conrad Dennis, bass; Raymond Lyons and Stephen Smith, guitar; and Atrill Morrison and 'Monarch' Smart, drums. When asked whether the saxophone was still a new instrument in Tobago in the 1930s, Henry Shade (b.1910) replied:

Oh, yes! You couldn't find another one! Two guitar, two cuatro and a flute is what you had when I was a boy growing up. … that was all the instruments we had.

Therefore they started the band because 'we wanted to do something better than what we had.'

Later, Conrad and Herbie Dennis and their children, and some of the children of Tom and Henry Shade formed Little Seven orchestra, a very popular band in the 1960s.[75]

At Parlatuvier in the 1930s a similar band appeared. Alfred Smart, who played the tenor banjo and the clarinet, said of the village band:

We had drum and strap, we had saxophone, we had trumpet and all dese things.[76]

Leo Solomon (1906–1999) from Thrilling Star recalled other music bands of the same period, with mainly young musicians:

LS: Mason Hall, Tom Shade band. And they had one in Belle Garden, Frederick Brothers. They had one in Scarborough, Stanley Skeete; tall, dark fellow. Then after years, after Stanley come and let go, then they had one Chris Alexander with … Leacock. George Leacock brother. They had a band in Whim too— Artiman Thomas, Sylvester Martin. Then we had one in Hope … the only one I can call the name is Purvis Caesar; he used to play in that band.

SCJ: So all these musicians were of your generation?

LS: Yeah; some was younger.[77]

Branford Williams confirmed that the majority of the musicians in the emerging bands with wind instruments were young men:

SCJ: So these bands that you mentioned—the Mason Hall band, Alexander band, Frederick band, your band—they were mainly young people, or older people?

BW: They was around the same type o' young fellas … young fellas about twenty odd and so on.

In 1933, according to the *Tobago Times*, there were six 'jazz bands' in Tobago.[78]

Leo Solomon also explained the musical preferences of people of different generations. He described the transition to clarinets, saxophones and other wind instruments, and referred to the saxophone that reached Plymouth from Maracaibo:

LS: And most of those [older] men those days, they couldn't dance the string music. They accustom to the reel dance [with tambourine music]. And I can't dance this tambourine dance. But with the string music, Oh man, I eat you on the floor now, now, now!

SCJ: So really, what you are saying is that there were different dances according to generations? The generation before yours [played the] tambourine, and your generation was much more [into] the string music?

LS: Yes. The brass instruments—saxophone. Well, they started first with fife, guitar, cuatro and violin, you know. Fife, cuatro, guitar and violin. And after this fife, guitar, violin, die out, clarinet came in. After clarinet, saxophone; then trumpet and trombone. Because the band I was playing in came from Patience Hill [Thrilling Star]. We had clarinet, saxophone, trumpet and trombone, with guitar, bass, banjo. It was eight of us playing in the band. And we used to go all about playing. We went into Charlotteville, we went into Parlatuvier; don't talk about around the area. …

SCJ: Your band, the Patience Hill band, was one of the first music bands?

LS: No. So far, well, we first had these blowing instruments. Then Frederick Brothers, and after that, well, the others came in. They had a band in Plymouth, but no blowing instrument. Was only guitar, fife and cuatro. A fella called Willington; Willington was from Les Coteaux, but he used to play; his son.

Then come, yes, 'e had saxophone. Willy Williams came from … Maracaibo, and brought a saxophone, and they had a band there in Plymouth. Well, they had in Canaan, but no blowing instrument—only guitar, fife, cuatro. Camillo Phillips and George Baird used to blow the fife.

Solomon explained why the saxophone was preferred to the fife:

LS: By the way, John Branford Williams have a fife home now. … It has keys, and they would make variation with these keys, you understand. It had one hole up here, and it has six holes down below; and it has keys over it. Now these fife made up in such a way, as to—during the course of the night, you find string instruments would climb up. After it get still in the night, and the string instrument draw the cold, they will raise gradually. So this fife man had to pump his fife to meet the height of the instrument.

SCJ: You mean the tone would rise?

LS: It rises. Where we take that first string, D, and you come G. A certain time after midnight, it would rise higher, a higher pitch; and sometimes you had to break the instrument down. You had to break down the high set. Because when you drop down that fife right away down, and it can't go higher, you had to break down the set to come to that.

Well, after years, you come to the saxophone business; that never happen. Saxophone, we play all through the night, because you had no pump to pump. So we going through all the night, only change the keys, you understand. Just change the keys.

If we start in G, well, sometime you had to play C, in order to pick up. When early in the morning, you play D chord, or F. … You play Ray Minor, Me Minor, C Minor, Sol Minor, Me Minor. And accordingly, when you get these sets, you go right through the night until three o'clock in the morning. If by chance the dance didn't score, well, after intermission, you call it off.[79]

Amelia Bovell (b.1912) explained the differences across the generations in the knowledge of the traditional music and dances:

AB: Well, de bouquet dance, deh used to get lancers, castillian an' all dese kinda tings. Pure old people, becarse dat time now, I was a young girl about tuteen, fo'teen years growin' up, o' smaller. My grandparents dem used to kerry me up in de place up deh had bouquet dance. Deh blowin'. Dem tambrine—dah is tambourine—an' dis Rufus Briggs, but he dead fuh years now, used to play 'e fife, and yuh heare dem a' play. De people dem a' dance cudrille [quadrille] an' all dese tings. But I was a young little chile growin'. Ah didn' get to *experience* it properly. …

Ah born in 1912. Suh dese tings now, dah is *years*. Because my big girl, deh doh know nutting about dat. Deh di' have—dem say what? wha' yuh call it—'eel an' toe polka, an' all dem ting. Buh yuh ha' to get somebody who was *playin'* dem music deh.

SCJ: So younger people like yourself never learned bouquet dance?

AB: Nuh, me never learn dat. Me learn de dance weh dem used to play wid *dis* music, saxophone business.[80]

She herself mastered the castillian, which was danced in dance halls and concerts, but none of the other older dances.

So important was the saxophone as a new instrument among popular musicians, that an unknown Canaan chantwel heralded its coming in a beautiful song, which shows the close interplay between the player, the music, and his audience. Mrs Cassie Homeward (1911–2003) recalled that it had been sung in Bethel in the 1930s:

Play, Bayliss, boy, play away
Play, Bayliss, boy, play away
Play, Bayliss, boy, play away
And he in de saxophone

Let de people dem come and see
Let dem, to come and see
Let de people dem come and see
We are playin' de saxophone

Play, Bayliss, boy, play away
Play, Bayliss, boy, play away
Play, Bayliss, boy, play away
We play on de saxophone

Let de people dem come and see
Le-et dem come and see
Play, Bayliss, boy, play away
And we play on de saxophone.[81]

Included in the music played by the youthful bands were popular tunes that they learned from gramophone records for waltz, two-step, polka, and other dances. An example of a gramophone song is 'You Got Me Crying Again', as sung by Branford Williams.

You got me cryin' again
You got me cryin' again
What is your love all about
I am in, I am out

Your kisses came from afar
Came from your lips, not your heart
It could be happy and den
Somebody new
Look good to you

You got me cryin' again
Just cryin'
For you.[82]

Another, for waltzing, was sung by Emeldalina Nicholson.

Time will tell how much I love you
Only with a smile and grace
Every day and every night
Only time will tell

Time will tell, time will tell
Only time will tell

Time will tell how much I love you
Ever the thought [inaudible]
Only because it's true
But only, only, only
Only time will tell.[83]

But these young musicians also drew upon the traditions of their elders, taking the older folk songs into the dance halls. One such song was 'Uncle Sam Say', which can be dated to the Spanish–American War in Cuba starting in 1895. It was also known in Grenada. In Tobago, to the generation born between 1900 and 1925, it was a children's song; and it was also sung to accompany traditional dances such as lancers. In keeping with the multiple contexts of folk materials, 'Uncle Sam Say' became also a dance-hall song in the 1930s, as sung by Emeldalina Nicholson.

Uncle Sam say
To get your gun in han'
Uncle Sam say
To get your gun in han'

Oh, Uncle Sam say
To get your gun in han'
For there is hot war
In Cuba tonight
My darling
Hot war in Cuba tonight

Oh, when you going, when you going around! [Sings.]

La la la la la la
La la la la la la
Uncle Sam say
To get your gun in han'
Oh, Uncle Sam say
To get your gun in han'
For there is hot war
In Cuba tonight
My darling
Hot war in Cuba tonight.

Thus, the influence of return migration, immigration and new popular genres, with the coming of talking movies and the gramophone, swiftly changed the style and repertoire of the young, male, Tobago musicians. By 1940 the string bands had been superseded by ensembles that had string instruments, clarinets, saxophones, trumpets, trombones and various percussion instruments, on the one hand. On the other hand, the steelband movement attracted an important segment of the young musicians.

5. MUSICIANS IN THE DOMINANT CLASS AND THE MIDDLE STRATA

In the late 1920s and early 1930s, a stellar gathering of musicians lived in and around Scarborough, some of them teachers and civil servants on transfer from Trinidad. They included Nelson Comma, guitarist, pianist and singer, for six months of 1924; Comma was the first Inspector of Schools to rise from the ranks of the teaching service in Trinidad and Tobago. Later came his daughter Olga and her husband, Fitz Gerald Maynard, from 1936; and Mrs C. M. Tull. All these were pianists. Mrs Tull also sang well. Olga Comma Maynard started the Nelson Comma Junior School in Scarborough c.1941 and taught music to her little charges; the school occasionally gave musical evenings.

The most admired of the migrants was John S. Donaldson, one of the nation's finest composers and pianists. His compositions included 'Boca Chimes', 'Gasparee', 'Wave, Cane, Wave', 'My Island Home' and 'Broken Things'. The words to 'Boca Chimes' were written by Mr Justice A. D. Russell, a retired judge and a *littérateur*, and Donaldson set them to music. Dr. J. D. Elder recalls that Donaldson collected, studied and played the local folk songs.

JDE: Anyhow, when he came up [to Port of Spain] on a Saturday, we would get together, and I would bring music from the bush; and he would play it on his— Oh, Lord, I can never, I don't understand why God should take away a good man like that! To hear that man play some of those folk songs on the piano, I wish to God I'd said to him, 'Look here, play all these, and let's put it on tape.' You never know. ... Donaldson made a contribution by writing up some of these things. I don't know where they could be found. ... But he used to play them for me.

SCJ: Play folk songs and write the music?

JDE: Yes, he used to arrange it, you see, and then play it. Most times, he arranged in his head, with the chords in his head. And he used to do it, I feel, as a pastime.[84]

These newcomers in the 1920s and 1930s met earlier gifted musicians. Volume I, Chapter 9 discussed the contributions of Archie John, S. J. Gordon and others. In the first years of the twentieth century, Scarborough's prominent accomplished pianists included Catherine Adesia McEachnie (later Mrs Fraser) (1883–1914), daughter of Henry H. McEachnie, a druggist, and his wife Catherine; and Ann Evelina Gordon (later Mrs Cordner, daughter of Sinai and Margaret Gordon). Dr. Thomas Kenny and Dr. Edwin Blanc, both transferred to Tobago from Trinidad, also played beautifully. Geraldine Prince (1874–1916), having qualified at the Royal College of Music, London, as a pianist, violinist and vocalist, was, from 1900, one of the foremost music teachers.[85] One of her students was Edwina Biggart (later Hutchinson), who by 1922 was an accomplished pianist, having also studied in Port of Spain under Miss Maillard. Edwina was the daughter of James A. A. Biggart, MLC, and his wife Marie. Some of the planters and their relatives were also very gifted, in particular, Mrs Lucy Latour (later Latour-Link), violinist; Miss Hamilton, pianist; Mrs Kernahan, a daughter of Dr. E. Blanc, pianist; Mrs Sworder, vocalist; and Mrs Nelly McCall, pianist and organist.

In Scarborough, Roundelle and Catherine O'Keiffe had a very musical family. Roundelle O'Keiffe (d.1902) was a particularly good singer. One of the sons was Gerald O'Keiffe, the outstanding chantwel discussed in this chapter. Another son, Hugh Bannister O'Keiffe, fought in Europe in World War I, underwent voice training in France after the war, and became an outstanding baritone. His only surviving song, a waltz composed c.1930, 'When Evening Shadows Fall', was well known, widely performed, and highly regarded in the colony. The words, as given by Jean O'Keiffe Daniel, his niece, are as follows:

The sun in all its splendour
Now is sinking in the west
O'er vale and hill, near dale and rill
The birds have gone to rest
And through the silent mystery
Of Nature's sweetest hour
I'm thinking of a soul so sweet
Even as the purest flower

The nightingale now carols forth
In strains so sweet and clear
I often wonder, dearest heart
If you too sometimes hear
Such melody at eventide
God sends to one and all
A gift of purest love and song
When evening shadows fall

Chorus
When evening shadows fall, sweetheart
I think then most of you
For in the garden as I pass
The roses touched with dew
Just waft to me a message sweet
A message and a call
From you, my dearest heart, to me
When evening shadows fall.[86]

One of the most influential of the Scarborough musicians was the well-beloved Dr. George Hilton Napoleon Theodore Clarke (1894–1941), a DMO. Clarke arrived in Tobago in 1919 from Toco in Trinidad, where he had so endeared himself to the populace that they had requested that he be not transferred. When their request was refused, they often travelled to Tobago by boat for medical attention from him. He was an accomplished cellist and baritone and, by 1922, had formed an orchestra in Scarborough, with W. F. O. Paul

(Clerk of the Peace and Sub-Registrar) as violinist; Egerton Blizzard, Scarborough Methodist Head Teacher, on the fife; and Miss E. Ferreira, whose instrument was probably the piano, of which she was a teacher. George Leacock knew the band in the late 1920s; he recalled:

> It had one Baird played the flute. Then it had John Solomon, played the cuatro. And it had another Baird, who played the guitar. Those were the men of the days. And somebody else played the violin; and he took all the jobs around.[87]

The Comfort and Happiness Promotion Club (CHPC), which met on Sundays at Mt. Parnassus, the home of L. A. Peters, also promoted music, with the young people with primary education as its target group. Its members included many of the best educators in Tobago, and John Donaldson was its Musical Director. Music and musical evenings were a part of its activities.[88]

Besides John Donaldson, several of the teachers were composing music. Most noteworthy was Thomas Aaron Telemaque who, after training as a teacher, became a Probation Officer and earned his MA in Social Science and a Diploma in Child Psychology by 1954. Telemaque composed several songs which were published in the USA, among them 'Take Me Back to Crusoe's Isle', 'Emile Dear', and 'Give Me Love', all of which were very popular among Tobago musicians. His brother, Harold Moses Telemaque (1909–1982), the distinguished poet, also composed songs; and the Telemaque brothers were members of the National Song Writers' Guild, Hollywood, USA.[89] Towards the end of his life Harold Telemaque composed hymns as well.

Mason Hall Government School, opened in 1938, was the first state school in Tobago. With its spacious, well-built facilities, it was the Government's showpiece, and they chose as head teacher, Benjamin J. Sealy ('Teacher Ben'), who quickly became the most popular teacher in Tobago. Sealy had been the champion Trinidad and Tobago athlete in 1920, and had represented the colony in intercolonial athletics in 1922. He was an excellent cricketer, both batsman and bowler, and had played in Test cricket for the West Indies against England in 1933. He was an outstanding teacher, and under his leadership Mason Hall Government School won the Madoo Medal, the first prize for efficiency among the

schools in the colony, in 1941 and 1942. Sealy was an organist, pianist and actor; and he was one of the artists in a dramatic group called The Tobago Players, which did a four-day tour of Tobago early in 1943, and took their performance of *Off Duty* to Port of Spain in February 1943. The producer was Captain Robert H. Harrower, a Canadian immigrant, who helped to build the Scout movement in Tobago; in 1949 Harrower was also President of the Tobago Amateur Football Association.[90]

Lionel Mitchell and L. A. Peters also composed songs in the 1930s. One of Peters' songs became known throughout Tobago as a rallying cry for staying on the land:

> Come boys, I have something to tell you
> Come here, I'll whisper it low
> You're thinking of leaving the homestead
> So don't be in a hurry to go
> The land has a lot to offer
> So think of the vices and sing
> And wealth is not made in a day, boys
> Don't be in a hurry to go
>
> *Chorus*
> Stay on the farm, stay on the farm
> Though profits come in rather slow
> Stay on the farm, stay on the farm
> Don't be in a hurry to go.[91]

So prolific was the outpouring of music and literature by the early 1940s that, at the Anglican Teachers' Get Together of 1942, the programme was mainly of items composed by the teachers themselves. Cecil Louis sang Thomas Telemaque's 'Give Me Love', accompanied by Ben Sealy.[92]

6. SACRED MUSIC-MAKING

Choirs as Village Tradition

Church and village choirs were an important part of the popular musical traditions, owing to the remarkable influence of the nineteenth-century missionaries like Dr. William Allen Purser and Rev. T. L. Badham, the teachers they raised up in Tobago, and those trained at the Mico and other Caribbean institutions. Purser, a Moravian lay minister, worked with churches of all denominations; Badham was also a Moravian. Testifying to the extraordinary impact of the musical traditions brought by Dr. Purser and other ministers, one of

Purser's students, Rev. Samuel E. Morris, stated in 1910 that as a teacher in Moriah Infant Day School from 1889 to 1891, he had taught 'every piece of music to be found in our present Tune Book from cover to cover.' Rev. William Melancthon Cornelius John, another former student of Dr. Purser, noted that Purser and the missionaries had shaped the musical taste of the people of Moriah.[93] This was also true of all the leeward villages, largely owing to the Moravian influence; and the combined influence of these musicians spread throughout Tobago. Some of the choirs were raised up under the auspices of the churches; others were village choirs, which were free to include people who had 'fallen' and were out of fellowship with the church.

These choirs and the sacred music they sang were strongly entrenched in the Tobago folk musical traditions. In the homes of many of the independent peasants there had been harmoniums since the nineteenth century, and the numbers multiplied in the twentieth; therefore they practised music in their homes. After 1915 a few also had pianos.[94] The teachers trained excellent school choirs, which became the seedbed of the adult choirs. The performance of sacred songs and cantatas for the major events in the church calendar and, indeed, throughout the year in each village, gave ample scope to the talents of these choirs. The lodges and friendly societies in the late nineteenth and early twentieth centuries also gave song services and cantatas. Competition between choirs was keen.

These traditions were reinforced by the work of certain ministers. Within the Anglican Church, Rev. A. B. Eastgate in May 1916 brought together fifteen singers from eight churches in a united choral service in Scarborough to stimulate 'vocal music'. However, the greatest influence came from Rev. Theodor Liley Clemens (1858–1933), a Moravian minister who served in Tobago from December 1888 to 1923, with only brief furloughs. Clemens was a gifted musician, and he composed and published the music for several anthems and hymns. His numerous publications included *Sunday Music*, a collection of 20 hymns that appeared in 1889; a musical rendition of the *Church Litany* for the morning service (1903); *New Music for Our Church Litany*, a liturgy of seven pieces for the Moravian Church (1904); *Andante in C Minor* (1905); *Eight Carols for Christmas* (1912);

Elegy in C Sharp Minor (1913); *Twelve Carols for Christmas* (1919); and *Rex Saeculorum*, an anthem for Lent and Passion week (1925).[95] In addition, he composed rounds to be sung by children, and songs and piano studies to mark special occasions or to honour outstanding individuals. Clemens worked closely with Rev. John E. Weiss, another Moravian pastor and musician, who arrived in Tobago in 1907.

Following in the tradition of Dr. Purser who had conducted a 100-voice choir singing Handel's *Messiah* in 1857, Clemens held annual concerts of combined Moravian choirs. This was the high point of the musical year in the leeward churches.

On 28 January 1904, Clemens staged the combined Moravian choirs at Montgomery; over 100 voices rendered pieces from famous composers. Mitchell J. Prince, himself a musician, commented in the *Mirror*:

> It is not often we hear such excellent singing when all the parts are delicately sustained, nor do we often listen to such an exquisite performance. Too much praise cannot be given to the choir for the very efficient manner in which they acquitted themselves, whilst nothing from us can add to the fame of such a brilliant performer as Mr. Clemens.

Among the singers was a Miss Simmons (probably Edith Simmons, sister of Herman Simmons), hailed as Tobago's Patti (after Anita Patti Brown, a famous African-American soprano singer at the time). Clemens conducted 120 voices in a similar concert in May 1906.[96]

On 7 October 1908, another concert of combined choirs with 100 voices, singing Handel's *Messiah*, was held at Moriah under the supervision of Rev. Clemens and Rev. A. G. Weiss. The performance lasted three hours. *The Mirror's* praise was fulsome:

> As far as memory goes, this has eclipsed every other Moravian concert given in Tobago except the first which was rendered at Fort King George in 1857 under ... the late Dr W A Purser ... Every thing was done in order and to time under the chairmanship of Mr T Thornton of Old Grange.[97]

The strength of this musical tradition in the villages cannot be over-emphasized. The singers, although humble village folk, were able to read music and to sing in four-part harmony, learning their parts in the tonic solfa. Some had been taught this at school, where the songs were first learnt in solfa, then with the words, as occurred at Delaford in the childhood of Mrs Henrietta Arthur (1899–1984).

> When he [the Inspector of Schools] to come to inspect, our teacher was Mr Ernest Branche, and he would practise us a song now to sing when de Inspector come. ... We would practise it in music. When de Inspector come, we sing it in music, and after we sing it in words.

Mrs Arthur sang the words of 'Beautiful Home', and then sang a part of it in tonic solfa.

> Our homes on the earth
> Are broken and sad
> For each has a loved one away
> On high in that beautiful home
> All are glad
> And rest be the beauty for aye
>
> *Chorus*
> Home, home
> Beautiful home
> Home, home
> Beautiful home
> Home, beautiful
> Home, beautiful
> Beautiful home
> On high
>
> Doh doh doh doh ray me
> Me fah fah lah ti doh
> Me soh fah ray soh fah ray me.[98]

Dr. J. D. Elder described the influence of the head teachers in the Windward District, who had been trained at the Mico Training College, Antigua. All these men were accomplished musicians.

> [S. E.] Thibou, [Jacob] Walters, Sam Charity, ... John Smith, four Mico men ... and all of them were great musicians. So, apart from what Purser and the Moravians could do, Thibou was this side, making musicians, singing out of *Singing Class Book*.

Elder also recounted how, in the late nineteenth and early twentieth centuries, the migrants to Charlotteville from the leeward villages, where the Moravian influence was strongest, helped to reinforce this musical tradition:

> But where they get dey music from? With dem people walking up [migrating to] this side from Dr. Purser, with big music, man. Everybody came with their *Singing Class Book*. ... Well, that book was the *Hansard* of those people. They came with a *Singing Class Book*;

they came with a *Pilgrim's Progress*; they came with a Bible; and they came with *The Coming King*, which is a Seven Days [Seventh Day Adventist] book.

> You see, that side [leeward Tobago] was music. And as they came up—Moriah people, Plymouth people, Les Coteaux people—they came with *Singing Class Book*, and singing tonic solfa.

Interestingly, Branford Williams, musician from the leeward village of Bethel, a Moravian stronghold, stated that he had learnt music from Timpson's *Singing Class Book*. And Rev. Samuel E. Morris, a Tobagonian missionary of the Moravian Church who had taught at Moriah under Rev. Clemens from 1889 to 1891, and who himself had been taught by Dr. Purser, wrote that Tobago was '*the* Moravian chorale-singing island of Eastern West Indies'.[99]

For Charlotteville, Elder continued:

> When I say music is central in the lives of these people, I really mean it, eh. When they coming home from fishing, in the evening, you hear ... it's a *whole* choir coming in; boatload by boatload, singing hymns. Tenor, alto, bass, treble, coming inside. And which boat could sing better, and which boat—Because, pretty often, a choirmaster is captain on one boat. One Seed is a fisherman, Sweet Williams is a fisherman, Old Reggie Murray is a fisherman.
>
> ... when you singing music notes, you know, they not singing any words. Is doh, ray, me, fah, soh, lah, te, doh, all the time. Is notes they singing, you know. The four lines on the staff and stave, they singing it note for note, out of their head. Is no joke. It doesn't matter what the hymn is. [Sings.] Sol doh me ray sol .... And they singing that hymn. And *everybody* singing. Tenor, alto, treble, bass. And you hear how bad note pass in such and such a boat; and by time they land, is bitterness. Bad note, and so on.
>
> Music is—wake, work, dead; like when dey making de coffin, like when dey digging de graves, is music, you see.[100]

Thomas Telemaque, educator and songwriter, described the singing meetings at wakes:

> ... the men hardly sing the words of the hymns. They sing the notes. Sometimes there is much controversy over a dotted note, a quaver, a slur, or a rest. Through this, many young men study vocal music with much enthusiasm so that they will not be found wanting at the wakes.[101]

Lionel Mitchell described the keen competition between choirs in the 1920s when he first went to Tobago.

SCJ: Each village would have a choir?

LM: Oh, yes, yes. And that is why, in those days, ... every Sunday you could find somewhere to go and sit down and listen to two choirs singing one against the other.

SCJ: Really? From different villages?

LM: Oh, yes. Different villages. You find this choir singing against that choir; this from this village and that from that village. And there'd be this kind of competition. ... They had their judges. But more or less, it was more again a question of the *meeting*. We mix. ... We meet. Because the people from one village moved with the choir to whatever village the choir was going.

SCJ: You met that in the '20s when you came here?

LM: Oh, yes! Oh, yes! ... In the church choirs, you had these tonic solfa masters, if you call them so, who were roped in to the church choirs because of their ability to teach from the solfa. That is why you were able to have church choirs in nearly all the villages in Tobago. And that is why, when you listen to a church service [with] most of these choirs, you don't hear just the melody, but you hear the *harmony* coming out there, because those old fellas who knew their tonic solfa well, they would teach parts. There was part-singing done. That is gone by the vogue now. ... You don't hear that *harmony*; you don't hear that coming out now.

But in those days, you had all those anthems and all that, where you have a lot of part-singing, and they used to be able to teach their choirs. Because the choir master who used to be able to get his choir to do the most parts—four parts, and he doing all four parts—he will always be regarded as the man, as against the fella whose choir will do two parts—soprano and alto. But you had these fellas who will give you the tenor and who will give you the bass, and you have the four parts going together there. If you listen to singing now in Tobago in the churches on a Sunday, it's not what it used to be at all. I mean, you were *enthrilled* [sic] to listen to the singing! Real harmony coming out there, and the voices blending. Not shouting. ... So the basic reason why Tobagonians are *so* musical, it is because of that solfa. I think so.[102]

In March 1931 the *Trinidad Guardian* noticed the popularity of 'Service of Song Competitions' in Tobago.[103] These competitions were entirely autonomous, organized by the villagers for their pleasure and recreation.

Fitz Gerald Maynard, recalling his first encounter with these traditions in 1922, stated:

They know a lot about this tonic solfa. You'd go to a service in the Mt. St. George church, not that they would sing in the tonic solfa, but you'd hear them singing the bass and tenor *correctly*, from the tonic solfa. ... I do know it was one of the things that I remarked upon in those Tobago days.[104]

Another keen observer, Oris Job-Caesar, writes:

It was wonderful to hear the intricate pieces which were mastered by these choirs and at times with only a tuning fork to give the pitch.[105]

In a 1948 essay, Harold M. Telemaque, describing the traditional serenading of the village choirs at Christmas, explained that they sang, not carols but 'Religious songs taken from a Cantata sung by a largn (sic) Choir':

The bases [sic] and tenors stand in the background and cover like a woollen canopy the sweet tones of the sapranos [sic]. Nowhere have I heard better bases [sic] more resonant, more accurate, more sedate.[106]

Elder's comments on Charlotteville apply to all Tobago:

Thus inside and outside the church, sacred music making became a constant feature of village life.[107]

These traditions influenced the calypsoes emerging from the 1950s onwards. Lionel Mitchell said of Calypso Rose (Macartha Sandy-Lewis), Tobago's foremost female calypsonian:

This girl, Rose, she's a wonderful person on tonic solfa. And again, she comes from Bethel. Again, the Moravian background down there with the tonic solfa. All her calypsoes, she could just sing them in tonic solfa for you. All! And when she's composing a calypso ... [hums] ... she sings it in the tonic solfa for you, and write it down. Oh, yes, she's wonderful.[108]

The Mighty Shadow (Winston Bailey), another outstanding calypsonian, grew up at Les Coteaux with his grandparents, Mr and Mrs Elvan Bailey. Elvan Bailey was a choirmaster.

Music and the Tobago Labour Movement

Choirs singing sacred music became an important part of the Trinidad Workingmen's Association (TWA) in both leeward and windward Tobago. In March 1931, a sacred concert in Scarborough was arranged 'to foster a better esprit de corps between the various sections, and to stir up the movement in Tobago.' Choirs from Scarborough, Black Rock and Glamorgan competed.[109]

In the Windward District, after the unfurling of the banner of the Delaford Section of the TWA in April 1931, a church service was held, followed by a service of 12 sacred songs by the choir of the Delaford Section, the choirmaster being Comrade James E. Clark, the branch Chairman. In the same month, the Delaford TWA choir competed with those of Canaan and Roxborough, with each rendering four items. Two months later, Clark invited John R. Wallace of Roxborough with his choir to competitive singing at St. Paul's School, Delaford, on Sunday 14 June. Roxborough won the competition, the audience having arrived from Roxborough, Speyside and Delaford. Combined choirs of the Delaford, Glamorgan, Scarborough and Roxborough branches of the TWA sang at St. Mary's School, Pembroke, on Sunday 19 July 1931. Some from the Delaford TWA went on Sunday 2 August to Speyside for a sacred song service in the Anglican school, in support of the Speyside Vicarage Fund. The following day, visitors arrived from Charlotteville, Roxborough and Delaford, and spent the day at Speyside, where the Delaford TWA members gave a grand concert and dance.

Although there were attempts to remove Clark from being Chairman of the Delaford branch in August 1931, because he 'spends most [sic] of his time in choir practice than in meetings', the deputy choirmaster of the Delaford Section, Ezekiel Richards, continued the work, leading the choir in support of church activities at Charlotteville in September 1931.[110]

The trade unions and the village choirs were also closely linked in leeward Tobago. To mark the second anniversary of its founding, the Scarborough branch of the Public Works and Public Service Workers Union (PWPSWU) celebrated in October 1939 with a song service by the Canaan village choir at the New Lodge Hall, Canaan. The union proposed to hold a singing meeting in each branch once per month to break the 'monotony' of regular business meetings.[111]

Similarly, when the Tobago Industrial Trade Union's (TITU) Bethel branch received 17 new members on 22 October 1939, they held a 'Sacred Cantata', which was rendered by a small choir conducted by Comrade M. Thomas; a silver collection was taken, while they sang 'Onward Christian Soldiers'.[112]

In 1940 the PWPSWU organized a Recreation Club with three sections, alphabetically named. Section A was for sports and dancing; B was for concerts, cantatas and song services; and C for orchestra. And at the island-wide conference of the union on 9 June 1940, Gaskynd Granger, the national secretary, suggested that a 'Choir of 100 voices should be encouraged to carry on Community singing.'[113]

The labour organizations had favourite hymns and anthems, which encouraged and uplifted the spirits of the workers; the anthem of the PWPSWU was 'We Meet Today in Freedom's Cause'. However, the choirs rendering sacred cantatas and anthems were highly appreciated, since they expressed the accomplishments and musical taste of the members.

An important labour activist was Sammy Peterkin, for decades Tobago's foremost popular singer and guitarist, who played his guitar at some of the workers' functions. Choral singing was integral to these; so too were the local orchestras with saxophones and the newer instruments, like Mayfair Jazz Orchestra, which played at workers' marches and parades.[114]

7. CONCLUSION

Return migration and immigration, in the context of a changing world with new mass media, especially the gramophone and the talking movies, expanded the repertoire of styles in the music of dance and entertainment. Returning migrants from Trinidad brought the Carnival arts, including the steelband, an extraordinary innovation created within the society. The steelband was embraced by many teenagers and young people in their twenties. It displaced the tamboo bamboo bands in the Carnival, and it was enjoyed in many social contexts.

String bands with guitar, violin, cuatro and flutes had been prevalent in the early twentieth century. As jazz music gained popular acclaim in the USA, the string bands were transformed by the rising generation of young male musicians into ensembles where pride of place was given to saxophones, clarinets and trombones. The new stylists played a wide range of music in school-rooms and dance halls, but they incorporated some of the older Tobago folk songs into their work. The tambourine music of the parents and grandparents of those born after 1910 became much less prevalent, although it was still an accompaniment for bongo, reel, jig and other traditional dances.

Thus, the changes in popular music help us to understand the dynamics of cultural change across the generations. They illustrate how each generation *inherits, selects, creates and transforms* its cultural heritage.

The Carnival arts offer useful insights on the complexities of creolization. Firstly, speech bands, ballads and oratorical calypsoes all displayed the importance of speech-making and mastery of the English language. The roots of this emphasis on oratory were African, European and local. The populace creatively appropriated from, and blended, different traditions to suit their purposes. In so doing, they embraced both the vernacular and Standard English, the two poles of the linguistic continuum. Secondly, although there was strong competition between singers, maskers and speakers from different villages, these performers displayed the communal values that undergirded the society. Competition was a creative form of social cohesion.

A native chantwel and calypso tradition was created in 'singing bands', each belonging to, based in, and supported by, its village or settlement. The Tobago chantwels sang on a range of topics with a variety of styles, and their best efforts were second to none. Some of the calypso singers composed ballads, chronicling events and celebrating Tobago. Regrettably, none of their music was recorded.

Among the intelligentsia, there was a great deal of music-making, with at least two composers, Thomas and Harold Telemaque, being members of the Song Writers' Guild of Hollywood, USA. Some of these individuals studied and appreciated the traditional folk musical forms and the folklore.

Sacred music, choirs, and singing in four-part harmony were embedded in the culture of the generations that had been schooled under the missionaries and the Mico-trained teachers up to 1920. At all social levels, four-part singing was a valued social accomplishment. Even at the heart of the early labour movement this was so, as the choirs of the TWA/TLP and the trade unions show.

But if the sacred pervaded the secular, the reverse was also true. By 1940 the authoritative hold of the church on the society was weakening. Over time, cantatas ceased to be important and frequent social events; they are now sung mainly at harvests for the minority who go to the churches. Although 29 choirs entered the competition for village choirs in 1954, they too were waning, and the weekly singing contests have long ceased. Thus, the sacred music tradition with its cantatas, anthems, singing class books, and four-part harmony became, like so many customs of the declining agrarian order, yet another tradition of the elders.

Notes

1 Jacob D. Elder, *Folk Song and Folk Life in Charlotteville* (Port of Spain 1971); *Folksongs from Tobago: Culture and Song in Tobago* (London 1994).

2 *TG*, 9 Jan. 1927, 11. The Charleston was a dance named after the city of Charleston, South Carolina, USA. Its rhythm is a traditional one from West Africa, made popular by a 1923 tune called 'The Charleston' by composer/pianist James P. Johnson, which became extremely well known in the USA and abroad. See 'Charleston (dance)', *Wikipedia Free Encyclopedia*, http://en.wikipedia.org/wike/Charleston_%28dance%29 (accessed 25 May 2006).

3 However, see Tony Hall, '"They Want to See George Band": Tobago Mas According to George Leacock', *The Drama Review* 42, no. 3 (1998): 44–53.

Tamboo bamboo: (French, *le tambour*, drum); percussion instruments made of bamboo. There were different sizes of bamboo and correspondingly different tones.

4 Elder, *Folk Song and Folk Life in Charlotteville*.

5 Gordon Rohlehr, *Calypso and Society in Pre-Independence Trinidad* (Port of Spain 1990), shows that a blending of folk traditions from migrants from the rest of the New World shaped the Trinidad Carnival. Chantwel: from French, *le chanteur*; Trinidad vernacular for a calypso singer.

6 Rohlehr, *Calypso and Society*, 41.

7 For Roxborough, *Mirror*, 2 Mar. 1903, 4; Charles Baird, 29 May 1905, 3, and 16 Nov. 1915, 5; Mason Hall, 8 Jan. 1906, 9, and 7 June 1913, 4–5;

Scarborough, 22 Aug. 1911, 1; Simmons' band, 6 Jan. 1912, 1; 30 Nov. 1912, 3; 18 Jan. 1913, 7; 14 June 1913, 9; 21 June 1913, 4; and 6 Apr. 1915, 10; Capt. Simmons, 8 Jan. 1909, 14; Mt. Grace, 19 Dec. 1910, 5; Lambeau, 31 Jan. 1916, 7; Plymouth, 7 June 1913, 4–5; Lyons', 20 Sept. 1913, 9, and 19 Nov. 1913, 1; Sylvestre, 2 Aug. 1913, 4–5; James Baird, 7 Aug. 1913, 9, and 6 Sept. 1915, 5; Forbes, 14 June 1915, 4, and 31 Jan. 1916, 7; Slaney, *TG*, 21 Apr. 1922, 5, reporting Slaney's death; Alleyne, *The Tobagonian*, May 1945, 5.

8   *POSG*, 9 June 1899, 7, for quotation; *Mirror*, 1 Mar. 1913, 8, and 1 May 1913, 4.

9   *Mirror*, 15 Feb. 1902, 11.

10 *Mirror Supplement*, 6 Mar. 1903, 5.

11 *Mirror*, 16 Feb. 1907, 7; 12 Feb. 1910, 6; 4 Mar. 1911, 4; 26 Feb. 1912, 1; 11 Feb. 1913, 6.

12 *TG*, 22 Feb. 1920, 11.

13 Cyril Wildman, interview, 5 May 1983.

14 Henrietta Arthur, interview with author, 13 May 1983.

15 George Leacock (1915–2005), interview with author, 30 and 31 Aug. 1985.

16 *TG*, 26 Feb. 1931, 3.

17 *TG*, 26 Feb. 1931, 3.

18 Elder, 'Evolution of the Traditional Calypso', 97–98.

19 *TG*, 18 Feb. 1923, 14.

20 The categories here overlap because neat classifications are not possible.

21 Samuel Moore (b.1902), interview, 17 Mar. 1985; James Frank (b.1902), unrecorded conversation with author, 27 Apr. 1983; Cyril Wildman, interview, 5 May 1983.

22 J. D. Elder, 'Evolution of the Traditional Calypso of Trinidad and Tobago: A Socio-Historical Analysis of Song Change' (Ph.D. thesis, University of Pennsylvania, 1967), 29; Rohlehr, *Calypso and Society*, 49.

23 As sung by Jane Ann 'Edna' Thomas (1894–2003), interview with author, 18 July 1992.

24 As sung by Alexandrina Watts (b.1909), interview with author, 2 Jan. 1985, and Annie Caesar (b.1908), 8 Jan. 1985.

25 As sung by Sislyn Craig (1921–1996), unrecorded conversation with author, 29 May 1983.

26 Sidney Gibbs (b.1906), interview, 29 May 1983; George Leacock, interview, 30 and 31 Aug. 1985.

27 Jules de Freitas (1906–1991), interview with author, 26 Apr. 1983; O'Keiffe is also credited with being the composer of a song that became popular in Trinidad: 'Run you run, Kaiser Wilhelm'.

28 As sung by George Leacock, interview, 30, 31 Aug. 1985.

29 Cassie Homeward (1911–2003), with Ivan Taylor and others, interview, 8 Jan. 1985.

30 William Shirer, *The Rise and Fall of the Third Reich: A History of Nazi Germany* (London 1960), 294.

31 As sung by Eileen Guillaume (1916–2004), unrecorded conversation, 22 Apr. 1983.

32 As sung by Eileen Guillaume, unrecorded conversation, 22 Apr. 1983.

33 As sung by George Leacock, interview, 30, 31 Aug. 1985.

34 Elton Arthur (b.1920), interview with author, 12 May 1983.

35 Dalton Andrews (b.1912), interview, 16 May 1983.

36 As sung by Alexandrina Watts, interview, 8 Jan. 1985. Allenby's resignation is reported in *TG*, 25 Dec. 1921, 3.

37 Verses sung by Sidney Gibbs, interview, 29 May 1983; chorus by Lionel Mitchell (1905–1992), interview, 27 Sept. 1984.

38 As sung by Noel Felix (b.1933), interview with author (with Rachel Eastman), 18 May 1983.

39 Hopestan: Hopeton; 'Ringe Hill: Orange Hill.

40 Typewritten in personal correspondence from Ms Alison Armstrong, Scarborough, March 2003; reproduced with minor corrections; reformatted into eight-line stanzas instead of four-line ones.

41 As sung by Leopold Solomon (1906–1999), interview with author, 17 Mar. 1985.

42 Jane Taylor (1912–1989), interview with author, 8 Jan. 1985.

43 As sung by Sislyn Craig, unrecorded conversation, 30 May 1983.

44 As sung by Eric Ottley (1910–1986), interview with author, 12 Mar. 1985

45 As sung by Keziah Solomon (1915–1995), with Leopold Solomon, interview, 17 Mar. 1985; on the date of the purchase, Bobby Smith, brother of Mrs Alefounder, unrecorded conversation with author at Grafton, 28 May 1983. Venture: probably Adventure, the name of a nearby estate.

46 Eric Ottley, interview with author, 12 Mar. 1985.

47 George Leacock, interview, 30, 31 Aug. 1985.

48 Rohlehr, *Calypso and Society*, 55–68. Sislyn Craig, unrecorded conversation, 30 May 1983; Lionel Mitchell, interview, 27 Sept. 1984; Jules Crooks (1903–1993), interview with author, 24 Apr. 1983.

49 George Leacock, with Cecile Leacock, interview, 30, 31 Aug. 1985.

50 Jules Crooks, interview, 24 Apr. 1983.

51 William Pope (b.1905), interview, 28 May 1983.

52 Alfred Smart (b.1915), interview with author, 18 May 1983.

53 Samuel Moore, interview, 17 Mar. 1985.

54 George 'Colonel' Holder (b.1911), interview with author, 17 Feb. 1985. On Kalinda and stick fights, see J. D. Elder, 'Kalinda: Song of the Battling Troubadours of Trinidad', *Journal of the Folklore Institute* 3, no. 2 (1966): 192–203.

55 George Leacock, interview, 30, 31 Aug. 1983. The first mention of maypole bands in Tobago's

Carnival in the *Trinidad Guardian* was on 26 Feb. 1928, 13.

56 Leopold Solomon, interview, 17 Mar. 1985.

57 Alfred Smart (b.1915), interview with author, 18 May 1983. Smart's village, Parlatuvier, was one of the places with a speech band but not a singing band.

58 Noel Felix, interview, 18 May 1983;

59 Roger Abrahams, *The Man-of-Words in the West Indies* (Baltimore 1983); Rohlehr, *Calypso and Society*, chap. 2.

60 Abrahams, *The Man-of-Words*, 8, 19, 121.

61 George Leacock, interview, 30, 31 Aug. 1985.

62 For more on the steelband, see George Goddard, *Forty Years in the Steelbands, 1939–1979* (London 1991).

63 Raw stick: Ellie Mannette, the celebrated pannist, later initiated the use of rubber to cover the tip of the sticks with which the pans were struck, so that the sound of the pans would have a softer tone.

64 To play mas: to be a masquerader in Carnival.

65 Alford Paul (b.1934), interview with author, 13 Feb. 2006.

66 George 'Josey' Richardson, interview with author, 19 June 1975.

67 Alford Paul, 13 Feb. 2006; Paul's emphasis.

68 Ibid.

69 At a sacred cantata, 'Star of Light', at Spring Garden in December 1902, cornets, saxophone and bass horn were instruments in the orchestra. *Mirror*, 5 Jan. 1903, 11.

70 The Plymouth band under Willy Williams who brought back the saxophone from Maracaibo is discussed in this section.

71 George Leacock, interview, 30, 31 Aug. 1983.

72 Leacock, 30, 31 Aug. 1983.

73 Leacock, 30, 31 Aug. 1983.

74 Branford Williams, interview, 9 Feb. 1985.

75 Henry Shade (b.1910), unrecorded conversation with author, 20 July 2005.

76 Alfred Smart, interview, 18 May 1983.

77 Leopold Solomon, interview, 17 Mar. 1985.

78 Branford Williams, interview, 9 Feb. 1985; *Tobago Times*, 7 Oct. 1933.

79 Leopold Solomon, interview, 17 Mar. 1985; Jane Ann Thomas also mentioned Sammy Willington from Franklyn in Les Coteaux as an excellent flautist.

80 Amelia Bovell with Branford Williams, interview, 9 Feb. 1983; Bovell's emphasis.

81 Cassie Homeward, interview, 8 Jan. 1985.

82 Branford Williams, interview, 9 Feb. 1985. The song is probably Charles Newman and Isham Jones, 'You've Got Me Crying Again', recorded by Victor 24255-A, New York, 14 Feb. 1933. Jones' orchestra was an important one for jazz and dance music. See

Tim Gracyk, 'Isham Jones and His Orchestra', http://www.redhotjazz.com/ishamjones.html (accessed 23 June 2006).

83 As sung by Emeldalina Nicholson (1901–2005), interview, 26 June 1996.

84 J. D. Elder (1914–2003), interview with author, 21 May 1983.

85 *Mirror*, 18 June 1900, 7; 17 July 1916, 12.

86 Jean O'Keiffe Daniel, niece of Hugh O'Keiffe, interview with author, 1 Aug. 1996. She states that O'Keiffe destroyed all his other compositions.

87 *LL*, 6 Jan. 1923, 10; 3 Feb. 1923, 2; 11 Oct. 1924, 13. George Leacock, interview, 30, 31 Aug. 1983.

88 *The People*, 24 July 1937, 2; 23 Oct. 1937, 10; Eric Ottley, former member of CHPC, interview, 12 Mar. 1985.

89 Aaron Telemaque was transferred from Tobago to teach at Forest Reserve, Trinidad, in 1941. *Teachers' Herald*, Nov. 1941, 34; *The Tobagonian*, July 1941, 24–25; *Teachers' Herald*, 16 Oct. 1954, 10.

90 *The Tobagonian*, Dec. 1938, 39–40; May 1942, 16; Feb. 1943, 18; July 1949, 16.

91 As sung by Eric Ottley, interview, 12 Mar. 1985, with corrections from Dorcas Henry, 21 Dec. 2002. For Mitchell, see Ann Mitchell-Gift, *Lionel P. Mitchell: A Biography* (Scarborough, Tobago 1996).

92 *Teachers' Herald*, June 1942, 25.

93 *Moravian Messenger* 20, no. 23 (1910): 358, for Morris' quotation; for John, *The Tobagonian*, Aug. 1941, 5.

94 For the most part, the Tobago populace knew only harmoniums before 1915; pianos were rare at all levels of the society.

95 *Mirror*, 15 May 1916, 7; *Moravian Missions* 2, no. 2 (1904): 31; *Moravian Messenger*, 10 Dec. 1903, 302; 24 Dec. 1903, 328; 30 Nov. 1912, 394; 31 May 1913. The above notices give bibliographical information on the following: Theodor Liley Clemens, *Church Litany* (London 1903); *New Music for Our Church Litany* (Liveredge, Yorkshire 1904); *Andante in C Minor* (London 1905); *Eight Carols for Christmas* (London 1912); *Elegy in C Sharp Minor* (London 1913); and *Rex Saeculorum* (London 1925). I am grateful to Albert H. Frank, Assistant Director, Moravian Music Foundation, who supplied information on *Sunday Music* (UK 1889) and *Twelve Carols for Christmas* (Bradford 1919).

96 *Mirror*, 9 Feb. 1904, 13. Some sources give the date of Dr. Purser's first concert as 1856. *Mirror*, 30 Apr. 1906, 10, with notice of the concert for 2 May 1906. Madame Anita Patti Brown performed in Trinidad in February 1913; because of her colour, she was refused accommodation at the Queen's Park Hotel, Port of Spain, about which she protested. *Mirror*, 11 Feb. 1913, 7; 15 Feb. 1913, 5; 16 Nov. 1914, 5.

97 *Mirror*, 16 Oct. 1908, 19; punctuation as in original;

and see *Mirror*, 5 July 1907, 10–11, for the 1907 concert.

98 Henrietta Arthur (1899–1984), interview with author, 13 May 1983.

99 Branford Williams, interview, 19 Feb. 1985; *Moravian Messenger*, 5 Nov. 1910, 358; Morris' emphasis.

100 J. D. Elder, interview, 21 May 1983; Elder's emphases.

101 Thomas Aaron Telemaque, 'Customs in Crusoe's Isle', *The Tobagonian*, June 1940, 9–13.

102 Lionel. P. Mitchell, (1905–1992), interview with author, 27 Sept. 1984; Mitchell's emphases.

103 *TG*, 29 Apr. 1931, 3.

104 Fitz Gerald Maynard (1900–1984), interview with author, 31 Mar. 1983.

105 *Tobago Times*, 3–9 Aug. 1984, 13.

106 *The Tobagonian*, Jan. 1948, 6, 8.

107 Elder, *Folk Song and Folk Life*, 17.

108 Lionel P. Mitchell, interview, 27 Sept. 1984.

109 *TG*, 29 Mar. 1931, 3.

110 *TG*, 29 Apr. 1931, 3; *LL*, 18 Apr. 1931, 2; 27 June 1931, 2; 15 Aug. 1931, 15; 22 Aug. 1931, 5; 19 Sept. 1931, 15.

111 *People*, 14 Oct. 1939, 9.

112 *People*, 28 Oct. 1939, 8.

113 *People*, 7 Sept. 1940, 9; 20 July 1940, 10.

114 Stanley Duke's Mayfair Jazz Orchestra from Rockley Vale played at their 1939 May Day celebrations; *People*, 6 May 1939, 11.

Part Two
Supporting Data

7

Demographic Trends and
Social Conditions in Tobago, 1844–1931

IN THIS chapter, the census data are used to examine Tobago's demographic trends and social conditions. Despite limitations such as inconsistent definitions and time-bound perspectives (both ours and the census-takers'), we assess those aspects of the social structure that are amenable to quantitative study. This is a necessary part of using all the available sources to provide a composite, though at times refracted and blurred, picture of Tobago society between 1838 and 1938. Because the 1844 census report was a very simple enumeration, on most issues the 1851 census provides the base data. Where necessary, data from the 1946 census are used.

1. MAJOR DEMOGRAPHIC TRENDS

The Origins and Composition of the Population

The origins and composition of the population for the period 1851–1891 have been discussed in Volume I, Chapter 7. In the twentieth century, the European population remained small. The Scots, who had been the largest subgroup of Europeans,

numbered only 8 out of 58 in 1946. The Africa-born steadily declined, and natives of India recruited mainly for work on estates, whose numbers reached 120 in 1921, declined in the next two decades. The main increases were the migrants from the BWI, whose numbers more than doubled between 1901 and 1946 (Table 7.1).

Only one census in the early twentieth century had classifications by 'race': that of 1946. From a population of 27,208, Whites numbered 169 or 0.6 per cent, which was the same proportion as in 1881; and the Mixed (including 105 Indian Creoles and 22 Chinese Creoles) were 1,323 (4.9 per cent), down from 2,862, 15.8 per cent of the population in 1881. Those classified Black were 25,408 or 93.4 per cent, in contrast to the proportion of 83.5 per cent in 1881. There were only 8 Asiatics in 1881 and no Syrians; in 1946 the relevant figures were: East Indians 231 (0.8 per cent); Chinese 42 (0.2 per cent); and Syrians 33 (0.1 per cent).[1]

The population had become somewhat more diverse between 1881 and 1946. While the White proportion of the population remained stable in that period, the Mixed showed a significant numerical and proportionate decline, and included people of Indian and Chinese descent.

TABLE 7.1 Origins of the Tobago Population, 1901–1946

Place	1901 No.	1901 Per cent	1911 No.	1911 Per cent	1921 No.	1921 Per cent	1931 No.	1931 Per cent	1946 No.	1946 Per cent
Tobago	17,241	91.9	18,865	90.9	20,941	89.5	23,035	90.9	24,520	90.1
Africa	132	0.7	80	0.4	30	0.1	11	0.0	1	0.0
BWI[a]	959	5.1	1,645	7.9	2,175	9.3	2,110	8.3	2,518	9.2
Barbados	—	—	*507*	—	*391*	—	*245*	—	*134*	—
Grenada and dependencies	—	—	*247*	—	*614*	—	*615*	—	*476*	—
Trinidad	*340*	*1.8*	*668*	—	*1,019*	—	*1,115*	—	*1,720*	—
Other BWI	—	—	*80*	—	*151*	—	*135*	—	*188*	—
Other WI	13	0.1	13	0.1	12	0.0	12	0.0	13	0.0
UK	48	0.3	60	0.3	46	0.2	32	0.1	57	0.2
Other Europe	5	0.0	6	0.0	10	0.0	3	0.0	1	0.0
India[b]	8	—	63	0.3	120	0.5	55	0.2	38	0.1
Rest of the world	3	0.1	11	0.0	52	0.2	87	0.3	60	0.2
Not given	2	0.0	6	0.0	4	0.0	7	0.0	—	—
Total	**18,751**	**100.0**	**20,749**	**100.0**	**23,390**	**100.0**	**25,352**	**100.0**	**27,208**	**100.0**

Sources: Calculated from Tobago Population Census Reports, 1851–1891; Trinidad and Tobago Population Census Reports, 1901–1946.

Notes:
[a] In 1901 Trinidad is not included in the figure for the BWI.
[b] In 1946 includes persons from Burma (today Myanmar) and Ceylon (today Sri Lanka).

Population Density

Throughout the century after Emancipation, the population density was low, by comparison with that of Grenada or St. Vincent. Table A2.1 compares Tobago in 1882 with the Windward Islands, of which it formed part until 1888; a comparison is also made with Trinidad for 1921, 1931 and 1946.

Population Growth

Although infant mortality rates were high, the major determinant of population growth was emigration to Trinidad and other nearby colonies. This, in turn, was determined by the state of the Tobago economy relative to economic conditions elsewhere. Overall population growth, which was 1.1 per cent per annum between 1861 and 1871, declined to insignificant levels between 1871 and 1901, owing to heavy emigration when the sugar industry collapsed in the 1880s. Only between 1901 and 1911 did the annual growth rate again reach 1.1 per cent. In the early twentieth century, return migration, coupled with labour recruitment and immigration from nearby colonies, contributed to population growth and the expansion of the cocoa industry. The growth rate remained steady until 1921, after which global depression and decline in commodity prices affected the main export crops. Emigration therefore accelerated after 1921, and for the next 25 years the annual population growth rate fell again to less than 1.0 per cent (Tables A2.2, 7.3).

Migration

Hundreds of British West Indians, mainly Barbadians, migrated to Tobago in the nineteenth century. While streams of emigrants went to Canada, Curaçao, Panama, Venezuela, and the USA between 1870 and 1920, Trinidad was a major destination for Tobago's emigrants. There are no records on Tobagonians in Trinidad before 1891. In 1891 there were 3,307 Tobagonians (1,774 males, 1,533 females) in Trinidad, and 16,942 in Tobago. In 1901 the comparable figures were 5,334 (2,948 males, 2,386 females) and 17,241 in Tobago.[2] Thus, between 1891 and 1901, persons born in Tobago living in Trinidad increased by 61.3 per cent; and, of the colony's natives of Tobago, the proportion living in Trinidad rose from 16.3 per cent to 23.6 per cent. Expressed another way, the increase of

Tobagonians in Trinidad between 1891 and 1901 was *five times* the increase of the Tobago population (398 persons) (Table 7.2).

Emigration occurred at a slower rate from 1901 to 1921, but the number of Tobagonians residing in Trinidad remained significant, being almost one-fourth of the Tobago-born in the colony. The expansion of the Trinidad oil industry in the 1920s and 1930s, coupled with Trinidad's need for labour to construct roads and the United States Bases during the Second World War, attracted renewed emigration from Tobago after 1921. In 1946 natives of Tobago living in Trinidad were 31.1 per cent of those in the colony (Table 7.2).

In 1901, the first year for which there are data, Tobagonians in Trinidad were clustered in Port of Spain, the capital, and the north-eastern Ward of Toco (County St. David), the nearest point to Tobago, with which there was constant traffic by steamer and small craft. There were smaller concentrations in County St. George—the urban area near the capital—and at Manzanilla on the east coast. Over time, however, the migrants to Toco declined numerically and proportionately, while the concentrations in Port of Spain/St. George and St. Patrick, the oilfield area of south Trinidad, became more significant (Table 7.2).

Growth of the Population and of the Working Force

One illustration of the heavy emigration is a comparison of the annual growth of the population with that of the working force, defined as the number of people enumerated in their usual main activity, paid or unpaid (Table 7.3).[3] Between 1851 and 1861, the annual growth of the working force was 0.3 per cent; in the succeeding decade it was 0.5 per cent, rising to 1.1 per cent for 1871 to 1881. For 1881–1891, however, the rate declined to -0.02 per cent, and further declined to -0.25 per cent for 1891–1901. Attesting to slower emigration rates, the immigration of labourers, and possibly higher fertility rates after 1901, the population grew by 1.1 per cent per annum between 1901 and 1911, with the working force outstripping it with an annual growth of 2.0 per cent. In the following decade both rates were the same (1.3 per cent). After 1921, however, both population and working force grew more slowly, with the latter declining absolutely by 1946.

189

TABLE 7.2 **Tobago-Born Population in Trinidad and in Tobago, 1891–1946**

Towns/Counties	1891	1901		1911		1921		1931		1946	
	No.	No.	%	No.	%	No.	%	No.	%	No.	%
Port of Spain		1,252	23.5	1,161	19.5	1,259	20.6	1,793	26.0	3,229	29.2
San Fernando		84	1.6	72	1.2	139	2.3	71	1.0	N. G.	—
Arima		162	3.0	108	1.9	78	1.3	258	3.7	N. G.	—
County of											
St. George		577	10.8	609	10.2	615	10.1	1,029	14.8	3,140	28.4
St. David		1,453	27.3	1,878	31.6	1,617	26.5	1,164	16.8	732	6.6
St. Andrew		630	11.8	653	11.0	682	11.2	585	8.4	423	3.8
Nariva		—	—	—	—	117	1.9	136	2.0	124	1.1
Mayaro		107	2.0	233	3.9	230	3.8	258	3.7	220	2.0
Caroni		439	8.2	356	6.0	417	6.8	276	4.0	315	2.8
Victoria		300	5.6	432	7.3	386	6.3	332	4.8	1,251	11.3
St. Patrick		320	6.0	441	7.4	554	9.1	1,020	14.7	1,609	14.6
Total in Trinidad	3,307	5,324	99.0	5,943	99.9	6,094	99.9	6,922	99.9	11,043	99.8
Total in Tobago	16,942	17,241	—	18,865	—	20,941	—	23,035	—	24,520	—
Stragglers		—	—	—	—	—	—	12	—	—	—
Colony's waters	—	10	—	13	—	16	—	7	—	—	—
TOTAL	20,249	22,575	—	24,821	—	27,051	—	29,976	—	35,563	—
Total in Tobago as % of Tobago-born	83.7	76.4	—	76.0	—	77.4	—	76.8	—	68.9	—

Sources: Calculated from Trinidad and Tobago Population Census Reports: for 1931, 24, and for 1946, Table 41, 48.

Note: N. G.: not given.

TABLE 7.3 **The Growth of the Population and of the Working Force, 1844–1946**

Census year	Population	Annual rate of change (%)	Working force	Per cent of population	Increase/ decrease	Per cent change	Annual rate of change (%)
1844	13,208	—	Not given	—	—	—	—
1851	14,378	1.3	8,469	58.9	—	—	—
1861	15,410	0.7	8,761	56.8	292	3.4	0.3
1871	17,054	1.0	9,190	53.9	429	4.9	0.5
1881	18,051	0.6	10,210	56.6	1,020	11.1	1.1
1891	18,353	0.2	10,194	55.5	-16	-0.2	0.0
1901	18,751	0.2	9,934	53.0	-260	-2.5	-0.2
1911	20,749	1.1	11,919	57.4	1,985	20.0	2.0
1921	23,390	1.3	13,421	57.4	1,502	12.6	1.3
1931	25,352	0.8	14,960	59.0	1,539	11.5	1.1
1946	27,208	0.5	14,088	51.8	-872	-5.8	-0.4

Sources: Calculated from Tobago Population Census Reports, 1844–1891; Trinidad and Tobago Population Census Reports, 1901–1946.

2. SETTLEMENT PATTERNS

Population Changes at District Level

For several of the censuses, the districts were deemed to be composed of parishes and towns, as follows. St. John, St. Paul and St. Mary were the Windward District; St. George, St. Andrew and Scarborough, the Middle District; St. David, St. Patrick and Plymouth, the Leeward District. In the early twentieth century, however, the area boundaries were either not given or were changed for the census enumerations, and only for 1946 are there data that are comparable with those for the late nineteenth century. (See Maps 7.1 to 7.3 for parish boundaries.)

The Leeward District experienced the heaviest loss from emigration in the last decades of the nineteenth century. In 1844, 19.6 per cent of the population resided in the Windward District, 40.8 per cent in the Middle, and 39.5 per cent in the Leeward. By 1891, the proportion for the Windward District had risen to 24.0 per cent, after a marked decline owing to internal migration in the 1840s and 1850s. The Middle District, in which Scarborough and its suburbs were situated, suffered a decline in its share of the population to 33.6 per cent in 1891; and the Leeward, which in 1871 accounted for 47.0 per cent of the population, had 42.4 per cent by 1891. Table A2.3 gives the district populations, and the intercensal population changes for 1871 to 1891 are shown in Table 7.4. In

both the Windward and Leeward Districts, particularly the former, rates of growth for males declined markedly in the decade 1881 to 1891 (Table 7.4).

TABLE 7.4 **Population Change by District and Sex, 1871–1891**

District	1871–1881		1881–1891	
	Increase/ decrease	% change	Increase/ decrease	% change
Males				
Windward	482	30.9	104	5.1
Middle	18	0.6	-11	-0.4
Leeward	-68	-1.8	-147	-3.9
Total	432	5.2	-54	-0.6
Females				
Windward	415	26.4	277	13.9
Middle	140	4.5	100	3.1
Leeward	10	0.2	-21	-0.5
Total	565	6.4	356	3.8
Both sexes				
Windward	897	28.6	381	9.5
Middle	158	2.7	89	1.5
Leeward	-58	-0.7	-168	-2.1
Total	997	5.8	302	1.7

Sources: Calculated from Tobago Population Census Reports, 1871–1891; based on Table A2.3.

In 1946 the Windward District accounted for 31.1 per cent of the population, while the Middle and Leeward Districts had 34.3 per cent and 34.6 per cent, respectively (Table A2.3). The increase in the share of the Windward District over its 1891 figure of 24.0 per cent was due to the collapse of sugar and the expansion of both peasant landownership and the cocoa industry after 1884, since the eastern half of Tobago was greatly suited to cocoa cultivation. Cocoa's ascendancy caused reduced emigration and a wave of internal migration from leeward to northern and windward villages. It also promoted immigration from Grenada, Carriacou and St. Vincent, and the recruitment of East Indian and other labourers to the Windward District in particular. After 1900 the windward settlements of Bloody Bay and L'Anse Fourmi, which had remained uninhabited between 1809 and the 1870s, were fully settled, and Roxborough became a thriving township. Thus, in the early twentieth century, there was the most even distribution of the population in the history of Tobago after 1763.

Population Changes in the Towns

In the nineteenth century, Scarborough and Plymouth were the two towns. In neither case do we know the boundaries used for the towns or their suburbs at each census. Assuming that they were the same over time, Table A2.4 presents the population of the towns by sex for 1844 to 1946.

In 1844 Scarborough's population was like that of most capital towns in the BWI after slavery. Such towns had low male : female ratios for three reasons. First, there had been a high urban demand for female domestic slaves. Second, there had been a high degree of female ownership of urban slaves; and third, women tended to own more female than male slaves. In the towns there were usually also high proportions of the Africa-born, and of Creoles from other colonies.[4] In 1844, 11.2 per cent of the population lived in Scarborough; and females far exceeded males, the sex ratio being 69.6 males per 100 females.[5]

The absolute and proportionate decline of the Scarborough population until 1881 does not indicate the decline of the town per se, but rather the growth of its suburbs, to which some freed people had resorted before 1838, and which became more populous thereafter. In 1861 the census gave the 'suburbs of Scarborough' as having 276 persons, 130 males and 146 females. In 1891, considering the suburbs of Scarborough to be those settlements within a radius of one mile from the town, their population was 1,331 persons.[6] The female preponderance was maintained over the years in both Scarborough and its suburbs; but the internal migration of the period after 1838, the age structure, the fertility and mortality rates of the urban and suburban population (on which we have no data), and the emigration beginning in the 1860s which was dominated by males, could have compounded the earlier patterns (Table A2.4).

Plymouth steadily declined in importance. Situated on Courland Bay with a deep harbour, Plymouth was the sole port of entry for the ships of the Royal Mail Steam Packet Company, which brought mail and passengers from Europe. However, from 1841 to 1881 there was great protest against this, since Plymouth was not a place of trade. Late in 1881, Plymouth ceased to be a port of entry. It was a fishing and agricultural village, and a centre for sea communication, some of it clandestine, with the northern villages and with nearby islands. None of the merchants did business there, and few of the propertied able to vote resided there.

In 1911 Roxborough was counted by the census as a town for the first time, reflecting its growth as the trading and administrative centre of the Windward District. The population of Roxborough and Betsy's Hope was 1,194 in 1911, increasing to 1,215 for Roxborough alone in 1921. In keeping with the downturn in the cocoa industry after 1920, Roxborough's population declined thereafter. Scarborough's population is given as 729 in 1911; it remained a small town, with only 908 residents in 1946. Plymouth experienced a trend of steady decline between 1891 and 1931, but its people trebled from 387 persons in 1931 to 1,180 in 1946 (Table A2.4).

Interestingly, by 1946 the population in the main towns was eclipsed by that of the large villages (Table 7.5). All of this indicates the minimal growth of Tobago's urban centres.

Population Changes at Settlement Level

There were 95 settlements, apart from Scarborough and Plymouth, in 1861, and 113 in 1891, the earliest and latest years in the nineteenth century for which there are data. In 1861, outside of the towns, only Rockley Vale, a suburb of Scarborough, had over 500 persons (503 or 3.3 per cent of the population), and 85.0 per cent of the population resided in settlements with fewer than 500 people. By 1891, 8 villages, with 4,746 persons or 25.9 per cent of the population, had more than 500 persons. These large villages were Riseland (563), Canaan (532), and Buccoo (511) in the Leeward District; Mt. St. George (800), Mason Hall (663), Adventure (616) and Indian Walk[7] (Moriah) (551) in the Middle District; and Roxborough (510) in the Windward District.[8]

There were two significant changes in the settlement patterns between 1861 and 1891.

Firstly, whereas 61.4 per cent of the population had lived in villages with fewer than 300 persons in 1861, only 46.4 per cent lived in such settlements in 1891.

Secondly, villages with over 400 persons, in which resided 11.6 of the population in 1861, had 30.7 per cent in 1891, the greatest shift being to the villages with over 500 persons with 25.9 per cent of the population.

Thus, by 1891 there were several very small settlements, flanked by a growing number of larger ones that accounted for an increasing share of the population (Tables A2.5, A2.6).[9]

Maps 7.1 and 7.2, in giving the spatial dimension to these statistics, show the development by 1891 of what may be termed 'conglomerate settlements', where two or more larger villages were close together, usually with smaller settlements nearby. For example, in St. Patrick parish, Canaan and Tyson Hall comprised one such grouping; Buccoo, Riseland, and Bethel/Bethlehem were another. Mason Hall (in St. George) had smaller satellite settlements in Adelphi and Concordia, and it was

TABLE 7.5 Population of Settlements with over 500 Persons, 1946

Place	Settlements with over 1,000 persons			
	No. of households	Males	Females	Total
Moriah	523	947	1,186	2,133
Les Coteaux	220	477	525	1,002
Charlotteville	277	656	704	1,360
Delaford	241	584	551	1,135
Mt. St. George	290	539	538	1,077
Mason Hall	239	502	550	1,052
Bethel	263	635	636	1,271
Plymouth	—	547	633	1,180

Place	Settlements with 500 but fewer than 1,000 persons			
	No. of households	Males	Females	Total
Bon Accord	184	380	436	816
Canaan	229	446	484	930
Whim	159	381	402	783
Speyside[a]	182	448	486	934
Glamorgan	136	241	285	526
Pembroke	143	279	298	577
Goodwood	151	303	305	608
Calder Hall	116	242	274	516
Scarborough	—	444	464	908
Roxborough	—	406	465	871

Sources: Trinidad and Tobago Population Census Report, 1946, 49; Central Statistical Office, Tobago Statistics (n.d., mimeographed), Table 6.

Note:
[a] In error, the census report gives the number in the Total column as 944.

closely linked by road with Mt. St. George. In St. David, Indian Walk (Moriah) with Woodlands, Culloden and Runnemede comprised another cluster. In St. David also, Plymouth, by 1891 a village of 636 persons, was close to Adventure with 616 persons. Only one of these 'conglomerate settlements' was in the Windward District: Roxborough and Betsy's Hope. The largest cluster was Scarborough and its suburbs, of which Rockley Vale was the biggest.

This pattern of development, which was already discernible in 1861 (Map 7.1), was directly related to the availability of land for village settlements, which in turn was affected by the pressure on the planters that the labourers exerted.

By 1946 the population in the largest villages exceeded that of the main towns.

MAP 7.1 **Tobago: Population of Settlements with more than 300 Persons, 1861**

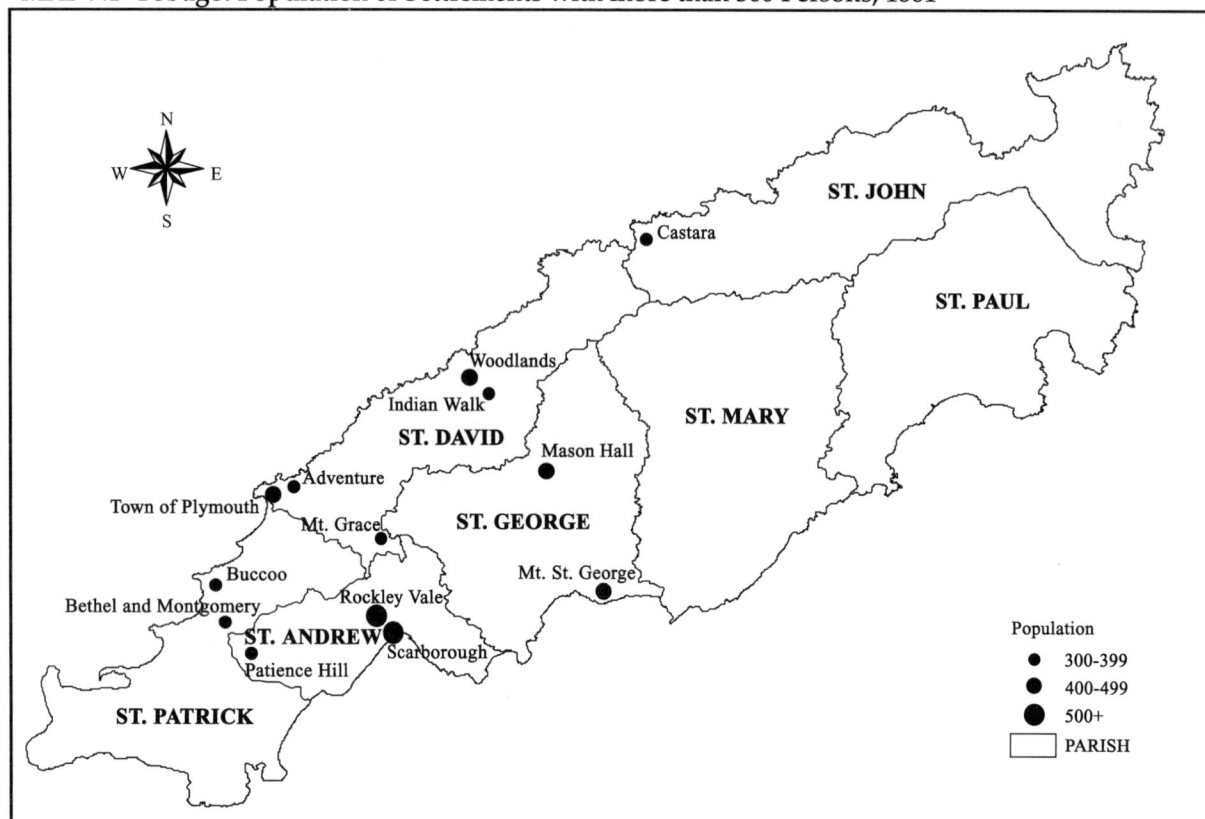

Source: Tobago Population Census Report, 1861.

In 1946 also, the main villages of the conglomerate settlements were among the largest. By then, in the Windward District new populous clusters had emerged: Charlotteville and its satellites; and Goodwood, Pembroke and Glamorgan (Table 7.5; Map 7.3).

TABLE 7.6 **Residents on Estates, Available Parishes, 1891**

Parish	Estate residents	Population	% of parish population
St. George	52	2,220	2.3
St. Andrew	42	3,022	1.4
St. David	92	3,985	2.3
St. Patrick	78	3,162	2.5

Source: Tobago Population Census Report, 1891.

Note: Parish population for St. Andrew and St. David excludes Scarborough and Plymouth, respectively.

Residents on Estates

The census distinguished residents on estates only in 1891, and they were given only for the parishes of the Middle and Leeward Districts, excluding Scarborough and Plymouth (Table 7.6). The estate residents recorded, 264 persons, comprised 1.4 per cent of the population.

3. AGE STRUCTURE, SEX RATIOS, FERTILITY

Age and Sex Structure

The population may be conceived of as comprising three basic age groups: the child population, the population of working age, and the elderly. These will be examined in turn.

MAP 7.2 Tobago: Population of Settlements with more than 300 Persons, 1891

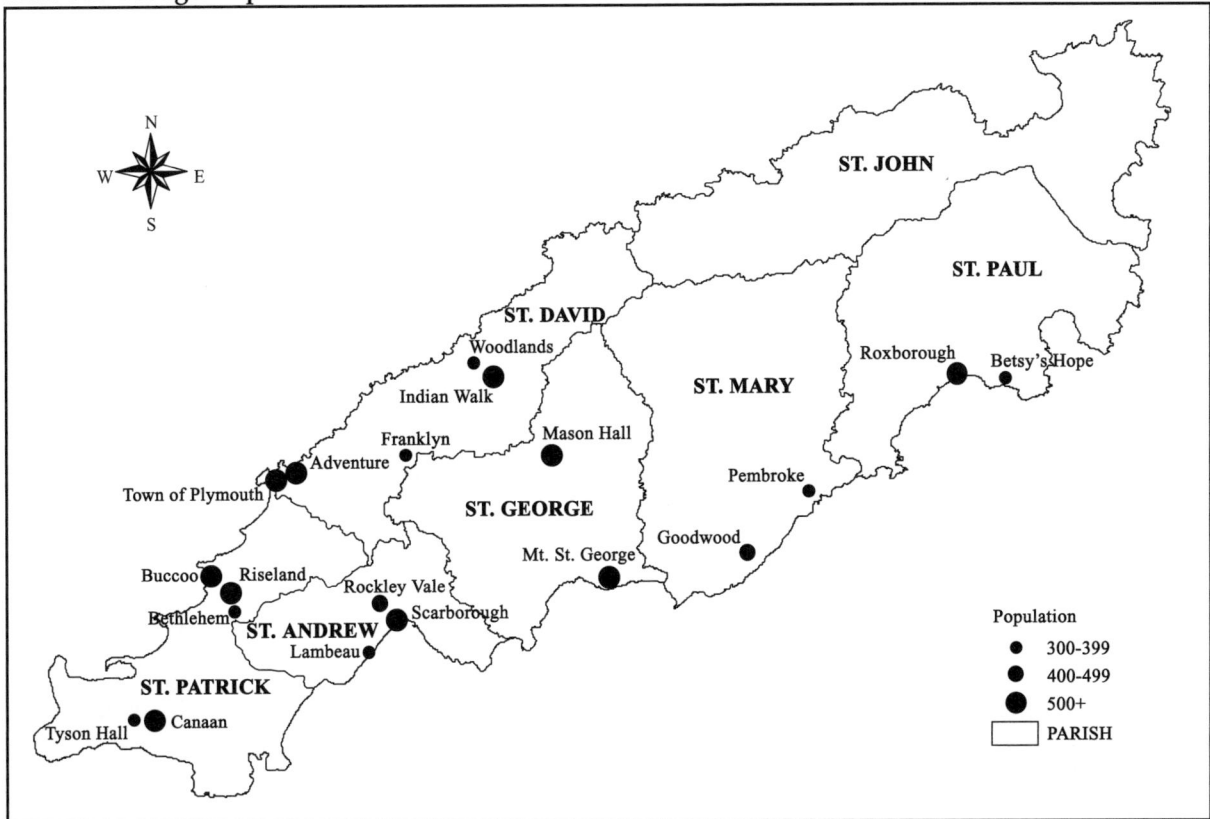

Source: Tobago Population Census Report, 1891.

The Child Population

The proportion of children aged 0–14 in the population moved from 35.4 per cent in 1851 to 41.5 per cent in 1901, mainly because of the high proportions of people of working age who emigrated in the late nineteenth century (Figure 7.1; Table A2.8).

The children born in each decade are an important component of population growth. Between 1861 and 1871, the average annual population growth was 1.1 per cent and the comparable figure for the cohort aged 0–9 was 1.6 per cent. From 1871 to 1881, the annual rate of increase in children aged 0–9 fell by almost one-half to 0.9 per cent, as the overall population growth similarly fell to 0.6 per cent (Table A2.7).

The heavy emigration of workers contributed to both falling numbers of children and declining rates of population growth. The 1891–1901 increase of 530 children aged 0–9 years was so

FIGURE 7.1 Age Profile of the Tobago Population, 1851–1931

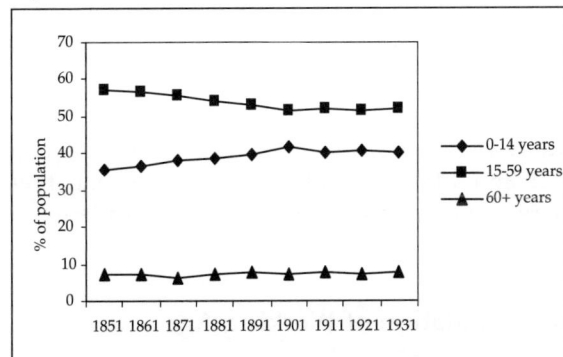

Sources: Calculated from Tobago Population Census Reports, 1851–1891, and from Trinidad and Tobago Population Census Reports, 1901–1931. Based on Table A2.8.

greatly eclipsed by emigration and death, that this number exceeded the net population growth of 398 persons.

195

MAP 7.3 **Tobago: Population of Settlements with more than 500 Persons, 1946**

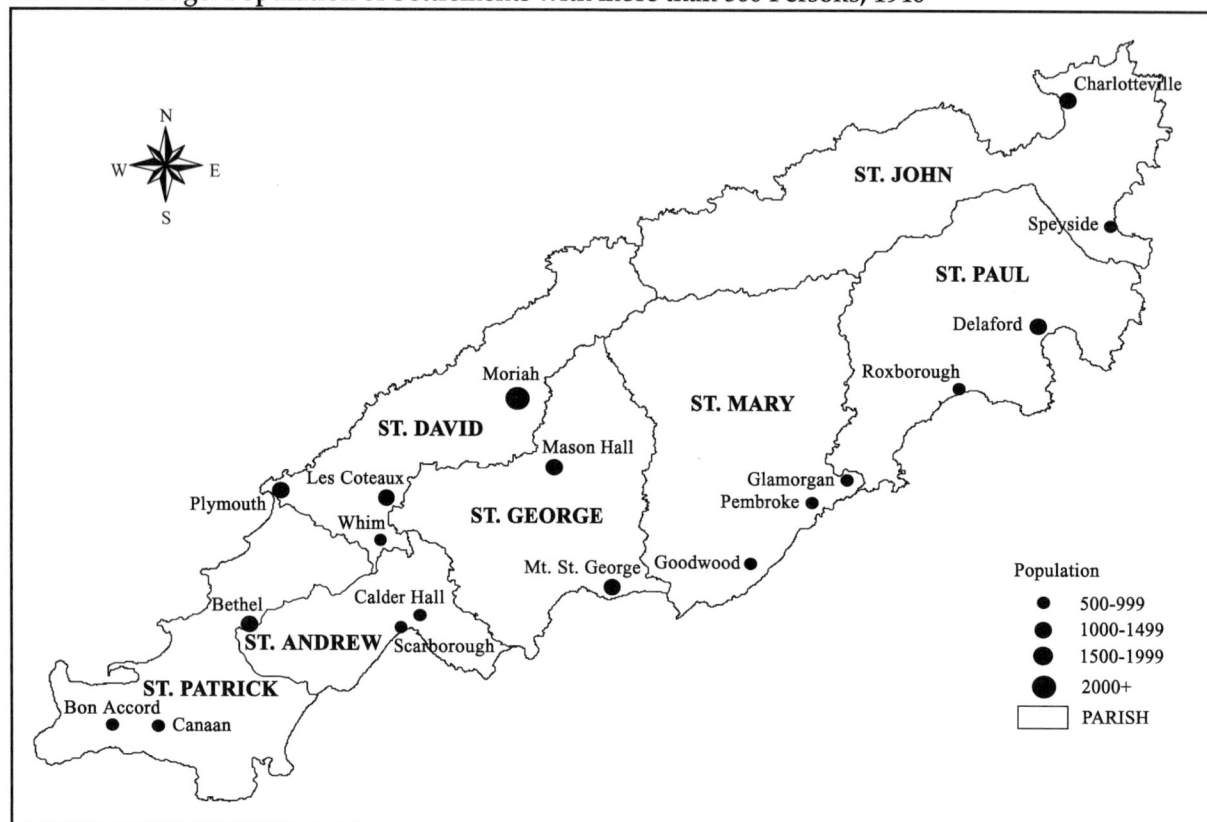

Source: Trinidad and Tobago Population Census Report, 1946.

From 1901 to 1931, the highest intercensal rate of increase for children aged 0–9 was 1.5 per cent per annum. This occurred between 1911 and 1921, when the contribution of children aged 0–9 to overall population growth was 32.1 per cent.

As emigration increased after 1921, the annual rate of increase of the children aged 0–9 between 1921 and 1931 was only 0.75 per cent, and their share of population growth for the decade fell to 25.0 per cent.[10]

The Population of Working Age

The population of working age is taken to be persons between ages 15 and 60. It declined from 57.2 per cent of the population in 1851 to 51.3 per cent in 1901, and hovered around 52 per cent from 1911 onwards (Figure 7.1; Table A2.8). This age cohort, particularly those aged 20 to 49, was the most affected by the heavy emigration of the late nineteenth century.

Between 1871 and 1921 the disparity in the sex ratios in the cohort aged 20–49 was marked; in 1901 it reached as low as 62 males per 100 females for persons aged 25 to 34. The severe attrition of males of working age by 1901 is shown in Figure 7.2.

The overwhelming impact of emigration on the age and sex structure of the population is evident from the statistics in Tables A2.7 and A2.9. Since the migration was largely of the able-bodied, the proportion of the population aged 20–49 declined steadily from 41.8 per cent in 1851 to 33.6 per cent in 1901, rising again slowly to 36.4 per cent in 1931.

Taking the population as a whole, there was a decline in the ratio of males per 100 females from 94.0 in 1871 to 86.0 in 1901, and thereafter only a gradual increase to 93.9 in 1931 (Table A2.10). All these trends reflected high levels of male emigration after 1871. In the context of exceptional male mortality rates during enslavement, they help to explain why females outnumbered males for many decades after Emancipation (Table A2.9).

196

The Elderly

This age group maintained a steady share (approximately 7.0 per cent) of the population (Figure 7.1; Table A2.8). Between 1881 and 1891, because of the emigration of younger people, it accounted for 43.7 per cent of the population increase: 132 out of a total of 302. By 1931 the elderly accounted for 13.9 per cent of the island's increase (Table A2.7).

Men aged over 60, who in 1851 had constituted 2.75 per cent of the population while the comparable figure for women was 4.6 per cent, comprised 3.5 per cent of the residents in 1931 (Table A2.9). The proportion of women over 60 in the population fell to 3.6 per cent in 1871, but fluctuated between 4.1 per cent and 4.4 per cent in the six decades following. Elderly men increased at the rate of 1.6 per cent per annum in the period 1851–1931, while for elderly women the rate was 0.8 per cent. It suggests that in the century after Emancipation increasing numbers of men enjoyed a longer lifespan, which was an improvement on the patterns of the slavery era.

The age and sex structure of the population is depicted in the age pyramids for 1861 (the only census in the nineteenth century with 5-year age intervals up to age 60), 1901 and 1931 (Figure 7.2).

Fertility

In the absence of a reliable, continuous series on births, a rough estimate of the fertility rate for each decade was derived. Table 7.7 gives the number of children under 10 alive at each census as a ratio of the number of females in the population aged between 15 to 49, since some census reports gave only 10-year intervals for the age cohorts above 20 years old. This measure is subject to changes in the age structure, and it falls short of the actual number of births, because of high infant and child mortality rates;[11] but it remains the best available estimate.

The rate of growth of females aged 15–49 declined steadily, from 10.5 per cent for the decade 1861–1871 to 6.9 per cent for 1871–1881, and 1.6 per cent for 1881–1891. The apparent increase in fertility rates in 1871 and 1881 may therefore be illusory on two counts: firstly, some of the children had mothers who had emigrated; secondly, the relatively small number of females in the denominators would increase the ratios. The

females of child-bearing age declined in number between 1891 and 1901, but increased thereafter, with the fastest rate of growth being 11.6 per cent for the decade 1911 to 1921.

Table 7.7 gives estimates of just over 1,000 children per 1,000 women aged 15–49 for 1871–1891, with an increase in 1901, fluctuating until 1931 between 1,109 and 1,150 children per 1,000 such women.

FIGURE 7.2 **Age Pyramids, 1861, 1901, 1931**

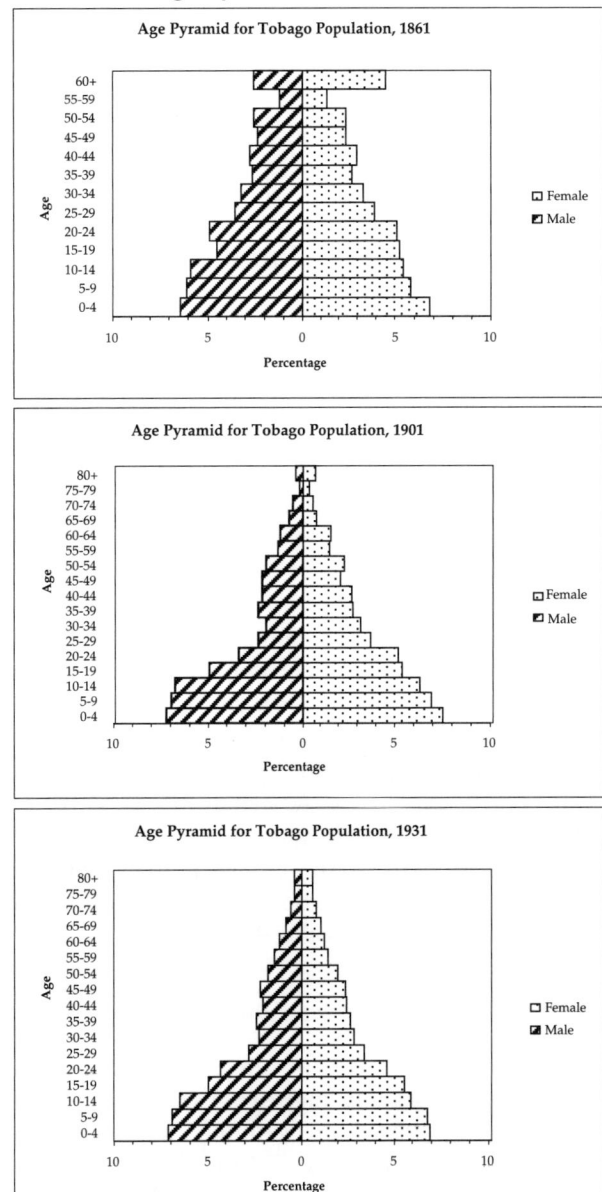

TABLE 7.7 **Surviving Children under 10 Years Old per Thousand Females Aged 15–49 at Census Years, 1851–1931**

Year	Children <10 years old	Females aged 15-49	Rate per 1,000 females	Year	Children <10 years old	Females aged 15-49	Rate per 1,000 females
1851	3,551	3,716	956	1901	5,347	4,703	1,137
1861	3,871	3,947	981	1911	5,674	5,114	1,109
1871	4,486	4,363	1,028	1921	6,523	5,710	1,142
1881[a]	4,867	4,664	1,043	1931	7,013	6,100	1,150
1891	4,817	4,737	1,017				

Sources: Tobago Population Census Reports, 1851–1891; Trinidad and Tobago Population Census Reports, 1901–1931.

Note:

a For 1881, the number of women aged 15–19 was estimated from the figure for the cohort aged 10–19 on the assumption of no change in the proportion of males and females in the cohort between 1871 and 1881. The proportion of both males and females among those aged 10–19 did not change.

4. SOCIAL CONDITIONS

Literacy and School Enrolment

The literacy rate is calculated as those able to read and write as a proportion of the population aged five years and over. Only for 1871 in the nineteenth century are there data. In 1871 the Middle District with Scarborough had the highest literacy rate of 48.5 per cent, followed by the Leeward and Windward Districts, in that order (Table 7.8).

By comparison with Jamaica where the gross literacy rate was 16.3 per cent in 1871, primary education had reached a wide proportion (at least 43.2 per cent) of the Tobago population.[12]

However, the education system was marked by low enrolment levels, especially of girls, before 1900, and attendance rates that were far below enrolment, particularly on Mondays (washing days) and Fridays, when produce had to be prepared for market (Table A2.11).[13]

Educational Advances, 1900–1931

For the twentieth century, however, Table A2.11 shows a remarkably high level of enrolment by 1912, when 94.5 per cent of the school-age population (children aged 5 to 14) were nominally at school; in 1931 enrolment reached 98.7 per cent. This indicates that by 1931 Tobago's children had greater access to education than those in many

TABLE 7.8 **Literates as Proportion of Population over Five Years Old by District, 1871**

District	'Can read and write'		Persons >5 years old	Literates as % of persons >5 years old
	Can	Cannot		
Windward	900	2,201	2,653	35.0
Middle	2,404	3,510	4,959	48.5
Leeward	2,904	5,105	6,838	42.5
Total	6,238	10,816	14,450	43.2

Source: Calculated from Tobago Population Census Report, 1871.

parts of rural Trinidad. In 1935 education was made compulsory only in Trinidad's towns, because some rural areas still had no schools. Moreover, the gender inequality in enrolment in Tobago ceased in the early twentieth century.

Average attendance remained at just over half the students enrolled in the period 1901–1921, and reached 66.2 per cent in 1931 (Table 7.9).

Expressed as a proportion of the school-age population, average attendance climbed from only 36.4 per cent in 1901 to 65.3 per cent in 1931 (Table 7.9). Unfortunately, attendance by sex was not given in the Blue Books.

The significant advances in access to primary education in the twentieth century were reflected in the gross literacy rates, which improved from 62.5 per cent of the population over 5 years old in 1911 to 77.7 per cent in 1931, compared with 47.0 per cent and 59.2 per cent, respectively, for Trinidad (Table 7.10).[14]

TABLE 7.9 **Average Attendance in Schools by Denomination, 1901–1931**

| Denomination | 1901 | | | 1912 | | |
	No. on roll	Average attend-ance	% of no. on roll	No. on roll	Average attend-ance	% of no. on roll
Anglican	1,318	723	54.8	2,143	1,191	55.6
Moravian	925	520	56.2	1,048	585	55.8
Methodist	842	420	49.9	1,375	790	57.4
Roman Catholic	278	163	58.6	497	248	49.9
Total	3,363	1,826	54.3	5,063	2,814	55.6
% School-age population	**67.1**	**36.4**	—	**94.5**	**52.5**	—

| Denomination | 1921 | | | 1931 | | |
	No. on roll	Average attend-ance	% of no. on roll	No. on roll	Average attend-ance	% of no. on roll
Anglican	2,319	1,287	55.5	2,826	1,884	66.7
Moravian	1,142	578	50.6	1,361	904	66.4
Methodist	1,539	783	50.9	1,670	1,097	65.7
Roman Catholic	659	363	55.1	665	431	64.8
Total	5,659	3,011	53.2	6,522	4,316	66.2
% School-age population	**91.2**	**50.2**	—	**98.7**	**65.3**	—

Sources: Trinidad and Tobago Blue Books and Population Census Reports, 1901–1931.

Note: For numbers in school-age population see Table A2.11.

Among those who could read and write, females slightly outnumbered males; but this was in keeping with the greater proportion of women in the population as a whole.

However, among those able to read only, women outnumbered men by a ratio of 1.5 : 1 in 1911 and 1.3 : 1 in 1931. Among those unable to read or write, males exceeded females between 1911 and 1931, the years for which data are available (Table 7.10).

The census reports for 1911 and 1921 noted that, outside of the colony's chief towns (Port of Spain and San Fernando), Tobago was the Ward with the highest proportion of those able to read and write. Despite the lack of resources, Tobago's dedicated teachers had achieved much.

TABLE 7.10 **Literacy in Tobago, 1911–1931**

| Year | Read and write | | Read only | | Neither | | Population > 5 years old | Per cent literate |
	Male	Female	Male	Female	Male	Female		
1911	5,375	5,724	1,062	1,663	3,485	3,440	17,749	62.5
1921	6,549	7,214	820	1,230	3,826	3,751	20,037	68.7
1931	8,094	8,856	585	776	3,596	3,443	21,801	77.7

Sources: Trinidad and Tobago Population Census Reports, 1911–1931.

Note: Literacy rate is persons able to read and write as a proportion of the population aged five and over.

Religious Persuasions

The religious affiliations of the population in the nineteenth century are available only for the years 1871 to 1891, as shown in Tables A2.12 and A2.13. Tobago in the period of our study was nominally Protestant, although African-derived religious beliefs and practices were maintained by many who attended the churches. The Church of England, to which approximately half of the population claimed affiliation, had congregations in all the districts, whereas the Moravians were concentrated in the Leeward and Middle Districts, and the Methodists in the Middle and Windward Districts. The decline of the Church of Scotland reflects the decline of the Scots and the closure of the Presbyterian ministry in 1841. The increase of Roman Catholics indicates the thrust which that denomination made from c.1885, which was intensified after the annexation of 1889. Seventh Day Adventists began to work in Tobago from 1890, and London Baptists from 1896.

In the early twentieth century, other religious groups such as the Christian Brethren (Gospel Hall Assemblies) arrived. The Seventh Day Adventists were to become one of the most important denominations in the twentieth century. Moravian membership, having peaked in 1891, declined in 1901, and never regained the 1891 levels, despite increases at the next three censuses. Methodist membership also peaked in 1891, but the increase in 1911 after the sharp decline of 1901 was not sustained. Emigration was certainly a contributory factor to these declines. Most of the Hindus and Muslims in the early decades of the twentieth century were immigrant labourers on the cocoa and coconut estates (Tables A2.12, A2.13).

Civil Status of Adults

Between 1861 and 1871, the married persons in the adult population more than doubled numerically and almost doubled proportionately (Table A2.14). The increases were in the Leeward and the Middle Districts, where the numbers trebled and almost doubled, respectively. The proportion married in 1871 was 39.4 per cent of persons aged 15 and over. In 1891 there were 3,981 married persons, down from 4,166 in 1871. Heavy emigration was a contributory factor to the apparent decline.

However, Tobago, with 37.9 per cent of its adult population married in 1901, was second only to Grenada with 39.8 per cent, among the neighbouring islands. The marriage rate in Trinidad was an underestimate, because only the Hindu and Muslim marriages that had been registered under the Immigrants Marriage and Divorce Ordinance, 1881, were recognized as marriages for the censuses of 1891 and 1901. For 1901, when East Indians are left out of the Trinidad calculations, the rate of marriage in Tobago (37.9 per cent) was higher than that for Trinidad (29.8 per cent).[15]

Many factors may account for the changing patterns and for the differences in proportions between Tobago and Trinidad. For example, the Registrar General of Tobago noted that the high costs of marriage licences and of the culturally approved elaborate wedding festivities were a deterrent to marriage in the 1880s, a time of severe economic hardship for the labouring class. Edith Clarke also observed that marriage rates tend to be higher in settled peasant populations than in highly mobile immigrant ones, which tended to have high proportions of single males. Tobago had an emerging peasantry and far smaller immigrant groups than Trinidad.[16]

Divorce was rare.

Types of Dwellings

The 1891 census was the first to describe the types of dwellings. Although the Registrar General saw the 1901 figures as only estimates, the pattern for Tobago is particularly interesting.

In 1891 there were 31 'barracks' with 106 rooms; in 1901 there were 6 of each. In 1891, 95.1 per cent of the occupied dwellings were undivided houses, and 3.0 per cent divided dwellings; in 1901 the respective proportions were 97.7 per cent and 1.4 per cent. Thus, by 1901 the overwhelming majority of the population lived in undivided dwellings. Tobago in the late nineteenth century had almost no estate barracks and urban 'barrack yards', which were integral to the development of society and culture in Trinidad (Table A2.15).[17]

After 1900, with the importation of labourers from neighbouring colonies, the number of barracks and rooms in yards increased. Even so, they accounted for only 3.9 per cent of the occupied dwelling units in 1931, and undivided houses were 94.2 per cent of the total units. The corresponding figures for Trinidad were 24.9 per cent and 65.8 per cent. The ratio of persons per room continued to be slightly higher in Tobago than in Trinidad (Table A2.15).

5. CONCLUSION

Tobago was a relatively homogeneous society, its people being mainly of African descent and Creole by birth, with very small numbers of Africans and Europeans by 1900. Chinese, Indians, Portuguese and Syrio-Lebanese were minuscule minorities in the early twentieth century. Migrants from nearby colonies were a small but important part of the population throughout the century after 1838.

The population lived at low density in small settlements, the most important of which became clusters of relatively large villages by 1891. This pattern continued into the first half of the twentieth century. Agrarian settlements of such sizes are noted for the primacy of face-to-face relationships.

Most people lived off the estates, at least in the Middle and Leeward Districts. Most of the population were concentrated near the estates and towns, within reach of roads and services.[18]

In the decades before 1880, population growth was 1.0 per cent per annum. The agrarian crisis of the 1880s led to heavy emigration in the late nineteenth century, negligible population growth, and a numerical and proportionate decline in the population of the leeward parishes, the centre of sugar production. Emigration affected family life, fertility rates, the age and sex structure, the size of the working force, and the ethos of the society. It also contributed to population growth in Trinidad, and to the cementing of family, trade, religious and other ties between the people of the united colony. In particular, emigration forged close links between Tobago's residents and the people in the north-east coastal villages of Trinidad throughout the twentieth century.

Urbanization, which had accelerated in the early years after Emancipation, halted between 1861 and 1946. Scarborough and its suburbs experienced no significant growth in the late nineteenth century, and Plymouth became a village.

In the early twentieth century, population growth accelerated with the expansion of cocoa cultivation in the north and east. There was a considerable redistribution of the population to the windward parishes, particularly St. John and

St. Paul, and Roxborough eclipsed Plymouth to become the second town. Major settlements emerged at Charlotteville and Moriah in the early twentieth century. Emigration increased after 1921 with the fall in prices of Tobago's major exports, and from 1921 to 1946 population growth again fell to less than 1.0 per cent per annum.

Where the social conditions are concerned, four important features were noted. First, in the nineteenth century, levels of school enrolment, particularly for girls, were low. For both sexes, enrolment and attendance improved considerably from 1911 onwards, and Tobago's gross literacy rates compared favourably with those of Jamaica and Trinidad. Second, the religious hegemony of the Anglican, Moravian and Wesleyan churches began to be eroded after 1890, through missions of the Roman Catholics, Seventh Day Adventists, London Baptists and other groups. Moravians and Methodists, the two main evangelical churches of the nineteenth century, recorded their highest membership in 1891 and declined thereafter, partly owing to emigration. Indeed, Moravian missions were started in Port of Spain in 1889 and at L'Anse Noire and Manantial in north-east Trinidad c.1896, to cater for the spiritual needs of Tobagonian and other Moravian migrants.[19] Thirdly, the prevalence of marriage in the adult population was relatively high by comparison with Trinidad, for reasons that are not fully clear. Finally, barrack housing was minimal before 1900, but increased thereafter with the expansion of cocoa and coconut cultivation. However, it was never as important as in Trinidad, and detached undivided housing units were the norm in Tobago.

The statistics outlined undergird our analysis of the society in remarkable ways. Firstly, the data on undivided housing give further significance to the observations in Volume I, Chapters 4 and 5, on home ownership as the first step in the quest for autonomy of the freed people, and on the salience of houses and homesteads in the pattern of property ownership by the 1880s. Secondly, the low degree of residence on the estates in the Middle and Leeward Districts corroborates the findings of those chapters on the decline in 'located labour'.[20] Thirdly, the data on the demographic transitions of the late nineteenth and early twentieth centuries enhance the analysis of the changing social structure in Volume I, Chapter 9, and Chapter 3 of this volume.

Notes

1 Tobago Population Census Report, 1881; Trinidad and Tobago Population Census Report, 1946. See discussion in vol. I, chap. 7. The population in 1881 was 18,051.

2 Trinidad and Tobago Population Census Report, 1901. The figure of 5,334 for the Tobago-born in Trinidad includes those on vessels in the waters of the colony.

3 In 1844 the compiler of the census examined the persons over 18 years and considered those at work and those 'having no employment.' In the subsequent censuses, the procedure was basically to describe the 'working force', as defined in the text. The working force is the concept mainly used in this and the following chapter.

4 B. W. Higman, 'Urban Slavery in the British Caribbean', in *Perspectives on Caribbean Regional Identity*, ed. E. Thomas-Hope (University of Liverpool, Centre for Latin American Studies 1984); Higman, *Slave Populations*, 118–19, 145.

5 Calculated from Tobago Population Census Report, 1844.

6 Calculated from Tobago Population Census Reports, 1861, 1891.

7 Indian Walk was the estate from which the ex-slaves bought land and built Moriah village after 1838. The 1891 census gives Moriah as having 10 persons, but this probably refers to the residents of the Moravian mission.

8 Mason Hall, Mt. St. George, Moriah and Riseland (near Bethel) were centres of smallholding activity in the 1840s (vol. I, chap. 4). Roxborough was the administrative centre for the Windward District.

9 Some of the larger settlements grew at the expense of the small. This is one reason for the increase in the number and proportion of settlements with fewer than 100 persons between 1861 and 1891 (Table A2.6). For example, *The News*, 10 June 1882, 3, stated that Petry (*sic*) Hill, a village equidistant between Mason Hall and Belmont Estate, had lost virtually its entire population of fewer than 50 persons. Some of the people had migrated to John Dial and Mt. St. George on the south coast, but the majority had gone to Mason Hall, one of the large villages identified in the 1891 census. For more on settlement patterns, see David L. Niddrie, *Land Use and Population in Tobago* (Bude, Cornwall 1961), 43–47.

10 Calculated from the figures in Table A2.7.

11 For example, in 1886 there were 675 births, of which 28 were still births. Of the 398 deaths, 36.9 per cent (147) were of children under 5 years. Report of the Registrar for Births, Marriages and Deaths for 1886,

The News, 14 May 1887. For the early twentieth century see, for example, George David Hatt's letter to James T. Rousseau, Warden, enclosing literature on infant care for public distribution; *Mirror*, 7 July 1908, 14–15.

12 Roberts, *Population of Jamaica*, 78.

13 See also vol. I, chap. 8 of this work.

14 The literacy rates for Trinidad in the census reports are computed over the total population. These figures differ because they are computed over the population aged 5 years and older. Figures for Trinidad include persons in vessels in the waters of the colony. A contributing factor to Trinidad's low literacy rates was the presence of large numbers of East Indian immigrants who were not literate in English, and whose education was neglected by the authorities. The comparable literacy rates for Jamaica were 47.2 per cent, 42.2 per cent and 67.9 per cent for 1911, 1921 and 1943, respectively, according to Roberts, *Population of Jamaica*, 78.

15 Trinidad and Tobago Population Census Report, 1901, 8–9. This report also includes the comparisons with neighbouring colonies.

16 See Registrar General's Report for 1885, *The News*, 3 Apr. 1886, 3. In 1885, 414 out of 753 births (55.0 per cent) were out of wedlock. Edith Clarke, *My Mother Who Fathered Me* (London 1957).

17 Bridget Brereton, *Race Relations in Colonial Trinidad, 1870–1900* (Cambridge 1979), and Donald Wood, *Trinidad in Transition: The Years after Slavery* (London 1968), show for Trinidad that the barrack yards were the crucible in which stick fighting, calypso, steelband and other folk traditions were forged.

18 Thomas C. Holt, *The Problem of Freedom: Race, Labor and Politics in Jamaica and Britain, 1832–1938* (Kingston 1992), 150, argues for Jamaica that if the ex-slaves had been oriented to marginal subsistence, as was believed by Colonial Office officials, they would have gone to the remote backlands. Sidney W. Mintz, *Caribbean Transformations* (Chicago 1974), 155, states that the creation of Caribbean peasantries was an act both of westernization and of resistance.

19 In the case of Port of Spain, there were also Moravian migrants from Barbados, Antigua and St. Kitts. The eight Moravian stations in Trinidad were established to meet the needs of immigrants. See 'Moravian Church 100th Anniversary Special', *SG*, 21 Oct. 1990, 11.

20 The 'located labour' system was one in which employment on estates was tied to access to houses, provision grounds and other amenities. See vol. I, chap. 4.

8

The Occupational Structure of Tobago, 1844–1946

To COMPLETE our statistical profile of Tobago society in the century after Emancipation, we must now examine the occupational structure. Such an analysis contributes to our understanding of the social structure and of occupational mobility through time.[1] First, the economic sectors are briefly discussed. Next, the 1844 census is examined, followed by a comparative analysis of the census data for 1851 to 1931. All the censuses from 1851 to 1946 used the 'gainful worker' approach (discussed in Section 3 below) to enumerate the economically active population. Because the 1946 census was the last to do so, we include its data in the tables and give it a short, separate discussion, since World War II (1939–1945) had a profound impact on employment trends in Tobago. Throughout, the limitations of the data are stated.

1. THE SECTORS OF THE ECONOMY

After Emancipation, 1838–1900

The Primary Sector

The sugar industry, which dominated Tobago's economic life until the 1880s, was both agrarian and industrial. The primary sector was predominantly concerned with growing sugar cane on estates, but smallholding agriculture with stock-rearing and small-scale fishing expanded in the decades after 1838. Bookkeepers, managers and overseers were the core supervisory staff on the estates. Metayers (sharecroppers), wage labourers, renters, and a small stratum of skilled artisans supplied the labour.

The Secondary Sector

Apart from muscovado sugar, molasses and rum, the main manufactured goods were handmade, using simple technology. They included clothing, boots and shoes, furniture and wood products, and the processing of foodstuff into products such as coconut oil, corn meal, farine (cassava flour), baked goods, confectionery, pickles, liqueurs and corned fish. All this was conducted as domestic and/or artisans' enterprises.

The Services Sector

The plantation system depended on the movements in international trade and commerce. It fostered production for export, with heavy emphasis on the consumption of imports. Therefore, commerce was the strongest segment of the tertiary sector before and after 1838.

After 1838 the local merchant factors continued to be influential, and many of them were planters. Retail shopkeeping expanded to serve the freedpeople on or near the estates, and itinerant hucksters, most of them female, bartered and sold both imported and local goods. The weekly markets, which attracted hundreds of vendors, were an important part of the distributive trades. Thus, there was continuity with the practices of the slavery era. The wholesale and retail trade was supported by merchants' clerks, writing clerks, shopmen, bookkeepers and porters. In the century after 1838, the distributive trades remained important sources of accumulation for people at all social levels. The smallholders also promoted increased trade in foodstuff and livestock with neighbouring colonies, especially Barbados, Trinidad and British Guiana.

There were few local financial institutions, apart from friendly societies and informal rotating credit/savings associations (*susu*) among the labouring class. There was no bank between 1847 and 1881, and the local one formed at the latter date was short-lived. The Government Savings Bank was the main banking institution from 1893 until two commercial banks opened branches in Scarborough in 1917, only to close them in 1923. In the nineteenth century, the leading merchants were usually agents for insurance companies based in the UK; real property and cargoes were the main items insured.

Because most construction was of wood, woodcutters and sawyers were valued tradesmen, as were carpenters, who remained the most numerous artisans until the mid twentieth century. Boat-building was done on a miniscule scale. Coopers, who constructed hogsheads and casks for the shipping of produce, were also important.

Owing to the poor roads, much communication was by sea. A major service was drogherage, the transport of goods to and from the outbays by sloops and open boats. Drogherage continued to be important until the 1930s. Sloops and schooners were also part of the trade with neighbouring colonies. On land, carts drawn by mules or cattle were the most important means of haulage. There were few traps and buggies, and horses and donkeys were the main means of transport.

In this context, mariners and boatmen, cartwrights, wheelwrights and blacksmiths provided valued services. Some of these artisans, as well as

millwrights and various mechanics, were also vital for the assembly and maintenance of estate machinery.

The next important set of services was domestic. Hundreds of men and women were employed as grooms, butlers, gardeners, maids, nurses, cooks and laundresses.

Before 1838, many of the services that are today financed mainly from public funds were performed within the domain of the plantation. Government administration, public works, education, and health services had all been minimal in slave society. The role of the state had to expand after 1838. Even so, it was far smaller than in some of the nearby colonies. The schools were either private or run by the churches with state assistance; the teaching service was small, with only 36 persons so employed in 1881, growing to 101 persons by 1901; and there were no public secondary schools or other training institutions. The police service was also small (only 12 constables in 1901), as was the staff in the general administration.[2] There was no hospital before 1876; and no public almshouse or asylum throughout the nineteenth century. Thus, the services employing the most persons before 1900 were provided by the commercial subsector and the skilled trades.

The Economic Sectors, 1900–1938

The Primary Sector

Tobago was annexed to Trinidad in 1889 and the closer Union of the two occurred in 1899. By 1900 the sugar economy had collapsed and was rapidly being replaced by new export crops—cocoa, coconuts, rubber, limes—for the foreign market, and livestock and foodstuff for local and inter-colonial consumption. The primary sector remained agrarian. In this period the peasantry, which had begun to expand in the last years of the nineteenth century, reached its apogee. Cocoa, coconuts and limes were both estate and peasant crops.

The Secondary Sector

Apart from the rump of the sugar industry, manufacturing continued to be dominated by artisans, mainly in clothing, furniture and food processing, as before. The new manufacturing activities included the production of copra and coconut fibre, and of lime juice and lime oil. A tobacco factory making cigars and a government cotton ginnery were started between 1908 and 1912, but both were short-lived. Most of these efforts produced semi-processed goods for export: to use Lloyd Best's term, the 'muscovado bias' continued.[3] There were also a few small enterprises for making ice and carbonated drinks, and for grinding cocoa beans and making, from the paste, balls which could be grated for the local chocolate tea.

The Services Sector

The tertiary sector expanded. With the hiring of pupil teachers, the teaching service increased. Although the state apparatus expanded, the Public Service was very small, and most of the heads of department were recruited from Trinidad or overseas. The greatest expansion was in the Public Works Department which, through permanent and casual labour, was, by 1938, one of the most important sources of wages in Tobago, particularly for men.

New groups of merchants emerged in the early twentieth century. Some were Portuguese immigrants in the rumshop and grocery business. Mainly from within Tobago emerged several traders with 'cocoa shops', who bought cocoa from the smallest producers and collected it for shipping to Trinidad. In general, however, these businesses did not survive into the succeeding generation. All suffered from the loss of direct shipping links with the rest of the world, starting in 1905, which helped to keep them subordinate to the Trinidad merchants, and curtailed much of the intercolonial trade with nearby colonies.

Itinerant vending, vending in the markets, and trafficking of local goods to Trinidad employed the majority of people in the services sector, many of whom were also part-time producers in the primary sector.

Artisans producing clothing and those involved in construction (tailors, seamstresses, carpenters and masons) continued to provide valued services.

Motor transport became increasingly important from the 1920s, and with it the emergence of private lorry, bus and taxi services. These changes produced new employment opportunities for drivers, conductors and motor mechanics.

Tourism had been pioneered by women who had started boarding houses in Scarborough in the 1880s, and the first hotel, Speyside Inn, was opened in 1924. In 1924 several boarding houses were also started, some of them built by planters. By 1938 the tourism industry was still a fledgling one, with five hotels and ten boarding houses.

By 1938, therefore, Tobago's economy was still agrarian, with rudimentary manufacturing of primary products for export, and production by artisans and domestic enterprises for local consumption. The services sector was expanding; but apart from the vending and bartering of foodstuff at the markets and in the villages, it too was small, in keeping with the small internal market, poor physical infrastructure, and minimal state functions.

2. THE 1844 CENSUS

The 1844 census recorded the occupations of persons 18 years old and over, dividing them into three categories. The first combined 'planters, agricultural labourers and cultivators of land for a livelihood'; the second was those 'deriving a living from trade or other business, profession or employment'; and the third was those 'having no employment'. Agriculture occupied 59.3 per cent of those 18 years old or over and 69.5 per cent of the employed; trade, business and professions occupied 26.0 per cent and 30.4 per cent, respectively. The unemployed were enumerated as 1,201 persons, or 14.7 per cent of those over 18, but these included the aged and infirm; women were 86.0 per cent (1,033) of this group, since those doing unpaid domestic duties were not distinguished (Table 8.1).

Despite the withdrawal of many women from estate labour after 1838, women were the majority among those in agriculture (51.9 per cent). There were no female professionals. Women comprised 43.4 per cent of the persons in trade, business and craft, and they outnumbered the men so employed in Scarborough and Plymouth, the towns. Employment in trade, business and craft for both sexes was most limited in the windward parishes, but in all parishes men greatly outnumbered women in these occupations, particularly in the leeward parish of St. Patrick (Table 8.1).

205

TABLE 8.1 **Occupational Categories by Sex, Parish and Town for Population 18 Years Old and over, 1844**

District, parish or town	Planters, agricultural labourers, cultivators of land for a livelihood				Persons living by trade, other business, profession or employment				'No employment'			
	Males	Females	Total	%	Males	Females	Total	%	Males	Females	Total	%
Windward												
St. John	205	229	434	71.6	68	24	92	15.2	11	69	80	13.2
St. Paul	212	213	425	70.5	64	43	107	17.7	14	57	71	11.8
St. Mary	168	208	376	78.8	40	21	61	12.8	6	34	40	8.4
Middle												
St. George	342	392	734	70.8	123	67	190	18.3	16	96	112	10.8
St. Andrew	343	433	776	54.2	254	205	459	32.1	44	153	197	13.8
Scarborough	49	78	127	15.3	264	325	589	71.0	9	104	113	13.6
Leeward												
St. David	629	511	1,140	61.6	194	109	303	16.4	45	362	407	22.0
St. Patrick	363	417	780	69.8	125	54	179	16.0	19	140	159	14.2
Plymouth	24	36	60	26.4	70	75	145	63.8	4	18	22	9.7
Total	**2,335**	**2,517**	**4,852**	**59.3**	**1,202**	**923**	**2,125**	**26.0**	**168**	**1,033**	**1,201**	**14.7**

Source: Calculated from CO 285/53: Tobago Population Census Report, 1844.

Note: The three categories comprise the total number of persons 18 years old or over in each locality; percentages are based on the figures for the localities.

3. THE CENSUSES FROM 1851 TO 1946

Methodological Issues

Limitations of the Data

From 1851, occupational titles were given. These are sometimes imprecise and say nothing about the relations of production in which the people were involved. Moreover, changing methods of enumeration at times make it difficult to understand the trends. Some occupations were also under-counted. For example, metayers (share-croppers) were first recorded in 1891, and the compiler observed that, probably in every instance, metayage was a secondary occupation.[4] The absence of metayers from earlier censuses reflected this occupational multiplicity, but there were certainly persons whose primary activity was metayage. Again, partly because of occupational multiplicity, 'peasant proprietors' were first mentioned only in 1891. Thus, important areas of income-earning and opportunity were hidden by the occupational data. Enumerations by sex were also rare before 1891. These limitations are taken into account in the analysis.

Key Concepts Defined

From 1851 to 1946 the censuses described the number of people in their usual main activity; neither age nor time references were given. Following George Roberts, we call the total number of economically active persons the 'working force', which he defined as 'that portion of the population usually engaged in the production of goods and services for the market'.[5]

The census-takers used what is called the 'gainful-worker' approach to understanding the economically active population. According to Harewood, this approach assumes 'a more or less stable functional role as a worker, a housewife … etc., and that this role is largely independent of, and more important than, his activity at any given time.' Thus the census data do not allow us to take into account widespread occupational multiplicity.

Both 'gainful workers' and 'working force' refer to those persons producing, or assisting in producing, marketable goods and services, whether paid in cash or an equivalent; and they usually exclude housewives. In Tobago, however,

most *households* produced agricultural goods or related products and services for sale or barter, *and we have therefore taken persons performing unpaid domestic duties to be part of the working force.*

In sum, the approach in the censuses does not capture the occupational multiplicity and the nature of what Vanus James calls the 'household-firms', which were features of the activities of the working population of Tobago.[6]

Harewood also notes that the 'gainful-worker' approach often does not yield direct estimates of the employed and the unemployed, although in principle the economically active population has both segments.[7]

In the light of the above concerns, in order to take into account

a. people doing unpaid domestic duties, who undoubtedly took part in household production and vending; and

b. the economically active who were unpaid or unemployed at the census dates,

the term 'working force' refers to *all economically active persons, paid or unpaid, employed or unemployed.* The unemployed were negligible before 1931. The 'working force' includes those given as 'living on private means', since the question asked in the censuses was greatly misunderstood, and many of these persons were actually workers. The 'working force' excludes the retired, aged and infirm, those otherwise dependent, and students.

For comparative purposes, we have provided worker participation rates for the 'working force' as herein defined (that is, including those in unpaid domestic duties, the unemployed and those with private means) and for the 'gainful workers', which excludes these groups (Table 8.8).

Classifying the Occupations

George Roberts states for Jamaica:

… in analysing occupational data we enter a domain in which census material proves often treacherous and unrewarding. Changing concepts of the working population, changing definitions of its major classes and the persistent attempts to fit the essentially simple occupational pattern of the island into elaborate classifications, more suitable to countries on the road to full industrialization, impose severe limitations on the available data.[8]

As for Jamaica, so for Tobago.

From 1851 to 1891, no official classification of the job titles was given. In keeping with the 'simple occupational pattern' of Tobago, this study classifies the occupations into three categories, based on the author's understanding of their income levels and general ranking in the social order. Where the titles were vague or difficult to interpret, they were placed in a fourth category called Other, Undefined. For the censuses from 1901 to 1946, we retained our classificatory scheme in preference to the changing official ones, because of its greater suitability to Tobago, and also to facilitate comparison through time. The term 'class', as used to name the occupational groups, means 'category'.

Class I

In Class I, two main strata were identified: planters, managers and merchants, on the one hand; senior officials, professionals, surveyors and clergy, on the other. The few hoteliers who were occasionally recorded were also placed in Class I.

Class II

Class II was deemed to be composed of four main strata. Teachers, governesses, minor officials such as constables[9] and clerks, and merchants' clerks, bookkeepers and 'shopmen' were considered one stratum. Teachers and minor officials were poorly paid. Yet persons so employed were highly respected and lived in a kind of genteel poverty. Printers were included here, because it was a trade to which greater prestige was given than to the other manual trades, since it required relatively high levels of formal education. Druggists and dispensers were also placed in this stratum.

Overseers and those in lower supervisory positions were taken to be the second stratum within Class II.

Shopkeepers, auctioneers and hucksters were considered the third stratum. Many of these were regarded as 'respectable', and some of the most successful shopkeepers became renters of 'coconut walks' and owners of substantial tracts of land; some even became planters.[10]

The fourth stratum in Class II is peasant proprietors and farmers. No definition of these terms was given in the censuses which used them,

but it is assumed that this was the main occupation of the respondents, and that they enjoyed a more comfortable standard of living than wage labourers.

Photographers, who were few, and mentioned only in 1871, 1931 and 1946, were placed in Class II, since their work required equipment and skill. Telephone and wireless operators, who emerged in the twentieth century, were also assigned to Class II.

No attempt was made to rank the strata in Classes I and II.

Class III

In Class III were placed, first, the skilled tradespeople, including butchers. Dressmaking is separately listed in our tables because, besides baking and making of confectionery, it was the main skilled trade in which women participated. Since the censuses before 1891 gave no employment data by sex, seamstresses were specially identified throughout, so that the occupational status of women could be better understood.

There was a wide range of skills among artisans, especially in trades where there were hundreds; and the demand for their services fluctuated with the economic cycles. However, they earned more than field labourers, and were among the first freeholders after 1838. The 'bespoke' tailors and seamstresses, master blacksmiths, carpenters and other skilled artisans enjoyed incomes that were far higher than those of labourers, *and belong in Class II*. However, the data do not allow us to distinguish them. *We therefore have to assume that the line between Classes II and III is not rigid, in keeping with the fluidity and ambiguity of the reality itself.*[11]

Mariners, boatmen and fishermen were placed together in Class III. Many of the mariners on census day worked on ships which happened to be in the harbours, and a few may have been master mariners—commanding officers, who should be in Class II. A few of the master mariners (especially those with transatlantic experience) even belonged in Class I, since they became planters in the late nineteenth and early twentieth centuries.[12] 'Fishermen and boatmen' included several categories of sailors on boats, sloops, droghers and other small craft. Although the grouping is heterogeneous, in the absence of more detailed information, mariners, fishermen and boatmen are treated as a stratum near the top of Class III. These are assumed to have been jobs that could have brought upward mobility, since the opportunity to earn from fishing and seafaring would have placed them above the standard of living of agricultural labourers. *Again, the fluidity of the reality, given the varied levels of skill and income and the lack of detailed data, must be noted.*

Agricultural labourers, general labourers, domestic servants, laundresses, porters and government messengers were placed in the lowest stratum of paid workers. Male domestic workers such as grooms and butlers earned more than field labourers, but in general these were the lowest-paid occupations.

For the censuses before 1901, midwives, who were often illiterate and trained by apprenticeship to older midwives,[13] were placed in Class III, as were the nurses enumerated in 1871, since neither public hospital nor formal training facilities existed then. After 1901, however, the nurses and midwives, who were usually trained public servants, were treated as part of Class II.

Unpaid domestic work was placed in Class III. Wives and daughters so employed were paid in kind, but would have enjoyed the living standards of the household. This category would have included women at all levels of the society; therefore these data are not given great weight in the analysis.

New groups of workers emerged at the 1931 census, most of them employed in transport and communications, given the advent of privately owned motor transport and a public telephone system by the 1920s. These workers, except for telephone operators, were placed in Class III. Workers in personal services outside of traditional domestic work, also emergent as a category in the census from 1931, were placed in Class II if they were in supervisory positions; the remainder—cooks, janitors etc—were counted in Class III.

Others, Undefined

Persons who claimed to be 'living on private means' were placed in this category and counted as part of the working force, because a high proportion of them were in fact at work. The census reports often stated that many of them had misunderstood the question. Those in occupations which were undefined or not clear were also included here.

Supporting Evidence

This understanding of the income levels associated with the job titles receives external validation from the jurors' lists and other historical evidence. In 1879 jurors were required to have a minimum income of £60, or freehold estate valued over £30; or to be managers of estates minimally valued at £100; or to be paying either a minimum yearly rent of £30 or annual customs duties of £50. The 1880 jurors' list had planters, managers, merchants, professionals, teachers, merchants' clerks, overseers, shopkeepers and a few master artisans: blacksmiths, mechanics and carpenters. All of these persons properly belong to what we call Classes I and II. From May 1886, all males who could read and write were eligible for jury service. Even so, the jury lists down to 1891 consistently show that persons in Classes I and II, and some in the upper reaches of Class III, were most likely to be called for jury service. These persons had incomes well above the basic agricultural wage of 8d per day, equivalent to a maximum of £10 8s per year.

The jury lists for the early twentieth century, based on income or property qualifications, also support this analysis. In 1902 only planters, merchants, professionals and middle-level civil servants qualified; in 1930 the list included also estate managers, owners of large holdings (not estates), one estate overseer and one master carpenter.[14] These were mainly persons from Classes I and II.

The policy on road repairs in the nineteenth century illustrates both the prestige ranking of occupations and the low status of females from the labouring class. The Road Act (Amendment) of 1849 obliged all males aged 16–50 to labour on the roads for 6d per day for two weeks per annum or to provide a substitute; the penalty was 4s for each day defaulted. Planters, merchants, professionals, senior officials, clergymen, teachers and clerks (groups in Classes I and II) consistently refused to perform such labour, because it was demeaning. They often paid women to do so. Many labouring men also sent their wives to the roads. There were changes to the Act over time, but statutory labour and penalties continued until 1887. By 1885, the workforce on the roads was mostly women from the labouring class.[15]

The jury lists and the official correspondence on the Road Acts support our ranking in broad outline, although they give no clue to the precise position of each job title. We assume therefore that, as a broad ranking in terms of income, this classification will serve.[16]

Main Occupational Trends, 1851–1881

After 1838 there was a redistribution of the population, spatially and occupationally. By 1851 the basic contours of the occupational structure were established, and they persisted for decades. Between 1851 and 1881, Classes I and II together accounted for less than 4.0 per cent of the working force, the remaining 96.0 per cent being in Class III (Table 8.2). Thus, mobility into Class II occupations via education, shopkeeping, huckstering and landowning was very limited before the sugar crisis of the 1880s.

Because of internal migration, population and economic activity were concentrated in the Middle and Leeward Districts; thus, there were important differences in the occupational distributions according to districts (Table A3.1). In 1851, 75.0 per cent of the merchants, 92.3 per cent of the clerks, and 71.4 per cent of the hucksters were in the Middle District, where Scarborough was located.

Since many hucksters were itinerant, they may have served the Windward District (where there was only 1), though residing outside of it.

In 1851, 16.3 per cent of the population lived in the Windward District (Table A2.3). Although 30.3 per cent of the shopkeepers were at Windward, most were likely to be owners or managers of shops on the estates. Therefore, of the occupations that were avenues of upward social mobility for the labouring class, only the skilled trades for men were proportionately represented in the Windward District, which had 16.5 per cent of the tradesmen. The teachers were too few to be significant. Of the seamstresses, only 7.8 per cent were in the Windward District. Thus, for the labouring population at Windward, whose landowning was insignificant in 1851, skilled trades for men were the major route to social mobility. Even fishing was concentrated in the Leeward District (Table A3.1).

Between 1851 and 1881, there was little change in this pattern. Merchants, clerks, shopkeepers and hucksters were concentrated in the Middle District. The Leeward District continued to have the majority of fishermen, although by 1881 they had increased in the Windward District (Tables A3.1, A3.2).

Since skilled trades, including dressmaking, fishing and seafaring, constituted the highest-paid jobs in Class III, Table 8.3 examines the percentages of these occupations in each district from 1851 to 1891. The few midwives reported were included, because this was one of the skilled female occupations in Class III, even though most midwives had no formal training in Western medical practices. The table shows a relatively stable pattern, with improvement in the positions of all districts by 1871, and decline thereafter.

The Censuses Marking the Collapse of the Sugar Economy, 1891–1901

The 1891 Census

In 1891 the job titles were given by the Registrar General of Trinidad and modified to suit Tobago's conditions. It is thus not always easy to make comparisons with certain categories at previous censuses. Metayers (sharecroppers) were enumerated for the only time between 1844 and 1901. The total was 798; but the occupational tables gave only the number for the Leeward District and part of the Middle District (503). However, for the first time after 1844, we are given the sex of the persons in each occupational group.

The working force numbered 10,194,[17] 16 less than in 1881 (Table 8.2). Class II increased dramatically, by 83.8 per cent. In part, this probably resulted from reclassification of some of the people in skilled trades. Skilled *men* were placed in a general category called 'mechanics and handicraftsmen',[18] which did not exhaust all the trades, since some of the bakers, for example, were females. The classification of bakers, who may have been itinerant or owners of small sales outlets, as hucksters and shopkeepers, is therefore a strong possibility, especially since these vendors leaped from 43 in 1881 to 169, an increase of 293.0 per cent, and since 85.2 per cent of them were females.

TABLE 8.2 Number in Occupations as Percentage of the Working Force, 1851–1891

Occupations	1851 No.	1851 Per cent	1861 No.	1861 Per cent	1871 No.	1871 Per cent	1881 No.	1881 Per cent	1891 No.	1891 Per cent
Class I										
Planters, merchants, managers etc.	124	1.5	97	1.1	79	0.8	105	1.0	138	1.3
Officials, professionals, clergy	38	0.4	29	0.3	30	0.3	41	0.4	39	0.4
Subtotal	**162**	**1.9**	**126**	**1.4**	**109**	**1.2**	**146**	**1.4**	**177**	**1.7**
Class II										
Teachers, clerks, shopmen, druggists	104	1.2	128	1.5	130	1.4	145	1.4	153	1.5
Overseers, foremen, supervisors	—	—	—	—	38	0.4	—	—	—	—
Shopkeepers, hucksters	62	0.7	56	0.6	51	0.5	46	0.5	169	1.6
Peasants, farmers	10	0.1	—	—	—	—	—	—	29	0.3
Subtotal	**176**	**2.1**	**184**	**2.1**	**219**	**2.4**	**191**	**1.9**	**351**	**3.4**
Class III										
Artisans, skilled tradespeople	908	10.7	920	10.5	1,178	12.8	1,195	11.7	1,070	10.5
Dressmakers and milliners	475	5.6	508	5.8	605	6.6	555	5.4	640	6.3
Mariners, fishermen, boatmen	185	2.2	209	2.4	239	2.6	219	2.1	314	3.1
Agricultural labourers	5,644	66.6	6,130	70.0	5,721	62.2	6,598	64.6	4,436	43.5
Metayers, agricultural contractors	—	—	6	0.1	—	—	—	—	503[c]	4.9
General labourers, porters	6	0.1	—	—	10	0.1	3	0.0	757	7.4
Domestic workers	799	9.4	487	5.5	899	9.8	1,099	10.8	754	7.4
Laundresses	—	—	182	2.1	175	1.9	194	1.9	195	1.9
Persons in domestic duties*	112	1.3	—	—	—	—	—	—	918	9.0
Others: sextons, midwives etc.	2	0.0	9	0.1	35	0.4	10	1.0	—	—
Subtotal	**8,131**	**96.0**	**8,451**	**96.5**	**8,862**	**96.4**	**9,873**	**96.7**	**9,587**	**94.0**
Others, undefined*										
Subtotal	—	—	—	—	—	—	—	—	79	0.8
Total	**8,469**	**100.0**	**8,761**	**100.0**	**9,190**	**100.0**	**10,210**	**100.0**	**10,194[d]**	**100.0**

Sources: Calculated from Tobago Population Census Reports, 1851–1891.

Notes: Percentages are subject to rounding errors. Categories marked * are not considered to be 'gainful workers' but are part of the working force.

[a] Managers and overseers were not distinguished from planters in the censuses for 1851, 1861, 1881, 1891 and 1921.

[b] The 868 'servants' in 1871 are taken to be domestic workers.

[c] These are 503 metayers, all of whom had primary occupations which were not given.

[d] The census statistics account for 10,194 of the 10,197 persons who are supposed to be in the working force.

TABLE 8.3 Persons in Skilled Trades, Fishing and Seafaring as Percentage of the Working Force in Each District, 1851–1891

District	1851			1861			1871		
	Number	Total in working force	Per cent	Number	Total in working force	Per cent	Number	Total in working force	Per cent
Windward	202	1,649	12.2	230	1,535	15.0	334	1,980	16.9
Middle	748	3,478	21.5	820	3,525	23.3	875	3,372	26.0
Leeward	618	3,342	18.5	593	3,701	16.0	831	3,838	21.7
Total	1,568	8,469	18.5	1,643	8,761	18.8	2,040	9,190	22.2

District	1881			1891		
	Number	Total in working force	Per cent	Number	Total in working force	Per cent
Windward	351	2,330	15.1	408	2,354	17.3
Middle	817	3,487	23.4	839	3,565	23.5
Leeward	812	4,393	18.5	777	4,278	18.2
Total[a]	1,980	10,210	19.4	2,024	10,197	19.8

Sources: Calculated from Tobago Population Census Reports, 1851–1891.

Notes: Persons in skilled trades are artisans except printers, plus dressmakers, milliners and midwives. Printers are treated as part of Class II. All the occupations considered here are designated part of Class III.
[a] In 1891, the census occupation table accounted for 10,194 persons, although its total was 10,197.

It is also possible that hucksters had been under-enumerated in 1881, when there were only 5. Moreover, in the crisis, waged employment being scarce, many women resorted to itinerant vending and bartering, which may help to account for the increase in hucksters in Class II. The teachers also increased from 36 to 55 persons, or by 52.8 per cent; and 20 (36.4 per cent) were women (Table 8.2).

In Class III there was, in keeping with the collapse of the sugar economy, a drastic decline in both agricultural workers and domestic servants. In 1881, together they accounted for 75.4 per cent of the working force; in 1891, 50.9 per cent (Table 8.2).

The 1891 census gave a new category, 'general labourers, porters etc',[19] numbering 757 persons. These general labourers and porters constituted 7.4 per cent of the working force. For the first time since 1851, 'wives and daughters in domestic duties' were enumerated, and they were 9.0 per cent of the working force (Table 8.2).[20]

There was a marked increase in fishermen, mariners and boatmen combined, from 219 in 1881 to 314 in 1891. The Windward District had 27.0 per cent of the combined group; and it accounted for 36.2 per cent of the boatmen and fishermen. All this suggests that fishing and seafaring became more important primary occupations there, as estate agriculture declined.

Occupations by Sex

Women comprised 56.4 per cent of the working force in 1891. When the occupations were classified by sex, only 6 women were in Class I, and women were slightly under-represented in Class II with 51.6 per cent of the jobs (Tables A3.3, A3.4). In Class III, both sexes were represented in keeping with their share of the working force.

Sex by Occupations

In the 'Sex by Occupations' classification for 1891 (Table A3.5), agricultural and general labour and paid domestic work occupied 62.4 per cent of females, with launderers bringing the figure to 65.8 per cent, while the comparable figure for men was 52.9 per cent. (Because metayers were inconsistently reported in the censuses, they were excluded from consideration here.)[21] The skilled trades, fishing and seafaring employed 31.2 per cent of the men, but only 11.1 per cent of the women were seamstresses, the most popular skill for women. Thus, 92.0 per cent of the men and 95.6 per cent of the women were in Class III occupations, but 52.9 per cent of the men were in the lowest-paid jobs, while 65.8 per cent of the women were so located, with another 16.0 per cent unpaid.

TABLE 8.4 Agricultural Labourers by District and Sex, 1891

District	Male No.	Female No.	Male Per cent	Female Per cent	Total No.
Windward	648	782	45.3	54.7	1,430
Middle	539	755	41.6	58.3	1,294
Leeward	656	1,056	38.3	61.7	1,712
Total	1,843	2,593	41.5	58.4	4,436

Source: Tobago Population Census Report, 1891.

Occupations by District

When the data are analysed by district, the female predominance in the agricultural workforce was most marked in the Leeward District (Table 8.4).

Further, the sharp decline in agricultural labourers between 1881 and 1891 was most dramatic (44.0 per cent) also in the Leeward District, the heartland of the sugar economy (Table 8.5).

Females comprised 54.6 per cent of the 'general labourers'. They were disproportionately represented in the Windward District, where they exceeded males by over 2 : 1. Males, however, were over-represented in the Middle District, being 55.7 per cent of this category (Table 8.6).

TABLE 8.5 **Agricultural Labourers by District, 1881, 1891**

District	1881		1891		1881–1891 Decline	
	No.	Per cent	No.	Per cent	No.	Per cent
Windward	1,736	26.3	1,430	32.2	306	17.6
Middle	1,806	27.4	1,294	29.2	512	28.3
Leeward	3,056	46.3	1,712	38.6	1,344	44.0
Total	6,598	100.0	4,436	100.0	2,162	32.8

Sources: Calculated from Tobago Population Census Reports, 1881, 1891.

TABLE 8.6 **General Labourers by District and Sex, 1891**

District	Male No.	Male Per cent	Female No.	Female Per cent	Total No.	Total Per cent
Windward	29	30.5	66	69.5	95	12.6
Middle	116	55.7	92	44.2	208	27.5
Leeward	198	43.7	255	56.3	453	59.9
Total	343	45.4	413	54.6	756	100.0

Source: Calculated from Tobago Population Census Report, 1891.

Note: Percentages are calculated within the districts in the Male and Female columns and over the total number of general labourers in the last column.

The 1891 Census: A Summary

The collapse of the sugar industry began to alter the occupational structure. Class II increased, mainly through what was classified as shopkeeping and huckstering, much of which today would be called the 'informal sector'. In Class III, there was a redistribution from agricultural and domestic labour into other lowly-paid or unpaid categories, especially 'general labourers' and domestic duties; and there was increased seafaring in the Windward District.

The 1901 Census

The enumerators used the following occupational classification: 'Official', 'Professional', 'Commercial', 'Agricultural', and 'General and Indefinite' for both Trinidad and Tobago. Since this obscures the gradations of rank and income that were integral to Tobago's occupational structure, our simple classification was kept. As in 1891, the sex distribution was also given.

The working force was 9,934,[22] a decline of 2.5 per cent from that of 1891 (Table A3.3). Class II showed further rapid growth (by 86.9 per cent),

and accounted for 6.6 per cent of the working force, up from 3.4 per cent in 1891 (Tables 8.2, 8.7). The steep increase is owed, firstly, to peasant proprietors, with a growth of 544.8 per cent (but these had been under-counted in 1891). Secondly, 'shopkeepers' (hucksters were not mentioned in 1901), advanced by 32.5 per cent, the majority (164 or 73.2 per cent) again being women; and thirdly, teachers, merchants' clerks and minor officials grew by 39.9 per cent (Table A3.3). The teachers showed the largest increase in this subgroup. Their number rose from 55 in 1891 to 101 in 1901, a growth of 83.6 per cent. One-third of the teachers (33) were women, as well as 27.2 per cent of the 92 clerks.[23]

Owing to the increases in both Class II and the Other category, Class III had 90.2 per cent of the working force, a decline of 3.8 percentage points.

In 1901 the skilled trades were fully enumerated; and for the first time we can see the importance of female participation among bakers and confectioners, 60 of the 66 (90.9 per cent) being women. Agricultural labourers continued to decline (by 8.0 per cent); and their proportion of the working force moved from 43.5 per cent in 1891 to 41.1 per cent in 1901.

The Wireless Station, Fort King George, c.1906. Tobago was one of the last places in the British Empire to receive the telegraph. As a result, Tobagonians commemorated the Coronation of King Edward VII on 26 June 1902, not knowing that the event had been postponed owing to Edward's illness. The Wireless Station began to function on 2 January 1906. *Reproduced by permission of the Syndics of Cambridge University Library.*

Bridge over the Louis d'Or River (also called the Delaford River), 1931. This river was unbridged until 1930. When the tide was high or the river was in flood, motor traffic had to wait hours, sometimes days, for the water to subside. Pedestrians and people on horseback, who had to wade through the water in all seasons, were also delayed when the river was impassable. Therefore the construction of this bridge in 1930 was a historic event for the people of windward Tobago. *Reproduced from CO 298/153 with permission from the Public Record Office, UK.*

Hon. George Horatio McEachrane II (*c.*1854–1908), merchant and planter, nominated Member representing Tobago in the Trinidad and Tobago Legislative Council from 1893 to 1903. *Reproduced by permission of the Syndics of Cambridge University Library.*

Hon. James Alphaeus Alexander Biggart (1877–1932), pharmacist, chemist, and activist in many spheres of social and political life. Biggart was Tobago's first elected Member of the Trinidad and Tobago Legislative Council (1925–1932). *Photograph courtesy Daphne Harper.*

Hon. Isaac Arbuthnot Hope (1865–1956), merchant, Tobago's Member of the Trinidad and Tobago Legislative Council (1932–1938). *Detail from a photograph courtesy Nydia Bruce Daniel.*

Hon. George de Nobriga, planter, director of several companies and sportsman, Tobago's Member of the Trinidad and Tobago Legislative Council (1938–1946). *Reproduced with permission from the Archivist, The National Archives of Trinidad and Tobago.*

Hon. Alphonso Philbert Theophilus James (1901–1962), businessman, trade unionist, and Tobago's Member of the Trinidad and Tobago Legislative Council for 1946 to 1961. *Reproduced with permission from André Phillips.*

Laurence Emmanuel E. Edwards (1893–1968), his wife Irene née Lord (1905–1975), and their two eldest children, Laura and Lloyd, c.1937. At far left is Enid Crosby. Laurence Edwards went to Tobago from Trinidad in 1919. He was a highly successful educator, and a tireless activist of the labour, peasant, and literary and debating movements. *Photograph courtesy William Edwards and Sylvia Herke.*

Gaskynd Granger (c.1915–c.1996), Guyanese-born trade unionist and labour activist. Granger lived and worked in Tobago as an organizer of the Tobago Peasants and Industrial Workers Union, founded by A. P. T. James in 1946. *Photograph courtesy Gaskynd Granger.*

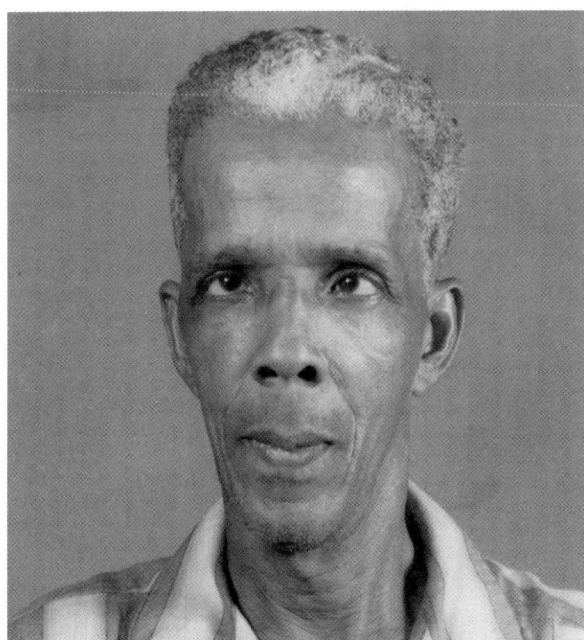

George David Hatt (1865–1924), merchant, amateur historian, social analyst and activist, with his wife Jane Anderson Hatt née Wilson, and the first six of their eleven children, at their home, Cinnamon Hill, *c.*1905. *Photograph courtesy Mr and Mrs Alec Hatt.*

Olive Sawyer (1914–1997), social worker and community activist. *Photograph courtesy Olive Sawyer.*

Eileen Guillaume née Armstrong (1916–2004), social worker and community activist. *Photograph courtesy Eileen Guillaume and Marjorie Tsoi-a-Fatt.*

Irma Crosby née Dalrymple (1907–2003), retired store clerk and bookkeeper. *Photograph courtesy Irma Crosby.*

Right: Jules Crooks (1903–1993), retired master tailor. *Photograph by Susan Craig-James.*

Tambourine and violin players at the wedding of David James and the author (under the arch), Tobago, 1977. *Photograph by Christopher Laird.*

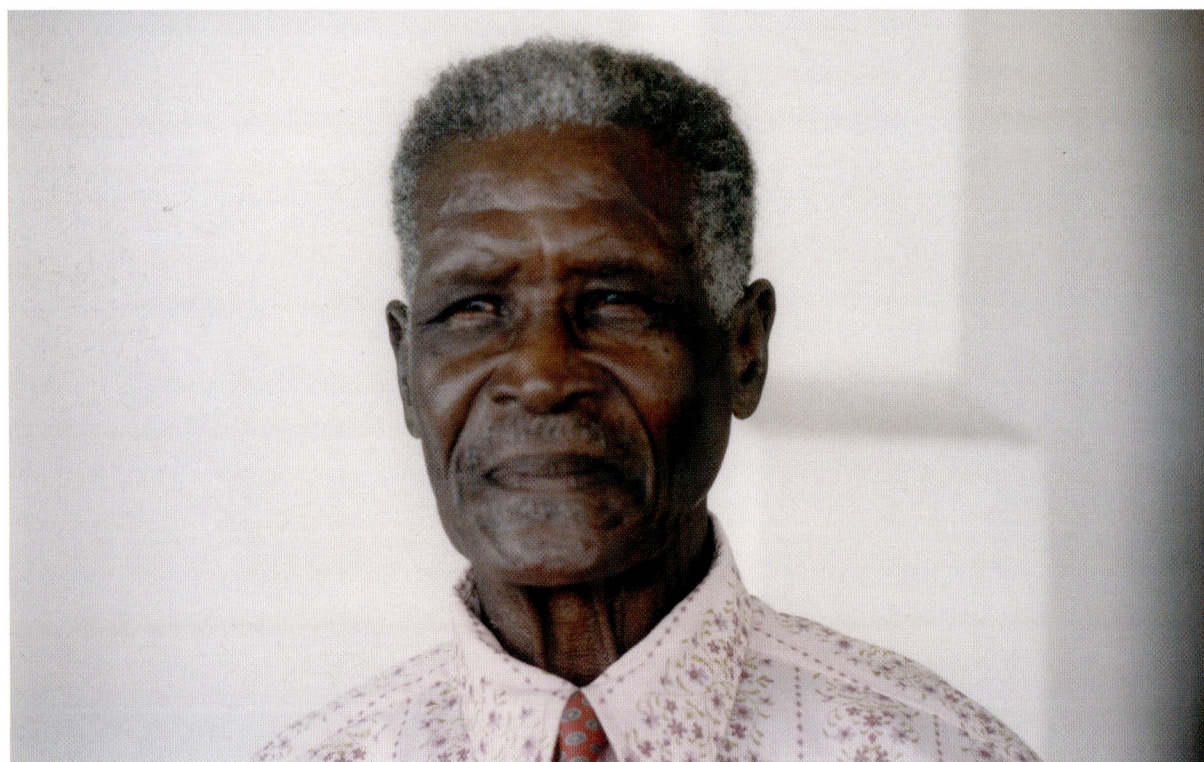

The author's parents, Sislyn Craig née Thomas (1921–1996) and Lionel Craig (b.1922); farmers and market vendors. *Photographs by the author.*

TABLE 8.7 **Number in Occupations as Percentage of the Working Force, 1901–1946**

Occupations	1901 No.	1901 %	1911 No.	1911 %	1921[a] No.	1921[a] %	1931 No.	1931 %	1946 No.	1946 %
Class I										
Planters, merchants, managers etc.	61	0.6	113	0.9	216	1.6	126	0.8	51	0.3
Officials, professionals, clergy	41	0.4	51	0.4	85	0.6	65	0.4	43	0.3
Subtotal	**102**	**1.0**	**164**	**1.4**	**301**	**2.2**	**191**	**1.3**	**94**	**0.7**
Class II										
Teachers, clerks, shopmen, druggists	214	2.2	360	3.0	363	2.7	520	3.5	627	4.4
Overseers, foremen, supervisors	31	0.3	44	0.4	—	—	5	0.0	134	1.0
Shopkeepers, hucksters	224	2.2	19	0.1	237	1.8	61	0.4	312	2.2
Peasants, farmers	187	1.9	416	3.5	786	5.9	933	6.2	1,870	13.3
Subtotal	**656**	**6.6**	**839**	**7.0**	**1,386**	**10.3**	**1,519**	**10.2**	**2,943**	**20.9**
Class III										
Artisans, skilled tradespeople	1,033	10.4	1,116	9.4	1,037	7.7	1,245	8.3	1,562	11.1
Dressmakers and milliners	686	6.9	965	8.1	923	6.9	478	3.2	707	5.0
Mariners, fishermen, boatmen	252	2.5	133	1.1	135	1.0	177	1.2	218	1.5
Transport, related workers	—	—	—	—	—	—	150	1.0	178	1.3
Agricultural labourers	4,082	41.1	4,531	38.0	4,501	33.5	3,950	26.4	1,445	10.2
Metayers, agricultural contractors	—	—	233	1.9	116	0.9	—	—	—	—
General labourers, porters	1,130	11.4	1,753	14.7	2,151	16.0	1,340	9.0	990	7.0
Domestic workers	729	7.3	746	6.3	1,009	7.5	701	4.7	278	2.0
Launderers, laundresses	266	2.7	181	1.5	138	1.0	70	0.5	86	0.1
Other personal services	—	—	—	—	—	—	16	0.1	213	1.5
Persons in domestic duties*	778	7.8	1,050	8.8	1,537	11.5	4,297	28.7	4,560	32.4
Others: sextons, midwives etc.[b]	11	0.1	3	0.0	—	—	—	—	35	0.2
Subtotal	**8,967**	**90.2**	**10,711**	**89.9**	**11,547**	**86.0**	**12,424**	**83.0**	**10,272**	**72.9**
Others, undefined										
'Living on private means'*	157	1.6	156	1.3	187	1.4	—	—	133	0.9
'Proprietors'	31	0.3	41	0.0	—	—	99	0.7	—	—
Others, not stated	21	0.2	1	—	—	—	9	0.1	5	0.0
Subtotal	209	2.1	198	1.7	187	1.4	108	0.7	138	1.0
Not retired, not gainfully employed*	—	—	7	0.1	—	—	718	4.8	641	4.5
Total	**9,934**	**99.9**	**11,919**	**100.0**	**13,421**	**99.9**	**14,960**	**100.0**	**14,088**	**100.0**

Sources: Trinidad and Tobago Population Census Reports, 1901–1946.

Notes:

Percentages are subject to rounding errors. Categories marked * are not considered to be 'gainful workers'.

[a] Managers and overseers were not distinguished from planters in 1921.

[b] In 1946 refers to unskilled factory workers.

General labourers increased by 49.3 per cent, and the proportion of women in this category grew also, from 54.6 per cent in 1891 to 59.9 per cent in 1901 (Tables 8.2, 8.7, A3.3 and A3.4).

When the occupations were classified by sex, males constituted only 41.0 per cent of the working force, and they were 44.4 per cent of the 'gainful workers'. Indeed, the general participation rates for both the 'working force' and the 'gainful workers' show a marked decline in male rates and an increase for females between 1891 and 1901 (Tables A3.4, 8.8).

There was an increase, by 40.3 per cent, of women in Class II; but male penetration of Class II advanced more rapidly than that of females—170 men in 1891, 402 in 1901, or 136.5 per cent growth. Men were 61.3 per cent of the persons in Class II, but in Class III, the proportions were reversed, with women constituting 61.0 per cent. The over-representation of men in Class II indicates that opportunities for social mobility via landowning, teaching and lower supervisory positions were greater for males than for females, whose major employment in Class II was in 'shopkeeping' (Tables A3.3, A3.4).

Within Class III, the relative positions of males and females remained unchanged. In the highest-paid jobs—the skilled trades and fishing—30.1 per cent of the men were employed, but only 12.7 per cent of the women were dressmakers and bakers, the two skills in which women are recorded. The comparable figures for 1891 were 31.2 per cent and 11.1 per cent, respectively. Among the lowest-paid workers—agricultural labourers, general labourers, domestic servants and launderers—36.4 per cent were males and 63.6 per cent females; of all the men, 55.4 per cent were in these jobs, and 67.3 per cent of all women (Table A3.5). For 1891, the proportions were 52.9 per cent for males and 65.8 per cent for females. Thus, at both upper and lower levels of employment in Class III, the estimates for males and females showed no appreciable change from those for 1891.

The Occupational Transition in the Sugar Crisis Summarized, 1881–1901

Between 1881 and 1901, there were three major shifts in the occupational patterns. The first was a sharp decline in participation rates for males and an increase for females between 1891 and 1901.

This was coupled with the concentration of women at the base of the occupational ladder, a feature for which there are data only from 1891 onwards. In 1891 and 1901, between 66 and 67 per cent of all women were in the least-paid jobs; the comparable figures for men ranged between 53 and 55.4 per cent.

The second shift was the clear expansion of Class II occupations, in which males were the greatest beneficiaries of teaching, clerical work and peasant proprietorship. In 1901 landowning was the least favourable Class II occupation for women, who constituted only 17.1 per cent of this group (Table A3.4). The beachhead which women sustained among hucksters and shopkeepers, among whom they comprised 73.2 per cent, is therefore noteworthy. The statistics are likely to have under-estimated the hundreds of women who vended and bartered at the weekly markets, and sold goods from village to village in the Windward District.

Thirdly, there was a shift in Class III employment out of agriculture and paid domestic work into 'general labour', and this was most marked in the Leeward District, the epicentre of the sugar industry. Women formed the majority of general labourers.

The Occupational Structure in the Heyday of the Cocoa Industry, 1901–1931

Participation Rates

Male participation rates in the working force rose sharply, from 67.5 per cent in 1901 to 78.6 per cent in 1931, in keeping with the changing age/sex structure in those decades; they declined again after 1931. For 'gainful workers', there was a decline of only two percentage points in the male rates for 1921–1931, and the sharpest drop was between 1931 and 1946, from 74.3 per cent to 68.7 per cent. For females, however, between 1901 and 1931, participation rates hovered around 80 per cent when unpaid domestic work is included; when it is excluded, the data for 'gainful workers' show a steady decline in female participation after 1901, falling sharply after 1921 (from 65.1 per cent to 36.0 per cent), in keeping with the trends for Trinidad and Tobago as a whole.[24] In general, the Tobago male participation rates were lower than those for the colony, since Trinidad had higher proportions of immigrant males of working age (Table 8.8). For both males and females in Tobago, rising rates of school enrolment and attendance in the early twentieth century helped to push worker participation rates downwards.

Main Trends, 1901–1931

Between 1901 and 1931, except for 1921 when Class I was inflated by the inclusion of overseers, Class I occupations remained at just over one per cent of all jobs. Four noteworthy changes occurred in the occupational distributions (Table 8.7).

Firstly, in contrast to the stability in Class I, Class II increased from 656 persons in 1901 to 1,386 in

1921 and 1,519 in 1931, or by 5.6 per cent per annum for the first two decades, tapering to an annual growth rate of 1.0 per cent from 1921 to 1931. Most of this increase was due, in order of importance, to the steady expansion of peasant proprietors, and to incremental increases of teachers, clerks and minor officials. In 1921 and 1931, Class II occupations formed 10.2 per cent of all enumerated, up from 6.6 per cent in 1901.

Secondly, within Class III, agricultural labourers as a proportion of the working force steadily declined, from 41.1 per cent in 1901 to 26.4 per cent in 1931, while the 'general labourer' category peaked at 16.0 per cent in 1921, and fell to 9.0 per cent in 1931 (Table 8.7).

TABLE 8.8 Worker Participation Rates for the Tobago Population 10 Years Old and over, and Comparison with Gainful Worker Rates for Trinidad and Tobago, 1891–1946

Year	Population 10 years old and over			Tobago: working force			Tobago: 'gainful workers'		
	Male	Female	Total	Male	Female	Total	Male	Female	Total
1891	6,239	7,695	13,934	4,439	5,755	10,194	4,439	4,837	9,276
1901	6,026	7,378	13,404	4,069	5,865	9,934	4,069	5,087	9,156
1911	7,024	8,051	15,075	5,458	6,461	11,919	5,453	5,409	10,862
1921	7,940	8,927	16,867	6,071	7,350	13,421	6,071	5,813	13,421
1931	8,730	9,609	18,339	6,859	8,101	14,960	6,488	3,457	9,945
1946	9,059	10,069	19,128	6,548	7,540	14,088	6,226	2,528	8,754

Year	Tobago: general worker rates			Tobago: 'gainful-worker' rates			Trinidad and Tobago: 'gainful-worker' rates		
	Male	Female	Total	Male	Female	Total	Male	Female	Total
1891	71.1	74.8	73.2	71.1	62.9	66.6	87.4	73.9	81.3
1901	67.5	79.5	74.1	67.5	68.9	68.3	85.0	67.6	76.4
1911	77.7	80.2	79.1	77.6	67.2	72.0	85.8	64.6	75.8
1921	76.5	82.3	79.6	76.5	65.1	70.4	85.4	62.7	74.4
1931	78.6	84.3	81.6	74.3	36.0	54.2	82.5	42.6	62.6
1946	72.3	74.9	73.7	68.7	25.1	45.8	78.6	26.1	51.8

Sources: Calculated from Tobago Population Census Report, 1891, and Trinidad and Tobago Population Census Reports, 1901–1946; Jack Harewood, *The Population of Trinidad and Tobago*, Table 5A, 133, for Trinidad and Tobago rates.

Notes:

[a] The working force in this study comprises the population over 10 years old in its usual main activity, paid or unpaid. It includes the unemployed, who were negligible before 1931; those in unpaid domestic duties; and those living on private means, most of whom were likely to be own-account workers. It excludes the retired, aged and infirm, the otherwise dependent and students. The 'gainful workers' are those in paid employment or apprenticeships, own-account workers, and those listed in 1946 as 'unpaid helpers' who were distinct from those in domestic duties. In 1946 the census counted 180 wage earners who were unemployed on census day as 'gainfully occupied'. All other unpaid or unemployed persons are excluded from the Tobago figures for 'gainful workers'.

[b] The general worker rate is the participation rate based on the working force; the gainful-worker rate is the participation rate based on the gainful workers in the population.

Thirdly, the most interesting figures are those for women in unpaid domestic duties. They increased by 4.6 per cent per annum between 1911 and 1921, and by as much as 17.7 per cent per annum in the next decade. Such women comprised 7.8 per cent of the working force in 1901 and 28.5 per cent in 1931.[25]

Fourthly, for the first time, in 1931 open unemployment was significantly reported in the Tobago census data, with 4.8 per cent of the working force 'not retired and not gainfully employed'.(See Table 8.7.)

Occupations by Sex

When the occupations were classified by sex, apart from the wives of the men who predominated in Class I, women were insignificant in positions of high authority and income. In Class II, the most substantial increases were in peasant proprietors, of whom over 80 per cent were men throughout the period. Shopkeeping and huckstering, particularly the latter in which women predominated, were not consistently enumerated, and it is difficult to discern the trends. Trading was often a secondary activity, which may account for its low enumeration. In teaching and clerical jobs, women were only one-third of the workers by 1931 (Tables A3.6, A3.7).

In Class III, the skilled trades, which had occupied 23.9 per cent of the male workers in 1901, employed only 17.0 per cent of them in 1921 and 1931 (Table A3.8). Certain trades related to the sugar industry and the era of horse transport—coopers, blacksmiths—declined, and the range of trades was limited in 1931: carpenters, masons, tailors, shoemakers, woodcutters and cartwrights accounted for 1,001 or 84.2 per cent of the 1,189 tradesmen. By 1931 the new tradesmen were mainly electricians and motor mechanics.[26] The number in dressmaking, the major skill of women, rose after 1901 but was almost halved between 1921 and 1931, accounting for only 5.9 per cent of women in 1931, down from 12.5 per cent in 1921. This was because of increasing access to ready-to-wear clothing.[27] Mariners, fishermen and other seafarers were 6.2 per cent of the working men in 1901; by 1911 they fell to 2.4 per cent, mainly because of the decline in the number of mariners owing to reduced activity in Tobago's ports after 1905, when most of the shipping was done by the coastal steamers. This combined group of seafarers remained at approximately 2 per cent of male workers until 1931 (Tables A3.6, A3.8).

There was a major shift in the composition of the agricultural workers. The male proportion in this group rose steadily from 40.7 per cent in 1901 to 65.7 per cent in 1931, but the percentage of all such workers in the working force fell from 41.1 per cent to 26.4 per cent in the same period (Tables A3.7, 8.7). By the same token, paid agricultural work, which had employed 41.3 per cent of female workers in 1901, accounted for only 16.7 per cent of them in 1931, having fallen sharply from 30.4 per cent in 1921 (Table A3.8). Thus, the general participation in estate agriculture fell; and while women had been the overwhelming majority of the plantation workforce in 1891, 1901 and 1911, thereafter there was a clear withdrawal of women from such work (Table A3.6, A3.8). The decline of females in estate labour was due primarily to the expansion of peasant activity in which they were partners and, secondly, to the reorganization of the estate labour force to ensure minimal dismissal of men after the slump of 1921.[28]

Domestic service attracted fewer people of both sexes by 1931. At the turn of the century, men in domestic service had been mainly gardeners, butlers and grooms, who formed approximately 20 per cent of such workers. By 1931 both numbers and proportions of these men were halved. In 1931 domestic service and laundering accounted for 8.7 per cent of female workers, down from 14.5 per cent in 1901. Laundresses in particular declined steadily among female workers, because of improved water supplies in Scarborough and the Leeward District from 1925, which facilitated laundering at home (Tables A3.6 to A3.8).

Even among general labourers there was a decline in females. Women accounted for 59.9 per cent of this group in 1901, and steadily dropped to 35.1 per cent in 1931 (Table A3.7).

Thus, by 1931 there was falling participation of women in all of the traditional areas of employment for females in Class III—agriculture, domestic service, general labour and even dressmaking. This was accompanied by steady growth in women in unpaid domestic duties. Such women rose from being 13.3 per cent of female workers in 1901 to 52.6 per cent in 1931, the most rapid increase being after 1921 (Table A3.8). These data suggest that the depressed economic conditions of the 1920s accelerated trends that had been emerging in female employment patterns from the early twentieth century.

The opportunities for waged employment in jobs that were not menial were limited for both males and females, and particularly so for females. Thus, by 1931 only 14 women were in Class I. Only 4.2 per cent of the women in the working force were in Class II, in contrast to 17.2 per cent of the men. The proportion of the female workers in Class III remained at over 90 per cent throughout the period 1901 to 1931, while the corresponding figure for men fell from 85.8 per cent to 74.2 per cent. In 1931 the lowest strata of Class III occupied 31.3 per cent of women in waged labour and a further 52.6 per cent of them were primarily in unpaid domestic duties; the respective figures for men were 51.7 per cent with 0.5 per cent in unpaid domestic duties (Table A3.8). However, despite the overall gains made by men, 55.7 per cent of the male workers were agricultural and general labourers, porters and domestic workers in 1901 and 51.7 per cent in 1931.

In an agrarian economy such as Tobago's, the censuses do not account for female labour on family farms and in other enterprises, and their sharing in family incomes as a result. They also understate the hundreds of women who huckstered and bartered from village to village and in the local markets; and they do not clearly account for the activities related to exports to Trinidad of poultry, vegetables, livestock, cocoa and other crops, on which the populace depended. When the low incomes from peasant farming and vending, and the closure in 1923 of the two commercial banks which opened in Scarborough in 1917 are taken into account, the employment patterns described bespeak widespread existence at near-subsistence levels for people of both sexes by 1931.

The 1946 Census

There were four noteworthy changes in the occupational structure between 1931 and 1946.

Firstly, the size of the working force and of the 'gainful workers' fell by 5.8 per cent and 12.0 per cent, respectively; and both male and female participation rates declined (Table 8.8).

Secondly, Class II occupations almost doubled in number and doubled their proportion of the working force, mainly because of the rapid expansion of small farmers through the Grow More Food campaign during World War II, which gave easy access to land. Women benefited from this, since their proportion of the peasant category rose from 13.7 per cent in 1931 to 23.3 per cent in 1946 (Tables 8.7, A3.7).[29] There was also important growth in the number of teachers and clerical workers, again to the benefit of women: indeed, for the first time, females were the majority in the teaching profession (136 females, 115 males). In reality, this attests to the low educational attainment of females in Tobago before 1920, since females outnumbered males in the Trinidad teaching service as early as 1901.[30] Moreover, as the tourism industry began to expand, and as the demand for certain urban services increased, for the first time the census reported restaurants and bars, of which there were 58, with as many as 40 owned by females; women also owned 9 of the 10 boarding houses. Interestingly, women constituted only 25.2 per cent of the 139 retail shopkeepers, but 75.2 per cent of the 105 hucksters.[31]

Thirdly, in Class III, agricultural labourers declined by 63.4 per cent, the rate of decrease among males being 55.7 per cent and among females, 78.3 per cent; by 1946 there were only 294 such females. There was also marked attrition of general labourers (by 26.1 per cent) and of domestic servants (by 60.3 per cent). However, there was a small group of workers in personal services, in particular cooks, cleaners, janitors and waiters, of whom women constituted 70.9 per cent (Tables A3.6, A3.7).

Fourthly, of the men in the working force, 29.1 per cent were in the better-paid Class III occupations, including transport, vis-à-vis 10.1 per cent for women, up from 22.0 and 6.6 per cent respectively, for 1931. Despite the apparent improvement since 1931, these statistics were approximately the same as for 1901, partly because of incremental decreases in the skilled trades (Table A3.8).

Because of the shrinking agricultural and general labour and the increase in smallholders in Class II, 32.5 per cent of men were in the least-paid jobs with 0.2 per cent doing unpaid domestic work, vis-à-vis 11.6 per cent and 60.3 per cent, respectively, for women. The corresponding figures for 1931 were 51.7 per cent and 0.5 per cent for men, 31.3 per cent and 52.6 per cent for women (Table A3.8).

Thousands of workers were not in *waged* employment in 1946, the first year for which the employment status of workers was given. Among Tobago's 6,226 gainfully occupied males, 36.1 per cent were own-account workers, as were 38.4 per cent of the 2,528 females. Sixty-one per cent of the gainful workers were wage or salary earners, with 49.5 per cent actually earning wages (as opposed to being apprentices or unemployed) on census day. In contrast, own-account employment occupied 21.1 per cent of Trinidad's males and 32.9 per cent of its females; 72.2 per cent of its workers were wage or salary earners, with 65.9 per cent actually earning on census day (Table A3.9).

However, it should be noted that wage earning in 1946 for most Tobago workers did not mean exclusive dependence on wages, since most employees on estates, public works and in private enterprises had land or other means of support.[32] Thus, we can confidently state that a proletariat did not exist in Tobago in the century after Emancipation. Further, when we consider the large number of people, especially women, who formed part of these own-account enterprises and who were not counted among the 'gainful workers', the own-account figures for Tobago would be much higher.

4. CONCLUSION

By 1851 an occupational structure was established whereby 96.0 per cent of the working force remained, for the next three decades, in occupations which we assigned to Class III. Between 1851 and 1881, the major avenues of upward mobility for the labouring class, as revealed in the occupational statistics, were skilled trades, dressmaking, fishing/seafaring, and 'shopkeeping'; and these opportunities varied from district to district, with the Windward District being least favoured.

Between 1891 and 1901, there was a steep decline in agricultural labourers and a redistribution of the lowly-paid into 'general labour', with 8 to 9 per cent of the working force in unpaid domestic duties. The disproportionate sex ratios resulting from emigration meant that women constituted 59.0 per cent of the working force in 1901. Women were the backbone of the agricultural, general and domestic workforce at the end of the nineteenth century. They had also been the majority in field labour in the 1830s[33] and in 1844, and the majority of road workers, a very menial form of employment, from 1838 to 1887. Throughout the period surveyed, the opportunities for both males and females were limited, but more so for females. Virtually all of the skilled trades, except baking, the making of confectionery, dressmaking and midwifery, were exclusively male.

By 1901 a significant breach into Class II occupations had been made, largely by males who had become peasant proprietors, teachers and clerks. Women, whose participation in teaching and clerical work also increased, predominated in what was recorded as 'shopkeeping', which was in unbroken continuity with their roles as hucksters and market vendors during the era of enslavement. By 1931, probably because vending was a secondary activity for many women, it was under-enumerated, but it was the only activity in Class II in which women predominated, being 70.5 per cent of the group. Men continued to consolidate their position in Class II.

By 1901 gendered differences in the distribution of jobs and related incomes were clear. At the top of the occupational ladder, women were rare. In the middle ranks, women were not usually employed as minor officials in the nineteenth century, and most teachers were men. In 1845 there had been 3 female teachers out of 19; in 1880 there were still only 3, out of 21.[34] By 1901 women had stormed the citadels of education and 'respectability' to become one-third of the teachers and 22.1 per cent of the store clerks; and they dominated petty trading; in 1931 they were 40.1 per cent of the teachers and 27.2 per cent of the clerical workers.[35] Even so, they were far behind their Trinidad counterparts, who in 1901 already outnumbered men in the teaching profession. This was not reported for Tobago until 1946. At the base of the occupational ladder in 1901, women predominated in all the least-paid occupations; they were the backbone of the agrarian workforce; and over 80 per cent of all women were either lowly paid or in unpaid domestic duties.

By 1931 there was little change in the relative position of the sexes, as reflected in the census data. However, two distinct trends were noticed. The first is the steady decline in female participation as 'gainful workers' after 1901, a process that sharply accelerated between 1921 and 1946. In contrast, there was an increase in male participation rates between 1901 and 1911; and although male rates declined after 1921, the process was much more gradual. In general, the participation rates of both males and females in Tobago were lower than those for the colony as a whole. Secondly, between 1901 and 1931, there was a marked withdrawal of women from estate agriculture and to a lesser extent from paid domestic service, laundering and general labour. There was another redistribution of female workers in Class III, this time into mainly unpaid domestic duties. In 1931, 52.6 per cent of women in the working force were so engaged, up from 20.9 per cent in 1921.

Despite the gains made by men, 55.7 per cent of the male workers were agricultural and general labourers, porters and domestic workers in 1901, and 51.7 per cent in 1931. These were the least-paid jobs. Manufacturing was mainly by artisans; and the range of male skills did not significantly increase, the new skills being those of electricians and motor mechanics. Machinists, fitters and even welders were rare in 1946. Yet the skilled trades remained important avenues for survival and social mobility. The proportions in skilled trades, both in the working force and among males alone, showed small but steady declines between 1901 and 1931, partly because of emigration to Trinidad and partly because the demand for certain skills, such as coopers and blacksmiths, was falling (Tables 8.7, A3.8).

The general conclusion to be drawn, in the context of the stagnation and decline of agriculture and the renewed pace of emigration after 1921, is clear. By 1938, a large part of the populace was surviving at close to subsistence levels, with restricted opportunities for upward social mobility, particularly for women in Class III.

The 1946 census recorded further changes. World War II, with the Grow More Food Campaign and the attraction of high wages in construction and other activities in Trinidad, created opportunities for many Tobago workers at home and in Trinidad. The cumulative effects of high primary-school enrolment after 1911 and increased access to secondary schooling were also noticeable. Thus, between 1931 and 1946, the main changes were the expansion of the peasants, teachers and clerical workers in Class II, with incremental gains to women in the process.

Women were also registering important gains as owners of restaurants, bars, 'snackettes' and other enterprises, while continuing to dominate the huckstering business; retail shopkeeping was conducted largely by males. Within Class III, agricultural labour continued its sharp decline with a severe attrition of women, who also continued to withdraw from general labour and waged domestic work, in favour of unpaid domestic duties, which accounted for 60.3 per cent of the female workforce. Small numbers entered services such as cooking in restaurants, boarding houses and other enterprises. The 1946 census for the first time allowed an estimate of those in own-account employment. The rates for Tobago were significantly higher than those for Trinidad, and the former are likely to be gross under-estimates, given pervasive occupational multiplicity and small agri-businesses in Tobago.

The census data in this and the preceding chapter confirm that gender was a significant factor differentiating the population and affecting its life chances, and is vital in analysing the social structure. Yet we enter a word of caution. Max Weber warned that interpretive understanding of the actors' meanings—'verstehen'—is a necessary condition of all sociological explanation, strong though the statistical data may be.[36] We have shown marked inequality in the employment patterns of males and females. However, this must be tempered by the fact that, for large segments of the populace, *households were units of production for subsistence and marketing, hence creating other roles and sources of income that are not reflected in these data.*

Nevertheless, the data tell of the extraordinary importance of low-waged female labour in Tobago's agrarian production in the century after Emancipation, after a history of female predominance in field labour during slavery. These facts give major significance to gender as a factor interacting with social class for any meaningful analysis of Tobago society.

The long, detailed view which this chapter takes has the advantage of showing both large and small shifts in the occupational patterns over time. These patterns are consistent with the main arguments of this work. The statistics confirm our analysis in Volume I, Chapter 5, on the differential ownership of land by sex. They also buttress and reinforce the analyses on the relatively late emergence of the peasantry.[37] Further, the expansion in Class II after 1891 supports our view that the crisis of the 1880s led to a restructuring of production and social relations, and to relative gains for the labouring class after 1889.[38] However, by the 1930s those gains were constrained by the general stagnation of agriculture and commerce, precisely the areas in which most progress had been made.

Notes

1 The distinction between social and occupational mobility is recognized.

2 Tobago Population Census Report, 1881; Trinidad and Tobago Population Census Report, 1901.

3 Lloyd Best, 'Outlines of a Model of Pure Plantation Economy', *SES* 17, no. 3 (1968): 283–326.

4 H. H. Sealy, Deputy Registrar General, to L. G. Hay, 31 Aug. 1891, with Tobago Population Census Report, 1891. Metayage was the chief means by which the sugar estates were cultivated between 1848 and 1948; see vol. I, chap. 8.

5 George Roberts, *The Population of Jamaica* (Cambridge 1957), 86.

6 Jack Harewood, *The Population of Trinidad and Tobago* (Committee for the International Co-ordination of Research in Demography (CICRED) Series 1975), 165. See also Rhoda E. Reddock, *Women, Labour and Politics in Trinidad and Tobago: A History* (Kingston 1994), 70. I had the privilege of working with Dr. Vanus James in 1998.

7 Harewood, *Population*, 166.

8 Roberts, *Population of Jamaica*, 85.

9 Constables, usually black, were not accorded the prestige given to clerks, bookkeepers etc, many of whom were coloured; their occupation suggests that they belong in Class II.

10 Coconut walk: a plot of land, usually smaller than ten acres in size, planted only in coconut trees. See vol. I, chap. 5.

11 Among teachers, skilled tradesmen and printers, the first labour organizations in the English-speaking Caribbean were formed in the late nineteenth century. See Richard Hart, 'Trade Unionism in the English-Speaking Caribbean: The Formative Years and the Caribbean Labour Congress', in *Contemporary Caribbean: A Sociological Reader*, vol. 2, ed. S. Craig (St. Augustine, Trinidad 1982). Angel Quintero Rivera, *Patricios y plebeyos: burgueses, hacendados, artesanos y obreros, las relaciones de clase en el Puerto Rico de cambio de siglo* (Rio Piedras 1988), 69–70, also shows that the earliest assertion of proletarian solidarity in Puerto Rico in the nineteenth century was among artisans.

12 In vol. I, chap. 9, master mariners are considered part of the middle strata; most of the occupations of the people considered the middle strata were from Class II. John Spicer, Harry Smith and William Hovell were mariners who became planters when estates were cheap. Spicer owned Shirvan and Bon Accord, and his wife Sarah owned Pigeon Point in 1884; Smith owned Caledonia from c.1896. Hovell, who also became a dry goods merchant, owned Pigeon Point in 1907. See Loraine Geddes Hay, *A Handbook of the Colony of Tobago* (Scarborough, Tobago 1884), xiii; on Smith and Hovell, see vol. I, chap. 9 and chap. 3 of this volume.

13 In 1884, under the 1882 Medical Ordinance, the DMOs examined the midwives and, if found qualified, each midwife was given a licence to practise. There were 51 midwives practising in 3 districts, and the number in the fourth was not given. Some had been practising for 40 years. The National Archives of Trinidad and Tobago: Administrator's Despatches, 1882–1885, Carrington to Browne, 20 Oct. 1884. In 1885, the two midwives who attended to Blacky Mamby who died in childbirth, Elizabeth Archer and Daphne Cudjoe, were illiterate (vol. I, chap. 6). Midwifery, usually accompanied by knowledge of herbal medicine, was a skill which, from the days of slavery, had been transmitted as part of the oral, African-based tradition.

14 CO 289/3: *Tobago Gazette*, Feb. 1880, n.d.; n. p.; cf. the 1875 jurors' list in CO 289/1: *Tobago Gazette*, 27 Mar. 1875; and for 1891, which included tailors, butcher, carpenters, blacksmiths etc., CO 289/6: *Tobago Gazette*, 30 Jan. 1891. *Trinidad Royal Gazette*, 18 Sept. 1902, 1291–92; and 8 Sept. 1930, 660–61.

15 *The News*, 31 Jan. 1885, Leader, 3. CO 321/103: no. 22, Sendall to Holland, 25 Mar. 1887, encl Llewellyn's minute, 17 Feb. 1887.

16 This classification ranks the three broad occupational groups. The skilled trades in Class III are considered to be in the upper ranks of the group (with master artisans, though not distinguished in the data, in Class II); no precise ranking *within* these occupational groups can be given.

17 The census occupational table gives 10,197, which is inaccurate.

18 The previous censuses listed the numbers in each trade or craft, without aggregating them. In 1891, this was not done.

19 Porters in the nineteenth-century censuses never exceeded 10; therefore most would have been 'general labourers'.

20 Because women in domestic duties were not reported for 1861–1881, we cannot discern the trends. However, had the 1851 figure of 112 increased at the same rate as that of the working force (20.4 per cent), the number of women in domestic duties in 1891 would have been 135, far fewer than the 918 recorded for 1891.

21 A number of metayers existed in leeward Tobago until the sugar estates ceased to make sugar in the 1940s. However, metayage was a secondary occupation for many of them.

22 The census occupational tables give a total of 9,946 as the working force, when the correct total is 9,934. When the children in and out of school are added, the census accounts for 18,409 persons; the total population was 18,751.

23 Trinidad and Tobago Population Census Report, 1901, App. E. Of the 92 clerks, shopmen and salespersons, 67 were males and 25, females in 1901.

24 Harewood, *Population*, 135–39; Reddock, *Women, Labour and Politics*, chap. 2.

25 Calculated from Table A3.6.

26 Trinidad and Tobago Population Census Report, 1931, Table B(1), Occupations.

27 Reddock, *Women, Labour and Politics*, 85.

28 On the latter point, see Reddock, *Women, Labour and Politics*, 72.

29 The 1946 census was also a census of farms; thus this is probably the most accurate enumeration of the smallholders in the early twentieth century. The census category 'farmers', which is distinguished from farm managers and farm labourers, is counted here as peasant proprietors.

30 In 1901 in Trinidad there were 589 female to 541 male teachers, when the respective figures for Tobago were 33 and 68. Trinidad and Tobago Population Census Report, 1901, App. E. Reddock, *Women, Labour and Politics*, 92–93, shows that most female teachers in Trinidad in 1901 were not certificated.

31 Trinidad and Tobago Population Census Report, 1946, Table 63.

32 In Tobago the wage was not a wage, in the sense of the sole means of livelihood, for most workers. See vol. I, chap. 4 and chap. 3 of this volume.

33 Cf. Higman, *Slave Population and Economy in Jamaica, 1807–1834* (Cambridge 1979), 208; and vol. I, chap. 3.

34 CO 290/29: Blue Book, 1845. All the female teachers were paid lower wages than the males in 1880; CO 290/64: Blue Book, 1880. In the nineteenth century, women were usually responsible for teaching the infant and sewing classes in the day schools.

35 In 1901, 33 out of 101 teachers, and 25 out of 113 clerical workers and salespersons were women. In 1931 they were 88 out of 219 teachers, and 82 out of 301 clerical workers. Trinidad and Tobago Population Census Report, 1901, App. E; Trinidad and Tobago Population Census Report, 1931, Table B(1), Occupations.

36 Max Weber, *The Theory of Social and Economic Organisation*, Translated by A. M. Henderson and T. Parsons; ed. with an Introduction by T. Parsons (New York 1964), 99–102.

37 See vol. I, chaps. 4 and 9.

38 See vol. I, chaps. 9 and 10.

Epilogue

9

The Post-War
Transition in Tobago, 1950–2000

I̶N THE post-war decades, the agrarian order that had been established after the demise of the sugar industry in the 1880s definitively collapsed. Tourism, which had been a minor industry in the early twentieth century, expanded after World War II. Its development was endorsed by the Planning Team reporting after Hurricane Flora in 1963.[1] Since then, tourism and ancillary activities have become an important sector of Tobago's economy, attracting large-scale foreign and local investment, particularly after 1987, when the Foreign Investment Act permitting foreign ownership of land in the country was passed.

The largest employer, however, became the state; and services of various kinds employed 92.3 per cent of the persons with jobs in 2000.[2] Services accounted for 98.4 per cent of Tobago's gross domestic product in 1997.[3] The minor economic activities are fisheries, the mining of aggregate for construction, livestock-rearing, and subsistence agriculture.

This chapter examines in broad outline the social transformation of Tobago between the end of World War II and the present. Most of it is based on the four census reports for 1960–1990, since the 1946 census data were used for several tables in Chapters 7 and 8. Data from the 2000 census, where available in 2006, are included.

The census reports for the decades 1960 to 1990 are in some respects incomparable because of changes in research questions, concepts, definitions, area boundaries and names. Due regard is paid to these issues throughout. At the outset, however, it must be stated that the 1990 census presents clear difficulties. In the earlier three censuses, the population in the Listing of Areas Register was the same as was published in the general tables of each report. In 1990 there were discrepancies between the totals given in the Listing of Areas Register (46,654), the age tables (46,435), the local and foreign-born population (44,647), and the Visitation Records cited by the *Tobago Region Physical Development Plan* (50,282). The *Annual Statistical Digest 1998/99* of the Central Statistical Office also gives the figure of 48,600.[4] The varying figures were used as needed.

After sketching the major demographic and other changes, this chapter outlines the accompanying changes in the social structure. The treatment is summary.

1. THE DEMOGRAPHIC TRANSITION

Origins of the Population

In 1960 Tobago's population was 33,333, having increased from the 1946 figure of 27,208. The proportion of the Tobago-born in the population hovered between 87 and 88 per cent until 1990, and the most important change was the increase of natives of Trinidad from 2,581 (7.7 per cent) in 1960 to 4,534 (10.2 per cent) in 1990. Migrants from other Caribbean territories were only 1.1 per cent of the 1990 population; in 1980 and 1990, they comprised 63 per cent of all the foreign-born. The rest of the foreign-born at each census accounted for less than 1 per cent of the population, and in 1990 they comprised 0.6 per cent. Tobago in 1990 was a society of predominantly Caribbean-born

people, with natives of Trinidad and Tobago comprising 96.9 per cent of the population (Table 9.1).

The age and sex distribution of the foreign-born is given for 1990 in Table A4.1. The majority of the Caribbean immigrants (68.8 per cent) were between ages 15-64, while 47.8 per cent of the others were in that category. Interestingly, in 1990, women outnumbered men among both groups of immigrants, the male : female ratios being 84 and 89 males per 100 females for Caribbean-born and other immigrants, respectively.

The *sociological* significance of immigrants from metropolitan countries with hard currency far exceeds their numerical smallness. This is particularly so in the light of the growth of a real estate market open to foreigners since the passing of the Foreign Investment Act (1987), which affected land values, social mores and other aspects of Tobago society.

TABLE 9.1 **Origins of the Tobago Population, 1960–1990**

	1960		1970		1980		1990 [b]	
	Number	Per cent	Number	Per cent	Number	Per cent	Number	Per cent
Tobago	29,487	88.8	33,494	86.4	34,779	88.1	38,713	86.7
Trinidad	2,581	7.7	3,963	10.2	3,384	8.6	4,534	10.2
Caribbean	719	2.2	—	—	483	1.2	509	1.1
India	—	—	—	—	14	0.0	9	0.0
Venezuela	27	0.1	—	—	13	0.0	14	0.0
UK	107	0.3	—	—	75	0.2	69	0.1
USA	45	0.1	—	—	78	0.2	86	0.2
All other	134	0.4	—	—	106	0.3	102	0.2
Not stated	99	0.3	—	—	—	—	—	—
Local born	—	—	51	0.1	553	—	597	1.3
Foreign born	—	—	—	—	2	—	14	0.0
Total	33,199	100.0	37,508	96.7	39,487	100.0	44,647	100.0
Total population	**33,333**	**—**	**38,754**	**—**	**39,524**	**—**	**46,435**	**—**

Sources: Population Census Reports, 1960, Vol. 3, Pt. A, Tables 5 and 6; 1970, Vol. 5, Table 1; 1980, Vol. 4, Tables 1 and 2; 1990, Vol. 4, Tables 2 and 3.

Notes:

[a] The migration tables seen for 1970 do not give the foreign-born.

[b] The figure for Trinidad is derived from Vol. 4, Table 2, and differs from 4,485 given in Tables 6 and 7 of the same volume on internal migrants.

Racial/Ethnic Composition

In 2000 the population was predominantly of African descent (88.8 per cent), with the Mixed group accounting for 6.5 per cent, and East Indians, 2.5 per cent. Chinese formed 0.1 per cent of the population, while Syrians/Lebanese and Europeans each comprised 0.6 per cent (Tables A4.2, A4.3). In 1990, the parishes of St. John, St. David and St. Paul had the highest proportions of Africans—97.7, 96.0, and 94.3 per cent, respectively—while the most ethnically differentiated parish was St. Andrew, where Scarborough is located, with 88.3 per cent. Portuguese, Chinese, Syrians and Lebanese, and Caucasians, most of whom were involved in business, were concentrated in St. Andrew. Of the 164 whites in 1990, 125 (76.2 per cent) were in St. Andrew and St. Patrick, as were 706 (73.4 per cent) of the 962 East Indians.[5]

Religion

The religious composition of the population became more varied, partly because of increasing ethnic differentiation, and partly because of the growth of new evangelical Christian churches and of groups practising African-derived religions. However, the census data after 1970 fail to reflect these changes. Moravians, a major influential denomination in Tobago, were not identified; neither were Spiritual Baptists, Rastafari, Orishas, and Buddhists. There is thus a large residual category, comprising 23.5 per cent of the population in 1990 and 20.5 per cent in 2000, whose religion is unknown.

Table A4.4 shows that Anglicans, Roman Catholics and Methodists all declined in their share of the population, while Seventh Day Adventists showed steady numerical and proportionate growth, increasing by 4.3 per cent per annum in 1960–1980 and 5.1 per cent per annum in 1980–1990, after which their annual growth rate was 0.6 per cent. Over the period 1960–2000, Anglicans suffered a net decline of 50.6 per cent in membership, and their share of the population shrank from 48.2 per cent to 17.9 per cent.

Pentecostals numbered 65 in 1960; they peaked at 9.3 per cent of the population in 1990 (4,189 persons) and declined to 7.1 per cent in 2000.

The small Presbyterian congregation, served by itinerant ministers from Trinidad, is composed largely of Indian migrants from Trinidad.

Hindus and Muslims remained small minorities. The most noteworthy change was the reversal of the prominence of Sanatan Dharma Maha Sabha (SDMS) adherents among the Hindus in favour of other Hindu groups, and a similar reversal for the Anjumaan Sunnat ul Jamaat Association (ASJA) in favour of other Islamic groups, between 1980 and 2000 (Table A4.4).

Population Growth

From 1946 to 1970, Tobago's annual population growth rate held steady at 1.6 per cent, falling to 0.5 per cent in the next decade. In the nation, the population grew at declining rates between 1970 and 2000, as a result of net migration and declining fertility rates. However, the patterns for Tobago and Trinidad differed. Trinidad's growth rates declined steadily after 1970, while in Tobago after 1980 they were higher than those of Trinidad, because major construction works and hotel expansion attracted immigrants, some temporary (Table A4.5). For Tobago in the decade 1990–2000, population growth was 1.1 per cent per annum, vis-à-vis 0.4 per cent for Trinidad and for the nation (Figure 9.1).[6] Tobago's population density in 2000 was 465 persons per square mile.

FIGURE 9.1 **Annual Intercensal Population Growth for Trinidad and for Tobago, 1960–2000**

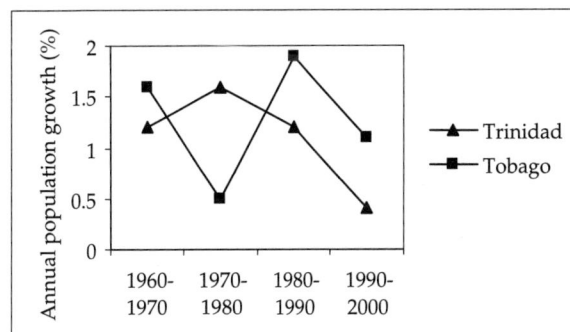

Sources: Calculated from CSO, *Population and Housing Census Reports*, 1960–1980; *Annual Statistical Digest, 1998/1999* (Port of Spain 2002), Table 11; *2000 Population and Housing Census: Preliminary Population Count* (Port of Spain 2001), Table 1. Based on Table A4.5.

229

Migration

Migration was the most important component of Tobago's population growth in the twentieth century. The number of external emigrants was first recorded in the 1990 census, which showed that 1,618 persons (644 males, 974 females) had left Tobago for foreign countries since 1980. Of these, 1,130 (69.8 per cent) went to the USA, 271 (16.7 per cent) to Canada, 99 (6.1 per cent) to the UK, and 52 (3.1 per cent) to the Caribbean. The full number of economically active emigrants is not known.[7]

The most fully documented migration streams are those between Trinidad and Tobago. Between 1931 and 1960, Tobago sustained 'considerable losses' to Trinidad, which Simpson regarded as conclusive evidence of 'push factors'.[8]

At census 1960, the net migration (loss) to Trinidad was 12,936, falling to 8,762 in 1970; after a decade of accelerated migration, it was 11,082 in 1980; but by 1990 it had fallen to 4,613. The net migration trends for 1960 to 1990 are given in Table 9.2.

The overall decline in the proportion of the Tobago-born residing in Trinidad indicates slower rates of migration to Trinidad, probably in favour of foreign destinations. The Trinidad-born in Tobago increased from 3,384 persons to 4,485 between 1980 and 1990 (or by 3.3 per cent per annum); and 63.9 per cent of these movers were aged 15–64 (Table 9.2).[9]

TABLE 9.2 Net Migration by Sex between Trinidad and Tobago, 1960–1990

	1960			1970		
	Male	Female	Total	Male	Female	Total
Tobago-born in Trinidad	7,644	7,972	15,616	6,126	6,650	12,776
Trinidad-born in Tobago	1,373	1,307	2,680	1,980	2,034	4,014
Net Migration (loss)	**6,271**	**6,665**	**12,936**	**4,146**	**4,616**	**8,762**
Tobago-born in Trinidad and Tobago	22,088	23,015	45,103	22,542	23,728	46,270
% of Tobago-born in Trinidad	**34.6**	**34.6**	**34.6**	**27.2**	**28.0**	**27.6**

	1980			1990		
	Male	Female	Total	Male	Female	Total
Tobago-born in Trinidad	7,226	7,240	14,466	4,511	4,587	9,098
Trinidad-born in Tobago	1,622	1,762	3,384	2,124	2,361	4,485
Net Migration (loss)	**5,604**	**5,478**	**11,082**	**2,387**	**2,226**	**4,613**
Tobago-born in Trinidad and Tobago	24,475	24,770	49,245	24,016	23,795	47,811
% of Tobago-born in Trinidad	**29.5**	**29.2**	**29.4**	**18.8**	**19.3**	**19.0**

Sources: Population and Housing Census Reports, 1960, Vol. 3, Pt. A, Table 5; 1970, Vol. 5, Tables 1, 2; 1980, Vol. 4, Table 1; 1990, Vol. 4, Tables 2, 6.

Age/Sex Structure

Age Profile

An outstanding feature of the age structure is the decline of the group aged 0 to 14 years from 45.8 per cent of the population in 1960 to 26.5 per cent in 2000, the decrease occurring after 1970 (Table A4.6). The greatest declines were in the cohort aged 0–4, which recorded an increase only between 1980 and 1990 (Table A4.7). The net decline in the children aged 0–14 between 1960 and 2000 was 6.2 per cent (or from 15,273 to 14,321 persons). (See Table A4.6; Figure 9.2.)

In Trinidad and Tobago as a whole, fertility rates were halved between 1980 and 2000. In that period, the number of births per 1,000 women aged 15–49 (*the general fertility rate*) fell from 108.2 to 51.8, while the number of births per 1,000 population (*the crude birth rate*) dropped from 27.7 to 14.4. The pattern for Tobago was similar to that for the nation.

FIGURE 9.2 **Tobago: Age Profile of the Population, 1960–2000**

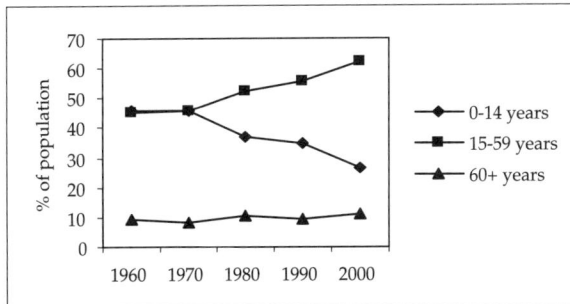

Sources: As for Table A4.6, on which it is based.

In Tobago the general fertility rate fell from 113.8 in 1980 to 51.0 in 2000. The crude birth rate also dropped from 26.8 to 14.0 per 1,000 inhabitants.[10] Since Tobago experiences heavy rates of emigration among its young adult cohorts, this, coupled with fertility declines in general, may account for the heavy attrition of the child population.

Although the age profile of Trinidad and Tobago reflects general fertility declines, the 0–14 age group contributed 36.3 per cent of the population in 2000, significantly higher than Tobago's 26.5 per cent. For the nation, the children's share of the population increased from 33.5 per cent in 1980, while in Tobago there was only steady decline.[11] For comparison with Figure 9.2, Figure 9.3 gives the national age profile.

FIGURE 9.3 **Trinidad and Tobago: Age Profile of the Population, 1960–2000**

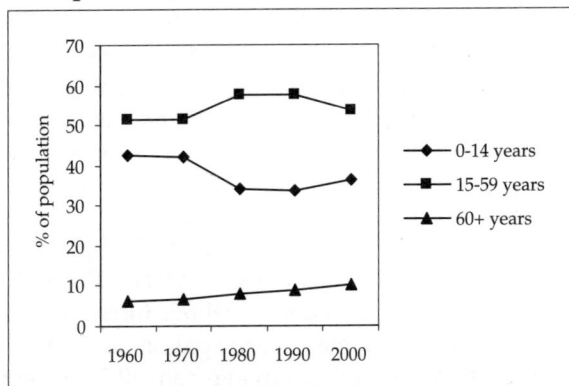

Sources: Calculated from CSO, *Annual Statistical Digest 1998/99*, Table 11; *Population and Vital Statistics Report 2000*, Table iv.

The group aged 15–59 constituted 45.1 per cent of the Tobago population in 1960 and 62.5 per cent in 2000 (Table A4.6; Figure 9.2). After growing by 1.7 per cent per annum between 1960 and 1970, it increased at the annual rate of 3.1 per cent between 1980 and 1990, and by 2.4 per cent in the following decade. The high rates of increase in this group were an important component of population growth, and cannot be accounted for by natural increase alone. How much of this growth is due to immigration, returning migrants, or a lower rate of emigration from these cohorts is not known.

The proportion of persons aged 60 and over remained relatively stable, fluctuating above and below 10 per cent (Figure 9.2). However, the annual rate of growth of the elderly increased in the past two decades, from 1.0 per cent in 1980–1990 to 2.8 per cent in 1990–2000, which may be influenced by Tobago's becoming a retirement destination. This has implications for the provision of health care and other services for the elderly.

FIGURE 9.4 **Tobago: Age Dependency Ratios, 1960–2000**

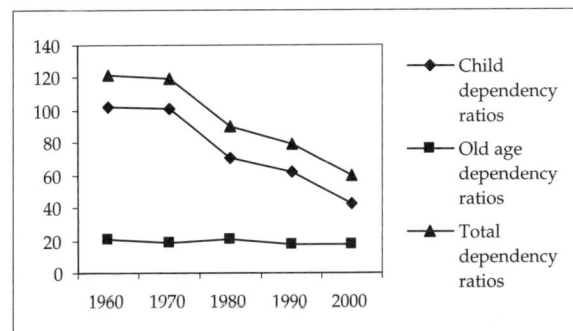

Sources: As for Table A4.8.

Age Dependency Ratios

The age dependency ratios of persons in the dependent age groups—under 15 and 60 years and over—to those in the economically productive ages of 15 to 59 years, are given in Table A4.8. Total dependency and child dependency ratios declined, the fall in the former resulting from the dramatic decline in the latter (Figure 9.4).

231

Sex Ratios

Despite high rates of male emigration and general imbalances in the sex ratios in the cohorts aged 20–49, the female predominance in the late nineteenth century was gradually altered in the twentieth. In 1990 males actually outnumbered females in the population for the first time since 1844, but in 2000 women were once more in the majority (Table A4.7). The age-specific sex ratios of the population for 1960 to 2000 are given in Table A4.9. How emigration and immigration affect the sex ratios has not been studied.

Settlement Patterns

There was a redistribution of population within Tobago after World War II. The windward and northern areas, which had attracted immigrants from Grenada, St. Vincent and the south-west of Tobago with the transition to cocoa and the opening up of Crown lands in the early twentieth century, lost population significantly, owing to the decline of cocoa and of agriculture in general. The leeward parishes of the south-west, particularly St. Andrew and St. Patrick, were the main recipients of the movements within Tobago, with 55.2 per cent of the population in 2000, up from 40.0 per cent in 1960 (Table A4.10). These parishes and St. David, which have been called the Western Region by the Policy Research and Development Institute (PRDI) of the Tobago House of Assembly (THA), accounted for 69.1 per cent of the population in 2000, up from 58.8 per cent in 1960.

However, despite these general trends in the parishes, Moriah in St. David and Roxborough in St. Paul displayed unusual patterns of growth. Their respective populations grew at the rate of only 0.2 and 0.4 per cent per annum between 1960 and 1990, but the corresponding figures for 1990–2000 were 8.8 and 6.2 per cent. In contrast, the annual increases in St. David and St. Paul parishes between 1990 and 2000 were 0.2 and 0.4 per cent, respectively—far lower than in these settlements.[12]

The most outstanding change was the growth of St. Patrick and St. Andrew parishes since 1960. The former increased by 103.2 per cent by 1990, and in 2000 its net increase for the 40 years was 174.2 per cent; the respective figures for St. Andrew were 53.4 per cent and 92.5 per cent. In contrast, the eastern parishes and St. David displayed much lower growth rates, with St. Mary

showing a net increase of only 4 persons in 40 years, while St. John had a net decline of 335 persons (Table A4.10).

The major determinant of these settlement patterns is economic. The growing sectors of the economy—the Public Service, tourism and other services—were mainly in the parishes of St. Andrew and St. Patrick. The data on employment patterns reinforce these findings.

Changes in Employment Patterns, 1946–1990

The Growth of the Working Population

The census data are not strictly comparable with the labour force data collected by the continuous sample surveys of the population. Therefore the censuses of 1946–1990 will be summarized, followed by a short statement on the labour force survey data for 2000. Because the period after World War II marks a major restructuring of the Tobago economy, statistics from 1946 onwards are used in this section.

The growth of the working population is shown in Table 9.3. Between 1946 and 1960, using the figures for persons with jobs in the week preceding each census, the annual increase was 0.3 per cent. After 1960, the definition of the working population was changed from persons 10 years old and over with jobs to persons 15 years old and over who were engaged in, or willing and able to be engaged in, producing economic goods and services; therefore the decline between 1960 and 1970 is a function of the changed definition. In Table 9.3, the annual rates of increase for women in the working population were significantly higher than those for men between 1970 and 1990.

Chapter 8 showed that 60.3 per cent of the female working force in 1946 were engaged in full-time unpaid domestic duties. The census data reveal that this situation changed significantly after 1970. Female participation rates moved from 24.0 per cent in 1970 to 37.7 per cent in 1980, and 41.7 in 1990 (Table A4.11). Throughout the following decade, the labour force surveys show increasing female participation in Tobago, with participation rates moving from 40.7 per cent in 1990 to 60.8 in 2004, while the comparable figures for females in the nation were 37.8 and 50.8 per cent.[13]

Table A4.11 also reveals high unemployment rates, in the context of structural adjustment in the 1980s, reaching 21.2 per cent in 1990.

Workers by Industrial Groups

As we would expect, the post-war data show a radical change in the distribution of workers by industry. In 1946, almost half the 6,226 gainfully occupied men (48.6 per cent) were employed in agriculture, fishing and related activities, as were 29.1 per cent of the 2,528 women. The chief industrial activities besides these were 'manufacturing', (which engaged 30.5 per cent of the women and 10.9 per cent of the men), construction (18.0 per cent of men, 1.5 per cent of women), and services, employing 9.9 and 28.5 per cent of the men and women, respectively. 'Manufacturing' referred

mainly to limited food processing, and to the making of shoes, clothing and furniture.

Thereafter, there was a steady decline in agriculture to account for 6.1 per cent of workers in 1990, when manufacturing employed 1.8 per cent. Construction in 1990 engaged 23.2 per cent of all workers (32.0 per cent of males); and public administration together with community, social and personal services employed 33.4 per cent. In general, services of various kinds, including transport, storage and communication, and construction services, employed 88.6 per cent of males, 94.8 per cent of females, and 90.8 per cent of the persons with jobs (Tables A4.12, A4.13). It should be noted that in 1946 only 27 women were employed in public administration, in contrast to their high participation in these and related jobs today.

TABLE 9.3 **The Growth of the Working Population by Sex, 1946–1990**

Year	Male No.	Male %	Female No.	Female %	Both sexes No.	Change % per annum Male	Change % per annum Female	Change % per annum Both sexes
1946	6,226	71.0	2,528	29.0	8,754	—	—	—
1960	6,765	74.4	2,322	25.5	9,087	0.6	-0.6	0.3
1970	6,357	74.4	2,184	25.5	8,541	n.a.	n.a.	n.a.
1980	8,403	68.2	3,908	31.7	12,311	3.2	7.9	4.4
1990	8,335	63.8	4,731	36.2	13,066	0.1	2.1	0.6

Sources: Population Census Reports, 1946, Table 52; 1960, Vol. 3, Pt. G, Table 3D; 1970, Vol. 4, Pt. 2, Table 2; 1980 and 1990, Vol. 3, Pt. 1, Table 1.

Notes:
The working population or gainfully employed in 1946 and 1960 was the population 10 years old and over with jobs; in subsequent years the labour force approach counted those members of the population 15 years old and over , who were engaged in, or willing and able to be engaged in, the production of economic goods and services. In all cases, the reference period is the week preceding the census. The statistics for 1946 and 1960 are not strictly comparable with those for succeeding years.
n. a.: Not applicable (because of incompatible definitions).

Types of Workers

The employment transition was also marked by changes in the types of workers. In 1946, 61.2 per cent of the working population were wage earners. Own-account employment, mainly in farming, petty shopkeeping, trade and huckstering, occupied 36.7 per cent (36.1 per cent of males, 38.4 per cent of females) (Table A3.9). However, wage earning in 1946 for most workers did not mean exclusive dependence on the wage, since most employees had land or other means of support.

The corresponding figures for wage earning and own-account employment for both sexes in 1990 were 86.1 and 10.5 per cent, respectively. Employers remained at just over 2.0 per cent of the working population from 1960 to 1990.

Government employment peaked at 62.2 per cent of the working population in 1980 and fell to 55.5 per cent in 1990, as a result of structural-adjustment policies. Even so, state employment was far higher in Tobago than in Trinidad. In 1990, for Trinidad and Tobago as a whole, the state employed 38.0 per cent of all workers.[14]

233

Workers by Occupation

Where occupational strata are concerned, the categories are not comparable over time, and the Tobago data were not given separately in the 1970 census. Nevertheless, the data show a clear expansion in persons in professional, administrative and managerial positions, reaching 7.3 per cent of the employed in 1990, which compared favourably with 8.4 per cent for the nation. At the lowest occupational levels in 1990, 31.8 per cent of Tobago's workers were in 'elementary occupations' (the term used by the Central Statistical Office), vis-à-vis 23.6 per cent at the national level (Table A4.14). For men in elementary occupations, the Tobago rate was 37.3 per cent, while the national figure was 25.5 per cent.

Employment Trends by 2000

The labour force underwent rapid changes after 1987, when major construction projects, many of them of three or four years' duration, were started. Tobago became, as it were, a 'growth pole' attracting hundreds of migrant workers from Trinidad and elsewhere. Tourism and related services also expanded. In the process, the labour force and participation rates showed rapid growth, and unemployment rates also fell rapidly. *The Medium-Term Policy Framework of Tobago, 1998–2000* stated that these patterns are cyclical, and are related to the many short-term projects.[15]

The labour force was 22,800 persons (12,600 males, 10,200 females) in 2000, up from 19,800 (11,600 males, 8,200 females) in 1995, an overall increase of 13.1 per cent or an annual growth of 2.6 per cent, which is twice the growth rate for the population.[16] Unemployment for both sexes in 2000 was 8.8 per cent (7.1 per cent for males, 10.8 per cent for females), down from 14.1 per cent in 1995 (10.3 per cent for males, 19.5 per cent for females). The declining unemployment rates are in keeping with general declines in the nation after 1994; even so, they fell rapidly, particularly for females.[17]

As regards the industrial groups in 2000, agriculture and fishing employed 4.3 per cent of persons with jobs. Altogether, services—electricity and water; transport, storage and communications; trade, restaurants and hotels; finance, real estate, and business; and community, social and personal services—employed 68.9 per cent of the persons

with jobs, while construction was the other major employer, with 23.4 per cent. Thus, 92.3 per cent of the persons with jobs worked in services including construction. The comparable figure for the nation was 78.5 per cent (66.0 per cent in services and 12.5 per cent in construction). The state is the major employer and is also responsible for the largest share of construction projects.[18]

As regards occupational groups in 2000, 32.0 per cent of persons with jobs were in 'elementary occupations', which engaged 37.6 per cent of the male workers and 25.0 per cent of the female. The figure for Trinidad and Tobago (both sexes) was 22.9 per cent. Of the persons with jobs, 18.7 per cent were senior officials, managers, professionals, technicians and associate professionals, which compares favourably with the figure of 20.6 per cent for Trinidad and Tobago.[19]

When the types of workers were compared with the national rates, government employment in Tobago continued to be significantly higher than in the nation (44.9 per cent in Tobago vis-à-vis 24.8 per cent), and correspondingly, private-sector employment was substantially lower (40.1 per cent vis-à-vis 52.0 per cent). There was also a significantly low proportion of men in private employment in Tobago (33.6 per cent), vis-à-vis 48.3 per cent for women; the national rate for men being 49.7 per cent, and for women, 55.8 per cent. Where own-account work was concerned, Tobago's female workers approximated the national rate (11.0 per cent, 13.9 per cent, respectively), but only 7.8 per cent of its male workers were so employed, by contrast with 17.7 per cent of male workers in the nation.[20] It may be that own-account work is underreported, since occupational multiplicity is widespread.

2. OTHER SOCIAL ISSUES

Education

Education is closely related to employment patterns. As late as 1997 Tobago had a very low transition rate (59.1 per cent) from primary to secondary education relative to the rest of the country (70.0 per cent average), and tertiary facilities on the island were minimal.[21] Since 1997 the Tobago Campus of the Trinidad and Tobago Hospitality Training Institute (renamed in 2005 the Tobago Hospitality Training Institute) prepares trainees for the tourism industry. The University of the West Indies provided facilities for tertiary study on a part-time basis from 1997, and in 2003 full-time study for the Bachelor of Education degree and the degree in Liberal Arts began. There are also various associate degree programmes and a community college, but many aspects of technical and vocational education and training are not available.

In 1990, for Tobago as a whole, 63.0 per cent of the cohort aged 11–19 were in secondary school, but in St. David and St. John, only 55.0 per cent and 53.0 per cent, respectively.[22] Moreover, when the entire resident population is examined, the highest attainment of 25,669 people (57.0 per cent) was primary education; another 12,453 persons (27.6 per cent) had secondary education; and only 497 (1.1 per cent) had university education.[23]

More secondary school places were provided from 1997, and the nation moved to full secondary schooling for all from 2000. Despite increased access to education, the question of quality remains. In 2000 an official Task Force appointed to enquire into poor secondary school performance in Tobago noted that 'more than half' of the students assigned to secondary schools were 'in serious need of remedial teaching'.[24] Special remedial programmes for the students have not been implemented in most schools which receive them, and they are expected to cope with the regular curriculum from Form 2. There is no known assessment of the efficacy of these measures. The comparable census data for 2000 were not available at the time of writing.

Conserving the Physical Environment and the Cultural Heritage

The bedrock of development is the people in their physical environment. Since 1765 Tobago has had the oldest protected forest reserve in the western hemisphere, the Main Ridge Rain Forest. This reserve won in 2003, 2004 and 2005 the World Travel Award for the World's Leading Eco-Tourism Destination. In 2005 the Buccoo Reef/Bon Accord Lagoon complex, comprising 1,287 hectares, was designated a protected wetland area under the Ramsar Convention.[25] However, there is yet cause for concern.

The tourism industry, coupled with high population densities and poor management of domestic and commercial waste, water, and sewage, resulted in severe degradation of the south-western marine environment. The presence of growing numbers of yachts whose waste disposal is unregulated compounds the issue. Much valuable agricultural land has also been converted to built development, a process that is irreversible. The construction of the north-coast road to replace the old bridle track from L'Anse Fourmi to Charlotteville in 2004–2007 was undertaken with considerable soil erosion and damaging effects on the marine environment. Sand mining of the beaches has also been common. In addition, little attention is paid to managing the growth of Scarborough, and to other aspects of physical planning and development control.[26]

Of equal concern is the fact that, despite the richness of Tobago's past, apart from the heroic efforts of the Tobago Museum and the annual Tobago Heritage Festival, there is almost no conservation through archives, recordings in all media, publications, and protection of the range of historic sites and buildings. Such resources can be translated into booklets, DVDs, displays and exhibitions, so that school children can discover, cherish, and desire to serve their island-home. These are intangible but important aspects of self-definition and self-knowledge for the process of nation-building.

This type of conservation would also greatly enhance the tourism product. Ironically, the THA's survey of cruise-ship passengers found that they were least satisfied with the historic houses/monuments and the handicraft/souvenirs aspects of Tobago's tourism.[27]

Serious Crime

Although the number of serious crimes has fallen since 2000, crime is the leading issue of public concern in the nation, because of increases in crimes against the person and generally low rates of detection, prosecution and conviction. Trinidad and Tobago is a transhipment point for narcotics destined for Europe and North America, and low surveillance of Tobago's coasts throughout the 1990s added to the island's vulnerability.

TABLE 9.4 **Serious Crimes in Tobago, 1990–2004**

Type of Crime	Number	% of crimes
Crimes against property	8,765	81.4
Crimes against the person	629	5.8
Narcotics offences	647	6.0
Fraud	233	2.2
Other	490	4.6
Total	10,764	100.0

Source: Calculated from Modus Operandi and Records Bureau, Trinidad and Tobago Police Service, unpublished tables, 8 June 2005; provisional data.

Serious crimes in Tobago rose from 481 in 1990 to 805 by 2004. Between 1996 and 2002, the more populous Western Region recorded 5,066 or 89.6 per cent of the serious crimes, while the East had 596 or 10.5 per cent. Thus, the more urban West, with 69.1 per cent of the population in 2000, had a disproportionately high share of the serious crimes. Tobago experienced a rising trend in cocaine seizures, from 1 kg in 1997 to 33 kg in 2003.[28]

As is the case at the national level, crimes against property are the most numerous of the reported serious crimes (Table 9.4).

Table 9.5, giving the rates of selected crimes per 100,000 persons, provides evidence of rising rates of serious reported crimes against both property and persons, with Tobago's rates for major and minor property crimes exceeding those for the nation in 2000 and 2004. (See also Table A4.15.)

In 2000 An Act to Amend the Dangerous Drugs Act, 1991, increased the amounts of narcotics that are deemed to be for the purpose of trafficking if found in anyone's possession. The number of serious narcotics crimes therefore fell after 2000 and, correspondingly, minor narcotics crimes increased in the nation. In 2004, Tobago's rates for both major and minor narcotics crimes exceeded those of the nation (Table 9.5).

One of the areas of public concern in the nation is the low forensic capacity of the criminal justice system, and the low detection and conviction rates. Detection rates for serious crimes in Tobago and in the nation for the period 1990 to 2004 are given in Figures 9.5 and 9.6, respectively.

Although detection rates in Tobago tend to be higher than in the nation, the general patterns for detection are the same. The lowest rates are for breaking in and burglary, robbery, larceny including motor vehicles, and larceny in dwelling houses—all crimes against property, which are the most numerous serious crimes (Figures 9.5, 9.6).

FIGURE 9.5 **Tobago: Percentage of Serious Crimes That Were Solved, 1990–2004**

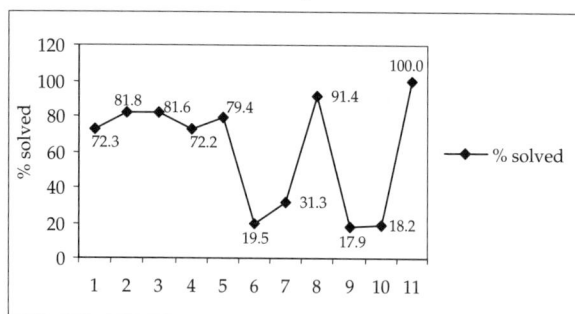

Source: Calculated from Modus Operandi and Research Bureau, Trinidad and Tobago Police Service, unpublished tables, 8 June 2005; provisional data.

FIGURE 9.6 **Trinidad and Tobago: Percentage of Serious Crimes That Were Solved, 1990–2004**

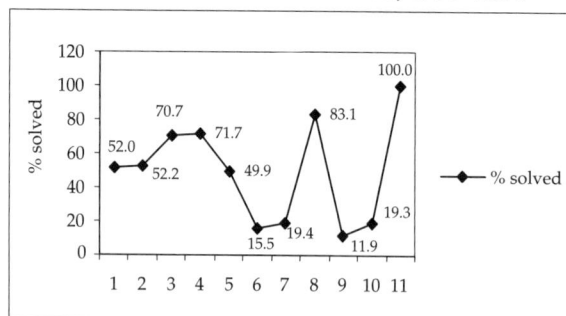

Source: As for Figure 9.5.

Notes to Figures 9.5 and 9.6:
1: Murder; **2**: Wounding and shooting; **3**: Rape, incest, sexual offences; **4**: Serious indecency; **5**: Kidnapping; **6**: Burglary and breaking in; **7**: Robbery; **8**: Fraud; **9**: Larceny including larceny of motor vehicles; **10**: Larceny in dwelling houses; **11**: Narcotics offences.

Crimes against property are also the majority of minor crimes, averaging in Tobago 498 per year out of 851 for 2000–2004. For unlawful possession, detection rates were 98.1 per cent, since every case of unlawful possession is by definition solved. If unlawful possession is excluded, the detection rate for minor property crimes in 2000–2004 was 18.1 per cent; if it is included, the rate was 19.9 per cent.[29]

Such very low detection rates contribute to the sense of insecurity in the population.

Possession of narcotics is treated officially as both a reported and a 'solved' case of narcotics possession, which explains why the police records show 100.0 per cent of narcotics reports as solved (Figures 9.5, 9.6).

The fact that the overall rates for property and narcotics crimes in Tobago surpassed those in the nation in certain years is cause for concern (Table 9.5), especially since Tobago is branded as safe and serene.

TABLE 9.5 **Rates per 100,000 Inhabitants for Selected Crimes, Selected Years, Tobago, and Comparison with Trinidad and Tobago, 1990–2004**

Category	Tobago			Trinidad and Tobago		
	1990	2000	2004	1990	2000	2004
Serious Crimes						
Crimes against property, of which:	763.3	1,381.2	1,165.3	1,093.6	1,042.4	999.0
Breaking in and burglary	567.9	878.3	720.8	621.0	445.4	404.0
Robbery	43.2	186.7	162.9	256.3	324.3	301.0
Larceny (including motor vehicles)	127.6	207.1	182.4	191.7	241.0	260.7
Larceny in dwelling houses	24.7	109.1	99.2	24.6	31.7	33.2
Fraud	0.0	136.8	8.9	20.2	41.4	25.5
Crimes against the person, of which:	45.3	90.6	106.3	63.9	108.9	132.8
Rape, incest, sexual offences	14.4	40.7	47.8	18.2	43.2	45.0
Serious indecency	10.3	11.1	8.9	5.5	13.2	4.0
Murder	2.1	9.2	7.1	6.9	9.5	20.2
Wounding and shooting	18.5	22.2	35.4	32.2	30.7	49.8
Kidnapping	0.0	7.1	7.1	1.1	12.4	13.7
Narcotics offences: serious crimes	125.5	83.2	69.1	99.7	97.0	45.6
Minor Crimes						
Narcotics offences: minor crimes	168.7	155.3	492.3	140.7	226.3	475.9
Crimes against property: minor crimes	903.3	1,229.6	742.1	1,416.5	813.8	623.4
Fraud: minor crimes	6.2	20.3	3.5	14.6	19.1	22.3
Totals						
Total serious crimes	989.7	1,763.9	1,425.7	1,332.9	1,357.3	1,269.7
Total minor crimes	1,331.3	1,682.6	1,578.0	1,803.7	1,238.6	1,331.0
Population totals	48,600	54,084	56,464	1,215,187	1,262,366	1,290,646

Sources: Calculated from Modus Operandi and Records Bureau, Trinidad and Tobago Police Service, unpublished tables, 8 June 2005, provisional data; and from population totals at 1990 and 2000 censuses and CSO, mid-year estimate for 2004.

Notes: For 2004, Tobago's population is estimated on the assumption of 1.1 per cent average annual growth since 2000, the same as had occurred between 1990 and 2000. This table is based on Table A4.15.

Minor crimes against property: Larceny receiving, Larceny in dwelling house, Praedial larceny and Unlawful possession.

Minor fraud crimes include embezzlement and false pretence.

3. OVERVIEW OF TOBAGO SOCIETY

The Changing Economy and Political Life

Economy

Tobago underwent both an economic and a demographic transition since the end of World War II. The most significant changes were the collapse of agriculture and the lack of a native economic base outside of tourism, with resulting high levels of emigration.

Since Tobago depends on imports for food and all other commodities, the cost of living there is appreciably higher than elsewhere in the nation. However, since 2005, new agricultural projects have been started to produce food crops for local and foreign markets.

From 2005, the introduction of state-subsidized fast ferries has made travel and trade between Tobago and Trinidad easy for the first time in ten decades. This is a signal improvement in the quality of life for Tobagonians.

The long decline in agriculture, together with expansions in education and in state activity generally since 1960, contributed to growth in public administration and state employment. By 1980, the state was the largest single employer in Tobago, to a degree that greatly surpassed its role in Trinidad.

Expansion in tourism and various ancillary services also boosted the significance of the service sector. The largest hotels and villas are owned by foreign capital or by conglomerates based in Trinidad. In addition, there was expansion in commerce and finance, but the biggest establishments are mainly branches of business houses based in Trinidad. The skilled trades, though important, have produced only one large construction firm. Small furniture-making establishments exist.

Although the world economy has experienced the enormous growth of services of all kinds since 1945, the trends in Tobago cannot simplistically be compared to the global. Tobago therefore faces two major challenges. The first is to move its services from the unremunerative to the more competitive end of the spectrum in the global market, while protecting its culture and environment. The second is to fully restore food production, since it is inconceivable that an island with such abundant natural resources should import almost all its food.

Given the nature of the Tobago economy, transfers from the central government are the main basis for the well-being of the population. It is not surprising, therefore, that contentions over Tobago's share of the national wealth and over the power vested in state organs in Tobago have become increasingly central in national life. The question of access to, and benefits from, the huge natural gas reserves off Tobago's coasts is also likely to become a matter of national importance.

Political Life

The gross neglect of Tobago, heightened by the closure of the Ministry for Tobago Affairs after the PNM under Dr. Eric Williams lost the two Tobago seats at the general elections of September 1976, strengthened nationalist sentiments within Tobago. In January 1977, Arthur N. R. Robinson and his colleague, Dr. Winston Murray, the two Members of Parliament (MPs) for Tobago, made a historic call for internal self-government for Tobago. After years of agitation, by Act No. 37 of 1980, the Tobago House of Assembly (THA) was established. The powers of this first THA since the old Assembly was abolished in 1876 were in effect minimal, and this provoked years of contention between the THA and the central government over the interpretation of the 1980 Act.

In 1995, at the general elections, the main parties in Trinidad won 17 seats each, and the two Tobago seats, won by the National Alliance for Reconstruction under Robinson, held the balance in the formation of a government. Robinson allied with the United National Congress (UNC) led by Basdeo Panday and, because of the strategic importance of the Tobago seats, was able to negotiate for the Government to revise the THA Act to give greater powers to the island's administration. The new Tobago House of Assembly Act, No. 40 of 1996, granted wider powers to Tobago, but many of these conflicted with existing legislation which gives decision-making power to agents of the central government (for example, on physical planning). These matters remain unresolved.

The new Tobago House of Assembly which came to power in December 1996 established in 1997 a Plan Team to devise a development plan for Tobago for the period 1998–2013. The fourth report of the Plan remained incomplete, but the initiative bore renewed witness to the importance of development planning for Tobago.[30] Another development plan was produced in 2005, entitled *A Comprehensive Economic Development Plan for Tobago (2006–2010): Tobago, Capital of Paradise: Clean, Green, Safe and Serene.*[31]

The general elections of December 2001, called by the UNC administration elected in December 2000 from which three ministers had defected, again gave Tobago strategic importance in the balance of power between the political parties. The UNC received 18 seats and the PNM, 18, including the 2 Tobago seats. The PNM was appointed to govern by the President, Arthur N. R. Robinson, who had been promoted to that office in 1997 by the UNC administration.

The Government in 2002 agreed to give Tobago its own natural gas pipeline to serve a small industrial estate at Cove in the south-west. Tobago is poised to gain direct access to offshore natural gas and other energy resources.

The Social Groupings Today

The old class structure has disappeared. Estate production, except for one coconut estate, is virtually extinct, and with it the influence of the planter class. Several of the estates are now State lands. Peasant agriculture is marginal. Planters and peasants, the two formerly predominant groups of producers, no longer have economic and political significance. The rump of the peasantry, however, are the main bearers of the traditional culture. The old Tobago merchants, mainly coloured, who had replaced the merchant-planters of the sugar era in the early twentieth century, also disappeared by the 1930s; by then Chinese and Syrians/Lebanese had established a foothold in commerce in Scarborough and Roxborough.

The new dominant class is segmented into three discernible groups. Firstly, there is a growing stratum of investors, managers and other high-level personnel, mainly from Trinidad and the metropolitan countries, working in tourism, finance and other services. Increasingly, they are being joined by permanent or temporary residents from Trinidad and the metropolis. Secondly, since 1970 there has been a small but significant return of Tobago-born professionals and persons of high

educational attainment to the island. This is reflected in the enlarged cadre of highly qualified persons in the upper occupational groups, as well as in an articulate and militant nationalist movement, which has pressed for change, particularly decentralized government and improved services. Thirdly, there is a small but important group of Tobago-born entrepreneurs in tourism, commerce, real estate and other services. This commercial group is itself segmented into Chinese, Syrians and Lebanese, whites/mixed, and blacks, although they share common interests. In the new elite as a whole, there is increasing racial and ethnic heterogeneity, mainly in the south-west.

Most of the coloured segment of the middle strata emigrated by the 1930s, to be replaced by an educated intelligentsia of teachers, clerical workers and sub-professionals, mainly black, with their economic base in salaried employment; some are landowners. Today, the intermediate social strata, in clerical jobs, sales, services and middle-income occupations, have expanded enormously, which is partly reflected in some of the housing developments in the south-west. An important segment of the middle strata is the expanding group of small entrepreneurs, most of whom are sole proprietors.[32]

For the labouring class, low-waged employment in 'elementary occupations' has increased. At the same time, although paid employment predominates, the modern society is grafted onto a cultural base shaped by independent own-account activity, widespread landownership, and subsistence agriculture. The wage is still not a wage, in the sense that other activities—subsistence farming, small business, skilled trades, property rental, taxi driving, fishing—usually contribute to the incomes of wage earners. Therefore, complaints about the poor work ethic in paid jobs are legion.

Integral to all this is the disadvantaged educational status of Tobago. Given the importance of education as an avenue to personal fulfilment and social mobility, and as a means of equipping the population to face the changing world, the corollary of Tobago's disadvantages was high unemployment rates before the 1990s, and expanding low-waged employment since then, along with heavy emigration in search of wider opportunities. The great dependence on employment in public works and 'elementary occupations', is a reflection of these conditions.

Although estimates of poverty from the Surveys of Living Conditions fell from 26.0 per cent in 1997 to 17.0 per cent in 2006, many workers would be very vulnerable, if employment created by the state should decrease.[33]

This is also the context for the increasing alienation of young underachievers, especially males, from the mainstream of social life, as shown by the increased incidence of crime, 'beach boys' and other forms of the sex trade, and drug abuse. The sex trade and drug abuse in such a mobile population help to drive the HIV/AIDS epidemic, which is mature in Tobago.[34] The main factors contributing to the epidemic are multiple sex partnering, inter-generational sex, a high prevalence of sexually transmitted infections, and substance abuse.

Without educational reform and efforts to revitalize the lagging regions and to encourage the participation of more Tobagonians in business activities, the development of a land market open to high-income newcomers in exclusive enclaves will mean increasing income inequality, crimes against property, and social turbulence.

Changing Village and Community Life

Many of the old traditions have been eroded or weakened, as the economic and social order in which they flourished is no more. Hurricane Flora of 1963 is widely perceived as the watershed between the old Tobago and the new, although the agrarian order had been waning long before World War II. Owing to the decline of agriculture, communal production in partnership groups is rare, and exchanges of gifts of foodstuff are less frequent. There is still help for deaths and weddings, but it is far less extensive than before. In 1994 there were 50 co-operatives comprising the following: 6 concerned with production and marketing, 1 in retail and distribution, 13 credit unions, 6 agricultural credit societies, and 24 junior co-operatives.[35] Their financial strength is not known. However, the general perception of Village Council activists is that the communalism of the past has given way since 1963 to increasing individualism.

In the Caribbean as a whole, there has been the growth of what Rosina Wiltshire-Brodber calls 'the transnational family', as a result of inter-island migration coupled with emigration to the metropolis.[36] There is scarcely a Tobago household that is not affected by these trends.

Although there are no known studies on the impact of these phenomena on Tobago family life, social workers and other observers in the field note clear consequences arising from looser family ties and responsibilities, in particular the need for state intervention, or for facilities provided by agencies external to the home, to assist with care for children and the aged. In the past, only the most destitute and the families of the few who went to prison relied on social welfare; today, as the economic base in agriculture of the former independence has been substantially reduced, state welfare provisions are both a right and a necessity. In the process, although family ties are maintained by telephone, e-mail, visits, periodic family gatherings, and gatherings for funerals and weddings, the attachments to wider kin have loosened.

At the same time, the pull of the south-west for work and school means that many families where the breadwinners and school children commute long distances, spending hours getting to and from home, have less time and energy to devote to activities in the localities.

The impact of 'modernity' as transmitted by the communications media has contributed to the erosion of the older, authoritarian and authoritative values, in favour of a more permissive society. Before 1938 when the first government school was built at Mason Hall, all the major schools were run by the churches. Even the private ones were usually started by people who were pillars of their churches. Churching and schooling therefore combined to encourage publicly acknowledged standards of uprightness, respect for self and others, and civic consciousness. These standards were upheld to varying degrees and were often honoured in the breach; but they were known and acknowledged. In addition, although the Church and the African-derived folk traditions were opposed on matters such as African culture, religious allegiances and sexual morality, the folk traditions helped to buttress the values that made for respect and order. Respect for elders was a cardinal principle of the African-derived norms, and in many families one could not even address older siblings without a prefix such as Brother, Sister, or Titty. Moreover, the communal traditions for work, savings and village support were all based on principles of hard work, reciprocity, trustworthiness and trust. Today, the strong influence of the mainline Christian denominations has waned, and the communal traditions have been greatly eroded.

All this has meant noticeable changes in the upbringing of the young. The 1997 Plan Team was told *by teenaged young people* in its consultation at Black Rock that compulsory education on parenting should now be given to parents. Similar concerns, not so strongly worded, but voiced nonetheless, were expressed at other public consultations, because of the perceived erosion of former values.

The loosening of social sanctions, both in the home and the wider society, in the context of inadequate coastal surveillance and low educational attainment, has contributed to the rising incidence of drug-related crime on the island. This too was a subject of public concern at all the public consultations of the Plan Team.

In the urban and suburban settlements, outside of the home, social ties are increasingly based on interactions at school, work, church, sporting and other interest-based organizations, rather than locality-based ones. Today, facilitated by the greater ownership of private motor cars, newer denominations and churches, located in or near Scarborough and its environs, attract congregations from a wide catchment area. Hence, in the settlements of south-west Tobago, even churchgoing is no longer exclusively village- or community-based.

Thus, all the major social trends suggest a loosening of ties at village level and a strengthening of the wider nexus of links within which individuals and groups map their lives. The village, for most people above age twelve, is no longer the place in which work, school, worship and recreation are mainly conducted. It may be that newer forms of 'community', displaying the criteria of participation, interdependence, communication, and ordered behaviour are emerging.[37] There is urgent need for anthropological research on these matters, as well as on the growing differentiation between localities in the parishes with high population densities and those with low.

The need to preserve social cohesiveness and community ties is particularly important, given the expanded nexus of social activities, the growth of amorphous conurbations in the south-west, the high number of young male underachievers, and the increase in crime.

Major Issues

Several major structural issues highlighted by this chapter are therefore interrelated. *First* is the small population size, and therefore the lack of skills, of community leaders, and of a 'critical mass' essential for many services and activities. This 'critical mass' will also be important for implementing the development plans. The severe and steady attrition of the child population is noteworthy. Given that population growth in some age cohorts is not by natural increase, overall population growth in the short term is likely to result from reduced emigration, returning emigrants and/or increased immigration.

Second are the large disparities between the lagging rural parishes and the south-west.

Third is the employment profile with its high dependence on state employment, miscellaneous services and low-wage jobs. Recent short-term improvements in the labour force participation rates have not shifted the emphasis from 'elementary occupations', although stated self-employment is increasing.

Until 1993, the *fourth* significant factor was the high unemployment among the young. Recent substantial decreases in the unemployment rates call for a close examination of the following: the geographical and occupational distribution of new jobs; and the role of migrant workers in these developments. Moreover, as the leading employer, the state should promote higher levels of productivity and an improved work ethic.

Fifth, the education system, in terms of scope, content, and access to post-secondary and technical/vocational education and training, needs continued reform. The smaller child population should facilitate the strengthening of the primary-school system. The provision of more resources for remedial learning is a vital need.

Sixth, the strengthening of village/community councils and related organizations as part of a strategy to increase civic participation and empowerment, and to educate and mobilize the population for social change, is absolutely essential. In this context, continued promotion of health awareness and changed lifestyles to curtail the scourge of HIV/AIDS is important.

4. CONCLUSION

The twentieth century began with a rosy dawn for Tobago. Sugar had collapsed; the old monopolies were broken. There was optimism about the development of Tobago's resources, particularly its agriculture and livestock. Despite the heroic efforts of Tobago's producers, those hopes could not be fulfilled after 1920.

After World War II Tobago underwent yet another economic and demographic transition. Agriculture declined and services became the economic base. The most important aspect of this is that central government transfers are the mainstay of the Tobago economy. Emigration accelerated, and major population shifts occurred from the northern and windward villages and townships to the settlements of the south-west.

Village life changed as a result. In the 1930s, the village was still the locus of most aspects of human life—work, school, worship, and much of the recreation took place there, in spite of interchanges with other settlements and with the rest of the world. Today, most aspects of life after primary school take place outside of the villages. Thus, village ties are loosening, and there is a greater reliance on a wider nexus of social ties.

In the process, the values that promoted respect and order have waned. The old order fostered social supports, but with sanctions, based as it was on the bedrock of churching, schooling, and communal traditions that had a certain moral strength and authority. These undergirding values have declined with little to replace them, especially in leeward Tobago. Such values and supports, which development specialists now call 'the informal and trust economy',[38] though intangible, are indispensable for the process of nation-building. They promote social cohesiveness and are most noticed when they are eroded, resulting in social disruption and human insecurity.

In 1984 Tobago produced its first television serial, a script written by Horace Wilson entitled *The Turn of the Tide*. Its title is symbolic of the mood and the reality in Tobago.

Certainly, the tide in its affairs has been turning. Previously a backwater, Tobago became in the 1990s one of the pools of growth in the nation's economy. As large resorts, public projects and guest houses increased, construction accelerated; and

immigration, in some cases temporary, boosted population growth, particularly of persons of working age.

However, the wider development crisis which Tobago faced in 1900 and at the end of the 1930s still remains to be addressed. Today, at the dawn of the twenty-first century, a major task is still to fashion economic bases that would sustain natural increase, support the flowering of the island's youth, and secure social equity.

In addition, the state and the statutory authorities, which are the largest employers in Tobago, will need to address the pervasively poor work ethic, on which complaints are legion.

Development planning initiatives face the challenge of implementation. However, since 1998 one area of progress has been the steps taken, in collaboration with the Central Statistical Office, to address the need for data collection and policy research on Tobago. In 1998, with Dr. Vanus James as consultant, the THA established a Policy Research and Development Institute, which conducted several important studies on the social and economic conditions, so giving a clearer understanding of the contemporary realities of economic and social life in Tobago. Another positive initiative is the preparation of *A Comprehensive Economic Development Plan for Tobago (2006–2010)* in 2005.

Despite the richness of Tobago's past, there is too little conservation, through archives in all media, recordings, publications, and protection of the vast range of historic sites and buildings. Tobago should not miss the opportunity to convert knowledge of her history and culture into forms that would benefit the population and enhance the tourism product.

Because of heavy emigration, Tobagonians have distinguished themselves outside of Tobago, providing leadership to the nation, the Caribbean and the world, in every field of human endeavour. Tobago needs the flower of this and future generations.

Over the centuries, as in the rest of the Caribbean, Tobago's resources and its labour have contributed to the wealth of groups and nations outside of its shores. Yesterday, sugar and cocoa; today, tourism; tomorrow, natural gas.

But as it was at the dawn of the twentieth century, two central issues face Tobago—

sustainable development with social equity, and popular empowerment. Today, one must add the phrase: within a stable social order.

The tide is turning. But the ship may yet founder on shoals such as: the loss of its moral moorings; the increase in serious crime; poor physical planning to protect the environment; too little conservation of the historical and cultural heritage; widespread underachievement in education especially among males; inadequate human resources in the Public Service; and the politics of the unitary state.

Notes

1   *Report of the Tobago Planning Team* (Port of Spain 1963).
2   CSO, *Labour Force Report 2001* (Port of Spain 2003), Table 17.
3   Policy Research and Development Institute (PRDI), *Tobago Business Register, 1997/98* (Scarborough 2000), Table 1.
4   Ministry of Planning and Mobilization, *Tobago Region Physical Development Plan* (Port of Spain 1991, draft); CSO, *Annual Statistical Digest 1998/99* (Port of Spain 2002), Table 8.
5   *Population and Housing Census Report, 1990*, vol. 2, Table 6.
6   The intercensal growth rates for Trinidad approximate those for the nation.
7   *Population and Housing Census Report, 1990*, vol. 4, Tables 17–18.
8   Joy Simpson, *Internal Migration in Trinidad and Tobago* (Mona 1973), 9.
9   *Population and Housing Census Report, 1990*, vol. 4, Table 6.
10 The rates in this and the preceding paragraph were calculated from CSO, *Annual Statistical Digest 1985* (Port of Spain 1987), Table 20; *Annual Statistical Digest 2000* (Port of Spain 2003), Table 18; CSO, *Population and Vital Statistics Report 2000* (Port of Spain 2005), Tables iv and 7.
11 Calculated from CSO, *Annual Statistical Digest 1998/1999* (Port of Spain 2002), Table 11, and *Population and Vital Statistics Report 2000*, Table iv.
12 The overall annual growth rates of Moriah and Roxborough for the period 1960–2000 were 2.5 and 2.1 per cent, respectively, while the parishes in which they are located grew by 0.5 per cent (St. David) and 1.6 per cent (St. Paul) annually in the same period. The population counts for Moriah in 1960, 1990 and 2000 were 943, 1,010 and 1,898, respectively; the comparable counts for Roxborough were 992, 1,118 and 1,812. Calculated from *Population and Housing Census Report, 1960*, vol. 3, Pt. D, Table 4; *Population and Housing Census Report, 1990*, vol. 2, Table 1; and *2000 Population and Housing Census: Community Register*, Tables 91–97.

13 The data collected by the Continuous Sample Survey of Population's labour force surveys are not strictly comparable with the census data, hence the small discrepancy in the percentages for 1990. CSO, *Labour Force Report 1992* (Port of Spain 1993), Table 3; *Labour Force Report 1995* (Port of Spain 1996), Table 2; *Labour Force Report 1997* (Port of Spain 1998), Table 2; *Labour Force Report 2000* (Port of Spain 2003), Table 2; and for 2001 to 2004, unpublished tables.
14 State employment refers to employment in both government departments and in public enterprises. Calculated from *Population and Housing Census Reports*, 1946, Table 53; 1960, vol. 3, Pt. G, Table 3D; 1970, vol. 4, Pt. 2, Table 1; 1980, vol. 3, Pt. 1, Table 6; 1990, vol. 3, Pt. 2, Table 4.
15 Tobago Development Plan, Report No. 2, *Medium-Term Policy Framework of Tobago, 1998–2000* (Scarborough 1998), 6–8. Cf. PRDI, *Review of the Economy and Policy Measures, Tobago, 2000* (Scarborough 2001), 1–7, which presents the data to 1999.
16 Tobago's labour force grew to 27,000 in 2004, an increase over the 2000 figure of 18.4 per cent or 4.6 per cent per year, which is far higher than the rates of natural increase. CSO, unpublished labour force tables for 2004.
17 CSO, *Labour Force Report 2001*, Table 3; *Labour Force Report 1996*, Table 3.
18 CSO, *Labour Force Report 2001*, Table 15.
19 CSO, *Labour Force Report 2001*, Table 16.
20 CSO, *Labour Force Report 2001*, Table 18.
21 *Education Policy Paper (1993–2003), White Paper* (Port of Spain 1994); Ministry of Education, *Report of the Task Force for the Removal of the Common Entrance Examination* (Port of Spain 1998).
22 *Population and Housing Census Report, 1990*, vol. 5, Pt. 1, Table 1.
23 *Population and Housing Census Report, 1990*, vol. 2, Table 8. The population total in the table is 45,050.
24 Trinidad and Tobago, Task Force Appointed by Cabinet to Enquire into the Poor Performance of Students in Secondary Schools in Tobago, *Report* (Port of Spain 2000), 8.
25 Republic of Trinidad and Tobago, Forestry Division, Biodiversity Clearing House, 'News and

Events', 25 Nov. 2005; http://trinbagobiodiversity.gov.tt/news/Trinidad _ramsar_sites.htm (accessed 14 July 2006).

26 Ministry of Planning and Development and Department of Regional Development and Environment, Organization of American States. *Planning for Sustainable Development: South-West Tobago Development Strategy* (Port of Spain 1996), chap. 1; Environmental Management Authority, *Trinidad and Tobago: State of the Environment Report 1996* (Port of Spain 1996), 39; Kairi Consultants Limited, *Environmental Data and Information Project: Socio-Economics*, Final Report (Port of Spain 1999), 49. A physical development plan was drafted for Tobago: *Tobago Region Physical Development Plan* (Port of Spain 1991). Draft.

27 PRDI with The Department of Tourism, THA, *The Cruise Ship Sector of Tobago's Tourism Industry, November 2000–April 2001* (Scarborough 2003), 19.

28 The figures for 1990–2004 were calculated from Modus Operandi and Records Bureau, Trinidad and Tobago Police Service, unpublished tables, 8 June 2005; provisional data. The data on serious crimes for 1996–2002 were calculated from PRDI, *Crime in Tobago, 1996–2002* (Scarborough 2003), Table 3. The trends in cocaine seizures are in PRDI, *Economic and Social Development in Tobago, 2003–2004* (Scarborough 2004), Table 14; the figure for 2003 is provisional.

29 Calculated from Modus Operandi and Research Bureau, Trinidad and Tobago Police Service, unpublished tables, 8 June 2005; provisional data.

30 The reports were as follows. PRDI and Department of Planning, Office of the Chief Secretary, THA, *Tobago Development Plan, Report No. 1: The Process of Development Planning in Tobago* (Scarborough 1998); PRDI and Division of Finance and Planning, THA, *Tobago Development Plan, Report No. 2: Medium-Term Policy Framework of Tobago, 1998–2000* (Scarborough 1998); PRDI and Division of Finance and Planning, *Tobago Development Plan, Report No. 3: The Tobago Strategic Plan* (Scarborough 1998); PRDI and Division of Finance and Planning, Tobago Development Plan, Report No. 4: The Integrated Plan for the Development of the People of Tobago in the 21st Century (Scarborough 1998). Unpublished. Draft. The author was a member of this team.

31 This latest Plan was prepared by The Task Force Appointed by the Government of Trinidad and Tobago to Prepare a Comprehensive Economic Development Plan for Tobago, and published by the THA, 2005.

32 See *Tobago Business Register, 1997/98*, Pt. I.

33 PRDI, *Tobago Survey of Living Conditions Report, 1997* (Scarborough, Tobago 1999). The high estimates of poverty in this report have been questioned by Michael Witter, 'A Review and Assessment of the Poverty Policy of the Tobago Development Plan' (Port of Spain 2000, mimeographed). According to Stanford Callender, Tobago Member of Parliament, The Survey of Living Conditions, 2006, gives 17.0 per cent as the estimate of poverty in Tobago; *Tobago News*, 14 Sept. 2007, 5. Whether the statistics for 1997 and 2006 are based on comparable methodologies is not known.

34 Cf. *Review of the Economy, Tobago, 2000*, 20, 40. Page 40 of this report states that in 1998 AIDS accounted for 18.5 per cent of Tobago's deaths. See Caribbean Epidemiology Centre, *Status and Trends: Analysis of the Caribbean HIV/AIDS Epidemic, 1982–2002* (Port of Spain 2004).

35 Thames Water International and ADeB Consultants, *Design of a Watershed Protection Programme for the Courland Catchment, Tobago* (Port of Spain 1994), App. H. Cf. Caribbean Network for Integrated Rural Development (CNIRD), *Tobago Profiles: A Survey of 14 Agencies/Groups Engaged in Rural and Community Development in Tobago* (St. Augustine, Trinidad 1990), App., which identified 6 organizations concerned with production and marketing, 13 with finance and credit, 6 agricultural credit societies, 6 associations of farmers or fishermen, 1 in retail and distribution, 2 service co-operatives, 12 devoted to production and development and 3 in multi-purpose activities.

36 Rosina Wiltshire-Brodber, 'The Caribbean Transnational Family', presented to a United Nations Educational, Scientific and Cultural Organization/Institute of Social and Economic Research Eastern Caribbean Sub-Regional Seminar, UWI, Cave Hill, 1986.

37 Thomas Bender, *Community and Social Change in America* (New Brunswick 1978), 3–13; David W. Minar and Scott Greer, eds, *The Concept of Community: Readings with Interpretations* (London 1970), x.

38 The quotation is from Tony Barnett, 'HIV/AIDS— The True Cost to Us All', *LSE* (The London School of Economics and Political Science) *Magazine* 17, no. 1 (2005): 6–8.

Appendix 1
Tables on Exports from Tobago

TABLE A1.1 Exports from Tobago, Quantity and Value (Pounds Sterling), 1916–1933

Exports	1916 Quantity	Value (£)	1917 Quantity	Value (£)	1918 Quantity	Value (£)	1919 Quantity	Value (£)	1920 Quantity	Value (£)
Cocoa (lbs)	1,634,465	47,672	1,313,885	32,847	1,829,298	45,732	2,114,710	88,112	1,627,909	66,080
Coconuts (no.)	645,285	3,361	47,652	1,671	488,400	1,953	2,072,368	16,578	2,132,883	20,048
Copra (lbs)	633,975	7,925	1,022,690	12,784	904,265	11,303	572,975	9,549	448,681	8,179
Other products	—	31,760	—	20,994	—	26,928	—	26,694	—	53,266
Total		90,718		68,296		85,916		140,933		147,573

Exports	1921 Quantity	Value (£)	1922 Quantity	Value (£)	1923 Quantity	Value (£)	1924 Quantity	Value (£)	1925 Quantity	Value (£)
Cocoa (lbs)	2,136,048	35,601	2,113,506	35,225	1,724,018	28,734	2,058,859	42,893	1,545,484	36,152
Coconuts (no.)	1,549,481	6,456	353,423	1,060	254,401	763	184,371	768	63,736	215
Copra (lbs)	821,492	10,269	1,293,896	10,782	2,078,216	21,648	1,531,941	19,149	1,885,262	19,638
Other products	—	39,757	—	26,440	—	26,178	—	28,323	—	31,815
Total		92,083		73,507		77,323		91,133		87,820

Exports	1926 Quantity	Value (£)	1927 Quantity	Value (£)	1928 Quantity	Value (£)	1929 Quantity	Value (£)	1930 Quantity	Value (£)
Cocoa (lbs)	2,314,181	57,855	4,495,258	140,477	4,573,860	114,346	3,026,680	75,667	3,401,200	70,858
Coconuts (no.)	67,861	170	95,800	200	240,600	722	195,670	489	508,386	1,272
Copra (lbs)	3,007,898	25,066	3,276,817	27,307	3,198,610	26,655	3,346,100	27,884	4,012,655	27,169
Other products	—	25,697	—	39,755	—	27,002	—	28,901	—	28,442
Total		108,788		207,740[a]		168,725		132,941		127,741

Exports	1931 Quantity	Value (£)	1932 Quantity	Value (£)	1933 Quantity	Value (£)
Cocoa (lbs)	3,091,895	40,534	3,001,721	40,254	3,560,344	29,670
Coconuts (no.)	389,607	677	112,131	236	918,715	1,914
Copra (lbs)	3,968,044	16,534	4,694,204	27,116	5,414,229	16,919
Other products	—	30,436	—	26,308	—	21,757
Total		88,181		93,914		70,260

Sources: Administration Reports of the Collector of Customs for 1920 to 1924, 1926, 1929, 1930, 1932, 1933. *Note*: [a] Total for 1927 is as in original; it should be £207,739.

Table A1.2 **Exports from Tobago, Quantity and Value (Trinidad and Tobago Dollars), 1933–1950**

Exports	1933		1934		1935		1936		1937	
	Quantity	Value ($)	Quantity	Value ($)	Quantity	Value ($)	Quantity	Value ($)	Quantity	Value ($)
Cocoa (lbs)	3,560,344	142,416	2,570,542	128,525	3,394,191	169,710	3,017,092	305,340	2,079,299	176,740
Copra (lbs)	5,414,229	81,211	5,233,874	68,040	3,485,535	73,196	4,991,883	137,970	6,342,496	190,275
Fresh vegetables	—	25,435	—	37,935	—	35,171	—	31,426	—	62,204
Livestock	—	66,456	—	59,678	—	77,754	—	82,907	—	67,445
Lime oil (gallons)	—	1,262	—	8,131	—	5,521	—	14,279	—	15,876
Leaf tobacco (lbs)	4,208	5,065	37,147	5,944	55,949	8,392	59,032	6,563	58,059	11,612
Coconuts (no.)	918,715	9,187	1,702,155	17,021	1,730,655	17,307	782,525	8,416	619,421	7,743
Coconut fibre (lbs)	—	—	—	—	—	—	1,050	31	160	6
All other products	—	6,216	—	7,558	—	7,462	—	8,154	—	6,432
Total		337,248		332,832		394,513		595,086		538,333

Exports	1938		1939		1940		1941		1942	
	Quantity	Value ($)	Quantity	Value ($)	Quantity	Value ($)	Quantity	Value ($)	Quantity	Value ($)
Cocoa (lbs)	3,681,882	184,094	2,584,760	180,933	3,257,784	236,189	3,197,506	290,682	2,490,746	249,074
Copra (lbs)	5,251,890	78,778	8,953,765	134,306	6,936,080	110,977	6,253,990	100,064	2,701,574	108,062
Fresh vegetables	—	68,645	—	57,920	—	52,746	—	57,866	—	100,731
Livestock	—	77,293	—	98,105	—	117,731	—	116,278	—	127,868
Lime oil (gallons)	—	8,085	—	11,311	—	27,089	—	10,350	—	6,930
Leaf tobacco (lbs)	41,614	4,994	40,528	4,864	61,657	12,331	59,241	11,848	25,360	9,129
Coconuts (no.)	92,040	920	3,125	31	40,250	402	38,700	387	8,410	59
Coconut fibre (lbs)	220	9	105,390	2,635	476,200	11,905	487,800	12,195	738,800	36,940
All other products	—	9,657	—	7,034	—	7,251	—	20,910	—	21,984
Total		432,475		497,139		576,621		620,580		660,777

TABLE A1.2 concluded Exports from Tobago, Quantity and Value (Trinidad and Tobago Dollars), 1933–1950

Exports	1943 Quantity	1943 Value ($)	1944 Quantity	1944 Value ($)	1945 Quantity	1945 Value ($)	1946 Quantity	1946 Value ($)	1947 Quantity	1947 Value ($)
Cocoa (lbs)	1,881,163	209,562	1,599,620	217,545	1,713,855	227,078	1,874,880	232,935	2,249,956	656,237
Copra (lbs)	2,357,730	111,982	6,830,811	324,463	7,908,120	553,567	9,489,844	664,286	8,536,670	597,563
Fresh vegetables	—	165,561	—	88,856	—	81,443	—	77,393	—	68,483
Livestock	—	87,779	—	53,284	—	89,785	—	83,478	—	75,934
Lime oil (gallons)	—	40,229	828	35,190	765	30,600	803	32,219	679	13,870
Leaf tobacco (lbs)	7,006	2,802	10,885	4,353	10,345	4,137	9,303	3,621	14,589	5,638
Coconuts (no.)	7,000	70	11,300	90	12,100	97	9,400	76	5,700	47
Coconut fibre (lbs)	1,018,600	50,930	713,800	85,690	1,014,000	50,700	1,150,800	57,540	804,400	40,220
All other products	—	64,644	—	57,842	—	61,376	—	59,835	—	64,922
Total		733,559		867,313		1,098,783		1,211,383		1,522,914

Exports	1948 Quantity	1948 Value ($)	1949 Quantity	1949 Value ($)	1950 Quantity	1950 Value ($)
Cocoa (lbs)	3,914,000	1,369,900	2,468,270	765,163	2,518,220	881,377
Copra (lbs)	5,200,740	364,051	7,439,040	520,732	5,766,480	490,150
Fresh vegetables	—	75,300	—	65,045	—	180,905
Livestock	—	96,000	—	118,800	—	260,712
Lime oil (gallons)	815	24,276	1,023	26,088	468	27,800
Leaf tobacco (lbs)	6,549	2,554	5,947	2,380	3,998	1,850
Coconuts (no.)	10,720	97	16,820	180	—	—
Coconut fibre (lbs)	836,400	41,850	982,000	49,100	914,200	40,710
All other products	—	55,200	—	66,531	—	140,888
Total		2,029,228		1,614,019		2,024,392

Sources: 1933: District Administration Reports for 1935, Council Paper No. 54 of 1936, 7; 1934–1935: Administration Report of the Collector of Customs and Excise for 1938, Council Paper No. 58 of 1939; 1936–1940: Administration Report of the Collector of Customs and Excise for 1940, Council Paper No. 33 of 1941, 3; 1941: Administration Report of the Collector of Customs and Excise for 1941, Council Paper No. 62 of 1942, 3; 1942–1944: Administration Report of the Collector of Customs and Excise for 1944, Council Paper No. 35 of 1945; 1945: Annual General Report on the Colony of Trinidad and Tobago for 1939 to 1946 (Port of Spain c.1947), 86; 1946–1950: Administration Report of the Comptroller of Customs and Excise for 1950 (Port of Spain 1951), 8.

Note: Trinidad and Tobago $4.80 = £1 sterling.

Appendix 2
Tables for Chapter 7

TABLE A2.1 **Tobago Population Density, 1844–1946, and Comparison with the Windward Islands, 1882, and with Trinidad, 1921, 1931 and 1946**

TOBAGO			WINDWARD ISLANDS, 1882			
Year	Population	Persons per square mile	Island	Population	Area: square miles	Persons per square mile
1844	13,208	114	Barbados	172,000	166	1,036
1851	14,378	124	St. Lucia	39,300	243	162
1861	15,410	133	St. Vincent	41,000	132	311
1871	17,054	147	Grenada	43,000	133	323
1881	18,051	155	Tobago	18,500	114	162
1891	18,353	158				
1901	18,751	161	TRINIDAD, 1921–1946			
1911	20,749	179	Year	Population	Persons per square mile	
1921	23,390	201	1921	342,423	184	
1931	25,358	218	1931	387,425	208	
1946	27,208	234	1946	530,762	285	

Sources: Tobago Population Census Reports, 1844–1891; Trinidad and Tobago Population Census Reports, 1901–1946; for Windward Islands, *Report from the Royal Commission …*, (1884; reprint, London 1971), Pt. II, 4.

Note: The area of Tobago was thought to be 114 square miles until the 1931 census, when it was given as 116.24 square miles. Trinidad's area in the same census report is given as 1,862.82 square miles. Except for the comparison with the Windward Islands, the population densities are computed using the areas given in 1931.

TABLE A2.2 **Tobago: Population Growth, and Comparison with the Windward Islands, 1844–1946**

	TOBAGO				WINDWARD ISLANDS	
Years	Population	Intercensal increase	Increase (no.) per annum	Per cent increase per annum	Census years	Per cent increase per annum
1844	13,208	—	—	—	—	—
1851	14,378	1,170	167	1.3	—	—
1861	15,410	1,032	103	0.7	1844–61	0.8
1871	17,054	1,644	164	1.1	1861–71	1.4
1881	18,051	997	98	0.6	1871–81	1.2
1891	18,353	302	30	0.2	1881–91	0.9
1901	18,751	398	40	0.2		
1911	20,749	1,998	199	1.1	1891–1911	0.8
1921	23,390	2,641	264	1.3	1911–21	0.4
1931	25,358	1,968	197	0.8	1921–46	0.9
1946	27,208	1,850	123	0.5		

Sources: Calculated from Tobago Population Census Reports, 1844–1891; Trinidad and Tobago Population Census Reports, 1901–1946; for the Windward Islands, George Roberts, *Population of Jamaica* (Cambridge 1957), Table 8, 50.

TABLE A2.3 **Population by District and Sex, 1844–1891, 1946**

District	Male	Female	Total	% of population	Male	Female	Total	% of population
			1844				**1851**	
Windward	1,227	1,364	2,591	19.6	1,205	1,144	2,349	16.3
Middle	2,439	2,955	5,394	40.8	2,866	3,287	6,153	42.8
Leeward	2,486	2,737	5,223	39.5	2,878	2,998	5,876	40.9
Total	6,152	7,056	13,208	100.0	6,949	7,429	14,378	100.0

District	Male	Female	Total	% of population	Male	Female	Total	% of population
			1861				**1871**	
Windward	1,358	1,321	2,679	17.4	1,559	1,572	3,131	18.3
Middle	2,995	3,398	6,393	41.5	2,835	3,079	5,914	34.7
Leeward	3,080	3,258	6,338	41.1	3,868	4,141	8,009	47.0
Total	7,433	7,977	15,410	100.0	8,262	8,792	17,054	100.0

District	Male	Female	Total	% of population	Male	Female	Total	% of population
			1881				**1891**	
Windward	2,041	1,987	4,028	22.3	2,145	2,264	4,409	24.0
Middle	2,853	3,219	6,072	33.6	2,842	3,319	6,161	33.6
Leeward	3,800	4,151	7,951	44.0	3,653	4,130	7,783	42.4
Total	8,694	9,357	18,051	100.0	8,640	9,713	18,353	100.0

District	Male	Female	Total	% of population
			1946	
Windward	4,166	4,287	8,453	31.1
Middle	4,537	4,805	9,342	34.3
Leeward	4,506	4,907	9,413	34.6
Total	13,209	13,999	27,208	100.0

Sources: Calculated from Tobago Population Census Reports, 1844–1891, and from Trinidad and Tobago Population Census Report, 1946.

TABLE A2.4 Population of the Main Towns by Sex and Sex Ratios, Selected Years, 1844–1946

	1844			1861			1881			1891		
	Male	Female	Total	Male	Female	Total	Male	Female	Total	Male	Female	Total
Scarborough												
Number	605	869	1,474	467	723	1,190	351	502	853	404	515	919
% male or female	41.0	59.0	100.0	39.2	60.8	100.0	41.1	58.9	100.0	44.0	56.0	100.0
Sex ratios		**69.6**			**64.6**			**69.9**			**78.4**	
% of total population by sex	9.8	12.3	11.2	6.3	9.1	7.7	4.0	5.4	4.7	4.7	5.3	5.0
Plymouth												
Number	178	222	400	250	249	499	355	412	767	297	339	636
% male or female	44.5	55.5	100.0	50.1	49.9	100.0	46.3	53.7	100.0	46.7	53.3	100.0
Sex ratios		**80.2**			**100.4**			**86.2**			**87.6**	
% of total population by sex	2.9	3.1	3.0	3.4	3.1	3.2	4.1	4.4	4.2	3.4	3.5	3.5

TABLE A2.4 concluded Population of the Main Towns by Sex and Sex Ratios, Selected Years, 1844–1946

	1911[b]			1921			1931			1946		
	Male	Female	Total	Male	Female	Total	Male	Female	Total	Male	Female	Total
Scarborough												
Number	320	409	729	730	733	1,463	367	466	833	444	464	908
% male or female	43.9	56.1	100.0	49.9	50.1	100.0	44.0	55.9	100.0	48.9	51.1	100.0
Sex ratios[a]		**78.2**			**99.6**			**78.8**			**95.7**	
% of Tobago's population by sex	3.2	3.8	3.5	6.5	6.0	6.2	3.0	3.6	3.3	3.4	3.3	3.3
Plymouth												
Number	238	297	535	194	236	430	178	209	387	547	633	1,180
% male or female	44.5	55.5	100.0	45.1	54.9	100.0	46.0	54.0	100.0	46.3	53.6	100.0
Sex ratios[a]		**80.1**			**82.2**			**85.2**			**86.4**	
% of Tobago's population by sex	2.4	2.7	2.6	1.7	1.9	1.8	1.5	1.6	1.5	4.1	4.5	4.3
Roxborough												
Number	581	613	1,194	598	617	1,215	404	420	824	406	465	871
% male or female	48.7	51.3	100.0	49.2	50.8	100.0	49.0	51.0	100.0	46.6	53.4	100.0
Sex ratios[a]		**94.8**			**96.9**			**96.2**			**87.3**	
% of Tobago's population by sex	5.9	5.7	5.8	5.3	5.1	5.2	3.3	3.2	3.2	3.1	3.3	3.2

Sources for all of Table A2.4: Calculated from Tobago Population Census Reports, 1844–1891; Trinidad and Tobago Population Census Reports, 1911–1946.

Notes for all of Table A2.4:
[a] Sex ratios are males per 100 females.
[b] The figures for Roxborough in 1911 include for Betsy's Hope.

TABLE A2.5 **Proportion of the Population in Settlements of Varying Population Sizes, 1861 and 1891**

Settlement size/type	0–	100–	200–	300–	400–	500+	Subtotal	Towns	Estates	Shipping etc.	Total
1861											
No. of persons	2,322	3,529	3,602	2,357	1,275	503	13,588	1,689	Not given	111	15,410[a]
Per cent of population	**15.1**	**22.9**	**23.4**	**15.3**	**8.3**	**3.3**	**88.2**	**11.0**	**—**	**0.7**	**100.0**
1891											
No. of persons	2,296	2,415	3,798	2,406	872	4,746	16,533	1,497	264[b]	59[c]	18,353
Per cent of population	**12.5**	**13.2**	**20.7**	**13.1**	**4.8**	**25.9**	**90.1**	**8.2**	**1.4**	**0.3**	**100.0**

Sources: Calculated from Tobago Population Census Reports, 1861, 1891.

Notes:
[a] Includes 22 persons not accounted for in the 1861 census tables on place of abode.
[b] Figures are for 4 out of 7 parishes.
[c] Includes 6 persons in a police station.
[d] Percentages are subject to rounding errors.

TABLE A2.6 **Settlements by Population Size (Excluding Towns), 1861, 1891**

	Population size (persons)						
	0–	100–	200–	300–	400–	500+	Total
1861							
Number of settlements	46	24	14	7	3	1	95
Per cent of settlements	48.4	25.3	14.7	7.4	3.2	1.0	100.0
1891							
Number of settlements	63	18	15	7	2	8	113
Per cent of settlements	55.8	15.9	13.3	6.2	1.8	7.1	100.0

Sources: Calculated from Tobago Population Census Reports, 1861, 1891.

TABLE A2.7 Population by Age, 1851–1931

Age group	1851 Number	1851 Per cent	1861 Number	1861 Per cent	1871 Number	1871 Per cent	1881 Number	1881 Per cent	1891 Number	1891 Per cent
0–4	1,910	13.3	2,035	13.2	2,604	15.3	2,593	14.4	2,616	14.2
5–9	1,641	11.4	1,836	11.9	1,882	11.0	2,274	12.6	2,201	12.0
10–14	1,539	10.7	1,732	11.2	2,002	11.8	3,964}	22.0}	2,423	13.2
15–19	1,306	9.1	1,497	9.7	1,759	10.3			1,864	10.1
20–24	2,541}	17.7}	1,534	10.0	3,176}	18.6}	2,970}	16.5}	1,558	8.4
25–29			1,154	7.5					1,273	6.9
30–34	1,971}	13.7}	992	6.4	2,064}	12.1}	2,235}	12.4}	1,058	5.8
35–39			819	5.3					1,031	5.6
40–44	1,505}	10.5}	880	5.7	1,339}	7.9}	1,577}	8.7}	952	5.2
45–49			731	4.7					810	4.4
50–54	905}	6.3}	744	4.8	1,159}	6.8}	1,181}	6.5}	694	3.8
55–59			380	2.5					484	2.6
60–64	1,060}	7.4}	1,076}	7.0}	624}	3.7}	1,257}	7.0}	480	2.6
65–69									297	1.6
70–74					445}	2.6}			244	1.3
75–79									139	0.7
80+									229	1.2
Total	14,378	100.0	15,410	100.0	17,054	100.0	18,051	100.0	18,353	100.0

TABLE A2.7 concluded Population by Age, 1851–1931

Age group	1901 Number	1901 Per cent	1911 Number	1911 Per cent	1921 Number	1921 Per cent	1931 Number	1931 Per cent
0–4	2,767	14.7	3,000	14.4	3,353	14.4	3,551	14.0
5–9	2,580	13.8	2,674	12.9	3,170	13.5	3,462	13.7
10–14	2,430	13.0	2,681	12.9	3,032	12.9	3,143	12.4
15–19	1,943	10.3	2,086	10.1	2,238	9.5	2,674	10.6
20–24	1,601	8.5	1,837	8.9	1,993	8.5	2,252	8.9
25–29	1,128	6.0	1,498	7.2	1,557	6.6	1,568	6.2
30–34	968	5.1	1,147	5.5	1,328	5.7	1,333	5.2
35–39	956	5.1	1,057	5.1	1,361	5.8	1,290	5.1
40–44	914	4.8	931	4.5	1,174	5.0	1,161	4.6
45–49	782	4.1	886	4.2	985	4.2	1,173	4.6
50–54	804	4.2	758	3.7	809	3.5	985	3.8
55–59	527	2.8	612	2.9	659	2.8	757	3.0
60–64	515	2.8	596	2.9	603	2.6	626	2.5
65–69	288	1.5	398	1.9	406	1.8	510	2.0
70–74	213	1.1	246	1.2	365	1.5	348	1.4
75–79	128	0.6	147	0.7	195	0.8	261	1.0
80+	207	1.1	195	0.9	162	0.6	258	1.0
Total	18,751	99.5	20,749	99.9	23,390	99.7	25,352	100.0

Sources: Calculated from Tobago Population Census Reports, 1851–1891; Trinidad and Tobago Population Census Reports, 1901–1931.

TABLE A2.8 Age Profile of the Population (Percentages), 1851–1931

Year	0–14	15–59	60+	Per cent of population
1851	35.4	57.2	7.4	100.0
1861	36.3	56.7	7.0	100.0
1871	38.0	55.7	6.3	100.0
1881	38.8	54.3	7.0	100.0
1891	39.4	53.0	7.6	100.0
1901	41.5	51.3	7.2	100.0
1911	40.3	52.1	7.6	100.0
1921	40.9	51.7	7.4	100.0
1931	40.1	52.0	7.9	100.0

Source: Calculated from the figures in Table A2.7.

TABLE A2.9 **Population by Age and Sex, 1851–1931**

	1851				1861				1871			
	Number		Per cent of population		Number		Per cent of population		Number		Per cent of population	
Age group	Male	Female	Male	Female	Male	Female	Male	Female	Male	Female	Male	Female
0–4	924	986	6.4	6.9	986	1,049	6.4	6.8	1,257	1,347	7.4	7.9
5–9	805	836	5.6	5.8	936	900	6.1	5.8	939	943	5.5	5.5
10–14	839	700	5.8	4.9	903	829	5.9	5.4	1,052	950	6.2	5.6
15–19	636	670	4.4	4.7	701	796	4.5	5.2	865	894	5.0	5.2
20–24	1,273}	1,268}	8.9}	8.8}	750	784	4.9	5.1	1,405}	1,771}	8.2}	10.4}
25–29					549	605	3.5	3.9				
30–34	959}	1,012}	6.7}	7.0}	487	505	3.2	3.3	1,070}	994}	6.3}	5.8}
35–39					405	414	2.6	2.7				
40–44	739}	766}	5.1}	5.3}	414	466	2.7	3.0	635}	704}	3.7}	4.1}
45–49					354	377	2.3	2.4				
50–54	378}	527}	2.6}	3.7}	379	365	2.5	2.4	589}	570}	3.4}	3.3}
55–59					184	196	1.2	1.3				
60–64	396}	664}	2.8}	4.6}	385}	691}	2.5}	4.5}	284}	340}	1.6}	2.0}
65–69												
70–74									166}	279}	1.0}	1.6}
75–79												
80+												
Total	6,949	7,429	48.3	51.7	7,433	7,977	48.3	51.8	8,262	8,792	48.3	51.4
	14,378		100.0		15,410		100.1		17,054		99.7	

TABLE A2.9 continued **Population by Age and Sex, 1851–1931**

Age group	1881 Number Male	1881 Number Female	1881 Per cent Male	1881 Per cent Female	1891 Number Male	1891 Number Female	1891 Per cent Male	1891 Per cent Female	1901 Number Male	1901 Number Female	1901 Per cent Male	1901 Per cent Female
0–4	1,347	1,246	7.5	6.9	1,320	1,296	7.2	7.0	1,354	1,413	7.2	7.5
5–9	1,107	1,167	6.1	6.5	1,112	1,089	6.1	5.9	1,291	1,289	6.9	6.9
10–14	2,014}	1,950}	11.1}	10.8}	1,232	1,191	6.7	6.5	1,253	1,177	6.7	6.3
15–19					894	970	4.8	5.3	925	1,018	4.9	5.4
20–24	1,333}	1,637}	7.4}	9.1}	653	905	3.5	4.9	629	972	3.3	5.2
25–29					535	738	2.9	4.0	433	695	2.3	3.7
30–34	991}	1,244}	5.5}	6.9}	433	625	2.4	3.4	371	597	1.9	3.2
35–39					495	536	2.7	2.9	433	523	2.3	2.8
40–44	733}	844}	4.1}	4.6}	419	533	2.3	2.9	402	512	2.1	2.7
45–49					380	430	2.1	2.3	396	386	2.1	2.1
50–54	648}	533}	3.6}	2.9}	335	359	1.8	2.0	364	440	1.9	2.3
55–59					228	256	1.2	1.4	242	285	1.3	1.5
60–64	521}	736}	2.9}	4.1}	241	239	1.3	1.3	219	296	1.2	1.6
65–69					134	163	0.7	0.9	135	153	0.7	0.8
70–74					92	152	0.5	0.8	97	116	0.5	0.6
75–79					59	80	0.3	0.4	46	82	0.2	0.4
80+					78	151	0.4	0.8	81	126	0.4	0.7
Total	8,694	9,357	48.2	51.8	8,640	9,713	46.9	52.7	8,671	10,080	45.9	53.7
	18,051		100.0		18,353		100.0		18,751		99.6	

TABLE A2.9 concluded **Population by Age and Sex, 1851–1931**

Age group	1911 Number Male	1911 Number Female	1911 Per cent of population Male	1911 Per cent of population Female	1921 Number Male	1921 Number Female	1921 Per cent of population Male	1921 Per cent of population Female	1931 Number Male	1931 Number Female	1931 Per cent of population Male	1931 Per cent of population Female
0–4	1,526	1,474	7.3	7.1	1,678	1,675	7.2	7.2	1,804	1,747	7.1	6.9
5–9	1,372	1,302	6.6	6.3	1,577	1,593	6.7	6.8	1,741	1,721	6.9	6.8
10–14	1,352	1,329	6.5	6.4	1,552	1,480	6.6	6.3	1,644	1,499	6.5	5.9
15–19	1,035	1,051	5.0	5.1	1,102	1,136	4.7	4.8	1,255	1,419	5.0	5.6
20–24	821	1,016	4.0	4.9	858	1,135	3.7	4.8	1,092	1,160	4.3	4.6
25–29	645	853	3.1	4.1	661	896	2.8	3.8	712	856	2.8	3.4
30–34	519	628	2.5	3.0	629	699	2.7	3.0	588	745	2.3	2.9
35–39	472	585	2.3	2.8	643	718	2.7	3.1	599	691	2.4	2.7
40–44	415	516	2.0	2.5	551	623	2.3	2.7	537	624	2.1	2.5
45–49	421	465	2.0	2.2	482	503	2.1	2.1	568	605	2.2	2.4
50–54	351	407	1.7	2.0	370	439	1.6	1.9	465	520	1.8	2.0
55–59	281	331	1.3	1.6	322	337	1.4	1.4	381	376	1.5	1.5
60–64	265	331	1.3	1.6	282	321	1.2	1.4	301	325	1.2	1.3
65–69	188	210	0.9	1.0	183	223	0.8	1.0	231	279	0.9	1.1
70–74	124	122	0.6	0.6	174	191	0.7	0.8	145	203	0.6	0.8
75–79	61	86	0.3	0.4	75	120	0.3	0.5	115	146	0.4	0.6
80+	74	121	0.3	0.6	56	106	0.2	0.4	97	161	0.4	0.6
Total	9,922	10,827	47.7	52.2	11,195	12,195	47.7	52.0	12,275	13,077	48.4	51.6
	20,749		100.0		23,390		100.0		25,352		100.0	

Sources: Calculated from Tobago Population Census Reports, 1851–1891; Trinidad and Tobago Population Census Reports, 1901–1931.

Note: The 1931 age tables account for 25,352 persons. Other tables in the 1931 census report account for 12,280 males and 13,078 females, a total of 25,358 persons.

TABLE A2.10 Age-Specific Sex Ratios (Males per 100 Females), 1851–1931

Age group	1851	1861	1871	1881	1891	1901	1911	1921	1931
0–4	93.7	94.0	93.3	108.1	101.9	95.8	103.5	100.2	103.3
5–9	96.3	104.0	99.6	94.9	102.1	100.1	105.4	99.0	101.2
10–14	119.8	108.9	110.7	103.3}	103.4	106.4	101.7	104.9	109.7
15–19	94.9	88.1	96.8	}	92.2	90.9	98.5	97.0	88.4
20–24	100.4}	95.7	79.3}	81.4}	72.2	64.7	80.8	75.6	94.1
25–29	}	90.7	}	}	72.5	62.3	75.6	73.8	83.2
30–34	94.8}	96.4	107.6}	79.7}	69.3	62.1	82.6	90.0	78.9
35–39	}	97.8	}	}	92.4	84.6	80.7	89.5	86.7
40–44	96.5}	88.8	90.2}	86.8}	78.6	78.5	80.4	88.4	86.0
45–49	}	93.9	}	}	88.4	102.6	90.5	95.8	93.9
50–54	71.7}	103.8	103.3}	121.6}	93.3	82.7	86.2	84.3	89.4
55–59	}	93.9	}	}	89.1	84.9	84.9	95.5	101.3
60–64	59.6}	55.7}	83.5}	70.8}	100.8	74.0	80.1	87.9	92.6
65–69	}	}	}	}	82.2	88.2	89.5	82.1	82.8
70–74	}	}	59.5}	}	60.5	83.6	101.6	91.1	71.4
75–79	}	}	}	}	73.8	56.1	70.9	62.5	78.8
80+	}	}	}	}	51.7	64.3	61.1	52.8	60.2
All ages	**93.5**	**93.2**	**94.0**	**92.9**	**89.0**	**86.0**	**91.6**	**91.8**	**93.9**

Sources: Calculated from Tobago Population Census Reports, 1851–1891, and Trinidad and Tobago Population Census Reports, 1901–1931.

TABLE A2.11 Children Enrolled in Schools by Sex and Denomination, Selected Years, 1850–1931

Denomination	1850			1860			1870			1880			1890		
	Male	Female	Total	Male	Female	Total	Male	Female	Total	Male	Female	Total	Male	Female	Total
Anglican	379	324	703	384	153	537	317	197	514	553	438	991	444	386	830
Moravian	261	266	527	407	292	699	513	372[b]	885	333	328	661	451	373	824
Methodist	264	160	424	217	214	431	298	220	518	299	279	578	407	419	826
Roman Catholic	—	—	—	—	—	—	—	—	—	—	—	—	16	23	39
Total	904	750	1,654	1,008	659	1,667	1,128	789	1,917	1,185	1,045	2,230	1,318	1,201	2,519
% of enrolled	54.6	45.3	99.9	60.5	39.5	100.0	58.8	41.2	100.0	53.1	46.9	100.0	52.3	47.7	100.0
School-age population[a]	1,644	1,536	3,180	1,839	1,729	3,568	1,991	1,893	3,884	2,218	2,178	4,396	2,344	2,280	4,624
Enrolled as % of school-age population	55.0	48.8	52.0	54.8	38.1	46.7	56.6	41.7	49.3	53.4	48.0	50.7	56.2	52.7	54.5

Denomination	1901			1912			1921			1931		
	Male	Female	Total	Male	Female	Total	Male	Female	Total	Male	Female	Total
Anglican	683	635	1,318	1,111	1,032	2,143	1,179	1,140	2,319	1,499	1,327	2,826
Moravian	466	459	925	574	474	1,048	564	578	1,142	694	667	1,361
Methodist	429	413	842	664	711	1,375	750	789	1,539	827	843	1,670
Roman Catholic	152	126	278	265	232	497	320	339	659	344	321	665
Total	1,730	1,633	3,363	2,614	2,449	5,063	2,813	2,846	5,659	3,364	3,158	6,522
% of enrolled	51.4	48.5	99.9	51.6	48.4	100.0	49.7	50.3	100.0	51.6	48.4	100.0
School-age population[a]	2,544	2,466	5,010	2,724	2,631	5,355	3,129	3,073	6,202	3,385	3,220	6,605
Enrolled as % of school-age population	68.0	66.2	67.1	96.0	93.1	94.5	89.9	92.6	91.2	99.4	98.1	98.7

Sources: CO 290 series: Tobago Blue Books for 1850–1880; CO 300/101, /111: Trinidad and Tobago Blue Books for 1890, 1901, respectively; Blue Books for 1912, 1921, 1931; Tobago Population Census Reports, 1851–1891; Trinidad and Tobago Population Census Reports, 1901–1931.

Notes:
[a] School-age population comprises children aged 5–14 at nearest census year. Percentages of school-age population are given by sex.
[b] Includes 42 girls in sewing school.

TABLE A2.12 **Religious Affiliations of the Population by District, 1871–1891, and for All of Tobago, 1901–1931 (Numbers)**

District	Church of England	Church of Scotland	Moravian	Wesleyan	Roman Catholic	Baptist	SDA	Other Christian	Hindu	Muslim	Other non-Christian	Not given	Total
1871													
Windward	1,895	10	16	942	6	—	—	—	—	—	1	261	3,131
Middle	3,453	15	281	1,965	27	—	—	2	—	—	8	163	5,914
Leeward	3,768	12	3,369	360	3	—	—	1	—	—	—	496	8,009
Total	9,116	37	3,666	3,267	36	—	—	3	—	—	9	920	17,054
1881													
Windward	2,527	2	27	1,416	1	—	—	[b]	—	—	—	55	4,028
Middle	2,520	8	975	2,297	10	—	—	7	—	—	—	255	6,072
Leeward	3,818	1	3,610	303	2	—	—	20	—	—	—	197	7,951
Total	8,865	11	4,612	4,016	13	—	—	27	—	—	—	507	18,051
1891													
Windward	2,696	1	43	1,610	38	—	—	2	2	—	—	31	4,409
Middle	2,553	13	1,189	2,268	113	1	—	3	—	—	—	22	6,161
Leeward	3,423	5	3,884	298	25	1	—	1	3	—	1	129	7,783
Total	8,672	19	5,116	4,176	176	2	—	4	5	—	1	182	18,353
1901													
Tobago	9,238	6	4,688	3,744	794	55	—	10	4	—	5	207	18,751
1911													
Tobago	10,792	30	4,904	3,972	855	45	54	13	47	23	11	3	20,749
1921													
Tobago	12,592	45	4,924	3,894	1,340	76	280	65	83	52	22	17	23,390
1931													
Tobago	13,202	27	5,001	3,878	2,077	57	713	264	54	26	7	48	25,354[a]

Sources: Tobago Population Census Reports, 1871–1891; Trinidad and Tobago Population Census Reports, 1901–1931.

Notes:
[a] The tables on religion in the 1931 census account for fewer than the total of 25,358. SDA: Seventh Day Adventists.
[b] For 1881, 'Other Forms of Worship' were put under the heading 'Other Christians'; the persons so enumerated could have included non-Christians for whom no figures are given.

TABLE A2.13 **Religious Affiliations of the Population by District, 1871–1891, and for All of Tobago, 1901–1931 (Percentages)**

District	Church of England	Church of Scotland	Mor- avian	Wesleyan	Roman Catholic	Baptist	SDA	Other Christian	Hindu	Muslim	Other non- Christian	Not given	Total
1871													
Windward	20.5	27.0	0.4	28.8	16.6	—	—	—	—	—	11.1	28.4	—
Middle	37.8	40.5	7.6	60.1	75.0	—	—	66.6	—	—	88.8	17.7	—
Leeward	41.3	32.4	91.8	11.0	8.3	—	—	33.3	—	—	—	53.9	—
Total	53.4	0.2	21.5	19.2	0.2	—	—	0.2	—	—	0.1	5.4	100.0
1881													
Windward	28.5	18.1	0.6	35.3	7.7	—	—	—	—	—	—	10.8	—
Middle	28.4	72.7	21.1	57.2	76.9	—	—	25.9	—	—	—	50.3	—
Leeward	43.1	9.1	78.3	9.0	15.4	—	—	74.1	—	—	—	38.8	—
Total	49.1	0.1	25.5	22.2	0.1	—	—	0.2	—	—	—	2.8	100.0
1891													
Windward	31.1	5.3	0.8	38.5	21.6	—	—	33.3	—	—	33.3	17.0	—
Middle	29.4	68.4	23.2	54.3	64.2	—	—	50.0	—	—	—	12.1	—
Leeward	39.5	26.3	75.9	7.1	14.2	—	—	16.6	—	—	66.6	70.8	—
Total	47.2	0.1	27.9	22.7	1.0	—	—	0.0	—	—	0.0	1.0	100.0
1901													
Tobago	49.3	0.0	25.0	20.0	4.2	0.3	—	0.1	0.0	—	0.0	1.1	100.0
1911													
Tobago	52.0	0.1	23.6	19.1	4.1	0.2	0.3	0.1	0.2	0.1	0.1	0.0	100.0
1921													
Tobago	53.8	0.2	21.0	16.6	5.7	0.3	1.2	0.3	0.4	0.2	0.1	0.1	100.0
1931													
Tobago	52.1	0.1	19.7	15.3	8.2	0.2	2.8	1.0	0.2	0.1	0.0	0.2	100.0

Sources: As for Table A2.12; calculated.

Notes: See notes to Table A2.12. Percentages for the districts give the proportion of the persons in the denomination who belong to the district. Percentages in the total rows give the proportion of persons in the island who belong to the denomination. Totals are subject to rounding errors.

TABLE A2.14 **Conjugal Condition of Tobago Population, 1861–1931 (Selected Years), and Comparison with Trinidad, 1901 and 1931**

TOBAGO

District	1861			1871		
	Adult population	Married	% of adult population	Adult population	Married	% of adult population
Windward	1,705	558	32.7	2,009	547	27.2
Middle	4,115	755	18.3	3,587	1,489	41.5
Leeward	3,987	668	16.7	4,970	2,130	42.8
Total	9,807	1,981	20.2	10,566	4,166	39.4

TOBAGO

	1891		1901		1911		1921		1931	
	No.	% of adults	No.	% of adults	No.	% of adults	No.	% of adults	No.	% of adults
Married	3,981	35.8	4,156	37.9	4,921	39.7	5,585	40.4	5,651	37.2
Unmarried	6,213	55.9	5,937	54.1	6,524	52.6	7,206	52.1	8,372	55.1
Widowed	919	8.3	881	8.0	946	7.6	1,037	7.5	1,170	7.7
Divorced	N.G.	—	N.G.	—	3	0.0	7	0.1	3	0.0
Total adult population	11,113	100.0	10,974	100.0	13,835	99.9	13,835	100.0	15,196	100.0

TRINIDAD

	1901[b]		1931	
	No.	% of adults	No.	% of adults
Married	32,973	29.8	67,686	26.3
Unmarried	69,255	62.7	175,161	68.0
Widowed	8,293	7.5	14,472	5.6
Divorced	N.G.	—	222	0.1
Total adult population	110,521	100.0	257,541	100.0

Sources: Calculated from Tobago Population Census Reports, 1861, 1871, 1891, and Trinidad and Tobago Population Census Reports, 1901–1931.

Notes:

[a] Adult population is number of persons aged 15 and over. N. G.: not given.

[b] For 1901, because of poor enumeration and non-recognition of many East Indian marriages, East Indians are excluded from the figures.

TABLE A2.15 **Types of Dwellings, Tobago, 1891–1931, and Comparison with Trinidad, 1931**

Type of dwellings	TOBAGO 1891		TOBAGO 1901		TOBAGO 1911	
	Number	Per cent	Number	Per cent	Number	Per cent
Dwelling houses	4,011	95.1	4,045	97.7	4,506	94.5
Divided dwellings	128	3.0	57	1.4	114	2.4
Barracks	31	0.7	6	0.1	150}	3.1}
Rooms in yards	49	1.2	29	0.7	}	}
Total dwellings occupied	4,219	100.0	4,137	99.9	4,770	100.0
Rooms occupied	7,026	—	7,083	—	7,742	—
Total population	18,353	—	18,751	—	20,749	—
Persons per room	**2.6**	—	**2.6**	—	**2.7**	—
Unoccupied houses	128	—	170	—	116	—
Houses under construction	91	—	112	—	93	—
Rooms unoccupied	304	—	372	—	286	—

Type of dwellings	TOBAGO 1921		TOBAGO 1931		TRINIDAD 1931	
	Number	Per cent	Number	Per cent	Number	Per cent
Dwelling houses	4,850	95.4	5,478	94.2	60,560	65.8
Divided dwellings	85	1.7	111	1.9	8,585	9.3
Barracks	91	1.8	120	2.1	10,304	11.2
Rooms in yards	58	1.1	105	1.8	12,562	13.7
Total dwellings occupied	5,084	100.0	5,814	100.0	92,011	100.0
Rooms occupied	9,876	—	10,533	—	209,927	—
Total population	23,390	—	25,358	—	387,425	—
Persons per room	**2.4**	—	**2.4**	—	**1.8**	—
Unoccupied houses	125	—	358	—	2,872	—
Houses under construction	64	—	90	—	699	—
Rooms unoccupied	323	—	699	—	7,866	—

Sources: Tobago Population Census Report, 1891; Trinidad and Tobago Population Census Reports, 1901–1931.

Appendix 3
Tables for Chapter 8

TABLE A3.1 **Selected Occupations by District, 1851 (Numbers and Percentages)**

Occupations

Districts	Planters		Merchants		Teachers		Clerks		Shopkeepers		Hucksters		Miscellaneous trades	
	No.	%	No.	%	No.	%	No.	%	No.	%	No.	%	No.	%
Windward	25	24.3	—	—	4	16.0	1	1.9	10	30.3	1	3.6	150	16.5
Middle	34	33.0	15	75.0	11	44.0	48	92.3	14	42.4	20	71.4	398	43.8
Leeward	44	42.7	5	25.0	10	40.0	3	5.8	9	27.3	7	25.0	360	39.6
Total	103	100.0	20	100.0	25	100.0	52	100.0	33	100.0	28	100.0	908	99.9

Districts	Seamstresses		Fishermen		Mariners		Agricultural labourers		Domestic workers		Laundresses		Total	
	No.	%	No.	%	No.	%	No.	%	No.	%	No.	%	No.	%*
Windward	37	7.8	13	11.2	2	2.9	1,328	23.5	70	8.8	—	—	1,641	19.4
Middle	278	58.5	22	19.0	50	72.5	1,992	35.3	468	58.6	—	—	3,350	39.6
Leeward	160	33.7	81	69.8	17	24.6	2,324	41.2	261	32.7	—	—	3,281	38.7
Total	475	100.0	116	100.0	69	100.0	5,644	100.0	799	100.0	—	—	8,272	97.7

Source: Calculated from Tobago Population Census Report, 1851.

Note: * Percentage of the working force of 8,469 persons. Percentages are subject to rounding errors.

TABLE A3.2 **Selected Occupations by District, 1881 (Numbers and Percentages)**

Occupations

Districts	Planters[a]		Merchants		Teachers		Clerks		Shopkeepers[b]		Hucksters		Miscellaneous trades	
	No.	%	No.	%	No.	%	No.	%	No.	%	No.	%	No.	%
Windward	22	23.4	—	—	11	30.5	7	12.3	3	7.9	—	—	234	19.6
Middle	28	29.8	11	100.0	14	38.9	45	78.9	22	57.9	5	100.0	458	38.3
Leeward	44	46.8	—	—	11	30.5	5	8.8	13	34.2	—	—	503	42.1
Total	94	100.0	11	100.0	36	99.9	57	100.0	38	100.0	5	100.0	1,195	100.0

Districts	Seamstresses		Fishermen		Mariners		Agricultural labourers		Domestic workers		Laundresses		Total	
	No.	%	No.	%	No.	%	No.	%	No.	%	No.	%	No.	%[c]
Windward	85	15.3	27	26.7	5	4.2	1,736	26.3	168	15.3	21	10.8	2,319	22.7
Middle	254	45.8	10	9.9	84	71.2	1,806	27.4	542	49.3	126	64.9	3,405	33.3
Leeward	216	38.9	64	63.4	29	24.6	3,056	46.3	389	35.4	47	24.2	4,377	42.9
Total	555	100.0	101	100.0	118	100.0	6,598	100.0	1,099	100.0	194	99.9	10,101	98.9

Source: Calculated from Tobago Population Census Report, 1881.

[a] Managers and overseers are not distinguished from planters in the census.

[b] Table 6 of the 1881 census report gives a total of 38 shopkeepers, but the subtotals add to 83. The smaller figure was used, since this agrees with the total for the table as a whole.

[c] Percentage of the working force of 10,210 persons. Percentages are subject to rounding errors.

TABLE A3.3 **Occupations by Sex, 1891, 1901 (Numbers)**

Occupations	1891			1901		
	Male	Female	Both sexes	Male	Female	Both sexes
Class I						
Proprietors, managers, merchants	132	3	135	56	3	59
'Public officers' and professionals	39	—	39	40	1	41
Hoteliers	—	3	3	—	2	2
Subtotal	**171**	**6**	**177**	**96**	**6**	**102**
Class II						
Schoolteachers, clerks and minor officials	118	35	153	156	58	214
Shopkeepers, hucksters	25	144	169	60	164	224
Submanagers, overseers	—	—	—	31	—	31
Peasant proprietors	27	2	29	155	32	187
Subtotal	**170**	**181**	**351**	**402**	**254**	**656**
Class III						
Skilled trades	1,070	—	1,070	973	60	1,033
Seamstresses	—	640	640	—	686	686
Mariners	96	—	96	48	—	48
Fishermen, boatmen	218	—	218	204	—	204
Agricultural labourers	1,843	2,593	4,436	1,662	2,420	4,082
Metayers [a]	346	157	503	—	—	—
General labourers, porters	344[b]	413	757	453	677	1,130
Domestic workers	165	589	754	142	587	729
Laundresses	—	195	195	—	266	266
Wives and daughters in domestic duties	—	918	918	—	778	778
Others	—	—	—	11	—	11
Subtotal	**4,082**	**5,505**	**9,587**	**3,493**	**5,474**	**8,967**
Others						
'Living on private means'	16	63	79	39	118	157
'Proprietors'	—	—	—	26	5	31
Others, not stated	—	—	—	13	8	21
Subtotal	**16**	**63**	**79**	**78**	**131**	**209**
Total	**4,439**	**5,755**	**10,194**	**4,069**	**5,865**	**9,934**

Sources: Tobago Population Census Report, 1891, and Trinidad and Tobago Population Census Report, 1901.

[a] The figure for metayers is only for the Leeward District and part of the Middle District.

[b] Includes 1 porter in addition to the 343 persons so classed in the census.

TABLE A3.4 Occupations by Sex, 1891, 1901 (Percentages)

Occupations	1891		1901	
	Male	Female	Male	Female
Class I				
Proprietors, managers, merchants etc.	97.8	2.2	95.0	5.0
'Public officers' and professionals	100.0	—	97.5	2.4
Hoteliers	—	100.0	—	100.0
Subtotal	**96.6**	**3.4**	**94.1**	**5.9**
Class II				
Schoolteachers, clerks and minor officials	77.1	22.9	72.9	27.1
Shopkeepers, hucksters	14.8	85.2	26.8	73.2
Submanagers, overseers	—	—	100.0	—
Peasant proprietors	93.1	6.9	82.8	17.1
Subtotal	**48.4**	**51.6**	**61.3**	**38.7**
Class III				
Skilled trades	100.0	—	94.2	5.8
Seamstresses	—	100.0	—	100.0
Mariners	100.0	—	100.0	—
Fishermen, boatmen	100.0	—	100.0	—
Agricultural labourers	41.5	58.4	40.7	59.3
Metayers	68.8	31.2	—	—
General labourers, porters	45.4	54.6	40.1	59.9
Domestic workers	21.9	78.1	19.5	80.5
Laundresses	—	100.0	—	100.0
Wives and daughters in domestic duties	—	100.0	—	100.0
Others	—	—	100.0	—
Subtotal	**42.6**	**57.4**	**39.0**	**61.0**
Others				
'Living on private means'	20.2	79.7	24.8	75.1
'Proprietors'	—	—	83.9	16.1
Others, not stated	—	—	61.9	38.1
Subtotal	**20.2**	**79.7**	**37.3**	**62.7**
Total	**43.5**	**56.4**	**41.0**	**59.0**

Sources and Notes: As for Table A3.3.

TABLE A3.5 Sex by Occupations, 1891, 1901 (Percentages)

Occupations	1891			1901		
	Male	Female	Both sexes	Male	Female	Both sexes
Class I						
Proprietors, managers, merchants etc	3.0	0.1	1.3	1.4	0.1	0.6
'Public officers' and professionals	0.8	—	0.4	1.0	0.0	0.4
Hoteliers	—	0.1	0.0	—	0.0	0.0
Subtotal	**3.8**	**0.1**	**1.7**	**2.4**	**0.1**	**1.0**
Class II						
Teachers, clerks and minor officials	2.6	0.6	1.5	3.8	1.0	2.2
Shopkeepers, hucksters	0.6	2.5	1.6	1.5	2.8	2.2
Submanagers, overseers	—	—	—	0.8	—	0.3
Peasant proprietors	0.6	0.0	0.3	3.8	0.5	1.9
Subtotal	**3.8**	**3.1**	**3.4**	**9.9**	**4.3**	**6.6**
Class III						
Skilled trades	24.0	—	10.5	23.9	1.0	10.4
Seamstresses	—	11.1	6.3	—	11.7	6.9
Mariners	2.2	—	0.9	1.2	—	0.5
Fishermen, boatmen	5.0	—	2.1	5.0	—	2.1
Agricultural labourers	41.5	45.0	43.5	40.8	41.3	41.1
Metayers	7.8	2.7	4.9	—	—	—
General labourers, porters	7.7	7.2	7.4	11.1	11.5	11.4
Domestic workers	3.7	10.2	7.4	3.5	10.0	7.3
Laundresses	—	3.4	1.9	—	4.5	2.7
Wives and daughters in domestic duties	—	16.0	9.0	—	13.3	7.8
Others	—	—	—	0.3	—	0.1
Subtotal	**92.0**	**95.6**	**94.0**	**85.8**	**93.3**	**90.2**
Others						
'Living on private means'	0.4	1.1	0.8	1.0	2.0	1.6
'Proprietors'	—	—	—	0.6	0.1	0.3
Others, not stated	—	—	—	0.3	0.1	0.2
Subtotal	**0.4**	**1.1**	**0.8**	**1.9**	**2.2**	**2.1**
Total	**100.0**	**99.9**	**99.9**	**100.0**	**99.9**	**99.9**

Sources: Calculated from Tobago Population Census Report, 1891, and Trinidad and Tobago Population Census Report, 1901.

Note: Percentages are based on the total numbers of males and females as given in Table A3.3.

TABLE A3.6 **Occupations by Sex, 1901–1946 (Numbers)**

Occupations	1901 Male	1901 Female	1911 Male	1911 Female	1921 Male	1921 Female	1931 Male	1931 Female	1946 Male	1946 Female
Class I										
Planters, managers, merchants etc	56	3	105	7	178	34	121	4	43	3
'Public officers' and professionals	40	1	51	—	76	9	55	10	42	1
Hoteliers	—	2	1	—	1	3	1	—	3	2
Subtotal	**96**	**6**	**157**	**7**	**255**	**46**	**177**	**14**	**88**	**6**
Class II										
Teachers, clerks, minor officials	156	58	240	120	236	127	350	170	354	273
Shopkeepers, hucksters	60	164	4	15	51	186	18	43	149	163
Submanagers, overseers	31	—	44	—	—	—	5	—	132	2
Peasant proprietors	155	32	333	83	643	143	805	128	1,435	435
Subtotal	**402**	**254**	**621**	**218**	**930**	**456**	**1,178**	**341**	**2,070**	**873**
Class III										
Skilled trades	973	60	1,064	52	1,037	—	1,189	56	1,511	1
Dressmakers etc.	—	686	—	965	—	923	—	478	—	707
Mariners	48	—	13	—	15	—	177[a]	—	3	—
Fishermen, boatmen	204	—	120	—	120	—	—	—	215	—
Transport, related	—	—	—	—	—	—	148	2	176	2
Agricultural labourers	1,662	2,420	2,127	2,404	2,263	2,238	2,596	1,354	1,151	294
Metayers	—	—	218	15	94	22	—	—	—	—
General labourers, porters	453	677	904	849	1,119	1,032	870	470	872	118
Domestic workers	142	587	157	589	198	811	71	630	44	234
Launderers	—	266	—	181	—	138	—	70	3	83
Other personal services	—	—	—	—	—	—	5	11	62	151
Domestic duties	—	778	—	1,050	—	1,537	33	4,264	11	4,549
Others	11	—	3	—	—	—	—	—	28	7
Subtotal	**3,493**	**5,474**	**4,606**	**6,105**	**4,846**	**6,701**	**5,089**	**7,335**	**4,076**	**6,196**
Others										
'Living on private means'	39	118	47	109	40	47	—	—	56	77
'Proprietors'	26	5	21	20	—	—	68	31	—	—
Others, not stated	13	8	1	—	—	—	9	—	3	2
Subtotal	**78**	**131**	**69**	**129**	**40**	**147**	**77**	**31**	**59**	**79**
Not retired, not gainfully employed	—	—	5	2	—	—	338	380	255[b]	386[b]
Total	**4,069**	**5,865**	**5,458**	**6,461**	**6,071**	**7,350**	**6,859**	**8,101**	**6,548**	**7,540**

Sources: Calculated from Trinidad and Tobago Population Census Reports, 1901–1946.

Notes:

[a] Includes fishermen and boatmen.

[b] Refers to those seeking their first jobs.

TABLE A3.7 **Occupations by Sex, 1901–1946 (Percentages)**

Occupations	1901		1911		1921		1931		1946	
	Male	Female	Male	Female	Male	Female	Male	Female	Male	Female
Class I										
Planters, managers, merchants etc	95.0	5.0	93.8	6.2	84.0	16.0	96.8	3.2	93.5	6.5
'Public officers' and professionals	97.5	2.4	100.0	—	89.4	10.6	84.6	15.4	97.6	2.3
Hoteliers	—	100.0	100.0	—	25.0	75.0	100.0	—	60.5	40.0
Subtotal	**94.1**	**5.9**	**95.7**	**4.3**	**84.7**	**15.3**	**92.7**	**7.3**	**93.6**	**6.4**
Class II										
Teachers, clerks and minor officials	72.9	27.1	66.7	33.3	65.0	35.0	67.3	32.7	56.5	43.5
Shopkeepers, hucksters	26.8	73.2	21.0	78.9	21.5	78.5	29.5	70.5	47.7	52.2
Submanagers, overseers	100.0	—	100.0	—	—	—	100.0	—	98.5	1.5
Peasant proprietors	82.8	17.1	80.0	20.0	81.8	18.2	86.3	13.7	76.7	23.3
Subtotal	**61.3**	**38.7**	**74.0**	**26.0**	**67.1**	**32.9**	**77.5**	**22.4**	**70.3**	**29.7**
Class III										
Skilled trades	94.2	5.8	95.3	4.6	100.0	—	95.5	4.5	96.7	3.3
Dressmakers etc	—	100.0	—	100.0	—	100.0	—	100.0	—	100.0
Mariners[a]	100.0	—	100.0	—	100.0	—	100.0	—	100.0	—
Fishermen, boatmen	100.0	—	100.0	—	100.0	—	—	—	100.0	—
Transport and related workers	—	—	—	—	—	—	98.7	1.3	98.9	1.1
Agricultural labourers	40.7	59.3	46.9	53.0	50.3	49.7	65.7	34.3	79.7	20.3
Metayers	—	—	93.6	6.4	81.0	19.0	—	—	—	—
General labourers, porters	40.1	59.9	51.6	48.4	52.0	48.0	64.9	35.1	88.1	11.9
Domestic workers	19.5	80.5	21.0	78.9	19.6	80.4	10.6	89.4	15.8	84.2
Launderers	—	100.0	—	100.0	—	100.0	—	100.0	3.5	96.5
Other personal services	—	—	—	—	—	—	31.2	68.8	29.1	70.9
Domestic duties	—	100.0	—	100.0	—	100.0	0.8	99.2	0.2	99.8
Others	100.0	—	100.0	—	—	—	—	—	80.0	20.0
Subtotal	**39.0**	**61.0**	**43.0**	**57.0**	**42.0**	**58.0**	**41.0**	**59.0**	**39.7**	**60.3**
Others										
'Living on private means'	24.8	75.1	30.1	69.9	21.4	78.6	—	—	42.1	57.9
'Proprietors'	83.9	16.1	51.2	48.8	—	—	68.7	31.3	—	—
Others, not stated	61.9	38.1	100.0	—	—	—	100.0	—	60.0	40.0
Subtotal	**37.3**	**62.7**	**34.8**	**65.2**	**21.4**	**78.6**	**71.3**	**28.7**	**42.7**	**57.2**
Not retired, not gainfully employed	—	—	71.4	28.6	—	—	47.0	52.9	39.8	60.2
Total	**41.0**	**59.0**	**45.8**	**54.2**	**45.2**	**54.8**	**45.8**	**54.2**	**46.5**	**53.5**

Sources: Calculated from Trinidad and Tobago Population Census Reports, 1901–1946.

Notes: Percentages are based on the figures in Table A3.6. [a] In 1931 fishermen and boatmen are included with mariners.

TABLE A3.8 **Sex by Occupations, 1901–1946 (Percentages)**

Occupations	1901		1911		1921		1931		1946	
	Male	Female	Male	Female	Male	Female	Male	Female	Male	Female
Class I										
Planters, managers, merchants etc	1.4	0.1	1.9	0.1	2.9	0.5	1.8	0.1	0.7	0.0
'Public officers' and professionals	1.0	0.0	0.9	—	1.2	0.1	0.1	0.1	0.6	0.0
Hoteliers	—	0.0	0.0	—	0.0	0.0	0.0	—	0.0	0.0
Subtotal	**2.4**	**1.0**	**2.9**	**0.1**	**4.2**	**0.6**	**2.6**	**0.2**	**1.3**	**0.1**
Class II										
Teachers, clerks and minor officials	3.8	1.0	4.4	1.9	3.9	1.7	5.1	2.1	5.4	3.6
Shopkeepers, hucksters	1.5	2.8	0.1	0.2	0.8	2.5	0.3	0.5	2.3	2.2
Submanagers, overseers	0.8	—	0.8	—	—	—	0.1	—	2.0	0.0
Peasant proprietors	3.8	0.5	6.1	1.3	10.6	1.9	11.7	1.6	21.9	5.8
Subtotal	**9.9**	**4.3**	**11.4**	**3.4**	**15.3**	**6.2**	**17.2**	**4.2**	**31.6**	**11.6**
Class III										
Skilled trades	23.9	1.0	19.5	0.9	17.1	—	17.3	0.7	23.1	0.7
Dressmakers etc.	—	11.7	—	14.9	—	12.5	—	5.9	—	9.4
Mariners	1.2	—	0.2	—	0.2	—	2.6[a]	—	0.0	—
Fishermen, boatmen	5.0	—	2.2	—	2.0	—	—	—	3.3	—
Transport and related workers	—	—	—	—	—	—	2.1	0.0	2.7	0.0
Agricultural labourers	40.8	41.3	39.0	37.2	37.3	30.4	37.8	16.7	17.6	3.9
Metayers	—	—	4.0	0.2	1.5	0.3	—	—	—	—
General labourers, porters	11.1	11.5	16.6	13.1	18.4	14.0	12.7	5.8	13.3	1.5
Domestic workers	3.5	10.0	2.9	9.1	3.3	11.0	1.1	7.8	0.7	3.1
Launderers	—	4.5	—	2.8	—	1.9	—	0.9	0.0	1.1
Other personal	—	—	—	—	—	—	0.1	0.1	0.9	2.0
Domestic duties	—	13.3	—	16.2	—	20.9	0.5	52.6	0.2	60.3
Others	0.3	—	—	—	—	—	—	—	0.4	0.1
Subtotal	**85.8**	**93.3**	**84.4**	**94.5**	**79.8**	**91.2**	**74.2**	**90.5**	**62.2**	**82.2**
Others										
'Living on private means'	1.0	2.0	0.9	1.7	0.7	2.0	—	—	0.8	1.0
'Proprietors'	0.6	0.1	0.4	0.3	—	—	1.0	0.4	—	—
Others, not stated	0.3	0.1	0.0	—	—	—	0.1	—	0.0	0.0
Subtotal	**1.9**	**2.2**	**1.3**	**2.0**	**0.7**	**2.0**	**1.1**	**0.4**	**0.9**	**1.0**
Not retired, not gainfully employed	—	—	0.1	0.0	—	—	4.9	4.7	3.9	5.1
Total	**100.0**	**100.0**	**100.0**	**100.0**	**100.0**	**100.0**	**100.0**	**100.0**	**100.0**	**100.0**

Sources: Calculated from Trinidad and Tobago Population Census Reports, 1901–1946.

Notes: Percentages are based on the total numbers of males and females as given in Table A3.6. [a] Includes fishermen and boatmen.

278

TABLE A3.9 **Employment Status of Tobago's Gainful Workers by Sex, and Comparison with Trinidad's Gainful Workers, 1946**

TOBAGO						
Employment status	Male	%	Female	%	Both sexes	%
Employers	75	1.2	7	0.3	82	0.9
Own account	2,247	36.1	970	38.4	3,217	36.7
Unpaid helpers	62	1.0	33	1.3	97	1.1
Wage earners	3,839	61.7	1,516	60.1	5,355	61.2
At work	*3,271*	*52.5*	*1,066*	*42.2*	*4,337*	*49.5*
Learners	*435*	*7.0*	*393*	*15.5*	*828*	*9.4*
Unemployed	*133*	*2.1*	*57*	*2.2*	*190*	*2.2*
In institutions	—	—	—	—	—	—
Not stated	3	0.1	2	0.1	5	0.1
Total	6,226	100.0	2,528	100.0	8,754	100.0

TRINIDAD						
Employment status	Male	%	Female	%	Both sexes	%
Employers	2,742	1.8	264	0.5	3,006	1.5
Own account	32,290	21.1	16,585	32.9	48,875	23.9
Unpaid helpers	2,451	1.6	1,148	2.3	3,599	1.8
Wage earners	115,320	74.9	32,328	64.1	147,648	72.2
At work	*105,693*	*68.7*	*28,960*	*57.4*	*134,653*	*65.9*
Learners	*2,445*	*1.6*	*1,190*	*2.3*	*3,635*	*1.8*
Unemployed	*7,182*	*4.7*	*2,178*	*4.3*	*9,360*	*4.6*
In institutions	906	0.6	24	0.0	930	0.4
Not stated	202	0.1	79	0.1	281	0.1
Total	153,911	100.0	50,428	100.0	204,339	100.0

Source: Calculated from Trinidad and Tobago Population Census Report, 1946, Table 53.

Note: Percentages are subject to rounding errors.

Appendix 4
Tables for Chapter 9

TABLE A4.1 Distribution of Immigrants by Age, Origin and Sex, 1990

| | Caribbean | | | | | Other countries | | | | |
| | Male | | Female | | Total | Male | | Female | | Total |
Age	No.	%	No.	%	No.	No.	%	No.	%	No.
<15	19	8.2	24	8.7	43	66	50.0	61	41.2	127
15–44	77	33.2	154	55.6	231	39	29.5	53	35.8	92
45–64	65	28.0	54	19.5	119	19	14.4	23	15.5	42
>65	71	30.6	40	14.4	111	8	6.1	11	7.4	19
Not stated	—	—	5	1.8	5	—	—	—	—	—
Total	232	100.0	277	100.0	509	132	100.0	148	100.0	280

| | Not stated | | |
| | Male | Female | Total |
Age	No.	No.	No.
<15	1	1	2
15–44	1	2	3
45–64	3	0	3
>65	2	3	5
Not stated	—	1	1
Total	7	7	14

Source: Calculated from *Population Census Report, 1990*, Vol. 4, Table 3.

TABLE A4.2 **Population by Ethnic Composition (Percentages), 1960–2000**

Ethnicity	1960 Per cent	1970 Per cent	1980 Per cent	1990 Per cent	2000 Per cent
African	93.0	94.5	93.5	92.0	88.8
Mixed	4.5	2.9	3.6	4.5	6.5
Indian	1.3	1.6	1.6	2.1	2.5
White/ Caucasian	0.8	0.6	0.4	0.4	0.6
Syrian/ Lebanese	0.2	0.1	0.1	0.0	0.6
Chinese	0.1	0.1	0.1	0.1	0.1
Other	0.1	0.1	0.5	0.2	0.1
Not stated	—	0.1	0.2	0.7	1.2
Total	100.0	100.0	100.0	100.0	100.0

Sources: Calculated from the sources for Table A4.3. Percentages are subject to rounding errors.

TABLE A4.3 **Population by Ethnic Composition and Sex, 1960–2000**

Ethnicity	1960 Male	Female	Total	1970 Male	Female	Total
African	15,302	15,673	30,975	17,980	18,635	36,615
Mixed	715	781	1,496	517	594	1,111
Indian	227	210	437	314	296	610
White/ Caucasian	146	127	273	106	132	238
Syrian/ Lebanese	28	24	52	20	23	43
Chinese	35	25	60	28	22	50
Other	28	12	40	28	15	43
Not stated	—	—	—	24	20	44
Total	16,481	16,852	33,333	19,017	19,737	38,754

Ethnicity	1980 Male	Female	Total	1990 Male	Female	Total	2000 Male	Female	Total
African	18,375	18,593	36,968	20,811	20,606	41,417	19,644	19,617	39,261
Mixed	703	723	1,426	983	1,037	2,020	1,371	1,525	2,896
Indian	303	345	648	463	499	962	522	583	1,105
White/ Caucasian	70	96	166	73	91	164	135	139	274
Syrian/ Lebanese	10	10	20	9	6	15	13	12	25
Chinese	17	17	34	22	24	46	24	17	41
Other	89	100	189	54	55	109	24	26	50
Not stated	40	33	73	152	165	317	287	251	538
Total	19,607	19,917	39,524	22,567	22,483	45,050	22,020	22,170	44,190

Sources: Population and Housing Census Reports, 1960, Vol. 3, Pt. D, Table 4; 1970, Vol. 7, Table 1; 1980, Vol. 2, Table 4; 1990, Vol. 2, Table 6; Central Statistical Office (CSO), *2000 Population and Housing Census: Demographic Report* (Port of Spain 2006), Table 7.

TABLE A4.4 **Religious Affiliations of the Population, 1960–2000**

Religion	1960 Sub-total	1960 Total	1960 Per cent	1970 Total	1970 Per cent	1980 Sub-total	1980 Total	1980 Per cent
Anglican		16,070	48.2	17,257	44.5		13,866	35.1
Baptist (Orthodox)		10	0.0	391	1.0		943	2.4
Jehovah's Witness		105	0.3	N.G.	—		289	0.7
Methodist		4,172	12.5	4,154	10.7		3,954	10.0
Pentecostal		65	0.2	N.G.	—		2,194	5.6
Presbyterian*		93	0.3	84	0.2		49	0.1
Roman Catholic		3,445	10.3	4,491	11.6		3,777	9.6
Seventh Day Adventist		2,245	6.7	3,176	8.2		4,199	10.6
Moravian		4,907	14.7	4,791	12.4		N.G.	—
Hindu—SDMS	22}	—	—	}	—	175}	—	—
Hindu—Other	95}	117	0.4	147}	0.4	2}	177	0.4
Islam—ASJA	11}	—	—	}	—	90}	—	—
Islam—Other	54}	65	0.2	98}	0.3	16}	106	0.3
Other		1,749	5.2	—}	—}		8,629	21.8
None/Not stated		290	0.9	4,165}	10.7}		451	1.1
Total		33,333	100.0	38,754	100.0		39,524	100.0

Religion	1990 Sub-total	1990 Total	1990 Per cent	2000 Sub-total	2000 Total	2000 Per cent
Anglican		10,641	23.6		7,932	17.9
Baptist (Orthodox)		1,823	4.0		5,981	13.5
Jehovah's Witness		444	1.0		668	1.5
Methodist		3,931	8.7		3,123	7.1
Pentecostal		4,189	9.3		3,130	7.1
Presbyterian*		111	0.2		100	0.2
Roman Catholic		3,867	8.6		3,335	7.5
Seventh Day Adventist		6,361	14.1		6,765	15.3
Moravian		N.G.	—		N.G.	—
Hindu—SDMS	12}	}	}	13}	}	}
Hindu—Other	314}	326}	0.7}	326}	339}	0.8}
Islam—ASJA	3}	}	}	8}	}	}
Islam—Other	160}	163}	0.4}	225}	233}	0.5}
Other		10,584	23.5		9,049	20.5
None/Not stated		1,031	2.3		3,535	8.0
Total		45,050	100.0		44,190	100.0

Sources: Population and Housing Census Reports, 1960, Vol. 3, Pt. D, Table 7; 1980, Vol. 2, Table 5; 1990, Vol. 2, Table 7; 2000 Population and Housing Census: Demographic Report, Table 8; for 1970, CSO, Annual Statistical Digest 1974/1975 (Port of Spain 1977), Table 20.

Notes:
[a] N.G.: Not given; SDMS: Sanatan Dharma Maha Sabha; ASJA: Anjumaan Sunnat ul Jamaat Association.
* Includes Congregationalists in 1980, 1990 and 2000.

TABLE A4.5 Population at Census Dates and Intercensal Growth per Annum (Percentages) for Trinidad and for Tobago, 1960–2000

Population (numbers)

Trinidad	1960	1970	1980	1990	2000
Males	395,099	440,495	519,336	581,996	606,283
Females	399,525	451,822	519,710	583,137	601,999
Both sexes	794,624	892,317	1,039,046	1,165,133	1,208,282
Tobago	**1960**	**1970**	**1980**	**1990**	**2000**
Males	16,481	19,017	20,304	24,392	26,768
Females	16,852	19,737	20,441	24,208	27,316
Both sexes	33,333	38,754	40,745	48,600	54,084

Intercensal growth per annum (%)

Trinidad	1960–1970	1970–1980	1980–1990	1990–2000
Males	1.2	1.8	1.2	0.4
Females	1.3	1.5	1.2	0.3
Both sexes	**1.2**	**1.6**	**1.2**	**0.4**
Tobago	**1960–1970**	**1970–1980**	**1980–1990**	**1990–2000**
Males	1.5	0.7	2.0	1.0
Females	1.7	0.4	1.8	1.3
Both sexes	**1.6**	**0.5**	**1.9**	**1.1**

Sources: Calculated from CSO, *Population and Housing Census Reports*, 1960–1980; *Annual Statistical Digest, 1998/1999* (Port of Spain 2002), Table 11; *2000 Population and Housing Census: Preliminary Population Count* (Port of Spain 2001), Table 1.

Note: The intercensal growth rates for Trinidad and Tobago approximate those for Trinidad.

TABLE A4.6 Age Profile of the Tobago Population, 1960–2000

Age groups	1960		1970		1980	
	Number	% of population	Number	% of population	Number	% of population
0–14	15,273	45.8	17,784	45.9	14,568	36.9
15–59	15,036	45.1	17,664	45.6	20,749	52.5
60+	3,024	9.1	3,306	8.5	4,207	10.6
Total	33,333	100.0	38,754	100.0	39,524	100.0

Age groups	1990		2000	
	Number	% of population	Number	% of population
0–14	16,793	34.6	14,321	26.5
15–59	27,157	55.9	33,809	62.5
60+	4,650	9.6	5,954	11.0
Total	48,600	100.0	54,084	100.0

Sources: Calculated from *Population and Housing Census Reports*, 1960–1990, age tables for given years; *2000 Population and Housing Census: Demographic Report*, Table 1.

TABLE A4.7 **Tobago Population by Age and Sex, 1960–2000**

	1960				1970				1980			
Age	Number		%		Number		%		Number		%	
	M	F	M	F	M	F	M	F	M	F	M	F
0–4	2,945	2,882	8.8	8.6	2,745	2,810	7.1	7.3	2,494	2,338	6.3	5.9
5–9	2,623	2,505	7.9	7.5	3,297	3,307	8.5	8.5	2,427	2,322	6.1	5.9
10–14	2,167	2,151	6.5	6.4	2,837	2,788	7.3	7.2	2,462	2,525	6.2	6.4
15–19	1,558	1,596	4.7	4.8	2,083	2,062	5.4	5.3	2,585	2,571	6.5	6.5
20–24	1,083	1,143	3.2	3.4	1,334	1,454	3.4	3.8	1,804	1,924	4.6	4.9
25–29	762	956	2.3	2.9	971	1,045	2.5	2.7	1,266	1,294	3.2	3.3
30–34	829	802	2.5	2.4	857	931	2.2	2.4	1,024	1,091	2.6	2.8
35–39	687	708	2.1	2.1	763	838	2.0	2.2	831	891	2.1	2.3
40–44	624	685	1.9	2.0	773	767	2.0	2.0	781	796	2.0	2.0
45–49	652	718	1.9	2.1	686	687	1.8	1.8	674	759	1.7	1.9
50–54	640	565	1.9	1.7	607	643	1.6	1.6	676	643	1.7	1.6
55–59	514	514	1.5	1.5	572	591	1.5	1.5	578	561	1.5	1.4
60–64	424	425	1.3	1.3	457	467	1.2	1.2	497	503	1.3	1.3
65–69	343	444	1.0	1.3	391	483	1.0	1.2	452	542	1.1	1.4
70–74	262	327	0.8	1.0	297	327	0.8	0.8	360	409	0.9	1.0
75+	368	431	1.1	1.3	347	537	0.9	1.3	392	553	1.0	1.4
N. S.	—	—	—	—	—	—	—	—	304	195	0.8	0.5
Total	**16,481**	**16,852**	**49.4**	**50.3**	**19,017**	**19,737**	**49.2**	**51.0**	**19,607**	**19,917**	**49.6**	**50.4**
	33,333		**100.0**		**38,754**		**100.0**		**39,524**		**100.0**	

	1990				2000			
Age	Number		%		Number		%	
	M	F	M	F	M	F	M	F
0–4	2,796	2,737	5.8	5.6	1,896	1,816	3.5	3.4
5–9	3,036	3,003	6.2	6.2	2,435	2,463	4.5	4.6
10–14	2,671	2,550	5.5	5.2	2,809	2,902	5.2	5.4
15–19	2,399	2,197	4.9	4.5	2,919	2,904	5.4	5.4
20–24	2,063	2,178	4.2	4.5	2,238	2,211	4.1	4.1
25–29	2,309	2,196	4.8	4.5	1,901	2,011	3.5	3.7
30–34	1,916	1,875	3.9	3.9	1,884	2,049	3.5	3.8
35–39	1,408	1,428	2.9	2.9	2,243	2,224	4.1	4.1
40–44	1,173	1,155	2.4	2.4	1,911	1,951	3.5	3.6
45–49	887	912	1.8	1.9	1,495	1,490	2.8	2.8
50–54	827	807	1.7	1.7	1,255	1,252	2.3	2.3
55–59	692	735	1.4	1.5	933	938	1.7	1.7
60–64	646	661	1.3	1.4	877	875	1.6	1.6
65–69	568	532	1.2	1.1	681	745	1.3	1.4
70–74	444	450	0.9	0.9	557	568	1.0	1.1
75+	557	792	1.1	1.6	734	917	1.4	1.7
Total	**24,392**	**24,208**	**50.2**	**49.8**	**26,768**	**27,316**	**49.5**	**50.5**
	48,600		**100.0**		**54,084**		**100.0**	

Sources: *Population and Housing Census Reports*, 1960–1980, age tables; CSO, *Annual Statistical Digest 1998/99*, Table 12; *2000 Population and Housing Census: Demographic Report*, Table 1.

Notes: M: Males; F: Females. Percentages are calculated on the basis of the total population.

TABLE A4.8 Age Dependency Ratios, Tobago, 1960–2000

Age dependency ratios	1960	1970	1980	1990	2000
Child 0–14 years	101.6	100.6	70.2	61.8	42.4
Old-age 60+ years	20.1	18.7	20.3	17.1	17.6
Total age dependency	121.7	119.3	90.5	79.0	60.0

Sources: Calculated from *Population and Housing Census Reports*, 1960–1990, age tables for given years;
2000 Population and Housing Census: Demographic Report, Table 1.

TABLE A4.9 Age-Specific Sex Ratios (Males per 100 Females), 1960–2000

Age cohorts	1960	1970	1980	1990	2000
0–4	102	98	107	102	104
5–9	105	100	104	101	99
10–14	101	102	97	105	97
15–19	98	101	100	113	101
20–24	95	92	94	94	101
25–29	80	93	98	104	95
30–34	103	92	94	101	92
35–39	97	91	93	98	101
40–44	91	101	98	101	98
45–49	91	100	89	97	100
50–54	113	94	105	102	100
55–59	100	97	103	94	99
60–64	100	98	99	97	100
65–69	77	81	83	105	91
70–74	80	91	88	99	98
75–79	81	76	71	84	90
80–84	75	66	71}	63}	72}
85+	110	47	}	}	}
Not stated	—	—	156	106	—
Tobago	**98**	**96**	**98**	**101**	**98**

Sources: Calculated from *Population Census Reports*, age tables for given years.

Note: Figures are rounded to the nearest whole number.

TABLE A4.10 Tobago, Population and Population Change by Parish, 1960–2000

Place	1960 No.	1960 % of population	1970 No.	1970 % of population	1980 No.	1980 % of population	1990 No.	1990 % of population	2000 No.	2000 % of population
East										
St. George	3,716	11.1	4,549	11.7	4,580	11.6	5,179	11.2	5,364	9.9
St. Mary	2,961	8.9	3,242	8.4	2,291	5.8	2,715	5.8	2,965	5.5
St. Paul	3,729	11.2	4,190	10.8	4,637	11.7	5,221	11.2	5,412	10.0
St. John	3,333	10.0	3,174	8.2	2,816	7.1	2,940	6.3	2,998	5.5
Subtotal	**13,739**	**41.2**	**15,155**	**39.1**	**14,324**	**36.2**	**16,055**	**34.5**	**16,739**	**30.9**
West										
St. Andrew	8,223	24.7	10,330	26.7	10,935	27.7	12,612	27.2	15,830	29.3
St. Patrick	5,109	15.3	6,154	15.9	7,859	19.9	10,383	22.4	14,011	25.9
St. David	6,262	18.8	7,115	18.3	6,406	16.2	7,385	15.9	7,504	13.9
Subtotal	**19,594**	**58.8**	**23,599**	**60.9**	**25,200**	**63.8**	**30,380**	**65.5**	**37,345**	**69.1**
Tobago	**33,333**	**100.0**	**38,754**	**100.0**	**39,524**	**100.0**	**46,435**	**100.0**	**54,084**	**100.0**

Parish	1960–1970 No.	1960–1970 Change %	1970–1980 No.	1970–1980 Change %	1980–1990 No.	1980–1990 Change %	1990–2000 No.	1990–2000 Change %	1960–2000 No.	1960–2000 Change %
St. George	833	22.4	31	0.7	599	13.1	185	3.6	1,648	44.3
St. Mary	281	9.5	-951	-29.3	424	18.5	250	9.2	4	0.1
St. Paul	461	12.4	447	10.7	584	12.6	191	3.7	2,133	65.1
St. John	-159	-4.8	-358	-11.3	124	4.4	58	2.1	-335	-10.1
East	**1,416**	**10.3**	**-831**	**-5.5**	**1,731**	**12.1**	**684**	**4.3**	**3,000**	**21.8**
St. Andrew	2,107	25.6	605	5.9	1,677	15.3	3,218	25.5	7,607	92.5
St. Patrick	1,045	20.4	1,705	27.7	2,524	32.1	3,628	34.9	8,902	174.2
St. David	853	13.6	-709	-10.0	979	15.3	119	1.6	1,242	19.8
West	**4,005**	**20.4**	**1,601**	**6.8**	**5,180**	**20.5**	**6,965**	**22.9**	**17,751**	**90.6**
Tobago	**5,421**	**16.3**	**770**	**2.0**	**6,911**	**17.5**	**7,649**	**16.5**	**20,751**	**62.2**

Sources: Calculated from *Population and Housing Census Reports*, 1960, Vol. 3, Pt. D, Table 4; 1970, Listing of Area Register; 1980, Vol. 2, Table 4; 1990, Vol. 2, Table 1; 2000 *Population and Housing Census: Community Register*, Tables 91–97.

Note: The 1990 population figures are from the age tables, while the overall Tobago population in 1990 was 48,600. The total population in the Listing of Areas Register was 46,654.

TABLE A4.11 **Labour Force Participation Rates and Unemployment by Sex, 1970–1990**

| | 1970 | | | 1980 | | | 1990 | | |
	Male	Female	Total	Male	Female	Total	Male	Female	Total
Adult population 15 years and over	10,138	10,832	20,970	11,920	12,537	24,457	14,509	14,644	29,153
No. with jobs	6,357	2,184	8,541	8,403	3,908	12,311	8,335	4,731	13,066
No. without jobs and seeking work or available for work	1,410	417	1,827	860	814	1,674	2,153	1,376	3,529
Total labour force	**7,767**	**2,601**	**10,368**	**9,263**	**4,722**	**13,985**	**10,488**	**6,107**	**16,595**
Gross participation rates (labour force as % of adult population)	76.6	24.0	49.4	77.7	37.7	57.2	72.3	41.7	56.9
Unemployment rates (% of labour force)	18.2	16.0	17.6	9.3	17.2	12.0	20.5	22.5	21.2

Sources: Calculated from *Population and Housing Census Reports, 1970*, Vol. 4, Pt. 2, Table 1; 1980 and 1990, Vol. 3, Pt. 1, Table 1.

TABLE A4.12 **Working Population by Industrial Group and Sex, 1946–1960, 1980–1990 (Numbers)**

Industrial group	1946			1960			1980			1990		
	Male	Female	Total	Male	Female	Total	Male	Female	Total	Male	Female	Total
Agriculture, forestry, fishing and hunting	3,026	735	3,761	2,488	438	2,926	730	104	834	692	102	794
Mining and quarrying	4	—	4	23	1	24	39	—	39	17	—	17
Manufacturing	676	772	1,448	519	273	792	170	61	231	134	100	234
Electricity, gas, water	—	—	—	221	10	231	472	33	505	463	64	527
Construction	1,119	39	1,158	1,563	101	1,664	2,999	496	3,495	2,667	361	3,028
Transport, storage, communication	293	31	324	360	49	409	725	160	885	808	227	1,035
Wholesale and retail trade, restaurants and hotels*	200	163	363	420	353	773	781	1,148	1,929	918	1,395	2,313
Services comprising	617	721	1,338	1,167	1,096	2,263	2,172	1,775	3,947	2,523	2,438	4,961
Financing, insurance, real estate, business	—	—	—	—	—	—	104	146	250	276	332	608
Police administration	—	—	—	—	—	—	652	457	1,109	873	638	1,511
Community, social, personal and other	—	—	—	—	—	—	1,416	1,172	2,588	1,374	1,468	2,842
Not stated/not adequately described	291	67	358	4	1	5	315	131	446	113	44	157
Total	**6,226**	**2,528**	**8,754**	**6,765**	**2,322**	**9,087**	**8,403**	**3,908**	**12,311**	**8,335**	**4,731**	**13,066**

Sources: Population and Housing Census Reports, 1946, Table 58; 1960, Vol. 3, Pt. G, Table 3D; 1980 and 1990, Vol. 3, Pt. 2, Table 6.

Notes: The 1970 census did not give the industrial tables by administrative area. * Treated as category called 'Commerce' in 1946 and 1960.

TABLE A4.13 Working Population by Industrial Group and Sex, 1946–1960, 1980–1990 (Percentages)

Industrial group	1946			1960			1980			1990		
	Male	Female	Total	Male	Female	Total	Male	Female	Total	Male	Female	Total
Agriculture, forestry, fishing and hunting	48.6	29.1	43.0	36.8	18.9	32.2	8.7	2.7	6.8	8.3	2.2	6.1
Mining and quarrying	0.1	—	0.0	0.3	0.0	0.3	0.5	—	0.3	0.2	—	0.1
Manufacturing	10.9	30.5	16.5	7.7	11.7	8.7	2.0	1.6	1.9	1.6	2.1	1.8
Electricity, gas, water	—	—	—	3.3	0.4	2.5	5.6	0.8	4.1	5.6	1.4	4.0
Construction	18.0	1.5	13.2	23.1	4.3	18.3	35.7	12.7	28.4	32.0	7.6	23.2
Transport, storage, communication	4.7	1.2	3.7	5.3	2.1	4.5	8.6	4.1	7.2	9.7	4.8	7.9
Wholesale and retail trade, restaurants and hotels	3.2	6.4	4.1	6.2	15.2	8.5	9.3	29.4	15.7	11.0	29.5	17.7
Services comprising	9.9	28.5	15.3	17.2	47.2	24.9	25.8	45.4	32.1	30.3	51.5	38.0
Financing, insurance, real estate, business	—	—	—	—	—	—	1.2	3.7	2.0	3.3	7.0	4.7
Public administration	—	—	—	—	—	—	7.8	11.7	9.0	10.5	13.5	11.6
Community, social, personal and other	—	—	—	—	—	—	16.9	30.0	21.0	16.5	31.0	21.8
Not stated/not adequately described	4.7	2.7	4.1	0.1	0.0	0.1	3.7	3.4	3.6	1.4	0.9	1.2
Total	100.0	100.0	100.0	100	100.0	100.0	100.0	100.0	100.0	100.0	100.0	100.0

Sources: Calculated from the sources for Table A4.12. Percentages are subject to rounding errors.

TABLE A4.14 **Persons Employed in the Past Week by Occupational Group and Sex, Tobago, and Comparison with Both Sexes for Trinidad and Tobago, 1990**

Occupational group	Tobago Male	Per cent	Tobago Female	Per cent	Tobago Both sexes	Per cent	Trinidad and Tobago Both sexes	Per cent
Legislators, senior officials, managers	333	4.0	282	6.0	615	4.7	14,779	4.7
Professionals	211	2.5	127	2.7	338	2.6	11,452	3.7
Technicians and associated professionals	422	5.1	704	14.9	1,126	8.6	33,822	10.8
Clerks	339	4.1	1,308	27.6	1,647	12.6	39,192	12.5
Service workers and shop sales workers	975	11.7	1,017	21.5	1,992	15.2	44,697	14.3
Agriculture, forestry, fishery and hunting	314	3.8	34	0.7	348	2.7	14,074	4.5
Craft and related workers	1,722	20.7	148	3.1	1,870	14.3	47,109	15.0
Plant and machine operators and assemblers	868	10.4	31	0.7	899	6.9	31,367	10.0
Elementary occupations	3,110	37.3	1,046	22.1	4,156	31.8	74,027	23.6
Not stated/not adequately described	41	0.5	34	0.7	75	0.6	2,639	0.8
Total	**8,335**	**100.0**	**4,731**	**100.0**	**13,066**	**100.0**	**313,158**	**100.0**

Source: Calculated from *Population and Housing Census Report*, 1990, Vol. 3, Pt. 2, Table 1.

TABLE A4.15 Reported Number of Selected Crimes, Selected Years, Tobago, and Comparison with Trinidad and Tobago, 1990–2004

Category	Tobago			Trinidad and Tobago		
	1990	2000	2004	1990	2000	2004
Serious crimes						
Crimes against property, of which:	371	747	658	13,289	13,159	12,893
Breaking in and burglary	*276*	*475*	*407*	*7,546*	*5,623*	*5,214*
Robbery	*21*	*101*	*92*	*3,115*	*4,094*	*3,885*
Larceny (including motor vehicles)	*62*	*112*	*103*	*2,329*	*3,042*	*3,365*
Larceny in dwelling houses	*12*	*59*	*56*	*299*	*400*	*429*
Fraud	0	74	5	245	522	329
Crimes against the person, of which:	22	49	60	776	1,201	1,714
Rape, incest, sexual offences	*7*	*22*	*27*	*221*	*409*	*581*
Serious indecency	*5*	*6*	*5*	*67*	*129*	*52*
Murder	*1*	*5*	*4*	*84*	*120*	*261*
Wounding and shooting	*9*	*12*	*20*	*391*	*387*	*643*
Kidnapping	*0*	*4*	*4*	*13*	*156*	*177*
Narcotics offences: serious crimes	61	45	39	1,211	1,225	589
Minor Crimes						
Narcotics offences: minor crimes	82	84	278	1,710	2,857	6,142
Crimes against property: minor crimes	439	665	419	17,213	10,273	8,046
Fraud: minor crimes	3	11	2	178	241	288
Totals						
Total serious crimes	481	954	805	16,197	17,134	16,387
Total minor crimes	647	910	891	21,918	15,636	17,178
Population totals	48,600	54,084	56,464	1,215,187	1,262,366	1,290,646

Sources: Calculated from Modus Operandi and Records Bureau, Trinidad and Tobago Police Service, unpublished tables, 8 June 2005; provisional data; and from population totals at 1990 and 2000 censuses and CSO, mid-year estimate for 2004.

Note: For 2004, Tobago's population is estimated on the assumption of 1.1 per cent per annum growth, the same as had occurred between 1990 and 2000.

Glossary

bake. (Noun); a type of bread, baked or fried.

bank. A tray in which **megass** was carried from the boiling house to the mill yard for drying, then to the megass house for storage, and from there back to the boiling house for use as fuel.

Belmanna war. The rebellion of May 1876 in Roxborough and other parts of the Windward District, Tobago, in which Corporal James Henry Belmanna was slain. 'To raise Belmanna war' in the Tobago vernacular is to become very angry.

bill. A tool with a long handle and a long concave blade, used for digging, pruning, and cutting; one of the most common tools used on BWI sugar estates from the period of enslavement to the early twentieth century.

boat basket. Large baskets of fish transported on either side of a donkey's back. Fishermen usually went at night from village to village with these baskets of fish in order to sell their catch cheaply and quickly, since they had no cold-storage facilities.

bobolee. Trinidad and Tobago vernacular for a large effigy made of cloth and stuffed with rags, usually beaten publicly on Good Friday.

bonito. A type of fish.

boule di fay. (From French, *la boule de feu*, bulb or globe of fire); this was a bottle of kerosene with a lighted cloth at the top to give light to travellers at night; also called *flambeau*.

bregedeh. A flat round bread about one inch thick, made with **leaven** as the rising agent; ingredients included butter and coconut milk.

cane 'ole; cane hole. The term used by metayers for the estate plots on which they planted canes.

cane liquor. Cane juice after it has been expressed from the sugar canes.

Caracas band. A group of workers working as **pardners**, who drank **chocolate tea** (also called **swag**) made from a variety of cocoa that came from Caracas, Venezuela.

cariso. Vernacular term for the Trinidad calypso; used between 1850 and 1920.

change. (Verb); Tobago vernacular for 'to exchange' or 'to barter'.

chantwel. Trinidad vernacular, from French, *le chanteur*, singer; an early name for a calypso singer.

chocolate tea. A hot drink made from unrefined cocoa with milk, sugar and spices; also called **swag** in Tobago.

choir girl. Tobago vernacular for smoked herring.

coconut walk. A plot of land, usually smaller than ten acres in size, planted only in coconut trees.

cocrico. A brown bird, akin to the pheasant, that is native to Tobago and Venezuela; one of the national birds of Trinidad and Tobago.

copper. A large vessel in which sugar cane juice was boiled to make muscovado sugar; also called a kettle. In the era of enslavement, there were usually five coppers, called a 'Jamaica train', and during the boiling process the liquid was ladled from one to another; in peasant production there was usually one copper.

copra. Collective noun for the dried kernels of the coconut.

crook. (Noun); a wooden device tied with ropes onto the backs of donkeys or mules, on which heavy loads are placed; also used as a verb, for example, 'to crook a donkey'.

crude birth rate. The number of births per 1,000 persons in the population.

drogher. Coasting vessel used to transport cargo between central ports and outbays. The verb **to drogue**, derived from drogher, is still used in the Tobago vernacular to mean to carry heavy loads.

esprit de corps. (French); pride and mutual loyalty in a group.

fanega. Measure used in the cocoa industry for 110 pounds weight.

farine. Cassava grated, strained to remove its water, and parched in a **copper** to make a coarse meal.

fireside. In Tobago this was three large stones placed apart to form a triangle. Fuel wood was put between the stones and lit with fire, and the cooking utensil was placed on the three stones.

flambeau. (French, torch); see **boule di fay**.

fo' day; fo' day mornin'. Before dawn.

general fertility rate. The number of births per 1,000 women aged 15–49 in the population.

grenne; grenne top. (From French, *le grenier*, granary, loft, attic or garret); a wooden shelf in Tobago kitchens above the **fireside**, from which salted fish and other items would be hung to dry; also called **lafter**.

hogshead. Large wooden cask in which sugar or other commodities were shipped.

Homo. (Latin); a man; used as a pseudonym herein.

Injin. Indian; usually used in Tobago to describe Amerindian baskets.

inter alia. (Latin); among other things.

Jab Jab. (From French, *le diable*, devil); one of the disguises in the Trinidad and Tobago Carnival.

jacks. A type of small fish.

King's Well. The King's Well at Cook's River was one of the few sources of water for Scarborough before 1925. Both the well and the nearby trough from which horses and donkeys could drink still exist.

lafter. See **grenne**.

laissez-faire. (French); letting things take their own course; used in this volume to mean minimal state intervention in the economy.

leaven. Flour and water mixed together and left in a calabash to ferment; used as the leaven or rising agent for baking before yeast was known in Tobago.

leeward. Places in the lee of the prevailing winds; in Tobago, facing away from the north-east.

len' han'. See **pardners**.

littérateur. (French); literary person.

massa. West Indian vernacular for master; refers generally to the dominant class.

megass; megasse. Also called **bagasse**, and in Tobago, **makash**: the tough fibrous residue of the sugar cane after the juice has been expressed. Megass was taken from the boiling house on trays called **banks** to the mill yard, where it was dried in the sun and then stored in the megass house, from which it was carried to the furnaces to be used as fuel during the process of boiling cane juice to make sugar.

métayage. (French); a form of land tenure in which the farmer pays a share of the produce, usually a half, to the owner of the land which (s)he cultivates; sharecropping; also called the *métairie* system. In Tobago both words were spelt without the accent.

métayer. A sharecropper in the **métayage** system; in Tobago it was spelt without the accent.

muscovado. Unrefined cane sugar; called 'wet sugar' and sometimes 'wood sugar' in Tobago.

pardners. Communal labour groups in which the participants pooled their labour on each other's behalf, so facilitating farming, metayer cultivation, house-building and other tasks; also known in Tobago as *day fuh day, day wuk, labour,* **len' han'**, and, where the members of the group were kin, as *bredders*. The practice is called *maroon* in Grenada, *coumbite* in Haiti, *coup de main* in St. Lucia, and *gayap* in Trinidad.

parting sugar. The term used in Tobago to describe the sharing of the sugar produced by the metayer; half was for the estate and half for the metayer.

pass the bowl; pass bowl. Tobago vernacular for the reciprocal sharing of prepared food by neighbours.

picong. Trinidad vernacular from French, *piquant*, prickly; a type of calypso in which witty barbs were thrown at other people.

pitch oil. Kerosene.

play mas. Trinidad and Tobago vernacular, meaning to disguise as a masquerader and to take part in the Carnival.

pound sterling. In this study, all references are to the historical pound. One pound (£) was equal in value to twenty shillings (s); one shilling was equal to twelve pence or pennies (d).

pulling coconuts. Removing the kernels from the coconuts.

reckonin'. The custom of confessing one's wrongs and seeking forgiveness on one's deathbed.

roti. A flat, soft bread of Indian origin, in which is folded curried meat or seafood and/or vegetables.

samblay. From French, *assembler*, to gather; refers to the act of gathering up the cocoa pods after they have been picked; the worker, usually a woman, was called a **samblayer**.

sans humanité. (French, without humanity); a refrain at the end of each stanza of some early calypsoes in Trinidad and Tobago.

shake han'. Gifts of money that were passed from hand to hand; the giver took care not to draw attention to the act of giving.

shanting. Competitive singing; usually used in the context of singing **picong** on Carnival days in Tobago.

sic. (Latin); thus, so; used to indicate that the preceding text is used or spelled as given.

simmy dimmy. Trinidad and Tobago vernacular for antics or strange behaviour.

sling. Cane juice when it has begun to coagulate during the process of boiling to make sugar. The task of the head boilerman was 'to bring the sling up to sugar'.

suit. 'A suit' was Tobago vernacular for bread and fish.

susu. (Yoruba, *esusu*); a rotating savings and credit association of African origin; in Tobago it was also called a 'throw-up', meaning that many people pooled (threw up) their funds together.

swag. See **chocolate tea.**

tamboo bamboo. (From French, *le tambour*, drum); percussion instruments made of bamboo, which were used to keep the rhythm in the Trinidad Carnival in the early years of the twentieth century, before the invention of the steel pan. Lengths of bamboo of different sizes were used to produce different tones.

tarmbrin; tambrine. Tambourine made with goat's skin.

trafficker. A person who bought commodities in Tobago and took them to Trinidad for sale there. The term is also used in this work to refer to similar trading between other islands. The term does not connote the selling of illegal goods as in the English usage.

truck system. Forms of employment in which consumption is tied directly or indirectly to the work contract, so causing workers to get into debt.

unofficials. Members of the Legislative Council who were not officials in the Civil Service.

watch house. A small hut, usually built on remote garden lands, since most people lived in villages.

watchekongs. Cheap shoes made of canvas with rubber soles, imported from Hong Kong.

windward. Facing the prevailing winds, which in Tobago are the north-east trade winds.

Bibliography

I. BOOKS, ARTICLES, THESES

Abrahams, Roger. *The Man-of-Words in the West Indies*. Baltimore: The Johns Hopkins University Press, 1983.

Alleyne, Albert E. 'Tobago Juvenile Farm Club'. *The Tobagonian*, February 1947, 7.

Anonymous. 'Tobago Revisited'. *Trinidad Guardian*, 22 February 1923, 5.

Armstrong, Eileen. 'A Study of Community Development in Trinidad and in Great Britain with Special Reference to the Work of Women'. Presented for the Associateship of the University of London Institute of Education, *c*.1955.

Baird-John, Anne Marie. 'The Life and Times of Mr Harold Moses Telemaque'. Caribbean Studies thesis, The University of the West Indies, St. Augustine, 1992.

Barnett, Tony. 'HIV/AIDS—The True Cost to Us All'. London School of Economics and Political Science *(LSE) Magazine* 17, no. 1 (2005): 6–8.

Bender, Thomas. *Community and Social Change in America*. New Brunswick, New Jersey: Rutgers University Press, 1978.

Best, Lloyd. 'Outlines of a Model of Pure Plantation Economy'. *Social and Economic Studies* 17, no. 3 (1968): 283–326.

Best, Wilfred. *The Student's Companion*. 1958. Reprint, 2nd edition, London: Collins, 1963.

Biggart, James A. A. 'Memorandum to the West Indian Sugar Commission', published as 'Tobago Needs a Land Settlement Scheme', *Trinidad Guardian*, 11 December 1929, 6.

Bishop, W. Howard. *Ex Post Facto* or *After the Deed Was Done*. Port of Spain: The author, 1907.

———. *The Magnificent Province*. N.p., n.d.

Brereton, Bridget. *Race Relations in Colonial Trinidad, 1870–1900*. Cambridge: Cambridge University Press, 1979.

———. *A History of Modern Trinidad, 1783–1962*. London: Heinemann, 1981.

Brown, Deryck. *History of Money and Banking in Trinidad and Tobago from 1789 to 1989*. Port of Spain: Central Bank of Trinidad and Tobago, 1989.

Brunner, Karl and Allan H. Meltzer. 'The Use of Money: Money in the Theory of an Exchange Economy'. *American Economic Review* 61 (1971): 784–805.

Campbell, Carl C. 'Tobago and Trinidad: Problems of Alignment of Their Educational Systems at Union, 1889–1931'. *Antilia* 1, no. 3 (1987): 21–27.

Caribbean Epidemiology Centre (CAREC). *Status and Trends: Analysis of the Caribbean HIV/AIDS Epidemic, 1982–2002*. Port of Spain: CAREC, 2004.

Caribbean Network for Integrated Rural Development (CNIRD). *Tobago Profiles: A Survey of 14 Agencies/Groups Engaged in Rural and Community Development in Tobago*. CNIRD: St. Augustine, Trinidad, 1990.

Caribbean Quarterly 4, nos. 3 and 4 (1956). Special Issue on *Trinidad Carnival*.

'Charleston (dance)'. *Wikipedia Free Encyclopedia*. http://en.wikipedia.org/wiki/Charleston_%28dance%29 (accessed 25 May 2006).

Chayanov, A. V. *The Theory of Peasant Economy*. Edited by D. Thorner, E. Kerblay and R. E. F. Smith.

Homewood: Irwin, for the American Economic Association, 1966.

Clarke, Edith. *My Mother Who Fathered Me*. London: George Allen and Unwin, 1957.

Clemens, Theodor Liley. *Sunday Music*. UK: Castle and Co., 1889.

———. *Church Litany*. London: Moravian Missionary Society, 1903.

———. *New Music for Our Church Litany*. Liveredge, Yorkshire: *The Globe* Printing Works, 1904.

———. *Andante in C Minor*. London, 1905.

———. *Eight Carols for Christmas*. London, 1912.

———. *Elegy in C Sharp Minor*. London: Novello and Co., 1913.

———. *Twelve Carols for Christmas*. Bradford: Bottomley Brothers, 1919.

———. *Rex Saeculorum*. London: Novello and Co., 1925.

Clifford, Hugh. 'Time and Tobago'. *Blackwood's Edinburgh Magazine* 178 (1905): 305–324.

Collens, James H., comp. *The Trinidad Official and Commercial Register and Almanack, 1893*. Port of Spain: Government Printing Office, 1892.

———, comp. *The Trinidad Official and Commercial Register and Almanack, 1894*. Port of Spain: Government Printing Office, 1893.

———, comp. *The Trinidad and Tobago Official and Commercial Register and Almanack, 1899*. Port of Spain: Government Printing Office, n.d.

———, comp. *Trinidad and Tobago Year Book, 1903*. Port of Spain: Government Printing Office, 1902.

———, comp. *Trinidad and Tobago Year Book, 1904*. Port of Spain: Government Printing Office, 1905.

———, comp. *Trinidad and Tobago Year Book, 1905*. Port of Spain: Government Printing Office, 1906.

———, comp. *Trinidad and Tobago Year Book, 1915*. Port of Spain: Government Printing Office, 1915.

Comma Maynard, Olga. *Carib Echoes*. Published in nine editions. Port of Spain: The author, 1929–1988.

———. *The Briarend Pattern: The Story of Audrey Jeffers OBE and the Coterie of Social Workers*. Port of Spain: The author, 1971.

———. *My Yesterdays*. Port of Spain: The author, 1992.

Comitas, Lambros. 'Occupational Multiplicity in Rural Jamaica'. In *Work and Family Life: West Indian Perspectives*, edited by D. Lowenthal and L. Comitas. Garden City, New York: Anchor Books, 1973.

Craig, Susan E. 'The Germs of An Idea'. Afterword to W. Arthur Lewis, *Labour in the West Indies: The Birth of a Workers' Movement*. 1939. Reprint, London: New Beacon Books, 1977.

———. 'Background to the 1970 Confrontation in Trinidad and Tobago'. In *Contemporary Caribbean: A Sociological Reader*, Vol. 2, edited by S. Craig. St. Augustine, Trinidad and Tobago: The editor, 1982.

———. *Smiles and Blood: The Ruling Class Response to the Workers' Rebellion of 1937 in Trinidad and Tobago*. London: New Beacon Books, 1988.

Craig-James, Susan E. 'The Evolution of Society in Tobago, 1838 to 1900'. Ph.D. thesis, University of London, 1995.

———. 'Agriculture and Society in Tobago: 1763–1963'. Prepared for the Tobago House of Assembly, Scarborough, Tobago, 1997.

———. 'Milch Cow or Hard Sucking Calf? The Joining of Trinidad and Tobago and Its Aftermath, 1884–1948'. Paper presented at a Conference organized by The University of the West Indies and the Policy Research and Development Institute of the Tobago House of Assembly on 'Tobago and Trinidad: 100 Years Together', Scarborough, October 1998. Mimeographed.

———. 'Modern Tobago Society: A Macro-Sociological Analysis'. Prepared for the Tobago Development Plan (1998–2013). Scarborough: Tobago House of Assembly, 1999. Mimeographed.

Cudjoe, Selwyn. 'Glimpses of Our Literary Past'. *Trinidad Guardian 80th Anniversary Supplement*, 31 August 1997, 88–92.

Cunard, Nancy, ed. *Negro*. London: The author, 1934.

Darlington, Levi A. *Calliope*. Port of Spain: The author, 1938.

———. *The Seven Great Monys*. Port of Spain: The author, [1935?].

Davies, Herwald R. [Rev.] 'Through Tribulation to Progress in Tobago'. *United Empire* 17 (1926): 553–556.

De Boissiere, Jean. *Cooking Creole*. Port of Spain: The author, 1943.

De Freitas, Charles. 'Vital Need Is to Revive Our Cocoa Industry'. In *Trinidad and Tobago's Agriculture*, edited by P. N. Wilson and J. B. Stollmeyer. St. Augustine: The University of the West Indies, n. d.

De Suze, Joseph A. *Trinidad and Tobago*. Port of Spain: Catholic News Office, 1894.

———. *Columbian Geography of the World*. Port of Spain, [189?].

———. *Little Folks' Trinidad: A Short Descriptive Historical and Geographical Account of the Island, compiled expressly for use in the schools of the colony*. 1901. Reprint, 11th edition, revised by Carlos C. Hart. Port of Spain: William Fogarty, 1956.

Elder, Jacob D. 'Kalinda: Song of the Battling Troubadours of Trinidad'. *Journal of the Folklore Institute* 3, no. 2 (1966): 192–203.

———. 'Evolution of the Traditional Calypso of Trinidad and Tobago: A Socio-Historical Analysis of Song Change'. Ph.D. thesis, University of Pennsylvania, 1967.

———. *From Congo Drum to Steelband: A Socio-Historical Account of the Emergence and Evolution of the Trinidad Steel Orchestra*. St. Augustine: The University of the West Indies, 1969.

———. *The Yoruba Ancestor Cult in Gasparillo*. St. Augustine: The University of the West Indies, 1969.

———. *Folk Song and Folk Life in Charlotteville*. Port of Spain: N.p., 1971.

———. *Song Games from Trinidad and Tobago*. 1965. Reprint, revised edition, Port of Spain: National Cultural Council, 1973.

———. *The Calypso and Its Morphology*. Port of Spain: National Cultural Council, 1973.

———. 'Tobago's Peculiar Culture'. Tobago House of Assembly, Scarborough, Tobago, c.1984. Mimeographed.

———. *African Survivals in Trinidad and Tobago*. London: Karia Press, 1988.

———. *Folksongs from Tobago: Culture and Song in Tobago*. London: Karnak House, 1994.

Elder, Jacob D., ed. *Ma Rose Point: An Anthology of Rare Legends and Folk Tales from Trinidad and Tobago*. Port of Spain: National Cultural Council, 1972.

Emmanuel, Patrick. 'Crown Colony Politics in Grenada: 1917–1951'. M.Sc. thesis, The University of the West Indies, Mona, 1967.

Erasmus. 'The Peasants of Tobago'. *The Tobagonian*, August 1944, 5–7.

Farrell, Terrence. 'Arthur Lewis and the Case for Caribbean Industrialization'. *Social and Economic Studies* 29, no. 4 (1980): 52–75.

Ferdinand, Prince. *A Handbook of Civilization*. Trinidad: The author, [193?].

———. *A Guide to Life*. Trinidad: The author, 1938.

Ferrer, Vernon O. 'Some Economic Aspects of Peasant Farming in Tobago, British West Indies, and the possible function of medium-term credit in the rehabilitation of low-income farming areas in Trinidad and Tobago'. M.Sc. thesis, Cornell University, 1945.

Figart, David M. *The Plantation Rubber Industry in the Middle East*. Washington, DC: Government Printing Office, 1925.

Fiske, Amos Kidder. *The West Indies*. New York: Knickerbocker Press, 1899.

Franklin, C. B., comp. *The Trinidad and Tobago Year Book* (for 1915–1941). Port of Spain: Franklin's Electric Printery, 1916–1942.

Goddard, George. *Forty Years in the Steelbands, 1939–1979*. London: Karia Press, 1991.

Gomes, Albert. 'Literary Clubs'. 1933. Reprint in *From Trinidad: An Anthology of Early West Indian Writing*, edited by R. W. Sander with the assistance of Peter K. Ayers. London: Hodder and Stoughton, 1978.

Gracyk, Tim. 'Isham Jones and His Orchestra'. http://www.redhotjazz.com/ishamjones.html (accessed 23 June 2006).

Guppy, R. J. Lechmere. *The Trinidad Official and Commercial Register and Almanack for 1890*. Port of Spain, 1890.

Hall, Tony. '"They Want to See George Band": Tobago Mas According to George Leacock'. *The Drama Review* 42, no. 3 (1998): 44–53.

Hammond, F. H. [Rev.] *A Tour around Tobago by Land and Sea*. Port of Spain: Franklin's Electric Printery, 1910.

Harewood, Jack. *The Population of Trinidad and Tobago*. N.p.: Committee for the International Co-ordination of Research in Demography Series, 1975.

Hart, Richard. 'Trade Unionism in the English-Speaking Caribbean: The Formative Years and the Caribbean Labour Congress'. In *Contemporary Caribbean: A Sociological Reader*, Vol. 2, edited by S. Craig. St. Augustine, Trinidad and Tobago: The editor, 1982.

Hatt, George David. 'Tobago Revisited'. *Trinidad Guardian*, 11 March 1923, 14.

Hay, Loraine Geddes. *A Handbook of the Colony of Tobago*. Scarborough, Tobago: Government Printer, 1884.

———. *A Handbook of the Island of Tobago*. Georgetown: The Daily Chronicle, 1899.

Higman, B. W. *Slave Populations of the British Caribbean, 1807–1834*. Baltimore: The Johns Hopkins University Press, 1984.

———. 'Urban Slavery in the British Caribbean'. In *Perspectives on Caribbean Regional Identity*, edited by E. Thomas-Hope. University of Liverpool, Centre for Latin American Studies, Monograph No. 11, 1984.

Hill, Errol. *The Trinidad Carnival: Mandate for a National Theatre*. 1972. Reprint, London: New Beacon Books, 1997.

Holt, Thomas C. *The Problem of Freedom: Race, Labor and Politics in Jamaica and Britain, 1832–1938*. Kingston: Ian Randle Publishers, 1992.

Howard, Esmé (Lord Howard of Penrith). *Theatre of Life: Life Seen from the Pit, 1863–1905*. London: Hodder and Stoughton, 1935.

Hyam, Ronald. *Elgin and Churchill at the Colonial Office, 1905–1908*. London: Macmillan, and New York: St. Martin's Press, 1968.

———. *Britain's Imperial Century, 1815–1914: A Study of Empire and Expansion*. London: B. T. Batsford, 1976.

Isaac, Annette. 'Unequal Development in Trinidad and Tobago: A Preliminary Study'. MA thesis, Carleton University, 1979.

James, Alphonso P. T., Louis A. Peters et al. 'Memorandum of Grievances and Complaints of the Inhabitants of Tobago, Presented to The Right Honourable Sir Arthur Creech Jones, Secretary of State for the Colonies'; also known as 'The James Memorandum'. Scarborough: The authors, 1948. Mimeographed.

Kairi Consultants Limited. *Environmental Data and Information Project: Socio-Economics*. Final Report. Port of Spain: Environmental Management Authority, 1999.

Lee, John M. *Colonial Government and Good Government: A Study of the Ideas Expressed by the British Official*

Classes in Planning Decolonization, 1939–1964. Oxford: Clarendon Press, 1967.

Lee, John M. and Martin Petter. *The Colonial Office, War, and Development Policy: Organisation and the Planning of a Metropolitan Initiative.* London: Maurice Temple Smith for the Institute of Commonwealth Studies, 1982.

Lewis, Gordon K. *The Growth of the Modern West Indies.* London: McGibbon and Kee, 1968.

Lewis, William Arthur. 'The Evolution of the Peasantry in the British West Indies', 1936. Mimeographed.

———. 'The Industrialization of the British West Indies'. *Caribbean Economic Review* 2, no. 1 (1950): 1–61.

———. *The Theory of Economic Growth.* London: George Allen and Unwin, 1955.

———. *Labour in the West Indies.* 1939. Reprint, London: New Beacon Books, 1977.

———. *The Evolution of the International Economic Order.* Princeton: Princeton University Press, 1977.

Luke, Learie B. 'Identity and Autonomy in Tobago: From Union to Self-Government: 1889–1980'. Ph.D. dissertation, Howard University, 2001.

Márquez, Gabriel García. *One Hundred Years of Solitude.* 1967. Reprint in English translation, Harmondsworth: Penguin, 1973.

———. 'The Solitude of Latin America'. Nobel Lecture, 1982. http://www.nobel.se/literature/ laureates/1982/marquez-lecture.html (accessed 14 June 2002).

Marshall, Woodville K. 'Notes on Peasant Development in the West Indies since 1838'. *Social and Economic Studies* 17, no. 3 (1968): 252–263.

Mathurin, Owen C. *Henry Sylvester Williams and the Origins of the Pan-African Movement, 1869–1911.* Westport, Connecticut: Greenwood Press, 1976.

Maynard, Fitz G. and Olga Comma Maynard. *The New Road: A Short Study in Citizenship.* 1961. Reprint, revised edition, Port of Spain: The authors, 1985.

Maynard, G. Oliver. *A History of the Moravian Church, Eastern West Indies Province.* Port of Spain: Yuille's Printerie, 1968.

Meikle, Hallis B. 'Tobago's Juvenile Farm Club'. *The Tobagonian,* September 1939, 13.

———. 'Tobago Villagers in the Mirror of Dialect'. *Caribbean Quarterly* 4, no. 2 (1955): 154–160.

———. 'Mermaids and Fairymaids or Water Gods and Goddesses of Tobago'. *Caribbean Quarterly* 5, no. 2 (1958): 103–108.

Meredith, David. 'The British Government and Colonial Economic Policy, 1919–1939'. *Economic History Review,* 2nd Series, 28, no. 3 (1975): 484–499.

Minar, David W. and Scott Greer, eds. *The Concept of Community: Readings with Interpretations.* London: Butterworth, 1970.

Mintz, Sidney W. *Caribbean Transformations.* Chicago: Aldine Press, 1974.

Mitchell-Gift, Ann, ed. *Lionel P. Mitchell: A Biography.* Scarborough, Tobago: Friends of the Tobago Library Committee, 1996.

Mole Brothers, comps. *The "Mirror" Almanack and General Commercial Directory of Trinidad and Tobago for 1901.* Port of Spain: Mirror Office, n.d.

———, comps. *The "Mirror" Almanack and General Commercial Directory of Trinidad and Tobago for 1903.* Port of Spain: Mole Brothers, n.d.

———, comps. *The Mirror Almanack and General Commercial Directory for Trinidad and Tobago for 1915.* Port of Spain: Mole Brothers, [1915?].

Morgan, David J. *The Origins of British Aid Policy, 1924–1945.* The Official History of Colonial Development, Vol. 1. London: Macmillan, 1980.

Niddrie, David L. *Land Use and Population in Tobago.* World Land Use Survey, Monograph No. 3. Bude, Cornwall: Geographical Publications, 1961.

———. 'Land Use and Land Settlement in the Caribbean: A Contribution to the Historical and Social Geography of the Lesser Antilles, with special reference to the Ceded Islands and in particular to Tobago'. Ph.D. thesis, University of Manchester, 1965.

Olivier, Sydney Haldane [Lord]. *Jamaica: The Blessed Island.* London: Faber and Faber, 1936.

O'Loughlin, Carleen. *The Coconut Industry of the West Indies.* Caribbean Development Bank Technical Report No. 9. Bridgetown: Caribbean Development Bank, 1972.

Orde, Thorlief. *Louis d'Or.* London: George Roberts, 1929.

Ottley, Carlton R. *A Historical Account of the Trinidad and Tobago Police Force from the Earliest Times.* Port of Spain: The author, 1964.

———. *A History of Place-Names in Trinidad and Tobago.* Diego Martin: The author, 1970.

———. *The Story of Port of Spain, Capital of Trinidad, West Indies.* 1962. Reprint, London: Longman Caribbean, 1970.

———. *Spanish Trinidad: An Account of Life in Trinidad, 1498–1797.* 1955. Reprint, London: Longman Caribbean, 1971.

———. *The Story of San Fernando.* Port of Spain: The author, 1971.

———. *Tall Tales of Trinidad and Tobago: Retold by Carlton R. Ottley.* Port of Spain: Horsford Printerie, 1972.

———. *The Complete History of the Island of Tobago.* 1965. Reprint as *The Story of Tobago,* Port of Spain: Longman Caribbean, 1973.

———. *Slavery Days in Trinidad: A Social History of the Island from 1797 to 1838.* Diego Martin: The author, 1974.

———. *East and West Indians Rescue Trinidad.* Diego Martin: Crusoe Publishing, 1975.

———. *A Guide to Trinidad and Tobago.* 1968. Reprint, Diego Martin: Crusoe Publications, 1979.

————. *Folk Beliefs, Folk Customs and Folk Characters Found in Trinidad and Tobago.* Diego Martin: Crusoe Publications, 1979.

————. 'Constitutional Changes in Tobago from House of Assembly 1770 to House of Assembly 1980'. Diego Martin: The author, 1980. Mimeographed.

————. *Creole Talk of Trinidad and Tobago.* First published in four volumes as *Trinibagianese*, 1965–1969. Reprint, 4th edition, enlarged, Port of Spain: The author, 1981.

Partap, Harry. 'The East Indian Experience in Media Development, 1845–1995'. In *In Celebration of 150 Years of the Indian Contribution to Trinidad and Tobago.* Edited by K. Ramchand, B. Samaroo et al. Port of Spain: Diane Quentrall-Thomas, 1995.

Pearse, Andrew, ed. 'Mitto Sampson on Calypso Legends of the Nineteenth Century'. *Caribbean Quarterly* 4, nos. 3 and 4 (1956): 250–262.

Pemberton, Rita. 'Towards a Re-evaluation of the Contribution of the West Indian Peasantry: A Case Study of Tobago, 1900–1949'. MA thesis, The University of the West Indies, St. Augustine, 1984.

Peters, Louis A. 'The Juvenile Farm Club: Its Birth and Growth and Usefulness'. *The Tobagonian*, December 1942, 19–20.

Phillips, André. *Governor Fargo: A Short Biography of Alphonso Philbert Theophilus James.* Scarborough: The author, 1993.

Phillips-Lewis, Kathleen. 'British Imperial Policy and Colonial Economic Development: The Cocoa Industry in Trinidad, 1838–1939'. Ph.D. thesis, University of Manitoba, 1994.

'Poems by E. M. Roach and H. M. Telemaque'. Scarborough, Tobago: Central Library of Trinidad and Tobago, 1973. Mimeographed.

Premdas, Ralph R., and H. Williams. 'Tobago: The Quest for Self-Determination in the Caribbean'. *Canadian Review of Studies in Nationalism* 19 (1992): 117–127.

Premdas, Ralph, and Eric St. Cyr, eds. *Sir Arthur Lewis: An Economic and Political Portrait.* The University of the West Indies, Mona: Institute of Social and Economic Research, 1991.

Punch, Lulworth D. *A Journey to Remember (39 Years in the Civil Service).* Port of Spain: The author, 1963.

Quintero Rivera, Angel G. *Patricios y plebeyos: burgueses, hacendados, artesanos y obreros: Las relaciones de clase en el Puerto Rico de cambio de siglo.* Rio Piedras: Ediciones Huracán, 1988.

Reddock, Rhoda E. *Women, Labour and Politics in Trinidad and Tobago: A History.* Kingston: Ian Randle Publishers, 1994.

Roach, Eric M. 'Ballad of Canga'. *Caribbean Quarterly* 4, no. 2 (1955): 165–68.

————. *Letter for Leonora.* Port of Spain: The University of the West Indies, Extra-Mural Department, 1966.

————. *Belle Fanto.* Port of Spain: The University of the West Indies, Extra-Mural Department, 1967.

————. *A Calabash of Blood.* St. Augustine: The University of the West Indies, 1971.

————. 'Growing Up in Tobago'. In *David Frost Introduces Trinidad and Tobago*, edited by Michael Anthony and Andrew Carr. London: André Deutsch, 1975.

————. *The Flowering Rock: Collected Poems 1938–1974.* Leeds: Peepal Tree Books, 1992.

Roberts, George W. *The Population of Jamaica.* Cambridge: Published by the Conservation Foundation at the University Press, 1957.

Roberts, Heather. 'The Life and Work of C. R. Ottley'. Caribbean Studies thesis, The University of the West Indies, St. Augustine, 1992.

Rogers, De Wilton. *Chalk Dust.* 1943. Reprint, Gasparillo, Trinidad: The author, 1973.

————. *Lalaja: A Tale of Retribution.* 1940. Reprint, San Fernando, Trinidad: The author, 1975.

————. *Blue Blood and Black.* Port of Spain: The author, n.d.

————. *Trickidad.* Port of Spain: The author, n.d.

————. *Silk Cotton Grove.* Port of Spain: The author, n.d.

————. *Parson Bailey.* Port of Spain: The author, n.d.

————. *The Poetry of Tagore in Comparison with a Few Poets of the West together with Kisagotami.* Port of Spain: People's National Movement Publishing Company, [197?].

————. *The Rise of the People's National Movement, Vol. 1, In the Beginning.* Trinidad: The author, n.d.

Rohlehr, Gordon. *Calypso and Society in Pre-Independence Trinidad.* Port of Spain: The author, 1990.

Ryan, Selwyn D. *Race and Nationalism in Trinidad and Tobago: A Study of Decolonization in a Multiracial Society.* Toronto: University of Toronto Press, 1972.

Saint de Lap. 'Tobago Juvenile Farm Club'. *The Tobagonian*, October 1941, 19.

Samaroo, Brinsley. 'Constitutional and Political Development of Trinidad, 1898–1925'. Ph.D. thesis, University of London, 1969.

————. 'The Trinidad Disturbances of 1917–20: Precursor to 1937'. In *The Trinidad Labour Riots of 1937: Perspectives 50 Years Later*, edited by Roy D. Thomas. The University of the West Indies, St. Augustine: Extra-Mural Studies Unit, 1987.

Sander, Reinhard, ed. *From Trinidad: An Anthology of Early West Indian Writing.* London: Hodder and Stoughton, 1978.

Schneider, Harold. *Economic Man: The Anthropology of Economics.* New York: Free Press, 1974.

Shephard, Cecil Y. *The Cacao Industry of Trinidad: Some Economic Aspects.* Port of Spain: Govern-ment Printing Office, Parts I and II, 1932; Parts III, IV, V, 1937.

————. 'British West Indian Economic History in Imperial Perspective'. Lecture to the Historical

Society of Trinidad and Tobago, 17 March 1939. In *Public Lectures Delivered under the Auspices of The Historical Society of Trinidad and Tobago during the Session 1938–1939*. Port of Spain: Government Printer, 1940.

———. *Peasant Agriculture in the Leeward and Windward Islands*. St. Augustine: Imperial College of Tropical Agriculture, 1945.

———. 'Report on Co-operative Cocoa Fermentaries in Tobago'. Port of Spain: Caribbean Commission, 1957. Mimeographed.

Shirer, William. *The Rise and Fall of the Third Reich*. London: Mandarin, 1960.

Simey, Thomas S. *Welfare and Planning in the West Indies*. Oxford: Oxford University Press, 1946.

Simpson, Joy. *Internal Migration in Trinidad and Tobago*. The University of the West Indies, Mona: Institute of Social and Economic Research, 1973.

Smith, Edwin W. *Aggrey of Africa: A Study in Black and White*. New York: Richard R. Smith, 1930.

Solomon, Patrick. *Solomon: An Autobiography*. Port of Spain: Inprint Caribbean, 1981.

Stover, Charles C. 'Tropical Exports'. In *Tropical Development 1880–1913: Studies in Economic Progress*. London: George Allen and Unwin, 1970.

Sturge, Joseph and Thomas Harvey. *The West Indies in 1837*. London: Hamilton, Adams and Co., 1838.

Telemaque, Harold M. *Nelson's Primary Geography for the Caribbean*. Revised edition. London: Thomas Nelson and Son, 1967.

———. 'An Anthology of Poems'. Trinidad: The author, n.d. Mimeographed.

Telemaque, Harold M. and A. M. Clarke. *Burnt Bush*. Port of Spain: The authors, n.d. [c.1947].

'The British West Indian Limes Industry', Report of an Extraordinary General Meeting and of the First Annual General Meeting of the West Indian Limes Association (Incorporated), Trinidad, April 1941. *Tropical Agriculture* 18, no. 6 (1941): 105–106.

The Drama Review 42, no. 3 (1998). Special Issue on the Trinidad Carnival.

The Gem. First issue. January 1937.

Thomas, Roy D. ed. *The Trinidad Labour Riots of 1937: Perspectives 50 Years Later*. The University of the West Indies, St. Augustine: Extra-Mural Studies Unit, 1987.

Walter, Karl. 'Revival in the West Indies'. In *Year Book of Agricultural Co-operation, 1930*, edited by The Horace Plunkett Foundation. London: George Routledge and Sons, 1930.

Webb, James L. A. Jr. 'Toward the Comparative Study of Money: A Reconsideration of West African Currencies and Neoclassical Monetary Concepts'. *International Journal of African Historical Studies* 15, no. 3 (1982): 455–466.

Weber, Max. *The Theory of Social and Economic Organisation*. Translated by A. M. Henderson and T. Parsons. Edited with an Introduction by T. Parsons. New York: The Free Press, 1964.

West India Committee Circular, No. 810, 17 Oct. 1929.

Will, Henry A. *Constitutional Change in the British West Indies, 1880–1903, with special reference to Jamaica, British Guiana and Trinidad*. Oxford: Clarendon Press, 1970.

Williams, Eric E. *Massa Day Done*. Pamphlet. Port of Spain: People's National Movement Publishing Co., 1961.

Wiltshire-Brodber, Rosina. 'The Caribbean Transnational Family'. Paper presented to UNESCO/Institute of Social and Economic Research Eastern Caribbean Sub-Regional Seminar, The University of the West Indies, Cave Hill, 1986. Draft.

Witter, Michael. 'A Review and Assessment of the Poverty Policy of the Tobago Development Plan'. Port of Spain: United Nations Development Programme and Scarborough: Policy Research and Development Institute, 2000. Mimeographed.

Wood, Donald. *Trinidad in Transition: The Years after Slavery*. London: Institute of Race Relations, 1968.

II.   OFFICIAL PUBLICATIONS

II.1   Barbados

Imperial Department of Agriculture for the West Indies. *Tobago: Hints to Settlers*. Bridgetown: Imperial Department of Agriculture for the West Indies, 1906.

Report of the Team Which Visited Tobago in March/April 1957. Development Plan for Tobago. Bulletin No. 34. Bridgetown: Development and Welfare in the West Indies, 1957.

West Indian Bulletin (Journal of the Imperial Department of Agriculture, Bridgetown) 12 (1912).

II.2   Trinidad and Tobago

Address of the Governor on the Opening of the Session of the Legislative Council on 8 November 1909, Council Paper No. 127 of 1909.

Administration Report of the Collector of Customs for 1920, Council Paper No. 103 of 1921.

Administration Report of the Collector of Customs for 1921, Council Paper No. 99 of 1922.

Administration Report of the Collector of Customs for 1922, Council Paper No. 71 of 1923.

Administration Report of the Collector of Customs for 1923, Council Paper No. 54 of 1924.

Administration Report of the Collector of Customs for 1924, Council Paper No. 56 of 1925.

Administration Report of the Collector of Customs for 1926, Council Paper No. 52 of 1927.

Administration Report of the Collector of Customs for 1927, Council Paper No. 68 of 1928.

Administration Report of the Collector of Customs for 1928, Council Paper No. 56 of 1929.

Administration Report of the Collector of Customs for 1929, Council Paper No. 67 of 1930.

Administration Report of the Collector of Customs and Excise for 1930, Council Paper No. 70 of 1931.

Administration Report of the Collector of Customs and Excise for 1931, Council Paper No. 42 of 1932.

Administration Report of the Collector of Customs and Excise for 1932, Council Paper No. 40 of 1933.

Administration Report of the Collector of Customs and Excise for 1933, Council Paper No. 62 of 1934.

Administration Report of the Collector of Customs and Excise for 1938, Council Paper No. 58 of 1939.

Administration Report of the Collector of Customs and Excise for 1940, Council Paper No. 33 of 1941.

Administration Report of the Collector of Customs and Excise for 1941, Council Paper No. 62 of 1942.

Administration Report of the Collector of Customs and Excise for 1944, Council Paper No. 35 of 1945.

Administration Report of the Comptroller of Customs and Excise for 1950. Port of Spain: Government Printing Office, 1951.

Administration Report of the Comptroller of Customs and Excise for 1958. Port of Spain: Government Printing Office, 1959.

Administration Report of the Customs and Excise Department for 1959. Port of Spain: Government Printing Office, 1960.

Administration Report of the Department of Agriculture for 1925, Council Paper No. 60 of 1926.

Administration Report of the Director of Agriculture for 1909–1910, Council Paper No. 115 of 1910.

Administration Report of the Director of Agriculture for 1938, Council Paper No. 71 of 1939.

Administration Report on the Department of Agriculture for 1911–1912, 1912–1913, Council Paper No. 152 of 1913.

Administration Report on the Department of Agriculture for 1917, Council Paper No. 122 of 1918.

Administration Report on the Department of Agriculture for 1924, Council Paper No. 52 of 1925.

Administration Report on the Department of Agriculture for 1925, Council Paper No. 60 of 1926.

Administration Report on the Department of Agriculture for 1930, Council Paper No. 79 of 1931.

Administration Report on the Department of Agriculture for 1932, Council Paper No. 33 of 1933.

Administration Report on the Department of Agriculture for 1934, Council Paper No. 72 of 1935.

Administration Report on the Department of Agriculture for 1935, Council Paper No. 51 of 1936.

Administration Report on the Department of Agriculture for 1936, Council Paper No. 47 of 1937.

Administration Report on the Department of Agriculture for 1937, Council Paper No. 50 of 1938.

Administration Report on the Department of Agriculture for 1942, Council Paper No. 57 of 1943.

Administration Report on the Department of Agriculture for the Year Ended 31 March 1911, Council Paper No. 161 of 1911.

Administration Report of the Director of Education for 1938, Council Paper No. 67 of 1939.

Administration Report of the Director of Education for 1945. Port of Spain: Government Printer, 1947.

Administration Reports of the Director of Agriculture for 1945 to 1957. Port of Spain: Government Printer, 1946 to 1959.

Administration Reports of the Medical Inspector of Health, Medical Officers of Health and the Port Health Officer for 1918, Council Paper No. 101 of 1919.

Agricultural Education: Circular from Joseph Chamberlain, Secretary of State, to Colonial Governors, Council Paper No. 119 of 1899.

Ali, Ridwan, et al. *Land Capability Studies Phase II, Report No. 8, Agriculture in Tobago.* Port of Spain: Key Caribbean Publications for Ministry of Planning and Development, 1973.

Annual General Report on the Colony of Trinidad and Tobago for 1939–1946. Port of Spain: Government Printer, [c.1947].

Annual Report of the Agricultural Services for the Year 1962. Port of Spain: Ministry of Agriculture, 1964.

Annual Report of the Agricultural Services for the Year 1963. Port of Spain: Ministry of Agriculture, 1965.

Annual Report of the Chief Manager of the Government Savings Bank for 1909–1910, Council Paper No. 96 of 1910.

Annual Reports of the Medical Inspector of Health and the Medical Officers of Health on Health Conditions in Trinidad and Tobago for 1917, Council Paper No. 121 of 1918.

Brown, Cyril B. et al. *Land Capability Survey of Trinidad and Tobago, No. 1, Tobago.* Port of Spain: Caribbean Printers, 1965.

Central Statistical Office (CSO). *Population and Housing Census Reports,* 1960, 1970, 1980, 1990. Port of Spain: CSO.

———. *Annual Statistical Digest 1985.* Port of Spain: CSO, 1987.

———. *Labour Force Report 1995.* Port of Spain: CSO, 1996.

———. *Annual Statistical Digest 1994/95.* Port of Spain: CSO, [1997?].

———. *Labour Force Report 1996.* Port of Spain: CSO, 1997.

———. *Labour Force Report 1997.* Port of Spain: CSO, 1998.

———. *2000 Population and Housing Census: Preliminary Population Count.* Port of Spain: CSO, 2001.

———. *Annual Statistical Digest 1998/99.* Port of Spain: CSO, 2002.

———. *2000 Population and Housing Census: Community Register.* Port of Spain: CSO, 2002.

Bibliography

————. *Annual Statistical Digest 2000*. Port of Spain: CSO, 2003.

————. *Labour Force Report 2001*. Port of Spain: CSO, 2003.

————. *Population and Vital Statistics Report 2000*. Port of Spain: CSO, 2005.

————. *2000 Population and Housing Census: Demographic Report*. Port of Spain: CSO, 2006.

————. 'Tobago Statistics'. Port of Spain: CSO, no date. Mimeographed.

Cocoa Industry of Trinidad: Report by S. M. Gilbert, Assistant Director of Agriculture, Based on Recent Economic Survey, Council Paper No. 4 of 1931.

Collens, James H., ed. *Handbook of Tobago*. Port of Spain: Government Printing Office, 1912.

Collens, James H. *Handbook of Trinidad and Tobago for the Use of Settlers*. Prepared by a Committee of the Board of Agriculture. Port of Spain: Government Printing Office, 1912.

Correspondence on Agriculture between the Government of Trinidad and Tobago and the Comptroller for Development and Welfare, British West Indies, Council Paper No. 23 of 1942.

Department of Agriculture. Annual Report for 1961. Port of Spain: Department of Agriculture, no date. Mimeographed.

Department of Agriculture. *Bulletin*, 1910–1917.

Department of Agriculture. *Rubber in Trinidad and Tobago*. Port of Spain: Government Printer, 1911.

Development Committee: Preliminary Report, Council Paper No. 50 of 1919.

District Administration Reports for 1899, Council Paper No. 102 of 1900.

District Administration Reports for 1926, Council Paper No. 53 of 1927.

District Administration Reports for 1927, Council Paper No. 82 of 1928.

District Administration Reports for 1928, Council Paper No. 74 of 1929.

District Administration Reports for 1929, Council Paper No. 58 of 1930.

District Administration Reports for 1930, Council Paper No. 50 of 1931.

District Administration Reports for 1932, Council Paper No. 55 of 1933.

District Administration Reports for 1935, Council Paper No. 54 of 1936.

District Administration Reports for 1936, Council Paper No. 78 of 1937.

District Administration Reports for 1937, Council Paper No. 82 of 1938.

District Administration Reports for the Year 1950. Port of Spain: Government Printer, 1951.

Education Policy Paper (1993–2003). White Paper. Port of Spain: Ministry of Education, 1994.

Environmental Management Authority (EMA). *Trinidad and Tobago: State of the Environment Report 1996*. Port of Spain: EMA, 1996.

Final Report of the Committee Appointed to Enquire into the Needs of the Cocoa Industry, with Memorandum by Sir Frank Stockdale, Agricultural Adviser to the Secretary of State for the Colonies, Council Paper No. 61 of 1940.

Forestry Division, Biodiversity Clearing House. 'News and Events', 25 November 2005. http://trinbagobiodiversity.gov.tt/news/ Trinidad_ramsar_sites.htm (accessed 17 July 2006).

Franchise Commission Report, Council Paper No. 90 of 1923.

Hart, J. Hinchley. *Report on the Agri-Horticultural Resources of Tobago*. Bulletin No. 12. Port of Spain: Trinidad Royal Botanic Gardens, 1889.

Governor's Address to the Legislative Council, Council Paper No. 4 of 1945.

Letter from Hon. H. L. Thornton Relative to the Expenses Incurred by the Member Residing in Tobago, Council Paper No. 68 of 1904.

Marshall, A. L. Report on the Transactions of the Tobago Branch of the Government Savings Bank for 1893, 8 July 1894. *Tobago Gazette*, 13 July 1894, 114.

Meaden, C. W. Report on the Grazing Capabilities of Tobago, Council Paper No. 77 of 1898.

Memorandum on Major Capital Works of Government Showing Progress of Work in Execution and Work Proposed for 1951. Approved by the Select Committee on Estimates, 1951. Port of Spain: Government Printing Office, 1951.

Memorandum Showing Progress of Certain Development Schemes in the Colony of Trinidad and Tobago up to 1948. Port of Spain: Government Printer, 1949.

Message of Governor Sir Hubert Winthrop Young to the Legislative Council, 29 November 1940, Council Paper No. 71 of 1940.

Message of His Excellency the Governor to the Legislative Council, 16 May 1941, and Supplement, Council Paper No. 17 of 1941.

Ministry of Education. *Report of the Task Force for the Removal of the Common Entrance Examination*. Port of Spain: Ministry of Education, 1998.

Ministry of Planning and Development, Town and Country Planning Division, and Department of Regional Development and Environment, Organization of American States. *Planning for Sustainable Development: South-West Tobago Development Strategy*. Port of Spain: Ministry of Planning and Development, 1996. Draft.

Ministry of Planning and Mobilization. *Tobago Region Physical Development Plan*. Port of Spain: Ministry of Planning and Mobilization, 1991. Draft.

Minutes of the Proceedings of the Legislative Council and Council Papers, 1898–1945. Port of Spain: Government Printer, 1899–1946. (Council Papers cited are listed by title, number and year herein.)

Legislative Council Debates, 1946–1962. Port of Spain: Government Printer, 1947–1966.

Parliamentary Debates (Hansard), 1962–1965. Port of Spain: Government Printer, 1962–1965.

'Patent Centrifugal Machine (Mr Harry S. Smith's) Complete Specification'. Trinidad and Tobago Department of Agriculture, *Bulletin* 9, No. 66 (October 1910): 219–221.

Petition to Governor and Legislative Council for Shorter Hours of Labour for the Clerks of Port of Spain, Council Paper No. 141 of 1909.

Policy Research and Development Institute (PRDI). *Tobago Survey of Living Conditions Report, 1997.* Scarborough, Tobago: PRDI, 1999.

———. *Tobago Business Register, 1997/98.* Scarborough: PRDI, 2000.

———. *Review of the Economy and Policy Measures, Tobago, 2000.* Scarborough: PRDI, 2001.

———. *Crime in Tobago, 1996–2002.* Scarborough: PRDI, 2003.

———. *Economic and Social Development in Tobago, 2003–2004.* Scarborough, Tobago: PRDI, 2004.

PRDI and Department of Planning, Office of the Chief Secretary, Tobago House of Assembly (THA). *Tobago Development Plan, Report No. 1: The Process of Development Planning in Tobago.* Scarborough: PRDI and Office of the Chief Secretary, 1998.

PRDI and Division of Finance and Planning, Office of the Chief Secretary, THA. *Tobago Development Plan, Report No. 2: Medium-Term Policy Framework of Tobago, 1998–2000.* Scarborough: PRDI and Office of the Chief Secretary, 1998.

———. *Tobago Development Plan, Report No. 3: The Tobago Strategic Plan.* Scarborough: PRDI and Office of the Chief Secretary, 1998.

———. Tobago Development Plan, Report No. 4: The Integrated Plan for the Development of the People of Tobago in the 21st Century. Scarborough: PRDI and Office of the Chief Secretary, 1998. Draft.

PRDI with The Department of Tourism, THA. *The Cruise Ship Sector of Tobago's Tourism Industry, November 2000–April 2001.* Scarborough: PRDI with The Department of Tourism, THA, 2003.

Report by the Surgeon-General on the Epidemic of Dysentery in Tobago in the Year 1912, Council Paper No. 11 of 1913.

Report of a Committee Appointed to Advise on the Trinidad–Tobago Coastal Steamer Service, with Appendices (Nicoll Report), Council Paper No. 3 of 1939.

Report of the Agricultural Policy Committee of Trinidad and Tobago, Parts I and II. Port of Spain: Government Printer, 1943.

Report of the Chief Manager of the Government Savings Bank for the Nine Months Ended 31 December 1915, Council Paper No. 76 of 1916.

Report of the Commission of Enquiry into the Recent Disturbances at Port of Spain, Trinidad. London, 1903; published as *Gazette Extraordinary,* 21 July 1903.

Report of the Commission of Enquiry on the Administration and Cost of the Government Steamship Service between the Islands of Trinidad and Tobago. Port of Spain: Government Printing Office, 1957.

Report of the Committee appointed by the Governor on 15 August 1918 to Consider Representations by the Royal Mail Company on Its Loss on the Coastal Service and to Advise, Council Paper No. 43 of 1919.

Report of the Committee Appointed to Enquire into the Medical and Health Policy of the Colony, Council Paper No. 65 of 1944.

Report of the Economics Committee. Port of Spain: Government Printer, 1949.

Report of the Estimates Committee on a Comprehensive Development Programme to be Carried Out within the Years 1939–1944, Council Paper No. 96 of 1938.

Report of the Franchise Committee of Trinidad and Tobago, Council Paper No. 35 of 1944.

Report of the Select Committee of the Legislative Council on Shorter Hours of Labour for the Clerks of Port of Spain, Council Paper No. 22 of 1910.

Report of the Tobago Planning Team. Port of Spain: Office of the Prime Minister, 1963.

Report of the Wages Advisory Board (1935–1936), Council Paper No. 88 of 1936.

Report on the Working of the Government Savings Bank for 1913–1914, Council Paper No. 135 of 1914.

Royal Commission on Trade Relations between Canada and the West Indies, Council Paper No. 123 of 1910.

'Rubber Cultivation in Trinidad and Tobago: Report of the Special Committee of the Board of Agriculture'. Trinidad and Tobago Department of Agriculture, *Bulletin* 16, Part 3 (1917): 115–116.

Rubber in Trinidad and Tobago. Port of Spain: Department of Agriculture, 1911.

Task Force Appointed by Cabinet to Enquire into the Poor Performance of Students in Secondary Schools in Tobago. *Report.* Port of Spain: Ministry of Tobago Affairs, 2000.

Task Force Appointed by The Government of Trinidad and Tobago to Prepare a Comprehensive Economic Development Plan for Tobago. *A Comprehensive Economic Development Plan for Tobago (2006–2010): Tobago, Capital of Paradise: Clean, Green, Safe and Serene.* Scarborough: Tobago House of Assembly, 2005.

Task Force for the Removal of the Common Entrance Examination. *Report.* Port of Spain: Ministry of Education, 1998.

Thames Water International and ADeB Consultants. *Design of a Watershed Protection Programme for the Courland Catchment, Tobago, Draft Final Report.* Prepared for the Water and Sewerage Authority. Port of Spain: Thames Water International and ADeB Consultants, 1994.

Tobago Financial and Other Returns, 1898, Council Paper No. 102 of 1899.

Tobago Metairie Commission Report with Evidence and Appendices. Port of Spain: Government Printing Office, 1891.

Tobago Producers' Association Ltd.: Report of an Inquiry into the Constitution, Working and Financial Condition of the Association, Council Paper No. 22 of 1938.

Tobago Region Physical Development Pslan. Port of Spain: Ministry of Planning and Mobilization, 1991. Draft.

Tobago Sea Communications Committee Report, Council Paper No. 44 of 1929.

Trinidad and Tobago Blue Book for 1912–13. Port of Spain: Government Printing Office, 1913.

Trinidad and Tobago Blue Book for 1921. Port of Spain: Government Printing Office, 1922. (This and the previous reference are available on microfilm in the West Indiana Division, The University of the West Indies, St. Augustine.)

Trinidad and Tobago Blue Book for 1931. Port of Spain: Government Printer, 1932.

Trinidad and Tobago Disturbances, 1937, Report of Commission. Port of Spain: Government Printing Office, 1938.

Wages Committee, 1919–1920, Preliminary Report, Council Paper No. 125 of 1920.

West Indian Census 1946. Part G. Census of Population of the Colony of Trinidad and Tobago. Report. Port of Spain: Government Printer, 1948.

II.3   United Kingdom

Colonial Office. *Development and Welfare in the West Indies, 1940–1942.* Report by Sir Frank Stockdale. Colonial No. 184. London: His Majesty's Stationery Office, 1943.

Hooper, E. D. M. *Report upon the Forests of Tobago.* Madras, 1887. (Available in CO 321/104).

Orde Browne, G. St. J. (Major). *Labour Conditions in the West Indies.* London: His Majesty's Stationery Office, 1939. C. 6070.

Parliamentary Debates, House of Commons, 1928, Volume 214; 1929–1930, Volumes 231, 232, 233, 235.

Parliamentary Papers, 1910, Volume XXVII. *Report of the Committee on Emigration from India to the Crown Colonies and Protectorates*, Part II, Minutes of Evidence. London: His Majesty's Stationery Office, 1910. Cmd. 5193.

Report by the Hon. E. F. L. Wood, MP, on His Visit to the West Indies and British Guiana, December 1921–February 1922. London: His Majesty's Stationery Office, 1922. C. 1679.

Report from the Royal Commission on Public Revenue, Expenditure, Debts and Liabilities of the Islands of Jamaica, Grenada, St. Vincent, Tobago, St. Lucia and the Leeward Islands. London: Her Majesty's Stationery Office, 1884. Reprint. Shannon: Irish Universities Press, 1971. C. 3840.

Report from the West India Royal Commission. London: Eyre and Spottiswoode, 1897. C. 8655.

Report of the West Indian Sugar Commission. London: His Majesty's Stationery Office, 1930. Cmd. 3517.

West India Royal Commission Report (Moyne Report). London: His Majesty's Stationery Office, 1945. C. 6607.

III.   ARCHIVAL RECORDS

III.1   Trinidad and Tobago

1. *Anglican Church Records, Tobago*
   Baptism, marriage and burial records housed at St. Andrew's Parish, Scarborough; St. David's Parish, Plymouth; St. Mary's Parish, Pembroke; and St. Patrick's Parish, Mt. Pleasant.

2. *Methodist Church Records, Tobago*
   Baptism, marriage and burial records housed at the Methodist Church Office, Scarborough.

3. *Moravian Church Records, Tobago*
   Baptism, marriage and burial records housed at the Moravian Churches at Montgomery, Moriah and Spring Garden.

4. *Roman Catholic Church Records, Tobago*
   Baptism, marriage and burial records housed at the St. Joseph Roman Catholic Church Office, Scarborough.

5. *The National Archives of Trinidad and Tobago, Port of Spain, Trinidad*
   Administrator's Despatches, Tobago, 1882 to 1885.

6. *Trinidad and Tobago Parliament Library, Port of Spain, Trinidad*
   a. *Trinidad Royal Gazette*, 1898–1940.
   b. Trinidad and Tobago Legislative Council Papers (1898–1950).
   c. *Minutes and Proceedings of the Legislative Council,* 1898–1945.
   d. *Proceedings and Debates of the Legislative Council (Hansard).* Port of Spain: Government Printer, 1946–1963.
   e. Sundry annual departmental reports published as booklets (1946–1960).

7. *Registrar General's Office, Port of Spain, Trinidad*
   a. Tobago Protocol of Deeds, 1842–1868.
   b. Tobago Protocol of Deeds, 1889–1890.

8. *The University of the West Indies, St. Augustine, Trinidad (The Main Library)*
   a. Andrew Pearse Collection, Folder 6.
   b. West India Royal Commission (Moyne Commission), 1938–1939. (Bound volume of memoranda and other evidence to the Commission.) Mimeographed.

III.2   United Kingdom

1. *Archives of the Library, Royal Botanic Gardens, Kew, Surrey*
   Sundry documents on agriculture in Trinidad and Tobago, including the Report by J. Hinchley Hart listed in II.2.
2. *Archives of the Main Library, Cambridge University, Cambridge*
   Photographic collection.
3. *Foreign and Commonwealth Office Library, London*
   Tobago Population Census Reports, 1851, 1881, 1891; Trinidad and Tobago Population Census Reports, 1901–1931.
   (The census reports for 1844 and 1861 are in the Public Record Office, CO 285 files for those years; the 1871 census report is in the House of Assembly Minutes, CO 286/26, 1871; the 1946 census report is listed at West Indian Census 1946, II.2 above.)
4. *Institute of Commonwealth Studies, University of London*
   West India Committee records.
5. *Methodist Missionary Society Archives, School of Oriental and African Studies Library, University of London*
   Wesleyan Missionary Society (WMS), Tobago Letters, 1817–1890.
6. *Moravian Missionary Society (MMS) Archives, Muswell Hill, London*
   Sundry newspapers and documents related to the West India missions.
7. *Public Record Office, Kew, Surrey*
   Several files in the series CO 285, CO 286 (Tobago); CO 295, CO 298, CO 299, CO 300 (Trinidad and Tobago), CO 700 (Maps of Tobago); CO 950 (West India Royal Commission (Moyne Commission) submissions and evidence) cited in the footnotes.
8. *Rhodes House Library, University of Oxford, Oxford*
   a. The Arthur Creech Jones Papers (ACJ).
   b. The Sir John Chancellor Papers, MSS. Brit. Emp. S.284.

III.3   United States of America

1. *The Moravian Archives, Bethlehem, Pennsylvania*
   a. *The Missionary Reporter*, 1870–1884; renamed *The Moravian Missionary Reporter and Illustrated Missionary News*, 1895–1902.
   b. *The Moravian Messenger*, 1890–1942.
   c. *Moravian Missions*, 1903–1952.
   d. *Periodical Accounts* relating to the Missions of the Church of the United Brethren, established among the Heathen. Second Series, Vols. 1–12, 1891–1927; and Nos. 138–178, 1930–1970.
   e. *Proceedings of the Society of the United Brethren for Propagating the Gospel among the Heathen*, 1864–1947.

IV.   NEWSPAPERS AND PERIODICALS

1. *The National Archives of Trinidad and Tobago, Port of Spain, Trinidad and Tobago*
   a. *The Labour Leader* (Port of Spain), 1922–1932.
   b. *The Mirror* (Port of Spain), 1898–1916; sporadic issues, 1917.
   c. *The People* (Port of Spain), 1933–1940.
   d. *Port of Spain Gazette* (Port of Spain), January–March 1937.
   e. *A Teacher's Annual* (Port of Spain), 1936–1937.
   f. *Teachers' Herald* (Port of Spain), 1934–1947.
   g. *Teachers' Journal* (Port of Spain), 1928–1934.
   h. *Tobago Herald* (Scarborough), 1953–1956.
   i. *Tobago News* (Scarborough), 2007.
   j. *Tobago Times* (Scarborough), 1933–1935.
   k. *The Tobagonian* (Scarborough), 1938–1950.
   l. *Trinidad Guardian* (Port of Spain), Oct.–Dec. 1919, Aug.–Dec. 1932, 1934, 1937–1940.
2. *The University of the West Indies, St. Augustine, Trinidad and Tobago (The Main Library, West Indiana Division)*
   a. *The Nation* (Port of Spain), Jan. 1959–Aug. 1962 (microfilm).
   b. *Port of Spain Gazette*, 1889–1892, 1895, 1898–1899, 1904, 1925 (selected issues), (microfilm).
   c. *Trinidad Guardian*, September 1917 to December 1934; May 1960 to January 1962 (microfilm).

V.   PRIVATE COLLECTIONS

Archbald-Doyle, Jennifer. Trinidad. Family papers and photographs.
Armstrong, Audrie, and Alison Armstrong. Tobago. Family papers and photographs.
Baptiste, Catherine Donaldson. Trinidad. Photograph.
Cordner, Margaret Ernestine. Trinidad. Family papers and photographs.
Daniel, Nydia Bruce. Trinidad. Documents and photographs.
Edwards, William, and Sylvia Herke. Canada and Germany, respectively. Family photographs.
Harper, Daphne. Trinidad. Family photographs.
Hatt, Alec, Mrs Hatt and Ms Patricia Hatt. Trinidad. Family photographs.
Granger, Gaskynd. Trinidad. Trade union documents and photograph.
Kelshall, Jack. Trinidad. Family archives.
Kendall, Carlos. Trinidad. Document.
Lambert, Gordon. Trinidad. Family papers.
Leacock, George. Tobago. Permission to photograph artefacts from the Scarborough Heritage Parlour.
Ottley, Myrtle, and Jason Ottley. Trinidad, and Tobago, respectively. Family photographs.

Bibliography

Phillips, Anna, and Diane Laguerre. USA. Family photograph.

Rajnauth, Arlene. Trinidad. Stamp collection, photographs, family papers.

Sawyer, Olive. Tobago. Personal artefacts and photographs.

Seaton, Olive. Trinidad. Family photographs.

Telemaque, Pearl. Trinidad. Family photographs.

The Turpin Family Papers on Charlotteville Estate, Tobago. Selected documents that the author was allowed to see in 1983.

VI.   INTERVIEWS

Note: All interviews were conducted by the author; all were tape-recorded. Unrecorded conversations from which notes were taken and typed or written up neatly the same day are indicated. Unless otherwise stated, all interviews were conducted in Tobago.

Adams, Samuel (b.1903). Retired peasant and metayer. Interview, Patience Hill, 3 January 1985.

Alleyne, Mary (1891–*c*.1985). Retired domestic worker, peasant and housewife. Interview, Craig Hall, 23 May 1983.

Andrews, Dalton (b.1912), and Ruth Andrews (b.1913). Mr Andrews, retired trade union and village council activist, and small businessman; Mrs Andrews, housewife. Interview, Belle Garden, 16 May 1983.

Arthur, Elton 'Bob Hope' (b.1920), and Lucia Arthur (b.1930). Retired agricultural worker; farmers. Interview, Louis d'Or, 12 May 1983.

Arthur, Henrietta (1899–1984). Housewife, landowner, former member of Delaford Carnival band. Interview, Delaford, 13 May 1983.

Bovell, Amelia (b.1912). Market vendor; former estate labourer and public works water-fetcher. Interview, with Branford Williams (b.1910), Bethel, 19 February 1985.

Carrington, Glycerie 'Vaso' (b.1914). Retired housewife; daughter of Henry Livingstone Rowley, master carpenter and farmer, and his wife Frances. Interview, Port of Spain, Trinidad, 20 January 2007.

Caesar, Annie (b.1905). Retired peasant, market vendor; former domestic worker. Interview, Mason Hall, 8 January 1985.

Cordner, Margaret Ernestine (1924–2007). Retired civil servant; former Commissioner of Guides. Unrecorded conversation, Diego Martin, Trinidad, 6 May 2002.

Christmas, Aurelia Moore (1903–1993), with Sylvena Nicholson and 'Sweetie' Nicholson, relatives. Mrs Christmas, retired peasant; folk artist; great granddaughter of Liberated African, Napoleon Murphy. Interview, Charlotteville, 26 May 1983.

Craig, Lionel (b.1922). Farmer and market vendor. Interview by telephone, 20 March 2007.

Craig, Sislyn (1921–1996). Farmer and market vendor. Unrecorded conversation, Whim, 30 May 1983.

Crooks, Jules (1903–1993). Retired master tailor. Interview, Scarborough, 24 April 1983.

Crosby, Irma (1907–2003). Retired store clerk and bookkeeper. Interview, Rockley Vale, 20 July 1993.

Dalrymple, Isabelle (1896–1997), and Auldith Cameron (b.1913). Retired seamstress and housewife, respectively. Interview, Scarborough, 15 July 1992.

Daniel, Jean O'Keiffe. Former store clerk. Interview, All Fields Crown Trace, 1 August 1996.

Daniel, Nydia Bruce (1917–2001). Retired training officer at the Trinidad and Tobago Telephone Company; former teacher; poet and debater. Interview, Port of Spain, Trinidad, 29 July 1996.

De Freitas, Jules (1906–1991), and Dorothy de Freitas (1913–1986). Mr de Freitas, former Works Department employee; Mrs de Freitas, former teacher. Interview, Government House Road, 26 April 1983.

Dillon, Charles (1895–1999). Retired shoemaker, sawyer, shopkeeper. Interview, Charlotteville, 19 May 1999.

Dillon, Marquis (1904–1995). Shopkeeper, carpenter; former cocoa contractor. Interview, Charlotteville, 25 April 1983.

Donaldson, Dolly (1897–*c*.1995). Retired store clerk. Interview, Bacolet, 3 September 1985.

Eastman, Moses (1921–2003). Government employee; fisherman, farmer, and former estate labourer. Interview, Whim, 9 January 1985; unrecorded conversation, with Rachel Eastman (1928–1992), confectioner and Government employee, Parrot Hall, 27 April 1983.

Edwards, Adina (b.1901). Retired teacher; Village Council activist and church worker. Interview, Roxborough, 25 April 1983.

Elder, Jacob D. (1914–2003). Ethnomusicologist and anthropologist; former Councillor and Secretary for Culture, Tobago House of Assembly; former educator. Interview, Scarborough, 24 May 1983; unrecorded conversation, 27 September 1984.

Felix, Noel (b.1933), with Rachel Eastman (1928–1992). Mr Felix, Works Department labourer, woodcutter and fisherman; son of Edward Felix (1881–1973), violinist. Interview, Parlatuvier, 18 May 1983.

Ferreira, Hugh (b.1915). Interview, Scarborough, 27 August 1985.

Frank, James (b.*c*.1902). Retired teacher; elder of the Methodist Church. Unrecorded conversation, Castara, 27 April 1983.

Gibbs, Sidney (b.1906). Retired hospital store-keeper. Interview, Rose Hill, 29 May 1983.

Granger, Gaskynd (*c*.1915–*c*.1996). Trade union organizer and labour activist in both Trinidad and Tobago. Interview, Port of Spain, Trinidad, 12 March 1983.

Guillaume, Eileen (1916–2004). Retired Community Development Officer. Unrecorded conversation,

Scarborough, with George Young, retired teacher, 22 April 1983. Interview, 29 April 1983.

Harris, O'Farrell (b.1908). Retired tobacco farmer and food-crop producer. Interview, Patience Hill, 16 February 1985.

Henderson, Holsey (1914–1997). Chairman, Adelphi Estate Limited; grandson of Ebenezer Henderson, merchant and planter, and of Gordon T. Macdougall I, planter. Interview, Cascade, Port of Spain, Trinidad, 29 June 1996.

Henry, Dorcas (b.1916). Retired District Nurse. Interview, Diego Martin, Trinidad, 9 July 1992.

Henry, Kadah. Retired Matron; great-niece of Joseph Francis Henry (1859–1945), educator and founder of the Middle School, Tobago. Interview by telephone, 28 June 1999.

Holder, George 'Colonel' (b.1911). Interview, Rockley Vale, 17 February 1985.

Homeward, Cassie (1911–2003). Peasant, market vendor; former domestic worker. Interview, with Ivan and Jane Taylor and Irene Cadiz, Bethel, 8 January 1985.

Inniss, Izzy (c.1891–c.1987). Former road worker, metayer, peasant, tobacco grower, market vendor, and midwife. Interview, Patience Hill, 9 January 1985.

James, Amos (1904–c.1999). Farmer, estate overseer, Methodist lay preacher, and community activist. Interview, L'Anse Fourmi, 24 July 1992.

Leacock, George (1915–2005). Folklorist and amateur archivist; co-founder with his wife Cecile (d.1988) of the Scarborough Heritage Parlour; former Carnival bandleader; retired businessman. Interview, 30, 31 August, 1985; unrecorded conversation with author, 3 February 1994; Scarborough, Tobago.

Lyons, Louisa 'Banty' (1904–2003). Retired farmer, shopkeeper and baker. Interview, D'Abadie, Trinidad, 10 August 1999.

McKnight, Ruby (b.1902). Former manager, Dornock Estate; retired small farmer. Interview, Castara, 20 May 1983.

Manning, Dora (b.1893). Former estate worker and cocoa contractor. Interview, Kendal Place, 13 May 1983.

Maynard, Fitz Gerald (1900–1984) and Olga Comma Maynard (1902–1999). Mr Maynard, retired head teacher; activist of the literary and debating movement, and of the Tobago District Agricultural Society, the Arts Festival, the Trinidad Youth Council, and the Association of Friendly Societies; founder, Trinidad Local Preachers' Fellowship; Mrs Maynard, retired educator; social worker; writer. Interview, Port of Spain, Trinidad, 31 May 1983.

Mitchell, Lionel P. (1905–1992). Educator, founder of the Tobago Institute of Education; social activist; bandmaster; scoutmaster. Interview, Scarborough, 22 April 1983, 27 September 1984.

Moore, Samuel (b.1902). Former employee, Trinidad Government Railway; retired estate labourer. Interview, Charlotteville, 25 May 1983.

Nicholson, Emeldalina (1901–2005). Retired trafficker, baker, storekeeper; former teacher. Interview, Petit Valley, Trinidad, 26 June 1996.

Noel, Lyttleton (b.1909). Estate owner. Unrecorded conversation, Les Coteaux, 24 May 1999.

Noray, Verna (b.1944). Domestic worker, confectioner. Unrecorded conversation, Whim, 10 August 2007.

Nurse, Percival (b.1915). Retired civil servant; amateur Tobago historian. Interview, St. Joseph, Trinidad, 17 June 1996; unrecorded conversation, 22 June 1996.

Nymn, Harold (1896–1986). Retired wireless operator. Interview, Spring Garden, 12 May 1983.

Ottley, Carlton R. (1914–1985). Retired Director of Community Development; historian; folklorist. Interview, Port of Spain, Trinidad, 8 June 1983.

Ottley, Eric (1910–1986). Retired civil servant; security officer; former calypso singer. Interview, Gonzales, Trinidad, 12 March 1985.

Paul, Alford (b.1934). Retired Public Health Inspector; Pastor; former member of the Les Coteaux steelband. Interview, Les Coteaux, 13 February 2006.

Peters, Edward 'Pappy' (1904–1993). Tobacco farmer; trafficker. Interview, Prospect, 28 September 1984.

Pope, William 'Sweetie' (b.1905). Retired estate worker; casual labourer on public works. Interview, Belle Garden, 29 May 1983.

Quamina, Barnabas (b.1893). Retired head teacher and political activist. Interview, Les Coteaux, 15 February 1985.

Richardson, Albert (b.1888), with Mrs Richardson. Retired estate labourer, road worker; farmers. Interview, Ten Chains, 24 May 1983.

Richardson, George 'Josey'. Steelband pioneer and pan tuner. Interview, Black Rock, 19 June 1975.

Rouse, Ivan B. J. (1906–1999). Retired head teacher, Inspector of Schools and social activist. Interview, Port of Spain, Trinidad, 8 March 1982.

St. Louis, Frank. Secretary, Tobago District Agricultural Society, and proprietor, Woodlands Estate. Unrecorded conversation, Scarborough, 22 June 1983.

Sandy, Agnes (1870–1987). Retired farmer, market vendor; former estate labourer and laundress; widow of Sawyer Sandy, fisherman and tambourine player. Interview, King Peter Bay Road, 16 July 1984.

Sandy, Cecil T. (1917–2004). Retired senior civil servant. Unrecorded conversation, Calder Hall, 17 July 1999.

Sawyer, Olive (1914–1997). Retired social worker and Community Development Officer. Interview, Calder Hall, 15 May 1983.

Scott, Jonathan (b.1934). Snackette proprietor; Captain, West Side Steel Orchestra; activist in Prime Minister's Best Village Competition. Interview, Patience Hill, 1 September 1985.

Sebro, Lytton (b.1921). Retired transport foreman, Health Department, Tobago, and Headquarters Commissioner for Scouts. Interview, Mason Hall, 23 May 1983.

Bibliography

Seukeran, Lionel F. (1908–1992). Retired businessman and politician; former member of the Legislative Council and of the Parliament; former trade unionist; activist of the literary and debating movement. Interview, San Fernando, Trinidad, 9 June 1975.

Shade, Henry (b.1910). Retired farmer; former saxophonist in the music band called Tom Shade and His Boys. Unrecorded conversation, Mason Hall, 20 July 2005.

Sinclair, George (b.1905). Retired teacher; son of Thomas Sinclair, Grenadian immigrant. Unrecorded conversation, Cinnamon Hill, 17 February 1985.

Smart, Alfred (b.1915). Retired road overseer; farmer; musician. Interview, Parlatuvier, 18 May 1983.

Smith, Bobby. Son of Harry S. Smith, planter; brother of Eleanor Alefounder, owner of Grafton Estate. Unrecorded conversation, Grafton Estate, 28 May 1983.

Smith, Hobson (b.1907). Retired teacher and writer. Interview, Moriah, 16 July 1992.

Solomon, Leopold (1906–1999) and Keziah Solomon (1915–1995). Mr Solomon, carpenter, guitarist and cuatro player, singer; member of Patience Hill band; Mrs Solomon, shopkeeper. Interview, 17 March 1985; unrecorded conversation with Leopold Solomon, Bethel, Tobago, 22 May 1999.

Stewart, Ethencer. Spiritual Baptist leader, midwife, former member of the Trinidad Labour Party. Interview, Woodlands, 29 April 1983.

Taylor, Egbert (b.1908). Former Tiger Patrol leader in World War II; retired senior field assistant, Department of Agriculture. Interview, Guinea Grass Estate near Plymouth, 23 May 1983.

Taylor, Ivan (1900–1993), with Jane Taylor (1912–1989), Irene Cadiz (b.1911), and Cassie Homeward (1911–2003). Mr Taylor, peasant, former estate worker; Mrs Taylor, former pupil teacher, peasant; Ms Cadiz, midwife and agricultural worker; Mrs Homeward, peasant, market vendor, former domestic worker. Interview, Bethel, 8 January 1985.

Taylor, William (b.1895). Former estate labourer and overseer; born at Castara, Tobago; migrated to Trinidad in 1911. Interview, Brooklyn Land Settlement, Trinidad, 19 May 1984.

Thomas, Jane Ann 'Edna' (1894–2003). Retired farmer and market vendor. Interview, Les Coteaux, 18 July 1992.

Thompson, Dolores. Writer and researcher on Tobago families. Unrecorded conversations, St. Augustine and Arima, Trinidad, 1, 9 April 1993.

Washington, Euclid (b.c.1910). Retired trade union organizer; former member of Tobago County Council. Unrecorded conversation, Mt. St. George, Tobago, 17 May 1983.

Watts, Alexandrina (b.1909). Former farmer; former domestic worker. Interview, Mason Hall, 2 January 1985.

Wheeler, Victor (d.2005). Retired school principal and Schools Supervisor; former close associate of the Hon. A. P. T. James; Anglican lay minister. Interview, Port of Spain, Trinidad, 13 March 2001.

Wildman, Cyril (1892–c.1984). Former planter and land valuator. Unrecorded conversation, 4 May 1983; interview, Port of Spain, Trinidad, 5 May 1983.

Williams, Branford (b.1910) and Amelia Bovell (b.1912). Mr Williams, public works foreman; musician and founder of Thrilling Star band; former estate labourer; Ms Bovell, market vendor; former estate labourer and public works water-fetcher. Interview, Bethel, 19 February 1985.

Wilson, Ruth (1886–1987). Retired seamstress. Interview, Mason Hall, 5 January 1985.

Yeates, Aubrey (1907–1997). Estate owner; former County Councillor; grandson of Dougald Yeates (c.1804–1884), planter and prominent Tobago civil servant. Interview, Crown Point, 16 July 1992.

Index

Note: Although this Index is very comprehensive, it does not include all the names given in this volume.